Economic Globalisation as Religious War

Economic Globalisation as Religious War argues that the theories and practises of economic globalisation are far from providing a new age of progress in contemporary international politics, but are more accurately seen as the predictable consequences which are experienced in times of religious wars.

Using a critical theory approach Michael McKinley traces the history and development of economic globalisation. Drawing on theories of neo-liberalism he demonstrates how economic globalisation is a form of war, specifically a religious war wherein the form taken is the imposition of a dogma upon non-believers of different persuasions.

McKinley argues that economic globalisation expresses itself in the present day as acts and fears of religious warfare and global terrorism. With the global expansion of economics and religion and the associated disappearance of nation state borders, these two seemingly diverse elements are juxtaposed and examined jointly. He does not take a stance against globalisation, but argues that there is a strong need that economic globalisation arises from democratic policies and that it is important to pay attention to local and temporal conditions if we are to avoid the increased spread of conflict of an essentially religious character. Acknowledging the importance of the United States as a prime mover and principal determinant of outcomes, this book has a strong US focus. It is divided into four parts that examine: the causes of neo-liberal war and the expanding global combat zone; Americanisation and Economics; university as a service to the empire; and the link between Economics and war.

Economic Globalisation as Religious War is a provocative and topical new book which would be of great interest to students and researchers of International Relations, International Political Economy and Security Studies.

Michael McKinley is Senior Lecturer in International Relations and Strategy, in the Political Science and International Relations Programme at the School of Social Sciences of The Australian National University.

Routledge Advances in International Relations and Global Politics

For 'Ria

sine qua non

Economic Globalisation as Religious War

Tragic convergence

Michael McKinley

Routledge
Taylor & Francis Group

LONDON AND NEW YORK

First published 2007 by Routledge
2 Park Square, Milton Park, Abingdon, Oxon OX14 4RN

Simultaneously published in the USA and Canada by Routledge
270 Madison Ave, New York, NY 10016

Routledge is an imprint of the Taylor & Francis Group, an informa business

© 2007 Michael McKinley

Typeset in Garamond by Minni Reis
Printed and bound in Great Britain by TJ International Ltd, Padstow, Cornwall

British Library Cataloguing in Publication Data
A catalogue record for this book is available from the British Library

Library of Congress Cataloging in Publication Data
McKinley, Michael.
Economic globalisation as religious war : tragic convergence / Michael McKinley.
p. cm. — (Routledge advances in international relations and global politics)
Includes bibliographical references and index.
1. International economic relations. 2. Globalization—Economic aspects. 3. Economics—
Religious aspects. 4. Neoliberalism. 5. Regional economic disparities. 6. War—Causes. I.
Title.
HF1359.M3892007
337—dc22
2007002906

ISBN10: 0-415-33266-4 (hbk)
ISBN10: 0-203-49571-3 (ebk)

ISBN13: 978-0-415-33266-8 (hbk)
ISBN13: 978-0-203-49571-1 (ebk)

Contents

Acknowledgments

This book had a long and difficult gestation. The research and the writing were always a delight, but the background was far from it: watching and experiencing the decline and self-harm of the neo-liberally embedded university system in Australia could not be anything else. This book, then, was written despite an environment hostile to traditional undergraduate teaching, postgraduate supervision, research, reflection, and overall scholarship. If this makes it an achievement, it is an achievement which must acknowledge the many Sherpas who lightened the load.

My university, the Australian National University itself, deserves mention for the financial assistance (particularly through the now defunct Faculties' Research Grant Scheme) towards research and the study leave which it still manages to provide despite influences to the contrary. Neither was ever enough, but honesty compels the admission that both were a great deal more than nothing, and nothing would probably have been the result without them.

My contacts as Routledge – in the early days through the RIPE series, and the extraordinarily encouraging anonymous reader of the early chapters – and then more recently, share in this achievement. No doubt I am missing some who contributed substantially, and to them I apologise, but to Heidi Bagtazo and Craig Fowlie I am especially thankful.

In similar vein, the manuscript finalising process was greatly facilitated by the generous financial assistance provided by both the ANU in general, and the Dean of the Faculty of Arts, Professor Adam Shoemaker in particular, and the equally generous collegial support extended by Professor Jenny Corbett, of the Australia-Japan Research Centre, who allowed me to take advantage of the excellent skills of Minni Reis. For this, many thanks.

At the personal level, here in Canberra, I need to recognise Jim George, outstanding theorist and national treasure in the Australian discipline of International Relations, and brother-in-arms in a thousand fights and skirmishes over two decades against the forces of darkness that lay siege to the modern university: without him, and put quite simply, intellectual winter.

Similarly, I am very glad to acknowledge Professor Barry Ninham, of the Department of Applied Mathematics in the ANU's Research School of Physical Sciences and Engineering: a brief enlightening conversation over a drink many years back sent me on a voyage of discovery which, hopefully, has been rewarded with fidelity in the relevant section of the following pages.

I was also blessed by just enough students at all levels who were genuinely interested in what I was writing about, and, within this generated and sustained optimism. Among them, undergraduates Lisa Barritt-Eyles, Judithe Lovick-Andrews and Richard Fairbrother, who, in the best sense, kept the faith. And for years now, so did certain postgraduates who came across the common path – most especially Malak Ansour and Dave Kennedy, friends beyond students and colleagues who always lighten the day. In the same light, friends who were never my students, and who probably do not know how their encouragement was so important must be named, and I do: Yin Qian and Clinton Fernandes.

And the days would definitely have been darker without the friendship, and the teaching, research, and bibliographic assistance provided from an unusual quarter – the Sociology Programme! – in the person of Judy Hemming, without a doubt, a shield of Achilles and scourge of mine enemies.

Beyond the shores of this Great South Land, many debts have also been incurred. So acknowledged are those to Mike Shapiro at the University of Hawaii at Manoa, forever a patient teacher of another teacher; Rod Alley at Victoria University in Wellington, New Zealand, exemplary academic whose influence is with me still; and Mick Dillon at the University of Lancaster, heady champagne in an arid climate. Though they do not know it, the debts to Robert Fisk and John Pilger must be recorded: their examples were always beacons, and thus I remember, too, Alfred Giannantonio, who, having read a piece by the latter, contacted me and became a source of solidarity.

As with scholars and friends, so with friends outside the university whose existence accounts for much that I have been able to do within it. This has been no more in evidence than in Dublin, a second home, and in the person of Tom Power – rugby *cognoscente*, listener, modern *shannachie*, co-rogue, and person of consequence in my life for over 30 years, throughout which he has been the personification of the old Irish greeting, *cead mille failte*. In the same country, I am indebted to Dr Deborah Condell, Consultant Histopathologist at Cavan General Hospital for patient assistance in reducing complex medical matters to the level at which it could be comprehended by a strategic analyst.

Finally, I must pay tribute to my co-panellists over many years, the Travelling Wilburys of successive International Studies Association Conventions: Annette Freyberg-Inan of the University of Amsterdam, Steve Rosow from SUNY, and Peter Vale of Rhodes University, RSA – all colleagues and friends in the collaborative effort to maintain sanity, optimism and cheer in a world bordering on, and frequently tipping over into the absurd. Over many years we have been privileged to meet and be guided in our deliberations by Danny Warner of the Graduate Institute of International Studies in Geneva, and for me, this too infrequent an observance could be forgone only through the same process by which I would contemplate the amputation of a limb. Much talk has been generated on the subject of 'the community of scholars' but, with all of these, I have been honoured to live in one. *Slainte*, and thank you one and all.

Michael McKinley
September 2006

Abbreviations

ANZUS	Australia, New Zealand and the United States of America
CEA	Council of Economic Advisers
FTAA	Free Trade Agreement of the Americas
GATS	General Agreement on Trade and Services
IMF	International Monetary Fund
GATT	General Agreement on Tariffs and Trade
MAI	Multilateral Agreement on Investment
MDGs	Millennium Development Goals
MTN	Multilateral Trade Negotiations
NAFTA	North American Free Trade Agreement
NAIRU	Non-accelerating Inflation Rate of Unemployment
NATO	North Atlantic Treaty Organisation
NGOs	non-government organisations
NICs	newly industrialising countries
OECD	Organisation for Economic Co-operation and Development
SAPs	(World Bank) Structural Adjustment Programs
TRIMs	Trade-related Investment Measures
TIPs	Trade-related Aspects of Intellectual Property Rights
UNCTAD	United Nations Conference on Trade and Development
WHO	World Health Organization
WTO	World Trade Organization

Introduction

Let us consider the times. Wealth is increasingly concentrated in the possession of a few, while poverty and declining standards of living are increasingly distributed among the many, who are, in any case, being exploited and dispossessed; in the hope of a better life the millions among this many enter into global migration and wandering – in many cases reversing, but also complementing the flow of capital; crime is ubiquitous, creating the need for legitimate violence as a corrective, and there is no shortage of powers, usually illegitimate, to carry it out in the service of megapolitical actors, who, despite their advantages of scale, are unable to eliminate pockets of the resistance.[1] And all of this is to the accompaniment of an aggressive insistence on religious observance by major actors, which is to say the obedience to, and reverence for certain controlling powers and truths by way of specified practices in honour of their efficacy and vindication is so commonplace that it is thought to be unremarkable.

If we take a step backwards, in effect to translate ourselves to another level of abstraction, we understand that this theodicy was conceived in destruction and renewal, born of hope, in the spirit of surrender, and the imperative of a new beginning which Heidegger captured as the realisation that '[o]nly a god can save us,' and Jung as 'the right moment... for a metamorphosis of the gods.'[2] We are bidden to be commanded by the Empire of the Good and to seek within its realm to establish the Utopia which will proceed from virtuously adhering to the imperial precepts. Little thought is given to the possibility, let alone the probability, that the entire movement might be regressive to past barbarisms, rather than progressive; that Utopia is not so much some place, but (and more strictly speaking) *no* place, and that other inversions and juxtapositions abound to the point where the revelations lack all credible provenance. Their truth is no more than, at best, an inferior religion, and the compulsion to do good no more than the conceit of Shaw's Caesar: the temptation to see one's tribal customs as the laws of nature.

Let us therefore examine the times more closely and their defining characteristics in somewhat greater detail. The power structure is essentially unipolar while never being able to stifle the emergence of challenges, the frequent cause of which is the scandalous state of the governance in, and of the predominant power – dynastic politics and patently corrupt personal lives being to the fore – though no one would excuse its putative rivals from their own excesses. For the dominant power, the threat is also constituted by those who take representative, if not totally democratic principles of government seriously; indeed, for many who are otherwise sympathetic to the reform project, the purging of the overall system of its debasing elements and its return to a more dignified existence in which its purpose is taken seriously, is seen as inescapably linked to precisely this acknowledgment. In any case, notwithstanding the essential worldliness of their concerns, protagonists are as one in their obsessional view that austerity, strict religious observance, and the education of community leaders at all levels according to a common, prescribed curriculum are integral to the arrest of the predominant power's declining authority and its rehabilitation and extension. More precisely, nothing less than disciplinary subjugation is demanded, and nothing less than an imperial reconstruction, indistinguishable from absolute rule, is envisaged, even if, as decorum might require from time to time and place to place, it must be served by treaties declared to be among equals in order to provide superficial concealment of what is undoubtedly the naked exercise of power. It is a time of monomania and aggression, and, where argument cannot justify the means and ends, faith is explicitly demanded and acts as the sufficient ordinance for the world missions to hand.

The times, then, are marked by 'fundamentalism' or what Karen Armstrong terms 'militant piety'; but they are also Gnostic – that is, the reformers who already substantially order the world, and would order it further, express the belief that they possess the redemptive knowledge of not only God, but of the origins and destiny of humankind. With those who have not experienced this *gnosis*, there can be no dialogue, only a bitterly antagonistic relationship which, by definition, can admit neither compromise nor coexistence. Where these confessional divisions are not coincident with the boundaries of nation states, the result is an exceedingly confused map, especially when the respective demographic and political characters of the world are superimposed on it.

More closely examined, this map reveals that the West – the 'Atlantic States' – is the most powerful bloc in what is virtually a three-zone division of the world. Of the other two, the Centre, which was once strong, is weakened as a result of civil war, national disunity, and fracturing; the East, on the other hand, is relatively isolated from the other two because of its religions and cultures (which include Islam), lack of political cohesiveness, primitive economies and deep internal ethnic divisions. Synoptically, the picture is one of conflicting interpretations for the simple reason that it is a period of contradictory forces and resists any possible singular understanding. Bourgeois enterprise, revolutions in science and technology, the flowering of literature and the performing arts, and struggles for constitutional representative government exist, and in many cases thrive alongside absolutism, famine, mercantilism, plague, political repression, poverty, slavery, and belief in the occult. Perhaps not surprisingly, population pressure and eroding living standards for the poor, who constitute the majority of the global population, are endemic. To be sure, it warrants Richard Dunn's description as, 'indeed a novel age.'

Honesty, however, now requires that I admit to it not being used in relation to the immediate past and the present, but to the period which began with the Augustinian friar, Gabriele Condulmero's election as Pope Eugenius IV in 1431, and continued for over two hundred years until the Treaty of Westphalia in 1648.[3] It is an age which encompasses splits in the temporal world rule effected by the Christian (Catholic) Church, its rottenness at so many levels, and the schismatic forces which this generated; it is the age, too, of counter-schism and dogmatic establishment and affirmation of the truth by which the world was to live, and die, and, above all, the attempt to restore Rome to the site of central power – directly over the body of the true Church, the consciences of Christianity's believers, but also, indirectly over the temporal world as well.

My deceit is only superficial. Although, in the construction of the foregoing narrative I used sources which were historically specific, I did so with a purpose – that of the dramatic effect which is achieved when the juxtaposition of eras is realised, and a sense of legitimacy – because each of the eras in question keeps calling the other into focus (provided, of course, you have a knowledge and understanding of both in the first place and find their juxtapositions as fascinating, illustrative, and persuasive). The journey to this position took just three turns. The first was almost banal, arising out of a consideration of the widespread death and damage done to humanity by economic globalisation. As someone whose academic education and training was in the specialisation of strategic, or security studies, the consequences were, and remain, those of war with but one exception: the magnitude of the consequences is greater. An interim finding was reached along the lines that something which was warlike, and indeed might very well be war itself, needed to be further explored to see if the appearances were sustained in other dimensions.

The second turn came, therefore, from a confrontation with the theoretical justification for these consequences in the body of thought popularly known to us as neo-liberalism, and more specifically its free-market core, neoclassical economics. What is so striking about this theoretical perspective, which is nothing less than a multi-level rationale for the allocation of resources defined as scarce, are the ways in which it replicates various strategic (security) theories by appeals to essentialist claims about human nature and rationality; indeed, when, as frequently happens, the theory is inadequate to its subject matter, almost identical forms of obfuscation and deferral are introduced to quell the rising doubt. Effectively, the disciplinary virtue required in these debilitating intellectual and lived circumstances – faith – invites a final turn by way of a consideration of both Economics and Strategy in religious terms, a recourse which, paradoxically, many critics within both areas of endeavour humorously, or tongue-in-cheek refer to but refrain from pursuing to the extent and depth which the move encourages. Thus, what at first seemed a plausible proposition worthy of further inquiry became a firm conclusion: economic globalisation is, for all of its representations as a liberating process for all of humankind, a form of not only war, but religious war – an obscenely destructive clash, sometimes between absolutes, wherein the form taken is the imposition of a dogma upon the *miscredenti* (non-believers of differing persuasions) – and which, even when translated into the late twentieth and early twenty-first centuries, satisfies the criteria for war laid down by successive schools of theorists of the subject as far back as 500 BCE, or as recently as the 1990s.

The more that the apparently discrete areas of Economics, Strategy, and Religion are interrogated, the more commonplace become these findings. Sometimes, what would hitherto have been understood as juxtapositions seem on further acquaintance to reflect a common, unified discourse which makes a nonsense of separation. We find, then, that this is an age when the business, economics, and finance shelves of major bookstores are incomplete without works which appropriate the term strategy in general, and offer the wisdom of the Chinese strategist, Sun Tzu, in particular, to mid-career military officers, seeking MBAs as their postgraduate degree of choice. Should they be thought of highly enough, they might even join select colleagues being trained in battlefield decision-making in the bear-pit of the stock exchanges; in time, as senior officers with successful combat experience, they will have superstar status on the highly lucrative corporate lecture circuit and be eagerly sought after as directors when they retire. And the credibility of it all is simply achieved by the interleaving of thought and deed, to the point where the convergence of national strategy with corporate strategy is such commonly asserted sense that it would be irrational to suggest otherwise. And all of this, it is emphasised, takes place in full public view despite the continued observation, in the popular, or public mind, as well as in the minds of the remarkably incurious in the academy, of there being a real, existing distinction between war and peace and the activities peculiar to both.

A willingness to 'rationally' tolerate not only juxtapositions but also inversions and contradictions is, therefore, imperative – which is another way of stating that the situation requires belief without evidence, let alone proof of the type normally demanded of others who would contest the revealed truths of neo-liberalism. Only under such a dispensation can thinking people simultaneously hold to the separation of the economic and the strategic and espouse the cause of the global revolution which is neo-liberalism given that the latter, as a matter of historical precedent (for example, the European conquests of Africa and the Americas) has only ever been attempted – indeed, was only ever possible – by violence and with catastrophic loss of life and culture over centuries. Only under such a dispensation could these same people forget that economies exist because people trade (not the other way round) and that a single global market economy without a global society, community, or single standard for the conditions under which capital is invested, labour is hired, and goods are produced is the work of deranged minds. And only under such a dispensation would inclusion and choice be trumpeted as benefits when all along the reality is that the former scarcely embraces Africa and Latin America while the latter cannot extend to the choice of economic system in the first place. The requirement, more specifically, of the denial of this 'disposition to war' as a natural dimension of the spread of the 'free market' is for the apprehension of divine truth and intangible realities which dissolve all obligations inherited from the realm of the profane.

Engagement with critical thinking has definite and foreshortened limits in such a milieu; indeed, it is no exaggeration to say that, when forced to face the absurdities of the ideology in action, the first preference is for responses which either attempt the denigration of such thoughts in favour of a technological reduction of society to an organism capable only of reflexive obedience to immutable 'natural' laws – what Jacques Ellul identified as the 'humiliation of the word.'[4] Some questions, it seems, are embarrassing. Failing that, a second recourse is to question the good faith and authenticity of the challenge, which is effectively to indulge a preoccupation with heresy so as to allay any widespread embrace of the idea that the world might just be multifarious and most probably uncertain. And the allowed tolerances here are somewhere between minimal and non-existent. As the Brazilian Bishop, Helder Camara famously reflected: 'When I give food to the poor, they call me a saint. When I ask why the poor have no food, they call me a communist.' Some questions, it seems, are not for now. Finally, and befitting a totalitarian movement, a heavy terroristic silence shrouds what is apparent to all who can see: if neo-liberalism is violent, then the violence is either denied, or held to be the fault of those suffering it, or transitional pending a wondrous future, or simply necessary, or all three. Some questions, it seems, ignore the nature of necessity and things. This is the essence of the Pontificate which Morris West concerned himself within so much of his writing – government by absolute regulation beyond effective appeal on the grounds of either: *non expedit* (it is not expedient); *non e opportune* (it is not timely), or (simply) *fiat* (let it be done thus).[5]

What is especially not covered by these proscriptions is anything to do with the fact that 'we live only in communion – not only with our present but with the past and the future as well,' that 'we are haunted by a whole poetry of living' which, *inter alia*, includes grief, love, understanding, fear, and even terror. Moreover, in every one of these remembrances authority of the type which we are asked by neo-liberalism to obey is incapable of illumination, and irrelevant, nothing more than 'the one-eyed man in the kingdom of the blind' because its sterile legalisms cannot command us in that which we most rejoice.[6] Against this, and in a first step towards a political economy in global politics which sensitively and authentically acknowledges that which illuminates our daily lives, this book is an explicit attempt to undermine the neo-liberal project as it is currently configured – that is, as a form of tyranny against the overwhelming majority of the world's people. Conversely, this is not what is sometimes called an exercise in 'anti-globalisation'; rather, I am in favour of economic globalisation (and any other form of globalisation for that matter) if it arises from democratic polities and is introduced according to local and temporal conditions which pay faithful attention to the need to adapt to the changing conditions according to a human rate – what Paul Virilio describes as 'metabolic speed.' But this is not the likely form that economic globalisation will take. Let me, therefore, declare something which I want to be clear from the very beginning: this book intends to hold economic globalisation in general, its framing ideology which is neo-liberalism, and their common core of neoclassical economics in particular, up to hatred, ridicule and contempt on the grounds that dialogue, argument and compromise with it are neither possible nor any longer desirable, and that all they now deserve is opprobrium. Thus, to remain with the metaphor central to this book, we are now at a Tridentine moment in economic globalisation. To the extent that the established powers of the world are willing to concede anything, it is only that, yes, certain excesses have been committed but that institutional and doctrinal reform will suffice; more drastic measures, undoubtedly warranted in light of the institutional disposition to these over time, are rejected out of hand, and no temporising between these positions is conceivable.

In days long ago, a work of this nature was accurately, but not pejoratively, described as a libel because it was a document which both contained a plaintiff's allegations and instituted a suit. More recently, of course, a libel became a defamatory, or malicious –

which is to say baseless accusation – with the same intent as its predecessor. The latter is not the case with this work; it is written and argued with fidelity to accuracy and in the public interest. Moreover, in the light of the carnage and pillage wrought by economic globalisation, it is a necessary contribution to its overthrow and replacement by a means of wealth creation which is respectful of human rights, social needs, and locally determined accountable and responsible forms of politics. Clearly then, this book is a catalogue of grievance, a corrective, and a plea for something other and better than neo-liberalism as an organising principle in global politics. Ideally, it would be addressed to friend and foe alike – to the former in solidarity and the offer of intellectual defence, and to the latter as a challenge and an invitation to dialogue – but the second of these is an ambition which can no longer be served.

Neoclassical economists and neo-liberals are almost touching in their reverence for the dogmas they have learned to repeat, but in point of fact, and in every area of knowledge construction with which they should be familiar and sensitive to, they are *persona muta*, lacking in both a language and an imagination with which they might communicate to a generally well-educated audience. What is worse, this injury is self-inflicted and self-willed, ignoring the obligation that a self-styled superior discipline has to justify its arrogation of power on pain of being relegated to the status of a modish, and only arguably, slightly superior superstition. This is a regrettable but inevitable consequence of Economics' attempt to appropriate the methods and, of course, the status of Newtonian physics as it departed from the study of political economy in, and after the late nineteenth century: in terms of a science that described the world as it was, that linear approach was a phantom, and could never give rise to any legitimate understanding of the world that relied on excessive abstractions and denied the extraordinary salience of initial conditions, dynamic feedback loops, and real, continuous time frames into the future. It marked the new discipline of Economics, therefore, as one which had been deaf to what Newtonian physics was, and where physics itself was going philosophically in the same periods, and, as if to demonstrate that it had not been inadvertence the first time, it repeated itself in relation to mathematics. So created, was a genus indifferent to listening or seeing, and thereby learning, and capable only of primal utterances – a discipline wholly deserving of Tom Nairn's dismissal (of another similarly inarticulate elite sub-culture): 'tongue-tied sons of bastards' ghosts.'[7]

From these introductory paragraphs it will be apparent that this book is written by an uncivil member of the aforementioned *miscredenti* and with all the risks that entails. These times are not convivial to serious disputation on questions about the conditions of life and death, the creation and distribution of wealth and poverty, and the relations between them in an era which trumpets the success of the West and of capitalism in the Cold War. In all probability, no times ever are, so, more precisely, what I mean is that prevailing opinion holds that it is eccentric, irrational, naïve, and ultimately, dangerous, to challenge the approved post-Cold War truths and doctrines which are currently holding sway. For all that, the risks are not those suffered by the likes of independent thinkers such as Giordano Bruno, who was burned at the stake for his recalcitrant caste of mind; rather, the contemporary fate is more likely to be dismissed out of hand, to be neither listened to nor read. Against this, though, Bruno's perseverance is exemplary:

I claim
no private lien on the truth, only
a liberty to seek it, prove it in debate,
and to be wrong a thousand times to reach
a single rightness.[8]

The method and path this disputation takes is through an examination of the consequences of economic globalisation in the first instance. It is this which drew my attention to the phenomenon and, appropriately, it is this which needs to be understood as the initial case which neo-liberalism has to answer. In any case, I am here following the example set by the classical thinkers, and more recently encouraged by Werner Dannhauser in a delightful essay of 1971 – of being exercised by a real problem in everyday life, and not that beloved of so many of my contemporaries aspiring to 'scientific' political science and international relations, who cannot abide beginning an analysis without 'interminable, abstruse reflections on methodology.'[9] This is not to denigrate theory – that is totally alien to a work such as this which relies on, and engages with one of the most powerful theories in world politics – it is simply to say that, when it comes to the approach I have adopted for this work, it is to be found in the body of knowledge called critical theory, and, to the extent that it is explicitly deployed here, it will be but lightly brushed across the work. In other words, the lightness of my explicit theoretical perspective in the following pages must not obscure what I take as a principle of intellectual activity and political action, namely, that '[t]he intellectual's weapon in the battle against power is theory, not abstraction or obfuscation but theory as a practice, as a struggle against power' because it sustains the political interrogations required by the grievances against neo-liberalism.[10]

The justification for this approach lies in my judgement that, because such theories are 'essentially reflective, reflexive, and ironic,' they allow for the emergence of a knowledge of social relations which has these characteristics at the same time that they repudiate a 'positivist mode of knowing tied uncritically to natural science models of investigation' which is exactly one of the central grievances against neo-liberalism. Conversely, therefore, the need is for the type of approach which Timothy Luke has so eloquently encapsulated as 'a way of seeing and a form of knowing that employs historical knowledge, reflexive reasoning, and ironic awareness to give people some tools to realise new potentials for the emancipation and enlightenment of ordinary individuals today.' By extension, a critical theory approach not only enables criticism, but also, by refining people's thinking, it facilitates a consciousness of 'what must be done and how to do it.'

The notion that works such as this are unwelcome and unhelpful because they do not suggest an alternative is rejected out of hand: in their radical critique of what society is told to believe is the 'only alternative,' they explicitly render this a broadly perpetrated nonsense which must be challenged and overthrown, and implicitly suggest that a myriad of alternatives are on the agenda. And throughout, they raise the possibilities of the emergence of democratic or responsible polities by demystifying 'how power, position, and privilege relate to class, group, and personal inequalities.'[11] Notwithstanding these qualities, it is an approach which is inherently fallible because resistance, too, must deal with the inertia of the existing reality, and so recognise that it is subject to what

Machiavelli called *Fortuna*, and Clausewitz identified as 'friction.' Thus, as any strategic analyst familiar with her, or his, own literature will attest, human action by even the most competent agents, and in even the best of causes, is marked by the unexpected and the unintended as reactions neither wholly nor partially under one's control exert their influences over fluctuating conditions and outcomes.

Sensitive to this caution, but not being intimidated by it, the immediate constellation of problems posed by neo-liberalism, and that which animates my analysis, are delineated in the two chapters which comprise Part I. The first deals with the causes of the neo-liberal war. All histories of particular conflicts begin with such an account, and include what is known classically as *casus belli*, the justification for opening and maintaining hostilities (usually an unredressed injury), and so it does here. When undertaken, the conclusion is that this war, though staggering in its casualties, is far from unique because it joins so many others in which the declared causes are patently fraudulent. The declared need, ostensibly, was to bring progress and prosperity to the South, yet a working familiarity with the succession of documents which outline US visions and doctrine over the last two decades puts the lie to this. Though vision and doctrine should be related; indeed, the latter should logically proceed from the former, but they are not, in this case, related in any meaningful sense, except inversely. And the reason is straightforward: the promise to the South is untenable if the North is to remain dominant, to enjoy its current standard of living. The promise, then, is only a declaration devoid of intent, a consoling word for the dying. Indeed, to the extent that the South registers upon the consciousness of the North, and the sheer magnitude of its pathologies determine that they must, they do so primarily and almost exclusively as a profound and chronic threat to Northern privileges and cultures ensuring that, at best, the global South constitutes an intractable security problem which, only with imagination and the deft administration of aid, but more accurately conceived of as alms, might be managed.

The second takes the form of a survey, principally in the global South of the territorially expanding global combat zone as it appears through the classificatory device of battlefield *triage*, where, for the great majority of cases under review, the prognosis is (according to the standard NATO criteria and related colour codes) black, or bordering on black: no expectation of survival, palliative care only, and then only according to the dictates of 'scarcity' which is contrived on the basis of the margins of resource comfort which the survivors require in order to bother with ameliorative conduct in the first place. *Triage*, therefore, brings into the foreground the cleavage through all areas of life between the top 20 per cent (and declining) of the world's population who live well, and the remaining 80 per cent (and expanding) who live in increasingly straitened circumstances and prospects.

The question as to exactly how such an irreconcilable world should come about, let alone be legitimised in the first place is, therefore, the first inquiry undertaken, as Part II. In the first instance, the concern, here, is to show how ideas of a certain type were authorised within the more general regime of 'productive knowledge' which is the US university system. What emerges simultaneously, however, is the very successful attempt by the United States, at a time of widely understood relative decline, to not only ensure their adoption by the global economy, but also to subordinate these ideas to the overarching strategic objective which was, and is the containment of possible challengers to its pre-eminent position in global politics. That such a strategy required considerably distorting and misrepresenting the historical record which ostensibly supported the American arguments was never considered a disqualification, nor was the fact that the 'new economics' which emerged reflected more than a century of religious and political straitjacketing of American economists operating in the university system. And that is because intellectual argument and academic freedom within that system, and especially within Economics, have always been restrained by prior requirements to keep sacred and extol a particular American identity, regardless of the consequences.

Part III examines in detail the disfiguring nature of these consequences for the university-as-institution as it probes the ways in which, under permanent national security mobilisation, and rewarded accordingly for its contributions to the cause of the moment, the university's *modus operandi* becomes 'reason in the service of empire.'[12] Once again, it is considered irrelevant by so many observers, commentators, and academic specialists either to mention that the reason for, and reason in, the academy is debased in this assignation, or that it would take something as equally bankrupt and disfigured in all of its claims as the discipline of Economics to thrive because of it. From Reconstruction onwards, if not before, the tryst with the state has been the condition for advancement within, and the condition of, legitimacy without a social category seemingly impervious to paradox and the lived requirements of an examined life.

To anticipate the question, 'why is there such a concentration on the United States?', the answer is that it has been the prime mover and principal determinant of outcomes in so many of the developments under the rubric of economic globalisation, as it was, and is in global politics more generally. This, it should be understood, includes the entire panoply of international relations theory-as-practice which, to put it simply and accurately, underwent a process of Americanisation following World War II. Furthermore, quite apart from the fact that the United States is capitalist, neo-liberal, and the sole superpower, it is the only global actor with the power to initiate and implement a revolution of the type which neo-liberalism demands; conversely, it is the only global actor with the power to effect a negative veto on such developments and to ensure that whatever regime might emerge without its blessing would be ineffective. Thus, though numerous other actors have supported the US in the neo-liberal project, and their support undoubtedly contributed to its progress, the contours of the neo-liberal world would have been questionably global and its regulatory regime virtually discretionary without the US as the motor of change.

Appropriately then, the purpose of the first two of the three chapters which make up Part IV is to develop the identity which Economics shares with strategies of war. The approach is from the more general to the particular, from equivalences and convergences through to congruencies, to the point where they exist side by side as discourses of authorised mass violence derived from an identical font of modernist certainty, yet also necessarily resting on, and requiring religious discipline. For this reason, the *romanita* – that imperialism over the mind drawn from a combination of authority, and acceptance of that authority on the grounds of faith which is found in both Economics and Strategy – becomes the final analytical focus. It is inescapable given that the tragic consequences which follow in these notionally distinct realms are nothing other than logical extensions of prescriptions that are juridically inhuman, politically oppressive and reactionary, and scandalously anti-intellectual. What is more, they are to be understood as intentional and not accidental, as an assiduously acquired disposition to distort and to refuse integration and recognition of the human.

A discovery of this nature leaves this writer with few places to go. A conclusion is, of course, required and the convention is honoured. Besides, it serves two purposes, being as helpful for the writer as it is for the reader, notwithstanding that it retains an air of incredulity that the world should be governed by preposterous ideas and the return to times, habits of mind, and political-religious violence that we, inheritors of the Enlightenment tradition, were encouraged to think of as irrevocably in the past. Yet that is where we are going, not inevitably, but out of an implied or expressed preference for the single theory which is neo-liberalism to dominate all others to the point of exclusion and at catastrophic cost to humanity. A prescriptive catechism for endless war is at work whereby all inquiries lead to elements of the same answer, and that answer requires repetition in the name of fidelity: there is no alternative. Surveying the rise and intellectual implacability of neo-liberalism it is useful to recall August Strindberg's counter of 1905:

What is philosophy?
A seeking of the truth.

Then how can philosophy be a friend of the upper classes?
The upper classes pay the philosopher, in order that he may discover only such truths as are expedient in their eyes.

But suppose uncomfortable truths should be discovered?
They are called lies, and the philosopher gets no pay.

What is history?
The story of the past, presented in a light favourable to the interests of the upper classes.

Suppose the light is unfavourable?
That is scandalous.

What is a scandal?
Anything offending the upper classes.

What is aesthetics?
The art of praising or belittling works of art.

What works of art must be praised?
Those that glorify the upper classes.
Therefore Raphael and Michaelangelo are the most famous artists, for they glorified the religious falsehoods of the upper classes. Shakespeare magnified kings, and Goethe magnified himself, the writer for the upper classes.

But how about other works of art?
There must not be others.[13]

The attraction to venture further is, however, irresistible because, if it is the case that violent and preposterous ideas inform the governance of the world, is it not perfectly logical to question – and let's name it directly – the 'mental health' of the people who embrace these ideas, who herald them as being without an alternative, and who, by their embrace of them, suggest that they are as preposterous as the wisdom the ideas are alleged to contain? The more that this is pondered, the more that two propositions evolve in the form of epilogues which revisit, but under a very different light, some of the analytical material found in the preceding chapters: according to the first, if we accord neo-liberals good faith, and accept at face value their claims that they know the world through a modernist, scientifically certain prism which, through the cumulation of knowledge, allows for control and prediction – what Yeats described as the 'gift to set a statesman right' – then how is it that the world is in *triage*? Either market economics is the problem (but it can't be because economists define the market as perfect and beyond reproach and they have mathematical truth and certainty to support them), or the world is the problem (which it is, but according to economists its unruliness is amenable to subjugation by science), or economists are incompetent, or all three are in fact true, the last-mentioned especially so since it requires a particular mind-set to believe the first two while ignoring the evidence of the third.

To this end, and within the thematic of economic globalisation-as-war, the first epilogue adapts a leading seminal work of military incompetence for the purposes of theorising *triage* as an illustration of global strategic economic incompetence. What is argued is that the people attracted to Economics are precisely the type of people who find the discipline's neurotic obsession with abstract order in the market, and the corresponding obsession with excluding the human whenever it appears, to be therapeutic for their own anxieties. Expressed differently, the very people attracted to this discipline which pretends to global advice are the very people who should be excluded from anything of the sort. To make this argument a certain speculative fancy is indulged; that is freely admitted, but it is not to deny the legitimacy of the flight if it strikes responsive chords.

Possibilities foreshadowed in the first epilogue are realised in the second – as a satire on the theme of Economics – as mental illness. This proposition, however, is less kind and proceeds from the assumption that, on the basis of the available evidence, and the insights which other disciplines in the social sciences offer, the good faith accorded neo-liberals is inappropriate. Fortunately, this is an approach which is considerably aided and abetted by those economists who, having observed the behaviour of their disciplinary community, have openly acknowledged defining aspects of its insanity. Moreover, the use of satire complements the common intention to 'send humour on a moral errand,' or to commit the crime of political arson, and even, as is my objective with regard to Economics, to seek 'death by ridicule'[14] for a set of ruling ideas which is not only riven with incoherencies, and the cause of widespread death and suffering, but which, in those which espouse them, inculcates deliberate indifference to the plight of billions. A brief passage by John O'Donohue captures the core of a doctrine so bleak that it was never fit for the table of human consumption and could only ever have been *bottled for the altar in a stone abbey / by an enclosed order.*[15]

Part I

1 Neo-liberal war

Casus belli, promises of progress, strategies of dominance, fraud

It is difficult to be original in describing the character, or the context, of the present. That it is a war that has been underway longer than the two World Wars of the twentieth century is not in doubt. That its *casus belli* was, and remains neo-liberalism is not in doubt: at every turn, on every available occasion, the belief is repeated among the world's major economic actors that this doctrine is both an imperative and the only acceptable principle on which to organise human – which is to say, social, political, and economic life. Indeed, so dogmatically is it affirmed that the steps to conducting an offensive in its name are virtually little more than reflexes, loosely automatic responses to the stimuli of power and opportunity. In time, and because of the scope of breadth and depth of the offensive, the physics of the vortex came into play. States, organisations, communities and people were irresistibly drawn into its constant round of frenetic activity, rapid change and destruction. Yet, at no stage did its strategists require it to undergo the one test of political action, namely, whether it made things better, or stopped them getting worse for the great majority of people who would have to bear its consequences.

This refusal constitutes a criminal abdication of command responsibility, not least towards the global South (though increasingly, if not with the same immediate consequences, in the global North as well). And the reason is clear: in the first instance, it must be understood that global inequality, that is, within and between states, is not just an issue in economic globalisation, it is the central, defining issue against which all grand strategies for humankind must perforce be judged. Absent efficacy on this issue and the strategy at hand is no more than a charade; should it make matters worse, it is an immoral charade. Thus, second, it is sufficient to recall that, what the North promised at the outset, and continues to promise to this day, at least in a declaratory sense, is that the South will enjoy a northerly transition from its current parlous state to a state of affluence and political reasonableness (always given sufficient time, pain, and if need be, menaces). If this were not the case, then it would be insulting to the South for academics, professionals, business people, international and non-governmental organisations, and commentators to arrange, convene and write on the theme of this division since it would make of its members little more than voyeurs, or worse, dilettantes.

It is, therefore, outrageous that any strategic assessment of the project must report that, having been constantly being put to the test, and found to be failing, the promise is subordinated to matters of more immediate concern to the North (and its adjunct, the West) which cause it to veer off into other directions, or even the familiar political void which attends the global political questions posed by the very mention of the term 'South.' The permanency of the South is thus ensured, thereby raising the question whether its ongoing existence is acceptable and even desired. But neither the dogma which is neo-liberalism, nor the offensive in its name ever abates; indeed, they comprise dreadful constants of chronic grand strategic fraud when it is realised that they pre-dated the Cold War, outlived it, and are operational now in a time in which two facts confront the North's declarations and promises: the relevant structures and trajectories of politics, demographics, geoeconomics, geostrategy, geopolitics, climate change and resource supply which are heavily weighted against the South's northerly transition, and the unwelcome but predictable rise of strong southern polarities within the North itself. Writing in 1944, but not about the war then underway for half a decade, but about the conflict which had sundered his own country's self-congratulatory notions about itself some sixty years earlier, the American poet and biographer, Carl Sandburg, captured the times with typical sensitivity:

> It had happened before in other countries among other peoples bewildered by economic necessity, by the mob oratory of politicians and editors, by the ignorance of the educated classes, by the greed of the propertied classes, by elemental instincts touching race and religion, by the capacity of so many men, women, and children for hating what they do not understand while believing they do understand completely and perfectly what no one understands except tentatively and hazardously.[1]

The present, then, as seen with the help of Sandburg, is as much, if not more than, any other time in history, a time of deceits, of opposites and oppositions, of reality masquerading as science, of unchallengeable wisdom, and of contradictions and paradoxes. But it is like no other war in many other ways as well. The Theatre of Operations, and thus, the Campaign, and thus, even the Front, is everywhere, recalling the boastful motto of the Royal Artillery – *ubique* – making it more truly a World War than either of its two named predecessors. The principal casualties are non-combatants, but that, too, is to commit an anachronism because no distinctions are apparent, certainly none are made, and in any case, none are possible, because everyone is in the line of fire. Moved by the possibility of such a state of affairs in the middle of the seventeenth century, Thomas Hobbes wrote his defence of absolute monarchy, *The Leviathan*, never conceiving of the possibility that, in certain forms, the governance he advocated might realise what he feared most – 'a known disposition' to fighting a 'war of every man against every man.'

The argument, in greater detail, takes the following form. It begins with a brief survey of the major 'vision,' 'guidance' and 'national strategy' documents, and broad-ranging, unclassified intelligence assessments starting in 1988, and coming through to 2006, which outline continuities, fractures and preoccupations in the US view of the global political world, now, and into the (apparently) foreseeable future of 2025. In effect, what this survey does is abstract from these documents a sense of the significance of the North–South divide in security terms; simultaneously, it reveals the nature of threats that exist in, and to global politics from the perspective of Washington, DC.

As the sole surviving superpower from the Cold War; indeed, the first ever military and economic hyper-power in many respects, an assessment of the quality and character of the view from the US is mandatory. In any case, the US has been the engine of change in economic globalisation to date and there is no credible alternative power that could suffice in this role for the time being. And this is not to ignore the profound problems which beset American power and severely qualify it, now and into the future. It makes little sense to appeal to 'the global North,' or 'the West' as actors which are internally constituted on an equal basis because, quite simply, they are not: for the most part, when they act effectively, they are led, and subordinate to the United States. Even less does it make sense to invoke the reality of an 'international community' which embodies the will to act because, when imperatives to do so have arisen, it has foundered on such challenges, as witness Bosnia, East Timor, Rwanda, and lately, Sudan. Though still in currency, its status is that of illusion, or an elaborate entity akin to The Keeper of the Privy Seal of Scotland,[2] content with an occasional, pious invocation and ceremonial honours. Similarly, the European Union, is to be viewed critically: possessed of an ageing population and stagnant levels of economic growth, it is additionally preoccupied with the process of expansion and tendencies which seriously reduce its cohesion, notwithstanding its ambitions to play a major role internationally. Post-Cold War political differences, exacerbated by US unilateralism on such issues as The Kyoto Protocol and the 2003 war against Iraq, have also undermined the solidarity once found in the Trans-Atlantic Alliance. As for the others thought to have, or be gaining influence, Japan remains with an uncertain economic future; China and India, both rising powers, have internal problems which require ongoing attention and resources, and Russia is admitted to the G8 summits as a pretender rather than on economic performance of the type needed. For the history of economic globalisation to the present, and for the foreseeable future, what Jeff Faux calls the 'Party of Davos' relies on US financial and military aid as the ultimate guarantors of the neo-liberal globalisation project.[3] Essentially, the recent and current global economic regime is, in John Gray's words, an artefact of American power and, as in its own hyperbole of self, found throughout the vision documents, the US would appear to be indispensable, as detailed by Barry C. Lynn, former executive editor of the magazine, *Global Business*:

> The global economy was created by the American state. Absent a clear-minded effort by the United States to manage this system – in ways amenable to the large majority of the peoples around the world who depend on it – it will slowly fall to pieces.[4]

What becomes apparent with even a brief examination of this literature is that 'guidance' and 'national strategy' are not necessarily correlated with 'vision,' and 'intelligence.' Furthermore, if due allowance is made for the common objectives found in all of them, and their paucity of political-economic analysis, there remains a radical disjunction between the documents describing the state of the world – the 'vision' documents – and those setting forth US national strategy. If, as logic would determine, the latter should proceed from the former via an explicit acknowledgment of the situation as a whole, the limits it sets to ambition, and action, then it must be concluded that the latter is not only radically incomplete but of uncertain provenance. And if, as is necessary, these visions are augmented with still wider and longer visions (as is done by way of a second investigation), then it is certainly that the doctrinal statements are incapable of expressing anything resembling a realisable grand strategy.

Accounting for this moves the inquiry into its third dimension which is best understood as a syndrome comprising Western and American pessimism, and its hard exoskeleton, strategic denial, in the face of an intractable world in general and a global South beyond both rescue and redemption in particular.[5] It is a disposition replete with its own support network of academically respectable accommodation, religious consolation (for those so inclined), political disenchantment, and distracting security priorities, though just one of the aforementioned is a necessary and sufficient cause to develop and sustain the prevailing mindset.

Finally, the Great Fraud. By extension, the very question as to whether the US and its western cohorts have a credible grand strategy for both its own future and the real and urgent material improvement of the global South, or is capable of expressing one, and this includes one that others might follow in relation to the latter, is redundant, and especially so if the mantra of solutions routinely proffered for its ills is examined, as they are by way of the third analytical foray. Not wishing to countenance defeat in public statements, nor endure the possibility of guilt for what is denied, the West and the United States enjoin the South to accept responsibility for what others, in the main, have done to it. More, it is to express contrition for its condition by positive acts indicating radical transformation. It is, therefore, to overcome its pathologies by exploiting the opportunities which present themselves in the guise of debt forgiveness, and to accept the salvific grace of neo-liberalism as sacramentally administered by the Bretton Woods institutions, the World Trade Organization (WTO) and various arrangements such as the regional free trade agreements. Universal education, as defined, and under conditions determined by these neo-liberal arrangements is to proceed alongside a determination to apply new technologies, develop good governance, and the embrace of market reforms.

In all, this is a project that requires the South to be inhabited and governed by people totally indifferent to public affairs which perforce concern them (those that, in ancient Greece, were known as the *idiotes*, or in current English, idiots), or charlatans. The reasons are straightforward: in the first instance all of the proposals which have the *imprimatur* of the US are, inferentially, direct and truthful in the expression of their primary objective, the maintenance of US hegemony in the face of various challenges, and the ways this will be effected, and these include all of the above measures; second, any acquaintance with the meaning attached to these means towards the ends of alleviation and improvement, and their consequences as so far experienced, would determine that not only are their protagonists lacking in good faith, in truth they comprise a blatantly dishonest subterfuge for ongoing subjection not least because, in the United States itself, neo-liberalism is steadily ensuring a southerly aspect throughout the country.

By any lights, this is a grand strategic farce. At the declaratory level, it is contemptible in its range of denials and rejections. It recalls Wilfrid Laurier's reproachful speech in Canada's House of Commons following the *Metis* Rebellion:

What is hateful... [are] the men, who, having the enjoyment of power, do not discharge the duties of power; they are the men, who, having the power to redress wrongs, refuse to listen to the petitioners that are sent to them; they are the men, who, when they are asked for a loaf, give a stone.[6]

Yet, it is insufficient to stop with dismissal. On the operational level the hollow pretence of grand strategy mocked actually fulfils the criteria for a successful grand strategy as much as any which come to mind when viewed *inversely* – thus, not as a genuine attempt to assist the South out of its pathological condition, but as a highly evolved science and art form which seeks, through the integration of policies, armaments and resources, to control and utilise the resources of a coalition of nations led, or dominated by the United States, to the end that its vital interests are effectively promoted and secured against all challenges so that the resort to war is either rendered unnecessary or is undertaken with the maximum chance of victory. In other words, it is possible to conclude on the basis of rigorous logic that the strategy is working perfectly. The predominance of farce is nevertheless inescapable. Put simply and crudely, grand strategic visions that are blind to grand strategic obstacles will result only in grand strategic failure. That is the prospect and it should be declared as such. It is within this understanding and this realisation that the following analysis proceeds. It begins with a discussion of how the world is seen, especially from the vantage point of the United States, because within that vision lies the explicit promise and presence of the fraud.

OF AMERICAN VISIONS, INTELLIGENCE, GUIDANCE, REVIEWS AND NATIONAL STRATEGY

The vision is to be found throughout eight selected documents, beginning with one that is produced at a time in which post-Cold War scenarios had to be taken seriously. Together, they constitute a representative, if not exhaustive body of material on how the US views, and most importantly, understands the world. They are interrogated, however, only for the light they throw on global inequality, as follows:

Discriminate Deterrence: Report of The Commission On Integrated Long-term Strategy (1988).[7]

Defense Planning Guidance (a draft Department of Defense Report, subsequently revised) published in *The New York Times* on 8 March 1992.[8]

Air Force 2025, A Report prepared by the 2025 Support Office, Air University, and developed by Air University Press Educational Services Directorate, College of Aerospace Doctrine, Research and Education, Maxwell Air Force Base, Alabama (1996).[9]

United States Space Command, *Vision for 2020* (1997).[10]

Global Trends 2015: A Dialogue About the Future With Nongovernment Experts (Publication approved by the National Foreign Intelligence Board under the authority of Director of Central Intelligence (2000)).[11]

The National Security Strategy of the United States of America, published by the authority of the President of the United States (2002).[12]

Mapping the Global Future: Report of the National Intelligence Council's 2020 Project (2004).[13]

QUADRENNIAL DEFENSE REVIEW REPORT (2006)[14]

As with Orwell's pigs, not all vision documents are equal and two inequalities are immediately apparent. The first is that if we are to plot the origins of current US strategy, then *Discriminate Deterrence*, in 1988, was the neo-conservative template for *NSS 2002* in particular and what is now identified as the Bush Doctrine. It established the line of pedigree which emerged, albeit slightly modified, in *DPG 1992* (which the Clinton Administration disingenuously withdrew from the public eye in the face of widespread criticism and temporarily replaced it with something more acceptable), and re-emerged in the prescriptions of the Project for the New American Century (PNAC), which then found doctrinal expression in the first Administration of George W. Bush. (Interestingly, this does not accord with the conventional wisdom which holds that the genesis of the Bush Doctrine was PNAC; on the contrary, it is not markedly discontinuous with the development of US strategic doctrine going back 14 years before *NSS 2002*, and it is worth noting, therefore, that one of the two Co-Chairmen of the Presidential Commission was Albert Wohlstetter a figure of seminal influence among some of the leading neo-conservatives).[15] The current relevance of individual vision documents, therefore, is gauged according to their philosophical fidelity to the central tenets of that 1988 Report from the Reagan Administration.

This is to say no more than that this line of documents reflect the traditional and consistent preoccupations of a pre-eminent power determined to remain one. Rising powers and possible threats (albeit with insufficient attention to political Islam) from the central unifying enemy, the Soviet Union, but also in Central Asia, Central America and the Middle East, satisfy the need for geostrategic anxiety globally and locally. Implicitly, Western Europe and the United Nations (UN) are downgraded as is the doctrine of deterrence. Quite explicitly, the solutions are to be found in the continuation of both US financial might and the technological superiority it will enjoy over all rivals. As would be expected from a unanimous report contributed to by Henry Kissinger, *Discriminate Deterrence* is a geopolitical manifesto of the type that could have been produced, and were, in the late nineteenth century. Clearly, then, it is the forebear of much that is current in US thinking and practice.

For this reason it is also worth concentrating on that for what it brought forth as regards the global South. It was an apparently unanimous document, produced by a group of 13 of America's leading experts in global politics and strategic analysis, who convened as the Presidential Commission on the Integrated Long-term Strategy under the co-chairmanship of (then) recently retired Under-Secretary for Defense, Fred Ikle and RAND Corporation nuclear strategist, Albert Wohlstetter, and included Zbigniew Brzezinski, Samuel P. Huntington, Henry Kissinger, and generals Andrew Goodpaster and John W. Vessey, in answer to questions posed by 'the changing security environment' of the time. Appropriately, it was described by the historian, Paul Kennedy, as 'one of the most important public overviews of what American grand strategy should be, as seen by its intellectual and policy-influencing elite, or at least an important part of it.'[16]

On Africa and Latin America, theatres of what *Discriminate Deterrence* describes as either 'Third World Conflicts' or 'low intensity conflicts' (the forerunner of 'asymmetric warfare'), the matter of their tragic economic, political, and social circumstances is simply not mentioned, either in themselves, or as a constellation of causes of the insurgencies, paramilitary crime, sabotage, terrorism, and other forms of intra-state violence.[17] Rather, the concern is with these effects and, thus, their causes, as permanent, implacable security threats to 'US interests' which, over the long term, will need to be managed and/or ultimately defeated in a *military* sense.[18] Expressed differently, though the Presidential Commission is fully versed in the minimal understanding that the 'new inequality' is, or might be, conducive to violence against US interests, it is insensitive to the prior reality that the condition itself is an ongoing act of violence by those interests against Africa and Latin America. Thus, the notion that the resolution of the condition and its consequences lie in radical economic reform and the establishment of regimes of real political and social justice, and that the predatory capitalism which has determined so much of Africa and Latin America's misery might be an appropriate site of investigation and understanding is totally absent. Absent is any sense of obligation towards the victims of power politics as victims, or in any other guise for that matter. Subsequently, there is little deviation from these themes and their treatment in successive vision statements with the exception that, post-9/11, Islamic radicalism and international terrorism occupy the category vacated by the Soviet Union.

The second is that, to the extent that these documents display an awareness of the need to factor global, non-territorial threats such as North–South inequality, or the anti-democratic tendencies of multinational corporations, into strategic planning as other than a management challenge (and admittedly this is rare), the less likely they are to be centred towards US operational strategy. Expressed differently, there is an inverse relationship between the emphasis they place on the need for non-geostrategic awareness and, crucially, the expression of this in contemporary doctrine. Accordingly, there is a need to differentiate between two evident lines in the documents – one that demonstrates an awareness beyond territorial threats, geopolitics and geostrategy, and another which cannot, or will not integrate this wider reality into its calculation and judgement but which nevertheless speak *ad authoritarium*. Hence only in *DPG 1992*, *NSS 2002*, and *QDDR 2006* is there no mention of any of the great global pathologies frequently, and sometimes prominently cited – such as accelerating inequality, burgeoning population, debilitating rates of change, and disease which are frequently foregrounded in the others.

One characteristic does change, however: after *Discriminate Deterrence* in 1988, the line gradually substitutes histrionics for meaningful action and their overall tenor becomes hysterical to the point of being an identifiable national 'personality disorder.' In the playing out of doctrine-as-strategy (and its reverse) this is demonstrated by observable, dominant characteristics which range from the tendency to overdramatise situations, to a lack of self-criticism, to manipulative behaviour and behavioural instability. Thus, whereas *Discriminate Deterrence* was 'traditional' in the sense that, notwithstanding its evasions and lack of imagination, it was pessimistic as to its expectations of global order and how it would be maintained, kept its technophilia almost under control, but nevertheless sober in its assessments, those that followed it in the 1990s substantially lost this ability as they increasingly incorporated such devices as the baffle-gab of management-speak and Alvin Toffler's sophomoric divinations of the future into their conclusions. From an examination of their formats over time, it is also hard to escape the conclusion that they were executive summaries of findings reached in isolation on the basis of information which had been hermetically sealed from comprehensive intelligence, in receipt of the official *imprimatur*, and no more than presentations designed to be delivered by PowerPoint rather than national security documents which need to be ventilated by dialogue and debate. With the appearance of *QDDR 2006* these impediments to meaning were present in indigestible quantities but they had by then been joined for nearly four years by the return of apocalyptic thinking which is the hallmark of the Bush Doctrine.

What was in 1988 expressed as a general concern regarding terrorism, is found in a more refined and elaborate form as the combination of 'radicalism and technology' (religious extremists in possession of weapons of mass destruction) assisted or facilitated by weak, and rogue states prepared to take the risks of retaliation. Extrapolating from 9/11, the threat postulated in early Bush Doctrine statements is, therefore, 'imminent, multifaceted, undeterrable, and potentially calamitous ...to the United States.'[19] By 2006 and the publication of *QDDR 2006*, these threats required a long war, a 20-year strategy, and the deployment of US troops in a host of countries, often clandestinely, fighting terrorism and other non-traditional threats in a theatre of war covering the entire world; essentially, the ambition of the US now extends to controlling global security on its own terms, with or without the cooperation of allies and friends.

Two conclusions follow. The first is that the Bush Doctrine is not so much a strategy as the neurosis of a self-pitying superpower raised to the level of a strategy. While in full accord with the judgement that the attacks of 9/11 (and other acts for which Al Qaeda is responsible) were obscene and unjustified mass murder, it cannot be the case that these reminders of common vulnerability that the US experienced justifies it in imposing its new and now persistent anxiety upon the rest of humanity by way of fiat since it does not share America's experiences nor its current circumstances (as much as many might want to enjoy the benefits of the latter). The second is that, as this condition has become entrenched, and the US has entered a fugue state, so too has the US dissociated itself from not only the intolerable situation of the world whose challenges are more comprehensively detailed, but also its responsibilities, among them the need to alleviate the situation of the South in other than in formulaic injunctions. Put another way, it is not as though the US is unaware of the situation, or that it lacks the intellectual and imaginative resources to identify it – several of the vision documents attest to the contrary; rather, it has deliberately chosen to exclude the various factors and trends in those documents when strategy and doctrine are promulgated. The reasons for this default will emerge after the closer audit which follows.

WIDER VISIONS, LONGER SIGHT

The first observation which might be made is that the world is faced with serious, non-traditional, non-geopolitical threats on a global scale considerably greater than tends to be acknowledged in the ignored vision documents. These comprise frequently interrelated environmental factors, or problems of not only great bearing upon global security and the possibility of improvements in the conditions of the global South, but of survival itself. And, while it is true that some were mentioned briefly in the vision documents, they required elaboration; crucially, others were simply absent. Numerous sources are available for an inventory but a consolidated account is found of twelve of them in *Collapse: How Nations Choose to Fail or Survive*,[20] a work by the biogeographer and evolutionary psychologist, Jared Diamond which, where appropriate, has been supplemented by related material.

Diamond divides these problems into four sub-categories, the first of which is the destruction, or losses of natural resources. So classified is the loss of natural habitats (which includes forests, wetland, coral reefs and the ocean bottom), the depletion of protein providing wild food stocks by over-exploitation, the decline in biodiversity, and the soil loss which is consequent upon the combined effects of unsustainable human agricultural practices: acidification, alkalinisation, desertification, erosion and salination.[21] Hunger is the immediate consequence and the present, let alone the future prospects are dismal; indeed, it is part of an emerging pattern in Africa, Central America, and South-east Asia, and is even being observed in Australia and parts of Western Europe according to reports by the United Nations Food and Agriculture Organisation's climate change group.[22] According to a 2004 estimate, 852 million people go hungry every day – equivalent to the combined populations of North America, Japan, and Europe – and this figure has been on the increase for the last decade.[23]

The second relates to the limits of supply for cheap energy in the form of fossil fuels, fresh water and what is termed photosynthetic capacity – the finite supply of sunlight for the purposes of growing crops and wild plants in those parts of the world with the necessary water and heat.[24] As a result of the sharp rise in the price of gasoline, it is the demand for fossil fuels that receives the greatest attention in the North because it is slowly being appreciated that this is the harbinger of something more critical, and it is. Notwithstanding the acrimonious debate between the protagonists and antagonists over 'peak oil' (declining availability of oil in general, or which is not economically viable to recover) there is a widespread, if not unanimous consensus among specialists that two drivers are responsible: one is a decrease in the growth of energy supplies at a time of accelerating demand, and the other is the increasing volatility of the existing supply as a result of the geopolitical competition for it. Exacerbating this is the absence of any real replacement for oil and gas among the candidate alternatives – synthetic oil, biomass, liquefied natural gas, wind, and solar power – that is credible, technologically developed, commercially available, and politically acceptable.[25] Scarcity is therefore a reality and so are, and will be for some considerable time, the conflictual consequences which go with a world addicted to oil for both its aspirations and the maintenance of its standards of living.

For now, this extant problem overshadows most, but certainly not all of the threats and issues which receive far greater prominence in the official US vision documents. By way of putting it in an easy-to-understand perspective, it dwarfs the 9/11 terrorist attacks; in fact, it might more accurately be compared to the casualties (dead and wounded) arising from the US-led coalition war against Iraq between 2003 and 2006 (by some authoritative estimates, well in excess of 100,000 dead) but *annually*. According to the data collected and analysed by the World Health Organization, and published in the journal, *Nature*, the Earth's warming climate is estimated to cause more than 150,000 deaths and five million illnesses each year, with these figures doubling by 2030.[26] Using the same data, health and climate scientists at the University of Wisconsin at Madison, who conducted one of the most comprehensive studies yet to measure the impact of global warming on health, noted that the rising temperatures caused by the affluent North disproportionately affect the poor countries of the South who are not responsible for them.[27] Left unaddressed, a catastrophe is in the making. According to the estimated projections by Christian Aid, and supported by Sir John Houghton, former co-chairman of the scientific assessment group of the Intergovernmental Panel on Climate Change, 182 million Africans will die from it by the century's end.[28]

The perversity of the Bush Administration provides additional grounds for understanding the security implications of climate change. As if it is not enough that the bare statistics are indicative of casualties never seen even in the wars between advanced industrial states, Sir David King, Chief Scientist for the British Government, and former Chief UN weapons inspector in Iraq, Hans Blix, both voiced their views that it is a threat greater than terrorism.[29] They were followed very closely by two independent, but almost identical studies commissioned by two of the most conservative institutions in global politics. The first was executed on the instructions of the World Bank, and concluded not only that 'global warming required immediate action,' but that the World Bank itself should 'aggressively increase its investments in renewable energies [and] should concentrate on promoting the transition to renewable energy' (away from its current lending policy of dedicating 94 per cent to oil and just 6 per cent to renewables). As the *Financial Times* reported in February 2004, the World Bank (WB) rejected the recommendations of the independent panel of experts that it had appointed.[30]

The second was a report commissioned by Andrew Marshall,[31] head of the Department of Defense Office of Net Assessment, which, on the basis of scenarios which are widely accepted as plausible, advised the Pentagon that climate change 'should be elevated beyond a scientific debate to a US national security concern' because of the potential it has for creating global anarchy as countries take unilateral action to defend and secure their dwindling food, water, and energy resources as conditions deteriorate.[32] By way of elaboration:

> Rather than decades or even centuries of gradual warming, recent evidence suggests the possibility that a more dire climate scenario may actually be unfolding.[33]

> By 2005 the climatic impact of the shift is felt more intensely in certain regions around the world. More severe storms and typhoons bring about higher storm surges and floods in low-lying islands such as Tarawa and Tuvalu (near New Zealand).

In 2007, a particularly severe storm causes the ocean to break through levees in the Netherlands making a few key coastal cities such as The Hague unlivable. Failures of the delta island levees in the Sacramento River region in the Central Valley of California create an inland sea and disrupt the aqueduct system transporting water from northern to southern California because salt water can no longer be kept out of the area during the dry season.... As glacial ice melts, sea levels rise and as wintertime sea extent decreases, ocean waves increase in intensity, damaging coastal cities. Additionally millions of people are put at risk of flooding around the globe (roughly 4 times 2003 levels), and fisheries are disrupted as water temperature changes cause fish to migrate to new locations and habitats, increasing tensions over fishing rights.[34]

In summary form, Schwartz and Randall foresee:

fishing wars between Spain and Portugal. Pakistan, India, and China – all armed with nuclear weapons – skirmish at their borders over refugees, access to shared rivers, and arable land. Bangladesh becomes uninhabitable. Drought hits the American breadbasket. Britain's weather begins to resemble Siberia. India, South Africa, and Indonesia are ripped apart by civil war. And ultimately, the report forecasts a decrease in the planet's human carrying capacity, leading to sharp reductions in the world's population due to starvation, disease, and war.[35]

As with the World Bank report, *An Abrupt Climate Change Scenario* was also suppressed by the Pentagon for some four months. When it was released – leaked in matter of fact at approximately the same time that a large body of respected scientists were criticising the White House for 'cherry-picking' science to suit its policy agenda – the decision had by then been taken to ignore it in terms consistent with comments by official spokespeople talking the following forms:

'I haven't seen it, I haven't read it and I don't want to make comments on the matter. As I understand it, this is a 'what-if' scenario – not a diagnosis, not a prophecy, and not a foundation for new policy.'

Dana Perino, White House Council on Environmental Quality

'Andrew Marshall is our *Yoda*, our big thinker who peers into the future. But it's all speculation. It was very ethereal, very broad in scope. It wasn't like, "Oh, wow, that totally debunks the President's stand on global warming," because *it was merely a thought exercise*.'

Lieutenant Dan Hetlage, USN, The Pentagon[36]

What needs to be appreciated is that, quite apart from the inference that, in the Bush Administration, the reading of evidence and broad thinking are inimical to policy formulation, but prophecy is not, the provenance of *this document* was virtually impeccable; indeed, almost from within a so-called policy community which is noted for its conviviality to the neo-conservative ascendancy. Marshall, for instance, is widely regarded as a

'Pentagon legend,' a senior official of long experience, who is given credit for being behind the policy of Ballistic Missile Defence development.[37] As for the consultants, Peter Schwartz is a CIA consultant and former head of planning for Shell Oil; Doug Randall is a senior member of the California-based think tank, Global Business Network. *An Abrupt Climate Change Scenario* was, therefore, no more welcome than a predecessor document, an Environmental Protection Agency report dealing with climate change which attracted so much interference from the White House that the Secretary for the Environment, Christine Todd Whitman, finally had to eliminate the section on global warming![38]

Human production and movement provide the third of Diamond's groupings: essentially this is the generation of toxic chemicals and atmospheric gases at rates which exceed the Earth's ability to degrade them, and the transportation of species from places where they are native and in balance to other places where they are, literally, alien and destructive of the local environment.[39] Notably, this problem illustrates the common phenomenon which is the intersection of one set of global problems with another, in this case the current and forecast use of burning fossil fuels, which produce the principal source of 'greenhouse gases,' with debilitating climate change. It also illustrates the Sisyphean nature of the condition overall: without alternatives to fossil fuels, rising global demand will continue to be satisfied within the limits of diminishing global supply and at increasing costs and growing political tensions – a process which will raise the level of 'greenhouse gases' by 60 per cent between 2002 and 2025.[40]

Finally, there is the constellation of population problems beyond those mentioned in the vision documents of simply having more people to provide for and the social and political incoherence this can result in – namely, their impact on the environment as increased numbers of people consume ever more resources and produce ever more waste and heat as the North continues its high-impact lifestyles, and the South aspires to the living standards of the North. Interleaving this are a less-than-understood counter-phenomena: according to Joseph Chamie, former Director of the United Nations Population Division, the population of the more developed regions of the world as a whole is almost certainly not going to increase beyond its current 1.2 billion whereas nearly half of the global population growth of 2.5 billion over the next 45 years will take place in just six countries – India, China, Pakistan, Nigeria, Indonesia, and Bangladesh.[41] Nor is it just a matter of numbers. Exacerbating them will be the effects of poor health in general, and epidemics in particular (and most particularly in Africa) – where increased mortality and morbidity due to lack of access to clean water and sanitation, coupled with the increasing prevalence of preventable diseases such as cholera, diarrhoea, malaria, measles, and pneumonia which currently are the causes of 11 million *infant* deaths.[42] HIV/AIDS infection, now globally at 78 million, casts an inescapable shadow over the future. In combination these pathologies dwarf even the 2004 Indian Ocean *tsunami* that killed 150,000 people.[43] The definite need for highly skilled and educated labour in the developed world (see immediately below) must also be seen as an intensifying force because, even now, it is estimated that half of the South's graduates are living abroad, with about one-third of research and development professionals residing in the OECD countries.[44]

In the same period, the populations of 51 countries are likely to be smaller than they presently are: among these are the Russian Federation (smaller by 31 million), Ukraine (down by 20 million or 43 per cent), and Japan (losing 16 million). In addition, on current and probable trends, 65 countries accounting for 43 per cent of world population will experience decline and/or ageing since they now have a well-established fertility pattern which is at, or below, the replacement level of 2.1 children per woman. With increased longevity in the developed world, by 2050, one person in three in many countries – such as Italy, Japan, and Spain – will be aged 65 or older, raising fundamental questions about how they will be supported, whether their respective pension schemes will be robust enough to provide for them financially, and what their level of disposition towards the rest of the world might be.[45]

More importantly, it is only when in possession of this injuriously brief list of parameters that we can begin to ask fundamental questions about arresting the transition of many states in the global South from being merely vulnerable, to the categories of failing, and ultimately, failed states (which is the current plight of countries home to 2 billion people), and of why some of them resort to underworld exports (terrorists, drugs and drug networks, and illegal arms).[46] To speak of the 'prospects for democracy' as a realisable outcome from current conditions in the global South is, therefore, meaningless rhetoric. Phrased differently, if questions about the carrying capacity of the planet are taken seriously, then questions about the very possibility of the numerically predominant global South being able to embark on a northerly transition under current and foreseeable modes of energy consumption and waste production which are not even sustainable for the North as it is, qualify as *non sequiturs* in both of that term's common meanings: they do not logically follow from any defensible premise, and they are absurd in the context of a comprehensive understanding of global realities.

EXPLORING GRAND STRATEGIC DENIAL: THE SYNDROME

It is often truthfully said that trend is not destiny, but the truth of the statement relies upon the trend changing because the theories which informed the original trend were revised as a result of discernment, or rejected and replaced as a result of dire necessity. This takes us back to grand strategy, or more precisely, how and why the US and the developed world in general do not have a grand strategy for the alleviation of conditions in the global South. Thus, if it is the case that the vision, guidance, intelligence, reviews and doctrinal statements are manifestly inadequate to the declared objectives of the North, not to mention deeply insulting to the history and daily experiences of the great majority of the world's population, then there is a need to account for what amounts to a grand strategic denial. Accounting for it, of course, might not change the North, but it might underline the great fraud which accompanies the denial for what it is. In this light, a start should be with the failure which higher (university-level) education brings to this deceit. This matter occupies Part III of this work and is there treated at greater length; for now, a few brief outlines of the problem require mention.

The suggestion is that there is merit in recalling Albert Camus who, in *The Rebel*, wrote: 'Man at bottom is not entirely guilty because he inherits history, nor is he entirely innocent since he continues it.' Inferentially, if continuation in the face of the need to change makes guilt inescapable, then continuation in the face of repeated failure, or in the name of status or wealth is a high crime. The modern, western, research university is the general site of such criminality with its particular locus to be found proximate to the Faculty of Economics and that sub-discipline of International Relations which is International Political Economy. Of course there are exceptions but it is the rule which must be indicted.

The university itself is now a ruined neurotic: when needing recourse to a defensive privilege for some reason or another, it proclaims itself to be a community of scholars; for the remainder of the time it operates as, and treats its staff and students accordingly, a large and frequently multinational corporation. Several historical influences were at work in this transformation but the end of the Cold War and its conjunction with the rise of neo-liberalism and economic globalisation were among the most significant.[47] As progressive tax cuts translated themselves into the abdication by government for adequate public education funding, the universities had to demonstrate their 'relevance' to those that would step into the breach. No longer funded by governments, or benefactors, or other corporations as a place which educates, they diversified into producing credentials for any sphere of activity that could be bent to a degree structure over three or four years and which, on the basis of a cost-benefit analysis, encouraged students to enrol in them. The transaction was, and remains an unhappy one: from the student perspective, students are clients; from the universities' perspective, they are income generators.[48]

How does this affect knowledge of the global South? Answer: in a profound way. Ask another question: do neo-liberal economic employers of graduates in Economics and International Political Economy actually demand educated, critical scholars with a nuanced and sophisticated understanding of global politics (broadly defined) when their preoccupation is with shareholder satisfaction? Another question still: which, and how many neo-liberal economic employers want to be reminded by their staff that, no matter what current and likely policies are for dealing with the mega-trends in global politics, they are utterly and hopelessly inadequate? In the belief that the respective answers are no, and very few, the question that then arises is: 'how are global politics addressed?' The answer is by relatively sophisticated denial, but denial nevertheless. It takes the form of endowing the discipline of Economics with scientific status and embracing its pronouncements as revealed truth – a form of religious consolation. Economics, however, modelled itself on a Physics which never existed in nature, and justly has become an Economics which doesn't exist in humanity.

For current purposes it is to be noted that the dominant narratives of Economics and International Political Economy are blind when it comes to recognising poverty in the South. As Tooze and Murphy have shown, the premises of Economics and the idealised rational economic actor at its core and so beloved of its theories are inapplicable to 'human beings *en masse* in a large, modern economy.'[49] To this must be added the problems which arise from ignoring that the Southern poor lack the power to make the type of rational choices which northern economists take more or less for granted in their calculations, and ignoring as well the fact that so much of economic activity in the South involves little, or no money, and is therefore invisible to empiricist disciplines at the macro level of analysis.[50] These disciplines in any case posit a simple, universal rationality which is defined through a specific Western, professional social science lens but which, for all of that, proclaims itself to be independent of time, history, culture and difference. By extension, economic life outside this frame, as economic life in the South undoubtedly is, must be denied since it cannot be recognised in the first place.[51]

But recognition might be worrying should it happen. Quite apart from the wilful use of disciplines that are blind, the North clings to everyday deceits that are comforting in their phrasing but outrageous. As Vandana Shiva reminds us, to accept that the poor 'are poor because they have been left behind,' or because they are 'lazy' is to accept a convenient absolution for the guilt which might accompany the truer accounts that the poor are poor because they have been deliberately excluded from access to their own wealth and resources, or because their wealth has been appropriated and their wealth-creating capacities destroyed.[52] Guilt, though, is not automatic and is probably better understood as fungible in the sense that it can be, and has been acceptably replaced by another condition, or rather, a concurrent group of associated opinions and behaviours – in this case, noble paralysis and queasy agnosticism, pervasive insecurity and the toleration of evil.

'NOBLE PARALYSIS' AND 'QUEASY AGNOSTICISM'

To explain these dimensions it is necessary to introduce the notions of political imagination and political will, or perhaps, their affine, political feasibility. Expressed briefly, the proposition is this: the abundance of information concerning serious trauma caused by economic globalisation – what some are calling 'the new inequality' – is inversely related to the willingness to act on it by those who can act on it because to act on it would require a radical reorientation by the United States in particular to the more significant issues in global politics. Certainly, in relation to political imagination, it would require that the traditional geopolitical approach be seen for what it is – an anachronistic obsession in the time of threats which cannot be described under that rubric. As Lewis Lapham wrote when *Defense Planning Guidance* was first reported:

> Nobody knows the language in which to ask or answer the questions presented by the absence of the Soviet empire. The old vocabulary of threat and counterthreat – all the acronyms, all the CIA estimates, all the computer printouts and satellite photographs, the whole archive of lovingly annotated paranoia – is as remote as the gibbering of apes.[53]

To persist with the obsession and its attendant concentration on orders of battle and weapons superiority in the face of their grand strategic obsolescence, therefore, is to seek solace in delusions of grandeur. Worse, it is indicative of the mental condition observed in the behaviour of Kaiser Wilhelm who, as Lapham reminds us, 'calmed his nerves and allayed his feelings of hysteria' about the world by proud displays of military bearing which, given their irrelevance, gave rise to a state which he describes with appropriate irony as 'noble paralysis.'[54]

We should understand this malaise as self-inflicted and more than a little convivial to the prevailing mindset of the North. Indeed, the proposition is that, in the absence of something approaching a *deus ex machina*, there are no grounds for any reliable predictions that the one billion (or so) which constitute the world's affluent population will undertake anything more serious than palliative care when it comes to attending to the needs of the five billion which constitute the world's impoverished population. They are not going to self-destruct and the reason is succinctly captured by Richard Rorty:

> Marx may have overstated when he identified morality with the interests of an economic class, but he had a point. That point is that a politically feasible project of egalitarian redistribution of wealth, requires that there be enough money around to insure that, after the redistribution, the rich will still be able to recognise themselves – will still think their lives worth living.[55]

Even less are they possessed of a good reason to continue the Enlightenment project of spreading liberty, equality and fraternity under the aegis of Western hegemony because that predominance is past, displaced by the deep pessimism that global social change along these lines is possible, or at least possible within the limits of bankruptcy. When it happened precisely, or how long the period of gestation is unclear but the attacks of 9/11 and the magnitude of the world's problems, both admitted in, and omitted from the statements of doctrine and the vision documents had their way with Western confidence. And it is an ecumenical dawning: for those of a religious bent, there are biblical reassurances which facilitate the disengagement of the affluent from the plight of the poor, a removal from responsibility which provides relief from the otherwise constant confrontation with an unpleasant world in which the former is complicit. Therefore, Jesus' advice that, 'The poor will always be with you' (Mark 14: 3–9) is as welcome as it is deployable because it endows the belief that poverty is inevitable with scriptural authority. Besides, the living of a good life within the dictates of religion in America is about acknowledging Jesus as a personal saviour, and directing one's devotion to Him above all, and not about directing one's life towards the alleviation of the poor, though this could be an optional activity. The poor, furthermore, are poor for a reason: somewhere, somehow, perhaps according to the divine will, they failed; and what are the promises of worldly success and eternal salvation if they are available to everyone regardless? Accordingly a veil of religiosity and mystification is drawn across the fact that there are other reasons for the condition of the global South, foremost among them being that it is both generated by the dominant economic system and a desired state for those seeking cheap labour.

The poor, though, are not forever lost and there is consolation for those among the rich who might feel a little bilious when they contemplate their abdication. It comes in the form of a type of divinely sanctioned *apartheid* whereby acceptance is found in the Gospel of John (14: 1–3) which recounts Jesus' promise that, 'In my Father's house are many mansions: if it were not so, I would have told you. I go to prepare a place for you.' Read by an eager and receptive optic, world class divisions are thereby aligned to, and anticipate the heavenly order of things and people: the divisions of the temporal world are insignificant since, at the Last Judgement, each person will stand before God to give an accounting of his or her life on Earth and will be rewarded, or not, with a place in heaven on the basis of what they had made of their talents and agency. If a person has lived a pious life, no matter in what circumstances, then ultimately it makes little or no difference that they were among the downtrodden and exploited in their initial phase of existence.[56]

But the moment can be shared with those who, never convinced of the promise of Heaven, and having once placed their faith in the service of an earthly, liberal transformation are now, in Rorty's words, seized by little other than a 'queasy, debilitating agnosticism.'[57] Gone is the inspiration to create a more just and equitable world – replaced only with the comfortable sense of thinking and acting locally. The transformation; more, the indictment is damning:

> The problem for good-hearted Westerners… is that they seem fated to live out their lives as idiots (in the old sense of 'idiot,' in which the term refers to merely a private person, one who has no part in public affairs). They are ingrates and dilettantes – ingrates because their affluence is made possible by the suffering of the poor and dilettantes because they are no longer able to relate thought to action. They cannot imagine how things could be made better.[58]

The practical implication of the fusion of these two belief systems into the life-world of America is a debilitating selfishness: for the latter, only the local matters any more. For the former, if all are in communion with God and loved by Him individually, and all are individually responsible for saving their own souls, then concerns with society, the alleviation of conditions in the South, not to mention the exhaustion which comes with both, are at best a detraction from the true object of worship, and at worst a form of idolatry, an unnecessary intrusion into the realm of the sacred. And while it might be the case that charity is practised, it is in the form of alms-giving and not in any way an attempt to redeem those who receive it; rather, it is to give them a chance to develop their own selfish relation with the Redeemer. If a reminder is necessary David K. Shipler recalls that, when Judy Woodruff of CNN moderated a debate among Republican candidates for the presidency in March 2000, she challenged Alan Keyes' pessimistic views of American morality by observing that, inter alia, welfare was down, as though 'welfare was an index of immorality.'[59]

'PERVASIVE INSECURITY' AND THE TOLERATION OF EVIL

This is a strategically constructed condition which relies, first, on US declarations that it is under attack. While, in its current manifestation it arises from the terrorist attacks of 9/11, its raiments were distinct in *Defence Planning Guidance 1992* with its objective of thwarting challenges to the superpower primacy of the United States through a form of global unilateralism which envisaged fighting sequential MRCs, or major regional conflicts (which clearly implied the rejection of collective internationalism and the United Nations). The plan was eventually described by the Pentagon as a 'win-hold-win' strategy in which, even when presented with a two-war situation, the US would cope with the continuing turmoil in the world by committing its full panoply of forces to achieve victory in one while committing air power to the other until the victorious forces were released from the first for the purposes of achieving victory in the second, and so on, and so on.[60] Sceptical strategists will note that the appeal of such a strategy depends inordinately on it not being operationalised, an avoidance which was successful until simultaneous deployments to Afghanistan and Iraq proved it to be just another faith-based initiative. The inference taken by society at large, however, requires no such leap. Permanent war was the logical conclusion drawn from these statements and the strategies which ensued. With the release of *QDDR 2006*, and its promise of a 20-year war against an unknown enemy and an abstract noun, the so-called Global War On Terror, there was no longer room for doubt.

Pervasive insecurity is also the product of a second, reinforcing determinant which is silenced in the strategic doctrine documents but given voice in *Mapping the Global Future.* There, in the Executive Summary of the chapter on 'The 2020 Global Landscape,' the term is quite specifically used in reference to a consequence of economic globalisation – namely as part of the 'enormous economic, cultural, and consequently political convulsions' which will follow as the middle classes across the developed world find their life prospects diminished and diminishing in the face of outsourcing their career positions on a large scale to the well-educated masses of low-cost labour in China, India and other emerging economies.[61] Coupled with the fact that populations in the West are enjoying, and presumably will continue to enjoy increasing longevity, the suggestion that a generous spirit will emerge and be sustained to underwrite programmes for those billions who remain excluded in the South is simply not credible. If anything, with technological innovation expanding the range of globally mobile occupations, the prospects are for economic and demographic divisions within countries, and races to the bottom between countries, as multinational corporations seek the most competitive source of labour and conditions of production.

Everyday life will be, indeed already is characterised by the politics of conflict and beleaguerment with the people of the global South being seen as an enemy which is more or less omnipresent and unlikely ever to surrender. The mood is captured in a series of profoundly disturbing lectures by the distinguished statesman and writer, Conor Cruise O'Brien, who likens the emerging forms of thinking to that which can prevail in 'a guarded palace in a city gripped by the plague' – in which even current survivors hear 'a frolicsome demon, gaily whispering in [their] ear: "You're damned!"'[62] Foremost among the casualties, presumed dead, will be the current categories of conceptual walking wounded at the operational level of international relations: obligations, duties beyond borders, the ethic of responsibility, and the needs of strangers. Although finding reasons to be inactive and deciding to be inactive in the face of evil are not peculiar to this age of neo-liberal globalisation, discerning the character of the age at least provides additional reasons for understanding why such inactivity will be further entrenched. It will explain, for example, why the genocides of Sudan and Rwanda, and the consequences of the resources war in Central Africa (which have claimed over four million people, 98 per cent of whom were killed by disease and malnutrition, and more than half of whom were children under the age of 5) will be tolerated, and perhaps, obscenely thought necessary if the developed world is to continue its high-technology-enhanced lifestyle. After all, the Democratic Republic of Congo holds 80 per cent of the world's reserves of *coltan*, a heat-resistant mineral from which is extracted *tantalum* which is engineered into the essential, tiny capacitors which control the flow of current in electronic devices such as cell phones and lap top computers.[63]

GRAND FRAUD

Fraud is not infrequently a strategy; thus, the proposition that Grand Fraud is the neo-liberal/neo-conservative grand strategy of choice, ought not to surprise. 'Grand' is used both because the fraud in question concerns a strategy of global intent and effect, and because the fraud is aggravated: it first denies the global problematics of global security and the relations between them by insisting on a restricted, authorised constellation of issues which are ostensibly within a geopolitical approach to solve, and then proceeds to impose solutions which are also, in and of themselves, frauds when exposed to questioning and countervailing evidence. In summary terms, the fraud is committed when the predicate conditions of global life are suppressed, and hence the predicate logic of the solutions themselves. For this reason the neo-liberal action programme analysed below comprises more of an overview than a detailed account of shortcomings and falsities.

Equally, for those executing the grand strategy, candour should never be extended to the point of conceding the proposition that their solutions are wanting, or even of permitting this to be put in the first place. Suffice to say that alms-giving and the gratuitous proffering of advice are quintessentially conservative measures and poses designed only to retain the *status quo*, not to overturn it. Nevertheless, there is a marked difference, another inversion, between the grand strategy of traditional definition and that which finds form through regnant neo-liberalism/neo-conservatism. Where the former consists of controlling and utilising the resources of a nation towards the objective of security, an art which implies actively using those resources, the North's grand strategy towards the South is more akin to an integrated, orchestrated withholding of those resources which would be most effective (economic, medical, intellectual), and deploying almost exclusively those that are coercive (military power) to the end that its vital interests will eventually come under siege and be undermined.

Nowhere is this more apparent than in the so-called answers which are proffered by the United States to the South for the latter's improvements or, as *QDDR 2006* frames the US mission, 'Shaping the Choices of Countries at Strategic Crossroads.'[64] Accordingly, in *The National Security Strategy of the United States of America*, we find there is but 'a single sustainable model for national success: freedom, democracy and free enterprise,'[65] and while it is difficult to take issue with the first two conditions, it is important to understand that they are heavily qualified by the third, or more specifically by the meaning that the third term gives to the first two (to which attention is given in the following pages). Above all, it is to be understood that there is to be no immediate surge in aid – the costs of the long 20-year war promised by *QDDR 2006* obviates that – and that free trade and free markets are not so much policy objectives of the Bush Doctrine as they are dogma, beyond challenge and argument. Parsed more closely the prescription for closing the have–have-not gaps is for the latter to 'pursue policies that support application of new technologies, such as good governance, universal education and market reforms.'[66]

Admittedly, for the poorest of the poor immediate debt relief by creditors in the North – 'forgiveness' in some lexicons – was promised, so perhaps this should be explored for what it indicates of goodwill to the South. If we leave to one side the absurdity of the South requiring forgiveness for loans from the North which should never have been made or required under the historical conditions that operated at the time, the outcomes to date of the heralded Millennium Development Goals (MDGs), which included halving extreme poverty, cutting child deaths, providing all of the world's children with an education, rolling back infectious diseases, and forging a new global partnership to drive results, all for delivery by 2015, are already revealing the weakness in commitment:

> the overall report card on progress makes for depressing reading. Most countries are off track for most of the MDGs. Human development is faltering in some key areas, and already deep inequalities are widening. Various diplomatic formulations and polite terminologies can be found to describe the divergence between progress on human development and the ambition set out in the Millennium Declaration. None of them should be allowed to obscure a simple truth: the promise to the world's poor is being broken.[67]

Faith, as externalised by adherence to the neo-liberal orthodoxy is nevertheless imperative merely for the extension of favour to be considered by the North. To be precise, this is nothing less than the reinvention of the Mosaic tradition in economic and philanthropic guise: just as the Hebrew prophet led the Israelites out of bondage in Egypt, the peoples of the South are to be delivered from their condition by accepting without qualification the transcending institutional authority of the new dispensation and its commands, applicable at the micro and the macro level, to privatise, marketise and deregulate. Where the Israelites were unified under the Mosaic Law, the current objective is global, as admitted by Renato Ruggiero, the first Director-General of the World Trade Organization (WTO):

> We are no longer writing the rules of interaction among separate national economies. We are writing the constitution of a single global economy.[68]

Evidently, all forms of economic thought and practice, and by extension, all forms of social and political thought and practice are to be not only homogenised but unified, notwithstanding the varieties of historical, social, cultural, economic and political experience. Evidently, too, the dream of a unified field theory which escaped Einstein's realisation in the world of physics, and the single belief system which eventually eluded post-Nicean theology are not thought to be discouraging precedents. On the contrary, perhaps the latter encourages the view that, for a while, belief can be imposed within an economy of indulgence, inquisition and excommunication?

Certainly there is the same institutional coordination which distinguishes the Mosaic and Christian projects, as well as what Paul Cammack describes as 'the clear and very cold authoritarian and monolithic logic which is central to the activity.'[69] And what is 'the activity?' Quite simply, it is the radical transformation of the South in such a way that it is ruled according to the dictates of 'deep neo-liberalism' towards the end that it provides the necessary pool of appropriately instructed and trained low-cost labour, including a 'reserve army of labour acting as a disciplinary force' for the multinational corporations of the North.[70] By way of extensive and annotated citations from World Bank reports on poverty reduction, Paul Cammack argues persuasively that all of the means noted above – universal education, good governance, market reforms and the application of new technologies – are, in the first instance, interrelated, and secondly to be understood as deriving their significance from the extent that neo-liberal objectives are served. Accordingly, in the neo-liberal lexicon, governance is only good if, and only if it behaves neo-liberally and is acknowledged as such in the form of private sector investor confidence, regardless of outcomes;[71] universal education is a public benefit if, and only if (in the words of World Bank President, James Wolfensohn), it creates the 'right kind of knowledge' in a labour force desired by neo-liberalism.[72] This was no more than a reprise of what the World Bank 1990 World Development Report, *Poverty*, made clear in 1990 with its unequivocal statement that the provision of basic social services to the poor was to be subordinated to the goal of increasing the productivity of labour:

> The *first* element [of the strategy] is to promote the productive use of the poor's most abundant assets – labour. It calls for policies that harness market incentives, social and political institutions, infrastructure and technology to that end. The *second* is to provide basic social services to the poor.[73]

As for 'the application of new technologies,' this is to accept the global order described without exaggeration by Peter Drahos and John Braithwaite as 'information feudalism,' and the re-inscription of borders through intellectual property rights and digitalisation in the name of 'free trade.' For the South it is to accept that membership in the WTO entails living under the strictures of an alien concept which defines one of the most egregious sources of North–South inequality. It is to accept that access to the knowledge and technology upon which development depends is to be rationed according to prices and supplies determined primarily by the net exporters of intellectual property, which is to say in, and by corporate interests, without any real consideration being given to the life-and-death health, or educational needs of the South. It is to accept, for example, that the health and longevity of populations of countries in which the state determines the cost of life's necessities – such as prescription medicines – are beholden to US pharmaceutical companies who pioneered and patented the drugs, but frequently with US government subsidies. Ultimately, it is to accept as legal, desirable and absolute a global property order and knowledge-elite which re-colonises the South through its control of access to educational tools, computer software, drugs, seeds, and even the human genome.[74]

Finally, to 'market reforms,' the move which requires a democratic state to arrange its society in the image and likeness of neo-liberalism (which frequently involves defection), to discipline this identity for waywardness, and then to deny accountability and responsibility for the consequences on the basis that the global economy is the cause (which frequently involves abdication). There is no single approach which indicates the magnitude of the fraud/crime, but the device adopted here is to cite, albeit in a very abbreviated form, the particular findings which relate to the consequences incurred by Mexico and the United States under the North American Free Trade Agreement (NAFTA), widely regarded as the neo-liberal constitutional template, in the first decade of its operation.

Abstracted from a wide range of assessments, under income distribution, wealth and political power all became more unequal despite an increase in total trade. Manufacturing wages declined by 11 per cent despite productivity increases of 50 per cent in 1994 to 2001, and income shifted from labour to capital. In Mexico, more than 1.5 million peasant-farmers were forced off their land, and 28,000 small to medium-sized businesses were destroyed as a direct result of NAFTA, and despite the predicted economies of scale which should have resulted from US agribusiness multinationals flooding the country to supply the market, retail food prices increased sharply. The migration to the cities of the displaced *campesinos* caused a glut in the labour market and industrial sector wages to spiral down by some 25 per cent. Poverty among households headed by women increased by 50 per cent; the rural poverty rate rose from 79 per cent in 1994 to 83 per cent in 1998, and the overall poverty rate rose from 51 per cent to 58 per cent in the same period. A damning indictment of the agreement was provided by a US Government report which found that Mexican manufacturing wages were considerably higher in 1981, under the old economic regime, than they were in 2000.[75]

By the end of 2005, in the United States, 2.5 million, or one-sixth of the manufacturing jobs in the US had disappeared with estimates varying as to the exact number for which NAFTA was responsible. Figures range from those in Department of Labour statistics, which concedes that 451,259 had either lost their jobs or had their incomes reduced substantially in 2002 to 2005, to other statistically consistent estimates by economists that, even by 2004, 900,000 manufacturing jobs were NAFTA casualties.[76] In all there is sufficient evidence to recall former Foreign Minister Jorge Castaneda's observation that NAFTA is:

> an accord among magnates and potentates: an agreement for the rich and powerful … effectively excluding ordinary people in all three societies.[77]

Evidently, the process is ongoing: since the admission of China into the WTO in 2001, and its replacement of Mexico as a source of cheap labour, Mexico, by early 2004, had lost nearly half a million manufacturing jobs.[78]

Yet we are also witnessing an increasing amount of what might be seen as inter-hemispheric mixing, most notably in the United States, where neo-liberalism has significantly contributed to the well-documented descent of living standards. On first acquaintance, this should be not just implausible and improbable, but preposterous. The United States is without doubt the great engine of change behind the neo-liberal transformation of the world, from which it follows that it owes to itself as much as the rest of the world the duty which falls to exemplars: to be, and be seen to be adherents in communion with the single truth it demands others to follow, regardless of their respective circumstances. Nothing less than exemplary practice is expected, therefore. If it is not, then there is a strong presumption of fraud. On the basis of the available and historically consistent evidence during the period since the neo-liberal ascendancy in the US, the presumption is more than justified. Indeed, the relevant evidence points to a neo-liberalism-induced decline which is contrary to the declared principles of a country which sees itself as 'the light on the hill' for the guidance and instruction of all others.

To begin with, we should understand that the US is not just an indebted country, but a prosperous country so heavily indebted that its economic way of life is unsustainable: by way of one indication, in 2005 alone, US external debt increased by 6 per cent of GDP, or US$725.8 billion, or US$7,200 per household, bringing the total US external debt to US$30,000 per household.[79] The year 2006 began, if anything, in a worse state, with January returning a deficit of US$68.5 billion, the largest monthly imbalance in US history.[80] For this, the US borrows US$2.6 billion per day. In response, Economics Nobel Prize-winner, Joseph Stiglitz spoke plainly: 'This can't go on forever – so it won't.'[81] He was preceded by another highly regarded economist, Stephen Roach, Chief Economist with the investment banking giant, Morgan Stanley, with a far more pessimistic assessment but for the same reasons: the US has no better than a 10 per cent chance of avoiding an economic 'Armageddon' because, eventually, the deficit and the value of the US dollar will be more closely correlated.'[82]

In parallel with this unchecked national profligacy are several trends which illustrate the probable future under neo-liberalism even for those countries which might experience temporary benefits for embracing it, with all its other costs, in an effort to be as American as possible. The first is a corresponding corporate profligacy which, in a central way, is nothing less than the reward system for entrenching and exacerbating inequality by the relatively small number of senior executives who either depress the wages of local labour forces, or just dismiss those who can earn them in the first place. Recent research findings by Ian Dew-Becker and Robert Gordon detail that, between 1972 and 2001, the wage and salary income of the top 10 per cent of income (which includes university graduates) distribution rose by approximately 1 per cent per year whereas the top 1 per cent rose by 87 per cent; the top .1 per cent (income of US$3 million per year in 2002) rose by 181 per cent, and the top .01 per cent rose by 497 per cent.[83] The example, *par excellence*, of this burgeoning plutocracy is Wal-Mart: in 2004, Scott Lee Jr., the company's CEO, was paid US$17.5 million, or more salary every two weeks than his average employee will earn in a lifetime.[84]

Those in work are, however, to be considered fortunate in relation to the second trend, which relates to those who are the casualties of neo-liberalism. Using Bureau of Labour Statistics on payroll data over the five years to January 2006, and with the analytical assistance of Charles McMillion of MBG Information Services, Paul Craig Roberts, former Assistant Secretary of the Treasury in the Reagan Administration, provides the following summary: the US failed by 7 million jobs to keep pace with population growth. Throughout the entire period in the private sector, 500,000 fewer jobs were created than one year's legal and illegal immigration. What employment growth existed in this period took place not in goods-producing activities (which actually experienced a net loss), but in the service sector – mainly in credit intermediation, health care and social assistance, waiters, waitresses, bartenders, and state and local government. The former were devastated as is shown by a summary of the workforce losses, in percentage terms: communications (43); semi-conductors and electronic components (37); electrical equipment and appliances (25); motor vehicles and parts (12); furniture and related products (17); apparel manufacturers (50); textile mills (43); paper and products (20); and plastic and rubber products (15). Roberts writes of this destruction:

Not a single manufacturing payroll classification created a single new job ....
The declines in some manufacturing sectors have more in common with a country undergoing
saturation bombing during war than with a super-economy that is 'the envy of the world.'[85]

Disturbing for those who advocate technical and professional qualifications as the price of admission to new sectors in the 'new economy' and a hedge against unemployment and poverty, were the percentage losses in the information sector (25), accounting and bookkeeping (4), and computer systems design and related areas (9). Managerial and supervisory positions declined by 209,000 and enrolments in engineering degrees declined in the knowledge that both positions for graduate engineers are themselves vanishing and there are 'several hundred thousand American engineers who are unemployed and have been for years.'[86] And the outlook is bleak: it is estimated that, by 2015, a total of 3 million US jobs will have been exported, mainly to China, as a result of 'out-sourcing' and 'off-shoring.'[87]

Finally, poverty. In such circumstances it is a logical and integrated consequence, or rather, bundle of consequences covered by a common descriptor. Nearly 13 per cent, or 37 million (including 13 million children) in the population of the US – the highest ratio in the developed world – are classified as living in poverty and, in most cases suffering from what is known as 'food insecurity.'[88] Even though most of the people classified as living in poverty have a job or, in some cases, two jobs, their condition is such that they are also known as 'the working poor.' Under the Bush Administration an additional 5.4 million have fallen into this category, not least because the minimum wage of US$5.15 has not risen since 1997 and, adjusted for inflation, is at its lowest since 1956.[89] In any case, as reported by the non-partisan Working Poor Families Project, one in every five jobs in the US pays less than a poverty-level wage for a family of four (US$18,810 in 2003).[90] The consequences of this consequence are also realised with nearly 46 million Americans lacking any health insurance in a country that does not guarantee basic health care.[91] The scale of the problem is to be gauged from the fact that, with the exception only of job loss, medical-related indebtedness is the largest single cause of personal bankruptcy in the US.[92] The model, then, is one replete with falling wages, accelerating wealth inequality, and increasing work insecurity – all with the associated stress and other pathologies which fall under Wallace Peterson's rubric of the 'silent depression' which affects 80 per cent of American families;[93] in sum, it is an example of the 'race to the bottom' between, and within developed countries, of social devastation, and the displacement of a debauched democracy by plutocracy and quite possibly something worse, something approaching fascism, if not fascism itself.[94] Of this James K. Galbraith writes:

Today, the signature of modern American capitalism is neither benign competition, nor class struggle, nor an inclusive middle-class utopia. Instead, predation has become the dominant feature – a system wherein the rich have come to feast on decaying systems built for the middle class.[95]

A conclusion is not necessary at this juncture, but more questions are. Why is there US strategy and US knowledge, and the two are manifestly neither the same thing, nor even necessarily related in any meaningful way? Why is there not even a glimmer of recognition that the North's dogmatic insistence on neo-liberalism as the required method of global economic, social and political behaviour is merely the prescription of the primary cause of the South's pathology as the cure which, if refused and resisted with sufficient energy, provokes the Bush Doctrine, the required method of punishment? Why, in the face of the intractability of human affairs – which number, inequality, environmental destruction and tyranny among its constituents – to geostrategic solution, is there only the unending exhortation to a single form of political belief as though by repeating it in a manner similar to the recitation of the Nicene Creed, all forms of opposition will be overcome?

The answers lie in asking these questions in a different way, specifically: how credible is the suggestion that the conditions of the poor South can be brought to a higher standard of living through the agency of the US-led North when the leader is in decline and faced with rising challenges, and the North itself insists on the maintenance of its own living standards in the full knowledge and understanding of the nature and extent of both the global pathologies and its complicity in them? So framed, it points to the blindness of US and Northern grand strategy as a wilful and desired result because, while the evidence in the vision documents is frequently suppressed, it would be incredible to suggest that it is unknown to the grand strategists themselves, within and without the United States. Within the same stream of logic, it points as well to the condition of the global South as a necessary condition of the North's *status quo*. In the global context of the war on terror and US leadership neither can be admitted. Nor can the condition of the global South as the principal casualty of this war.

2 *Triage*

A survey of casualties in the neo-liberal combat zone

Triage, briefly defined, is the process of sorting the deserving from the undeserving according to predetermined priorities directed to predetermined ends. It is the process which attends any overwhelming medical disaster, and so is commonly, if not exclusively associated with the treatment to be accorded to battlefield casualties, under conditions of limited (medical) resources. But it has wider applications, being utilised as a system to allocate any scarce commodity, such as food, only to those capable of deriving the greatest benefit from it. Traditionally, the categories used are (1) those beyond help in the present situation, (2) those in need of immediate attention, and (3) those capable of surviving with no additional ill effects until treatment can be provided. Bear in mind that *triage* is a double-edged instrument: for those who are most directly involved, it is not about classifying human trauma for its own sake; rather it is about selecting those who will survive, who will return in a functional way to their respective units, and who will maintain the effectiveness of that unit or system. In the longer term, however, the classifications (and what they include in a substantive form) are important because they tell us more completely what happened than does the catalogue of what was allowed to remain. The recourse to such an approach is, therefore, also initiated as an alternative, less accommodating approach to that offered by mainstream analyses in the hope of challenging the latter's well-refined habit of remotely viewing that which should be viewed more immediately, and giving names which are more proper and truthful.

TRIAGE CATEGORIES

Recently, under the Conventional NATO Triage Classification, the three categories noted above have been expanded to four, but remain defined according to resources and immediate prognosis, and further defined, by colour, also according to resources and prognosis. The intention here is neither to agree nor disagree with the various classifications; rather it is to dramatise the plight of the world's people's which are neo-liberal casualties by placing them within one or another of the classifications on the basis of their condition and the treatment they received, the latter being clear evidence of the former, as follows:

> T1: Immediate surgery to save life or limb. Minimal operating time. Expected good-quality survival.

T2: Delayed. Time-consuming surgery. Life not jeopardised by delay. Stabilisation minimises effects of delay.

T3: Minimal. Minor injuries. Managed by minimally trained staff.

T4: Expectant. Serious, multiple injuries. Treatment is complex and time consuming. Treatment consumes considerable personnel or resources.

Additional triage *classifications*
• *Red/Emergent:* Priority 1
Critically ill patient that may survive with intervention that does not consume significant resources and personnel.
• *Yellow/Urgent:* Priority 2
Likely to survive and remain stable for several hours with stabilisation.
• *Green/Non-urgent:* Priority 3
Minor injuries that may be treated by those with minimal training and may wait until other injured patients are cared for.
• *Blue/Variable urgency:* Priority 2 or 3
Patients with severe injuries not expected to survive unless time-consuming care is almost immediate. These patients may take too many resources from more viable patients and may have to have low priority due to limitation of resources.
Note: This colour is sometimes used in place of black because many providers have difficulty placing a patient into the category of palliative care only.[1]

It is important to note that where the unit's potential contribution is degraded, so too, is its *triage* priority. In global politics the example of Western non-intervention – which, nevertheless, was highly influential – in the Rwandan genocide was apposite: because that country was regarded as geopolitically and geo-economically insignificant, it was consigned to a category even beneath Black/Expectant. Not only was Rwanda accorded no obvious priority; 'comfort measures' were withheld from the mutilated and dying ethnic groups who numbered in the hundreds of thousands.

Rwanda, moreover, indicates a variation in scale of traditional *triage*. Previously, it was an essentially local practice; indeed, the need to sort was imperative in the context of the unavoidable scarcity of medical services in, or near, a relatively restricted geographical area such as a battlefield, or the scene of an unforeseen natural civil disaster. But *triage* is now global, determining that the choice which attends it is also global; the effect is to reduce whole classes of people within otherwise bountiful countries, and whole countries themselves, and whole regions in some cases, and even continents, to one or other of the hopeless, blue/black categories. Herein lies the second variation: though the geographic scale has expanded, the categories have essentially contracted.

As for the systemic imperative, one, rather arresting, 'reality check' so popular in the current vernacular is provided by the (then) International Monetary Fund (IMF) Managing Director, Michel Camdessus' proposition that, in 1998, the time was nigh for the introduction of a 'second generation of reforms' which might require the '*sacrifice of a generation*.'[2] And the latter, it should be noted, was being advanced at a time of full knowledge that, chronically, Africa and Latin America had already been devastated by exactly the type of political-economic ideas and practices he wished to perpetuate, and acutely, that the Asian financial crisis was but the latest reproach to any notion of an *idée maitresse.*

For all of that it was at least an explicit acknowledgment that the intention existed to conduct a renewed offensive, and, as the following survey indicates, an offensive indistinguishable from those undertaken in major wars – but with one exception. For sound strategic reasons, it is an uncontestable truth accepted by military forces around the world that multi-front wars are to be avoided if at all possible, yet the character of this campaign is defined by being not so much multi-front as all-front, but executed with varying intensity according to the significance attached to the region in question. To this end, as was outlined in the previous chapter, it is sometimes necessary to control territories (vast tracts of Africa and Latin America, for example) while conceding that their condition makes integration within the overall coalition of forces impossible; in this event, they are to be managed in such a way that they do not become a security threat to that coalition. To establish the basis for the argument that economic globalisation in theory and practice is an instrument of destruction at least commensurate with major war it is necessary, in the first instance, to take stock of the world in terms of the relevant conditions, conditions wrought by neo-liberalism, their trends, and their likely consequences.

ROUNDS OF THE *TRIAGE* TENT

In human terms it is a bitter legacy of trends, instruments, and overall state of the world which frames this inventory. By way of the commanding trends which can be observed, the principal casualties are the collectivities – nation, state, society and community, and the ideas which hitherto sustained them – which, for better or worse, previously informed, authorised, and gave meaning to individual life in all its multifarious expressions. In their place, essentially, the dominant ideology of neo-liberal economic thought substitutes the central construct of neoclassical economics – Rational Economic Man – an acquisitive, traumatically-stressed and isolated individual whose decisions are less exercises in free choice than they are responses to an overly simplified, unchanging world devoid of meaningful relations and reciprocities. Proceeding in parallel, however, the second phase of the assault is executed by the Third Industrial Revolution, fuelled, as William Greider notes, 'by invention and human ingenuity and a universal aspiration to build and accumulate,'[3] and catalysed by 'thinking machines' which increasingly displace human agency from not only all levels of communication, production, marketing, and distribution, but also conceptual, managerial, and administrative functions. Thus the collectivities and their roles, including of course, government-by-states, continue to exist but in a regime of redistributed power: where the state has abdicated certain political-economic roles, its prerogatives have become the reserved powers of the unaccountable institutional instruments of globalisation, foremost among them being those cited in the foregoing, the WTO, WB, and the IMF – which are now the *de facto* government of the economies in some 30 countries in sub-Saharan Africa[4] – and numerous agreements organised around the principle of free trade, such as the North American Free Trade Agreement (NAFTA).

Expressly because of the extant expansion, permanence, and tangibility of such pathologies in the global political economy Robert Cox admits to Antonio Gramsci's 'pessimism of the intellect'[5] – or, as it might be expressed in the present context, the tendency to see the world in the *triage* colour categories of blue and black. The evidence he and a great many others marshal is grounded in a certain type of 'new capitalism' which, embodying the 'distinct system of values, pattern of consumption, social structure and form of state' that it does, has also produced its own distinctive 'socially destructive consequences' which are indicative of a mounting crisis in the global political economy.[6] Surveying the vectors and the wreckage, he is moved to describe the present by recalling Karl Polanyi's analysis of an early moment in capitalism's past: we have now returned to Polanyi's first phase – in which the state is 'evacuated from substantive economic activity,'[7] and, by and large, are 'reduced to the role of adjusting national economies to the dynamics of an unregulated global economy.'[8] 'Unregulated' in this context needs to be qualified so as to include the surrendering of national prerogatives regulating the mobility of capital and goods and services, but not labour, which is to remain localised, domiciled within the geographical territory of traditional nation-states, or selectively encouraged so as to undermine the benefits won or negotiated over the last century by trade unions. This is the qualitative change which needs to be kept in mind throughout the following discussion: it is not that international, or global trade is a new phenomenon – it isn't – but, as Robert Heilbroner has discerned, there has been a fundamental transformation from a capitalist political world, dominated by state actors, which contained competing economies, to a capitalist economic world, in which states, though they are competing political entities, are also subordinate actors.[9] So understood, the war which is economic globalisation has the character of revolution; it does not involve a transformation to anarchy – as a crude understanding of 'unregulated'– as the-absence-of-law could imply; rather, it is a transformation to a system of governance in which states facilitate government by, and in the interests of corporate capital.

The casualty list at this point, which already includes nation, state, society, and community, all of whose vital signs are compromised by symptoms of profound morbidity, is extended to include the notion and reality of a nation-state economy, not the least reason for which is the fact that it is fast becoming a concept without a referent. As the renowned economist, Robert B. Reich, Secretary of Labor in the first Clinton Administration wrote in 1991:

> As almost every factor of production – money, technology, factories, and equipment – moves effortlessly across borders, the very idea of an American economy is becoming meaningless, as are the notions of an American corporation, American capital, American products, and American technology. A similar transformation is affecting every other nation.[10]

To this, Cyrill Siewert, chief financial officer of the US-based conglomerate, Colgate–Palmolive, provides an additional political dimension with his advice that: 'The United States does not have an automatic call on our resources. There is no mind-set which puts this country first.'[11]

In the absence of a national identity, and a declared independence from the fortunes or otherwise of a particular national economy, global corporations are, nevertheless, integral to understanding the performance of national economies for the simple reason that, first, control over the former is virtually impossible once the requirements of economic globalisation have been formally recognised by the state; in so doing, states effectively ceded whatever residual abilities they possessed in this regard at the time. Indeed, the ultimate commercial organisation that was ushered in with this development has become known as the 'virtual corporation' – 'a quick-witted corporation so dispersed that it resembles the ganglia of a nervous system, a brain attached to many distant nodes but without bodily substance at the centre.'[12] It is in this light that the phenomenon of intra-firm trade and its distorting effects are easy to grasp. By this is meant that, in most countries, components or affiliates of non-indigenous multinationals account for one quarter of all economic activity. Taking the US as an example, transactions between a firm and its foreign affiliates or components accounts for 40–50 per cent of total imports and 35–40 per cent of total exports.[13] Thus the distinction needs to be made between such goods which travel within the closed, internal channels of companies, and those which travel in the open marketplace, in order to understand the emptying of the term 'national economy':

> All of this intrafirm traffic is counted in the national trade statistics, but national trade identities are increasingly irrelevant to the buyers and sellers. Nation-to-nation trade flows are driven more and more by the proprietary strategies of the multinational corporations organising their own diversified production, less and less by traditional concepts of comparative advantage among nations or the economic policies of home governments.[14]

According to these demonstrated abilities to alter national economies, therefore, corporations are the states' arbiters in a system from which there is no escape; moreover, at this level of analysis, the power of national governments might be regarded as having been redistributed among global corporations and institutions who serve their interests.

Such examples, however, are only suggestive of corporate power *vis-à-vis* the state. What they lack is an appreciation of finance capital, what for some is the 'basic mechanism of globalisation.'[15] To account for this view it is necessary just to record the scale, and secondly, the relation of finance capital to the global trade in goods and services. In turn, both may be approached through a small number of observations which, effectively, detail the death of governmental control over conventional money: between the early 1950s, when global foreign exchange trading was negligible, and the early 1990s, the international electronic transfer of funds reached a rate which dwarfed the amounts exchanged globally for goods and services – US$2 trillion against a mere US$20–30 billion per day.[16] Expressed another way, the annual Gross National Product of the world – some US$23 trillion in 1996 – was traded through the fibre-optic network of New York every 10–12 days.[17] And conducting this business is no more than 50 banks and a very much smaller number of major brokerage houses.[18]

Taking the United States in the 14 years to 1994 as an example, US$1.5 trillion was expatriated and invested in foreign stocks, representing both a 16-fold increase of foreign investment and a decrease of significant proportions in the capital available for domestic enterprises and, hence, domestic employment.[19] Unremarkable in this context is the statement by a former chairman of Citicorp, who described 'as a kind of global plebiscite on the monetary and financial policies of the governments issuing currency' the verdicts which are passed by the network of currency traders who are seated in front of '200,000 monitors in trading rooms all over the world.' More specifically, he recalls how, in 1981, 'the market' successfully moved to disabuse France's President François Mitterrand of his socialist values, and reverse his socialist policies, by a six-month campaign of capital flight from his country.[20] But the schedule of states which have had to defer to the regime of 'global speculators' includes many more than France, even in the industrialised world; indeed, the United States, the European Union, Sweden, and Spain have all experienced its force, as have Mexico and Malaysia among the industrialising nations.[21] On the other hand, the favoured, investee nations also have cause to reflect on their good fortune, if recent Indonesian experience is typical: between 1991 and 1996 the value of shares traded on the Jakarta Stock Exchange grew by 1,000 per cent, but over one-third of it is foreign-owned.[22] On the bases of such demonstration effects of national economic impotence Greider, in 1996, provided a conclusion not markedly different from an epitaph:

> In the advanced economies, most governments have become mere salesmen, promoting the fortunes of their own multinationals in the hope that this will provide a core prosperity that keeps everyone afloat. The clearest evidence that this strategy is not working is the condition of labour markets in the wealthiest nations: either mass unemployment or declining real wages (nominal pay adjusted for inflation), and, in some cases, both of these deleterious effects.
>
> The more subtle evidence of the dilemma of leading governments is their deteriorating fiscal condition: most are threatened by rising, seemingly permanent budget deficits and accumulating debt.
>
> The general fiscal crisis of rich nations is driven by the same fundamental – disappointing economic growth that, year after year, fails to generate the tax revenues needed to keep up with... public obligations [and] to ameliorate the harsh conditions of industrial capitalism.[23]

That this demise was made possible by computers creating what Kurtzman terms the 'neural networks of money,' and facilitated by state legislation, predominantly in the interests of finance capital, serves less to confirm the impact of the Third Industrial Revolution than it does the near inversion of the role of the states themselves.[24] In the interim, of course, the Asian financial crisis further demonstrated, for those that might have been sceptical, the possible consequences that financial speculation can wreak in an unregulated environment, when the currencies of even quite efficient economies can fluctuate by 100 per cent in only a matter of months.

This judgment needs to be only slightly modified, if at all, in the case of the World Trade Organization (WTO), established on the completion of the Uruguay Round of the General Agreement on Tariffs and Trade (GATT). Based on treaty documents which run to more than 22,000 pages and weigh 395 pounds, the World Trade Organization, in matters under its jurisdiction, is sovereign; indeed, it is officially described as having a 'legal personality' equivalent to the United Nations. Its power is exercised through secret panels of three experts whose members review laws of member states that have been denounced by other members as impediments to trade. Thus, these panels may challenge national, but also local and regional standards, on matters such as environmental and consumer protection, occupational health and safety, food security, plant-closing legislation, restrictions on foreign ownership, and many other matters, under the rubric of 'non-tariff barriers to trade.' Member states will then be obliged to change their laws or face trade sanctions if their standards are *higher* than those set by the WTO, but not if they are lower.[25] Among the US laws already challenged (by the European Union) under WTO auspices are the Marine Mammal Protection Act, the Nuclear Non-Proliferation Act, and California's Safe Drinking Water and Toxic Enforcement Act. On these, as in all disputes, neither individual citizens, nor their organisations, have any right to observe, let alone appear before the panels to testify.[26]

In these terms, it is both curious and significant, therefore, that in the United States Congress (and some other legislatures), the Agreement creating the WTO was ratified via the new 'fast-track' process which evaded the constitutional requirement for a two-thirds majority. As Ralph Nader has warned, although the WTO has been represented as an instrument for the elimination of regulative barriers to global trade, it also formalises 'a world economic government dominated by giant corporations, without a correlative democratic rule of law to hold this economic government accountable.'[27] The WTO, therefore, centralises what national governments surrendered under the GATT, but under conditions incapable of being scrutinised by those it 'governs.'

As this regime of conceded and usurped power extends, so too does the schedule of collateral damage. Since national political institutions were the first target, democracy – real, imagined, or potential – enters a natural decline. As well as being relegated by a centralising of power in the various extra-national formations of global capital, they are also reduced by the domestic requirement of capital, to which they have in any case acceded, to deregulate, privatise, and otherwise dismantle instruments of state intervention and protection (even for the most vulnerable members of society). As a consequence of these general developments, multinational corporations have been free to pursue their related goals of maximising both profit and corporate control of the known universe. In this they have succeeded to an extraordinary degree: in the assessments of the United Nations Centre on Transnationals, they have increased in number from 7,000 in 1970 to some 35,000 in 1991, to 63,000 in 2000.[28] Supplemented by the profile of the 200 largest transnational corporations published by the Institute of Policy Studies in 2000, the phenomenon comes into sharper focus:

1   Of the 100 largest economies in the world, 51 are corporations; only 49 are countries (based on a comparison of corporate sales and country GDPs).

2   The Top 200 corporations' sales are growing at a faster rate than overall global economic activity. Between 1983 and 1999, their combined sales grew from the equivalent of 25.0 per cent to 27.5 per cent of World GDP.

3   The Top 200 corporations' combined sales are bigger than the combined economies of all countries minus the biggest 10.

4   The Top 200s' combined sales are 18 times the size of the combined annual income of the 1.2 billion people (24 per cent of the total world population) living in 'severe' poverty.

5   While the sales of the Top 200 are the equivalent of 27.5 per cent of world economic activity, they employ only 0.78 per cent of the world's workforce.

6   Between 1983 and 1999, the profits of the Top 200 firms grew 362.4 per cent, while the number of people they employ grew by only 14.4 per cent.

7   A full 5 per cent of the Top 200s' combined workforce is employed by Wal-Mart, a company notorious for union-busting and widespread use of part-time workers to avoid paying benefits. The discount retail giant is the top private employer in the world, with 1,140,000 workers, more than twice as many as No. 2, DaimlerChrysler, which employs 466,938.

8   US corporations dominate the Top 200, with 82 slots (41 per cent of the total). Japanese firms are second, with only 41 slots.

9   Of the US corporations on the list, 44 did not pay the full standard 35 per cent federal corporate tax rate during the period 1996 to 1998. Seven of the firms actually paid less than zero in federal income taxes in 1998 (because of rebates). These include: Texaco, Chevron, PepsiCo, Enron, Worldcom, McKesson and the world's biggest corporation – General Motors.

10   Between 1983 and 1999, the share of total sales of the Top 200 made up by service sector corporations increased from 33.8 per cent to 46.7 per cent. Gains were particularly evident in financial services and telecommunications sectors, in which most countries have pursued deregulation.[29]

Subsequently, it continued almost unabated, as Stephen Lendman observes:

> US corporations have never had it better. It's been so good that 82 of the largest 275 companies paid no federal income tax in at least one year from 2001–2003 or got a refund; 28 of them got tax rebates in all 3 of those years even though their combined profits totalled $44.9 billion; 46 of them, earning $42.6 billion in profits, paid no tax in 2003 and got $4.9 billion back in tax rebates. And the average CEO pay for these 46 companies in 2004 was $12.6 million.[30]

Additionally, it has to be reported that the tax base in many countries, especially the US, has been in a more or less permanent state of erosion as this evasion has proceeded. Thus, whereas, in the 1950s, corporations contributed 23 per cent of the all-federal income taxes collected, by 1991 it had eroded to 9.2 per cent,[31] thereby transferring the burden for necessary services to other parts of society, which frequently acted as a catalyst for their reduction, if not their elimination. And this leaves to one side the fact that the tax system is so corrupt that the bidder who won a round of golf with Tiger Woods for US$30,100 at a 2004 Buick charity auction could deduct all but US$200 of it; or the fact that the fifth leading philanthropist in the US, Texas oilman and corporate raider, T. Boone Pickens, received his rating in part due to a 100 per cent deductible gift of US$165 million to the golf programme of Oklahoma State University (which, within an hour of receiving it, then reinvested it in a hedge fund controlled by Pickens).[32]

Global corporate power, though, is nothing if not absolutist in its ambitions. Having suborned governments, it has then sought the destruction of trade union power as a possible counter to its own. The attack effectively is from two directions, from below and from above. From below, a three-stage sequence induces weak unions by, in the first instance, the practice of corporations laying off large numbers of workers in response to the opportunities to reduce production costs which are presented by automation and cheaper foreign labour. Increasingly, this then creates a pool of workers who are either intimidated by this example, or simply unemployed, yet desperate for work. The former, accordingly, accept pay freezes, or reductions in pay and conditions previously 'unheard of in the unionised sector of the economy in the 1960s and 1970s.' Ultimately, workers understand that unions are demonstrably unable to safeguard and promote their interests; in the short term at least, unions are seen as an impediment to survival in a Hobbesian labour market.[33] In 1994, less than 12 per cent of the US workforce in private industry was organised for collective bargaining, a proportion smaller than at any time since the New Deal labour reforms of the mid-1930s;[34] by 2005, according to the US Bureau of Labor Statistics, the corresponding figure had declined further, to 7.8 per cent.[35]

From above, as the International Confederations of Free Trade Unions has documented, attacks increased on a global scale as the WTO became operational. The 1995 survey of violations of trade union rights, via a conservatively estimated schedule of breaches of just two of the International Labour Organisation's Conventions – those pertaining to the rights to collective bargaining, and freedom of association – indicated abuses in more countries (98) than ever before across a spectrum which ranged from harassment and dismissal through to detention, violence, and the murder of workers attempting to exercise these rights.[36] The United Kingdom and the United States were countries typical of those where interference was of a type towards the non-lethal end of the spectrum, with official-attitudinal, legislative, or other discriminatory practices in evidence. But from there violence against trade unionists escalated to the arrest of 4,300, and the murder of 528,[37] representing a 65 per cent increase in interference in just three years.[38]

But this reduction of workers to commodities is only the most immediate consequence, or the most shorthand expression of the total domination of life driven by the principle of private profit maximisation. Put differently, as an organising principle it cannot but erode other values which elevate collectivities and caring above individual gain. Thus the loss of democracy entails a syndrome of decline in 'broad human interests' which include: environmental protection, social caring, equality, human solidarity, community stability, individual and family security, long-term public and private planning and investment, dignity in the workplace, goods and services consumed collectively, and cultural diversity.[39] As a corollary, collective action by workers is further inhibited, if not rendered impossible, by their geographic, national, ethnic, and religious, and gender divisions.[40] Moreover, in this loss, which is understood as radical disempowerment by those most affected, and they are a growing number, what Robert Cox refers to as 'depoliticisation' sets in. By this he does not mean an absence of politics, which would be absurd, so much as 'a disillusionment of people with political leadership, a turning away from politics with a certain disgust, an association of politics corruption, [and] a sense that politics doesn't really matter except to the politicians ... [because] what determines the condition of people in their everyday lives is removed from their control, [they are] left in the futility of alienation.'[41]

The prognosis reveals no relief, only the acuteness in the hierarchies and inequalities of wealth to match the chronicality of the basic condition. Framing this are stark overall conditions, as revealed by the 2005 United Nations *Human Development Report*: by 2003, 18 countries with a combined population of 460 million had gone so far backwards in terms of their human development that their plight was worse than in 1990 – an 'unprecedented reversal.'[42] It also reports that one billion people live on less than US$1 per day, 40 per cent of the daily subsidy paid for every cow in the European Union and 10.7 million children die under the age of 5. But for a truly obscene comparison in this area, the amount the US spends on foreign aid – US$10 billion annually – is estimated to be equal to the amount that its citizens spend on pornography in the same period. Unsurprisingly, life expectancy in general has fallen, and child mortality in particular has increased to the point where the former (with HIV/AIDS at the core of the problem) is now at levels that are only comparable with the Black Death (Bubonic Plague) in fourteenth-century Europe which killed an estimated 25 million people in five years, or the 'Spanish Flu' pandemic of 1918 to 1919, which killed between 20 and 40 million. Expressed starkly, the average Japanese woman can expect to live to be 84 whereas the average Botswanan will die at 39; someone living in Zambia has less chance of living to age 30 than someone born in England in 1830.[43]

The key to understanding this phenomenon of the dynamic nature of the global distribution of wealth within and between countries, regions, and hemispheres under regimes of economic globalisation are the generically (and euphemistically described) 'adjustment' programmes which have been imposed on the South as a condition of assistance in the first place. Under such measures they were told, prosperity would eventually follow. What followed, however, was not prosperity but another depressing confirmation – this time of a decade of research on the World Bank by Patrick Markee, who showed that:

> structural adjustment programs failed to increase GDP growth or foreign investment and only marginally increased exports. What they did accomplish, however, was a radical opening of developing economies to the world market, a general reduction in wages and protections for workers, and intensified poverty.[44]

Nor is this likely to change. Structurally and economically, it is precisely the outcome which the 'rigid and rigidly orthodox, view of free-market, infrastructure-driven, export-oriented development' determines – so much so that it requires an inversion of the conventional understandings of what is underway; in the words of one World Bank critic, structural adjustment 'isn't a development strategy, it's a corporate strategy.'[45] Attitudinally, the World Bank is unrepentant: as one of its former vice-presidents expressed it, 'you can't have development without somebody getting hurt.'[46]

And 'getting hurt' is certainly the outcome. As the World Health Organization reported in 1995, 'Poverty is the biggest single underlying cause of death, disease and suffering worldwide,' and the patterns of disease and mortality confirm this conclusion: 40 per cent of deaths worldwide are due to communicable diseases, 99 per cent of which occur in the Third World, and to maternal, perinatal, and neonatal causes from which the rich countries are almost immune. In such a world the poor are not only excluded from the benefits of health care systems that are available to the affluent, they are also restricted from participating in, or incapable of taking, decisions that affect their health. If we then consider that ill health in turn leads to an inability to work, unemployment thus intensifies poverty and a vicious circle of descent is created which then spins off into disability, starvation, mental illness, suicide, family disintegration, and substance abuse.[47] What can, and frequently does, emerge then are incubator states, regions, or systems, and a world of contagions, as has happened and continues to happen, for example, with HIV/AIDS in Africa and drug-resistant tuberculosis in Russia.[48]

Using related data from the same period, the United Nations World Food Program has detailed another of the more significant consequences: hunger for some 830 million people, including 200 million children, mainly in large swathes of territory in sub-Saharan Africa and Asia, where 33 per cent and 17 per cent of the respective populations are deprived of sufficient food to provide the nutrients for active, healthy lives.[49] In Latin America and the Caribbean, the proportion is 11 per cent of the population. Officials within the Program, moreover, say that their research reveals that the scope of the problem is such that, since 1997, it has either not improved, or is getting worse.[50] This is affirmed by numerous studies and commentaries throughout the period of neo-liberal ascendance.

Africa, in the present context, is the most pathetic continent or, as Robert D. Kaplan has astutely observed on the basis of a wide range of economic data and reports, it is a continent 'falling off the world economic map.' Thus, though nearly 720,000,000 people, 13 per cent of the world's population, inhabit it, it contributes just 1.2 per cent of the world's gross domestic product, and the trend is a diminishing one. Even in the 1990s, according to the extraordinarily optimistic estimates of the World Bank's long-term projections for African economic development, it was going to take 40 years for Africans merely to regain their 1970s income levels; if Nigeria is excepted, the period of wait blows out to 100 years. If sub-Saharan Africa is the focus, the figures are even bleaker: population grows at double the planet's mean growth rate, while 28 of the 46 countries in the region have declining economies. In the 1994 *Human Development Report*, which rated 173 countries on the basis of literacy, schooling, population growth, per capita gross domestic product, and life expectancy, 22 of the bottom 24 countries were in sub-Saharan Africa.[51]

Latin America, though generally better off than Africa, is none-the-less ravaged by what is described as the 'worst plunder since Cortez.'[52] Per capita income in 1990 was virtually unchanged from 1980 levels, the number of those living in poverty rose from 130 million to 180 million, and income inequalities worsened in the same period, underlying the fact that underemployment and unemployment are rife. Even in the 1996 *Human Development Report* it is noted that income distribution improved in only three countries while it deteriorated in five. Accompanying these developments are not only the directly related effects of poverty itself, but also the intermediate, yet central, nexus between 'adjustment' and pathology: intra-state violence; the rise, or re-emergence, of refugees, and the internally displaced; the rise of hunger and malnutrition; the return of serious diseases (such as tuberculosis and cholera, once thought to have been banished by modern medicines), and thus, death, in what can only be described as holocaust proportions.[53]

Overshadowing all is death. The toll in the global South from the encroachments of globalisation reaches 13–18 million annually, most of them children, according to James Gustave Speth, president of the World Resources Institute; it is 12 million children under the age of 5 years according to the 1996 *Human Development Report*; and at least six million children under 5, each year since 1982, according to estimates by the United Nations Children Fund and the United Nations Economic Commission for Africa.[54]

Essentially the same findings are confirmed by the World Bank economist, Branko Milanovic, who, for the first time, used household survey data in over 100 countries and published his report under the title, *Worlds Apart: Measuring International and Global Inequality*.[55] In summary form, he concluded that developments over the last two decades of the twentieth century produced consequences that were 'remarkable' for the following reasons:

1   They have reinforced the position of the West as the club of the rich. Not only because at the end of the century there are only nine non-Western countries that are rich (compared to 19 in 1960), but because the 'threat' of non-Western contenders has all but disappeared.

2   The hope of non-Western countries catching up has effectively been dashed over the last quarter of a century...

3   While the West reinforced its control of the top, being an African country became synonymous with being very poor, much more so than probably ever in history. There was an uninterrupted slide downwards...

4   The downward mobility of the countries – of which Africa is the most striking example – is reflected in the fact that while the number of the rich countries and contenders decreased between 1968 and 1998, the ranks of the Third and Fourth World swelled.

Of particular significance is the fact that Milanovic finds that, with few exceptions (mainly in Asia) which have been upwardly mobile, the dramatic tendency is for the already poor Third World to 'bifurcate' into those that remain poor and those that became even poorer, descending to the Fourth World. He also confirms that the rule of the World Bank and International Monetary Fund is plutocratic and that the bilateral aid available from the North is simply not focused on the poor.[56] At best inequality is reducing only marginally, and even then, in only a handful of countries, a conclusion which the *Human Development Report 2005* is alive to because it cautions readers not to exaggerate these gains.[57]

PTSD: PERMANENT TRAUMATIC STRESS DISORDER

For those in work, any sense of achievement or relief that they have survived 're-engineering,' for the present anyway, is compromised by what the American Management Association term the 'heavy price' of damaged morale.[58] The climate of the workplace, according to the US Office of Technology Assessment, is becoming increasingly Orwellian because of the introduction of non-human agents as either monitors of performance, or arbiters of second-by-second efficiency in processes which the volume, flow, and pace of information have accelerated at speeds derived from computers rather than human capabilities. Non-human agents in environments which approach the description 'electronic sweatshops' are monitoring 20–35 per cent of clerical workers. Immediately induced by this surveillance are stress, physical and mental fatigue, and creative 'burnout.' Over a longer period, absenteeism, depression, tension, extreme anxiety, and workplace accidents result. And over an extended time frame, the consequences include serious health-related problems (ulcers, high blood pressure, heart attacks, strokes, and alcohol and drug abuse) and, ultimately, death.[59]

For the unemployed, the damage is different, although frequently the long-term effects are not easily distinguished. Both categories share anxiety and depression which, even if they are derived from disparate apprehensions, nevertheless frame their respective regimes of material suffering. More noticeable, therefore, are the effects which result from the withdrawal from a cash economy. Since the unemployed, especially the long-term unemployed, are without an income, various manifestations of poverty which take the form of an incapacity to provide for necessities at the level of survival are imposed in quite quick succession, and profoundly. Thus, homelessness was the plight of some 7 million at some time in the 1980s in the US; currently (2006), the figure is 3.5 million, or 1.3 per cent of the population, of whom 39 per cent are children (nearly half of whom are under the age of 5) in this state in any given month.[60]

Inadequate food and a lack of access to health care exacerbate this condition, but are in any case major causes of misery in their own right. In 1992 more than 10 per cent of the US population depended on food stamps, despite the fact that 40 per cent of the poor were engaged in some form of employment. By 2005, a comparable 25.7 million Americans were receiving food stamps, a 49 per cent increase since 2000.[61] But even this assistance was insufficient in the light of statistics showing that, as well, over 50,000 private food banks, pantries, and soup kitchens were also distributing food to the needy, who include, disproportionately, the old as well as the very young.[62]

Lacking adequate and nourishing food, and not being able to afford or to have access to health care produces predictable pathologies across society, but specifically in the most vulnerable groups. Low-birth-weight infants, and malnourished children, for example, are more likely to develop serious long-term health disorders which militate against both their employment prospects and, ultimately, their life expectancy. The significance of this for the United States might be gauged from studies which reveal that one out of every eight children under the age of 12 doesn't get enough to eat (and an almost identical number suffer from nutritional deficiencies), and nearly 30 per cent of the poor have no health cover of any kind.[63]

In the light of this morbidity it is not surprising that studies have established a link between unemployment and increased risk of death. In the US a University of Utah study conducted by two economists, Mary Merva and Richard Fowles, discovered that, for every one percentage point rise in unemployment, there was a 3.1 per cent rise in deaths resulting from strokes and a 5.6 per cent rise in deaths resulting from heart attacks, or an additional 2,771, and 35,307 deaths in the 1990 to 1992 period respectively.[64] Wider afield, these findings are confirmed according to studies whose reports were published in the *British Medical Journal*. In Britain, in the years 1981 to 1991, though death rates generally tended to fall, they actually rose among the poor – especially among men in the 15 to 44 age group. The unemployed, moreover, have a significantly greater chance of contracting cancer and heart disease, and overall, have a mortality rate twice that of the employed (when corrected for initial medical condition). And, in many ways overshadowing all such accounts, there is the work of the social epidemiologist, Richard Wilkinson who, in two major compilations of studies, of advanced 'market democracies,' published in the mid-1990s and 2005, respectively, confirms that health and inequality are inversely related, that where socioeconomic differentiation exists, life is shorter and more stressful. In other words, mortality closely correlates with inequality – it decreases among the poor when there is a more egalitarian distribution of income, and increases with impoverishment.[65]

WAR CRIMES, WAR CRIMINALS, AND PRISONERS OF WAR

To belabour the obvious, these pathologies are redolent with implications for security if it is understood in holistic and human terms. Certainly, the situation as it applies in the United States is understood by the wealthier and more powerful elements of that country to be a threat to their security. James K. Galbraith, one of the more astute observers in these matters, now writes of the 'new dialectic' in most advanced industrial societies which embodies a 'profound change in the nature of class conflict.' In his view the traditional, 'all-embracing struggle between capital and Labour' has suffered redundancy in the face of the 'more relevant dialectic ... between the haves and the have-nots.' The former are those who now combine political power with relative well-being – the surviving powerful and still affluent members of the business community who are now in company with the 'large and wide-ranging professional, academic, cultural, and entertainment communities, the great modern rentier class, and the vast numbers of the retired' who regard recession and the failure of society to produce enough jobs as 'discomforts for others to suffer.' These classes – 'the comfortably endowed and the relatively or specifically deprived'– now, and in the future, will define the antagonists of political and social conflict.[66]

Both classes, evidently, are fulfilling their allocated roles in a more-or-less traditional pattern of behaviour. In Europe, specifically in Germany, Italy, Russia, and France, forms of aggressive and frequently violent neo-fascist politics are pursued by the mobilisers of the grievance which results from economic dislocation unaccompanied by any hope of likely, or timely redress.[67] Group dynamics in the US, however, favour the formation of gangs at both the under-class, and middle-class, levels to the point where, in the early 1990s, up to 130,000 illiterate and unemployed teenagers in Los Angeles were members of the former, and more than 70 of the latter have emerged in the relative affluence of Westchester County.[68]

In the US, too, the prison population has grown spectacularly: in mid-2005, US Bureau of Justice statistics revealed that the rate of incarceration in the country was 1,000 new inmates per week as the total number behind bars nationally reached 2.2 million, or one in every 136 people in the country.[69] Explaining this carceral state, Rifkin writes that, '[j]ust outside the new high-tech global village lie a number of destitute and desperate human beings, many of whom are turning to a life of crime and creating a vast criminal subculture.'[70] By the evidence he adduces from numerous sources that this is not an exaggeration: the aforementioned Merva and Fowles study, by way of example, was based on a 5 per cent increase in wage inequality, over the period 1979 to 1988, across 30 metropolitan districts, revealed coincident percentage increases in motor vehicle theft (2.2), larceny and theft (2.0), robbery (1.0), property crime (4.2), aggravated assault (3.1), violent crime (2.1), and murder (4.2).[71] Similarly, between 1987 and 1993, according to the FBI's Uniform Crime Report, the victims of chronic unemployment and poverty increasingly turned to crime to survive with corresponding increases in shoplifting, convenience store robberies, bank robberies, commercial business robberies and violent crimes ranging from 18–50 per cent.[72]

So great is the state of civil anxiety induced thereby that a 1993 *Time*/CNN poll reported that 30 per cent of those surveyed thought that suburban crime is at least as serious as urban crime. Accordingly, it is estimated that 3–4 million Americans then chose to live inside walled residential communities, and, in 1992 alone, more than 16 per cent of US home-owners installed electronic security systems. In addition, suburban architecture now includes the concept of 'stealth buildings' – homes which are effectively 'private fortresses' constructed of steel and concrete, and surrounded by fences 12 feet high and monitored by security-camera systems, whose facades are 'plain and even grim, masking an opulent interior.'[73]

But the wider order of battle extends beyond the deprivations of 'desperate human beings' and the time-honoured reflex of their targets thinking in terms of siege and defensive circles. It remains significantly incomplete unless it is extended to include other, also time-honoured reflexes derived from radically straitened economic circumstances and their various consequences, but which receive less attention at all levels of analysis. This is to concentrate on the development of the pervasive and ominous binary which, in the work of Samuel Bowles, David M. Gordon, and Thomas E. Weisskopf, is constituted by 'guard,' and 'threat,' labour.' 'Guard Labour' is those people who not so much produce goods as enforce the rules under which production takes place. These include workplace supervisors, police, judicial, and corrections employees, private security personnel, the armed forces and civilian defence employees, and producers of military and domestic security equipment. To be sure, some 'guard labour' must be considered inevitable, but, in large numbers, it attracts attention to itself – both as a charge against production and because it raises questions about the conditions which it polices.

This is not the case with 'threat labour,' although it is, like 'guard labour,' unproductive, but about which other questions are more appropriate. 'Guard labour' is made up of the unemployed, those discouraged from seeking employment, and prisoners who, together, make credible the threat of dismissal from whatever employment is being enjoyed, and by providing salutary examples of life on the industrial heath. Between 1966 and 1989 in the US, the combined trend of these components rose from nearly 33 to nearly 37 for every 100 employed in production. In absolute terms this represented a population of 34 million Americans, or 'over a third more people ... than all those employed in manufacturing industries at all occupational levels.'[74] Perhaps no more striking an example of this trend towards the securitisation of daily life is the rise in the number of private security guards which, to say the least, has matched the trend in incarceration: in 1993, in the US, they outnumbered publicly employed police by 73 per cent; by 2005, however, their strength was conservatively estimated at 1.5 million, or 2.5 times the number of federal, state, and local police officers in a US$52 billion per year national industry with prospects of a 7.7 annual growth rate.[75]

Alive to the wider potential of such a social structure the war historian, Martin Van Creveld, locates it within the process he identifies as 'the transformation of war' itself, in which states and their military forces are rendered increasingly questionable as sources of order. In particular, he writes of the advent of new modes of conflict – murder, car-bombings, kidnappings, and massacres – conducted by bands of outlaws which increasingly resemble what has traditionally been called crime.[76] From another perspective the endemic structural violence in the situation is consistent with Paul Virilio's notion of endo-colonisation – a state of existence in which the conditions of life are those inflicted upon a vanquished people by an army of occupation, and the responsibility for it all is deferred to some imposing externality such as (in this case) 'the market.'[77] But, whatever the perspective, the condition which is viewed and experienced appears most accurately to be described in terms of war in general, and defeat in war more specifically.

CONFRONTING THE EVIDENCE: GLOBAL STRATEGIC FAILURE

Triage, by its very nature, can only ever be cursory; it always proceeds on the self-conscious assumption that much is omitted because only the most serious, and, to be honest, only the most obvious conditions can be addressed contemporaneously. But, when the dead, the wounded, and the damage are counted and named even as cursorily as they have been in the preceding pages, one inference is virtually inescapable: the strategy that caused them is a not only a failure, but a deadly failure. And this goes some way to explaining why, adjacent to the *triage* tent, there are frequently found two other tents – one for isolation, and one for the morgue. Indeed, what the more obvious casualty lists point to is confirmed by a wider reference to historical records which can only be alluded to here: the scope of the failure is global, encompassing not only the so-called 'millennial losers' – Africa and Latin America – but also, as detailed in the previous chapter, the free trade arrangements which constitute neo-liberalism's alliance equivalents (such as NAFTA), and the great engine of the ideology which is the United States.

The failure then expresses itself as comprehensive and accelerating inequality, where inequality is experienced by the great majority of the world's people as the steady decline, in many cases to zero, in the prospects for living a full, long, and secure life as generally defined and accepted by values which are local and temporal. On this besetting condition there is little serious argument which contests it; indeed, continuing a trend established in the 1980s with *Discriminate Deterrence*[78] it is accepted as a predicate circumstance in two principal US security planning documents for the early twenty-first century – the United states Space Command's *Vision for 2020*, and the Central Agency's *Global trends 2015*.[79] But whereas they see a burgeoning world economy and the widening gap between 'haves' and 'have-nots' side-by-side, there is no evident understanding that the nature of the former – predatory, turbo-charged and increasingly unregulated capitalism – is in fact the cause of the latter. Ironically, however, it is an implicit admission of an enduring feature of global economic life that certain economic strategies, because of the way they mal-distribute wealth and costs (not to mention the way their consequences are measured) logically produce economic growth and extraordinary benefits for the few on the one hand, and declining conditions of life for the many on the other hand.

What none of these documents concede, however, is the fact that the logic of the form of capitalism which is being globalised is not, and cannot be arrested at state borders, even at the borders of the United States, despite 'the impact of US hegemony' on [other states'] domestic and foreign policies,' and despite the unanimity of the elite analytical view which holds that the US is the 'global driver' and 'preponderant power' in world politics.[80] By extension, there is no awareness that either the neo-liberal alliances, or the like-minded neo-liberal allies of the US promoting economic globalisation, are similarly suffering from this particular variant of 'blowback.' And while there is no doubt that the growing gaps within the developed world are not of the same magnitude as those between the global North and the global South, there is hardly a case for rendering the world's fracture zones invisible, yet this is the inference to be taken. In sum, the world that *triage* foregrounds needs to be admitted as the schedule of consequences which attend neo-liberalism.

TRIAGE BLUE AND BLACK

Should this, albeit brief, survey of existing and deepening catastrophe leave any doubt as to the unrelieved grip of the 'new capitalism' on the minds of policy-makers, and their incapacity to think in any other terms, no matter the context, it is surely dissolved by two examples, one on each side of the Atlantic, of its status as *idée fixe*, as monomania. As though the developing global South has not been pillaged enough, it was the suggestion of Lawrence Summers, then with the World Bank, that low-wage countries be targeted for toxic waste dumping on the ground that the potential for income loss and environmental injury were relatively lower in such places.[81] And in the United Kingdom, wherein one might expect that *any* concessions to human decency would be encouraged if they had the potential to reconcile the minority Republican community (discrimination against which catalysed over 25 years of civil strife) with the Unionist majority in Northern Ireland, it was reported that Baroness Denton, the Environment Minister, described *fair employment legislation* as a burden which had to be lifted in order to encourage investment – as though wage rates 33 per cent less than the US, and 60 per cent less than Germany were not incentive enough![82]

There are many ways, no doubt, to understand economic globalisation, but understanding it as a form of non-teleological revolutionary, or simply counter-revolutionary, violence achieves a measure of intellectual, economic, political, and social justice. Intellectually, because it is a self-evidently violent re-ordering on the basis of the abstract principles and practices of corporate capitalism, which, notwithstanding the revulsion one experiences on making their acquaintance, comprise a readily identifiable discourse; a discourse, moreover, entirely unreflective when it comes, for example, to knowing the world through the medium of 200,000 monitors, or 200 'data points,' and promoting, in turn, 'the renewal of once-forbidden barbarisms.' At the same time, it is economically, politically, and socially revolutionary because it effects an extraordinary vanishing: as the economy globalises, so too does the point where, traditionally, the geography of privilege and wealth was separated from the world of necessity and poverty. In the foregoing survey, therefore, conditions in the Third World and the United States were interleaved, not to imply anything approaching an overall equivalence between them, but, rather, to introduce through the US as exemplar a persistent reminder of the ubiquitous nature of the effects wreaked by economic globalisation, here described by Greider:

> The global economy divides every society into new camps of conflicting economic interests. It undermines every nation's ability to maintain social cohesion. It mocks the assumption of shared political values that supposedly unite people in the nation-state.[83]

But, given the chasms of global differentiation, what 'mocks the assumption of shared political values' is more than the intensification of intra-state conflict – it is the daily complicity of those who live in the pockets of wealth and privilege throughout the world in the untimely deaths and misery of the great majority who are being 'globalised.' It is the inescapable consequences of a process – economic globalisation – which is but vaguely understood, if at all, even by the majority of its beneficiaries. And where they are aware, a disposition comprised substantially of apathy and cognitive dissonance is ascendant, as illustrated in Ted C. Fishman's tongue-in-cheek account of his plan to provide for his children's education using global, or international, investment funds. Thus, he acknowledges that, given the structure of the funds in question, his laudable objective and family responsibility inevitably incriminates him in the support of 'tyranny, authoritarianism, and latter-day feudalism' (and, just possibly, gun-running and murder).[84] At one level this is a direct consequence of the fact that his portfolio embraces 1,000 foreign companies in dozens of countries; at another, it is the result of not having the time or the inclination to investigate the sources of what are proving (for him) to be high returns; at another level still, the continual confrontation with a reality that challenges one's self-respect.[85] Reading it recalls the story Albert Camus frequently recounted, of the concierge in the Gestapo headquarters who went about her everyday business in the midst of torture explaining, 'I never pay attention to what my tenants do.'[86]

What 'mocks the assumption,' therefore, is a lack of even a liminal, let alone a confrontational, and visceral, understanding of the processes and their consequences, the proposition being that inattention on the part of thinking people would be extremely difficult, if not impossible, if they investigated their situations because they would necessarily discover that a reaction was unavoidable. For now, and briefly, that is because 'economic globalisation' is deprived of an adequate understanding, even within the term 'revolution,' within which it should be explored. In the interim, it has been suggested that a generic term, and its context, will suffice in this account – combat zone, and war, respectively.

The inductive leap here is not demanding given what has preceded. The pathologies of a globalising world, surely, are the equal of anything found in times defined as the 'clash of arms.' If 100 million have been killed in the formal wars of the twentieth century, why are they to be privileged in comprehension over the annual toll of five million children from structural adjustment programmes since 1982? Put another way, short of nuclear holocaust, what destruction and death could war bring to Africa that the World Bank and IMF have not already brought? Or even another: if the threshold of understanding the economic globalisation project as something other than another cycle of recession is indicated by Lester C. Thurow's view that no country has ever experienced America's recent maldistribution of wealth without a revolution, or a military defeat and subsequent occupation, then it is entirely reasonable to regard the wider tragedy afflicting humanity as neither metaphor, nor simile, of war, but war itself.[87] That it is so accords with more than the empirical evidence; it resonates with the genealogy of globalisation in Cold War power politics, and its legitimation in understandings of both modern scientific thought as authorised by the contemporary university, and religious dogma which the university ostensibly displaced. In this light any exploration must begin with an understanding of how the dialectic of the economic predominance, and later decline, of the United States generated a countervailing strategy of restoration, which not only conflated war and economics, but was, equally, informed by Clausewitz's famous dictum that war, and thus economics, was an 'act of violence intended to compel our enemy to fulfil our will.'

Such a reflection might, indeed should, return the gaze to the most pitiful of globalisation's casualties, the global South. By any ethical standard worthy of the term, its plight requires serious redress but, if the Report by the US Presidential Commission On Integrated Long-term Strategy, subsequent pronouncements by Jacques Attali, former head of the European Bank for Reconstruction and Development, and the raft of vision and doctrine documents analysed throughout this chapter are indicative of elite views over the last decade or so in the industrialised North, then quite the opposite is the prospect.

Attali, in *Millennium: Winners and Losers in the Coming World Order,* voices the same anxiety, albeit in the interests of 'modernity' and the 'beleaguered North,' but extends the logic as he makes the categories of threat more obvious. Africa is, thus, a 'lost continent' while Latin America is undergoing a transformation to 'terminal poverty.' To both continents and to the South in general, moreover, he applies the same condemnation – 'millennial losers.' But they are losers whose dispossession, envy, and consequent reactions – 'true world war of a new type of terrorism that can suddenly rip the vulnerable fabric of complex systems' – recall for Attali an historical precedent – 'the barbarian raids of the seventh and eighth centuries;' implicitly, therefore, their condition is seen as both beyond hope and demanding of eternal vigilance.[88] And, as with *Discriminate Deterrence* and its successors, it is the provenance of the pronouncements that is both significant and depressing: Attali, at the time, was a leading French Socialist Party intellectual and a member of the European policy-making elite; he was not, as Walden Bello made clear, a 'reactionary' so much as a 'liberal' who was, with relative ease, seduced into the belief that the interests of the 'rich, white North' and the 'poor, coloured South' are irreconcilable.[89] The grand strategic fraud which is the promise to the global South of faithfully adhering to neo-liberalism under all circumstances thereby discloses its character: upon already wounded combatants, it strikes further blows which are lethal, but the patients are denied the truth of their condition for fear of spreading panic, and even resistance. They are, therefore, lied to under a warped interpretation of the dispensation permitted in *Triage* Black/Expectant which it is appropriate to recall here:

- *Black/Expectant* No obvious priority.
Overwhelming injuries with little chance for survival or already dead. Only priority is comfort measures to those dying.
Note: With regard to patients who are categorised Expectant, chaplains may be present and circulate throughout the *triage* and treatment areas to render comfort and administration.

Part II

3 American decline and the ascendancy of Economics
Neo-liberalism as new containment doctrine and theory of globalisation

Central to understanding the contemporary globalisation of the world economy is the role of the United States in the process. In general terms, it is necessary to understand the objective and provenance of globalisation because they mirror the habits of mind and attendant practices with which the record of US strategic leadership in the Cold War is replete. The objective – invulnerability – actually predates the Cold War and can be found as far back as the War of 1812, while the habits of mind and practice which constitute provenance – deciding in isolation and acting unilaterally (which frequently involves leaving allies and friends with little choice in the circumstances but to follow) – though developed since that time also, have been increasingly prominent this century, becoming defining characteristics following World War II.[1] Not surprisingly, this creates a United States that is, essentially, estranged from the world it seeks to order and to lead, and it cannot be any other way. The ideas from which it draws its identity and mission are the result of a self-defined exceptionalism which is then used as a rationale for, first, intervention, and then, the liquidation of alternatives, be they ideological, philosophical, political, economic, or strategic. Given the objective, security can only proceed from universalising the exception, a contradictory project if ever there was one.

Credibility is, nevertheless, extended to this enterprise by the fact that the United States became, and remains, the most powerful country in world history. At the same time, whatever indulgences this might grant cannot obscure the fact that the US is not as exceptional as it would like to represent itself; indeed, of crucial importance for the empirical case that the US makes on its own behalf as an exemplar model of development is that its appeal is contingent upon, first, tolerating a conscious and premeditated US imperium; second, accepting US accounts and understandings of the way the world works; third, consenting to the elaboration of American myths as an accurate historical portrayal, not least concerning the nature of its economy since 1940; and finally, submitting to the indignity which is the self-willed amnesia present in exhortations to adopt the American model. To this end, it is the argument of the following pages that, by and large, the international community has complied with its obligations, and hence, the US has achieved its aims, effecting them through a combination of its outright dominance of the global economy and the institutions which police it. The present situation is, however, even more impressive than that in which the containment of the Soviet Union and the Eastern Bloc operated: in the absence of the economic equivalent of a military stalemate, there is now neither the need for accommodation with alternatives to neo-liberalism nor the room for them to manoeuvre. And paradoxically, this move was undertaken precisely at the moment in recent US history when observers of all complexions were conceding what had been obvious since at least the mid-1960s: the US was in decline.

UNDERSTANDING AMERICAN DECLINE

The indications, or evidence of this condition are not all that difficult to marshal, especially if they are approached through that body of contemporary literature which emerged around the time of Paul Kennedy's *The Rise and Fall of the Great Powers*, in 1988, through a succession of works such as Valdas Anelauskas' *Discovering America As It Is*, in 1999, to the current cascade of similarly oriented analyses which, if only indicatively, must include the recent and very recent works of Morris Berman, Jane Jacobs, Eric Larsen, and Robert Pollin.[2] Notwithstanding that such writings, though numerous and by scholars of diverse backgrounds and intellectual persuasions, are attracted to different foci in these and related works, all are unified to a remarkable extent by their engagement with the well-documented development of the pathologies of US society to such an extent that their accounts now constitute a significant area of American Studies, broadly defined.

Their concerns, moreover, were shared at the time by significant figures who had served at the highest levels of the US Government. Consider just two examples: the first was an article which appeared in *Foreign Affairs*, the prestigious organ of the Council on Foreign Relations, by Robert Hormats, former Assistant Secretary of State for Economic and Business Affairs, in which he writes of 'cities [which] are in some parts indistinguishable from Third World slums,' inhabited by an 'already large underclass,' which includes large numbers of 'minorities [who] fall outside the productive economy,' and will continue to do so because of the 'profound neglect' of the secondary education system.[3] The second was a similar request to reflect upon the same America and was described by Robert S. McNamara, US Secretary of Defense from 1961 to 1968, and President of the World Bank from 1968 to 1991, as a country marked by:

> destructive rates of illiteracy; unacceptably high levels of unemployment among blacks and teenagers; a rapidly growing underclass – in the capital of the richest nation in the world, Washington, DC, 51 per cent of all births are illegitimate; high and rising rates of drug abuse and drug-related crimes; a failure to adequately address the problems of the poor and disadvantaged; severe distortions in sectoral and regional growth patterns; and a significant deterioration of our physical infrastructure. I make these statements not in a partisan way. *This is a function of our society.*[4]

This is not to claim a spurious unanimity between these two former high-ranking officials, or the schedule of writers which could be marshalled beyond those already cited to support them; rather it is to state that there were, within the corpus of their works, threads and patterns which justified, internally, the concept of a 'gulf' war in the United States, with its own MIAs – those Missing In America – and externally, the need for those who would follow the US example to reconsider their object of imitation. In brief, they provided thoughtful, balanced accounts of the contemporary successes, but mainly excesses of the United States. More critically, what they pointed to, each in a different way, was the unravelling of a society. And there was a litany of its manifestations which, in their exacerbation over the last two decades, have the most profound implications for the US, both as a civilisation and as the sole remaining superpower.

In this context only a few of the more telling of them need be named here: the growth of crime and violence, crowded prisons, an accelerating drug culture, the breakdown of the justice system, rising unemployment in the already underprivileged classes, corporate high crime and insider trading, ecological crimes of commission and omission, increasing functional illiteracy, decreasing quality of intellectual life, high levels of litigation, intolerance and racial hatred, declining industrial productivity, the growth of poverty and homelessness, a scandalous lack of access to medical treatment for over 40 million people, and a crumbling transportation infrastructure. These existed in a society whose per annum debt was then running at 8 per cent of GNP, a figure sufficient to have turned the US spectacularly from the world's largest net creditor to its largest net debtor nation. Moreover, it was being incurred not so much for investment or development but to finance consumption. The consequences of these 'open and highly visible pathologies,' as Robert Heilbroner termed them, was both 'silent depression' and tangible decay,[5] not to mention what John Lyons discovered to be a 'confused, divided and afraid' society.[6] And, incredible as it might seem, the widely respected economics commentator, Felix Rohatyn, was writing that the financial independence of the United States 'has come to an end.'[7]

Similarly, surveying the wreckage within four categories – economic performance, political system, social and economic policy, and social pluralism – the renowned political scientist, Ted Robert Gurr, was most sceptical that the US was a valid model for the world:

> there [should] be a boldface Surgeon-General's warning on all prescriptions for instituting an American-style political economy: *it can be hazardous to your social and economic health.*[8]

The appeal of the model, however, persisted then as it persists now because, as Gurr astutely observes, America has appeal if you are on top and within it, or outside it and prefer it (albeit in ignorance) to a rejected regime. But if you are 'looking up from the bottom' (Gurr's term), and increasingly Americans were, then you discovered Jean Beaudrillard's paradox: 'America is powerful and original. America is violent and abominable.'[9] For those who delighted in the former, any sense that the pathologies are precisely the consequences guaranteed by the strategies in force was, and remains absent; indeed, it was, and remains imperative for both the confidence of the United States in itself, and the confidence of those who would follow it, that this state of inattention and loss of consciousness be maintained in perpetuity if the model is to serve its purposes of regeneration at home and exhortation abroad.

And it was maintained. In the United States, the critical faculties of the American mainstream were simply overcome by celebration as the country bent itself to an inevitable return to a position of preponderant power, as alien as its pursuit and appearance ought to have been with the passing of the Cold War. Notwithstanding that this event, in itself, was worthy of celebrating, in the wider scheme of global politics, it and the Gulf War which followed within a year, served only to emphasise the ease with which decline could be eluded: resolutely, the US refused to consider that it might, like Greece, Rome, and Britain before it, be on an historical trajectory in which the points of passage necessarily included descent. One such defining moment was 28 January 1992, when President George Bush gave his annual State of the Union message to the US Congress and quickened a previously nascent apprehension into alarm. George Bush, it seemed, had succumbed to the pornography of unipolar triumphalism and its accompanying masturbatory reflex:

> Much good can come from the prudent use of power. And much good can come of this: a world once divided into two armed camps now recognises one sole and pre-eminent power: the United States of America. And they regard this with no dread. For the world trusts us with power – and the world is right. They trust us to be fair, and restrained, they trust us to be on the side of decency. They trust us to do what's right.[10]

To hear, and then read such self-congratulation less than one year after *Desert Storm* – an event accurately described by Richard Falk as that 'cruel, merciless, and vengeful war in the Gulf' – realised the fear bordering on alarm that the New World Order, in which name it was rationalised, was indistinguishable from an imperial vision.[11] Global politics, it seemed, were not to be sustained on the basis of new, future possibilities. As Bush was making explicit, the traditional practices of power politics were too much with the United States, affirming once again a variation on the Zen paradox which teaches that, though all possibilities are open to the US, the US is not open to all possibilities. It was not even aware of the general truth in the remark of the Goncourt brothers in the role of pornography in the state: 'One tames people as one tames lions, by masturbation.'[12]

Thus, just because the 'declinist' school of scholarship in international relations and international history had rightly, and, in some cases profoundly, illustrated its theses, it was too often assumed that what was on offer was epitaphic, even eschatological, rather than forms of diminution. Forgotten, furthermore, was just how limited the imagination of the US was, yet how powerful it was even as its predominant status had eroded; even more forgotten was how powerful it would remain, not just as the sole surviving superpower, or leading economic power, or as a still predominant (but reduced) alliance partner throughout much of the post-Cold War world, but as the strategic and intellectual hegemon of the West.

At the most obvious, and traditional, level – military-strategic – the US clearly retained both its status, and habits of hegemonic mind. As the leaked draft of the 1992 Pentagon document, *Defense Planning Guidance*, indicated, global domination was not to be surrendered merely on the grounds that the Cold War had deprived the US of global leadership against a global enemy. Indeed, continued domination of 'a market-oriented zone of peace and prosperity that encompasses more than two-thirds of the world's economy' was the objective even if it meant 'discouraging' the advanced industrialised nations, many of whom were allies of the US, 'from challenging [US] leadership or even aspiring to a larger global or regional role.'[13]

Subsequently, the 'draft' nature of this document was emphasised and provided a basis for disavowals that it represented US policy. But subsequently, too, there were indications that were difficult to reconcile with the disavowals. Among these were the military's declared mission of possessing the capabilities to fight two Gulf Wars at once; a refusal to place US forces under UN command even if they were engaged in UN operations; a level of national expenditure in 1995 (approximately US$280 billion) which was more than the rest of the world combined; and, in combination with its allies, a level of expenditure representing 90 per cent of the world's military budget.[14] Other indicators supported the same view: expressed as a ratio of the combined military spending of the nine next largest national budgets, US spending was 120 per cent; as a ratio of the military budgets of all regional adversaries (Cuba, Iran, Iraq, North Korea, Libya, and Syria), it was 1,600 per cent.[15]

Economically, as well, comparable margins of advantage or superiority were still to be observed, and, significantly, to be maintained insofar as possible: only a jaundiced eye would see Bush's State of the Union vision in 1992 as excluding the economic realm. To this end, Agnew and Corbridge argue that there is considerable evidence to the effect that the policy-making elite in the US still see the international political economy in state-territorial terms to a marked degree and are prepared to act so as to reduce relative advantages accruing to America's rivals. And for this task it is uniquely placed through the combination of strategic capabilities in its possession – a modal point for information in a world economy highly determined by information flows, 'the world's leading reserve currency,' and a single economy which is greater than two of its closest rivals, Germany and Japan, combined. In a global economy framed by the WTO and NAFTA, furthermore, this situation is unlikely to change since free trade and interdependence will advantage US firms at least as much as those within rival states. There are solid grounds, therefore, for avoiding the conclusion that the decline of the US is synonymous with its demise.[16]

Moreover, while no rival currently has the resources to challenge the global leadership role of the US in the areas canvassed, it is also the case that an enhanced capacity to exercise hegemonic power is realised times without number on an everyday basis as a result of the transformation of global power to include, in addition to those categories, US cultural dominance which Joseph Nye celebrates as 'soft power,' and critics of the same phenomenon, such as Richard Barnet and John Cavanagh, have derided as 'Coca-colonisation.'[17] At issue here is the so-called 'second face of power' by which other states comply with US wishes, without being directly commanded, or coerced, to do so because of the institutionalised and universalised 'attraction of one's ideas or the ability to set the political agenda in a way that shapes the preferences that others express.'[18]

Finally, but very much to the point, regardless of the perpetuation of hegemonic vitality in, and of, the US itself, there are now serious disincentives to challenging the US. In a world environment characterised by issue areas of a transnational nature, which is to say by common problems unamenable to single-nation remedies, the incentives among the small number of leading industrialised countries to cooperate with the US, and with each other, rather than to engage in an expensive (and perhaps futile) attempt to displace the US, and which potentially could undermine the common rules which have emerged between them as regards security, trade, and investment, now determine a certain acceptance of the extant international hierarchy. Indeed, in a world in which the very notion of hegemon is increasingly *passé* and redundant to all but the United States, which is habituated to it, the question of who might succeed the US only begs the question of why such an inquiry is necessary in the first place.[19]

Thus, it was the irony of the juncture of history covered by the closing two decades of the twentieth century that the US was relatively less powerful in objective terms than at any time since 1945, yet the domain over which its ideas ruled was greater than at any previous time in its history as a nation. As Felix Rohatyn observed, though the end-of-Cold War revolutions in Bulgaria, Czechoslovakia, Hungary, and Poland had as their objectives, not German economic efficiency or Japanese economic discipline, but (an Eastern European understanding of) American political democracy as their objective, there was cause for asking whether they were in fact 'seeing the light of a distant star, which some time ago, may have ceased to shine so brightly.' In other words, Rohatyn saw their quest in terms of 'becoming what they think we are.'[20] But the Eastern Europeans are not alone in this. We find the Australian Foreign Minister, Senator Gareth Evans, as late as 1995, proclaiming the United States still to be 'the exemplar of the Western model' [of economic development].[21] Moreover, the model in question is that of scientific rationality, in political economy as in all other aspects of life, which had moved Ralf Dahrendorf, some 30 years earlier, to describe the US as the 'Applied Enlightenment.'[22] Between the two statements it is almost as though nothing of historical importance had happened to challenge either assessment.

Earlier, the United States was the source of a scientistic rationality which, if adopted unreservedly and practised wholeheartedly, provided a comfort second only to religion in its ability to allay the existential anxieties of 'the peril of living in the uncertainty of time.'[23] Then, it was a Fordist cafeteria for the Western Cold War mind-set, providing an 'overarching geopolitical discourse' which created, justified, and compassed the defeat of a common communist enemy.[24] Then, all of this was the unremarkable present and future, to be accomplished through the familiarity, utility, and method of traditional Western social analysis which the US propagated within that discourse.[25] Then, it remained impervious to virtually every reproach it encountered, be it intellectual, strategic, or political, or combinations thereof.

Nothing, it seems, has changed – at least not if the former Eastern Bloc and Gareth Evans' considered views are any indication. Despite the overwhelming evidence that, by any criteria befitting something as canonical as the 'exemplar of the Western model,' this discourse stood, and fell irredeemably, with the events which signalled the end of the Luce's 'American Century' in general, and the US record in the Vietnam War and the emerging awareness of decline in particular . Whereas North Vietnam's formal victory in 1975 was the final punctuation in an American defeat which had been foreseen by policy-makers as early as 1964, and obvious to a wider critical audience since the Tet offensive in 1968, the economic auguries were no less ominous. By the 1970s the US had discovered the realities of a world economy which was increasingly interdependent, one significant indication of which was the dollar crisis of 1971 which caused President Richard Nixon to withdraw the dollar from the gold standard. At the same time America was beginning to experience a measure of technological decline (from its peak in the 1950s and 1960s), and was facing a global environment characterised by an oil crisis (caused by the 1973 OPEC 'oil shock'), deep recession, and rising protectionism. And, so as to be clear, what was at stake in these developments was not so much various discrete reversals to America's interests, but the givenness of the economic underpinnings of Western strategy as codified in the Bretton Woods agreements of 1944.

These established nothing less than the *quid pro quo* by which, in return for US military commitment to defend the 'free world' against communism – and this leaves to one side the dubious propositions that all of the former were indeed free, and that the Soviet Union was bent on military expansion – world trade was to be not only opened up, but also denominated in US dollars which were redeemable against gold; the dollar effectively became the world's main reserve currency, the linchpin of international finance. It was an arrangement designed to give the United States unique advantages, which, early in its existence, were realised, both financially and cognitively. Any real opposition to the agreements was dissolved by both the US commitment and the relative weaknesses of those who disagreed. US corporations, through their wartime expansion, were of such a scale and scope that their competition, domestic and foreign, was relatively impotent – in fact so impotent in the case of the latter, that imports into the US averaged only 5.6 per cent of GNP in the 'boom years' of 1948 to 1966; in addition, between 1946 and 1949 the US share of world gold reserves rose from 60 per cent to 72 per cent.

Conversely, in Britain, the normally conservative, and pro-American journal, *The Economist*, complained bitterly of the terms which Washington imposed for settling war debts under Bretton Woods: 'It is aggravating to find that the reward for losing a quarter of our national wealth in the common cause is to pay tribute for half a century to those who have been enriched by the war.'[26] Such bitterness remained recessive, however, so long as the economic advantages of the agreements flowed to the United States and the American commitment allowed the West to interpret both as a satisfactory transaction which need not be revisited despite the fact that it required an acceptance, *in perpetuum*, of Western subordination to the United States.

In time, though, the success of Bretton Woods collapsed on its principal architect. In the US itself the wealth created in this period encouraged domestic competition to the US corporations, which, when accompanied by a distrust of big business and corresponding effective antitrust activity, resulted in an overall decline in corporate profitability.[27] More significantly, as a result of the overvaluing of the dollar which Bretton Woods encouraged, the effect of the economic reconstruction of Western Europe and Japan (which also brought with it increasing challenges to US corporations from abroad), but also developments such as American foreign investment, a surge in imports (and consequent damage to exports), and currency speculation, was to create foreign holdings of dollars which exceeded US reserves of gold, resulting in Nixon's abandonment of the convertibility pledge.[28] Thus, in the space of 30 years in military terms, and 27 years in economic-financial terms, the US designs for a post-World War II global order incorporating what was, in essence, the first phase of contemporary grand-strategic, and thus economic globalisation, had come seriously undone.

Of these defeats, and much more importantly, their lack of recognition by certain policy elites (as evidenced above) it has to be acknowledged that the US possesses a seemingly incorruptible appeal which countermands the insolence of its failures. Both, nevertheless, disclose two extremely relevant aspects of the more immediate origins of economic globalisation which are accessible with the benefit of an even tighter focus than used to this point. The first is the particularity of the capitalism which is being served by the theories and practices which attend the globalisation process. As Cox has described it, this is a capitalism which 'proclaims a universality exclusive of other types,' but is, nevertheless, 'historically specific and of fairly recent origin in the USA and Britain.' What is sometimes known as 'Anglo–American' economic thought is, therefore, to be differentiated from those other forms of capitalist theory, found more often in Europe and Japan, but, whereas the latter's cultural and historical moorings preclude them from proselytising on a global basis, the former 'radiates a worldwide influence,' not least because its abstract, scientific pretensions are incapable of acknowledging any such inhibitions.[29]

The second, and related, aspect helps explain just why the US proposed a radically expanded GATT mission – first, during the Tokyo Round of Multilateral Trade Negotiations (MTN) which ran from 1973 to 1979, and then, with the even more expansive and radical proposal of the WTO, during the Uruguay Round of MTN, which began at Punta del Este in 1986 and were concluded in 1993. Significant is the fact that the Tokyo Round was launched in a period when the US was confronting the changing nature of the global economy, and its declining role in it. With what Stephen Toulmin identifies as the 'nostalgia' for a world ordered to its advantage, and instinctive to a superpower, it sought to bring under the purview of GATT a range of new areas for trade liberalisation – such as non-tariff barriers, safeguards (e.g. the use of unilateral measures such as voluntary export restraint agreements), tropical products (which were of interest to developing countries), and agriculture.[30] It was, therefore, a period in which, to prevent further erosion and to exploit existing advantages, especially in technology, the US sought to ensure guaranteed access to new markets by way of means which were entirely familiar to anyone with a critical understanding of Bretton Woods. To the fore, then, was not imagination, but 'institutional sclerosis,' an attempt to reclaim certainty in the form of hegemony by revisiting, and relying upon, a previous arrangement now out of time.[31]

In other words, if the scholarly accounts on US decline are taken seriously, then, at the very time that their implications for US hegemony were being understood by US policy-makers, the movement towards globalisation effected what Brecher and Costello term a 'daring global *coup d'état*' for US capital and capitalism.[32] It represented, therefore, a change in the character of the strategic arena, from one whose surface manifestations were, for the most part, dominated by the possession, disposition, and deployment of the military instruments of power, to one in which such measures are but companions, robust companions admittedly, to the institutional and legal instruments of wealth-creation. At the risk of overemphasis, nothing in this transformation was alien to the strategic values and vision which the United States brought to the task of ordering the world following World War II. In the initial stages of this project, the euphoria of victory, delight in peace, and engrossment in the tasks of reconstruction meant that it might have been less obvious, or less commonly known, that is all. But, after three decades of the project, it is surely a compelling feature of US strategy that, when emerging, albeit friendly, forces from within the Western alliance posed a challenge to the institutional foundations of US capital, its responses were built upon 'hierarchical relations of domination and subordination which could not be easily abandoned.'[33]

PREPONDERANT POWER

The character of any 'solution,' therefore, was virtually predetermined. Thus, despite the US government's antitrust activity against big business in the late nineteenth century, there were clear indications from the earliest days that the free market in ideas, as well as goods, was not to pursue to the point of indiscretion, or, to put it another way, to the point where there would be an obvious correspondence between declared and operational policy, at least in the international arena. Quite simply, what made sound sense within the United States was not to be adopted within the community of states, or even within a community united against a common economic, political, and strategic adversary. George Kennan, the leading architect of US foreign policy in the early Cold War, succinctly outlined the principles involved as follows, in 1948:

> We have about 50% of the world's wealth, but only about 6.3% of its population. … In this situation, we cannot fail to be the object of envy and resentment. *Our real task in the coming period is to devise a pattern of relationships which will permit us to maintain this position of disparity* without positive detriment to our national security. To do so we will have to dispense with all sentimentality and daydreaming; and our attention will have to be concentrated everywhere on our immediate national objectives. We need not deceive ourselves that we can afford the luxury of altruism and world benefaction. *We should cease to talk about vague … and unreal objectives such as human rights, the raising of living standards, and democratisation.* The day is not far off when we are going to have to deal in straight power concepts. The less we are hampered by idealistic slogans, the better.[34]

Evidently, the advice was taken to heart (and to purse). The US decided its strategy would be one of 'a preponderance of power,' in which economic and strategic concerns would operate in tandem so as to ensure that the US would be virtually invulnerable.[35] US capital's recourse, within this, was to defend its steadily eroding position with 'guard,' and 'threat,' labour; indeed, this tactic, and the growth of 'military Keynesianism,' grew to such proportions that it justified the description of the US as a 'garrison state.'[36] As the *Bulletin of Atomic Scientists* has estimated by way of various comparisons, if the Defense Department was classified as a state, its land holdings would make it the twenty-ninth largest in the union; in population terms, its employees – civilian and military (including reserves) – would make it the third-largest US city.[37] Or, there's Rifkin's more fulsome account, complemented by Marilyn Waring:

The war economy continued after V-J day in the form of a vast military-industrial complex, a labyrinth of Pentagon-financed endeavours that came to dominate the American economy. By the late 1980s, over 20,000 major defence contracting corporations and an additional 100,000 subcontractors were working on Pentagon projects. The military share of total goods consumption was more than 10 per cent during the Reagan–Bush years. *The military-industrial complex had swelled to such monstrous proportions that if it were a separate nation, it would rank as the world's thirteenth largest power.* In the 1980s the United States spent more than [US]$2.3 trillion on military security. *Nearly [US]$46 out of every [US]$100 of new capital went to the military economy.*[38]

The US military budget [in 1986, US$1 billion per day] …is larger than the GNPs of all but eight countries in the world …[and] is the largest centrally planned economy outside of the Soviet Union.[39]

Because, essentially, what was being sought was the preservation of American privilege, domination, and good fortune at the expense of all others, friends and allies included, US policy was, again essentially, not so much a strategy as an exercise in wish fulfilment. Because of that it was also indiscriminant in its targets, embracing many national economies that were essential to the strategy of Containment which was being pursued simultaneously. Thus, even in what is arguably the United States' most important alliance, NATO, underlying tensions were so great that a Chicken War was followed by a Spaghetti War (both with the European Community) until, in 1987, the North Atlantic Assembly published a document which described the intra-alliance trade wars as a direct threat to NATO itself.[40]

Similarly, as newly industrialising countries (NICs) in the Asia-Pacific region – Japan, South Korea, Taiwan, Singapore, and Hong Kong foremost among them – developed economically and became in fact the main competition to the US economy, their status, too, was revised in line with the US economic imperatives of the day. Whereas, earlier, their 'distinctively statist policies [including import and investment restrictions] … were overlooked by Washington's containment liberals and advocates of realpolitik' in the interests of the US corporations who operated in them very profitably, and the global struggle against communism. But eventually their very success, which included the ability to compete successfully in the US domestic market, lowered the threshold of US capital's tolerance to the point where unrestricted access to their domestic markets for, *inter alia*, the purposes of dumping surpluses – 'Free Trade' – was the only condition that would suffice. Effectively, this amounted to a pre-emptive attack on the state in the NICs in the hope that the US would not have to face a proliferation of economies successfully modelled on Japan.[41]

No NIC, no matter how precarious its position, was beyond being targeted by the US in its mission of economic irredentism. Indeed, the inability of countries to retaliate seems only to have encouraged the United States in its campaigns. Thus, Bangladesh, Fiji, Myanmar (Burma), and Papua New Guinea were all subjected to US discipline in what proved to be a an 'eminently successful trade offensive.'[42] Of course, as with most successful offensives, success was not an objective to be achieved for its own sake, but rather as the basis for the ongoing relationship, in this case the recolonisation of the subordinated countries through the universalising of certain economic priorities established unilaterally by the United States. Conversely, this renders illegitimate all other economic models, especially those which provide for development within a culturally specific sensitivity, an example of which occurred in 1983, when President Reagan ordered 6,000 US troops to invade a British Commonwealth country, the West Indian mini-state of Grenada, whose defence forces numbered less than 1,000, in order to reverse a popular local movement towards a revolutionary non-capitalist form of development.[43]

Under the aegis of the Uruguay Round of the GATT, the US offensive was expanded, in 1986, to include Trade-Related Aspects of Intellectual Property Rights (TRIPs), Trade-Related Investment Measures (TRIMs), and the services sector which will also serve to re-establish Northern hegemony over Southern countries. A broader front still was established subsequently by the 1994 North American Free Trade Agreement (NAFTA), which is to be reinforced by the Free Trade Agreement of the Americas (FTAA), described by many as 'NAFTA for the Americas,' and the expansion of the General Agreement on Trade and Services (GATS) which came into force in 1995, launched by the World Trade Organization in 2000. (The mid-1990s also saw the introduction by the Organisation for Economic Cooperation and Development, of the Multilateral Agreement on Investment (MAI) – effectively constitution for the global economy – the adoption of which was curtailed by a growing awareness, even among neo-liberal governments, that its powers within domestic jurisdictions were simply too intrusive.)

In the case of TRIPs, by extending and reinforcing the practice of patenting, Third World users of recent technological and biotechnological advances in the North will be hostage to the patent holders despite the fact that, in the case of biotechnology, for example, many of the breakthroughs are derived from resources which are freely available in the South. In short, what is being implemented is, in the words of a United Nations Conference on Trade and Development (UNCTAD) analysis, the privileging of 'monopolistically controlled innovation over broad-based diffusion.'[44] The Third World is to develop, it seems, but under conditions primarily determined by the United States. Moreover, they are conditions which preclude an 'imitative path of technological development' – using such techniques as reverse engineering, the adaptation of foreign technology to local circumstances, and the improvement of existing innovations – in other words, which preclude the possibility of Southern countries following Japan, South Korea, or Taiwan, and so competing with the US like them.[45] It is appropriate, therefore, to investigate these measures at somewhat greater length for the light they throw on economic globalisation, its instruments, and the strategies and values both incorporate.

TRIPs, in the first instance, are to be understood as less a Western, but almost exclusively an American, imposition in direct line of strategic pedigree from Bretton Woods. At its heart was 'a centuries old tradition of intellectual property consciousness' complemented by a 'doctrinal knowledge and the juristic and judicial refashioning of that knowledge' as to how US intellectual property was to be asserted, accepted by the global membership of the GATT, and entrenched within its legal framework. (This was in contradistinction to Third World countries with which the concept found little, or no sympathy, or even Europe, which, according to the US, was guilty of 'an excessively cultural perception' of it.)[46] The objective was threefold: to create an intellectual property rights (IPR) order, which would effectively render permanent the existing monopoly privileges of the US, the world's only net exporter of global property, by as Peter Drahos frames it, 'the control of material objects [such as are produced in manufacturing processes] ... through the control of abstract objects [such as algorithms implemented in computer software].'[47]

What the US proposed, and achieved with TRIPs under the GATT, was both the reconceptualisation, and revaluation, of information, globally, and a corresponding modification in the domestic laws of most GATT members as regards information. In turn, information became propertised by law; by law, also, it became the subject of newly created rights, and thus regulated, and thus more expensive; and by extension national and international legal and administrative structures were established which mandated the domestic policing of compliance with a global privilege enjoyed primarily by the United States.[48] In the process the US, as patent hegemon, even succeeded in claiming that life forms freely found in nature and, in some cases, accessed for centuries by Third World peoples, could be patented 'so long as some artificial means are involved in isolating them.'[49] As a result, traditional methods which are less technologically intense are defined as unpatentable.[50] As Brian Martin has observed: 'This has led companies to race to take out patents on numerous genetic codes. In some cases, patents have been granted to covering all transgenic forms of an entire species, such as soy beans or cotton.'[51] It is the case, for example, that World Patent No. 9208784, or 'human t-lymphotropic virus type 2 from Guyami Indians in Panama' is claimed by the US Department of Commerce, which has demanded 'global acquiescence to the patenting of life forms.'[52]

Given that the US objective in the matter of TRIPs was to preserve US dominance by protectionist means and, notably, within a negotiating framework ostensibly devoted to 'trade liberalisation,' it is important to understand how their recognition was achieved. This need for this explanation is a pressing one in terms of formalising a monopoly, but becomes acute in the realisation that three related aspects of TRIPs quite specifically question their intellectual and ethical integrity. The former is best approached through the common aversion of many countries to such a concept as 'intellectual property.' Put bluntly, the record, according to Drahos, shows that the US position relied, first, on an assertion that such a thing both existed and required global regulatory protection, and second, that the argument in support thereof relied on (as noted above) 'a centuries old tradition of intellectual property consciousness' complemented by a 'doctrinal knowledge and the juristic and judicial refashioning of that knowledge' possessed almost entirely by the US, whose negotiators wielded it with 'disciplining effect.'[53] In which case, the TRIPs relied on a closed, self-referential argument which any person with a passing exposure to elementary logic would have found contemptible.

The question of ethical integrity arises from the silences in the dominant discourse on TRIPs, particularly in the area of life-forms. If the US Department of Commerce can hold World Patent No. 9208784, or 'human t-lymphotropic virus type 2 from Guyami

Indians in Panama,' and the US National Institutes of Health can hold patent No. 5.397.696, comprising genetic information contained in cells which once belonged to a 20-year-old Hagahia man from Papua New Guinea, and if both patents endow their holders as the exclusive owners of the respective information, the question of appropriation is surely to be answered. By what proprietary process short of conquest, or feudal prerogative, is it possible to claim invention of that which already exists, discovery of that which is already known, and ownership of that which is held in common, especially if invention and discovery were made possible only with the help and guidance of those whose contributions will be unacknowledged? If, however, the scientists who collected the information did not reveal that it might subsequently be used for private commercial gain, the question turns from the circumstances in which something is freely donated or made over, to one of arbitrary deprivation and dispossession, otherwise known as expropriation – in a word to 'biopiracy.' This is obviously the case if, as in the case of the Guyami of Panama, for example, their willingness to assist with medical research for the general improvement of the human condition, and their belief, as elaborated by the President of their National Congress, that the patenting of life-forms is 'fundamentally immoral and contrary to the Guyami view of nature and our place in it.'[54]

What this record implies, therefore, is an explanation susceptible to neither logic, nor ethics, nor common decency, alone, or in combination. According to Drahos: 'The US and US business succeeded …because they pushed the issues relentlessly at all possible levels, in all possible fora, using all possible agents.'[55] But the primary instrument he identifies in this commitment was, quite simply, coercion, in conjunction with sophisticated forms of surveillance mounted by the US business community, and 'consciousness raising campaigns' designed, as it were, to capture the 'hearts and minds' of target populations in countries in which breaches of copyrights held by US companies were rife.[56] Specifically, it was a strategy undertaken by a highly coordinated alliance constituted by the US Administration, US corporate interests, and the Congress, which deployed as a weapon what is known as the '301 process' of the Trade Act of 1974, which provides for graduated responses of US sanctions against countries, firms, and individuals found wanting in their legislation and/or compliance according to US standards.[57]

In practice the 301 process has resulted in some of the worst fears that economic globalisation is but a mule for American enculturation being realised. In recent times it has been triggered against: Brazil, because it limited the scope of its patent legislation and its term of protection for computer software to 25 years; Spain, because its legal remedies in the copyright area precluded owners of copyright from conducting *ex-parte* searches of a defendant's premises based only on the court submissions of the plaintiff; and Australia (a developed, industrial democracy in which some 90 per cent of all patents are foreign-owned) and the European Union, because their electronic media broadcast quotas, designed as minimum safeguards of national culture and identity, were held to discriminate against the US motion picture industry.[58] As implied, the 301 process was a successful bilateral strategy, which, because it isolated target countries who were in every case vulnerable to US sanctions, virtually guaranteed outcomes favourable to the US. It even precluded effective action by such countries at the multilateral level because 'resistance to US negotiating objectives at a multilateral forum could itself trigger the 301 process.'[59] In other words the inevitability of agreement at multilateral fora reflects their status as the coerced extension of coerced bilateral relationships.

In the interests of completeness, however, coercion, and more particularly, biopiracy, should be extended to the wider context of Western scientific imperialism in the developing countries, and specifically, the use of such countries for medical research. The suggestion, then, is that TRIPs were both part innovation, and part Western customary practice. In acknowledging the latter it is noteworthy that the principal lobby group set up in the United States to establish a pro-TRIPs climate among the leading GATT members, the Intellectual Property Committee, included, *inter alia*, the pharmaceutical corporations Bristol–Myers, Du Pont, Johnson and Johnson, Merck, Monsanto, and Pfizer (whose CEO, Ed Pratt, was chair of the Advisory Committee for Trade Negotiations, as well as an adviser to the US Official Delegation at Punta del Este).[60] And one of the customary practices in question is that which the (Australian) Medical Lobby for Appropriate Marketing repeatedly criticises, namely, marketing policies which do not treat developed and developing countries equally, as exemplified in the practice of marketing drugs in the latter which are denied a product licence in the former because of a lack of efficacy, or safety, or both. Another is the practice of conducting research projects in Africa and Asia which 'do not conform to the Declaration of Helsinki *and could not be conducted in the developed world.*'[61] The reasons for doing so are familiar:

> lower costs, lower risks of litigation, less stringent ethical review, the availability of populations prepared to give unquestioning consent, anticipated under-reporting of side effects because of lower consumer awareness, the desire for personal advancement by participants, and the desire to create new markets for drugs.[62]

Moreover, because the volunteers in such projects are poor, and because early clinical research is conducted in an atmosphere of secrecy as regards safety and dose ranging, 'much preliminary research is unpublished, particularly when adverse effects are high and further development is abandoned.'[63] The result is that people who are too poor to buy the effective treatment for their illness, and thus too poor to buy whatever product is marketed from the project they contributed to, are being exploited as little better than laboratory objects whose value is determined by a corporate utility function not significantly different from the role they served under explicit regimes of colonialism.

TRIMs should be seen as an assault in parallel with TRIPs. They have the same deleterious effects on the developing world by seeking to abolish local requirements that foreign investment contributes to national development by way of minimum levels of domestic content or equity, or levels of production by foreign concerns for export. At the same time, there is only silence on the practices of multinational corporations which include transfer-pricing, price-fixing for subsidiaries, and closed purchasing arrangements. The magnitude of these deliberate exclusions is to be gauged from estimates that over half of international trade is transnational, and between two-thirds and 80 per cent of that is between one subsidiary and another of the estimated 18,000 multinational corporations and their 104,000 affiliates.[64]

What TRIPs does by monopolistic control, and TRIMs achieves by making the South into no more than an opportunity for exploitation, the opening-up of the service sector to foreign penetration completes by driving local skills development into recession in the face of a transnational presence with all the benefits of scale, not to mention the advantages which accrue from TRIPs and TRIMs. This is done by requiring that foreign service-providers receive the same treatment accorded to their domestic competitors. Since up to 67 per cent of foreign investment in recent years has been in fields such as transport, construction, telecommunications, financial services, and legal services, the potential for the Third World countries to become substantially beholden to foreign interests for the cost, design, building, quality, and maintenance of their infrastructure is obvious, as is the corresponding retardation of their own service resources.[65]

Almost anything left uncovered by these measures was to be covered by the GATS 2000 negotiations, somewhat conservatively, though accurately, described as 'comprehensive and far-reaching' by Nicola Bullard:

> The current [1994] rules seek to phase out gradually all governmental 'barriers' to international trade and commercial competition in the services sector. The GATS covers every service imaginable – including public services – in sectors that affect the environment, culture, natural resources, drinking water, health care, education, social security, transportation services, postal delivery and a variety of municipal services. Its constraints apply to virtually all government measures affecting trade-in-services, from labour laws to consumer protection, including regulations, guidelines, subsidies and grants, licencing standards and qualifications, and limitations on access to markets, economic needs tests and local content provisions.[66]

To these, further advantages to corporate capital were envisaged by way of:

1 Imposing new and severe constraints on the ability of governments to maintain or create environmental, health, consumer protection and other public interest standards through an expansion of GATS Article VI on Domestic Regulation. Proposals include a 'necessity test' whereby governments would bear the burden of proof in demonstrating that any of their countries' laws and regulations are the 'least trade restrictive,' regardless of financial, social, technological or other considerations.

2 Restricting the use of government funds for public works, municipal services and social programmes. By imposing the WTO's National Treatment rules on both government procurement and subsidies, the new negotiations seek to require governments to make public funds allocated for public services directly available to foreign-based, private service corporations.

3 Forcing governments to grant unlimited market access to foreign service providers, without regard to the environmental and social impacts of the quantity or size of service activities.

4 Accelerating the process of providing corporate service providers with guaranteed access to domestic markets in all sectors – including education, health and water – by

permitting them to establish their Commercial Presence in another country through new WTO rules being designed to promote tax-free electronic commerce worldwide. This would guarantee transnational corporations speedy irreversible market access, especially in Third World countries.[67]

By any interpretation government action was to be rendered extremely limited since three concepts at the heart of the agreement – services themselves, the trade in services, and measures which affect the trade in services – are so broad that it is difficult to see what might be excluded from its aegis especially since test cases of the existing agreement in Europe, where it has been challenged, have all been decided in favour of the former. In this light, virtually all services provided by governments as a result of taxation and local, democratic decision-making, some of which are non-profit and many of which are culturally diverse and culturally sensitive and in the hands of government for these reasons, were to be reduced to new economy sectors in which for-profit, and probably foreign-owned, organisations will operate at the expense of development among the domestic service providers. Indeed, it was inevitable: since developed countries account for 70 per cent of the export market in services, the strategic objective is more properly understood as the opening up of already vulnerable areas of the economy to multinational, for-profit penetration. Effectively then, what the GATS proposed was an onslaught against public services and the deeper entrenchment of an already existing subordination of the South to the North.[68] It came as little surprise, therefore that, in 1999, the European Commission reached the conclusion: 'The GATS is not just something that exists between Governments. It is first and foremost an instrument for the benefit of business.'[69]

Since early 2000, this view has enjoyed a growing, but still minority consensus which, if nothing else, at least indicates that the costs of the GATS are increasingly being understood on the basis of experience to date and anxieties concerning the future. In evidence is a widespread critique which has been mounted by NGOs, parliaments and developing country governments with the aim of cancelling, or postponing indefinitely any further expansion, if not the repeal of the GATS according to the following outline:

1   The negative impacts on universal access to basic services such as health care, education, water and transport.

2   The fundamental conflict between freeing up trade in services and the right of governments and communities to regulate companies in areas such as tourism, retail, telecommunications and broadcasting.

3   The absence of a comprehensive assessment of the impacts of GATS-style liberalisation before further negotiations continue.

4   An understanding of GATS in the same terms as the European Commission – namely that it is primarily about expanding opportunities for large multinational companies rather than providing for the developing countries' development and needs, defined in their own terms.[70]

Yet throughout, the offensive continued, seemingly immune to the experience and deaf to the pleas of the casualties it was creating. Indeed, one of the more significant examples of this indifference is provided by the initiatives external to these WTO projects but no less integral to the 'daring global *coup d'état*' noted by Brecher and Costello – namely, the campaign undertaken by the United States in the name of the FTAA, but in the context of the NAFTA, then in operation for seven years. The question that arose, moreover, and which is even more relevant today, is why, given a critical understanding of that precedent (and the information for this was to hand from the very early years of NAFTA's operation) over the first seven years of its operation, could an argument outside nothing more than pure neo-liberal ideology be made for undertaking a 'NAFTA-on-steroids' agreement? The case it seems rested on the benefits imputed to Mexico: a compliant government had made the country more appealing to foreign investors (by allowing free entry and exit of investment in all sectors), and, by lifting trade barriers, made production there for export to the US more profitable; in addition, the number of Mexicans employed in the *maquiladoras* has, accordingly, increased by more than 100 per cent while Mexican exports to the US have risen by 122 per cent.

The problem was that the calculus of the agreement ignored, or excluded from these benefits, the costs of their realisation, which were as widespread as they were profound. The investment freedoms caused financial volatility entailing a 39 per cent loss of purchasing power and an increased debt burden which cost between US$24 billion and US$44 billion per annum to service as the result of a 40 per cent decrease in hourly wages and the number of Mexicans living in the categories of severe and moderate poverty increased by 47 per cent, and by 2001, constituted more than half of the population. Industry-related pollution and accompanying public health problems have increased dramatically, and the country's constitutional guarantees of rights to communal land ownership had been either curtailed or eliminated.[71]

Not dissimilarly, in Canada and the United States the principal casualties were workers and their conditions: though definitive figures appear not to have been available, indicative data was and it was not encouraging. Robert Scott of the Economic Policy Institute estimated that some 760,000, mainly manufacturing job opportunities had been lost to Mexico, whereas a more conservative number of 260,000 was indicated when the number of workers who had qualified for the special NAFTA retraining programme made available to those whose employers moved their operations to Canada or Mexico was considered. North of the border the substantial decline in manufacturing which began under the Canada–US Free Trade Agreement of 1989 was also accompanied by a massive increase in the polarisation of wealth between the top, and bottom, deciles (from 50:1 to 314:1), and an almost as dramatic reduction in social programmes, especially unemployment insurance – from 87 per cent to 37 per cent.[72] (Reliable data confirming the extent of costs in all three signatory countries, based on the first decade of NAFTA's operation, is presented in the relevant section of Chapter 2, *Triage*.)

For these reasons the April 2001 Quebec City meeting of the leaders from 34 countries of the Western Hemisphere to negotiate the FTAA was understandable only as the advent of a corporate dream in the making. With NAFTA as the template, the proposed FTAA was to surpass NAFTA in its scope and power. It would encompass a population of more than 800 million and a combined GDP of US$11 trillion. As well, it would incorporate the measures already mentioned in the GATS 2000 proposals – in addition to those of the failed MAI. In short, it would embody the most ambitious elements of every global trade and investment agreement – existing and proposed – into one hemispheric pact, with sweeping authority over every aspect of life in the Americas. And, by proposing it as what President George W. Bush calls 'a moral imperative,' within a 'hemisphere of liberty,' the impression is created that free trade *is* both democracy, and therefore ethical, when clearly the grounds exist for construing the vision of corporate control vested in the various agreements as the antithesis of both.[73]

The FTAA is designed to give transnational corporations unequalled new 'rights' to challenge and compete for every publicly funded service now provided by governments – from health care and education to social security, culture and environmental protection. If adopted, it will remove the ability of every government to create or maintain laws and regulations protecting the health, safety and well-being of their citizens and the environment they share.[74] Worse, the FTAA will then be a model, or template in its own right for future world trade agreements, eventually confirming current trends which are rendering domestic health, environmental, and other laws around the world subservient to those of international trade. To this end, and quite explicitly, the FTAA is to be viewed as not so much about trade as about placing democracy under corporate control, and, in general, removing governments from their *raison d'être* of serving the public interest.[75]

Given this brief survey of US initiatives under the guise of 'Free Trade,' Chakravarthi Raghavan's description of the Uruguay Round's potential to create 'recolonisation' of the Third World rather than global prosperity was both prescient and an accurate portrayal of the form and substance of globalisation over the last 30 years.[76] If anything, the collapse of the Soviet Union and the Eastern Bloc allowed the US the latitude, or space, to express its imperial desires globally, regardless of opposition from friend and adversary alike, in a manner which the Cold War impeded. Faced with undeniable evidence that its military leadership role is no longer seen as desirable, or as necessary, or even as possible, as it once was – Somalia, Bosnia–Herzogovina, Iraq, and Afghanistan are but four examples – the US has steadfastly remained faithful to the precepts of 'preponderant power' advanced by the Truman Administration by redressing the situation through a renewed emphasis on the more explicitly economic and the related global institutions which it can control.

PREPONDERANT UNDERSTANDINGS

Among the components which have not changed, however, is the systematic articulation of the desirable world order through the global imposition of an Enlightenment tradition of scientific rationality upon the study and understanding of the world itself. For this inquiry, the most potent form of that imperium resides in the discipline of Economics which emerged in the United States after the publication, in 1890, of Alfred Marshall's *Principles of Economics*.[77] From then on, both Adam Smith's political economy-centred description of the study as 'the nature and causes of the wealth of nations,' and Karl Marx's 'a critical analysis of capitalist production,' were eschewed in favour of a supposedly neutral and unadorned term, 'economics,' and an approach which emphasised a legacy of Descartes. In their stead came Lionel Robbins' definition of the new economics as 'the adaptation of scarce means to given ends,' and the replacement of the labour theory of economic value with 'a subjective calculus of individual preferences.'[78] Ostensibly captured in this process was certainty in the study of wealth, through mathematics; resurgent was a discourse which saw nothing remarkable about a 'free market,' which settles competing demands solely on the basis of money rather than needs. Or, as the discipline of Economics became, the 'perfect coincidence between science and cupidity,' through the appropriation of mathematical forms.[79]

It was a takeover, an appropriation of the endowments of natural science for the use of Economics without understanding, or even caring for, the intellectual permissions that both required. Thus, nothing more true can be said about the late nineteenth-century origins of the discipline of modern Economics than that it was an unmistakable case of (Newtonian) 'physics envy.' What impressed economists of the time were the notions upon which the classical Cartesian–Newtonian cosmology had been built, and which had lent to science in general, and physics in particular, the capacity to not only know the world through what Richard Tarnas describes as its 'supreme cognitive effectiveness,' but also to explain it with 'rigorously impersonal precision.'[80] In these terms physics had developed over two centuries to the point where it was the exemplar, *par excellence*, of the belief that it was possible to observe the world objectively; that the world was to be understood as, essentially, a machine; and that, therefore, a strict mechanistic causality governed all phenomena.

By extension, if the world accorded to what was, essentially, Newtonian mechanics, it was also, essentially, static; and being static, it was also, with the expenditure of sufficient scientific effort, subject to prediction and control. Above all, it was, as near as could be imagined in human temporality, an entity in perpetuity, existing for all time – where 'for all time' conveyed an existence co-terminous with that of the Earth and its solar system itself. The modern discipline of Economics was thus naturalised, and heralded as but another instance of the unity to be found throughout the universe, in the life of humans as in the ways of the non-human world.

And there is nothing more paradoxical about these origins than that, though they reflected the historical development of natural science, they were embraced as universally valid for all forms of social inquiry by economists. Which is another way of saying that, by borrowing a tool-box from the natural sciences in order to understand human interaction and relationships, Economics embarked on an enthusiastic and dogmatic path to fundamentally misunderstanding its own subject matter. Nor was this predicament in any way alleviated by revolutionary developments in the theoretical foundations of physics which, in the very period that Economics was co-opting it, caused in physicists, according to Werner Heisenberg's prophetic words, 'the feeling that the ground would be cut from science.'[81] Indeed, for a long time prior to the quantum revolution, effectively throughout the nineteenth century, scientists drawn to such new subjects as historical chemistry, historical geology, systematic biology, physiology, ecology, and evolution found themselves to be poorly served by methods or forms of explanation whose relevance was most appropriate only to 'objects and systems that were in fact inert, inanimate, and unthinking. In the study of these new phenomena, the *practices* of the natural sciences required and embodied such crucial departures from the mechanistic theories of seventeenth-century physics – including historiographical reflection, and questions of good and bad modes of bodily operation – that their results could not truthfully be described as the 'coldly factual products of "value-free" reason.'[82]

In a foretaste of the discipline of Economics' habit of cognitive dissonance when faced with a universe of facts which does not accord with its most cherished intellectual constructs, the new discipline of Economics adopted the only course available to it if it was to maintain its pretensions as a science in Cartesian and Newtonian terms: it ignored the challenges to certainty as if they were no more than epiphenomenal. Economics was not alone in either the habit of avoidance, or the obsession with its status; as Dorothy Ross has argued, persuasively, and in reference to sociology, political science, and history, as well, American social scientists after the Civil War made strenuous efforts to sustain fixed laws of nature and of history, and, when that was found not to be possible, to subject capitalism, democracy, and science to both scientific and technological control, and America's millennial identity, known more widely as American Exceptionalism.[83] In the context of this analysis, the fusion of American Exceptionalism with the American discipline of Economics is of extraordinary significance because not only does it locate the embeddedness of the latter in the specific historical experience of the United States, but the other social sciences are to be understood as intellectual reinforcements for Economics, as complementary components of a shared meta-narrative.

In any other discipline idiosyncrasies of this type would in a short time incur a compelling disqualification from being treated seriously on any topic of political significance, let alone having a privileged voice on virtually all of them. But Economics has not only avoided such opprobrium, but flourished to the point of being the dominant social science in late twentieth-century America if the displacement of other types of social scientists by economists from major positions of bureaucratic and political authority is any indication.[84] Explaining this seemingly outrageous success is not difficult, but it does require an extraordinarily high tolerance of further paradoxes which compound those already existing – of a putative science arising from a combination of intellectual vanity, ahistoricism, and a metaphysical commitment to universalising a model which is exceptionalist in its own terms. Thus, it needs to be understood that, from the 1930s on, the status of Economics in the United States was less influenced by the intellectual content of its theories than it was by historical developments and ideologies which reproach the corpus of beliefs which gird neo-liberalism.

PREPONDERANT MYTHOLOGY

Essentially, there is a juxtaposition featuring the discipline of Economics and the historical context in which it is held that it proved itself. The former claims an explanatory power in relation to the rational behaviour of an individual in the market, bound by such law as is necessary to maintain the market's autonomy, but otherwise free from both government intervention and, of course, war. On every count, however, the very economic theory which is being globalised is derived from a totally alien historical experience because the rational actor/free market ideal simply never existed in either the New Deal, or World War II, or the Cold War, nor could it have, given the demands which were made on the US economy during their respective periods; indeed, while it is undeniable that different levels of economic success attended all of them, it is equally undeniable that they were a tribute to strong, centrist, and statist responses which, ideally, precluded the very outcomes which are celebrated.[85]

Of greatest significance for this imperialism of the intellect is the fact that American Economics had a 'good war'; indeed, in Bernstein's formulation it was the requisite discipline of 'American power in an American century,' or, as Paul Samuelson referred to it, World War II was the 'economist's war.'[86] World War II became, therefore, a constellating event in its own right for post-war Economics, and a salutary example of the means by which to theorise the United States' rise to world pre-eminence after 1945. Indeed, the lustre of the defeat of fascism, and the political-economic regime which attended that victory, ensured that what should have been a temporary, 'hostilities-only' arrangement of the US economy became routinised as an operational norm. But what was being routinised was not so much an economy fit for peace, but the theory of economics and consequential industrial capacity which had made a great war effort possible in the first place, and which in turn mandated the same wartime effort, rationalisation, and capacities in peacetime. What Michael A. Bernstein calls the 'theoretical trajectory' of post-1945 Economics became, therefore, a 'necessary product' of the War Department's need for guidance from the Economics discipline in the area of resource allocation competitive decision-making in the period 1941 to 1945. And since the Truman Administration's strategy of 'preponderant power' gave rise to resource allocation problems and estimations of adversary action not significantly different to those conceived of during the war itself, the same theoretical techniques, including 'activity analysis' and 'linear programming,' remained to the fore – 'and profoundly affected research protocols and pedagogical agendas in the Economics discipline as a whole.'[87]

As the neural transmitters across the synapse between the American state and American society, the universities were the first non-governmental institutions to embody the wartime-routine-operational mind-set as the wartime-routine-operational professoriate returned to the academy. Full of wartime-routine-operational insights, values, proselytising zeal, and grace, no area of the economy, government or private, military or civilian, it seemed, was thought to be beyond their 'operationally useful methods.' Nor should this have been surprising; they possessed, in the words of Barry Katz, 'a concrete sense of the embeddedness of their ideas – and themselves – in history.'[88] Within a handful of years, a melding of game theory (whose mathematical demands were identical with linear programming) with the concerns of the American security state created a united study of constrained maximisation, or minimisation, framed by competitive behaviour, allowing some to believe they had developed a calculus for assessing the costs and benefits of nuclear war.[89] As US self-confidence in general grew under the strategy of 'preponderant power,' so, too, did the self-confidence of the Economics profession in the US which was charged with not only effecting US responses, but concomitantly, of prescribing paths of non-communist development and modernisation in the non-industrialised world which would advantage US capital.[90]

These latter efforts involved not only *the vetting of individuals for appointment to resurgent foreign institutions of higher learning,* but also *the articulation of new programs of instruction, even reading lists.* New subfields of the discipline, such as growth and development theory, garnered attention and resources owing to the interests of the government in fostering decentralised market growth in developing nations as a means both *to further US foreign policy interests* and to forestall Soviet and Chinese initiatives around the world.[91]

For a discipline less than half a century old in formal and collegiate terms, this was status indeed, or, as Bernstein has reflected upon it, 'a poise represent[ing] the seasoning of a powerful new field.'[92] The year 1946 saw the creation of the Council of Economic Advisers (CEA), a three-person policy advice group of professional economists appointed upon the consent of the Senate, which, with the Office of the Surgeon General, is one of only two executive branch units 'that, by the terms of its enabling legislation, represents a *specific* professional entity in the White House.'[93] But it was no more than reflecting the orthodoxies of the new economic dispensation which the war had brought into being and which, as the Cold War progressed, affirmed that war was central to the new status of Economics. Where the interests of the security state and Economics discipline coincided, research was 'nurtured and sustained;' where they departed, certain tendencies were regarded as 'dangerous, wrong-headed, or even treasonous' and 'actual suppression' was effected by a spectrum of intimidation which ran from administrative discouragement through financial deprivation for research, to the denial of employment and promotion.[94] The economic orthodoxy so established became, under these conditions and in time, a tradition, widely appreciated by the private as well as the public sector, but it was a tradition acutely aware of the contingencies upon which its privileges depended, if the bitter account of one its victims, Sam Bowles, is any indication:

> Not satisfied with being once removed from power, many economists – a good portion of the senior faculty of the Harvard Economics Department among them – have gone into the lucrative and gratifying business of directly advising corporations, government bureaus and presidents. 'Relevance' in economics has come to be synonymous with service to governmental policymakers. Not surprisingly, conventional economists have proven of more service in hiding the costs of the Vietnam War than in ending it; they have done better at explaining away poverty than in eradicating it. In their advisory roles, conventional economists have reflected the bias of their theories as well as the political requirements of remaining 'in favour' by at best accepting and more often justifying the institution of capitalism as the framework within which decisions are made.[95]

So inured was the discipline in the very disposition to which it stood accused by Bowles that one of the foremost against whom it was directed, the Chair of the Harvard Economics Department, James Duesenberry, when challenged as to why, in view of the indefensible nature of the Vietnam War, he had not resigned his appointment to the CEA, defended his ongoing involvement in the very terms which, as we will see, are the defining characteristics of academic professionalisation – ego maintenance, bureaucratic effectiveness, narrow techno-rationalism, and a cynical intolerance of those who acted outside these parameters:

> I figured they weren't going to stop it, so I might as well stay in the meantime and work for the most stable financial policies. What good would it have done if I had resigned? There would have been an article on page three of the *New York Times* one day and forgotten the next. I am the kind of man who puts one foot before the other. *I have no use for these paper humanists.* At least I got the tax program and some housing legislation through. *As an economist I was not concerned with the big picture.*[96]

As a self-denying ordinance and hubristic discipline Economics became so effective that economists were duly celebrated (by other equally constricted disciplines it has to be said) as exemplary social scientists; indeed, the RAND Corporation saw them as ideal intellectual foils to the large number of physical scientists they employed because 'economists could act as the generalists and integrators in analyses of general war.'[97] And the Council of Economic Advisers was tasked accordingly, its members contributing to discussions on such matters as 'mobilisation of the national economy in the face of atomic attack,' 'economic stabilisation after attack,' 'the economics of national security,' 'economic preparedness,' and 'emergency economic stabilisation.' As one Assistant Director for Stabilisation in the Office of Defence Mobilisation envisaged their role in the post-atomic war period:

> I do not envisage someone crawling out of the rubble waving a price regulation, but I do suggest that certain minimum and simple rules of economic behaviour may properly supplement other survival rules when it is time to move behind the first instinctive or pre-arranged measures.[98]

In the global context of the Truman Doctrine which called for the containment of all aspects of possible Soviet influence, and hence, of the development of corresponding macro-economic policies and military-industrial infrastructures, imitations of the CEA were ample testament to the understandings of its status beyond the United States. Canada, Japan, West Germany thus all flattered the CEA directly, which is to say institutionally, while, to varying degrees, India, Poland, Singapore, Turkey, and in a most ironic tribute, the Soviet Union and Yugoslavia, sought to be apprised of its wisdom.[99] As Bernstein writes in reflection of this triumph, 'American Economics had, in a wide variety of ways, made itself an essential part of both American governance and the evolution of the discipline and policy practice world-wide.'[100]

In other words the prescriptive power which mainstream economic theory enjoyed through to the advent of the Reagan Administration (at the latest) could never have been derived from its record of peacetime management of the American economy – because such an economy was impossible during World War II and simply never came into being after it. On the contrary, its success depended on masterminding a Cold War economy which could out-spend and out-produce the Soviet Union and the Eastern Bloc by creating, in the words of William Appleman Williams, the material basis for, 'empire as a way of life.'[101] In many circles the growing dependence of the economy on

the state's military budget, which this involved, was known as 'military Keynesianism' –
effectively, a Cold War intervention in the market which, with good reason, appeared to
have almost limitless potential as an economic pump-primer:

> Excluding its multiplier and accelerator effects, as well as the 3.4 million service men
> and women, defence work directly accounted for 4.1 million jobs or 5.9 per cent of
> total civilian employment in 1967. These jobs were distributed as follows: 16 per
> cent in the aircraft industry; 7.5 per cent in the radio, television and communications
> equipment industries; 6.2 per cent in the ordnance industry; and most of the
> remainder in the service industries. Some industries were more dependent on these
> jobs than others: 64 per cent of the jobs in the ordnance industry were dependent
> on defence contracts, as were 59.1 per cent of the jobs in the aircraft industry and
> 10.5 per cent of all jobs in manufacturing. In 1965, 55 per cent or [US]$7.8 billion of
> all industrial research and development funds were provided by the federal
> government, and of this fully 80 per cent was used for military purposes.[102]

In the late Cold War, and the post-Cold War period since, the imperial mission of US
economic thought has remained essentially undisturbed, the exception being that, with
the advent of what some call the 'Leninist Extinction,' the tribute which capitalism paid
to socialism in the form of liberal-capitalist-democracy has lost its imperative character.[103]
The consequences have not only included an accelerating pace of state withdrawal from
market regulation in the West, but a triumphal insistence that the economies of the
successor states to those of the former Soviet bloc, and the newly industrialising countries
(NICs), institute free-market systems of such pristine purity that they have never existed
in the West. Exactly why, or how, either movement continues to survive even a cursory
examination of US history or contemporary conditions is mystifying. It is as though the
internal decline of the United States is a fabrication and not a verifiable reality.

PREPONDERANT AMNESIA

It is on the basis of such mythologising that John Kenneth Galbraith has reserved
some of his most stinging rebukes for those 'arch exponents of free enterprise' who
have, and are, advising the former communist states on economic and social programmes
involving an 'acceptance of – even commitment to – unemployment, inflation, and
disastrously reduced living standards' as the essential therapy out of which will come 'a
new revitalised work ethic, a working force eager for the discipline of free enterprise.'
Moreover, he notes, their 'primitive' ideological construct, which insists that 'self-
mortification is the path to righteousness,' exists all but entirely in their minds rather
than in any identifiable economic reality, past or present. He is equally scathing of their
rejection of both liberal-pluralist power structures and ethics for the simple reason that
the appeal of the market economy for the former communist states is derived from
understanding it in the very terms – imperfect, to be sure, but social democratic
nevertheless – which the neo-liberals are bent on destroying. Of such a programme he
writes: 'This, I choose my words carefully, is insanity.'[104]

In similar vein, in the course of a lecture at the University of Edinburgh in January
1990, he specifically addressed the glib notion that a return to the free market of Adam

Smith as being 'wrong to the point of a mental vacuity of clinical proportions.'[105] And the source of the animus is straightforward, namely, the ignorance which such advocates have of the foundations for their own wealth – the Keynesian revolution:

> In fact they owe, or have owed, their eminence to earlier generations of socially minded leaders who made their citizens economically and socially more comfortable and secure.[106]

But this is no unequivocal celebration of capitalism before neo-liberalism; rather, Galbraith becomes only deeply ironic, recording the failures of the former in the context of their proposed exacerbation:

> It is a grim but wholly unshakeable fact ... that no one in search of a better life would wisely move from East Berlin to the South Bronx. Not even in search of liberty, for nothing so represses freedom as an effective absence of money, food, and a place to live.[107]

Objections to these and similar formulations on the basis that, as the unifying power of a common enemy was progressively denied to the West in general, and the US in particular, by the *détente* which followed upon, first, Mikhail Gorbachev's accession to the Soviet leadership, and then the collapse of the Soviet imperium, the status of Economics is more appropriately determined by its record of confronting the different world of the last decade ignores at least four principle elements of theory-as-practice in the record of the period. In the first instance, it was in the late 1960s – that is, well in advance of the fall of the end of the Cold War – that the US entered a period of economic decline, especially with regard to its performance relative to the European Community, Japan, and the NICs. Second, its response to that decline was to mount an offensive against its adversaries – internally, dismantling the New Deal 'social contract' between corporate capital, corporate Labour, and the federal government, so as to remove what were seen as barriers to competitive efficiency; and externally, by instituting a 'free trade' regime which, given the already existing advantages enjoyed by US transnational corporations, both re-subordinated the NICs to a global economy still dominated by the US, and finessed an attack on Japanese economic power. Third, as was documented earlier in this analysis, whatever material abundance has been created by the practice of neo-liberal economic theories has been achieved at the expense of environmental destruction, human suffering, political and social freedom, and cultural diversity. And fourth, neither American economic decline, nor the unilateral cancelling of the New Deal 'social contract,' nor the attack upon the NICs and Japan for the undisguised purposes of subordinating them to US domination, nor any of their attendant pathologies, is remotely consistent with a sensible understanding of the 'successful,' 'peacetime' theory of Economics which is propounded by the US mainstream, but they are conditions of existence entirely consonant with, respectively, imperial excess, wartime economic life, and a theory of economic war.

Nevertheless, it is conceded that an appreciation such as this is either unknown to those who continue to be attracted to Economics, or irrelevant to their objectives and ethics. It is otherwise impossible to explain the well-documented authority of American economists and business people throughout the former Soviet Union and Eastern Europe since the end of the Cold War.[108] Somehow or other, an absolution is extended to the fact that the victorious US regime was possible only by the simplification of society's objectives inside the disposition to war which the Cold War entailed.[109] Or that US geopolitics required the toleration of state intervention in Third World economies (provided the overall complexion of the government in question was anti-communist).[110] Or that, in many cases, 'free-market economics' was, and is, compulsorily or coercively imposed on states as a condition of their economic development.[111] Or that its legacy has been widespread impoverishment and environmental devastation.[112] Or, finally, that the resultant condition of the economic South after half a century of subjection to the economic wisdom of the United States is now thought by such authorities as Jacques Attali (former head of the European Bank for Reconstruction and Development) and the US Presidential Commission on Integrated Long-Term Strategy (and its neo-conservative successors) to be so irreconcilable with the now beleaguered economic North that they both share a view of it as a possible source of implacable future threat.[113]

Absent, therefore, is any sense that the global economic condition is an amalgam of precisely the consequences guaranteed by the strategies in force. And this, in itself, is interesting because it lends a certain nuance to the argument being advanced here – which is that, though it is the case that the economic strategies of the United States are becoming indistinguishable as between the domestic and external realms, because they are both developed and executed in the same way, it is also to be recognised that the engulfment of economists in general, and economic policy-makers in particular in a common, largely uncontested intellectual background determines an almost identical outcome. In other words, the background is the independent variable.

The question that then arises is why so many nominally sober-minded, intelligent people who, it should be expected, are neither easy to fool nor credulous, should espouse neo-liberal Economics with the conviction of a biblical revelation. Bear in mind that the advocates in question are popularly regarded by society as people of superior ability, intensive and sound training, and high ideals who, nevertheless, are seemingly undisturbed by significant doubt and dissent in the face of evidence, at home and abroad, in the developed and industrialising, as well as Third World countries, which is of a chronic nature, and in any religion, let alone an overwhelmingly proud scientific discipline, would guarantee defection – in the form of apostasy and heresy – rather than conversion to it.

4 The Americanisation of the new Economics
American Exceptionalism and American religion

Questions which seek to locate the sources of American conduct in the intellectual structures and power relations of American society are covered by the general attitude to such inquiries throughout the West: they are unwelcome because they run the risk of disclosing just how essential the intelligentsia is to political power. In the formulation of Regis Debray: 'the sociology of real capitalism ignores (or marginalises) the intelligentsia in order to conceal it as an active political force and to perpetuate the illusion that it does not exist.'[1] That illusion, successfully established and maintained is, moreover, dangerous because it allows space and legitimacy to the notion that ideas associated with 'the intelligentsia' are either basically irrelevant to the common people and the everyday life of a nation, or relevant only to the extent that they are the common-sense response to the challenges and provocations of an anarchic world. Just how dangerous is the refusal to uncover these ideas is clear once the consequences of actually pursuing a manifold line of inquiry into what might be called American intelligence and American knowing.

Several questions come to mind. How does the United States make the world as an object of knowledge? How did the United States get where it is intellectually? What is the intellectual character of the United States? How is American knowledge produced? What does this knowledge tell America about the world? And what does this knowledge tell the non-US world about the United States? – because the world *is* informing the United States, too, but the information passes through the filter of the agents of production. The project, then, produces an intellectual mirror: *knowing* America becomes an attempt to understand how America understands the world.[2]

It is, moreover, a project with historical and contemporary ramifications. America, since its European settlement, identified itself through an organic cosmogony of exclusivity and exceptionalism; during the Cold War it became, without question, the most powerful actor in history, and thus for many, realised its own prophecy. And now that extended crisis is over, it is the sole remaining, and again for many, victorious superpower at what is arguably an historic juncture (or a reasonable approximation thereto). It is necessary, therefore, to relate America in its evolving, predominant and contemporary moments to the destiny foreseen at its founding; to relate its culture and society, in their particularities, to the universe of non-American history and experience. In greater detail this involves both connecting the cosmogony in its various parts to the historical development of American understanding, and then characterising that understanding as it becomes, ultimately, the national intelligence which informs American global strategy.

Because the terms 'America' and 'the United States' are totalising abstractions in the context of this analysis, the logical, inner focus will be upon, first, establishing the atmospherics of American culture, and second, the production and deployment of knowledge – upon how information is selected, processed, understood, informs policy and is made, eventually, into material 'fact' in the name of those abstractions. Effectively, then, the focus is on US strategic intelligence, but of a type in which strategy is envisaged as 'the art of controlling and utilising the resources of a nation [military, non-military – economic, psychological, moral, political, and technological] ... to the end that its vital interests shall be effectively promoted and secured against enemies, actual, potential, or merely presumed.'[3]

Accordingly, strategic intelligence becomes the epistemological basis for strategy, and strategy, in turn, becomes intelligence-in-action. But, importantly, what is in action, and what the term 'security' psychologises and launders, is a preoccupation with threat which is, at times, constructed as being no less than a global danger and which necessitates no less than an aggressive, vigilant mode of surveillance which then orders the world in terms of the threats it poses. Indeed, it will be argued that this outcome is ubiquitous, existing in a relatively unbroken form in all of the sites examined, each site, moreover, not only contributing to the intelligence outcome but reinforcing and intensifying the vectors of the others. The overall concern, then, is to disturb the sedimentation from which extend the more visible roots of American security praxis. It is *not* to examine the various operating environments of what is euphemistically called the 'intelligence community' so much as it is to present an account of the reciprocal embeddedness of that 'community' and American strategic culture.

The initial approach to explaining such behaviour is by way of a loose adaptation of Bruce Wilshire's 'mimetic engulfment' – 'the prerational structures of involuntary imitation of others'. His argument, which influences the analysis at hand, is that:

> the formation of identity of self – and education – occurs largely at an archaic level of engulfment in the moody background world of everyday experience.... Adults in their own groups typically do not realise the extent to which they are undeliberately modelling themselves upon others around them in the foreground and the background world... the typical condition of human identity is one of more or less compromised individuation... whole societies move together along lines of least resistance, because it is directly and dumbly felt that the world tilts in a certain direction.[4]

Operationally, this results in individuals (intelligence analysts, economists, academics, policy-makers, decision-makers, advisers, and even those who have earned the accolade of 'leader') locating themselves, insistently, within a *world* which authorises both their place within a particular 'purified group,' *and* the 'phobic exclusions of potentially polluting others.'[5] By extension, critical distance is chimerical and empathy with the Other (who is a pollutant) unlikely, perhaps impossible. Furthermore, the intellectual character of the product, in this case mainstream economic thought and strategy, will be just another manifestation of the interests of the dominant, authorising community.

Implied in such an approach, which not only embodies 'a theory about how the world works,' but also 'authorises certain kinds of speaking, writing and analysing,' and now made explicit, is the salience of the concept of 'discourse' and its operational mode of 'discursive formation.'[6] This warrant, it should be noted, includes both *what* is to be spoken, written, acted, and analysed as well as *who* is to 'occupy the position of a subject.'[7] Discourse, then, encompasses more than speech, text, and act; it is the very order under which such disciplines and exercises are made possible, and institutions established; hence the need to study intellectuals, the disciplines they are bound to, and (by way of example) the universities in which they are located and produced. Discourse, therefore, is not solely a form of representation, but also a *material condition* which 'enables and constrains the socially productive imagination,' not least because it 'regulates our forming of ourselves' according to the criteria of 'truths,' or 'conditions of possibility,' which are themselves discursively produced.[8] Discourse is, moreover, as Agnew and Corbridge emphasise, such a dialectically integrated weaving of thought and practice that notions of discourse as 'a manifestation of thought prior to practice,' or 'a set of ideas either determined by practice or functional to its reproduction' only obscure the absolute and unreserved nature of its accepted tenets.[9] Thus, adapting and following closely the contours offered by them, but in relation to the discourse of economics (as opposed to geopolitical discourse), the former involves 'the deployment of representations of "the market" which guide the economic practices central to a political-economic order.'[10]

To uncover a discourse, then, is to provide an account of the linkages, the 'relatively stable techniques' which permit what can be written, said, or thought 'only in specific ways and not others,' and which provide protocols for the way in which such knowledge changes, if at all.[11] The 'truths' proclaimed by a discourse are, accordingly, 'perspectival:'

> all truths are relative to the frame of reference which contains them; more radically, 'truths' are a function of these frames; and even more radically, these discourses 'constitute' the truths they claim to discover and transmit. ...

> [A]ll that exists are discrete historical events, and the propositions which claim to tell the truth about them have no reality beyond that acquired by being consistent within the logic of the system that makes them possible.[12]

The immediate purpose, thus, is to undertake an inquiry which is designed to challenge the 'commonsensical' and the 'self-evident' and to breach what Paul Bove describes as 'the privilege of unnoticed power' and its attendant 'instruments of control.'[13] It is to understand that, where the common etymological roots of discourse and (academic/ intellectual) discipline intersect, namely, in the systematic control of conduct, reason, and argument, they also give rise to common political consequences for society's 'most basic categories of understanding and thought' including the hierarchising of identity and difference, and authority and subservience, and the shaping of aesthetic, moral, and political value judgments.[14] Ultimately, to critically examine discourse is to abide by Michel Foucault's recommendations that it should be approached – not as a commentary produced by a particular form of thought, mind, or subject and obeying certain laws of construction – but as a 'monument' whose conditions of existence, character-disposition, and practical field of deployment in local struggles are a rebuke to its self-effacing tactics.[15]

On the face of things this analytical course is encouraged by just three observations of reliable provenance made in respect of American cultural, intellectual, and political life. The first is that made by an English observer, Alan Ryan, who is, nevertheless, supported by American counterparts, Louis Menand, and Barry Alan Shain, to the effect that the United States is 'astonishingly group-minded'[16] and lacking in real cultural diversity.[17] In this light Ross has observed that, in relation to the dominant discourse of social science which is responsible for providing the officially sanctioned accounts of how America is, and works, and how the world is, and works, one is struck by its double confinement – to the epistemologies of natural science, and to an intolerant liberal ideology. Proscribed, as a consequence of the former, are social sciences capable of historicist understandings of the world, and, as a consequence of the latter, an enhanced spectrum of political thought minimally defined by the 'organicist poles' of conservatism and socialism. Most striking, therefore, is a consensualising and homogenising American social science characterised by 'historical vacuousness and narrow political vision.'[18]

Commentaries on what might be regarded as the natural epistemological affinity which exists across the spectrum of the analytical community, be they intelligence analysts or university professors, provide the second; the Harvard historian of Russia, Richard Pipes, provides a relevant testimony:

> [The CIA's] analytic staff, filled with American PhDs in the natural and social sciences along with engineers, inevitably shares the outlook of US academe, with its penchant for philosophical positivism, cultural agnosticism, and political liberalism. The special knowledge which it derives from classified sources is mainly technical; *the rest of its knowledge, as well as the intellectual equipment which it brings to bear on the evidence, comes from academia.*[19]

Similarly, Michael Shafer, in his search for an explanation of the failure of US counter-insurgency policy, based as it was upon a world view more than a military-strategic problematic, turned to the question of why, in the American realms of theory and practice, the intellectual differences between academics and policy-makers were of degree rather than kind despite the obvious institutional distinctions between them which might otherwise suggest more profound divergences. Indeed, at this level his task is no less than an explanation of the unity of theory and practice characterised by the persistence of ideas, 'so appealing – even though wrong... which distort reality or cripple efforts to respond to it.' What he discerns, ultimately, is the nature of that appeal: the 'comfortable homeyness' afforded by an intellectual tradition of social science which asserts its accounts in universalised terms, based on abusive simplifications which, nevertheless, are prescriptively useful – which is to say, policy permissive in a world of embarrassing specifics.[20]

And Edward Said's subsequent account of the strong conformity which reigned in policy circles during the 1990 to 1991 Gulf War against Iraq is the third observation:

What prevailed was an extraordinary mainstream consensus in which the rhetoric of the government, the policymakers, the military, think tanks, media, and academic centres converged on the necessity of United States force and the ultimate justice of its projection, *for which a long history of theorists and apologists* from Andrew Jackson through Theodore Roosevelt to Henry Kissinger and Robert W. Tucker *furnished the preparation.*[21]

Knowledge, as it is described in the above, accords very much with the Nietzchean formulation of it as a mode of power or, in William E. Connolly's description, 'a distinctive tool of power' which renders the world in such a way that it is made comprehensible.[22] We return, therefore, to discourse as a producer of knowledge, and thus, a practice done unto things; a voluntaristic practice, moreover, which is carried out 'despite resistances' which might be offered by the thing being rendered.[23] In the analogous way that strategic intelligence gives understanding to strategy, discourse, as a strategy in its own right, makes intelligence possible in the first place. In a discourse, therefore, are to be found practical rules for the functioning of the discursive system and a resulting regularity in the practices which ensue and then give rise to a finished text.[24] Just as clearly, discourse is a practice of construction, easily institutionalised, and all the better facilitated if it is so located.

Thus constructed is a framework of interplay between engulfment and discourse in which the former holds the status of an intellectual ambience, an object of purely intellectual intuition akin to the Kantian category of *noumenon*, and the latter a culture-specific catalyst, or *phenomenon* essential for producing reliable, which is to say predictable, outcomes. And, to maintain the Kantian analogy, it is an interplay which brings to the fore the basic thrust of both components: namely, the presupposition and eventual self-fulfilling vindication of a mind–world correspondence. In these terms, it is the relevant accounts of God, nation, society, and state which warrant investigation because, in the context of questions relating to the processes by which the world is known and their nexus with grand strategy, of which economic policy is a sub-specie, it is these institutions, groupings or qualities and their agents which, overall, claim responsibility for, embody, and articulate the various notions of national identity, ideology, and culture. To this end the remainder of this chapter is organised in terms of the successive foci which become sharper as they move from the atmospheric, or vague, background influences upon global intelligence in general to those which are more immediate and causal as regards economic globalisation.

American Exceptionalism and American religion, therefore, deserve first consideration as they are conceived of as general, natural pressures upon the more specific intelligence-related discourse they support. Between them and it, however (and the boundary is extremely porous) lies American capitalism which, in the late nineteenth and early twentieth century, became such an extraordinary solvent of tradition and traditional values that it changed almost beyond recognition – in fact subjugated – the established ideals and practices of commerce, community, religion, and intellectual life and university education. This fourfold dialectic occupies the second level of analysis. But, by extension, it proceeds to a third and final level, an exploration of the particular implications for intelligence about the world which result from the effects of professionalisation and segmentation of the university, and its co-option by the state as the principal disseminator and legitimator of the latter's orthodoxies.

AMERICAN EXCEPTIONALISM, AMERICAN RELIGION – GLOBAL IMPLICATIONS

To understand the ideas of national identity which prevail in the United States is to understand an 'historical consciousness,' expressed less as a philosophy and more as a 'set of attitudes... in the articulate discourses of educated classes as well as in the *mentalité* of cultural groups.' It is to understand a particular meaning being given to historical events and the power of cultural formations which determine that meaning.[25] It is also to understand the power of the world view derived from these processes which is riven with totalising and hierarchical dichotomies at every level – be it the national ontology (and the metaphorical constructions which buttress it), or the pre-eminence accorded to patriarchy, individualism and the country's unchanging Anglo-Saxon heritage and lineage – to the point where Others have little saliency.

In terms of the logic involved, of course, nor could they be recognised. The idea of America was, from the beginning, one embodying an 'inexpungible uniqueness' beyond the common conceits of national identity found universally.[26] Since America was constructed and defined in oppositional terms to Europe and its entrapment in history, America was to be 'the land that left Europe and history behind' because it was both outside of history, and the end of history.[27] Change, in any qualitative sense, was thus not only impossible, but unnecessary (although Richard Hofstadter once observed that this logic did not preclude eruptions of the belief that America was the only country that was born perfect and continued to progress[28]). And since Europe's own exaggerated imagination held that continent to be the repository of civilisation, 'America' effectively degraded the culture from which it fled on the basis of knowledge, and rendered all other cultures and experiences worthless by two stages of remove.

Inseparable from an understanding of this fantasy is the meaning given to the land which was America and its method of seizure. It was a continent of virgin land, abundant in natural resources, and without the structures which gave rise to history as understood by the European settlement. When, in time, a successful revolution led to the establishment of republican government, and the ample opportunities for wealth creation which the land afforded, the mythic views of the new world which were first expressed in the old, European world blossomed: America was part of God's eternal plan which by definition meant 'America' was ahistorical, and which, accordingly, rendered human history, as experienced in Europe, chronopolitically impossible and theologically inadmissible for America.

Disturbances or perturbations, rather than revolutions, were nevertheless allowed, but not so as to change the qualitative nature of America; hence 'change' in this sense was reduced to a 'quantitative multiplication and elaboration of its founding institutions.'[29] Moreover, America was removed from the one great, inescapable, ordering, 'given' of existence – death – since, in the views Americans held of their country, America moved only 'in space rather than differentiated development in time.'[30] Not for nothing, then, were these views invested as American Exceptionalism, nor similarly was it productive of metaphors wich represented America as 'an unchanging realm of nature' – the ocean, whose perpetual movement yielded tides, and even storms, yet could never deny the reign of a timeless and general equilibrium.[31]

To portray American identity in this light is not to ignore the crises it has faced from events whose historicity imposed themselves upon an inhospitable national consciousness, or from intellectual perspectives generally rooted in historicist understandings of the world. On the contrary, that such confrontations took place is admitted, as is their total failure to seriously subvert the object of their attack. Whether it be the American Civil War's insistence on America's presence in history, or the subsequent variations on an identical theme provided by the rapid industrialisation and rise of class conflict in the period of the Gilded Age (1870–1900), or the disorienting pace of change in general in the 1920s, the obligation to develop an historicist understanding of the United States was evaded in favour of particular reformulations of American Exceptionalism which were increasingly beholden to the scientism which was driving economics, history, political science, and sociology.[32] Indeed, in view of the way in which such changes have determined modifying prefixes in Economics and politics (neoclassical, and neo-conservative or neo-liberal, respectively), the refashioning of American Exceptionalism in the face of developments which demanded a revision if it was to continue to be taken seriously as the continuing basis for American identity gave rise to a variant which correspondingly deserves to be thought of, and known as, American neo-Exceptionalism.[33] This concept will be developed in the following pages, especially where the nexus between it and the 'new economics' is argued.

What emerged as neo-Exceptionalism, then, was a discourse which overcame the intruding and threatening historicism. Socialism, for example, exerted a claim in response to the conditions of the Gilded Age just as a form of modernism, which accentuated a radical discontinuity with the past, responded to those of the 1920s. Nevertheless, they were so alien to the predominant culture that they were placed in the position of having to overthrow it, whereas other ideas had the comparative advantage of offering co-option for the acceptable price of revision. If, as in the 1850s and 1860s, wage-labour impoverishment was the problem, it was, at the same time, only a temporary problem to be overcome by the promise of continued westward expansion which would in sufficient time deliver economic independence. Later, towards the end of the century, when the same problem had not succumbed, the individual ownership of economic resources was sacrificed on the altar of marginal economics in general, and a utilitarian theory of value in particular, which proclaimed the market to be a 'beneficent social organism.'[34] Finally, when modernism-as-perpetual transition was the cause of Exceptional discomfort, the recourse was just an intensification of habits learned in the 1890s – change would not be denied, but it would be controlled, and social *science*, in the form of the quantitative methods available to political science and sociology, would provide the basis for the necessary manipulation, prediction, and control.[35]

At each turn, an exceptionalist argument won the day. Westward expansion carried with it the refutation of Malthusian pessimism which confined the growing populations of the lower classes to increasing misery, given that the land available for cultivation was fixed; elevating the market to the status of an ordering device, and relegating those within it to atomistic, competitive, freely calculating consumers, who thereby maximised their goals, was both an idealisation of a liberal world, and, more importantly, a scientistic representation of the 'natural' character that was America. The contributions of the scientised disciplines of political science and sociology only further entrenched this view as they made of America an object of aggregation, constituted by a population of smaller aggregations and individuals which was, by the appropriated science of the day, susceptible to the manipulative techniques of the laboratory, and hence capable of being designed as a perpetual engine of liberal change.[36] It was never the case, therefore, that historicist movements were forgone in America's understanding of itself, but that historicist movements were incapable of providing, externally, the necessary undermining of a national identity so strong that it could invert and subvert itself internally without apparent penalty.

Taken together, the elements of American Exceptionalism have induced in the United States a discourse of unique sensibilities, not just of nationalism, but of national mission – a tendency to universalise the American experience and to either export it, or impose it, or both. Naturally these options can only be realised if the non-American Other does with its history what American Exceptionalism effectively demands: ignores it. Either way, it makes the United States impatient with those states slow to grasp the 'truth' and even hostile to other forms of social and political revolution and development.[37] David Mayers, in his professional biography of George Kennan, is therefore, correct to identify the 'white man's hubris' which imbued the American world view, a presumption, evidently, of which his subject was aware in the following terms:

> to see one's self as the noble big brother and protector, the object of admiration, appreciation, and gratitude on the part of people weaker and darker than ourselves, uninitiated, as yet, into the sacred mysteries of the American outlook.[38]

And, as Todd Gitlin put this still-prevailing view many years later, 'we are not so much a nation as a mission. … We are the people who think we have been chosen to choose.'[39]

With a sharper focus, this dispensation is, of course, to be recognised as the imperialistic sub-set of exceptionalist beliefs which comprise, in the words of John O'Sullivan's 1845 catch-cry, 'manifest destiny,' defined, in Anders Stephanson's account as 'a particular (and particularly powerful) nationalism constituting itself as prophetic but also universal.'[40] From which spring numerous consequences, most of which are subject to the judgment of Stanley Hoffman, who wrote that the strategic culture which American Exceptionalism bequeaths to American policy-makers causes them to 'ask the wrong question, turn to the wrong analysis, and thus in the end provoke the wrong results.'[41] More specifically, since the contradiction between being 'exceptional' and asserting the universal relevance of the US is never resolved, the US is continually in collision with a world of adversaries and enemies. On the one hand it is, in its own estimation, an 'exemplary state' and thus should exist '*separate* from the corrupt and fallen world, letting others emulate it as best they can'; on the other, being providentially chosen, it is sanctioned to engage in regenerative *intervention*.[42]

Believing it is 'exceptional,' it believes it is also invincible; believing it is 'exceptional' and the instrument of a universal mission, it tends neither to compromise nor to trust diplomacy (for that has a basis in compromise). It tends, therefore, to decide in solitude, and to act unilaterally. Caught between the 'truth' of its own exceptionalism and the world's non-American realities, it is ethically adrift, which is to say only pragmatic. But since pragmatism is a poor excuse for war, conflict, when it occurs, requires that 'Americans must define their role... as being on God's side against Satan.'[43] Accordingly, in the matter of security America truly pursues the impossible dream (and an imperial fantasy) because its security problematic is the world and its goal is invulnerability, as James Chace and Caleb Carr have observed:

> The territorial integrity offered the new nation [the US] by the Treaty of Paris in 1783 did not provide sufficient security for the war hawks of 1812, who tried to remove the British presence from North America altogether; an expanded but still uncertain western border was unacceptable to James Polk, who established the American presence on the California coast and the Rio Grande; well-defined continental boundaries meant little to men such as Henry Cabot Lodge and Theodore Roosevelt, who viewed an American presence in the Pacific as vital to the nation; and predominance in the Western Hemisphere, in much of Europe and in parts of the Western Pacific and East Asia proved too little to quiet America's fears during the Cold War.[44]

Of equal significance is that to all such adventures are attached an indulgence, a special favour rather than a legal right which provokes no guilt for the harm caused. Because the language of exceptionalism is absolutist, it is an ideal and most reliable prophylactic against thought, and because absolutism and absolution are unified in their sense of freedom, or release from imperfection and punishment, respectively, at worst there is only shame that the mission is as yet not accomplished with the requisite perfection. The denials involved suggest hypocrisies of monumental dimensions, proclaiming as they do:

> rose-coloured images of the American paradise shaped by the milk-white hand of Providence, the citadel of virtue and the ark of innocence, a nation so favoured by God... that it never killed a buffalo or a Cherokee Indian, never ran a gambling casino or lynched a Negro or bribed a judge or elected a President as stupid as Warren Harding. And because it had behaved itself so well (always doing right, always dressed for church), it had become a land entirely overgrown with honeysuckle, where the urban poor go quietly off to reservations in Utah and nobody... fornicates on Sunday afternoons.[45]

Parsing this ideology for slightly more detail and greater extension it is apparent that the imperialism which it embodies deserves attention, if for no other reason than that it is a framing ethic. American Exceptionalism and its successor ontologies of indulgence and self-justification – Manifest Destiny, *Pax Americana*, Containment, and Roll-back – were, it should be noted, at first conceded in terms of this character, hence the term 'liberal empire.' That the adjective was more a tactic to bestow a certain benignity, even benevolence, upon the noun and its concomitant practices, than it was a statement of fact, should not obscure a continuity which was expressed, in contiguous, territorial terms, until the potential therein was exhausted, and in extra-hemispheric and colonial terms when the possibility was first presented – in the course of the Spanish–American War – and opportunistically in the years since 1945.[46]

In this light the question that comes to mind concerns the role of ideas, specifically, the source or inspiration of those ideas which could breathe life into, and subsequently support, an oxymoronic concept such as 'liberal empire.' Here, two general origins can be identified: the City of God and the City upon a Hill. In the context of this chapter the former is not intended to be a direct, Augustinian application so much as an appropriation of an idea designed to convey the potency of religious beliefs which, *inter alia,* hold that the state is based on self-love, that the state is an ethical community which has as its chief end the happiness of mankind, and that the state is, therefore, a terrestrial and temporal site in which the Church (as the worldly incarnation of the City of God) is to be supreme over the state.

As for the latter, it is a seventeenth-century term redolent with an informed self-awareness of an America as historical world exemplar, 'set like a... light unto the Gentiles as they sit in immemorial darkness.'[47] Whereas the former embodied the unreconciled tension in Augustine between love of self and love of God imposed by living in the world, wherein the first-mentioned could drive out the second, the latter's temptation, as noted by Daniel Boorstin, was more the tendency over time to become 'mere self-consciousness, conceit, or even self-flagellation,' the symptoms of which he catalogues as 'demagoguery in politics... [and a] timid conformity' in all spheres of public and private life.[48] What Boorstin, the twentieth-century Professor of History, shares with Augustine, Bishop of Hippo in the fourth century, is that both of their pessimisms were realised.

The catalyst, if specific catalyst there be, is America's civil religion, a confessional adherence not totally congruent with the formal denominations – Catholicism, Judaism, Presbyterianism, etc. – but comparable with them inasmuch as it shares 'certain common elements of religious orientation.'[49] Among these in a general sense are those dogmas outlined by Jean-Jacques Rousseau in his concept of the civil religion (in *The Social Contract*): a belief in God and a life to come, the reward of virtue and the punishment of vice, and religious tolerance. In particular they share an activist theme that 'lies very deep in the American tradition, namely the obligation, both collective and individual, to carry out God's will on earth.' As suggested, both religions co-exist separately, and are institutionalised in the American collectivity, with the civil religion being the more public expression of the political realm, while the 'church' or 'synagogue' religion provides for the more personal expression required in the private sphere.[50] Overall, Richard Hofstadter's observation that becoming American involved a particular political engagement is very much to the point: 'It has been our fate as a nation not to have ideologies, but to be one.'[51]

Where differences exist in the creed, they are not of the order of mutual exclusivities so much as mutual reinforcements. As Robert Bellah notes, for example, at every point behind American history, as reflected in the American civil religion, lie biblical archetypes: Exodus, Chosen People, Promised Land, New Jerusalem, Sacrificial Death, and Rebirth.[52]

Indeed, in conjunction with the equation of America with ancient Israel, there is a justificatory role for virtually every demarche undertaken in the name of the national interest.[53] Given the ideology of the Puritans, as witnessed by Governor Winthrop's explicit invocation of the 'ominous precedent of Israel,' and their belief that they were 'chosen' to undertake a sacred 'errand' across the length and breadth of the American continent, it could hardly have been otherwise.[54]

Religion, civil and denominational, therefore, constitutes discourses, profoundly so when the clear functional division between them is understood. In Bellah's calculus, the former's God is 'on the austere side, much more related to order, law and right than to salvation and love,' and who is, moreover, 'actively interested and involved in history, with a special concern for America,'[55] thus sponsoring a practice, according to Seymour Martin Lipset, that became 'predominantly activist, moralistic, and social rather than contemplative, theological, or innerly spiritual:'[56] to the churches are delegated 'personal piety and voluntary social action.'[57]

We are, then, to understand America as, in Harold Bloom's bold descriptions, a 'religion-soaked' and 'a religion-mad country.'[58] Broadly speaking, the religion in question is primarily Protestant, but 'especially evangelical'; it embodies a confessional tradition of what Garry Wills terms '[America's] native fundamentalists.' And of that general tradition he also notes that 'nothing has been more stable in our history, nothing less budgeable, than religious belief and practice.'[59] Politically, it was significant, particularly in the nineteenth century when it was, according to George Marsden, both 'the dominant force in American life,'[60] and the 'unofficial religious establishment' of American politics; then, too, it 'tolerated when it did not encourage anti-Semitism and anti-Catholicism,'[61] integral components of the contemporary forces for social stability.[62] Related is the fact that religion in the United States was, and remains both monotheistic and patriarchal,[63] which, historically, had the effect of adding to the two aversions already mentioned those of anathematising the worship practices of the Native Americans and the Africans who were transported to the continent as slaves.[64] The confessional tolerance demanded by the Rousseauean dogmas of civil religion, it seems, had ethnocentric, at least European, limits.

A greater appreciation of the political significance of religion is, moreover, facilitated by reference to the knowledge and/or beliefs which it entailed. The exclusivist mind-set outlined by Wills was indeed only the immediate consequence of a confession which Bloom identifies in summary form as American Gnosticism.[65] The essence of this form of believing and 'knowing' – of, in Bloom's description, their 'fusion' into the 'American Religion' – is represented as follows:

> [Americans are] believers in a pre-Christian tradition of individual divinity. Americans believe that God knows and loves them in a personal way, and that something inside them, deeper even than a soul, is already in contact with God. The American self stands outside of creation, as old as God, of which it is a part. In the American religion, to be free is to be joined in solitude with God or Jesus.[66]

Poll data, collected on a nationwide basis by George Gallup, Jr., and Jim Castelli, provide and affirm the tenets (and the attendant strength of observance) of this dispensation, as does, ironically, a different reading of it by Andrew M. Greeley, undertaken on assignment from the Social Science Research Council, which assumed, *a primo*, that the data would reveal a trend towards secularisation in the American population.[67] Thus:

> 94 per cent of Americans say they have never doubted the existence of God; 90 per cent of Americans pray; nearly 90 per cent (88 per cent) of Americans say they believe that God loves them; eight Americans in ten say they believe they will be called before God on Judgement Day to answer for their sins; eight Americans in ten say they believe God still works miracles; seven Americans in ten say they believe in life after death; 50 per cent of Americans say they believe in angels; 37 per cent of Americans say they believe in a personal devil; 40 per cent of the American population attends church in a typical week (i.e. more people attend church on a weekly basis than go to all sports events combined); internationally, Americans are second only to Malta in terms of rating the importance of God in their lives.[68]

Finally, if to Bloom's and Wills' analyses is added Richard Hutcheson's study of religion and the Presidency, then together, but from strikingly different perspectives, a certain historically valid three-component consensus emerges. This states that America is, first, not willing to become a secular state – on the contrary, it is not only religious, but 'insistently religious in its outlook;'[69] second, the religion which Americans profess is not only decidedly fundamentalist, but also peculiarly ('exceptionally') 'American' in a theological sense; and third, that religion is at the same time not only of the right ideologically but also potent politically.

The City on a Hill is of course embodied in this tradition yet part of something else as well. And that 'something else' is the tradition of the Enlightenment, or the Age of Reason, which stressed tolerance, reasonableness, common sense, and the encouragement of science and technology. In effect, this saw the tyranny of religious dogma challenged by the prejudices of a universalised reason and inevitable progress in all things. In very many ways it was the ideal intellectual framework in which a City on a Hill could be located. On the other hand, given the scope and nature of American religious belief, it is immediately possible to understand why the two realms of thought could not be conjoined without contradiction, without infecting each other in manners inconsistent with the canons each espoused.

CAPITALISM, PROFESSIONALISATION, AND ACCOMMODATION

The intervening variable which explains this transition was Capitalism. And it could only flourish in a 'City on a Hill' by overcoming the indigenous resistance offered by the contemporary prevailing ideologies. In turn, this meant obtaining the surrender of Puritanism, Agrarian Republicanism and, somewhat later, Liberalism, none of which offered assured succour to capitalism in their own terms, but all of which contained vulnerabilities (material anxiety, conceptual poverty, and a preoccupation with property acquisition, respectively[70]) which capitalism could exploit for its own purposes. As they fell, so too, did the prospects for emergence and survival of non-capitalist alternatives.

Thus emerged religion-as-personal-piety-and-voluntary-social action: it was a caricature to any audience familiar with the generality of traditional religious belief and practice;

indeed, it could, without a great deal of injury, be said to be indistinguishable from the concerns of a community service organisation such as Rotary. Moreover, this analogy is even more appropriate on closer consideration of the history of consumer capitalism in the United States throughout the period (1880–1930) in which the transformation was greatest. In brief, we might understand it via the 'strategies of enticement' which followed the establishment of the modern department store. As William Leach details them, the presence of a critical mass of putative purchasers, the advent of the mass market in conjunction with the abundance of consumer goods, and their presentation within promotional spectaculars created a new ethic of desire based on acquisition and consumption as a means of achieving happiness and fulfilment.[71]

Essentially, this was a life-threatening challenge for the American churches which also had the most far-reaching consequences for American knowing. As regards the former, they could either resist absolutely the encroachments of consumer capitalism by a traditional reaffirmation that materialism and its wiles were anathema – in which case they would undoubtedly lose much of their membership, not to mention financial support for the clergy and infrastructure. Conversely, they could embrace consumer capital and its benefits by a plausible argument for both in terms of God's blessings upon the faithful – in which case they would not only betray the Christian Gospel's proscriptions against the pursuit of wealth and the things of this world, but ironically, for both Catholics and Protestant denominations alike, also rely upon a type of rationalisation not noticeably different to that which marked the egregious apologies for power and privilege which gave rise to the Reformation. The horns of this dilemma, then, were survival and capitulation. But there was a third alternative and, in general, the churches took it with alacrity: they accommodated to consumer capitalism in the name of survival, in the process becoming less the churches they had been and more like agents of cultural unity and social amelioration. They became, also ironically, victims of the Reformation's anti-intellectualism and its emphasis, in moral and theological questions, on the individual and the private. So routinised along institutional lines did this occur that the churches' historical identification with criticism, dissent and resistance gave way to a religious passivity that was 'finally so sympathetic to America's new culture and economy as to form yet another pillar upon which the new order rested and was sustained.'[72]

As such, moreover, it became a defining, even *the* defining discourse of American culture, uniting a country that was at the time as ethnically diverse as any in history. The attenuated and universalised conception of the consumer-self, possessed of limitless desires, became the 'reigning American concept,'[73] enthroning, in the process a belief that the world of consumption was the domain of freedom, thus ennobling American patterns of global gluttony which demand that 5 per cent of the world's population be serviced with 30 per cent of the world's energy, and 40 per cent of the world's mineral resources. Enthroning as well, and by extension, a belief that any threat or interruption to this level of consumption was a threat to the security of America rather than an occasion for reflection upon the unequal distribution of global wealth.

An intellectual abdication of this magnitude, and its direct consequences for international politics, is possible only with the complicity of those responsible for the exegesis of the dominant discourse (of capital). And we might note in that case that, historically, the librettos of American political and social culture – Democracy, Individualism, New Deal Liberalism, Narcissism, New Conservatism, and so on – were all scored to the 'marching hymn' of capitalism.[74] Yet, maintaining the metaphor, the composers and librettists which did so assumed a centrality previously denied to intellectuals as a class because previously there had never existed such an acute need to reconcile the irreconcilable, or defend the indefensible. For example, many of the civil religion's biblical archetypes – Exodus, Chosen People – were communal, but they were to be displaced by capitalism's individualistic ethic, and, as regards church religion, capitalism and capitalists were capable of being celebrated only if the immiseration of the masses they were responsible for were instead portrayed as part of a divine plan or natural order. Whatever the argument, it required an heroic sophistry to finesse its transgressions against logic, God, humanity, and the traditional formulations of identity. The drawing of the intellectual class to the bosom of the state, then, was the result not of the former's intellectual rigour (with which it was associated), but conversely, of it committing apostasy by rendering the service of not pushing rigour to the point of indiscretion. And it was to be a harbinger of the intelligence and security discourse which emerged in the Cold War.

The starting point is the need to proceed with analysis in the face of a dominant, university-sited epistemology for establishing and producing 'truths' – which, in so many ways, is impoverishing, incomplete, inadequate, and alienating. Briefly, indeed very briefly stated, this is the result of the fact that, for the most part, the modern, Western university and its modes of inquiry are embedded in seventeenth-century scientific thought and philosophy. In sum, these are riven with hierarchical and totalising Cartesian dualisms many of which are now so commonly accepted as to have acquired the status of 'givens': subject–object; mind–body; self–other; now–then; culture–nature; male–female; and weightless mind–material body.[75] Hierarchical here refers to the first-stated member of the pair being 'thought to be superior to its companion,' and totalising because 'they are thought to exhaust the alternatives within the parameter in question.'[76] Missing from this state is 'any sense that anything is missing' when, in fact, what is missing is the understanding of relation – what John Dewey warned of when he wrote: 'The world seems mad in preoccupation with what is specific, particular, disconnected.' Or Martin Buber expressed it in positive terms: 'Inscrutably involved we live in the currents of universal reciprocity.'[77]

Yet there is still more than reciprocity; there is the need to acknowledge, as have thinkers apart from Buber and Dewey, as ostensibly disparate as Albert Einstein, Alfred North Whitehead, William James, and Ignazio Silone that 'reality' is always observed contingently by a man or woman 'of a certain region, a certain class, and a certain time.'[78] To recapitulate, what this hints at, even if it does not require, is the 'formation of identity of self' which occurs 'largely at an archaic level of engulfment in the moody background world of everyday experience.' Within this condition, for which Wilshire's description is 'mimetic engulfment,' people are typically but 'undeliberately modelling themselves upon others around them' to the extent that individuation is only ever a compromised quality.[79] In a special way consistent with these, professionals (academics, for example) are recognised and authorised within their 'purified' (vocational) group at the same time as they phobically exclude those that would pollute them, namely, those not accorded, or who have rejected the status of 'professional;' or those whose interventions into professional life disrupt it, undergraduate students being the perfect example in the category 'research university.' [80]

And what does all of this signify? In a line: there exists no objective reality independent of the observer's understanding of it. It means, also, as per Werner Heisenberg and others, that the very act of observing is simultaneously the act of participating. The need exists, therefore, to admit Whitehead's 'withness of the body' which, as William Irwin Thompson argues, allows observers to 'at least comprehend [history] through the relevance of [them]selves.' [81] In so doing the conclusion is inescapable that, despite urgings and inclinations to the contrary, the world is never meaningfully experienced by way of a series of confrontations directly with nature or events, but rather, these experiences are mediated by the science of nature, or the history of events, respectfully.

In relation to the university, what Wilshire argues is a consequence of professionalisation, and describes at its macro-institutional and meta-theoretical levels – moral collapse – many others have proclaimed at the strategic and disciplinary levels from perspectives which appear to punctuate the American political spectrum. It is not the intention here, however, to enter into a review of these offerings so much as it is to extract from them those critiques which are telling in terms of their implications for the quality of American strategic intelligence about the world upon which it has all manner of designs. Accordingly, the initial progression must be to the intellectual requirements of understanding the world strategically which, inappropriately and therefore regrettably, is approached, where the attempt is made at all in the modern university, through 'strategic studies' (a.k.a. 'international security studies' in some quarters), and then to a consideration of the university itself as a site for its acquisition.

To state it most plainly, strategic studies is interdisciplinary but, as John Garnett has argued, it is still 'a subject with a sharp focus – military power – but no clear perimeter, and it is parasitic upon the arts, science and social science subjects for the ideas and concepts which its practitioners have developed.' [82] It also reflects the administrative division of knowledge in the university (of which, more below) at the same time as it shares the central philosophical question asked by the major disciplines contributing to it. And these questions concern, *inter alia*, justice, identity, glory, power, war, peace, stability, and order. By this count, strategic studies, and its application in strategy at the level of policy, is an intellectually demanding and socially relevant activity which requires a holistic study of societies and cultures beyond (the disciplines of) anthropology and sociology.

The pity of it is, however, that the university is operationally incapable of discharging anything as demanding as an education function described in these terms. *Intellectually*, this was effected when it attempted to solve the perceived opposition between the rational and the irrational, between (say) history and poetry, or literature and science, by imposing administratively convenient divisions upon the academy. Accordingly, intellectual problems were to be solved by a form of reverse calculus: whereas in the mathematics of calculus (of Newton or Leibniz) infinitesimal amounts are manipulated so as to provide for the eventual *integration* of a phenomenon, the study of societies and cultures in the university was rent asunder by its reduction to small, derivative functions which then admitted no unifying institutional logic or rule. Popularly understood, calculus's advantage was that it called into being the rigorous mathematics of change and gave to its parent discipline additional real content and a literally dynamic mode of thought; the university, as the principal repository institution for education, established only the fragmentation of knowledge, a managerial class which decides upon the structure of that knowledge, and studies which are characterised by their unrelatedness.

Perhaps, just perhaps, this process was inevitable for, as William Irwin Thompson has cautioned, 'short of divine illumination, there is simply no way to study "the whole of things" without a careful analysis of some distinct pieces.' ('Some,' I take it, is the operative term which implies that there should be limits to the atomisation of human experience.) In any event, atomisation did occur and, as a consequence, so, too, did the fragmentation of students to the extent that mutual exclusivity developed between the formal disciplines in even the social sciences which by definition are of human relevance. To opt for one required sacrificing the other.[83] The result is that 'reality,' always elusive, is even more difficult to perceive and understand.

In the normal course of events an institution so divorced from a truly educational project would have ceased to attract funding, students, and staff, or at least be ignored by those concerned to do something serious and worthwhile with their lives beyond the age of compulsory schooling. That this has not been the case is due largely to the 'professionalisation' of the university. As universities became less relevant intellectually their declining status was more than compensated for as the source of vocational licences in the fields of medicine, law, engineering, computer operations, economics (narrowly defined), business, and management (*in vacuo*). This gave the university a second-order, socially relevant function inasmuch as it provided benefits which were derived, in however an attenuated process, from the basic theoretical tradition of inquiry which was previously part of its primary function. As professional instruction and training eclipsed education, university departmental behaviour also became 'routinised along highly specific professional norms.'[84] People – academics – became what they did. Coterminous with this development the university increasingly realised itself as a business, or as the founding president of York University, Murray Ross, phrased it, 'a large public corporation.'[85] It did so, however, so that it continued to *sound* as much like a community of scholars while *behaving* just like any other organisation.[86]

Lost in this metamorphosis is what David Halberstam terms 'civility of discourse' at the elite level. Even in Lewis Perry's discussion of intellectual life in America, where he excepts only New York, with its 'freelance world of letters' from the dominance of the university in this field,[87] but where the latter situation is represented as exercising a 'positive, consolidating power,' it eventually turns out that this is for no other reason than that they lured intellectuals to 'positions of prestige and security within their walls,'[88] whence, he concedes, most lost 'the sense of obligatory dissent and criticism 'implicit in the status as members of the intelligentsia.'[89] In turn, the 'prestige and security' accorded them were a function of the availability of corporate and government funding for the solutions they could apply to immediate, short-term problems, particularly in the period from the 1940s to the 1970s. But it was also a reward for providing 'solutions' which were seen in one way or another as appropriate, even where they weren't successful. Moreover it was a tribute from communities of 'credential-consumers' whose continued operations were predicated on a steady supply of techno-rationally trained graduates whose mind-set was indistinguishable from those they had studied under.[90]

'Rampant segmentation' (as Perry describes it[91]) achieved other objectives, too, which though they might not have been articulated at the beginning of the process, could hardly have escaped the notice of those that were effecting it as it proceeded. The consolidation and complicity of intellectuals within the segmenting university, for instance, removed them from 'most common discourse'[92] – effectively, silencing an entire class of critics who might otherwise be concerned with the plight in and of 'the whole of things.' Thus detached, and their detachment compounded by the professional certainty derived from the problem-solving mode of intellectual life, academics became less disposed to engage in discussions of 'ethics, history, [and] political and aesthetic ideals' which, invariably, meant discussions characterised by inconclusiveness, irony, and ambiguity.[93] Accordingly, their ongoing prestigious and secure existence was determined by the maintenance of that very divorce since it beggared the imagination to propose that funding of the type available from corporate and government sources would ever be available in the same amounts merely for studies which had produced nothing but contestation since the time of the Seven Sages (around 700 BC). Indeed, in an article in *Daedalus*, in 1978, no less an authority than the president of America's first modern university, The Johns Hopkins University, Steven Muller, bemoaned this fact and the impoverished quality of research which resulted.[94]

Muller might also have bemoaned the strategy which was in evidence, but perhaps this would have been redundant since Edward Shils, of the University of Chicago, had already done so, and Perry's precis of that account locates 'segmentation' in an entirely different, and altogether sinister light:

> [Shils]... identified the prevailing strategy: neutralise and accommodate the dissenters, but recognise that 'the stability of the larger society depends... on the maintenance, within the culture and the institutional system of the intellectuals, of the predominance of that element which accepts an objective discipline and the integration of academic institutions into the central institutional system of American society.'[95]

Given the role which academics from Harvard, MIT, Yale, Berkeley, Chicago, Stanford, and Columbia can be confirmed to have played in American government (from intellectual histories of the United States), and the links they have with the more prestigious 'think-tanks' such as Rand, the Hudson Institute, the Heritage Foundation, the American Enterprise Institute, the Center for Strategic and International Studies, and the Institute for Contemporary Studies, the strategy would appear to have been most successful.

PROFESSIONALISATION OF THE UNIVERSITY AND ITS CONSEQUENCES

One of the problems associated with detailing what is effectively the prostitution of the university-as-institution is that it is frequently taken to imply that there was once a 'golden age' of the university. Unfortunately, nothing written about the academy could be further from the truth since it would also posit a more general 'golden age' of society in which knowledge, inquiry, and criticism – the endeavours of intellectuals, in brief – were respected as necessary activities in their own right for any civilised and self-respecting society. And there is no body of research in general, and certainly not in regard to the United States, which supports this proposition. As David Ricci has noted, in the post-Civil War period, for example, American universities did not so much *defend*, or *apologise* for the established order as legitimate its advent, a development subsequently seen as creating the basis for the 'entire complex of professions in the new order.'[96]

In so doing the universities provided the discursive foundations for the American state and its authority. In the particular case of the American social sciences, even in their infancy, this was especially so: as Dorothy Ross has argued at length, they have 'consistently constructed models of the world that embody the values and follow the logic of American exceptionalism,' of which the 'most striking outcome has been scientism' and, with it, a single-mindedness on the part of those who practise it that 'cannot notice the qualitative human world their techniques are constructing and destroying.'[97] Elsewhere she has written that Exceptionalism 'was the discursive frame within which the social sciences worked, the language which set their core problem and shaped the logic of their solutions to it.'[98] Thus, she sees the two most influential paradigms of the present to be instrumental positivism and neoclassical economics,[99] both of which are among the pantheon of scientism's manifestations which 'command the mainstream of American social science… [due mainly] to the complicity of heterodox social scientists and their failure to develop a fully historicist understanding of their task.'[100]

And 'complicity' is the appropriate term since it involved an associative jealousy, sometimes termed 'physics envy,' for the predictive and manipulative status which the most lustrous of the 'hard' sciences enjoyed within the Enlightenment project, especially in the late nineteenth century. In the collective desire to emulate the Newtonian paradigm in matters social and political, the discursive strategy of choice was, and had to be, positivism. Within a proliferation of areas of inquiry, there could be no other way if the recalcitrant phenomena were in any way to be controlled and amenable to policy 'solutions.' Occluded, where they were not lost immediately, were the contexts of the data – institutional, cultural, and historical – and by extension, any credible claim to an understanding of the whole. In their stead scientism, itself only a bastardised version of an administrative method for understanding nature, triumphed by way of the 'language within which people understand the world… [and] necessarily construct worldviews.'[101] In this light it is mandatory, but perhaps all too obvious to note that any strategy of global human significance which deliberately excludes an appreciation of historical difference and complexity is intellectually bankrupt and dangerous.

The university by these accounts is a principal, institutional, yet bifurcated locus of intellectual power. The power within – to shape minds – is licensed by the discursive consistency of the graduates – who, in turn, shape the world – not, however, in any idiosyncratic manner, but, as Alan Ryan has it, 'according to rules of rationality compatible with the rules of the social system.'[102] Reason, therefore, is inseparable from the institutions in which it is preserved and transmitted just as the institutions themselves are inseparable from the states and societies which sustain them. Within this relationship education is a mode of social production.[103] The product, though, acquires power only through acceptance, after which, in a Gramscian sense, it is diffused and disseminated so thoroughly that it displaces and wins out over others so thoroughly that it achieves hegemony over the world of 'commonsense.'[104]

To recall Said's 'extraordinary mainstream consensus' on US foreign policy is now to understand 'the twinning of power and legitimacy' as well as how the rationales for imperial doctrines – the Monroe Doctrine, Manifest Destiny, Massive Retaliation, Containment, Roll-back, etc., and now, Free Trade – were couched in terms of a moral imperative, 'world responsibility,' of which coincidence Said writes, 'exactly correspond[ed] to the growth in the United States' global interests after World War Two and to the conception of its enormous power as formulated by the foreign policy and intellectual elite.'[105] It is also to understand the professionalisation of the university in Wilshire's definition:

> a way of life which provides a livelihood through the practice of a skill valued by society; this requires a 'cognitive base' of expert knowledge which can be acquired only through protracted training in a special field.[106]

Central to professionalisation, therefore, is a particularisation of discourse – what William H. Epstein refers to as a process through which 'a professional practice assumes and resumes authority... by attributing it to a disciplinary authority' supposedly external to the process itself.[107] Thus textual critics authorise their interpretation by attributing it to, say, the author's intentionality, the textual structure, or generic conventions. This 'gesture' is an attempt both to deny that they are engaged in interpretation at all, and to present the unadorned meaning of the text, whereas, in reality, it is merely the substitution of one set of interpretive principles by another, which, all along, denies that that is what is happening.[108] In the human sciences, as Jane Flax reminds us, a similar discursive strategy operates: a fictive but persuasive account of 'Man' is created whose 'nature' can be investigated for its regularities and norms and, hence, its laws, via the methodology and techniques of that same discourse. These sciences, Flax continues, claim merely to 'discover,' and not create, such laws; and, since they are the product of 'experts,' their discovery 'will be considered authoritative and final.'[109] This conclusion, which implies that there is no appeal from the writ of 'experts', is inescapable since their discourse is, by definition, the embodiment of reason and rationality, from which it follows that to reject it is to renounce the rational and to enter, effectively, a plea of deviance and/or insanity.

Entirely consistent with these modes of the seventeenth-century university, the principles of disciplinary professionalisation affirm Dewey's 'mad' world, preoccupied with the 'disconnected,' and deny the 'universal reciprocity' of Buber. Moreover, since the 'gesture' attempts to transfer authority from the critic to the author, or the text (or whatever is thought to be the most potent externality), it allows for the assumption of identities in order to infiltrate the discourse of the Other, determining, *inter alia,* that literary critics, area specialists, and intelligence analysts are involved in projects of common interpenetration so long as they are each committed to a professional discourse.[110] Yet, since interpretation is what is afoot, the declaratory project, in Pierre Bordieu's suggestion, reduces to 'a lie which would deceive no one were not everyone determined to deceive *himself.*'[111]

To the extent that the university gives its identity to the processes and objectives of the state it might better be understood as a site of 'establishment intellectuals' whose outlook is characterised by an infatuation with state power rather than engagement with the issues that power inexorably creates, and whose specific location is within any one of a number of groupings which deserve less the appellation 'department' than they do Wilshire's 'interlocking directorate.'[112] It might also better be understood as the site of lost vocations in the sense that the 'gravity of history and individual responsibility… [to] public matters, and to public discourse' is dissolved as the norms of the state are internalised.[113] In their place, more precisely, reigns a commitment to addressing problems in the only way allowed by professionalised, segmented university disciplines; in other words in 'a piecemeal, ameliorative fashion.'[114]

TRANSCENDENCE

To understand this politically centripetal, if not vertically intellectual mobility of the intellectual, it is necessary to understand four relevant characteristics of American intellectual life which were evident from the earliest days of the nation. First, to the extent that reason in America required 'quiet literary research,' it did not exist. Second, to the extent that reason implied or pursued secularism, it was heresy, and an unappealing heresy at that. Third, to the extent that reason was practised by a 'realist' who, in Emerson's famous reference, 'converses with things,'[115] it was legitimate and flourished, although, as Curti observed, the popular tendency existed for the scholar to be viewed as an 'impractical recluse.'[116] But this prejudice passed somewhat when it was understood that the scholar could be enlisted, and willingly enlisted to the point of complicity, to intellectualise what religion and privilege alike ordained – captured neatly in the subtitle of John Trumpbour's edited critique of Harvard University's involvement in government: 'reason in the service of empire.'[117] What needs to be emphasised is that the 'turning' to intellectuals and the university by the state in the early years of American history became a habit, and then proved to be an incurable reflex. Through history there were always enough problems – massive social change, economic disaster, nuclear deterrence, and world orders (old and new) – which, seemingly, demanded the attention of the university.

Hence the fourth emerges, because, to the extent that the pursuit of reason in the university transcended 'cognitive rationality,' to use the concept developed by Talcott Parsons, 'merge[d] with nonrational ways of knowing' and became a way of 'attaining the vision of divine truth, of ultimate reality,' it became an accomplice to American civil religion. And one with a classical genealogy at that: was it not Plato who claimed that 'all education is initiation,' Aristotle who argued that what 'contributes most to preserve the state is… to educate children with respect to the state,' and Alfred North Whitehead who added, 'all education is religious'?[118] University education thereby acquires a pragmatic, manipulative character at the same time that it imparts, somewhat indeterminately, a metaphysical appreciation of matters incapable of being fully understood within the operational-intellectual environment thought to be typical of the academy. As has been argued previously in this work, such transcendence is a general and characteristic condition found in the scientism and embedded American Exceptionalism of the American social sciences. Moreover, it is the possessing spirit of the neo-liberal economic theory driving the globalisation of the world economy.

The university, by this account – which is to say by its internal conformation with the configurations of power external to itself in the so-called wider community – indicts itself as a transmission system for conservative interests. As noted earlier, this is less a departure from tradition in the West than it is a continuation of an orthodox tradition of service to the state which goes back to the origins of the modern academy. But what demands further attention is the profundity of its moral abdication and philosophical transformation – from a locus of education and learning in which, simply put, students are led out of ignorance and prejudice into liberation in accordance with their knowledge and understanding – to an institution which, by definition, is primarily concerned to install in its students the requisite information, techniques, and answers which are held to be sufficient to a chosen 'discipline,' and hence which minimise, where they do not obviate, the possibility and potentials of education. Surely, it stands to reason, education-as-a-leading-out is impossible where the instruction to be received takes the form of knowledge which is, for all intents and purposes, unproblematic: non-ambiguous, clear, and determinable – in a word, finished.[119]

Should this be thought an unduly jaundiced appreciation of the presence and role of professionalised disciplines the following chapter is devoted to a drawing of a fuller face of the university which even the foregoing does not entail. This is a drawing which sketches in the unfamiliar, and frequently concealed, lineaments of a face not only turned away from education but towards power; and even then, not only towards power but, more specifically, towards servicing the dominant political-strategic interests of the US through the provision of sympathetic exegeses and advice, no matter the obscenities committed in their name. Of necessity, therefore, the following drawing is abstract in style, but not because it lacks reference to specific circumstances; rather, because it takes a summary form which is derived from a real, tangible world which frames as it contextualises the overpowering of education, and the overdetermining of instruction.

Part III

5   *Suprema a situ*[1]
Economics in the university and the world

Of all the academic 'disciplines' which are representative of the modern, seventeenth-century university's pathologies and status as authoriser, creator, repository, and transmitter of productive truths – and virtually all are candidates – the discipline of Economics, or, more precisely, its dominant mode of neoclassical economics, is the exemplar *par excellence*. It is, at heart, unselfconscious and insufficiently self-critical, but also a vision-less, masculine and male-dominated discourse in such a state of disarray that it can only think of reform and improvement in terms of the very causes of its current condition – ever increasing levels of theoretical rigour – rather than a serious consideration of the principal fault which is its theoretical bankruptcy. Specifically, in its obsession with maximising behaviour as a foundation of human activity, it is crudely Newtonian and Darwinian in a Quantum age in which extremal theories of survival are, to put matters bluntly, wrong. Accordingly, its constructs are as disfiguring of the human condition as they are totalising; its habits, ethics, and disposition are marked by some of the worst traits historically found in professions which have given themselves to an ideology – intellectual evasion and predatory practice bordering on, where it does not unambiguously entail, insanity and criminality. The consequence for Economics, though it might also be justifiably seen as the cause of its malaise, is a crisis in which understandings provided by the discipline are inadequate to the phenomena it seeks to analyse.

In no other discipline is there found a discourse so dominated by putative certainties derived from seventeenth-century rationality (fused with the unacknowledged naturalisation of capitalism, and cryptic claims of Western superiority in general and US dominance in particular), and yet so undermined by its confrontation with empirical and theoretical challenges mounted from the world over which it seeks authority. It is a discipline, therefore, *in partibus infidelium* – a discipline whose claim to knowledge has been extinguished (in this case) by rigorous inquiry, by being, in other words, incompetent, where it is not mistaken. In its confidence and trust in the revelatory powers of science, its prizing of discipline ahead of thought, its confusion and disorder in the face of the world – and its attempts to reconcile the latter on the unrelenting terms of the former – it is best understood as a doctrinal system of thought, rigidly administered, and authoritatively held and taught by a professionalised clerisy; in other words a form of dogmatic theology.

These words, and the conclusions they describe, have all been chosen carefully because what saves Economics is that it remains, through a process of discursive entrenchment, in demand by the community, and hence by the students who would serve the community as graduate-professionals. But, to emphasise the situation, it does so without the necessary purchase on understanding that rightly should license its teachings. In the absence of a disciplinary willingness to undergo a Copernican revolution, it remains neurotically persistent and anti-intellectual, reproducing itself through the instructional and miseducation projects that the modern university is accustomed to harbouring, and proffering policy advice which is inevitably inappropriate.

Justifying this, it is sufficient to revisit, in greater critical detail, the theories and practices of neoclassical economics and the challenges to both of them which have been made *in the discipline's own terms*, which is to say from within the discipline itself, broadly defined – from its axioms and concepts, from its bodies of shared or common empirical data, and, most significantly, from the area of mathematical economics, by whose formal rigour Economics laid claim to the status of a science. Of necessity, such a project is an incidental critique of Economics' pretension to be integrated within the Cartesian-rationalist dream of modernity which holds that society, a diverse, even disparate entity, is incoherent without having imposed upon it a logic external to itself. At the same time, and more generally, it is also a refracted critique of the logic and rationality defined by modernity, overarching constructs which should be briefly recalled.

Modernity's claim is that logic or rationality comprises an evocative, integrated trinity of rational method, unified science, and exact language which, correctly applied, in Stephen Toulmin's words, 'are designed to "purify" the operations of human reason by decontextualising them.'[2] Erected thereby are the three pillars of rationality in the modern world: by way of the first two (rational method and unified science) *certainty* and *systematicity* arise; and through decontextualisation, the mind is wiped clean of the historical and cultural frictions which would otherwise impede the birth of, and distort the transition to, the truly rational state.[3]

Two other features attend this project that must be noted. The first is that 'the world' unreconstructed modernity creates through its rationality reflects the authority – some would say the hubris – thought to reside in mathematics as a pure, frugal, and formal language and logic. By definition, therefore, it is engaged in a three-stage process in order to function. Initially, it abstracts from the world only the data it can recognise, and that means a denial of whatever legitimate uncertainty, ambiguity and disagreement which exist concerning both the data and the context it is located within. It then renders the data usable by simplifying it in a form amenable to translation into the symbols of mathematics. In this process many important assumptions about the world are obscured but one, at least, is explicit: abstraction and simplification are, it is held, essentially, not injurious to the scientific method, nor to understanding the world, for the reason that complexity is, at most, a superficial manifestation which conceals an intrinsic order in all things, universally. Finally, the metaphysical commitment to a 'naturalised' cosmopolis based on the understanding that nature is without history but is, nevertheless, a system in equilibrium is accomplished: as suggested by the Newtonian mechanics from which this view derives, it is constant, permanent, simple, static, and invulnerable.

Within the modern rationality, therefore, we can identify ideals that are 'intellectually perfectionist, morally rigorous, and humanly unrelenting.' Absent is any notion that the world of humanity might render modernity's methodology 'unrealisable and practically irrelevant' for all but those with a vested interest in the *status quo*.[4] Absent, too, is any notion that science is a mediation, in favour of the belief that science describes the operations of the world, a default of monumental proportions if one takes seriously Werner Heisenberg's caveat that 'the science of nature does not deal with nature itself but in fact with the *science* of nature as man thinks and describes it.'[5] Holding to the former, he warns, 'man finds himself in the position of a captain whose ship has been so securely built of iron and steel that the needle of his compass no longer points to the north, but only towards the ship's mass of iron,'[6] a condition Erwin Schrodinger likened to atrophism and ossification, in which 'joyfully isolated groups of experts' engage in 'virulently esoteric chat.'[7]

By preferring to ignore Heisenberg's insights, Economics within this discourse is thereby provided with the solvent for society and, thus, community obligations, a disappearance notoriously expressed in Margaret Thatcher's fiat: 'there is no such thing as society' – all that exists is the aggregate of individuals on their particular vectors. Equally, since the world is the realm of unchanging nature, in which all constituent parts are determined in terms of their contribution to the overall equilibrium, nature, so understood, is quintessentially conservative. Attempts to change the *status quo* are against nature and the 'wretched of the earth' are cautioned against revolution no more than the upper classes are reassured of their innate, organic superiority.[8]

Understandably, one popular metaphor for modernity's cosmopolis which emerged was that of the ocean, as much constitutive of the system of nature as any that might be imagined and it was found to be appropriate to not only the economy, but, in the United States and within the discourse of American Exceptionalism, to America itself, since both demanded a concept fluid enough to permit dynamic atomistic movement, within the confines of what Ross terms a 'larger stasis.'[9] The symbiosis here was no mere historical coincidence or appropriation of images; on the contrary it reflected the crisis-challenge to American Exceptionalism posed by destabilising socioeconomic change in the 1890s which threatened to sunder the nation, and with it, the national myth, and the escape from this fate promised by the new, scientific theories of economics.[10]

By the prevailing logic, both the economy and America were known to be ordered in accordance with 'natural' laws. Since Economics, courtesy of developments in mathematical economics, was in possession of a scientific paradigm which could guarantee certainty, predictability, and control, it remained only to discover the corresponding scientific paradigm for America, but that paradigm had to eschew historical change of a non-exceptionalist character if it was to remain faithful to the exceptionalist dispensation. Thus conditioned, historical change was permitted but only to the extent that it was defined as perpetual liberal change subject to scientific control.[11] And, to complete the circle, that control was to be realised, in significant part, by the 'marginalist revolution' in neoclassical economics (see below for greater detail). For the present, it is sufficient to understand that the marginalist world vision of the market as articulated in the US by

John Bates Clark was a 'beneficent social organism' in a state of natural equilibrium – conditions which resonated strongly with the basic tenets of American Exceptionalism.[12]

In its claim and dimensions, therefore, modernity's rationality, with its requirement of humble subordination to a system of unrelieved determinism, is a totalitarian monologue. Obliquely, neoclassical economics even concedes the point in its preoccupation with eliminating all barriers to the 'free market' where 'all barriers' is defined as trade unions, or 'almost any kind of human institution or group of actors' which absent themselves from, resist, constrain, or attempt to modify its operations.[13] It is appropriate, therefore, to refer to the new Economics by the more politically precise appellation, 'the new capitalism:'

> Its basic instinct is to free itself from any form of state or interstate control or intervention. Its thrust is deregulation, privatisation, and the dismantling of state protection for the vulnerable elements of society. It preaches that the unregulated global market is good for everybody, although some may reap its benefits earlier than others. The state retains a function as enforcer of contracts and as instrument of political leverage to secure access to resources and markets world-wide. It is also at times expected to salvage reckless enterprises, if they are big enough, and to compensate an innocent public for plunder by unscrupulous financial operators. But, by and large, the state is conceived as subordinate to the economy. Competitiveness in the global economy is the ultimate criterion of public policy.[14]

Such an inversion of the role in government, effectively from protector of the majority against the excesses of the unregulated greed, to arbiter of last resort in such a system, necessitates an opening up of Economics to the vulgar gaze of critique. What follows, therefore, is an examination of the discourse which begins in the broadest terms and gradually reduces to quite specific foci on its foundational concepts. At this level the purpose is to highlight the prejudicial framing of Economics which is the result of its obsession with mathematics intertwined with its corresponding need to engage in abstractions which only parody the human condition. To emphasise, the concern here is to establish general cases of critique from which perspectives the specific analyses will be more easily understood, since so many of them are variations on an original approach or theme.

COVETING SCIENCE, PRACTISING SCIENTISM

A disciplinary yearning that is most accurately captured by the term 'physics envy' seduced political economy away from its roots in society towards the end of the nineteenth century. The success of science, particularly physics as an exemplar of the ability to control conditions and predict outcomes, promised a rational understanding of the economy through the eye of mathematics (with which physics was braided), which, of course, required a reconfiguration of the study in terms of the methods by which it was to be understood. In the prevailing view, mathematics was to give to Economics, and thus to economists, the relevance and, therefore, the professional status with government, industry, and community, which had progressively been accorded to scientists since the age of Newton. Since, in modernity, mathematics was the highest distillation of truth – exact, unshakeable, and infallible – all that remained for the transformation to be effected was to establish the necessary axioms, isolate the relevant variables, and apply the appropriate mathematics which would reveal economic truth with clarity without historical precedent. It would, additionally, render Economics a double layer of security: since mathematics was widely thought to admit no appeal, its disciplinary security was directly proportional to their use (this was especially true in the case of differential calculus, which could be deployed in the service of the central concept of the maximising behaviour of individuals central to economic activity); and it was a powerful means of excluding from Economics the non-mathematically trained scholars from other disciplines in the social sciences.[15]

As already noted, the turn to physics was ironic because physics was itself beginning its turn to a world much less congenial to the type of professional, policy-oriented certainty that was Economics' objective. Even more ironic, however, was that the associative jealousy which obsessed Economics not only occluded an awareness of the quantum revolution in physics, but also the nature of, and uncertainties in, mathematics as a multi-discipline itself. It was as though, in the process of becoming something that was, by definition, an ahistorical area of inquiry according to its adherents, Economics was excused from seriously investigating the intellectual history of its new habitat for signs of contradiction and decay. Had it done so it is possible that the embrace of mathematics – specifically, 'the maths of nineteenth century engineers' with which economists are so fixated[16] – might have been less warm, because, throughout the nineteenth century, a revision of its claims and pretensions, themselves a reflection of its strange evolution since classical times, most notably in the development of 'strange geometries' and 'strange algebras,' had become imperative. Destroyed in the process was one of mathematics' principal conceits – that the mathematical laws of science were truths and that mathematical design was inherent in nature; indeed, also under challenge was the imperial appeal of mathematics based on its claim to be not only true, but also universal. Thus, like Newtonian physics in the face of the quantum revolution, mathematics was suffering a long-overdue debility of identity, forced on it by the accumulated contradictions in the behaviour of mathematicians which were no longer tenable. Reflecting on this, the historian of mathematics, Morris Kline, writes:

> mathematics had developed illogically. Its illogical development contained not only *false proofs, slips in reasoning, and inadvertent mistakes* which with more care could have been avoided. Such blunders there were aplenty. The illogical development also involved *inadequate understanding of concepts, a failure to recognise all the principles of logic required, and an inadequate rigor of proof,* that is, intuition, physical arguments, and appeal to geometrical diagrams had taken the place of logical arguments.[17]

Nineteenth- and early twentieth-century mathematicians, moreover, were not only aware of this, but published their misgivings. Of ideal concepts such as proof and absolute rigour, Alfred North Whitehead lectured that they had 'no natural habitat in the mathematical world.' And throughout the last 200 years, the consensus seems only to have grown, with a foremost American mathematician, E.H. Moore, concluding in 1903 that mathematics was a function of the historical epoch in which it was constructed, a view essentially shared previously by Hermann Hankel, Richard Dedekind, and Karl Weierstrasss, and subsequently by some of the greatest mathematicians in the last 100 years – Hermann Weyl and, irony of ironies for Economics, Nobel prize-winning physicist, Percy W. Bridgman.

To put the argument directly and succinctly, mathematics is a product of society and develops in a social context which is usually narrow and particular; and has a social role that is usually defined by dominant social groups. These social interests, historically, have not only determined the practices, fashions, and uses of mathematics by the judicious use of funding and patronage, but have even extended to the 'social organisation of the production of mathematics: the training of mathematicians, patterns of communication and authority in mathematical work, professionalisation, specialisation and power relations.'[18] Within these categories, and identically determined, mathematics is both the beneficiary of the male domination of the dominant social institutions, and the site of ongoing male domination within the discipline – the latter, of course, being an outcome which is itself legitimated by the construction of the requirements of science as suiting only those who are emotionally detached, instrumental, and competitive.[19] Thus, when mathematical science is subjected to a rigorous sociological investigation of the type undertaken by David Bloor, the much-vaunted 'objectivity' of mathematics is seen to deal *not* with physical reality but with social creations and conventions which must be adhered to only because mainstream academic mathematics has institutionalised an obligatory set of beliefs *through social negotiation*.[20] By extension, mainstream academic mathematics is but one conception of a mathematical world which is rich in alternative concepts driven out by the social interests vested in the former.[21]

An example from theoretical physics (which Economics has been at pains to simultaneously emulate and ignore) can illustrate these findings in action. If it is accepted that mathematics finds its foremost application in theoretical physics, it is a revelation to understand that, in the development of quantum theory in Weimar Germany, explanations for the phenomena were chosen on the basis of their physical, social, and political desirability: specifically, in the prevailing climate opposed to rationality and causality, quantum physicists chose to present their accounts by way of a mathematical formalism which could be interpreted as non-causal. Nor was this an atypical scientific recourse, as Brian Martin writes of the various schools of thought ('statistical,' 'hidden variable,' 'splitting universe,' and 'realist') trying to make sense of it all:

> The case of quantum theory is intriguing because, in the decades since the establishment of the orthodox or Copenhagen interpretation, a number of alternative interpretations have been put forth. Some of them use the same mathematical formulations, but interpret their physical significance differently, while others use different mathematical formulations to achieve the same result.[22]

And this is a relatively expurgated view of the discipline's confusion. In Nick Herbert's examination of the eight models of quantum reality he concludes that:

One of the best-kept secrets of science is that physicists have lost their grip on reality. ...

If we take [their] claims at face value, the stories physicists tell resemble the tales of mystics and madmen....

An astonishing feature of these eight quantum realities is that they are experimentally indistinguishable. For all presently conceivable experiments, *each of these realities predicts exactly the same observable phenomena....*

Some of these quantum realities are compatible with one another....

But other quantum realities are contradictory....

Not only can physicists not agree on a single picture of what's going on in the quantum world, they are not even sure whether the correct picture is on the list....

They may, however, all be wrong....

All of them without exception are preposterous.[23]

Physics' inability to develop a 'single picture' of reality is not peculiar, historically or scientifically: in mathematics, in 1931, the Austrian mathematician, Kurt Godel, effected what Kline terms a 'débâcle,' by demonstrating that, while mathematics consisted of several schools, each in disagreement with the others, none of the logical principles accepted by the several schools could prove the consistency of mathematics. Even worse for the status of mathematics was an emergent character of confusion in which disagreement between the various constructions attended both the question of what might properly be designated as mathematics, and, within the constructions, of what might be the proper superstructure.[24] Expressed another way:

No formal system satisfactorily describes itself.
... axioms are unprovable in a system on which they are based. That is what makes them axioms, rather than inferences... [and] the system will always throw up questions which the axioms, even if admitted, are insufficient to decide.[25]

To what should have been the deep professional embarrassment of economists for at least the last 70 years, mathematics and physics were not what they were coveted for; indeed, they were its opposite – the former, courtesy of Bohr and Heisenberg 'stranded in indertiminacy,' the latter, along with logic, 'on the beach.'[26]

Of particular importance for Economics was the particular status of two branches of mathematics which, it is widely agreed, have made seminal contributions to the development of the discipline – differential calculus (in relation to the extremal nature of economic theory), and statistics (the manipulations of which are at the heart of macro-economic predictions of probable states of the economy as a result of policy change). Neither, it has to be said, have been treated more kindly than mathematics in general, nor, logically, could they be, in the search for certainty. Calculus, as the result of its faults, became the focus of 'rigorisation' in the mid-nineteenth century and after, but the efforts ultimately failed to achieve this end. Even the best efforts by David Hilbert failed to establish its predicate, or first-order logic. Of this Kline notes that the search for certainty has produced only an 'unending' process of undecidable propositions.[27]

Statistics also underwent a developmental phase in the nineteenth century – from being seen and used in an ancillary role, as servants of argument, to being accorded the dominant role in the search for the laws of nature. Eventually they were thought capable of deciding 'whether the universe was a deterministic system of law, or whether it was the product of the operations of blind chance.'[28] The answer, if it qualifies as such, is that nature is 'not at all determined, but rather chaotic.' The best approach to certainty in nature that statistics can provide is by way of predicting a most probable state under specified conditions, but, for all of that, nature remains independent of mathematical laws.[29] In any case, statistics do not, in themselves, explain why certain states are more, or less, probable. In the end, as Mary Douglas highlights in Ian Hacking's work, statistics are historically sensitive; they cannot be divorced from the political culture and the associated style of reasoning in which they are manufactured, the neglect of which caveat he demonstrates with many examples, effectively attributes 'autonomy' to statistics and results, *inter alia*, in the 'reckless use of the law of large numbers for finding facts about human behaviour.'[30]

For all of its existence, therefore, mathematical economics has relied on the certainty and scientific status of a discipline whose troubles constitute, according to Kline, 'a mockery of the hitherto deep-rooted and widely reputed truth and logical perfection of mathematics.' Neoclassical economics has, therefore, throughout its lifetime and of its own volition, proceeded into serious error and ridicule since it insists on fate-sharing with a form of science, which we are reminded is endangered and, because of this, dangerous:

> the lack of a proof of consistency still hangs over the heads of mathematicians like the sword of Damocles. No matter which philosophy of mathematics one adopts, one proceeds at the risk of arriving at a contradiction.[31]

In this light the criticisms which social critics and some critical economists make of Economics, to the effect that it privileges the mathematical over the material and the interpretive, equivalence over difference, quantity over quality, and numbers (which are held to be value-free) over figurative language (which is held to be excessive), are somewhat beside the point because they imply that, in general, the status of science as a producer of knowledge is unassailable, and that, in particular, mathematics is beyond reproach as a judge in the field of Truth and Knowledge. What eludes them is a prior matter of extraordinary importance, the logical and philosophical exhaustion of science, which Bruce Wilshire outlines in the following terms:

> the term good 'talks' to us on the inner level of the self. But it cannot be taken in as a whole by science and defined in the required precise and predictive sense, so it cannot figure in the truths that scientists discover. Science by itself cannot tell us how to educate, not even how to educate as persons those who are to be scientists. In fact, although science is considered the paramount way of knowing, it cannot establish what nearly everyone assumes: that it itself is good.[32]

Thus, the extremely valid charges against Economics made by Tony Lawson – that the discipline is guilty of, uncritically and in a widespread manner, appropriating mathematics for systems or conditions for which they are not suited – is a fourth-, and only fourth-order criticism, being degraded, if you will, by the need to understand the long-standing and significant critiques which attend, in descending order, science, mathematics in general, and the prevailing, conventional attitude of economists to mathematics.[33] Thus, fourth is significant because it locates the misappropriation within a third-order critique which, in simple terms, is the foregrounding of a disciplinary disposition best described as a form of contemptible anti-intellectualism.

The basis for this claim is that, historically, Economics has contrived successfully, and at the highest levels to celebrate itself as an 'unworldly,' area of mathematical inquiry at the same time as its adherents lower down in the professional hierarchy represented their knowledge as essential to sound government. Nobel prize-winning economist Gerard Debreu, in his 1990 presidential address to the American Economics Association, provides one of the more outstanding contemporary examples of the former, proposing an 'acid test' for articles in economic theory, namely 'removing all their economic interpretations and letting their mathematical infrastructure stand on its own.'[34] For others, outsiders, such a criterion is warranted on the basis that, for all of Economics' immersion in virtually every area of state policy, 'the theory and its development have been as insulated from empirical influences as geometry ever was before Einstein,' implying thereby that, since it fails by the criteria of policy utility, it might as well be given residence in the neighbourhood it most covets and, accordingly, be regarded as 'a branch of mathematics.'[35] But contempt is also courted because the abnegation of the world, so dear to Debreu's 'acid test,' has been joined not only with exhortations to use mathematics but, at the same time and in the recommendation of Frank Hahn, to 'avoid discussion of "mathematics in economics" like the plague.' Such advice, furthermore, is proffered on the basis of assertion rather than argument, but appears to have succeeded for the most part none the less.[36]

Through such habits Economics became a casualty, not so much of science – because, as this brief account indicates, the best science was replete with warnings as to its confusions and limitations – but scientism, that naive acceptance of science as the source of absolute truth, and hence, the equally naive belief in the applicability of the methods and techniques of the physical sciences to the study of human behaviour. Even worse, for Economics, the besetting consequence was a discipline which, in Fred Block's critique, 'has never provided a fully adequate understanding of the economies it seeks to analyse.'[37] Economics in these terms is a parody of science, a poor or enfeebled imitation which, in its attempts to satisfy only the dictates of pure reason, ignores or extracts from economic life almost everything that gives it meaning, while reifying the remainder.

A SCIENCE OF *AD HOC* STRATEGEMS

It is at this entry point that the fourth-order critiques come into their own. As previously noted, those undertaken in considerable analytical detail by Tony Lawson in his recent study, *Economics and Reality*, which consolidate the numerous, telling, and more celebrated criticisms of neoclassical economics are particularly valuable, the more so when the focus is on the extensive and enduring dysjunctions between economic-theoretical perspectives and analytical practice. Of these Lawson identifies three exemplary levels of inconsistency

– method, social theory, and methodology. As regards the first he refers to that habit of economists to 'frequently employ methods, practices and techniques of enquiry and modes of reference, that are inconsistent with the theoretical perspectives on method which they claim to draw upon.' In econometrics, for example, R.E. Lucas has drawn attention to several practices within its ambit, including the 'indifference of econometric forecasters to [certain sub-sets of available] data series;... the frequent and frequently important refitting of econometric relationships; [and]... most suggestively ...the practice of using patterns in recent residuals to revise intercept estimates for forecasting purposes,' all of which contravene accepted theory.[38]

Such transgressions, moreover, are widely tolerated, as witness the testimony of the highly respected econometrician, E.E. Leamer:

> The opinion that econometric theory is largely irrelevant is held by an embarrassingly large share of the economics profession. The wide gap between econometric theory and econometric practice might be expected to cause professional tension. In fact, a calm equilibrium permeates our journals and our meetings. We comfortably divide ourselves into a celibate priesthood of statistical theorists, on the one hand, and a legion of sinner-data analysts, on the other. The priests are empowered to draw up lists of sins and are revered for the special talents they display. Sinners are not expected to avoid sins; they need only confess their errors openly.[39]

But, according to Leamer, this is not the limit to the departure from science: frequently; indeed usually, it is the same people who espouse theoretical virtue and practise analytical vice, leading Lawson to comment that the result is the presence of sanctioned incongruities in the discipline.[40]

The second level of inconsistency speaks of profound inadequacy rather than incongruity. Specifically, it is the inability of the various neoclassical economic theories to include the necessary substantive content to sensitively embrace such basic economic categories as choice, institutions, market, money, social relationships, uncertainty, and change. Since some of these categories will be revisited further on, it will suffice at this point to dwell briefly on the exemplar offered by Lawson, namely, that of choice, the rhetoric of which suffuses the Economics discourse. For Lawson the central notion that 'economics is all about how people make choices' is contradicted by no less than what is, perhaps, the central axiom of the discipline:

> In the formal 'models' found in mainstream journals and books, human choice is ultimately denied. For if real choice means anything it is that any individual could always have acted otherwise. And this is precisely what contemporary 'theorists' are unable to allow in their formalistic modelling. That is, although the reality of choice appears to be widely acknowledged by economists in their more informal discussions and public pronouncements, the exercise of choice is a phenomenon that is always absent from the substantive analyses that are conventionally reported. Instead, individuals are represented in such a way that, relative to their situations, there is almost always but one preferred or rational course of action and this is always followed. Despite some suggestive rhetoric, human beings, as modelled, could not have been otherwise.[41]

Effectively, this is no more than the logical conclusion to an illogical approach because the 'lack of attention to elaborating the nature of (social) being, or existence,' what Lawson also refers to as the 'neglect of ontology,' is a direct consequence of 'an implicit and uncritical reliance upon various results of positivism.'[42] More comprehensively understood, the phenomenon at hand is the injurious abstraction required of an approach which, when it is 'operationalised,' must exclude from consideration any recognition that economic arrangements are social arrangements and, therefore, historically contingent; that, when change occurs, the parameters, and even the nature, of economic activity change by definition; and that economic arrangements are inseparable from the society (including its legal rules and enforcement mechanisms) in which they exist.[43]

Equally, the over-determination of human choice outcomes is an inescapable consequence of, in Rosenberg's description, the 'extremal' character formulation of core economic principles, itself an atavistic reminder of Economics' Newtonian (and Darwinian) ancestors. Both proclaim that certain systems, mechanical and biological, respectively, are to be understood in terms of their minimising and maximising behaviour, and by doing so, 'provide the explanation of all of their subjects' behaviour by citing the determinants of all their subjects' relevant states.' Accordingly, extremal theories are total theories; when evidence contrary to that predicted by the theory is to hand, the response is to challenge the formulation of the test conditions, but not the extremal nature of the theory. They remain, therefore, unfalsifiable in terms of the scientific method that ostensibly produced them, or, in Rosenberg's words, 'untouched by apparent counterinstances.'[44] For this reason, numerous philosophers of science have felt compelled to either dismiss those pretensions of Economics which are derived from the extensive analogising of the discipline with Newtonian physics, or to qualify them in such a way that the difference hardly matters. T.W. Hutchison is to the fore in this regard:

> but the mathematical 'revolution' in economics has been one mainly (or almost entirely) of *form, with very little or no empirical, testable, predictive content involved.*... Not only has nothing genuinely describable as 'a Newtonian revolution' taken place in economics, it is reasonable to suggest that it is not probable that anything of the sort is going to occur in the foreseeable future.[45]

In this light it should not be surprising that the third level of inconsistency which Lawson identifies is constituted by a most pervasive area of ignorance – basically, the extension of Hahn's injunction to avoid the discussion of mathematics in Economics to the more encompassing realm of methodology, or philosophy, in Economics. It is variously, seen as either a 'waste of time,' or contrary to common sense; in either case, methodology is discouraged 'explicitly and boldly.' As well, there is a 'clear reluctance' on the part of mainstream economic journals to publish articles in the area, and funding agencies to underwrite relevant research. As Lawson writes of the situation in the UK, 'the training currently provided and recommended for Economics students tends to be more or less devoid of any explicit methodological content.'[46] Given the insubstantial nature of its foundations this might be thought an appropriate response, a method of avoiding an embarrassing acquaintance with doubt, akin to those communities and societies which discouraged their lower echelons from acquiring excessive education for fear that it would encourage challenges to the established order by redistributing knowledge, and hence, power. Indeed, the degree to which mainstream economic analysis excises from its professional deliberations the inescapable context of its being recalls John Ralston Saul's view that its 'greatest desire is to generalise and institutionalise a syndrome resembling Alzheimer's disease.'[47]

EXCEPTIONAL (AMERICAN) ECONOMICS

All that remains at this point is to recall that Economics has an American dimension which, through the operations of its modernist, scientistic rituals sacralised the economy. In particular, Descartes' concern with rationality triumphed in the US over his equally insistent search for causality, not just because the survival of Economics demanded it, but because, in a maelstrom of social change, prediction and control were being sought in the name of establishing attitudes and values in which American Exceptionalism would endure.[48] There, accordingly, the injury to a comprehensive understanding of life is more apparent and, naturally, more pronounced because, immediately following World War I, quantitative method became the 'hallmark of the new science' and, with it, the predominance of statistical analysis – which incorporated behaviouristic premises, replicable, exact measurements, and prescriptions as to what was to be studied and how. In Ross's account the statistical turn was but another embodiment of what should, by now, be a familiar congruence:

> [Statistics] configured every object of study as an aggregate of individuals and every field of inquiry as the statistical study of aggregate behaviour. In form, if not in name, it reconfigured the liberal, exceptionalist ocean, in which no structure impeded the flux of atomistic movement.[49]

Given the overcoming of religious objections and reservations about capitalism which was underway at this time, and the transformations of these resistances into an accommodation, the nearer one was to the American ideological mainstream, the nearer one was to the concept that the economy was godly and that the pursuit of material comfort and bodily well-being – total happiness for many – via consumption, was divine. In the final analysis commerce and religion were in harmony, and God and Mammon were co-deities in an expanded pantheon. Bizarre as it might seem, this was exactly what was proclaimed; recall again, this was a period of intended and unintended inversions and reversals. It began following the American Civil War and lasted until (say) 1930, and saw, *inter alia*, the extra-continental expansion of the United States to the Philippines, which were 90 per cent Roman Catholic, to the end of 'Christianising them,' as President William McKinley recounted it to an incredulous adviser. It saw the rise of monopolistic and oligopolistic capital, and their entrenchment under the Sherman Antitrust Act of 1890 – which was designed to limit their power. And it saw the rise of the modern theatre of consumption, the department store, with its objective of creating 'organised dissatisfaction' for standardised objects of desire, effecting, in William Leach's description, 'the metamorphosis of consumption from vice to virtue.'[50] In all it was a period which ushered in a new commercial culture to match the spirit of the new Economics.

That spirit was captured by some of its more notable celebrants, in their injunctions to:

> Wake up and stretch yourself.... The only thing that keeps us from taking plenty of either money or air is fear. All you desire is YOURS NOW.... *You are born to dominion and plenty.*

And equally, the repugnance for it is unambiguously reflected in Thorsten Veblen's lament that 'the ancient Christian principles of humility, renunciation, abnegation ... had been virtually eliminated from the moral scene,' and replaced by nothing representative of workmanship or human service so much as 'an indefinitely extensible cupidity.'[51]

In general terms, then, the legacies of the 'new Economics,' particularly as they are expressed in the 'new capitalism,' might be described as excessive abstraction in relation to the individual, personal satisfaction, and the market, and disingenuousness as regards the ongoing exemplar which the United States is held to be. Any conception of the human being which considers its reduction to the level of an 'insatiable, desiring machine,' or 'an animal governed by an infinity of desires,' as the essence of a human science has clearly decided to engage in fractional distillation and abusively deny the myriad integrative and creative aspects which are in evidence.[52]

Similarly, the proposition that ever-increasing levels of personal consumption are positively correlated with happiness, that the market, therefore, is infinite, is prescriptive of little else but narcissism and imperialism (no matter that these conditions are finessed as personal fulfilment and modernisation, respectively). While this justifies American Exceptionalism's desire to (contradictorily) universalise itself, and thus to 'develop' global recalcitrants, it says nothing of the revision undergone by that discourse nor, more significantly, of the testimony it provides to the power of that which it is most concerned to deny – history and culture. It thus reformulated itself in response to the crisis of Gilded Age change by exploiting the opportunity presented by scientism in Economics, to the extent that the new variant was neo-Exceptional in the way that classical political economy became neoclassical economics; both required political and systemic revolutions, and both effected an escape from history. But what it reformulated to was never addressed yet is of fundamental importance for the subsequent analysis of modern economic theory in this chapter. And that is because American Exceptionalism was never, in itself, *exceptional* – in fact, it was the understandable national fantasy of a people who confused their migration, from tyranny to a new continent, with a beginning outside of history. What the organisation of their fantasy obscured was its origins in the concepts and hopes of a reformed, virtuous, and religiously tolerant England. Thus, it was less a unique creation of the intellect than nostalgia for a purified *status quo ante.*[53] In other words, at the very heart of the conjunction of the discourse of the United States with that of modern Economics there lies an atavistic presence which denies the denial of history and is, given high levels of interdependence between American Exceptionalism and neoclassical economics, suggestive of the other, philosophical and theoretical embarrassments which reside in the latter.

To develop this argument it is necessary to visit the principal economic sites of theory from which are derived modern Economics' claim to be a science and a repository for policy advice. This is no more than a continuation of the analytical focus of this book, a steadily tightening progression from the broader to the increasingly specific. Accordingly, the constructs and theories which underpin Economics, such as Rational Economic Man, The Market, Competitive General Equilibrium (which was introduced to economic discourse via the 'marginalist revolution'), Rational Expectations, and Non-Accelerating Inflation Rate of Unemployment, will be the principal foci. But other theories – relating to the relationship between economic growth and employment, for example – and their linear/Newtonian character and/or the empirical problematic they provoke will also be examined.

The utility of empirical critique is, of course, non-existent unless it is accompanied by an understanding of facts as constructed entities which are *given* their meanings discursively; they do not, in other words, exist (have a meaning) independent of the observer's understanding of them. Thus, the intention in this section of the inquiry is not to confront one set of data with another for the purpose of claiming that one is superior to the other, and thereby demonstrate the falsity of the theory of competitive general equilibrium. Rather, it is to suggest that the proliferation of non-conforming and conflicting data prompts the need to reflect upon the palpable inadequacy of a theory which essentialises and universalises a single view of the human condition outside of time. The empirical critique, then, is not a closeted obsession for the theory to become more rigorous, and thereby lay claim to more accurate, more specific data, but the basis for the explicit proposition that it is the search for just such a theory and its data which is the underlying problem. But there is a second, practical, and more immediate objective in mind as well given the pre-eminent status of Economics and economists in the policy communities of the industrialised, or developed democracies. The almost daily confutation of their abstract theories by events not foreseen, and their inability to agree within their own professional, ostensibly scientific discourse, provides a form of intellectual self-defence for those who, in societies dominated by instrumental positivism – hence, in the absence of philosophical acuity in the political leadership and, perhaps, themselves – need to resist mainstream economic prescriptions and their tragic consequences by the most effective means.

RATIONAL ECONOMIC MAN

At the core of modern economic theory lies *Homo Economicus,* also known as Rational Economic Man, a construction, in aggregate terms, who *is* the economy because the economy is defined as the sum total of the activities of all such individuals. But Rational Economic Man is a contradictory beast if the new capitalism is taken seriously. Simultaneously, he is held to be the untrammelled, self-sufficient, competitive individual whose tastes, preferences, and behaviour are fixed, and whose 'every transaction, every act of social intercourse, must take place within the nexus of cash and of maximising self-interested individualism;' and the actor whose behaviour will nevertheless maximise human welfare in society, always presuming that such an actor finds that Thatcher's denial of it is unpersuasive – in other words, suspends his belief in the everyday theories by which he lives and prospers.[54] Psychologically, such a person is the dubious beneficiary of a multiple personality disorder; in his community, he is unreachable; politically, the minimum that might be said of him is that he is unreliable, but mathematically, he is, as noted earlier in this chapter, the character actor made imperative by differential calculus.

Fortunately, the nonsense that is Rational Economic Man is undone very easily. The immutable, or dogmatic, nature of his tastes is denied by logic and plain common sense alike if it accepted that any individual human agent has three choices – to adhere to a previous decision; to make an alternative decision of his/her own choice; or to be persuaded to another decision on the basis of social interaction.[55] This spectrum of possibilities serves at least to complicate what is an otherwise simplistic account. The nonsense then takes more of a tumble to the extent that the choices of men and women tend towards simple cooperative behaviour, and the avowed rationality of neoclassical theory is not only put aside, but, as Robert Axelrod's work on the benefits and domination of collaborative endeavours indicates, the very status of neoclassical theory to explain anything except conservative behaviour, conservatively defined, in a world in which agony, horror, drama, tragedy, and the imagination which is stimulated in their presence, is in doubt.[56] The pessimism of this conclusion deepens when, for example, the work of the French Nobel laureate, Maurice Allais, is factored in: the long-delayed effects of his 1950s research has been to draw attention to the fact that certain 'systemic patterns of behaviour which run directly counter to the maximisation hypothesis.'[57] When joined by the more recent research conducted by the British economist, Graham Loomes, and published in the *Economic Journal* in 1998, the demise is complete, as Paul Ormerod observes:

> Loomes concludes that the postulates of conventional theory are fundamentally flawed. The quest … to model individuals as if they were characterised by some set of fully formed and highly articulated preferences, which they can and will apply consistently to any and every form of decision problem, is doomed. *Not just difficult: doomed.*[58]

Clearly, neoclassical economics is aware of such conditions but is offended by them; more, it cannot speak to them since they occupy the realm of the 'irrational,' and anything 'irrational' has no meaning (where it is not madness itself). But if one accepts that agony, horror, drama, and the imagination which is stimulated in their presence are causal of all behaviour, then neoclassical economics' obsession with idealised actors acting ideally, conforms to a rationality which is lacking in seriousness. In the knowledge that Adam Smith, the metaphorical father of modern Economics, and Alfred Marshall, and John Maynard Keynes all recognised the philosophical and moral dimensions to economic life and the primacy of society (as evidenced by their education in philosophy and/or their writings), it is a disfigured, and disfiguring tribute which Economics pays to modernity for survival as a science.[59]

Exploring this travesty further, it will be found that the expanded critique of *Homo Economicus* has much to learn from the standpoint of a feminist understanding of Economics. To this end there is a need, in the first instance, to understand it as a male-dominated discipline, a discipline which faithfully, but mistakenly, extends the masculinised world view which overtook science in the sixteenth and seventeenth centuries. Surveying the aspirational literature of the time by such luminaries as Henry Oldenburg (an early secretary of the Royal Society) and Francis Bacon, as well as offerings which represent the historical development of Economics, and then drawing upon numerous recent analyses employing literary criticism, historical interpretation, and psychoanalysis, Julie Nelson produces abundant proof of both the gendered nature of Cartesian thought and the 'identification of science with masculinity, detachment, and domination, and of femininity with nature, subjectivity, and submission.' The critical issue of individual choice illustrates this character admirably: the material world, and the existence of real persons and things within it – such things as childhood, bodily needs, human connectedness, and nature – are displaced in favour of the detached *cogito*, possessed only by man.[60] Such a theoretical eccentricity then isolates Economics from one of the most easily verifiable facts of life, as expressed by Diana Strassmann: 'human beings begin (and often end) life in a state of helplessness and unchosen dependency.'[61]

Whether as a consequence of this orientation, or other factors, it is nevertheless the case that male domination of Economics is also in evidence demographically. At the mundane level of awards it can be gauged by 'the extent to which women have been absent from the ranks of prestigious economists who have played a significant part in shaping the discipline' and, more widely, by the under-representation of women among those who receive advanced degrees in Economics, or who are appointed to the faculties of colleges and universities, especially to senior positions.[62] Further testimony in support of the general proposition appears to be manifest in a recent claim by a leading philosopher of Economics, Donald N. McCloskey:

> It is a fact that there is not a single prominent economist who is also an avowed homosexual, although, given the reported percentages of men and women with homosexual experiences, there must be hundreds upon hundreds of gays and lesbians in our field.[63]

What McCloskey is raising in this unusual critique (the more so because, within it, he announces his intention to become, 'under medical supervision,' a woman) is that the discipline to which he has given his professional life is, *prima facie*, a discipline of oppressive silences. It demands, or easily imparts the requirement, that the subjective 'I' exists in straitened conditions if that identity needs to be understood in terms which it has decided are feminine – bodily needs, human connectedness, and nature. As Donald/ Deirdre contemplate it: 'It makes you wonder whether a discipline that ignores love and friendship might be a little nuts.'[64]

The gendered nature of economic thought which follows from the gendered nature of Cartesian thought provides little support for those who would defend Economics against McCloskey's suggestion. Indeed, one of the most immediate consequences of this genealogy ought to be the replacement of *Homo Economicus* with *Vir Economicus*. The explanation here is simple: although the former literally means 'economic human,' the gendered nature of Economics demands that a more accurate, or more truthful term be used to cover the male-dominated phenomena in question: the suggestion, accordingly, is the latter, where *vir* is the Latin word for 'male adult' or 'husband.'[65] Deploying the term *Vir Economicus* would, therefore, capture the stereotypical male celebrated in market Economics: 'rule-driven, simple-mindedly selfish, uninterested in building relations for their own sake. A cross between Rambo and an investment banker.'[66] It might also be a first step to countermanding the deception resident in the current description by a degree of long-overdue honesty.

Meanwhile, Economics continues to make women invisible through an incomplete treatment of the economy in which women as subjects of economic study are absent, through approaches which are blind to the family and household work, two areas in which, traditionally, women, as uncompensated domestic labour, are economic producers, but within a social, rather than an individual framework that requires the particular models in use to exclude them. And this says nothing of the need to not only include women, but to do so in terms of the contexts in which they are most likely to be located – dependence, interdependence, tradition, and power (although these same dimensions could, with advantage, be introduced to mainstream, male-oriented economic analysis).[67] The partiality of the dominant mode of economic representation, therefore, is incomplete, but it is more than that as well: it is preferential and, in the injury it does to women's labour, vicious. It compounds their degrading within Cartesian science with the arbitrary refusal to hear, see, and speak the obvious role of women in the economy, an inclusion which, as Block argues, radically potentialises Economics as an area of social inquiry.[68] Moreover, the self-absolving plea that the assumptions of Economics are only assumptions, and relatively innocent ones at that, fails, as Diana Strassmann demonstrates, because these same assumptions disguise the value judgments inherent in the decisions, policies, and ultimately, the views of the world and the material conditions, which flow from them.[69] In the denial of this nexus is found another instance of the confusion between the popular addiction to a narrow self-knowledge framed by professional self-consciousness, and a deeper awareness of the self and its relations afforded by an understanding of the origins of historical and social habit – a refusal which, far from being harmless, recalls Jung's verdict that it merely 'adds stupidity to iniquity.'[70]

THE MARKET

The basic principles of this device are quite straightforward, for which we might refer to John Kenneth Galbraith:

> The Market Economy is based on the unplanned, uncontrolled response of individual producers and of corporations, small or large, to the will and the purchasing power of the consumer at home and abroad. The purchasing power that drives this mechanism originates from the productive activity to which the purchasing power responds. A closed circle. This is the essence of the market system.[71]

Of this closure, and the familiar totalising mind-set which accompanies it, Robert Kuttner additionally reminds us:

> There is at the core of the celebration of markets relentless tautology. If we begin by assuming that nearly everything can be understood as a market and that markets optimise outcomes, then everything leads back to the same conclusion – marketise!

> If, in the event, a particular market doesn't optimise, there is only one possible conclusion – it must be insufficiently market-like. ... Should some human activity not, in fact, behave like an efficient market, it must logically be the result of some interference that should be removed. It does not occur that the theory mis-specifies human behaviour.[72]

Needless to say, for Galbraith and Kuttner, as for countless other critics of the market which Economics idealises, there is much about it which not only 'mis-specifies human behaviour,' but either trivialises altruistic actions, or is invasive of values on a higher plane than the market, or produces sub-optimal outcomes, or is (in common parlance) immoral.[73] As regards the first, mis-specification, Block, for example, points to the foundational myopia ever-present in the methodology of Economics, which naturalises the economy as a timeless entity – that is, seeing the economy as 'an analytically separate realm of society that can be understood in terms of its own dynamics,' and the individual actors within that economy as rational maximisers of utilities – without realising that all such constructs are cultural creations.[74] To this end he introduces the anthropological studies of bourgeois society undertaken by Marshall Sahlins showing that economic necessity is no predictor of actual social arrangements, either in tribes of hunter-gatherers or more complex, modern societies.[75]

Effectively, what Block is critical of is the differentiation accorded only one dimension of the economy (the micro-economic choices that are available to individuals) from the two with which it needs to be integrated – 'the state actions that structure an economy ...[and] the vast area of social regulation ... that condition and shape microeconomic choices.')[76] Indeed, his critique is that, given the high level of abstraction involved, 'there is remarkably little discussion in the literature of the workings of actual markets,' and that 'markets of the kind exalted in theory are rare.'[77] Similarly, Kuttner cites the pioneering work of psychologists Daniel Kahneman and Amos Tversky, within the analytical school of experimental economics, which demonstrates that normal, real, people engage in countless acts of unselfish regard for others: in other words, far from being the rational, utility-maximising individual operating in an institutional vacuum, their life practices are informed by 'general norms of fairness' in the expression of their 'civic and social selves.'[78]

These same people have also demonstrated an extraordinary and chronic resistance to both 'efficiency' by taking free market choices which, rationally, were 'not the best, but the worst'. Here, Ormerod instances the demise of the Betamax video cassette recorders at the hands of the technologically inferior VHS machines, the continuing success, in the computer age, of the QWERTY typewriter keyboard – a nineteenth-century invention that was deliberately designed to be inefficient; the failure to adopt the more economically efficient and ecologically sound system known as Integrated Pest Management in favour of chemical pesticides, and the geographical clustering of industrial firms in Wales (for example) contrary to the conventional market criteria for the location of industry.[79]

At the same time, the expression 'civic and social selves' leads into the second profound critique of marketisation: 'In a political community, some things are beyond price.'[80] Among the myriad that come to mind are human and political rights, one's person, one's fellow human beings, one's vote, and political office. Certainly this is not to deny that attempts have been, and continue to be made to subject all areas of life to market Economics, but it is to say that, even in societies in which market Economics are found to a marked extent, there is a popular revulsion at the suggestion that they should be the determinant of, to put it simply, life and death. Interlinked with this view is an equally popular understanding, doubtless approximate and inchoate at times, that a pure, or doctrinaire reliance on markets will produce sub-optimal outcomes. Those espousing such a view are conscious of the fact that, in the financial world, panics and depressions resulting in political chaos have been the legacy of this dogma; but more than this, their scepticism is derived from a knowledge of history in which such public goods as free, secular, and compulsory education, extensive infrastructure development, health, and environmental protection, were never valued properly by, and seldom on the agenda of, the market. Neither, too, was the need to redress the more egregious excesses of the market which result in gross inequality, always a serious impediment to the emergence and development of democratic politics.[81]

It is for this reason that John Ralston Saul offers the cautionary advice: 'The history of the marketplace has been repeatedly written by its actions.'[82] And for the same historically informed reasons, Galbraith advocates public intervention where the stakes embrace the contemporary and long-term protection of the planet, the protection of the vulnerable from the adverse effects of the economy, quality control of goods, and the economy's own tendencies to self-destruct with appalling consequences.[83] Finally, it should be appreciated that what is true of national markets is also true globally: every country in human history which has entered into the strong, sustained growth which distinguishes industrial, and post-industrial societies from all others, 'has done so in outright violation of pure, free-market principles.'[84]

It is manifest nonsense, therefore, to propose that the free, or unconstrained market is organisation which maximises liberty, justice, and efficiency for the great majority of its actors, and hence, is the most moral of economic arrangements if that term is understood as encompassing and imposing an ethic of care and responsibility for others. Given that individual income and wealth are the prerequisites for freedom in the market, the presence of extremes of wealth and poverty relegate the poor to what Kuttner accurately describes as 'the paltry freedoms of a meagre income.'[85] For some, mainly the wealthy, this is just, reflecting, ultimately, the positive correlation of reward and ability, as though extenuating circumstances such as birth and fortune were irrelevant. But, as was documented in an earlier chapter, the quality of life provided is not far removed from Thomas Hobbes' description of man in the state of nature – nasty, poor, brutish, solitary, and short.

Cynically interpreted, therefore, the avoidance of discussion of 'the workings of actual markets' could well be the result of disciplinary prudence. Since the pathology of the market is a concept and undertaking far removed from Economics, it would be an alienating experience to have to confront, as a matter of daily professional experience, the confounding of all received notions of the market with an unambiguous empirical record that it 'accords wealth and distributes income in a highly unequal, socially adverse and also functionally damaging fashion.'[86] Equally, it might well be devastating for professional confidence to encounter – that is, to come upon adversarialy – the defiant lived experiences of the great majority of people with the central tenets of market discourse. Yet this is the prospect.

THE MARGINALIST REVOLUTION AND COMPETITIVE GENERAL EQUILIBRIUM

As problems of income distribution and economic cycles came to the fore in the late nineteenth century and threatened established orders throughout the industrialised world, serious attention was turned to theories of value in an attempt to refute the growing relevance of the writings and predictions of Karl Marx. The emergent principle in micro-economics, which carried this burden, though historically ancient in its genealogy, was heralded as revolutionary when it (re-)appeared as 'marginal utility.' Its underlying assumption was psychological, namely, that satisfaction would decline as greater amounts of a product or service were consumed, and it held that the value of a product or service is established by individuals who carry out rational calculations and consume units of a product or service according to the utility derived from the last – marginal – unit purchased, such utility being equal to the cost of obtaining it. Conversely, when applied to companies, who were assumed to be small, produce identical products, and incapable individually of manipulating the market, it was held that the given rate of profitability resulting from a given level of production and inputs will only diminish with successive increases in inputs and production. In such a world the market is efficient in itself: without any form of state intervention whatsoever, supply exactly equals demand, costs and benefits are weighed precisely, no certain net benefit is ever forgone, and all resources are fully utilised.

Implicitly, therefore, it formulated an ideal liberal world of free-willed individuals, competing and choosing in a market which admitted transient fluctuations of price but inevitably reverted to a stable system of natural values. This had to be the case because prices would determine supply and demand as individuals and companies realised their optimal utility, at which point satisfaction and rationality alike determined that equilibrium would prevail. It thus served to legitimate the naturalised world view of modernity, timeless and certain, in general, and American Exceptionalism in particular. Understandably, in this light, Robert Heilbroner and William Milberg write that 'general equilibrium has come to dominate the marginalist approach to economic analysis.'[87]

Overarching as this is, it does not explain the extraordinary attraction which the theory of competitive general equilibrium has exerted since it first surfaced. Thematically, these may be categorised in terms of their endogenous, or organic, appeal within certain policymaking communities, and the esoteric, or somewhat more restricted appeal the theory has among the initiated, that is, within the discourse of modern Economics. Of course, this organisation does not imply total separation between the categories; on the contrary, it intends to exemplify the obverse relationship of political, to economic life. Thus, in considering the endogenous variables it is necessary, in the first instance, to admit the continuing legacy of modernity in the form of 'the imperialism of psychology.'[88] By defining Rational Economic Man in terms of her/his quest for satisfaction, by affirming this concept in the discourse of national identity, religion, higher education, and the widespread intolerance of alternatives, especially in the world's most powerful economy, the popular culture in the industrialised democracies was effectively colonised by a single understanding. Furthermore, this, again in the United States, was the avowed objective of such leading political psychologists as Charles E. Merriam and Harold D. Laswell in the 1920s, the latter of whom advocated propaganda as not only necessary, but salutary, because it would promote the 'engineering frame of mind' upon which depended 'the management of collective attitudes' through the manipulation of symbols that would not so much resolve economic, social, and political conflicts as render them harmless.[89]

If the deserved contempt that such influential but wrong views warrant is put aside for the moment, however, scholarship and intellectual fairness alike demand that the real economic problems of the 1970s and since, and the impetus they provided for the turn to the global (neo-liberal) variant of neoclassical Economics, receive their due. Here, at least seven arguable, if not compelling, sub-cases are found in the literature. Their enumeration is no more than a recital of the uncertainties brought on by the decline of the United States and other formerly pre-eminent industrial powers in the face of global capitalist competition which they themselves promoted as an antidote to communism, and the dissolution of the Cold War. If a musical metaphor is permitted they sound the *pibroch* – the Scots-Gaelic lament for the passing – of theories and practices once fervently believed to be progressive in every way, and conducive to certainty, but now just as fervently held to be mistaken, if not discredited, and a source of policy debilitation.

Thus, the welfare state economies which found themselves in various states of crisis, and other economies which concluded that the Keynesianism they had been practising was not yielding the expected benefits at the same time that entrepreneurship was declining, all turned towards a coherent paradigm that promised to reverse these conditions. The breakup of, first, the Eastern Bloc, and then the fracturing of the Soviet Union into a still undecided morphology only exacerbated the despair for left/socialist alternatives, especially in the contemporary knowledge that, in matters economic, the communist world concurred in the prevailing Western view of itself as a failure. Similarly, in much, but certainly not all of the developing world, the failure of centrally planned economies and the corruption often associated with it had created a receptive constituency for theories which, at the market level, pledged equality of opportunity, and hence, empowerment, while at the individual level the same benefits, by logical extension, would realise the local control of destinies.[90]

But it was also the case that the Modernist view of a world subordinate to modern science was as vital as it had ever been in the discourse of economic policy-makers. According to the exegesis, it was no mere coincidence that Western market economies had produced greater levels of material well-being to their citizens over the last two centuries; on the contrary, this was the result of their development according to a general, scientific theory of Economics that represented a formidable intellectual achievement in its own right, and becoming, collectively, 'the most successful form of economic organisation yet invented.'[91] Experience, logic, and prudence therefore determined that, where the system had fallen into disrepair, the most appropriate remedial actions were those which were consistent with the scientific spirit of the discipline's origins, namely, *scientific* refinements.

At this juncture, clearly, experience and science interpenetrate so completely that the endogenous motivations are virtually congruent with the esoteric motivations and no useful purpose is served by attempting to present one set or the other in sharp relief. But where this inquiry asks a question beyond the economic declines outlined – such as 'who benefits under the new theoretical regime?' it is forcibly returned to John Kenneth Galbraith's understanding of the emergence of both neoclassical economics (and the neo-liberal variant) in terms of the services rendered to privilege by theorists. Specifically, what the latter performed for the former was what might be called restoration therapy. Here a redefinition of the complaint is called for: while it might be acceptable in some literatures to describe the downturn in the Western economies as a 'decline,' it was *experienced*, most particularly in the United States, as a fall from hegemonic power, which is something altogether different; it was the loss of control, prediction, and certainty in economic matters which enjoyed the status of a 'given' prior to the 1970s. It was, as well, an anomic condition which left the afflicted in need of accustoming itself to, and learning the norms and compromises of, reduced potency. Alternatively, a creative physician could treat the patient and not the condition, thus ensuring that the treatment would be acceptable to the latter. Correspondingly, the former had to promise no less than a return to hegemony (with attendant benefits being welcome) – a not insuperable task given the therapeutic role of the Economics profession for more than a century.

From the very birth of neoclassical economics in the late 1800s, it should be noted, the 'stake' – the condition – which its adherents defended was the *status quo*, based as it was on the doctrine of *laissez-faire*. That the theory provided the promise of the possibility of material advancement to all individuals equally, in addition to the ideological justification for already existing economic privilege was not a disadvantage either. (Indeed, it is relevant that in the contemporary period the globalist version of neo-liberal economics, transnational liberalism, is embraced by what Agnew and Corbridge describe as a 'set of interlocking interest groups' across First and ex-Third World elites.)[92] That it has always required both dehumanising its essentially human subject matter, and conjoining the metaphysical with the physical, is apparently irrelevant; ultimately it allows both an illustration and a rare (for this writer) endorsement of an observation by Allan Bloom, namely, that like 'nothing else' studied in the university, modern Economics is the 'perfect coincidence between science and cupidity.'[93]

Galbraith terms this 'the economic accommodation' which results from the need by those who are very well-off to have their status receive an intellectual benediction, a condition of longing he finds so historically consistent that it is among phenomena which justly deserve the description 'lesson;' hence:

> The most nearly invariant [lesson] is that individuals and communities that are favoured in their economic, social and political condition attribute social virtue and political durability to that which they themselves enjoy. That attribution, in turn, is made to apply even in the face of commanding evidence to the contrary. The beliefs of the fortunate are brought to serve the cause of continuing contentment, and the economic and political ideas of the time are similarly accommodated. *There is an eager political market for that which pleases and reassures. Those who would serve this market and reap the resulting reward in money and applause are reliably available.*[94]

Elsewhere he is even more specific in enumerating the three basic requirements of the discipline of mainstream Economics in terms of the needs of the fortunate which its practitioners must serve, none of which are in any way socially or intellectually responsible: the defence of the principle of limited government involvement in the economy; the 'need to find social justification for the untrammelled, uninhibited pursuit and possession of wealth'; and a similar justification for a reduced sense of responsibility for the poor.[95]

To the end outlined, therefore, Galbraith cites the Yale University economist, William Graham Sumner, who, in 1914, wrote that '[t]he millionaires are a product of natural selection.... They may fairly be regarded as the naturally selected agents of a society for certain work. They get high wages and live in luxury, but the bargain is a good one for society.'[96] In the present he instances the writing of George Gilder and Professor Arthur Laffer, the former of whom was forced to appeal to 'the necessity for faith' among his readership so as to reconcile what was, in fact, irreconcilable in his arguments; and the latter of whom had arguments on taxation so removed from even the fantasies of Economics that 'it is not clear that anyone of sober mentality took [them] seriously.'[97] Which, it has to be said, and Galbraith emphasises as much, misses the point: Gilder's *Wealth and Poverty* acquired 'near biblical standing' in the early 1980s while Laffer will be commemorated for demonstrating that a 'justifying contrivance, however transparent, could be of high practical service' to a 'gilded constituency.'[98] All of which provides a suitable preface for a critical investigation into the theory of competitive general equilibrium *in its own terms*, in both empirical and theoretical modes.

Accordingly, a comparison between the six principal assumptions and implications specific to the theory of competitive general equilibrium and the world in which it operates is revealing. For a start, mathematical convenience is advanced if the theory assumes, first, a 'continuum of traders' which is infinite; that is to say, limitless, in which, second, all traders produce identical products, yet none are of sufficient size to influence the market price of the product being sold.[99] Third and fourth, and by extension, government intervention is both unnecessary – because the price mechanism will create the optimum values of all goods thereby clearing every market (in goods and labour); and unfair – because such interventions will make at least one actor worse off.[100] Thus, fifth, to state what should be obvious, 'theoretically,' *there is no unemployment*, and thus, sixth, the market is in a state of timeless equilibrium since no rationality exists for it to depart from the optimal conditions it has created.

Empirically, however, there is no infinite continuum of traders, because such a thing is no more than an abstract mathematical artefact, physically impossible to realise. Moreover, contrary to the marginalist revolution, economic history (even at the time it was advanced) provides abundant evidence that economic dominance was possible 'by exploiting the unprecedented and massive *increasing* returns to scale of production and distribution.'[101] In the United States, for example, just one thousand firms produce two-thirds of the country's industrial production, the consequences of which, writes Galbraith, are that 'the prices negotiated with suppliers and trade unions have no theoretical relation to what occurs in the competitive market.' Neoclassical economics' response to this is only disingenuous: it concedes the point, but then relegates it to the status of an aberrant condition, conceding also, presumably, that no more than a maximum of one-third of economic activity is addressed by its core theory.[102]

Nor do markets appear to be efficient or sensitive to the lack, or presence, of government intervention: over the last 140 years unemployment in Britain has averaged 5 per cent; in peacetime Germany since 1920 it has averaged 4 per cent; and in peacetime USA since 1900 it has averaged above 6 per cent.[103] Even in the economy of pre-World War I Britain, which existed under conditions closer to the free-market ideal than any Western European country since 1945 – minimal workers' rights, extensive use of casual labour, and the virtual non-existence of maternity leave and redundancy payments – unemployment averaged 5 per cent and rose frequently to 8, or even 10 per cent.[104] Significantly, nothing seems to have changed nearly a century later: in the early 1990s, radically deregulated Britain 'enjoyed' virtually the same high levels of unemployment as regulation-bound France and Italy.[105]

Similarly, the price mechanism has a most imperfect history, and prospect, of efficacy. In a major work on exhaustible resources, which by definition ought to exemplify an equilibrium formed from rising prices, dwindling supply, exploration, and the advent of replacements or substitutes, Partha Dasgupta and Geoffrey Heal demonstrated that, because of the 'impossibility of fully informative price systems,' it was equally impossible to prove the existence of the information necessary to prevent a resource from becoming exhausted, and to accept that the pricing mechanism was likely to provide correct incentives for exploration activity.[106] Important as these general findings of likely market failure are, the conditions under which Dasgupta and Heal established them were more important because they drew attention to two interdependent evasions of the competitive equilibrium theory: radical uncertainty, and the future (real time), the conditions under which everyday human decision-making takes place.

Even before considering the implications of a static, timeless environment, it is salutary to turn for just a moment to the general consciousness of the individual who is making these decisions. Consider, specifically, this description by John McCrone of the brain, an organ which takes all of half a second to produce a fully realised state of awareness:

> It follows an arc of activity that begins with the establishing of plans and expectations, then passes through a preconscious stage before eventually flowering as an organised, tightly focused state of response. In other words, *each moment of consciousness has a hidden structure....*

> [It] is turning out to be the most complex system that science is ever likely to encounter. It has not just complexity, but complexity of an almost alien form. It has rococo dimensions of structure and process *unimagined even in other complex systems like economies, ecosystems, and living cells.*[107]

McCrone's account, furthermore (relying on the work of David Chalmers), is at pains to point out the ways in which human consciousness is not merely a form of robotic recognition – which is to say, that, unlike the latter, human consciousness understands the colour red (for example) as possessing 'an inescapable and apparently irreducible mental quality ... [which] no amount of careful description could convey' to a person possessing only a black-and-white sense of vision.[108] For this reason, and also because 'there are an infinity of types of conscious moments that a brain can have,' he advises that: 'consciousness as it is experienced from the inside looks likely to lie forever beyond the grasp of scientific theory.'[109] At the mundane level, economic theory, if it were sufficiently self-aware and self-critical, would have to concede that the task of explaining the transformation of a physical state into a mental state is beyond the capacities of the borrowed toolbox which is nineteenth-century engineering mathematics.

It chooses, however, to increase the distance between its own disciplinary requirements and a fuller understanding of the limits which science imposes by locating its canonical actor in a static, or timeless environment which recognises neither past nor future. The advantage to this fictional place is that there can be no uncertainty if all relevant information is known; on the other hand, if the future exists, then, by definition, both time and uncertainty exist, and knowledge is imperfect (to say the least). And even then the advantage accruing to predictive certainty is slight and questionable. Indeed, it is held by Dasgupta and Heal to be possible only under 'extremely restrictive' conditions. Furthermore, as David Newbery and Joseph Stiglitz have proved, in the competitive equilibrium which exists in the more frequently experienced world of prevailing uncertainty, the Pareto optimum curve is reduced to the status of an exception rather than the rule.[110]

But this is, perhaps, to honour the model overmuch, because if we take seriously its timeless character competitive equilibrium theory becomes another nonsense, as explained by Gerald O'Driscoll and Mario Rizzo (with a little assistance from William James and Alfred North Whitehead):

> The denial of time consciousness is inherently self-contradictory from the perspective of the agent. This is because the instantaneousness (or mathematical) present is 'specious.' 'Where is it, this present? It has melted in our grasp, fled ere we could touch it, gone in the instant of becoming' [James]. We simply cannot perceive a present apart from memory and anticipation. The perceptible present, on the other hand, 'is the vivid fringe of memory tinged with anticipation.' Thus, '[t]here is no sharp distinction either between memory and the present immediacy or between the present immediacy and anticipation' [Whitehead]. Time consciousness or real duration must be a flow because, without the *continuity* associated with the span of memory to anticipation, there is no temporal perception, no action, and hence no subject-matter for economics.[111]

Proceeding one step further, the non-existence of real time posits an instant in which cause and effect are simultaneous rather than sequential. Taken further still, there is no possibility of action because action is predicated on causal efficacy. The conclusion is bizarre – the static model of competitive general equilibrium contains two concepts 'implicitly at war with each other: the specious present and action.'[112]

The persistence of the theory of competitive general equilibrium at the core of modern Economics, despite the corrosive impact of empirical evidence upon six of its core theorems, requires, therefore, an heroic credulity in those who would be informed by it. In others of a more sceptical nature, as Ormerod accurately observes, it makes its adherents close relations to one of Lewis Carroll's characters in *Alice in Wonderland*, the Red Queen, who admits to often believing six impossible things before breakfast.[113] Wry reflections aside, its official, mainstream standing appears to fall less under the rubric of science than it does under *scientism* – an attempted use of Cartesian/Newtonian scientific method as an end in itself.

To credulity we might as well add obstinacy because it is not as though the leading articulators of the discourse were unaware of its inadequacies. In the United States, John Bates Clark, that country's metaphorical father of neoclassical economics, turned to equilibrium theory and the celebration of capitalism from socialism as much because of the escape it provided from both the need for worker revolution (in his view) and the conservative reaction to leftist social thought, as he did because of its intellectual rigour. To this end his university appointments and standing were secure in comparison to others, such as Richard T. Ely and Henry Carter Adams, whose oppositional Christianity and more extended advocacy of socialism he actively discouraged and cautioned them against on pain of the harassment they duly received in their university posts until such time as they capitulated to the paths sanctioned by American Exceptionalism.[114] But the condition of succour was intellectual disfigurement: as he freely admitted, in order to maintain the concordance between American Exceptionalism and an American political economy undergoing destabilising change, he put *'actual changes out of sight, intentionally and heroically.'*[115] Then, some 60 years ago the British economic theorist, John Maynard Keynes, expressed the basis of his aversion to it if it included what Clark was so adamant to excise: 'its teaching is misleading and disastrous if we attempt to apply it to the facts of experience.'[116] Thus, Ormerod concludes, long before the appearance of Dasgupta and Heal's work – indeed from the previous 100 years of economic history – 'the weight of evidence [was] against the validity of the model of competitive general equilibrium as a plausible representation of reality.'[117]

At which point it is surely no exaggeration to note that, even in the tolerant, liberal societies of the West, persistent recourse to ideas which are held to be descriptive of its past and prescriptive for the future of the developed world, yet inadequate to its reality by commonly agreed epistemological criteria, would attract the attention of some of the medical specialisations which cluster around the specialisation of psychiatry. This, needless to say, has not been the case, for reasons which are beyond the scope of this project. But Galbraith's suggestion might suffice in passing. In his survey of the history of economic thought and practice, he appears to establish the principle that the default to engage in serious economic discussion in the face of at least an intellectual need to do so springs from the fact that those whose material interests are being served – the rich, in other words – do not demand and promote such activity until they perceive a serious economic problem.[118] Serious intellectual problems about economic theory, presumably, are at an even greater remove, encompassed, if at all, within Schrodinger's 'virulently esoteric chat.'

In the theory of competitive general equilibrium they exist nevertheless, in the form of debilitating challenges and critiques mounted since no later than 1933 when John von Neumann asked: 'what mathematical assumptions are necessary in order to prove that a set of prices ensuring that supply equals demand in every market exists at all?'[119] Then, following his mathematical proof that 'assumptions could indeed be made which would guarantee the existence of a set of prices for any set of equations describing the behaviour of a competitive economy,' subsequent work in the early 1950s by Kenneth Arrow explored the implications of his findings. Briefly, these revealed, through mathematical logic, the 'stringency of conditions' which are required if the guarantee of equilibrium is to exist.[120]

For 'stringency of conditions' in this context, read, *inter alia*, 'a proliferation of markets which concern *future* events.' Notwithstanding the empirical inadequacy-to-reality of all of the assumptions of the theory of competitive equilibrium, according to the assumptions determined in the theoretical-mathematical research, it is additionally necessary to assume that there is 'a very large number of futures markets, *transparently more than exists in reality.*' As well, according to Arrow, all participants in the market must possess 'a complete list of all future states of the environment which might obtain,' and 'everyone must hold identical and correct beliefs regarding the prices which would exist in each potential state of the world at every point in the future.'[121]

While these conditions might be regarded as unachievable, addiction to competitive equilibrium among mathematical economists was such that considerable effort then went into investigations as to whether the theory could be accommodated to the uncertainties of the future. The most significant response to the problematic was provided by Roy Radner, who, while relaxing Arrow's assumptions, reaffirmed the existence of competitive equilibrium, even if the participants in the market held different beliefs about the future. But the conditions under which it existed in Radner's world were that 'everyone in the economy needs to have an infinite amount of computational capacity – not just access to a Cray super-computer, but *literally an infinite amount of capacity.*'[122] Radner, therefore, concluded that the theory of competitive general equilibrium 'is strained to the limit by the problem of choice of information. It breaks down completely in the face of limits on the ability of agents to compute optimal strategies.'[123]

While this is certainly the reappearance of uncertainty, it is more than this upon a closer look. Since Radner's findings may be said to embody two varieties of uncertainty – the future environment and the behaviour of others – then an individual's behaviour will be influenced by her/his uncertain expectations about the future of the economy as a whole. But though the whole economy comprises the aggregate behaviour of the individuals who make it up, those individuals are learning how to act and react at the micro (individual) level by observing and understanding their behaviour at the macro (aggregate) level. In such a cognitive and purposeful relationship, the postulates of Rational Economic Man are, once again, demonstrably inadequate because the reciprocal processes it involves lead to behaviour which cannot be reduced to multiples of simple individual behaviour.[124] Or to express it in the words of James Coleman's interdisciplinary (Economics/sociology) *Foundations of Social Theory*, social and group norms are so pervasive that the entirely independent behaviour of the individual, Rational Economic Man is a 'broadly perpetrated fiction.'[125]

Arrow and Radner's work should also be understood as something other than virtual epitaphs for their subject. In spirit they are also revealing illustrations of the attempts which have been made to refine, and thus salvage, the theory of competitive general equilibrium from the predations of theory and practice, and to retain its centrality in policy advice. Ironically, however, the more that refinements are introduced, the greater is the awareness of, and attention attracted to, its inadequacy in both realms. To this end Joaquim Silvestre's work has shown that even 'negligible violations' of some of its assumptions can have results which are 'far removed' from the equilibrium which is predicted.[126] Effectively, this 1993 finding only confirms the earlier research undertaken 40 years ago by Richard Lipsey and Kelvin Lancaster on the conclusion drawn from the theory, and held as holy writ in neoclassical policy communities – namely, that all moves towards a deregulated economy are, *ipso facto*, beneficial to the economic competitiveness of the economy in question when, in fact, there is no basis for such a general presumption to be made.[127] And several scholars, among them Richard Day, have reached constructed 'plausible examples' which demonstrate the impossibility of discovering prices which will clear the markets.[128] Finally, the whole notion of a general equilibrium is held hostage to the known existence of multiple solutions, or 'multiple equilibria' to the price problematic, a conclusion that corrodes the very notion of a stable economic system under market competition.[129]

As the provenance of the overwhelming majority of these challenges comes from within the Economics discourse itself, they must be presumed to be relatively common knowledge among informed economists. But this is not to imply that the disqualification from policy advice the profession should incur is acknowledged. As with most discourses there is a defensive privilege – an evasion – which allows it to recover authority otherwise ceded to rigour. In the case of Economics it travels under two banners. The first is a concession that, of course, failures have occurred, but they have to be seen as the result of design flaws in the relevant policies, themselves a consequence of adulterating a science with vested – social, political, cultural, and moral – interests. The second is equally insidious, consisting of the phrase 'as if' which licenses the profession to proclaim that it is essentially irrelevant that its theories have been devastated one way or the other because the economy actually works *as if* they were all intact.

In both cases the demand is for a suspension of the critical faculties that minimally insist on internal consistency within theories, and practices which claim to improve the lot of the great majority of people. That is to say, neoclassical dogma has to be accepted as though the challenges to it were irrelevant, insubstantial, or non-existent. Indeed, it is through this demand that we might begin to understand why Galbraith so frequently characterises this commitment to abstract theory as 'theological' and above any need for empirical support according to those who follow it.[130] Thus, in terms of the first defence, we are asked to believe that design perfection according to pure theory will realise the ideal economy even if the partial but substantial measures already taken towards that end are counter-suggestive. And, regarding the second, another 'as if' is imputed – this time to critics who, on the same counter-suggestive foundations are asked to accept the ultimate triumph of neoclassicism 'as if' this was an intellectually and morally responsible decision to take in the circumstances.

In the final analysis this is no more than the worship of (what is seen as) a crowning theoretical construct whose splendour is thought to warrant the tolerance of well-intentioned transgressions that are committed, and the indulgences that are permitted, in its name. But given the nature, extent, and magnitude of the challenges outlined, this is really a demand for cognitive dissonance, complicity in corruption, and organised amnesia on a scale notorious in the pre-Reformation Church and denounced at the Council of Trent. Equally, in its willingness to propose self-serving rationalisations as being in accord with theory, and to contemplate no more than refinements to theory where its abolition is justified, speaks more of hubris than it does of a proclaimed modern science.

THE CONCEPT OF RATIONAL EXPECTATIONS AND ECONOMIC FORECASTING

This construct, sometimes described as a nuance, is to macro-economics what Rational Economic Man is to micro-economics – a solvent for the theoretically inconvenient persistence of men and women to behave in ways unacceptable to the synoptic abstractions of neoclassical economics. In turn, the concern with macro-economics is driven by its claim to understand 'the world' where 'the world' is defined by the macro-economic activity and trends of the (mainly) industrialised countries: understanding the world, of course, being the *sine qua non*, for policy formulation and implementation, and the production of forecasts. And it is correct, furthermore, to infer from the relative recency (less than 20 years) of the concept of rational expectations that its introduction was the result of a profound dissatisfaction with the accuracy of previous models. Indeed, this was the case: different models provided contradictory answers to the same question, they were untrustworthy on their own, and poor indicators of future states of the economy.[131] Thus, more or less sequentially since 1960, the advent of the multinational corporation, the rise of Japan as a major economic power, the emergence of inflation as a chronic problem in all industrial nations, the decline of productivity suffered by the Western powers in the 1970s, the decline of US global economic leadership, the Japanese recession of the early 1990s, the German recession of the same period, the strength of the American recovery in 1992, and the decline of the same in 1993 were all missed.[132]

By way of refinement, therefore, rational expectation was introduced to the end of establishing macro-economics as a theoretical construct comparable with micro-economic theory, in which attempt, given the weaknesses of the latter, there was no little irony. Nevertheless, what emerged was the belief that:

> 'rational' economic agents – people and companies – will not just learn from their mistakes in forming expectations, but that the learning process will enable them to identify the true model determining the behaviour of the economy. They will then use this model in order to form expectations. It is as if (that favourite phrase of economists) everyone not only has his or her own personal macro-model, *but everyone has the same model and, to stretch credibility even further, a model which happens to be a true and correct representation of how the economy behaves....* By definition, economic agents are 'rational,' so they should use this rational method of forming expectations.[133]

This style of elaboration is familiar. Like the concept of the market before it, rational expectation possesses an 'unavoidably tautological property' because what is being proposed is that 'the market's movements could not have occurred had marketers' expectations-guided actions not been what they were.'[134]

In essence this is the modernist dream of the fresh start – Rene Descartes' shared basic concepts/'clear and distinct ideas,' or John Locke's shared evidence/'ideas of sense' which was held to be 'equally available to reflective thinkers in all epochs and cultures.'[135] It rests on assumptions that such ideas are found in humanity universally, and that they are learned through repetition, both regardless of cultural diversity.[136] It rests, therefore, on concepts which, ethnographically, have been overturned by research into that which macro-economic theory denies is relevant – enculturation and diversity. At two of the most basic levels of understanding the world, spatial relations and colour, this has been documented: not only do some cultures perceive spatial relations differently from the Euclidean ideal in modern industrial cultures, but also, through differing ideas of reflection, talk or think about colours, or colours of objects, in ways which reflect cultural specificity.[137]

Rational expectation as a universally realisable concept is thus bankrupt in its genesis, notwithstanding the difficulties it gives rise to in the realm of economic analysis, and the conservative political ideology in which it is deployed. And it is salient that in Galbraith's and Ormerod's excoriating treatments of the economic forecasting industry, in whose service rational expectation is a front-line unit, all three explanations of failure may legitimately be considered direct consequences of its universalist assumptions. Thus, Galbraith cites the way in which human judgment is over-determined by statistical data and precedent in a world in which the conditions of the precedent no longer exist, and the unpredictable future course of change initiated by current decisions, while Ormerod, a former forecaster himself, points to the endemic ignorance of how the economy works.[138]

Ormerod's observation deserves further investigation because it underscores an extraordinary contradiction inherent in the concept. To repeat, the theory postulates that, with sufficient exposure to, and consequent reflection on the experience of, the economy, actors in it will converge on an identical and correct view of its operations. In certain theologies this is famously known as 'an act of faith,' and it is an act of extraordinary generosity in the deposit of the faith that it required if it is understood that, even among people in the developed economies there are indications that a minimum of 57 per cent of the population are incapable of correctly processing simple arithmetic information.[139] Absent this competence and the requirement of economic theory that the future consequences of a current decision be understood in terms of its economic efficiency is open to a profound interrogation.

The question, specifically, is why this can even be suggested, let alone tolerated, in even the greatest economy in history, that of the United States. Why, in an age in which one-third of its adult population is functionally illiterate, and another one-third is functionally a-literate, should this be allowed as a credible assumption (given the reasonable proposition that macro-economic ideas are complex ideas, and the transmission and understanding of complex ideas requires reading)?[140] Why, when the well-documented US experience of public knowledge of significant everyday events is so abysmal and distorted should a theoretical concept emerge and be rapidly incorporated into the relevant discipline's mainstream which requires knowledge that can only be described as esoteric?[141] Why, given the prevalence of quite bizarre beliefs about the world – including the belief expressed by one-third of American citizens surveyed that the US government is in regular contact with aliens – should it be assumed that knowledge of the economy comprises a unique category of competence?[142] And why, in a world in which knowledge of the economy eludes economic forecasters, causing their models and forecasts to seriously disagree (when they do not contradict each other), should that very knowledge be in the possession of untrained laity?[143]

And it does elude the professionals, as was indicated earlier. Just how much might be gauged from the survey of economic expectations in the United States and Britain, conducted by Lovell, and Holden and Peel, respectively, which assess their compliance with the tenets of rationality. After what Ormerod terms 'careful examination of the evidence,' they conclude that 'the hypothesis of rational expectations did not appear to be consistent with the data.'[144] Confirming these findings was a subsequent study by Baghestani and Kianian which examined 75 American macro-economic forecasts over the period 1981 to 1991. Their conclusion was that no fewer than 73 of them were inconsistent with the concept of rational expectations.[145] Of significance in terms of the US findings is that forecasters in that country are funded on a predominantly commercial basis, meaning that they have every incentive to perfect, and provide, reliable assessments of the future, yet it is the case that, by this criterion, their reports are indistinguishable from those of a European provenance, which tend to be funded by government.[146] Significantly, the government-funded Federal Reserve has produced the best (of admittedly poor) offerings which attempt to predict the short-term movements in the overall output of the US economy.[147]

More recently, the IMF, the OECD *Economic Outlook*, the Treasury in the United Kingdom, and the government agencies of the other G7 countries more generally have all provided examples in the macro-economic field of both of what Ormerod terms 'spectacular failures' or 'systematic failure.' The former includes the 1997 collapse of the Asian economies in 1997 while the latter takes in estimates of GDP growth which contain errors so large that, arguably, it would have been better to predict a following year's growth and inflation simply as being the same as the current year.[148] The unacknowledged problem in this context is one of ambition: policy-makers require short-term forecasts in order to possess the data which will allow them to control and 'fine tune' the economy; the economy, for its part, is just not amenable to being known in this way by the 'esoteric mathematical techniques' of current science. While they may be elegant and intricate, it is less the linear phenomenon that it is held to be, and significantly more a non-linear system in which small, random, and even imperceptible influences within its initial conditions inevitably defeat attempts to produce consistently reliable forecasts based on highly imperfect abstraction.[149]

Such a demonstrated lack of progress in the ability to understand or predict the economy ought not to obscure the preposterous logic which is inherent in taking economic forecasts seriously. Imagine, if you will, that the gift of prophecy in economic matters exists: why, then, should it be available to the public when it represents a patent for an invention from which untold wealth will follow? In other words, since economic forecasts are available to the public, such access to them is the foremost evidence that they enjoy an inverse relationship with reliability. In Galbraith's phrasing of their status, the choice is between an 'act of unimaginable generosity,' or 'questionable information … confidently offered.'[150]

For all of that, forecasts and forecasters are not without their uses. Political-economic power is diffused in them, uncertainty about the future is reduced to plausible parameters by them, and executive anxiety is assuaged with them; and, because of all these palliatives, economic professionalisation is maintained through them. Through the obeisance to rational expectation, and the articulation of the so-called policy-ineffectiveness proposition, they also reassure conservative forces in government and society of the scientific probity of abstaining from ameliorative efforts to improve the lot of those disadvantaged by the practice of neoclassical economics. Consider Daniel Fusfield's account of this service:

> As people learn that stimulation of aggregate demand demands leads to inflation [through other neoclassical laws dealt with below], they adapt more quickly. Instead of a reduction in unemployment followed by an increase in unemployment back to the 'natural' level, the time sequence is compressed until, after several experiences, the intermediate steps are eliminated. The economy responds immediately to increased aggregate demand with inflation, while unemployment is unaffected.[151]

Thus, in almost the same way that Rational Economic Man was conservatively defined in conservative interests, the concept of rational expectation follows suit; indeed, it is exemplary as an attempt to install a self-fulfilling and self-generating, virtually Pavlovian reduction into economic theory in the guise of scientific understanding. What is being insinuated in the process is the imperviousness of the independent economy to human will, volition, and influence, especially as exercised by government and, correspondingly, the reduction of such categories to epiphenomena.[152] No less does it deserve Lawson's wary approach:

> In the open social system in which we live, characterised as it is by fundamental uncertainty, the hypothesis of rational expectations is hardly realistic. Although human beings knowledgeably and skilfully negotiate their every day tasks, the knowledge actually possessed is obviously a far cry from the requirements of this particular hypothesis about expectations. Indeed, the suspicion must always have been that the resort to such a hypothesis is little more than an act of desperation.[153]

It would be unfair, however, to put the failure of macro-economic prediction entirely down to the inadequacies of rational expectation, especially when it is better understood as a collaborative endeavour with that branch of macro-economics known as econometrics. At the mundane level, econometrics sets itself the task of analysing macro-economic data using statistical techniques; on more exalted planes, however, the purpose of its product is to act as a source of advice to government and organisations as regards the economic consequences of changes in policy and to predict future states of the economy. It even defines itself as being in the position of an arbiter of the various contending schools of macro-economic theory.[154] Intellectually, if the (American) Econometric Society's statement of purpose is a fair example, it is just a little pretentious (to which might be added masculine, and lacking in point of scientific fact):

> The Society shall operate as a completely disinterested, scientific organisation, without political, social, financial or nationalistic bias. Its main object shall be to promote studies that aim at the unification of the theoretical-quantitative and the empirical-quantitative approach to economic problems and that are penetrated by constructive and rigorous thinking similar to that which has come to dominate in the natural sciences.[155]

The difficulty is that, for econometrics, the omens are poor for it being able to discharge its functions. As was noted earlier in this chapter, it shares with the discipline of Economics in general certain debilitating inconsistencies between theory and practice. More devastating still is one of the central findings of the extremely powerful critique of econometrics made by Lucas, namely, that what it presumes – the stability of econometric relations under alternative policy rules – is refuted by '*everything we know about dynamic economic theory* [and] *indicates that this presumption is unjustified.*'[156] Worse, if that is possible, is the fact that the theory–practice intersection in econometrics has most of the distinguishing features of a major intellectual crash site. A compelling schedule in explanation of this has been compiled by David Hendry using, in the main, the criticisms of John Maynard Keynes, but also himself:

> using an incomplete set of determining factors (omitted variables bias); building models with unobservable data variables (such as expectations), estimated from badly measured data based on index numbers ...; being unable to separate the distinct effects of multi-collinear variables; assuming linear functional forms not knowing the appropriate dimensions of the regressors; mis-specifying the dynamic reactions and lag lengths; incorrectly pre-filtering the data; invalidly inferring 'causes' from correlations; predicting inaccurately (non-constant parameters); confusing statistical with economic 'significance' of results and failing to relate econometric theory to econometrics. (I cannot resist quoting Keynes again – 'If the method cannot prove or disprove a qualitative theory and if it cannot give a quantitative guide to the future, is it worthwhile? For, assuredly, it is not a very lucid way of describing the past.') To Keynes' list of problems [i.e. the above], I would add stochastic mis-specification, incorrect exogeneity assumptions ..., inadequate sample sizes, aggregation, lack of structural identification and an inability to refer back uniquely from observed empirical results to any given initial theory.[157]

Adding to even this catalogue Oskar Morgenstern has shown that econometrics' problems precede its theoretical shortcomings if the matter of collecting and interpreting economic statistics is taken into account.[158]

Not surprisingly, the ambience of critical treatments of econometrics is funereal where it is not only contemptuous. Lawson's scholarly conclusion exhibits the former:

> The most telling point against [the overwhelming bulk of the] econometrics project is the *ex posteriori* result that significant invariant event regularities, whether of a probabilistic kind or otherwise, have yet to be uncovered in economics, despite the resources continually allocated to their pursuit.[159]

The recidivist pretence, nevertheless, deserves the latter, provided succinctly by John Ralston Saul: 'Econometrics, the statistical, narrow, unthinking, lower form of economics,' he writes, 'is passive tinkering, less reliable and less useful than car mechanics.'[160]

THE NON-ACCELERATING INFLATION RATE OF UNEMPLOYMENT (NAIRU)

As implied immediately above, the critique of macro-economic theory necessitates an awareness of the interrelationships between various sub-theoretical areas. One of the more significant of these, raised by rational expectation, is that of the Non-Accelerating Inflation Rate of Unemployment (NAIRU), which, far too often, and misleadingly at that, is referred to as the 'natural' rate of unemployment for a particular economic state as though anyone but an economist captured by a discourse from which ethics had been excluded could find it 'natural' that some people should be deprived by an abstraction from one of the prime means of a purposeful life. Nevertheless, if the trip to the other side of the looking glass is ventured, the NAIRU is found to be based on the work of William Phillips who, using British data for the period 1861 to 1913, discovered a statistical relationship of a negative character between rises in money wages and unemployment. The Phillips Curve, as its graphic representation was known, and subsequent research by Paul Samuelson and Robert Solow which refined the original by relating high unemployment to low inflation, ultimately appeared to suggest a known relationship between inflation and unemployment.[161] Based on rational expectation, the implication of this work was that, 'for any particular economy at any point in time, there is a unique level of unemployment at which inflation will neither accelerate, nor decelerate,' and furthermore, 'deviations from this unique rate of unemployment would be purely temporary.'[162] Equilibrium was, once again, reaffirmed, in the form of the more technically accurate NAIRU, which, given the metaphysical proclivities of the discourse, was understandably translated into a naturalised referent.

It was embarrassing, therefore, that Robert Solow felt moved to observe that the naturalness of the rate of unemployment corresponded closely to the political requirement to account for increased levels of unemployment in the USA and Western Europe; the natural, it seems, was unique, but only in a temporal and local context.[163] But this was not so much the limit, as the start of many such postmodern interventions. The data which was thought to support the NAIRU simply did not exist if the base for it was a wide range of economic history across many Western countries over a 40-year period. Disturbingly, for adherents of the 'natural rate' hypothesis, the US evidence pointed to a plurality – at least three, and as many as five – 'unique' rates of unemployment. Further, in the terms of Ormerod's summary of the evidence, in most Western economies, 'the general relationship is not in fact between the rate of inflation and the level of unemployment, but between the *rate of change* of inflation and the *rate of change* of unemployment.[164]

Of equal significance is the finding that specific historical events – for example, the oil-price shock of 1973 to 1974 – and specific reactions to them, determine the nature and levels of subsequent unemployment.[165] Taken individually or together, these findings are less than reassuring for one of the central theorems of macro-economics. That which was scripted out, history, intrudes as an independent variable; forecasts, as a consequence, proliferate on the basis of the same statistical data for countries with different historical experiences; and the plural term, 'equilibria,' needs to be deployed to describe what is meant to be a single and unique condition. Moreover, though these findings are revealing in themselves for the concept at hand, their true ramifications are more apparent within neoclassical economics' understanding of the general relationship between economic growth and unemployment.

ECONOMIC GROWTH AND UNEMPLOYMENT

To state that Western governments believe with theological commitment that there is a necessary, positive, and universal relationship between economic growth and employment is to be guilty of a truism. Nevertheless, it is their mantra and mandala, symmetrical psalm of praise and design symbolising the universe. For others, the *miscredenti*, such views are as ignorant as they are vagrant, which is to say, lacking in any visual means of support. In summary form, this opposition is derived from studies which attest to the relatively poor correlation, over the last two decades and internationally, between the rate of economic growth and either the growth in employment, or the level of unemployment.[166] These studies, additionally, have discerned a certain organic quality to the economy – 'the ability, when prodded or stimulated, not simply to wobble around a fixed position, but to jump to a different position altogether.'[167] Note, at this position, that output might be greater than previously, but the consequential benefits economic orthodoxy predicts for employment/unemployment will, in all likelihood, be absent, as will an inevitable return to the *equilibrium ante*.[168]

It was quantum behaviour of this nature that gave rise to the findings of equilibria (rather than an equilibrium) in the foregoing discussion. And, to partially repeat, the causes of this behaviour are twofold: first, historical, structural, and qualitative changes within economies, and their associated political-economic institutions, are economically relevant forces in their own right; and second, the behaviour in question is more appropriately defined, and understood, as essentially *non-linear*.[169] While the former reinforces the poverty of neoclassical positivism (even as it allows economic professionalisation through formal models and theories), the latter undermines the entire Cartesian/Newtonian project which the discourse has adopted, and hence requires a further word.

LINEARITY

As a modernist discourse neoclassical economics has always been, and remains, inescapably linear in that the core theory, competitive equilibrium, assumes the simple linear aggregation of individuals' behaviour, while the exclusions, history (especially in the form of constellating events) and society, are the types of entities which would guarantee non-linear intrusions and irreversible transformations. Real complexity is, therefore, sacrificed in the interests of a scientific aesthetic. All of this continues, moreover, as orthodoxy despite the overbearing evidence that 'market efficiency,' the predicted consequence of equilibrium theory, is invalid.

In financial markets, for example, one of the most important sources of industrial investment and widely regarded as a litmus test of efficiency (defined narrowly as the balancing of supply and demand on the basis of all known information) no rule has yet been discovered which will enable consistent profits to be made from trading in the shares of a particular company. To put this another way, at any given time, the price of shares in a particular company reflects nothing more than a simple supply–demand situation, and the belief that everything that should be known about the company by actual and potential shareholders is known (which is a far more restrictive definition than Rational Economic Man is entitled to if she/he is to act true to specie); from this it follows that only unpredictable news will change the share price, and since unpredictable news is effectively random news, forecasting is impossible. Sophisticated research over many years confirms this character in the financial markets.[170]

More recently, however, this finding has been modified, but certainly not challenged outright, by Fujitsu in Japan, and Fidelity in Boston, whose approaches suggest the utility of non-linear mathematical techniques for understanding the direct management of funds, or the advice they give to other fund managers. But, to underscore the point at issue, the simple linear techniques embodied in equilibrium theory are, according to this litmus area of economic activity, plainly wrong to the extent that they posit a market efficiency-cum-equilibrium which has not been discerned and refuses to come into being.[171] Moreover, if, as critical scholarship increasingly reveals, economic activity is to be constituted by what might be called non-linear operations, themselves functions of multiple inputs and complex feedback loops, then the postulates of neoclassical economics no longer apply.

ECONOMICS ... 'THAT RAVING SLUT WHO KEEPS THE TILL'

A more extensive categorisation of Economics' inadequacies than that already adduced could be elaborated at will if this treatment was to satisfy itself with nothing more than a gratuitous indictment of the tragic flaws in neoclassical economics. While that project is not without its merits in Western societies dominated by the neoclassical discourse to the near-exclusion of its critiques, it is the case that such an indictment could itself be gratuitously indicted, but only in parts. It might be proposed, for example, that the critique fails to take into account the extraordinary *mathematical* achievements found in the discourse, or that, for extended periods of recent history, the discourse provided a 'workable' description of economic reality. But this only forces a return to, and a reinforcement of, the entire schedule of criticisms of those core theorems which are included, and of which there are too numerous, philosophically and empirically, to legitimate a dismissal on any intellectual or political grounds.

It forces, as well, a return to the Alzheimerian condition of contemporary Economics – one in which the very roots of the discipline and the familial cautions that they acknowledged are wiped from daily memory in a way which discloses an entire mental set. Where, for instance, in the uncritical acceptance of mathematics, is there even a minimal understanding of the wisdom of neoclassical founding father, Alfred Marshall, who wrote:

> I had a feeling in the later years of my work on the subject that a good mathematical theorem dealing with economic hypotheses was very unlikely to be good economics: and I went more and more on the rules – (1) Use mathematics as a shorthand language rather than an engine of inquiry. (2) Keep to them until you have done. (3) Translate into English. (4) Then illustrate by examples that are important in real life. (5) Burn the mathematics. (6) If you can't succeed in 4, burn 3. The last I did often.[172]

Indeed, we look in vain for even a practical vestige in Economics of Marshall's only confident dogma – 'that every short statement on a broad issue is inherently false.'[173] And as for an understanding of Economics as a 'study of the economic aspects and conditions of man's political, social and private life; but more especially of his social life,'[174] the discipline is vigilantly ignorant.

Instead, critical analysis of Economics involves an almost inevitable, and certainly haunting, return to its modernist origins – those 'intellectually perfectionist, morally rigorous, and humanly unrelenting' ideals which were to provide the basis for a world of certainty and systemacity, cleaved anew from nature, and sundered from history. What this dream produced, of course, was what it most detested – an understanding of the human condition which required a deposit of faith in a professional magisterium of the type which Galileo eventually bowed to and Giordano Bruno was burned at the stake for refusing. Its instruments, too, reproached it because physicists themselves, in their attempts to explain the natural world, were increasingly rendering irrelevant the foundations of the physics which it turned to. Subsequently they have been joined in this turning away by biologists and chemists to the point where, intellectually, the full offence which the nakedness of Economics should give is saved by its residence in a near-deserted neighbourhood, as though it, and it alone, is unaware that the assumptions and foundations of the Newtonian world view have been overturned.

This is no minor derangement; this is *folie de grandeur;* a luciferan refusal to serve the scientific rationality which allowed the dream of the 'science' of Economics in the first place. It is the unwillingness to adopt a befitting humility in the face of repeated revelations that the world refuses reduction, and is multifarious besides. In misappropriating physics to itself, neoclassical economics made three inductive leaps – that the data it would abstract was accurate and complete in the sense that laboratory data may be so defined; that the data was additive, commutative,[175] and associative;[176] and that physics shared its myopia for linear relationships – which it did once, but was in the process of surrendering.[177] Thus, by excluding history, Economics refused to 'know itself,' ignoring in that denial that it was closer to palaeontology, astrology, and climatology to the extent that the data of greatest importance to its understanding of the world are incomplete, prone to error, and based on a single experience.[178] In Economics the insistence that it was a science because it was mathematical became a belief in the absurd for the same reason, and because it also refused to know mathematics and physics.

Ironically, physics had much to teach Economics, especially in the years after the first publication of Marshall's *Principles of Economics*. Among these lessons would have been: that, following Heisenberg, and of relevance to forecasting, we cannot know, as a matter of principle, the present in all of its details; that, by extension, small emergent phase, radically contingent events are of extraordinary importance over time (which definitely exists) and, accordingly, unpredictability is inherent; that, just as science is not to be confused with nature (but the way we describe nature); Economics is not human behaviour, but only a poor, synoptic abstraction of human behaviour; that these lessons, taken individually and collectively, indicate a non-linear, sometimes chaotic world which turns standard theories upside-down, and that, returning to Heisenberg, not learning them creates only an 'incomprehensible mumbo jumbo.' In other words, the difference between physics and Economics is that while the most critically aware of the physicists know how to use quantum mechanics, they invariably agree with such luminaries as Richard Feynman and Murray Gell-Mann who confess that neither they, nor anyone else, really understand it, or how it could be what it is, whereas, in Economics, the antecedent understandings are confident, but delusional, and the applications are devoid of the empirical success which quantum physics is capable of.

When Economics followed Cartesianism by rejecting the timely, the local, the concrete, the oral, and the 'reasonable uncertainties and hesitancies' of the sixteenth-century sceptics, it is no exaggeration to say that it inflicted upon itself a condition of aggravated autism. It became incapable of speaking to the dreams, fears, and visions of society because it could not hear them in the first place; at the same time it was totally absorbed in its own aestheticism, an organic proof of not only Heisenburg's compass which is a slave to the ship's mass, but J.H. Woodger's finding that the theoretical imagination is frequently the casualty of the obsession with formal logic.[179]

The consequence for Economics is, in a word, disarray, what Heilbroner and Milberg find it necessary to call 'the crisis of vision in modern economic thought.' In their work, modern Economics is characterised by an 'extraordinary indifference' to the problem of its disconnection between its theory and 'reality'; its analyses are, therefore, unguided by the psychologically, perhaps existentially necessary, presence of such entities as values, and political hopes and fears which are unavoidably present in other approaches to the study of society such as political science and sociology.[180] Thus, not only are economic forecasters failing to provide forecasts which are sufficiently accurate to be of use to those who need them, the work of economic theorists is riven with tensions, incongruities and even arbitrary explanations; worse, since the criticisms which both are attracting are being suppressed, there is no widespread acknowledgment of the discipline's incoherence.[181] Furthermore, to the extent that Economics remains committed to its Newtonian *form*, if not in a corresponding set of substantive empirical phenomena, and committed, as well, to the abstract concepts it has developed, this situation only 'constrains the pattern of acceptable disagreement in a way that silences serious challenges' of the type which would provide the necessary reform.[182]

Forgone, accordingly, is more than the restoration of an area of inquiry into human relations, because, in the inability, or refusal, to come to terms with its own pathologies, Economics ultimately declines self-knowledge. Significantly, it declines to know what it is *not*. Thus, being incapable of seeing itself, it is to be expected that it is incapable of seeing beyond itself. For Saul, this is exemplary 'unconscious' behaviour, but the extent to which Economics is truly, pathologically, unaware is no better illustrated than by Heilbroner and Milberg's unearthing of the lack of appreciation of its own embeddedness in a distinctive social order comprising exhibiting three mutually reinforcing characteristics – the drive to accumulate capital, the coordination of production and the regulation of distribution by the market, and the coexistence of public and private realms (in which the latter must obey the laws of the former) – which defines it: capitalism.[183] For Economics to be concerned with the 'real,' therefore, it must delimit itself from its singular obsession with 'representative agent rational choice for thinking about modern organised capitalism' and construct a 'conceptual vocabulary and analytical repertoire' appropriate to the historical contingency and complex social order under which the variants of capitalism develop and operate. At the very least this would render explicit what is now unmentioned in economic discourse – 'that economics cannot be learned or used without speaking of capitalism.'[184] It would, as well, re-historicise, re-socialise, and re-politicise Economics in a way which is as far beyond the extant discourse as it is beyond, its exemplar, pre-quantum physics.

In turn, the historicity of this imitation is a timely reminder of the crisis reactions which have marked the development of neoclassical economics itself, the most recent being its resurgence in times of right-wing ideological ascendancy as evidenced in the period of the Reagan and Bush administrations in the United States, and in the Thatcher and Major Conservative governments in the United Kingdom. They are, of course, finessed as something other than convenient hypotheses, and a great many intellectual achievements are held to be represented in their formulations and laws, just as a multitude of benefits are not infrequently recorded, and heralded, in their name. But all these claims are as irrelevant as those which justified the selling of indulgences in the pre-reformation church, or legitimated monarchical rule according to Divine Right because the elegance of their apologetics is, in the final analysis, insufficient to defend the indefensible. In 'The Circus Animals' Desertion' William Butler Yeats has, though preoccupied with something else, captured both the imperative of Economics, and the reasons for its demise as well as any might in a few lines:

> Those masterful images because complete
> Grew in pure mind, but out of what began?
> A mound of refuse or the sweepings of a street,
> Old kettles, old bottles, and a broken can,
> Old iron, old bones, old rags, that raving slut
> Who keeps the till. Now that my ladder's gone,
> I must lie down where all the ladders start,
> In the foul rag-and-bone shop of the heart.

The question, then, is 'why, in the university, does the modern discipline of Economics prosper when it relies on both an unrealisable methodology and an intellectual foundation that is held to be 'unconditional, independent of circumstances and decontextualisable' when philosophical and empirical demonstrations alike indicate it is no more than 'hypothetical and substantial?'[185] The answer, which, in terms of this inquiry, is more suggestive than definitive, imposes a return to the discourse leader, the United States, and the power over thought which its economic-theory-as-practice has achieved. Barry Alan Shain talks of this in terms of America's 'intellectually monolithic environment' with its 'multilayered insulation that guards its most cherished myths.'[186] In support of this view he quotes Joseph Schumpeter's observations of the American people during the 1930s, when, if ever, a fracturing of the American Exceptionalist consensus was as warranted as it was probable; but no: not only business people 'but a very large part of the workmen and farmers thought and felt in the terms of the bourgeois order ... [they] did not really have a clear conception of any alternative.'[187]

That lack of other possibilities, in the universities' case, is the result of an intentional assault on, but something less than an overwhelming defeat of, the institution. Recall, there is a consensus as to the role of the universities in society, and a common view held by both 'radical teachers and business technocrats' (to use Michael Ryan's description) that, in any formational contest, it is a site *sans pareil*. To Antonio Gramsci it was 'a pocket of the memory ... a total reservation for the ethics of the truth.'[188] And, more expansively, in the words of the Port Huron Statement:

> The university is located in a permanent position of social influence. Its educational function makes it indispensable and automatically makes it a crucial institution in the formation of social attitudes. In an unbelievingly complicated world, *it is the central institution for organising, evaluating, and transmitting knowledge.*[189]

For intellectuals within the academies of the industrialised West it provides something else as well – both the incomparable opportunity to oppose injustice and oppression by exposing them, and the temptation to serve the capitalist economy and the state (which find some of their many unions in the university). To serve the former is to anticipate a life of professional disregard and loneliness; the latter, one of affluence and prestige.[190] In this, the discrimination suffered by critics in the United States, who, historically, were denied funding, and were the subject of other intimidatory experiences of the Cold War, the punitive measures undertaken by the university-as-institution in relation to criticism defined as un-American, and the advantages available to those whose activities fell within the narrow tolerances of American Exceptionalism and anti-communism must be seen as inducements to conform of no small order.[191]

Here, the lengthy and prestigiously published work, *Anti-Americanism*, by Paul Hollander, a professor of sociology at the University of Massachusetts, Amherst, and a Fellow of the Russian Research Centre at Harvard University, provides one of the most extraordinary examples of the intellectual sanctions made possible by the mainstream consensus. To be anti-American (for an *American*) is to be driven by 'unrealistic expectations'; to engage, therefore, in 'less than fully rational' critiques of the United

States, and to possess the necessary 'excess liberty' in which to write them; in the final analysis, it is to be anti-capitalist, and thus, anti-modern.[192] Given this context, it is no doubt possible to prefer the less fraught option because the alternative, for an academic, is to be defined anathematically. A further rationalisation is spawned by the effect that, on occasions, this accommodation might allow for the humanising of 'the exercise of power by the "significant classes." It is not surprising, therefore, that Chomsky found the reason academics devote themselves to such projects as preserving imperialist ideology 'is that they do so out of their free choice.'[193]

By this account the university embraces one of the more dangerous disciplines for organising the lives of this planet's six billion (and rapidly growing) souls. Historically located, Economics' *state*, as distinct from its status, is that of a medieval orthodoxy in the trappings of sixteenth-century formalism. Conversely, its *status* rests not on the efficiency of its explanations and predictions, but on its authority, which is contiguous with that of the modern, Western university. In this, the university is only reaffirming the distinction between the needs of a theory according to the prevailing modernist definition, and the needs of society – in effect, the needs of the theory's victims – and its institutionalised preference for the former.[194]

Part IV

6 Equivalence and convergence

Neo-liberal globalisation as war and militarisation

REFLECTIONS ON THE 1990s

It was, perhaps, analytically unfortunate that the Cold War came to an end in such close propinquity to the year AD 2000. By this is meant that the understanding of the events, ideas, and tendencies which comprised the termination of the greatest economic, ideological, and strategic stand-off in history were excessively influenced by not only the numerical sense of transition from one millennium to another, but also the heightened anxiety such processes are said to entail. Moreover, they worked to this end upon extant conditions unrelated to the millennium – the hubris which a foolishly declared triumph in the Cold War was thought to justify, and paradoxically, the anxieties which attended any honest self-evaluations of the material and psychic state of the victors. The result was not so much a loss of 'reality' from our understanding of the world (though that has to be acknowledged as a casualty), but an intensification of the palpable confusion which the last decade or so of the twentieth century in global politics produced. Consider just some of the indications of this period:

- The President of the United States celebrated victory in the Cold War in general, and the massacre which became *Desert Storm* in particular, with the claim that it was all God's will; in the same period a former Secretary of Defence and a former Assistant Secretary of State for Economic and Business Affairs both testified to the country's profound decline.

- Indicative of certain types of decline, senior US officials of the Strategic Defense Initiative Organisation propose converting the 10-warhead Russian SS-18 intercontinental ballistic missile into a launch vehicle for the US *Brilliant Pebbles* sensory interceptors. The Russians, for their part, from a base on the outskirts of Moscow, began selling mock dog-fights in MiG-29s to wealthy American tourists (who act as co-pilots) for US$12,000.

- The so-called 'Leninist Extinction' gives rise to popular and, for some, persuasive (albeit contested) accounts of: 'the coming anarchy'; the undesirability of exporting liberal democracy to the non-Western world; the reduction of the people of Africa and Latin America to a Nietzchean category – a 'misfortune to higher men' – and, the need, above all, to manage whatever conflicts they have among themselves and, especially, with the 20 per cent of the world's population that is consuming 80 per cent of its resources.

- Where war was the subject of analysis there was a widespread consensus that, wherever it might be fought, it would strongly resemble warfare of the types which pre-dated the modern state system, although it will also tend to be concentrated in the cities rather than the countryside, and in the Third World rather than the First.

- War, in metaphorical terms, suffused the discourse on the global economy, where competition between the United States and Japan was increasingly portrayed in terms of conflict and the stakes nothing less than national survival; the market/theatre of operations was, therefore, the source of discipline to which all efforts were bent – even in some cases to the point of advocating the 'Japanisation' of the US.

- Contradicting Japanese experience, however, there was a widespread consensus that governments (and the societies which generate them) and markets are mutually exclusive, despite the fact that, historically, the need to redress the excesses of the latter comprised one of the most compelling reasons for the former.

- At the heart of Western questions to which the 'market' and/or 'Japanisation' was the answer lay the unambiguous evidence of Western decline – understood as a fall from hegemony – and the anxiety which attended it, in conjunction with an intransitive suspicion that traditional claims upon Western understanding derived from the Enlightenment are frail.

- Governmental control, let alone prediction, was chimerical, and a recourse to the bizarre abounded as the Central Intelligence Agency admitted to employing psychics; in certain documented instances, it was evident that the Reagan White House ran on astrological time.

- Governments nevertheless continued to maintain that they ruled sovereign, territorial entities – indeed, this very obsession lay at the heart of British recalcitrance on the subject of the European Monetary System – yet daily practice confounded such claims: US$2 trillion were transferred electronically every 24 hours, and the cross-rate of currencies had more to do with assessments made by rating agencies and finance houses than with the determinations of central banks.

- Corporations paralleled, and in many cases, surpassed nation states as economic powers in their own right: of the largest 100 economies, 47 were corporations, each with more wealth than the 130 nation states which comprise the lower end of the wealth table; in 1995, for example, 161 countries had GNPs less than the worldwide turnover of Wal Mart, a corporation whose total number of American employees is equal to the population of North Dakota. Harvard University's annual budget was equal to the GDP of Rwanda.

- Diseases (such as *mycobacterium tuberculosis*) once thought to be either localised or in retreat were found to be not only multidrug-resistant but also globalised by that epitome of globalisation, the long aeroplane flight, while, conversely, commuters in Western cities were estimated to spend three months of their working lives stationary, at traffic lights, and were fortunate if, in the 1990s, they travelled any faster than their predecessors did in 1900.

• At the level of the prosaic in Western cities, it was cheaper to buy 30 sets of underwear than to pay to have them laundered; since 1970, an additional 293 million tons of clothing and footwear per year were disposed of at landfills or incinerators in the US. Bottled water cost more than gasoline, and Americans spent US$2000 per second on legal drugs.

• In Haiti, the worker who sewed a pair of Pocahantas pyjamas received 0.06 per cent of the US retail price; for similar work in Burma, workers were paid 6 cents per hour; and in Indonesia, it would take a Nike worker 44,492 years to earn Michael Jordan's annual endorsement fee.

• Elsewhere in the predominantly non-Western world, where the population was expected to double (to between 5 and 6 billion) by 2030, 500 million were homeless, or living in housing described as life-threatening – conditions which produced a current annual death-toll of 10 million.

Many would no doubt say of these manifestations that they indicated, at the very least, 'a world turned upside-down,' and quite probably, chaos. At the precise moment that the greatest adversarial relationship in history dissolved and at the time of spectacular productive capabilities in goods and services, global politics remained enthralled to war to the point where daily life was subjugated to its theories and practices, even in Economics, to such an extent that no less than half of humanity was condemned to misery on the basis that it will otherwise impinge on the enjoyment of the most fortunate fifth. Even for this select quintile, however, life was discontinuous with the easily remembered past since, increasingly, the ameliorative role once undertaken by government was rapidly being abdicated, as was, more generally, the decisive political role that once defined government. So profound was the erosion of certainty that peoples who once considered themselves quintessentially modern, and thus above superstition, sought shelter in metaphysics.

This was the transitional world, or rather significant abstractions from it, that preoccupied visionaries, promoters, and believers alike – such as Francis Fukuyama's and his 'end of history' thesis,[1] and Samuel P. Huntington's vision of the 'clash of civilisations.'[2] Best read as paeans, these provide, each in a distinct way, acclamation, commendation, and reassurance for anxious policy-makers because they argued that no profound change was necessary to the dominant modes of Western thinking and acting. For Huntington, the prescription was, effectively, a *re*scription: in a world of conflicting cultural interests-as-national interests, he advised that Western security will be determined by the traditional European resort, balance-of-power-politics, contemporarily in the guise of balance-of-civilisations. For his part, Fukuyama assumed the role and incumbent duties of industrious court metaphysician to a superpower haemorrhaging in capabilities and confidence – Rasputin to Huntington's Pere Joseph. Through the self-hypnosis achieved by rendering and inverting Hegel (principally via the medium of Kojeve), he staunched the flow by nothing less than claiming that actually existing liberal democracy not only brought its rivals down, but is, in the final analysis, the highest point of human development, and the condition which is being globalised. Yet, interestingly, as regards the conditions of actual life, he conceded in the round what Michael Rosen and David Widgery portray and develop with greater acerbity – namely, that it is also unexciting and bleak:

> At the end of the twentieth century, some of us fondly imagine ourselves as emancipated from superstition simply because we shop in supermarkets, have electronic TV channel changers and a wide choice of newspapers all saying more or less the same thing. In fact, religion, often of an extremely irrational kind, is spreading as fast as the radio waves, thanks often to philandering puritans. Our main sources of information are controlled by a handful of multimillionaires ('we have a free press because it is owned by free millionaires'); people who have nothing to sell but their ability to work are still served up a diet of bread and circuses to keep them poor but ignorant, while the middle class imagines itself intellectually independent because it reads a newspaper of that name. …We still worship the car and pay extravagant homage to the military-industrial machine while putting on red noses once a year in an attempt to stop famine. We accept as unquestioned the right of various unelected policemen, civil servants and financiers to govern the fine details of our personal life. Yet we noisily boast about our democracy because every five years we can fill in an election ballot, making as many as ten crosses in our political lifetime.[3]

Few, nevertheless, even well into the first decade of the twenty-first century, identify these offerings as variations on the related characteristics of equivalence and convergence, of, and towards respectively, war and economics as they apply to the processes of globalisation. Yet they are. Indeed, by way of those narratives in which primary colours are ascendant over pastel shades, this is exactly what is being implied within the processes captured by the term *globalisation*.[4] If equivalence is understood as a movement towards a common conclusion, and by convergence is meant equality of value, or significance, or effect, then, in the transitionary world of today these two relationships are framed as follows: what military thinking (strategy) and practice are to war and the disposition to war, economic theory and practice is to globalisation. Both give rise to identifiable and equivalent structures and conditions on the one hand, and consequences which are convergences on the other, some of which are absent from, or seen as irrelevant to, the mainstream understanding of globalisation. Interwoven with this analysis, therefore, is the dual awareness that, while the military dimension of a war, and the economic dimension of globalisation dominate their respective processes, it is misleading to believe that either is sufficient to explain their character or significance.

THE ORIGINS OF EQUIVALENCE AND CONVERGENCE

By way of an easement into this thesis, consider the surveys undertaken in the previous pages. War by the industrialised countries is justified in the defence of economic privilege; interdependently, economic life – effectively the enjoyment of economic privilege, as privilege, is therefore dangerous, and necessarily takes on the character of the system which succours it. Thus, like major war traditionally, it is to be understood as nothing less than the struggle for national survival. In the liberal democracies, then, daily existence is purchased at the price of a chronic sense of impending danger, and bears a stronger resemblance to life framed within the Hobbesian definition of war – that is, by 'the known disposition thereto during all the time there is no assurance to the contrary.' But given the character of its global economic dimensions this understanding may be further nuanced by Daniel Bell's formulation of economics as the continuation of war by other means. In all, it is a life totally other in its experiences than those intuitively associated with victory.

Searching for the principal cause of this regnant malaise is a fruitless labour, but in order to make sense of the present a brief excursion into recent history, in particular the years immediately following World War II, is both necessary and revealing. In this period any notion that the purpose of the war was, in the final analysis, to establish an equable and durable peace was explicitly overruled by the objective of the United States, underwritten by the victorious allies to varying degrees, to extend one of the dominant characteristics of the victory – that is, the relationship of American superiority over both its one-time allies and the defeated countries of Europe and Asia – by way of geo-strategic alliances, supranational financial arrangements, and a particular way of life (the last-mentioned being, arguably, as much a cause of the first two as it was independent of them). It was an objective requiring a grand strategy, and it was a grand strategy which required, as Melvyn Leffler has persuasively argued, the possession and pursuit of a 'preponderance of power' by the United States.[5]

Yet it was not a strategy in response to anything approaching an immediate threat, nor could it be: Leffler demonstrates that, at the time, the Soviet Union was vulnerable, and in no way constituted an acute threat. As well, John Lewis Gaddis' analysis of the Cold War provides additional support for viewing US strategy as a preoccupation with geopolitical control within his overall view that US officials developed a 'generalised sense of vulnerability… in the absence of threat', which led them to 'regard preservation of a global balance of power as a vital interest even before specific challenges to that balance had manifested themselves.'[6] Thus, it is in the working-out of this grand strategy that contemporary globalisation is to be understood, rather than as a post-Cold War innovation.

To serve the first, geostrategic, objective, the United States, in 1949, relied heavily on the fruits of wartime collaboration in the Manhattan Project, atomic weaponry, and abandoned its historical aversion to 'entangling alliances' with the establishment of the North Atlantic Treaty Organisation (NATO) and its associated and complex structures designed to develop and execute policies, provide for the command structure of the NATO forces themselves, secure the logistics requirements of those forces, and effect and maintain consultation between the member states. Subsequently, a certain promiscuity was in evidence as the US formed alliances throughout the world, initially in the name of the 'containment,' and then (by mid-1949), the 'roll-back,' of communism. Procuring the geoeconomic objective was assured in the immediate sense by the productive capacity of the US and its possession of the greater share of the world's gold reserves.

Beyond the immediate, however, such a grand strategy was, and could only be, predicated on sub-strategies of a global economic nature which promised, or appeared to promise, the indefinite extension of the *status quo*. Indeed, this objective is thought by some leading scholars to have been an imperative in its own right, determined by the opportunity which a devastated Western Europe presented for refashioning the post-war global economy according to American economic power and needs.[7] Accordingly, America demanded that Western Europe not only move away from its traditionally closed markets towards a global trading system, but also institute economies that pursued fast growth-through-debt, and thus were more prone to inflation (which discounts debt) – conditions which were ideal for American manufacturers, producers, and financial institutions. Created, in the words of Walter Russell Mead, was 'an unprecedented global boom' and a 'debtors paradise'[8] which the rest of the world was powerless to resist even if it wanted to.

Of the two pillars of the grand strategy, the demand for a debt-driven, fast-growth, global trading system was, without doubt, the more subtle yet the more aggressive. The more subtle because, unlike alliances and balances of power, which were explicitly associated with war in recent memory, it offered a novel turning away from the imperial trading blocs which had historically generated so much conflict; the more aggressive because it was an offensive against the traditional European reliance upon thrift and inherited wealth, and consequently democratised desire, dissatisfaction and consumption, a development pregnant with inescapable consequences, and attested to by the experience of the United States.[9] Of greater significance, however, was that both pillars were riven by a common contradiction which, succinctly expressed, was a belief in the infinity of resources in a finite world. To elaborate, it is necessary only to recall that containment and roll-back were essentially non-strategies because they abrogated a fundamental principle of strategy, namely that they described an open-ended commitment to secure the non-communist world against all threats – real, imagined, or merely presumed. Given a Western world of more or less sovereign states, this made US security, and the finite resources which contributed thereto, hostage to a multitude of forces beyond both its control, and its national interests, strictly defined.

Correspondingly, the Americanisation of economic theory and practice relied upon, in the rubric of Simon Patten, the creation of 'standardised' wants by 'standardised' consumers who would be accorded 'standardised' satisfaction.[10] Crucially, though, this desire had necessarily to be created and then unleashed: in the words of Emily Fogg Mead's celebrated defence of advertising, in 1901, 'the ability to pay' was not a concern; rather the task was to stimulate 'the imagination and emotion to desire' in people 'with the ability to want and choose.' As Katherine Fisher, an early advertising copywriter, expressed matters in 1899, 'Without imagination, no wants.... Without wants, no demand to have them supplied.'[11] In simple terms this required the reduction of consumers to a state of chronic insatiability and high levels of indebtedness; indeed, Charles Kettering's (General Motors) formula for economic prosperity was expressed in such terms – 'the organised creation of dissatisfaction.'[12] By extension, if desire was limitless, prosperity was also limitless, and resources had to follow suit. Moreover, this was exactly what was promised by the America negotiators at Bretton Woods in 1944, as instanced by David C. Korten:

> At the opening session, US Secretary of the Treasury Henry Morgenthau advocated rapid 'material progress on an earth infinitely blessed with natural riches.' He asked

participants to embrace the elementary economic axiom ...that prosperity has no fixed limits. It is not a finite substance to be diminished by division.[13]

In these terms, Bretton Woods, as the institutionalisation of postwar American ideology, was to early globalisation what the Manhattan Project was to the Western Alliance. It provided the means for ordering the greater part of the world along lines established by the United States. Those lines, furthermore, were vectors to a vanishing point, to the form of annihilation entailed by the willingness to apprehend (by which is meant the capture and understanding) infinity, to surrender the self without hope of release as collateral for participation in an enterprise out of keeping with the immediate circumstances. For all of that the inevitability of failure was disguised on the basis of equivalent and naturalised appeals: where nuclear weapons promised 'peace' in an anarchic world on the basis of a mutual genocide pact (and thereby required the global population to live in terror), through the Bretton Woods institutions, the global population was offered infinite, blameless consumption for the price of a chronic, clinically defined neurosis. The nuclear balance of terror, and the economic life of desire are, accordingly, equivalent, not only as separate instances of infinite deferral, but, given their nature, also variations of life under a regime of permanent war, or disposition to war, where, at best, the fighting conforms to the Burkean phrase, 'an unpitied sacrifice in a contemptible struggle,' and at worst, to war for its own sake.

War of this type was, of course, a pandemic of life in the ages before the modern state, when honour, pillage, revenge, and a delight in violence were among the first line of a feudal society's motivations. In feudal systems, more particularly in the clan system of Scotland until the Battle of Culloden (1746), for example, war – its rationale, declaration, and the means by which it would be fought – was the customary prerogative of the sovereign or the clan Chief. Service in such wars was similarly ordained, being owed on the basis of economic allegiance for tenure on land in the gift of the Chief. The social and political structure, therefore, determined that the clan was a military tribe in which all men would do battle. Unfortunately for posterity, and because of what John Prebble fittingly captures as 'romance lusting after fact,' a great deal of nonsense has attached to perceptions of this ancient blood contract since 1746, and hence detracts from, and distorts its considerably less idealised state which has much to offer by way of provocations and interrogations of the conditions of everyday life which raise globalisation to the status it enjoys.

GLOBALISATION AS THE UNIVERSALISING OF THE LOCAL

Life in a clan was a life of servitude to a master well described as a 'civilised savage,' who, if the circumstances were propitious, could deny his foster-brother, or sell his tenants to the plantations in the Americas.[14] Making due allowance for minor details, he was, by all accounts, strikingly familiar to contemporary portrayals of the putative Renaissance businessman in charge of a multinational, or transnational corporation, especially in the light of their common quasi legal authority, resulting then, as increasingly now, from governmental abdication which only confirmed instead of constraining their 'right' to act without challenge:

He could speak Gaelic and English, and very often French, Greek and Latin as well. He sent his sons to be educated at universities in Glasgow and Edinburgh, in Paris or Rome. He danced lightly, his own Highland reels and southern measures. He drank French claret and wore lace at his throat. ...He swore oaths in which God and Celtic mythology were mixed ...but his allegiance to Kings was quixotic. In his glens he was king, and there was no appeal higher than him among his clan. ...[He] believed in the blood feud and the Holy Trinity. A man of wild and ridiculous poetry, harsh and remorseless principle ...an uncomfortable anachronism.[15]

Equally significant is the fact that he ruled with the approval of his clan over a life which was accepted as fitting even by those most degraded by it. Since, by tradition immemorial, clansmen understood, in John Prebble's words, that their Chief was 'halfway between them and God,' any refusal to answer the call to arms took on luciferan dimensions and was punished accordingly.

Life in globalisation is remarkably similar. War, in its economic guise, is still declared by sovereigns or chiefs, without recourse to, but in the name of, the wider polity whose well-being they are thought to understand by virtue of their imputed successes and positions of political-economic power. Prebble sees this as 'wild music calling up the rant and the red reminders' of courage and glory,[16] while, in John Kenneth Galbraith's contrapuntal observation, it is the conjuration of three factors: a 'euphoria' which inhibits reflection when new and easy access to wealth is a prospect, 'extreme brevity in the financial memory,' and the 'specious association of money and intelligence.'[17] Notwithstanding these defaults, hostilities are opened in the name of national competitiveness, from which it is a short inductive leap to national survival. By this logic the competitiveness of the economy is implicitly fused with the combat-readiness of the military forces as one of the bi-conditions of existence when it ought more properly to be seen as an idiosyncratic dictate, or a profound misunderstanding of both economics and the nation state. The reasoning here is straightforward: countries, as Paul Krugman has been insisting in some of his most excoriating (albeit persuasive) analyses, might have unhappy or unsatisfactory economies, but they do not, as do corporations, 'go out of business' because they are uncompetetive;[18] indeed, the initial claim that they do should be understood only as a response to the threat, or actual onset of, the loss of economic dominance; in other words as but a *casus belli* for a declining clan. To this end it is noteworthy that, when so many analyses by discourse-framers and leaders in international economics become heralds of 'economics-as-war,' and seek mobilisation of the nation through publication, they engage in a late twentieth-century ritual commensurate with the sending of the fiery cross tied with blood-stained linen through glen, loch, strath, or clachan to gather the clan.[19]

The feudal obligation to serve also remains relatively intact for reasons which, if the US is any indication, are unchanged. By the early 1990s, personal indebtedness to financial interests, as evidenced by an average ownership of three to four credit cards, runs to US$1 billion, with the result that Americans then carried more consumer credit than all other peoples in the world combined.[20] Total consumer debt ran at 96 per cent of total disposable income – a factor which no doubt explained why, in 1990, more than 700,000

Americans (approximately 1 in 250) filed for bankruptcy.[21] The obligation to discharge indebtedness in these circumstances is assured since the only thing worse than the debt itself is being consigned to the fate of not being able to incur it in the first place, a status akin to homelessness and internal exile, much as befell those who dishonoured their clan's call (because there was no concept of a life worth living beyond the land which gives personal identity and meaning to daily life).

To this point the claim of equivalence possesses at least a suggestive legitimacy, sufficient to warrant venturing a further analogical step. This will be in the direction of ecology. To begin with, the Highlands of Scotland were isolated by their unwelcoming geography until well into the seventeenth century, denying outside penetration but permitting, by way of a familiar conceit, a sense of superiority over the southern Other. Topographically, they were covered by only shallow soil, which perforce made clansmen into herdsmen (that is, when they were not engaged in raids, or could be stirred from their indolence); clansmen lived, therefore, according to the dictates of the environment and the economy it allowed – in rough, cold, badly lit one-room cottages which, seen from afar, appeared as lumps of mud.[22] They were seen as 'barbarians who spoke an obscure tongue,'[23] because their language was neither of Scotland in general, nor of the mountainous region north of the Tay in particular (in the sense that it did not originate in these places); it was, in fact, Irish Gaelic, the vernacular of an earlier colonisation.[24] But this should not imply a spurious unity; indeed, as between clans, 'the natural jealousies of men who live remote and primitive lives made common cause impossible.'[25] By way of consolation they commemorated a savage past in music and song, and abided by an ethical system that seemed no better than a catalogue of permissible crime.[26]

The clan, obviously, was a closed military-social system, and this was of profound importance for understanding its longevity and psychic purchase on its members. With perhaps the notable exception of the Chief and the possible exception of the small number of more prosperous and high-ranking functionaries in the clan, it was in every respect a proudly ignorant society. Had it not been so driven in on itself it is difficult to see how the Highlands of Scotland, an Iron-Age agglomeration of tribes, would have survived to the mid-eighteenth century considering that, 400 miles south, the world of towns, capitalism, and national rule were relatively developed concepts and practices. To understand the Highland exception, it is necessary to advance the inquiry into a slightly more detailed accounting for the ignorance which prevailed there.

It was, in the first instance, a *willed* ignorance, but it was something more, an ignorance which was also ignorant of the fact that it was ignorant. [In more cosmopolitan circles this is sometimes known as the state of mind in which a Socratic Fool reposes – the lack of knowledge (and an indifference to it) about one's own lack of knowledge.] Hence, a question: how could this exist over time, and through what device? Of the ignorance Prebble replies:

> there was no schooling, nor did the people need any. In their pipes, their songs and bardic legends, they had a hard and relevant culture that matched and explained their life to them. Their Irish tongue sang sweetly on their lips, and spoke their emotions through its lilting cadences. God had found a way into the mountains before

Christianity came to the south, and had declared an amicable armistice with the Celtic mythology of giants, witches, precognition and stones that spoke with the voices of men.[27]

But his description of the clan order-of-battle is also relevant:

Each family… stood… according to its importance in the clan, so that the common humbly, the raw thighed, half-naked sub-tenant of a sub-tenant would find himself in the rear rank of all, and think it no more than his right. Brother fought beside brother, father by son, so that each might witness the other's courage and valour and find example in them.[28]

In these two passages Prebble is recounting what Bruce Wilshire, in his much later work, identifies as 'mimetic engulfment,' by which he means 'the prerational structures of involuntary imitation of others …at an archaic level of engulfment in the moody background world of everyday experience.'[29] Clan men, from the time they were young boys, therefore, were engaged in a process in which they were involuntarily, without self-awareness, and almost osmotically, 'undeliberately modelling themselves upon others around them in the foreground and the background world.'[30] They are engaged, in nothing less than the making of reality in a way that produces and regulates knowledge, hierarchises that knowledge as it relates to its most basic categories, presents it as transparent, naturalised, and self-evident, generates and legitimates its own questions and leaves 'no place for any of us to stand outside of it' – the process of discourse.[31]

A second question may now be put: how might the clan, its theories and practices, find equivalent expressions of a heuristic nature in globalisation? The answer, briefly, is to be found in the role of the modern university, most particularly in its teaching of the mainstream discipline of economics. What this approach posits is an equivalence between the ubiquitous clan forms which instructed its members in all aspects of life, and the training provided by the twentieth-century research university, which in reality remains fervently seventeenth century in its approach to knowledge – and which is constructed around the totalising, hierarchical dualisms of Descartes and the principles of Newtonian physics.[32] In no area of study is the latter more pronounced than in the discipline of neoclassical economics, graduates in which are subsequently celebrated in so many walks of political life, and whose discourse is, in most cases, dominant within the globalisation process even where economists, *per se,* are not present or speaking. In this formulation, the university in general, and the discipline of economics, in particular, are the clan, and the family within the clan, respectively, and it is the latter, accordingly, which deserves closer attention at this juncture.

The clan was, pre-eminently, poorly accommodated and closed – patriarchal, arrogantly superior in its self-estimation, offering little welcome to 'any soft-breeked creature living south of its hills,'[33] and speaking a language which only confirmed its unique identity. All of these are significant identifiers of economics. Its often-observed 'physics envy' speaks eloquently of a study acutely aware that, notwithstanding its scientism, it has yet to escape what Albert Camus called the 'tradition of humiliated thought' and remains within the shadow of natural, predictive, *science.* [34] In the meantime the chilly draughts of criticism which ventilate its pretensions drive its inhabitants ever closer towards its disciplinary centre of warmth; only here, in orthodox consensus, can they celebrate their provincialism as truth, affirm the value of their profession to the world, and renegotiate, in the words of Magali Sarfatti Larson, their 'cognitive exclusiveness.'[35]

In the debates over economic globalisation there is probably no more pungent exemplar of this defensive privilege than Paul Krugman, introduced in one article by (an admittedly unsympathetic) Robert Kuttner as a 'card-carrying neoclassical prodigy.'[36] In one recent attempt to repel outside, critical thinking from its attacks on classical economics' theories of international trade, he bemoans the fact that so many people conceptualise the globalising economy as a new Cold War (an interesting denial for someone prepared to use 'collateral damage' to describe the harm he sees done by the outsiders); effectively, they have adopted Daniel Bell's aphorism. This, most would agree, is Krugman's right as a respected and well-published academic economist; indeed, on the basis of his knowledge and standing he should be among the front rank of dissenters able to engage, *inter alia*, Lester Thurow, Robert Reich, Jeffrey Garten, Clyde Prestowitz, Ira Magaziner and Mark Patinkin, and the World Economic Forum, in robust debate. His terms of debate, however, are the terms of the clan: those who are persuaded that economic globalisation resembles the late Cold War fail to understand 'even the simplest economic facts and concepts,' engage in discussion of international trade issues which is 'marked by deep ignorance – all the deeper because it poses as sophistication,' and peddle visions based on not only 'shadows and mirages,' but frameworks which are derived from sources external, and unacknowledging of the canonical texts of mainstream academic economics. Thus bemoaned, it is not just error, but the fact that 'among policymakers, business leaders, and influential intellectuals – that is, among the people who matter …*economists have lost control of the discourse.*'[37] Worse, they have lost it to a cabal of politically successful, but self-deluded men who, in contradistinction to himself and his kin, lack that 'real understanding' of economics which is grounded in 'crisp, tightly argued models,' are mere 'policy entrepreneurs,' or 'policy intellectuals.'[38]

This still does not explain the defeat of the economists so much as describe it. For that, Krugman is equally clannish, adopting the professional equivalent of the 'wild charge which was [the clan's] only battle tactic.'[39] Witness the following: (i) *global economics* has a romantic ring to it and in any case touches so many 'real-world concerns' that a large number of non-economists feel they have the right to talk on the subject; (ii) the more people in category (i), the more that non-economists are encouraged to speak, leading to 'strength in numbers'; (iii) 'serious economics is often intrinsically difficult,' whereas economics written by non-economists often sounds more persuasive than the real thing; (iv) 'there is a lot of bad-mouthing of economists'; (v) bad-mouthing of economists is well-received by non-economists, a fact which reinforces economists' poor reputations; and (vi) 'serious people talk mostly to each other and tend to believe what they hear.' In Krugman's overall view, 'there is a circular process by which bad ideas drive out good.'[40]

Engaging with Krugman point for point, therefore, is not required; one cannot very well argue with a practitioner of a *disciplina arcana* if one does not accept whispers and concealment as terms of the debate, or, above all, with pique. But one can argue with the objective of the charge, which is the exorcism of pollution and the restoration of purity to the regime of truth which Krugman sees as imperiled. For this, he turns to the university to provide the necessary prophylactic, seeking in it an unapologetic acculturation of the type military 'boot camps' are notorious for. In this, he is wrong in terms of the ideals which the university is thought to embody, but not mistaken in terms of what the university has become, the latter being intuitively plausible given that Krugman espouses it confidently and without any sense of unease, let alone betrayal. Thus, he essentialises a curriculum for economics undergraduates which, despite all of what has happened in the last 190 years to change human life and our understanding of it, reduces to 'the insights of Hume and Ricardo.'[41] And even this canon is selective as to David Hume, whose 200-year-old work on equilibrating forces in international trade is cited with approval as a 'classical analysis,'[42] whereas Krugman is silent on Hume's epistemological scepticism and his major conclusion on empiricist-based claims of knowledge (which Krugman as a neoclassical economist is dependent upon), namely, that they can be defended only in metaphysical, and not in their own terms.[43] Krugman's response is to impose closure, and thereby, ignorance, even within the texts of the sanctified few who receive his *imprimatur*. It comes with a venerable precedent, nevertheless. In 1746, the clans which went to their defeat at Culloden were rejecting the Hanoverian George II ('German Geordie') as their King, on the basis of a 'tired' and 'mildewed,' 60-year-old claim, by the House of Stuart, with an outnumbered force armed with obsolete weapons.

Where the clan saw itself as being complete unto itself for the perpetuation of what is, in Paul Bove's terms, a 'naive dream vision,'[44] Krugman's university will fulfil the same function by its corresponding default as regards education, and its metamorphosis into an instrument of instruction concerned with installation. It follows, then, that if education is defined according to its etymology, as a drawing, or leading out, and is constituted by both a 'moral relationship between persons devoted to truth,' and a continuing process by which people become 'basically well-functioning,... knowledgeable concerning our common fate and eager to learn more,' that the university under Krugman's dispensation will produce archetypal clansmen, as in Clifford Geertz's phrase, 'highly trained barbarians.'[45]

Note, they will not be without morality, rather they will observe the morality that neoclassical economics in general, and capitalism in particular, sanctions. Their morality will, in other words, 'exonerate the activities and results of market activity' on the same grounds that pillage was absolved in the Highlands – that since the interests, material well-being, and happiness of the political unit are given legitimate goals, they necessarily outweigh challenges to their pursuit on other grounds.[46] For this reason Geertz's description is used advisedly. Krugman's explicit programme which, at its core, is the neoclassical programme personalised for this analysis, is extraordinarily adept at producing and reproducing three additional dimensions of clan life which promote its bellicosity.

In the first instance, it is an anti-intellectual exercise in the costume of education. What it promotes, above all else, is professionalism and professional judgment. What counts is not the educated understanding of an issue, but the ability to focus on nothing more than its immediate parameters so that it might be 'solved.' An example in the recent work of the Harvard economist, Richard B. Freeman, whose concern with the complex problems causing, and resulting from, inequality in the United States, is tragic in this regard.[47] Freeman, like Krugman, brings a great deal of clarity to contemporary debates on the effects of globalisation and, within his disciplinary self-confinement, is an authentic public intellectual. Thus, on inequality, he asks the question 'who's responsible?' and then proceeds with a multi-factor analysis which lays the blame (so to speak) with certain policies and structures. His recommendation for improving matters is, accordingly, with new, improved policies and structures; explicitly it is not with any attempt to redress the underlying causes of inequality. That is because:

> there is no necessary link between the causes of a problem and potential cures. When someone has myopia, a largely genetic disease, we cure it with glasses or contact lenses. *We do not mess with the genes, although they may be the root cause. When you have a headache, you take aspirin rather than go into a long exegesis about where the headache came from.*

> The same reasoning applies to the problem of rising inequality and stagnant real wages.... *The heart of the matter is not how we got into the inequality fix* but whether we should care about it and what we can do about it.[48]

Freeman, in these passages, leads us to the second dimension of bellicosity. His attempt to ensure the survival of his own authorising group is a mannerism reminiscent of the clan's organic regard for itself; the deliberate ignorance of the 'root cause,' and its depiction as an illegitimate area of study, can be seen in no other way than a strategy which will countenance the death and immiseration of others, his countrymen and countrywomen included, so long as economists are recognised as elite advisers. And it is clan-professional survival which is at stake, for at the very moment economics ceases to be defined by its highly fractionated abstractions and opens itself to things it now holds to be 'externalities' it becomes, in its own terms, disreputable and polluted.

The obsession with the disciplinary purity is therefore integral to economics as a discipline as it was to the clan: both hold intrusions to be taboo. And it forces Economics to disclose its phobias in identical terms to those of the clan – which is to say, governed by what James Hillman speaks of as 'the long sharpened tool of the masculine mind' which, alone, determines the worthiness of areas of study.[49] Ultimately, as Wilshire speculates, it is Hamlet's obsession, the will dominated so as to obey, remember, and avenge, his father:

> Remember thee?
> Yea, from the table of my memory
> I'll wipe away all trivial fond records,
> All saws of books, all forms, all pressures past
> That youth and observation copied there,
> And thy commandment all alone shall live
> Within the book and volume of my brain,
> Unmixed with baser matter. Yes, by heaven![50]

Thirdly, bellicosity is to be found in the hatred for other ways of knowing that both the clan and the discipline of Economics proclaimed and institutionalised through a regime of instruction. Whereas the clan universalised itself as the focus of all things meaningful, and thus was on a permanent war footing, Economics excised self-delight from humanity by the same process of abstraction, and produced rational economic man. Both because they have a single energy of identity oblivious to others, have effectively no path to a wider identity, and thus but one path to unity, and that is hatred. In their fragmented consciousness, might they not be thought of as within the sources of Swift's 'savage indignation,' as both 'yahoos, who hate one another more than they hate any different species, and the abstract rational houyhnhnms who, for all their rationality, do not love'?[51]

In their clannish defences of Economics Krugman and Freeman leave us with important insights, but not because they reconcile great tensions in their discipline; rather, it is because their remedies to these tensions are symptomatic of the confusions which attend them. They make available, in the words of Warren Samuels's study of the discipline, 'a cosmology, a metaphysics, a set of goals, an apologia, a vision… which defines existence.'[52] We are privy to 'a definition of reality which mediates between man and man and between man and the unknown.'[53] Unintentionally their vision and their reality are cautionary tales of the contemporary salience of Venetian politics in the last decade of the sixteenth century, and the enormity of their consequences as expressed by one who was about to experience them:

> They need hobgoblins, too – a fear
> To hold the hunt together, so they eat,
> Drink, sleep and breed, a single tribe,
> Protective of itself, self-justified.[54]

Feudal thinking, unchallenged, begets feudal action, and the accounts of its existence in globalisation are copious. The presence of one, the propensity to equate the competitiveness of a national economy with national survival, when what is at stake is, rather, the hegemonic or dominant power status of a national economy, has already received sufficient attention for now, except to note that it is probably one of the most powerful examples of discourse creating the conditions of existence. The feudal-economic discourse in globalisation, however, is also marked by one of the besetting failures of strategic thought in history – inflexibility. (Here Culloden is but a single case among many, and could, arguably, be thought inferior in comparison with the trench warfare of World War I.) At Culloden this was apparent in myriad ways but none so obvious as the persistence in a relatively effective, traditional form of attack, the mass charge, which, against the Duke of Cumberland's modern army, was an exercise in mass suicide.

In economic globalisation the equivalent elision of understanding is found in the unfavourable transformation of the macro-economic conditions of the American economy in the early 1970s in conjunction with the end of the Cold War. If the tendencies towards greater socioeconomic equity were to be maintained at the levels which existed in the three decades following World War II, both of these developments required an economic response which recognised that the limits of US capabilities had been not only reached, but exceeded, and an acknowledgment that history 'had robbed mainstream economic theory of both its conceptual raison d'être and the material contexts within which its analytical apparatus made the most sense.[55] Yet, because of the development of twentieth-century Economics in professional terms, and the intimate relationship between the economics profession and the government during the rise of the United States as a superpower, the economics mainstream became, and remains, arrogantly unreceptive to alternative views.[56] *Mutatis mutandis*: this was the conundrum faced by most countries in the industrialised world.

In the prevailing structures of a war-generated, centralised economic command structure, this was an exclusion easily effected by hierarchy and decision-making rather than intellectual merit. But this should not imply that there were possibilities for what is, after all, a form of dissent being treated as other than a breach of 'good order and (military) discipline.' More generally, it is not to suggest that pluralism, in whatever form it might take, is tolerable in either the military or the economic context; indeed, if the legitimate scrutiny of the operations of multinational, and transnational organisations, the role of finance houses and ratings agencies, and the existence of trade unions as legitimate representatives of workers' interests provide typical indications, the attitude, in common parlance, is close to one of 'zero tolerance' (though admittedly it is a habit of mind in response to challenge common to more organisations than the clan).

Intuitively and empirically, the corporations which operate on a global scale would appear to deserve scrutiny. Consult the body of literature which they have attracted and the justification is immediately apparent in the magnitude of their activities: some – ITT's role in the overthrow of the Chilean government in 1973, for example – have been blatant agents of imperialism; over 25 per cent of world economic activity is conducted between the largest 200 corporations; up to one-third of all world trade takes place between different units of a single global company; they openly disavow national loyalties, and, as if to prove the point, in 1993, the General Accounting Office reported that more than 40 per cent of the corporations doing business in the United States with assets in excess of US$250 million or more, paid income taxes of less than US$100,000 (where they paid any at all). As well, they are one of the principal instruments of unemployment in the countries in which they are nominally domiciled – in the three years 1991 to 1994, just five corporations (IBM, AT&T, GM, Sears Roebuck, and GTE) announced lay-offs totalling nearly one-third of a million workers, but, in the same period, corporate chief executives were rewarded obscenely, as evidenced by the total income, which includes salary, bonuses, and stock options, of Disney's Michael Eisner (US$215,911,000) and H.J. Heinz's Tony O'Reilly (US$114,177,000).[57] Even Louis V. Gerstner, chairman and chief executive of IBM, which announced lay-offs of 30,000 for 1994, received a package of US$8 million for the year.[58] In brief, there were abundant reasons to justify the establishment and continuing operation of the 35-person United Nations Centre on Transnational Corporations limited though its resources were by comparison with its subjects, and also for it to be concerned, as it was, with the development of a code of conduct for their global operations. They were not sufficient, however, to prevent it from being run down as a result of pressure by the corporations being brought to bear through various conservative lobby groups they funded in the US with the result that, in 1993, it was phased out of existence.

The logic of capital as mediated by the boardroom is reproduced in the matter of national currencies, specifically in the mechanisms by which the policies of democratically elected governments are hostage to unelected, non-(publicly) accountable currency traders. As one adviser to President Clinton has remarked, the value of the US dollar at any given time may be reduced to 'a snapshot' of the discussion which such interests are having in relation to the policies the administration is following. Similarly, in France, where, in 1981, 'the markets' were hostile to the socialist policies of President François Mitterrand, they set in train an exodus of capital until such time as he changed them. In both cases two wartime military characteristics were in the ascendant (and acknowledged as such by Walter Wriston, former chairman of Citicorp) – the discipline being imposed is inescapable and draconian. Recalling the words of Giordano Bruno, it is 'protective of itself, self-justified' to the extent, conceded by Wriston, that the real power over currency lies not with national governments or central banks, but with traders seated in front of '200,000 monitors in trading rooms all over the world' who conduct 'a kind of global plebiscite on the monetary and fiscal policies of the governments issuing currency.'[59]

In the matter of unions, 'zero tolerance' is an accurate description of the closed structures of global corporations in the overwhelming majority of cases, if not all. Because corporations now possess the ability of military rapid reaction forces, and, more significantly, some mercenary armies – effectively to *globalise* their operations anywhere on the planet as a result of modern technology and 'free trade' agreements – the workers are increasingly analogous to members of elite units: if they have work, they are respected and their self-esteem is high, but both are bought at the cost of accepting a spartan discipline in the face of increasing levels of deprivation and provocation. Thus, as wages and conditions have deteriorated in the United States, the proportion of the workforce organised for collective bargaining has dropped to under 12 per cent, lower than at any time since 1936, when the Wagner Act, the principal New Deal labour reform, was enacted.[60]

To compound their plight, in globalisation they serve without benefit of whatever mitigation comes from the legal regulation of conflict. Neither are non-combatants excused this regime. In this the feudal-clan dimension of conflict reasserts itself. To recap, the clan was a military organisation, and war between clans punctuated its existence. Notions that war should be fought only for the purpose of self-defence, and that some weapons were, even then, prohibited, as embodied in Article 51 of the United Nations Charter, or that Rules of Engagement should control or restrict military operations were alien. Contemporary globalisation exhibits a regression to this view and it is found nowhere more prominently than in two neoclassical components of globalisation. The first is, of course, the requirement that the 'free market' be given full rein for ascertaining outcomes, the corollary of which is the removal of as many, if not all forms of state intervention as can be agreed between capital and government. The second is Margaret Thatcher's redefinition of the polity in her denial 'there is no such thing as society' explicitly refusing, therefore, the propensities which generate an awareness of commonality, and the influences upon self-control and restraint it has been held to exercise over individuals.[61]

A popular term for the former approach is 'winner-takes-all,' which allows the logic of acquisitive individualism within capitalism to exhaust the entire category of logic in its own name and, as seen above in relation to the rewards for chief executives, examples of it proliferate in the corporate world, as does its consequence of radical inequality. The latter, on the other hand, is the obverse of the former; it merely asserts a particular condition sought within the ambit claim of deregulation. If globalisation is war, both would appear to be covered by nothing more than the atavistic appeal of war for plunder. Thus, both find ready analogues in feudal life.

But there is a rupture in the comparison, too. Both must also be seen as comparable to a modernist development in warfare – the imposition of unconditional surrender on a defeated enemy which is the prerogative only of a state or alliance possessing annihilationist power and the determination to express it strategically. The 1990 to 1991 Gulf War with its consequential murder of hundreds of thousands of infants and the destitution of its population for the purpose of forcing Saddam Hussein into *absolute* compliance with the term of the cease-fire agreement is a leading case in point. What this suggests is that, instructive though the establishment of equivalences might be between the discursive structures of the feudal clan system and globalisation, they are limited; more, in order to delimit the terror of globalisation they require a re-visioning in the light of consequences which are indistinguishable from those of war.

CONVERGENCE: THE INTEGRATION OF WAR WITH GLOBALISATION

The tendency of globalisation towards a common conclusion, or result, associated with war is initially quite easily apprehended if it is seen as occurring through what might be termed the relationship of cross-appropriation. By this is meant that, as the discourse of Economics, particularly global economics developed, a tendency to treat itself militarily (as witness the plethora of works on globalisation-as-war), military strategy has found a corresponding resonance in both the command and high-risk echelons of economic life. This relationship exists, moreover, extensively, *and* as an integration, which is to say closer than the composite military-industrial network of President Eisenhower's renowned anxiety. And we find it in expressions such as 'geoeconomics,' which Edward Luttwak elaborates as the 'logic of conflict, grammar of war,' and in 'The Enterprise,' the term of corporate genus used by the 'privately funded' mercenary force which served as the secret arm of the National Security Council during the US destabilisation campaign against the Sandinista government in Nicaragua in the mid-1980s.[62]

Nor should this be a surprise because the mind-set from which these practices were derived is, effectively, the unreconstructed theoretical basis of international relations which guarantees the preparation for war and, ultimately, war itself, fused with the need to redress the relative economic decline of the United States. As Jim George has demonstrated, ever since the US defeat in Vietnam, successive attempts by mainstream international relations scholars to rehabilitate their discipline's policy use while simultaneously providing a theoretical legitimation of US hegemony have, instead of overturning the core realist perspective which led to that débâcle, achieved little more than mottling it with the concerns of international political economy.[63] Strategy and economics were accommodated accordingly in what became known as neo-realism, although, strictly speaking, there was much about it that took the form of a reacquaintance rather than an introduction.

As early as 1817, the United States Military Academy's fourth superintendent, Sylvanus Thayer, introduced to the academy the 'grammatocentric principle' – defined as organisation through, or around, writing – and with it the overthrow of direct, visible command in favour of indirect, hierarchical, and centralised control on the basis of daily, weekly, and monthly written reports in the manner, observes Postman, of a modern Chief Executive Officer.[64] As Thayer's graduates advanced their careers, so too did his ideas: in 1832, 60 years before the advent of Frederick Taylor's techniques of 'scientific management,' time-and-motion studies, including surveillance of workers, and the establishment of 'objective' norms of individual productivity, had been introduced to the Springfield Armoury.[65]

It was a continuing tradition, operationally as well as administratively, as the 1930 memoirs of a senior military officer remind us:

> I spent thirty-three years and four months in active service as a member of our country's most agile military force – the [United States] Marine Corps. I served in all commissioned ranks from a second lieutenant to major-general. And during that period I spent most of my time being a high-class muscle man for Big Business, for Wall Street, and for bankers. In short, I was a racketeer for capitalism....
>
> Thus I helped make Mexico and especially Tampico safe for American oil interests in 1914. I helped make Haiti and Cuba a decent place for the National City Bank boys to collect revenues in.... I helped purify Nicaragua for the international banking house of Brown Brothers in 1909–1912. I brought light to the Dominican Republic for American sugar interests in 1916. I helped make Honduras 'right' for American fruit companies in 1903. In China in 1927 I helped see to it that Standard Oil went its way unmolested.
>
> During those years I had, as the boys in the back room would say, a swell racket. I was rewarded with honours, medals, promotion. Looking back on it, I feel I might have given Al Capone a few hints. The best he could do was to operate his racket in three city districts. We Marines operated on three continents.[66]

By the time of the Vietnam War, the hold of internalised corporate-business norms on the United States Army was pernicious. A six-month in-country assignment became 'career-enhancing' to the extent that, via one, officers could reach the rank of major in only six years. As legatees of Thayer's principles, and by embracing the entrepreneurial spirit with which the Army was infused, some even 'invested' the lives and well-being of their soldiers in missions for the purpose of a still more accelerated promotion. The formalisation of this ethic was illustrated by the fact that, in this period, for each graduate history degree held by a serving officer, there were ten in business administration, management, and economics.[67] In a more recent example of the symbiosis 15 leading oil and gold traders on the New York Mercantile Exchange have been charged with instructing 12 Marine Corps generals in information processing and split-second decision-making, on the grounds that the Exchange offers the same information and stakes environment experienced by senior officers in modern war.[68]

Evidently it is an example to be emulated in a world transiting from, in Heilbroner's view, a capitalist-political, to a capitalist-economic, complexion.[69] Even in Australia in the 1990s, the advertisements for the Royal Military College, Duntroon, emphasised 'the edge' which the acquisition of leadership skills, management techniques, and self-discovery would provide, while never once mentioning the military's combat obligations. Those obligations were, however, to the fore in: Colombia, where both British Petroleum and the drug cartels hired units of Colombian soldiers to guard against guerrilla attacks; Haiti, where former soldiers formed private forces to protect the wealthy; Liberia, where industrial gangs contracted by multinational corporations engaged in resource extraction; Croatia, where Military Professional Resources Inc – a firm of retired US Army generals – prepared that state's army for its 1995 summer offensive against the Serbs; and Bosnia, where the same company trained that state's army.[70]

The most noteworthy of such cases has probably to be found not so much in, but in relation to, Papua New Guinea: there, in response to nearly a decade of civil strife on the mineral-rich island of Bougainville, and frustrated by the PNG Defence Force's failure to subdue the Bougainville Revolutionary Army, the government of Sir Julius Chan turned to a 'military consultancy' for its remedy. That organisation was a Pretoria-based subsidiary of the Strategic Resources Corporation trading under the name of Executive Outcomes, then the only incorporated private mercenary army in the world: among the 'advisory,' 'training,' and 'equipment' services it provided were clandestine warfare, combat air patrol, armoured warfare, basic and advanced battle handling, and sniper training. Given that its chief executive, Eben Barlow, was, under South Africa's apartheid regime, the commander of a notorious special forces battalion before he moved to another unit specialising in assassination, disinformation, gun-running, espionage, and sanctions-busting, and that its workforce consisted mainly of former elite commandos of the same regime, it was clearly an organisation capable of, and devoted to, an extensive honouring of its logo, the paladin (popularised by the old television series, *Have Gun Will Travel*). To this end it had also been contracted to the governments of Angola, South Africa, and Sierra Leone, and the De Beers diamond cartel.[71]

Informed by Heidi and Alvin Toffler's book, *War and Anti-War*, regarding the changing nature of war and especially who makes it, the company's economic philosophy was both neoclassically correct, and a confirmation of Martin Van Creveld's view that the transformation of war – effectively the 'privatisation of violence' – involved a return to war for individual profit, otherwise expressed as payment for performance. According to Barlow, only a company like Executive Outcomes could dispense with the restrictions placed on national forces (who get paid even if they are unsuccessful) and operate according to the law of the marketplace.[72] Indications are that it was an ideal with considerable appeal beyond the cases cited to this point. In November 1996, the US National Security Council was at least prepared to entertain, if not endorse, the idea of using Executive Outcomes to secure a humanitarian corridor for fleeing Hutu refugees in Rwanda on the grounds of economic efficiency (when compared to a UN peacekeeping mission) and the lack of political repercussions which follow from the privatisation of casualties.[73]

Although the term seems not to have been applied, it is nevertheless the case that what is being created in this synergy are new instruments of coercion – market forces. And, just as they are exemplary of the unification of globalisation and war, they are also indicative of the unification of consequences, otherwise known as casualties and battle damage. Under virtually every heading common to war analysis – theatres of operation, killed-in-action and wounded-in-action (including the sub-categories of 'friendly fire'/ 'amicide'), non-combatants, prisoners of war, forces-of-occupation, environmental degradation, and psychopathy (including war crimes) – the magnitude of destruction in globalisation only confirms it is war's *alter ego*. With the purpose in mind being more to create an intellectual space, rather than to provide an exhaustive inventory of convergence, and because such an account would be a work of major proportions in itself, the demonstrations of this relationship will be limited to examples which, hopefully, will be seen as indicative of a wide spectrum of identity.

The notion of a geographically contained war zone, a so-called 'theatre of operations,' provides a start for the reason that, in globalisation, the distinction between territories of safety and territories of danger cannot be sustained intellectually or geostrategically. Expressed another way, given the forces, purposes and logics of globalisation, especially to denationalise territory, then the most that might be said is that some areas are more or less globalised, but that they are so characterised has predominantly more to do with the interest that globalisation has in them than in their interest in globalisation, or their capacity to resist it. In effect this translates the world into a single theatre of potential operations, limited in their incidence and intensity only by the calculations of return on investment which apply to different locales (which are, therefore, likely to be tightly defined with little respect for precedent or national sentiment). In the commodification which accompanies globalisation, value is apportioned according to a 'stateless' calculus, which, expressed in the principles of former Paramount Communications chairman, Martin Davis, means 'you can't be emotionally attached to any particular asset.'[74]

Thus, globalisation is an offensive against which there is no defensive perimeter, and certainly no protective border. Indeed, in terms of its ability to strike without meaningful warning, and to contaminate its surroundings, globalisation is frequently commensurate with intercontinental ballistic missiles. On other occasions the analogy is more appropriate to an attack by a guerrilla army against relatively isolated and weak outposts of a fading metropolitan power. By way of the former, it has been estimated that, under globalisation, about one-third of all jobs in the United States are at risk due to the growing productivity and low-wage labour of such countries as China, India, and Mexico, while those remaining in work will suffer a deterioration of their wages and working conditions for the same reasons. In these countries, however, the 'threat' is not from Chinese, Indian, and Mexican companies *per se,* but from corporate operations chartered in the United States – *Fortune 500* companies that comprise the US–China Business Council – and a well-funded China lobby in the Congress.[75] In this case US labour is attacked from its own territory by those flying its own flag, and that is an irony as well:

China, alone among the nuclear powers, was, in the early years of its strategic development, the only one that developed a missile attacking its own territory (the implication being that, by demonstrating the willingness to severely damage itself, potential aggressors would be under no illusions about a Chinese response). The latter's presence, guerrilla capitalism, on the other hand, is to be judged from the record of states and municipalities in the same country and even the same state bidding against each other as they offer subsidies to multinational corporations to set up locally, as did Alabama with Mercedes–Benz (US$253 million), and Illinois (US$240 million) for Sears just to remain.[76] The 'front' is as fluid as it is ubiquitous.

Casualties, by which name those killed and wounded are collectively known, follow the 'front.' As in all wars they are regarded as the single most important consequence; at the same time they are also regarded as inevitable although the particular level of casualties which is inevitable is contested. In neoclassical economics their number is held to be described by the Phillips Curve (a product of various core assumptions in the discipline) which produces a unique forecast for the given conditions. Jesuitical care is taken, nevertheless, to ensure that casualties are understated by adopting methodologies which will guarantee a conservative outcome; in the post-Vietnam War era, revulsed by infamous 'body-counts' (and perhaps by Herman Kahn's invention of the term 'megadeaths' in relation to the consequences of nuclear war), a certain care is also taken to efface the level of carnage being inflicted upon the enemy (the US Gulf Wars with Iraq being acute cases in point). A need exists, therefore, to employ a realistic and reasonable system of description capable of disclosing the casualties actually caused by the hostilities under-way. In this study, that criterion can be met by acknowledging the consequences for the general population of the 'state of war' which everything we know about the subject tells us is as much a 'state of mind' arising from daily life as it is a contest between weapons and armed forces.

An example might assist this proposal. It is widely accepted that the Vietnam War produced in the region of 60,000 US combat deaths; what is less well-known, yet needs to enter the record is the fact that, by 1981, almost 25 per cent of those who saw combat in Vietnam had been arrested on criminal charges, mainly drug-related, and, by 1990, the number of suicides among Vietnam War veterans exceeded combat fatalities.[77] These deaths are not recorded on Maya Lin's otherwise profoundly eloquent Vietnam Veteran's Memorial in Washington, DC, yet it is undoubtedly the case that, even were they to be corrected by already existing tendencies in the population as a whole, a significant number would have to be the direct result of the Vietnam experience. The intention, accordingly, is to factor in 'immiseration,' a term of common usage in contemporary political-economic analysis, to describe the globalising condition which followed upon the abandonment of Keynesian economics in the 1980s in favour of neo-liberal economics. Immiseration includes deterioration of the conditions in, and threats to, full-time, adequately paid employment; underemployment and/or unemployment; increasing economic poverty; socioeconomic inequality; poor physical health; psychological sickness; and the overall wretchedness of the great majority of people which results as the theories and practices of globalisation intensify their hold on societies throughout the world on the grounds that these conditions are not only consequences, but also the more proximate causes of, and morbidity under globalisation. Used in this context, 'immiseration' encapsulates and joins globalisation's state-of-war with its state-of-mind.

Of the above factors, inequality and poverty are the most important since they are both significant determinants of the others and, historically, of membership of the common soldiery. It is also undeniable that they are defining features of the Third World, that their incidence has increased since the onset of globalisation (though the 'development' and 'modernisation' variants were earlier contributors), and that they are now common pathologies in the First World.[78] Given this, and the accounts and analyses which are to hand, immiseration under globalisation has to be seen as framing greater destruction in the Third World than any war has wrought, while in the First World, the levels are those of major war, although the respective magnitudes in each are not comparable.

In a world still unable to understand the Holocaust, figures provided by the United Nations Children's Fund and the United Nations Economic Commission for Africa compound the sense of incomprehensibility: in the decade following 1982, in Africa, Asia, and Latin America, at least six million children under the age of 5 have died as a result of IMF–World Bank Structural Adjustment Programs (SAPs); the same programmes are also estimated by reliable studies to be responsible for a 100 per cent increase in infant mortality in some countries in Africa.[79] On these figures alone, the convergence of war and economic globalisation is demonstrably proved while at the same time throwing into shadow the two world wars which produced 11 and 55 million deaths respectively. While World War I resulted in less than two years of infant SAP mortality, World War II's figures include deaths from all causes and across all age groups – the suggestion being that, if total SAP-induced mortality is factored in, the total deaths in globalisation for just one decade would be at least comparable with World War II. Even as it stands without such a correction, current rates of SAP-induced infant mortality render globalisation one of the two or three deadliest forms of war in human history. From another perspective they exceed by a factor of two the total number of deaths attributed to wars in the period of the Cold War (40 to 50 million). In the final analysis they confirm a phenomenon of twentieth-century warfare, which has undergone such a radical transformation in the ratio of combatant to non-combatant deaths (from 20:1 in World War I to 1:13 in Vietnam), that the phrase 'the civilianisation of war' is no exaggeration.[80]

Western death-tolls, while considerably less, are also historically revealing. In the various studies of the relationship between socioeconomic differentiation and mortality, especially the relationship between unemployment and risk of death such as was undertaken by economists Mary Merva and Richard Fowles of the period 1990 to 1992, the results are consistent with substantial war. On the basis of the discovery that every one percentage point rise in unemployment produces a 3.1 per cent increase in deaths resulting from strokes, and a 5.6 per cent increase in deaths resulting from heart attacks, the overall death-toll was calculated at 38,078, or just over 19,000 per year. In absolute terms this renders the two years of globalisation covered in the Merva and Fowles study the fifth most costly war fought by the United States – behind the Civil War, the two World Wars, and Vietnam, but ahead of Korea (34,000). Annually, it is more deadly than Vietnam on the basis that the combat death-toll in that conflict would be reached within only three years and two months (as opposed to eleven years in Vietnam).

As with all wars, globalisation is no exception to the high incidence of deaths by 'friendly fire,' or, as it is otherwise known, 'amicide' – defined as the unintentional killing of one's own forces in the course of war.[81] One area which serves well to indicate this seemingly inescapable pathology of war is the use of highly toxic pesticides. It can, moreover, be regarded as globalisation's particular convergence with one of the more egregious practices of the Vietnam War, the use of chemical defoliants such as 2, 4, 5-T and Agent Orange, and the long-term effects on those contaminated by them. In both cases, it should be noted, the chemical agents in question were deployed in order to increase operational efficiency, and both are now strongly linked to sickness and death. Accordingly, in a study of the pesticide compounds endosulfan, dieldrin, toxaphene, and chloradane in the Columbia River Basin, the findings of which appear in an article published in *Science* in June 1996, it is reported that not only is there a link between them and breast cancer and male defects, but a significant probability that, when combined with other pollutants, the damage is increased by up to 1,000 times.[82] In Sinaloa, Mexico, different findings attest to the deadly effects of pesticides: in the Culiacan Valley it is 'normal' for 3,000 workers per year to be hospitalised for pesticide intoxication, a result of aerial spraying in the course of daily work; similarly, the Huichole Indians working the tobacco fields of Nayarit State are dying at an alarming rate which is now thought to be the result of working and sleeping in close proximity to leaves coated with pesticides such as Hamivel and methomyl.[83]

Brazil, however, is the major user of pesticides in Latin America, and one of the largest in the world, in its attempt to develop cash crops for export in line with World Bank and IMF Structural Adjustment Programs. There, in 1989 alone, a total of some 25,000 tons of pesticides, including Aldrin, a known carcinogen, and Folidol (which, under even the most stringent of conditions, is still known to attack the nervous systems of organisms) were applied in the states of Bahia, Minas Gerais, and Parana. According to extremely conservative toxicological studies at the poison control centre in Campinas, São Paulo, at least 2 per cent of the population (or 280,000) Brazilians are contaminated by pesticides each year.[84]

Brazil's experience strongly reflects Vietnam's. In the latter, in the eight years to 1970, when the use of Agent Orange and 2, 4, 5-T was severely restricted because of their teratogenic (foetus-damaging) properties which were discovered in studies conducted for the National Cancer Institute, 100 million pounds of herbicide (or six pounds for every inhabitant at the rate .75 of a pound per year) were sprayed on South Vietnam; in Brazil, the annual rate is 56 million pounds, or at least four times higher. And while the current annual rate per inhabitant is less (.35 of a pound per year), the period of exposure is at least three times as long, suggesting that contamination is probably greater.[85] Furthermore, the war is hardly being won, as was the case in Vietnam: the list of species resistant to at least one pesticide is growing – from 182 in 1965 to more than 900 currently, thereby creating a demand for an even greater volume of deadlier agents.

Economic combat, under the general conditions of inequality and poverty, and in the specific circumstances of markedly decreased probabilities of survival, produces at least two alternatives for many at the front line – desertion, and surrender (or capture) as a Prisoner of War (POW). In globalisation, especially for the less skilled members of the population in the United States, these options are effectively coterminous with the resort to crime, and, for many, subsequent incarceration. The rates of incarceration, however, exceed those of wars in recent memory and are ludicrously expensive. In comparison with the Korean War, in which 0.5 per cent of US forces became POWs, by 1995, more than 2 per cent of the US male workforce – over one million men – was in prison, and almost another 5 per cent was under some form of supervision by the criminal justice system. The state of California in the same year was in the position of budgeting more for prisons than for higher education, as well it might have given that incarceration is nearly as expensive as the fees for sending a student to Harvard.[86]

Thus two objectives are served. Crime is reduced at the same time as a deterrent, of sorts, operates. Of the two, the former is the more appreciated because it allows one of the great historical prerogatives of war, looting or pillage of the defeated peoples and territories by the forces of occupation, to proceed with a minimum of impediments. In globalisation a predominant form of this privilege, and it must be understood it is a commander's privilege we are speaking of, is the tendency, in Britain's family-owned, personally managed companies most noticeably, to seek immediate, personal gratification of the spoils of victory by consuming the profits of whatever operation is at hand. Where pension funds or other forms of finance institution have taken over the effective ownership of companies, whether it be in Britain or the United States, the pattern remains constant. Basically, the 1980s created a demand for short-term performance in financial institutions comparable with that on offer, until October 1987 anyway, in industrial companies, with the result that long-term investment became hostage to the imperative of consumption. In turn, this led to various forms of speculative, financial engineering by the financial institutions and the sort of catastrophes in that sector which followed as a result of over-exposure to failed ventures.[87] In sum, it is a form of looting which is, clearly, closely related to the concept of 'winner-takes-all' but is to be distinguished from it inasmuch as the principal beneficiaries are stock-holders as opposed to senior executives.

Of greater significance is the distinctly Clausewitzian character, overlaid, it must said, with German strategic urgency, which the relevant financial engineering makes necessary. If it is recalled that, for Clausewitz, the art of war called for the objective to be attained by choosing the 'shortest way to it that you dare to go,' while simultaneously bringing to bear the utmost concentration of force, and if it is also recalled that, for Germany in both world wars, the speed with which it could secure its rigidly sequential objectives was of paramount importance, then contemporary 'profit-taking' is understandable. Because of the need to service shareholders with dividends in quick time, exceedingly bold and therefore risky 'strategies of decision' are called forth in the manner of the Schlieffen Plan and *blitzkrieg* which, if they fail, and failure has closely attended their pursuit, converge on the financial version of the classic German dilemma of a two-front war – 'over-exposure.' In both cases what is present is identical: to cite Clausewitz on this form of war, it is 'an innate propensity to extreme hazards,' while, in the financial realm, John Kenneth Galbraith refers to it as 'a serious commitment to error.'[88]

In view of the record of destruction canvassed in the foregoing, these phrases might more widely be seen as the leitmotiv of the entire globalisation project itself. And nowhere would it be more applicable than in the environmental devastation it wreaks. The problem which immediately presents itself in a study such as this, however, is one of choice from the spectrum of possible inclusions posed by, *inter alia,* the toxicity of modern agricultural and industrial practices, energy supply and usage, declining biodiversity, deforestation, ozone layer depletion, global warming, biological extinctions, and population growth. Thus, inadequate though it might be, a relatively mundane selection has been made which, hopefully, exemplifies the problematic: meat-eating, the appropriateness of which is suggested by the fact that the growth of albeit small middle classes in countries formerly designated as overwhelmingly poor almost automatically results in the diversification of diet involving a more meat-centred, grain-burning mode of life which is a boon to the traditional sheep and cattle-exporting countries such as Argentina, Australia, and New Zealand, and an encouragement to others to follow suit, even if it means burning off their rainforests to do so. For all exporting countries, traditional and recent, it will inevitably mean waterway pollution from pasture run-off, and a contribution to global warming through the methane produced by animals (the latter being more accentuated in cases where forests have been cleared).

Notwithstanding these costs, three other aspects of red meat-eating should be considered in brief, namely, that it is dangerous to health, wasteful of scarce resources, and an extraordinarily excremental scourge besides. The indictment of meat as life-threatening is now on substantial foundations: reports by the Surgeon-General of the United States in 1987, and numerous studies, including those conducted by the American Cancer Society, the American Heart Association, the National Academy of Pediatrics, and the National Academy of Sciences have established that it increases the risk of contracting the 'diseases of affluence' – heart disease, cancer, and diabetes – through the consumption of large amounts of fatty acids and cholesterol present in, especially beef.[89]

In relation to inefficiency, the 1991 Worldwatch paper *Taking Stock: Animal Farming and the Environment,* which assesses outputs on the basis of the inputs of fossil fuel to plant, protect, harvest and transport the grain used to produce meat, is to the point: it takes 6.9 kilograms of grain (or 30,000 kilocalories of fossil fuel), the equivalent of four litres of gasoline, to produce one kilogram of pork, and 4.8 kilograms of grain (or 17,000 kilocalories of fossil fuel) to produce one kilogram of beef in the US, whereas (US) chickens require only 13,000 kilocalories per kilogram, and eggs and cheese can be produced for 10,000 kilocalories per kilogram. European Union figures are higher than the US because of the increased use of fertiliser, and Japanese figures are twice as high as the US because double the amount of grain is fed to the cattle. To produce one kilogram of boneless steak in (say) California, it also takes over 24,000 litres of fresh water.[90] Overall the 1.3 billion cattle populating the Earth take up nearly 24 per cent of the land mass, and the methods of farming they have attracted are responsible for both the consumption of one-third of the world's grain harvest (enough to feed hundreds of millions of human beings) and for much of the planet's increasing desertification.[91]

Meat-eating-as-excremental-scourge should need little explanation if it is appreciated that the organic waste produced by a typical 10,000-head feed lot (around 500,000 pounds per day, or 2 billion tons per year) is equivalent to the human waste generated in a city of 110,000 people. In Holland, pig farming is even more destructive because the industry is producing around 215 million tons of excrement per year, which includes 94 million tons of manure – of which only 50 million tons can be absorbed into the land without prejudice to the water supply and vegetation. The result is that, absent a market for excess manure, the country is on the brink of an ecological disaster, the financial costs of which are reckoned at over US$500,000 annually.[92]

We have, therefore, the basis for a comparison with the Vietnam War (including Laos and Cambodia) and the Gulf War of 1990 to 1991. On the basis of the militarised environmental destruction in the former the term 'ecocide' was introduced into the lexicon of war, as well it might have been:

> Over the course of the war, the United States dropped more than 25 million bombs on Vietnam. Almost half the forests in the southern half of the country were soaked with defoliants. Over half of the country's coastal mangrove swamps were destroyed, and nearly 5 million acres of forests – almost 17 per cent of the entire country – were damaged, many irreparably so. The ecological catastrophe wrought by the war has snowballed as a war-numbed people try to eke out a living in a poisoned land. Lacking forest cover, soil quality has deteriorated. Flooding has increased dramatically. Farmers, trying to grow food on degraded land, have turned to heavy pesticide use to try to boost production; as a consequence, chemical run-off from agricultural pesticides is now poisoning much of Vietnam's water supply. The health of Vietnamese women, more so than men, has suffered from the poisoning of their land…. Vietnamese women today have the highest rate of spontaneous abortion in the world and cervical cancer rates among the highest.[93]

Indeed, the magnitude of destruction of wild plants and animals in their natural habitat prompted, first, US Senator Claiborne Pell, and then Professor Richard Falk, to propose that ecocide be defined as a crime and, accordingly, outlawed by an international convention against ecocide in virtually the same manner that genocide was outlawed by the international community.[94]

Even allowing for the fact that Protocol 1, *Article 55: Protection of the Natural Environment* [Additional to the Geneva Conventions, 1977] embodies these intentions, Operation *Desert Storm* is a recent reminder of the political unwillingness to operationalise them.[95] As a result of the wartime destruction of Iraq's chemical warfare stockpile and ammunition dumps, attacks on, and sabotage of, the oilfields and tankers by both Iraq and the US, and the hundreds of fires which ensued, the Gulf and its environs were inundated with chemical contamination and toxins (including cyanide, dioxin, and PCBs). Additionally, an oil spill equal to the largest in history produced massive levels of destruction in the marine and bird life. While the 600 fires raged at their peak, more than one million tons of sulphur dioxide and 100,000 tons of nitrogen oxides were released into the atmosphere each month; according to the US Environmental Protection Agency, roughly ten times more pollution was being created from this source in Kuwait in

March 1991, as was being emitted by all US industrial and power-generating plants combined.[96]

The question might therefore be asked as to whether there is any significant distinction to be made between environmental destruction in peace and war; specifically, might it not be appropriate to find that they both constitute ecocide? Certainly, this must be as defensible a proposition as arguing that the environmental consequences of a short 'event' such as the Gulf War, which admittedly will exist for decades to come, is more, or less, destructive than the perennial release of greenhouse gases which account for 25 per cent of the global warming trend, and the colonisation of land and resources for the purpose of defending the exclusive privilege of a declining minority of the global population to eat themselves to early, criminally unnecessary, expensive, and indulgent deaths.[97]

The reality that ecocide is a war crime, that it is psycho- or sociopathic behaviour within economic globalisation would seem to warrant further reflection on whether the overall project itself might not require, or at least encourage, these very crimes. De Tocqueville's observation that, 'in democracies nothing is greater or more brilliant than commerce,' because those who practised it did so 'not only for the sake of the profit it holds out to them, but for the love of the constant excitement occasioned by that pursuit,' is a pointer to a tradition of commentary which has remained constant.[98] Richard Hofstadter drew similar conclusions, but supplemented them with a hint of the predatory: 'business in America at its highest levels appealed not merely to greed and the lust for power but to the imagination; alluring to the builder, the gamester, and the ruler in men, it offered more sport than hunting and more power than politics.'[99] Similarly, economists, in which persons the study and acquisition of wealth are unified, did not escape excoriation, and by none less than John Maynard Keynes, when the subject of financial markets was the issue. In Paul Ormerod's account:

> Many individuals attracted to these markets, Keynes argued, are of a domineering and even psychopathic nature. If their energies could not find an outlet in money making, they might turn instead to careers involving open and wanton cruelty. Far better to have them absorbed on Wall Street or in the City of London than in organised crime.[100]

The problem with dichotomous thinking is simply that: in Keynes' view it was Wall Street *or* organised crime, as though the one precluded the other, as though General Butler's memoirs were not evidence of a resolution, a bi-presence. Consider the annual five million SAP-induced infant death-toll in Africa, Asia, and Latin America referred to earlier, and then add to it the material devastation reported by a UN advisory group: 'health systems are collapsing for lack of medicines, schools have no books, and universities suffer from a debilitating lack of library and laboratory facilities.' Consider, as well, that Latin Americans regard the financial flow from their continent as the 'worst plunder since Cortez.'[101] Finally, consider elite, Western reaction to this, as found in the writings of Jacques Attali, former head of the European Bank for Reconstruction and Development, and the US Presidential Commission on Integrated Long-term Strategy. For Attali, impoverished, immiserated Africa and Latin America are irredeemable 'millennial losers' and, thereby, threats to be guarded to be kept beyond the vale of European prosperity, whereas, for the Presidential Commission, they constitute an implacable and permanent post-Cold War source of conflict which has to be managed as a new addition to 'the menu of defence planning problems.'[102]

What we have in globalisation, therefore, is nothing less than (to use terms which are common to the very relevant work of Kelman and Hamilton) authorised and routinised dehumanisation, and sanctioned massacres; globally, it is John Kenneth Galbraith's war between the Haves and Have-nots in the mode of 'Charlie' Company's attack at My Lai on 16 March 1968.[103] Should this be thought an outrageous claim, reflect on whether Attali or the Presidential Commission could survive even a single murder charge (i.e. as opposed to the charge of genocide) under the US Uniform Code of Military Justice, Article 118 (murder), given that it provides for conviction if an accused:

1   has a premeditated design to kill;

2   intends to kill or inflict great bodily harm;

3   is engaged in an act which is inherently dangerous to others and evinces a wanton disregard for human life; or

4   is engaged in the perpetration or attempted perpetration of burglary, sodomy, rape, robbery, or aggravated arson.[104]

And if we further reflect on the fact that the discipline of neoclassical economics which is realised as the practice of globalisation, celebrates compartmentalisation of both human life and human beings by the technical distancing afforded by its rational-scientific approach to 'problems' which must by definition be 'solved' (to all of which its practitioners are devoutly loyal), the situation which comes to mind exactly is the type of totalitarian order which contemplated, and then ordered, the Holocaust and total war bombing offensives of World War II.[105]

7 Congruence

Economics as war

To subdue the enemy without fighting is the acme of skill.
Sun Tzu, *The Art of War*, 500 BC

That cannot be called war where men do not kill each other, cities are not sacked, nor territories laid waste.
Niccolo Machiavelli, *Istorie Fiorentine*, early sixteenth century

The nature of war consisteth not in actual fighting, but in the known disposition thereto during all the time there is no assurance to the contrary.
Thomas Hobbes, *Leviathan*, 1651

The fundamental principles upon which rest all good combinations of war have always existed.... These principles are unchangeable; they are independent of the nature of the arms employed, of times and places.
Henri Antoine de Jomini, *Traite des grandes operations militaires*, 1807

War therefore is an act of violence intended to compel our opponent to fulfil our will.
Carl Philip Gottlieb von Clausewitz, *Vom Kriege*, 1832

Economics is the continuation of war by other means.
Daniel Bell, cited by Samuel P. Huntington, 1991

War, evidently, is understood in remarkably different ways by its leading philosophers. All agree, however, that war is most frequently violent; most, quintessentially so. Similarly, there is a consensus that war is a strategy, an instrument of attainment – of territory, wealth, honour, or some other such political objective. And there is a widespread acknowledgment that the nature of war waged by particular states is determined by the nature of the state itself; that, in other words, war cannot be divorced from its social and political origins: guerrillas fight small wars using bands of armed irregulars, whereas developed nations prosecute industrialised mass slaughter. There is a natural tendency for available resources to be used to their utmost, political considerations permitting.

Modern economic theory and practice is no different. Indeed, it is the argument of this chapter that, if 'economics' were to be substituted for 'war', nothing in the above claims would lose its validity. Thus, though there are now substantial differences between the classical and neoclassical economists as to the dimensions of economics, both schools converge on its strategic, or instrumental status. Moreover economists would take no issue with the claim that the type of economics pursued by a state reflects its social and political nature, or that the economics in question will move to occupy the entire space of whatever market has been established. Where economists would no doubt discover error is in a claim that, though war is violent, economics cannot be, since the latter is defined as the activity of free and rational peoples in a free market, underpinned by the absence of war and the rule of law. But, as with many a 'discovery' in economics, this is at best a partial truth relying on an impoverished imagination for its status, or at worst, an indulgent consolation for those who, in the recesses of their neo-liberal consciences, suspect their own complicity in processes of destruction. Consider the brief, yet evocative vista of neo-liberal violence summoned up by Ricardo Trumper and Lynne Phillips:

> The neo-liberal discourse is quite straightforward: it attempts to reinstate the discourse of the primacy of capitalism as a form of life and of economic policy. It does so by giving new breath to previously discredited theories of the advantages of unencumbered capitalism, of completely free markets, and of comparative advantages. As well, it champions the importance of reduced state intervention in the economy, the privatisation of economic activities, and the cancellation of government-run social programs. It vehemently promotes the primacy and morality of competition and profit-seeking and equates freedom with freedom of ownership and business, while decrying unionisation as a monopoly practice....
>
> Put simply, neo-liberalism theorises and legitimises the capitalist counteroffensive of local conglomerates and of neo-liberalism – the rights of multinational corporations to do business anywhere regardless of borders, the welfare of the population, or environmental degradation.[1]

If this passage is not sufficiently specific as to the violence which abounds in neo-liberalism, recall that its origins lie in the philosophical reformulation of economic life as the pursuit of wealth in a world of scarce means, implying thereby that, since humankind's objectives are given, *a priori*, conflict necessarily follows. In tone and substance, this approach to economics is remarkably similar to the point of congruence with the classical approach to grand strategy, in peacetime as well as in wartime, defined by Edward Mead Earle in 1943 as being 'the art of controlling and utilising the resources of a nation ... to the end that its vital interests shall be effectively promoted and secured against enemies, actual, potential, or merely presumed,' and in a world in which (unsurprisingly) war is 'inherent.'[2]

Moreover, in a more immediate way, neo-liberalism might be understood as violent in terms of the consequences it produces by refusing to acknowledge that which it proclaims as a foundation, namely the global finitude of available resources. Certainly, on the one hand, it has constructed an entire discourse around the belief in the form of what Michael Pusey reports as 'a Darwinist relation between system and environment.' In parallel, however, its refusal to adapt to its own definition of the physical environment – indeed to the very environment itself – by advocating and pursuing *infinite* growth creates not only a 'violent rupture between nature and culture,' but the antithesis of the original, a 'model of the self-destroying system.'[3]

But it is no different in the 'inner environment' of the socio-political. It, too, is objectified, and its residual constituents from former times, such as 'church, remembered inheritance, extended family, and neighbourhood,' subjected to the corrosive forces of neo-liberal rationality in the assumption that their replacement, 'the market,' will provide the same conditions, resources, and levels of social stability and meaning that existed previously. In all, this is a virtually impossible task, since it is among neo-liberalism's perverse achievements that it has managed to increase the *a priori* objective, wealth, while systematically reducing employment, adhering in the process to David Ricardo's notorious 1819 absolute elevation of the former and disregard for the latter. Again, Pusey's characterisation of this process is most salient:

> In setting itself into this relation between the economic system and the social environment, the state apparatus [promoting neo-liberalism] takes on a form of rationalisation which looks more like *aggressive nihilism* than reason and which seems to endanger the reproduction of society itself.[4]

Thus, as closer inspection is undertaken, and as it is increasingly understood that the withdrawal of state protection for the vulnerable elements of society is required by neo-liberalism in its most dogmatic form, it is no coincidence that some critical economists have turned their interest to, and acquired their understandings from, the natural sciences which inspired it.[5] Given the interdependence of economic system and physical environment, and state and society, the Lotka–Volterra non-linear mathematical system which, *inter alia*, has been found so useful in analysing and understanding symbiotic relationships has demonstrated its considerable utility. Significantly, among its more notable achievements are contributions in the field of predatory biology.[6]

By insights such as these an appreciation emerges that classically defined war is not the only mass violence committed against states, societies, peoples, cultures, and the environment in the world today. Moreover, given the scope and intensity of neo-liberalism's destructiveness, which is recognised here in terms of self-destruction and annihilation, the suggestive case that modern economics is indistinguishable from classically defined war in so many of its manifestations is made. Do not these terms and insights recall processes every degree as destructive as Machiavelli's prescription, a disposition every degree as bellicose as Hobbes, tactics and strategies every degree as instrumental as Clausewitz's, and a theoretical basis every degree as universalist as Jomini's? And is not economics' successful evasion of being seen more widely in Bell's formulation war due to its having finessed its domination in obedience to Sun Tzu, by, more precisely, putting the outcome of resistance for most people so beyond doubt that fighting is unnecessary? In other words, though the form of war might change, the conclusion remains that the phenomena in question are, for all of that, war.

This said, the enterprise of discovering congruences is a fraught one. As Oliver MacDonagh observed: 'Nothing is easier, or more historically debauching, than to manufacture historical analogues from disparate sets of material; and the oftener one particularises, the more likely one is to err.'[7] Hence, the category of congruence is not to be understood in terms of Euclidian exactitude. That would be to understand the propositions regarding a broad correspondence between economics and war in a manner reliant upon identical, but politically insignificant detail – which is to say, pedantically – when what is intended, and legitimately intended at that, is an understanding which comes from seeing anew a normalised, sanitised, theory-as-practice: through the lens of what is commonly regarded as abnormal and obscene, the theory and practice of war.

GENERAL CONGRUENCES

If congruence is understood in two ways – as deriving from both a broad correspondence each to the other, and in terms of a common, comparable relationship to the Enlightenment – then the most appropriate beginning for this analysis lies in the more proximate origins of the dominant theories of modern war, and new economics, as they have been articulated over the last 170 years and 100 years, respectively. Both arose as consequences of earlier scientific revolutions fused with historical experience, and proceeded to their most developed, or contemporary, forms, after a period of unpopularity, catalysed by the exigencies of Cold War politics, though at different times, and under different stimuli. More specifically, the works of Carl von Clausewitz and Antoine Henri Jomini were philosophically inspired by the Enlightenment (although Clausewitz was also influenced by the German Movement that was hostile to it), and the opportunities its ideas allowed for understanding the Napoleonic Wars, Each enjoyed separate and distinct periods of international prominence at the expense of the other in the period between 1820 (approximately) and 1918, and were rehabilitated in the early nuclear age to satisfy different requirements.[8]

Similarly, though neoclassical economics emerged in the late nineteenth century as an emulation of both Newtonian physics and the industrial wonders it wrought, it lay fallow, particularly in the United States, in the face of the greater appeals generated by New Deal 'progressivism' (which favoured central planning, corporatism, and welfare payments to the needy) in the context of the benefits offered by a 'permanent war economy.' It was turned to only in the late 1970s as the global and domestic decline of the US induced the revocation of the previously tolerant attitudes towards ameliorative and regulative measures.[9]

Interestingly, in both bodies of theory – war and economic – the principal contending theories were at one on their respective central issues, the normality of war and capitalism, yet both were diametrically opposed philosophically. For Clausewitz, Jomini's proclamation of a timeless, universal military theory was, quite simply, illegitimate, ignorant, and unreal, whereas, within neoclassical theory, the opposition is between a declaratory position in which a totally 'free market' operates, and an operational policy which is little more than an offensive against business regulation and the rights of labour, and the defence of the state-produced status quo as regards the incentives and privileges of capital – military Keynesianism, for example.[10] In economics, as in war, the revisionary catalyst was a crisis in, or challenge to, either the global dominance of the West in general, or the dominant political-economic regime of the United States in particular, or both. To appropriate John Kenneth Galbraith, serious theoretical endeavour requires, first, that there be a serious political problem.

That there were problems was never in doubt; indeed, they were expressed in terms – Containment, Massive Retaliation, Balance of Terror, Mutual Assured Destruction – which connoted a purpose of truly historical, even apocalyptic, dimensions. For the war theorists, it was the need to theorise war in a manner appropriate to the nuclear age, to which end Jomini's operational thesis that war could be studied, understood, and conducted as a science via knowledge of its unchanging rules and mathematical formulae served the interests of nuclear deterrence and its game-theoretic foundations. But Clausewitzian philosophy had even more scope: fundamentally 'realist' in its understanding of the state, its sovereignty, its power aspirations, and above all, the normality of war in the relations between states, its resurrection was determined by the guidance it offered on both the relationship between war and policy, and, most notably, limited war – in other words, on the type of wars which Western powers, especially the United States and its allies, were determined to fight in those arenas (e.g. the Third World) not directly covered by theories of a Jominian character.[11] War theorising, therefore, was bifurcated: on the one hand it provided the intellectual rationale for a type of war which, hopefully, would never be fought, and on the other, it justified the undoubted willingness of the US to use force in the pursuit of national interests under conditions thought unlikely to lead to nuclear war.

With the exception of the contradiction between the declaratory and operational variants of the same (neoclassical) theory, economics admitted less tensions between its constituents. In fact it is probably more accurate to describe the comparison between significant parts of the two bodies of thought as one of inversion. Whereas, from abstract principles of human behaviour, nuclear deterrence theorised a war which, hopefully, would never come, neo-liberalism, from the same equally abstract principles of human behaviour, sought the establishment of a condition which had never been. Moreover, the embrace of the previously unpopular doctrine of neo-liberalism was remarkably similar to the extent that it was a response to the domestic and global challenges to extant regimes of US economic hegemony in the Cold War. Thus, while each body of thought contained a speculative, or fantastic objective (deterrence/pure neoclassicism) without direct correspondence in the other, each was also derived from a common abstraction, and existed alongside a justification for strategies of immediate significance (limited war/the privileging of capital) which had identical, hegemonic aims, and thus, imparted a definite unity to the pairing. In the era of the Cold War, both exalted, as they defended, capitalism and possessive individualism, on the basis of axioms derived from a set of initial assumptions within a discourse of human behaviour dominated by a naive fundamentalism which accepts Newtonian science as the basis of truth even in the political realm.

That natural science had begun to reject this form of fundamentalism towards the end of the nineteenth century, and was adamant about it by the 1930s, was irrelevant; indeed, to develop the critique any further around this point is to collude in the disingenuousness of which is at issue. Neither in war nor economics was the relevant theorising about significantly more than what John Kenneth Galbraith calls the Economic Accommodation, and Alan Ryan derides as 'the [Panglossian] politics of business as usual.' Within them both is found the reconciliation of intellectual accounts with economic and political interest, and, in an overarching way, the comfortable and conservative consolation that the particular state of the world in which the West in general and its rich in particular enjoy extraordinary privileges at the expense of the great majority of people on the planet has been ordained by an unappealable history.[12]

If this implies a somewhat extreme formulation, and such a formulation is willingly conceded, it should be understood that it is an extremism consistent with the theories in question. In Clausewitzian theory, war, by its very nature as an act of violence which is intended to compel one belligerent to fulfil the will of another, necessarily entails not only escalation, but a movement towards extremes. Negatively put, the introduction of moderation is an absurdity. Accordingly, war is profoundly predisposed to the absolute, being contradicted in this course by the influences of politics. Of itself, war extends its application of violence to the entire territory of the enemy, and the enemy's population, even while being directed by a strong central authority.[13] Moreover, as the tendency towards extremes becomes pronounced, absolute war tends to dominate and regulate every realm of life, as in Aron's assertion that: 'Total mobilisation approaches the totalitarian order.'[14] The question that need not be pursued, therefore, is whether neo-liberal economic theory, which subordinates the individual rationality to that of Rational Economic Man, the nation and the state to the single criterion of competitiveness in the global economy, and disfigures all forms of human behaviour but the most conservative, could possibly be an exception to the same tendency and its destructive consequences.

Nor is there difference to be discerned in the self-absolution which absolutism grants for these consequences. In both cases moral culpability is rendered soluble by 'right' intention, philosophical certainty, and, ultimately, the recourse to 'paradox' – as though self-contradiction possessed a sacralising power akin to the indulgences which the medieval church bestowed upon the crusaders. Thus, the permission to commit certain otherwise proscribed acts – mass killing foremost among them – is enjoined with not only the forgiveness of the act itself, but also the remission of temporal punishment which it warrants. The unacknowledged basis for such casuistry is the principle of the double effect which holds that, when faced with a choice between evils, the lesser may be chosen without prejudice to one's moral standing.

In war and economics the general form this indulgence takes is the 'healing-killing paradox.'[15] In fact, twentieth-century war is littered with claims that the evil which has resulted from some of its more horrific forms was an 'unintended' consequence of the need to achieve a certain laudable strategic objective, even where, to accept this disclaimer, it requires a concomitant idiocy (classically defined) of commonly used weaponry and its probable, more often inescapable, consequences. Nevertheless, in the period between the World Wars, air power theorists of the like of Giulio Douhet, Billy Mitchell, and Hugh Trenchard captured the spirit prevailing among them when he argued that, because it was necessary in war to break an enemy's means of resistance, it was also necessary to extend war to 'objectives selected as most likely to achieve this end,' and that meant 'centres of production, transportation, and communication,' which, if it resulted in civilian deaths, would lead to a speedy conclusion of hostilities.[16] Strategic war, in this light, was heralded as more humane than previous modes; more, it underwrote conventional deterrence to a significantly increased degree.[17] Virtually identical views were held among British and US air power policy-makers and commanders in World War II, with the additional view being argued that it reduced the level of casualties in the ground war which would otherwise need to be fought.[18] Of the last-mentioned rationale, the dropping of the atomic bombs on Hiroshima and Japan are the most obvious, if also the most problematic, strategic examples; the Holocaust, without doubt, is the most obvious and notorious, period.[19]

As innumerable accounts of the imposition of neo-liberal economic theory-as-practice attest to, precisely the same exegesis is employed in the justification of comparable levels of death and destruction. Can it be seriously argued, for example, that the certain and modernist attitude struck by Gines de Sepulveda in his *De la causa de la contra los indios* of 1550, with its antecedents going all the way back to ancient Greece, is other than the continuing spirit of global neo-liberalism today?

> This war and conquest are just first of all because these barbaric, uneducated, and inhuman [Indians] are by nature servants. Naturally, they refuse the governance which more prudent, powerful, and perfect human beings offer and which would result in their great benefit (*magnas commoditates*). By natural right and for the good of all (*utriusque bene*), the material ought to obey the form, the body the soul, the appetite the reason, the brutes the human being, the woman her husband, the imperfect the perfect, and the worse the better.[20]

When, subsequently, Sepulveda locates the root cause of the Indians' barbarity in their culture, with its ignorance of private possessions and subjective liberty, and its overall refusal to capitulate to the ways of the *conquistador*, do we not discern in this rationale, as does Dussel, 'the definitive and classical' articulation of the myth of modernity? Consider the argumentative progress of the *conquistador* case that: (1) European civilisation is superior to all others; (2) the abandonment of those aspects of a culture defined as barbaric by the superior civilisation through, and in favour of, European civilisation, implies progress, development, and emancipation for that culture; (3) European domination and its binary partner, indigenous anguish, is, therefore, doubly necessary – in the first instance as pedagogic violence whose means are justified by the ends, and in the second, as the necessary price to be paid by the indigenous culture for its current civilisational progress and previous 'culpable immaturity;' (4) the European, therefore, remains not only innocent, but virtuous in this process; and (5) the victims, having had the opportunity to cede their barbarism, on first acquaintance, by persuasion and voluntarily, have only themselves to blame for the consequences of what is, manifestly, their own irrationality in the face of modernity's bounties.[21] Is it not, in its own terms, another case of the healing-killing paradox; is it not a virtually identical prefiguring of the ethical evasion required by the Holocaust and strategic bombing by some four centuries, and does it not propagate what Dussel defines as a '*sacrificial paradigm* which calls for the sacrifice of the victim of violence for human progress'?[22]

Objections that the connection between the *conquistadors* and neo-liberalism must surely be attenuated by the elisions of time, that distinctions must be made between the adoption of neo-liberalism within, and between, Western democracies, and its concomitant adoption within and between the rest of the world, and that the incidence and scale of 'anguish' is of a different – which is to say, a significantly diminished – order, constitute similar refusals to contemplate the logical consequences for what Toulmin described as the modernist obsession with beginning again from a 'clean slate.' As regards the possibility of attenuation, it is instructive to turn to a recent, quite typical account by D. C. North, a leading exponent of the international variant of neo-liberalism, who in the manner of his identification of the perfect and the imperfect, cannot but recall Sepulveda:

> [The] modern Western world provides abundant evidence of markets that work and even approximate the neoclassical ideal ... Third World countries are poor because the institutional constraints define a set of pay-offs to political/economic activity that do not encourage productive activity.[23]

Moreover, if Eurocentrism is understood to have been supplanted in terms of its global dominance by American Exceptionalism, which, try as it might, contained from its earliest formulations, and retains to this day, irreducible residues of *conquistador* thinking, then reservations about the relevance of Columbian ideology to neo-liberalism are misplaced. And there is probably no better example of the fusion of such atavism with current pretensions than Francis Fukuyama's consoling paean to the United States at the very time its most astute observers were discovering its serious decline:

> What we may be witnessing is not just the end of the Cold War, or the passing of a particular period of postwar history, but the end of history as such: that is, *the end point of mankind's ideological evolution and the universalisation of Western liberal democracy as the final form of human government.*[24]

As Mehmet observes, what distinguishes this passage is not only its 'total dismissal of Islamic, Confucian, or non-Western cultures, which, after all, constitute the great majority of humanity,' but the presumption that they must disappear because other, *Western*, constructions such as Marxism–Leninism have lost their footing.[25]

What is worse, there is a view in certain elite circles that the transformation from (Sepulveda's) 'barbarism' to Euro-American civilisation is simply not possible for the great majority of 'barbarians.' Thus, in the formulations of the former head of the European Bank for Reconstruction and Development, Jacques Attali, the poor of the southern hemisphere are, in neo-liberal discourse, to be consigned to the role of 'millennial losers.' Africa is to be a 'lost continent,' while Latin America is to slide into 'terminal poverty' – their peoples having no greater prospect than 'migrating from place to place looking for a few drops of what we have in Los Angeles, Berlin, or Paris.'[26] Nor is this forecast alone in its profound pessimism: the US Presidential Commission on

Integrated Long-Term Strategy is at one with it, especially as it relates to the most likely outcome – conflict with Third World peoples by way of a 'form of warfare [mainly terrorism] in which "the enemy" is more or less omnipresent and unlikely ever to surrender.'[27] In a series of profoundly disturbing lectures, the distinguished statesman and writer, Conor Cruise O'Brien, likens such forms of thinking to that which can prevail in 'a guarded palace in a city gripped by the plague' – which even current survivors hear 'a frolicsome demon, gaily whispering in [their] ear: "You're damned!"'[28]

Concurrently, however, the North is subject to beleaguerment from within as its own populations are reduced in their circumstances; indeed, this process is already underway – as, *inter alia*, the rise of crime, incarceration, state law enforcement and private security establishments, and the xenophobic right in the developed West testifies. For these early casualties of the 'coming world order,' neo-liberal theory-as-practice is equally the origin of their condition as it is in the South. Where once their ability to obtain paid employment which would satisfy reasonable demands of necessity and comfort was a right, it is now the case that their skills, and their attitudes towards the redundancy of these skills in an automating, globalising, world, has reduced them to the status of 'internal barbarians'– the principal difference being that, even if they accept their status like Third World subjects, there is no modernist cultural transformation available for their further 'development' or 'progress' not only because they already reside in that end state, but it is precisely that state which has rendered their present without a future.

This, to emphasise the point, is precisely the conclusion guaranteed by a discourse which valorises 'the economy,' the political order, and the social order, in that order, and then discloses its full intent by representing society, with its traditional notion that it is a subordinating variable, as 'some sort of stubbornly resisting sludge, as a "generic externality" and even an idealised opponent of "the economy."'[29] This 'death of society', no less, is the conclusion guaranteed by thinking imperially in the first place: the incubus which now increasingly oppresses parts once defined as the Self, commenced life as the colonisation of the Other (who was also territorially distinct), but the dominant understanding of modernity homogenised the two even as it exhausted the need for subjects. The unrequired components could then only be thought of in neo-Darwinian terms – a once necessary, but now economically redundant, class, like an army from an earlier age, whose campaigns are remembered but not honoured, and whose growth and decay have begun to threaten the remaining, but shrinking comity. Should this be thought an exaggerated formulation it is worth recalling that it is not to the biologist, Charles Darwin, but the sociologist beloved of economists in America's so-called Gilded Age, Herbert Spencer, that we owe the term 'survival of the fittest'; and it is to his most distinguished disciple, William Graham Sumner, that we owe the advice that 'millionaires are a product of natural selection' whose wealth and power is socially beneficial.[30]

In these circumstances, the underlying 'givens' of both international relations realism and neo-liberalism are virtually identical – anarchy in a world of primary actors (states and transnational corporations) in which war between them in the pursuit of profit and power is a natural state. In the interstate realm it is, obviously, the recourse to alliances and balance-of-power, orchestrated by great powers, which *homo strategicus* pursues in an attempt to deter would-be aggression; in economics, the domesticated market solution is sought through not dissimilar arrangements whereby collusive associations of enormous enterprises are, formally or informally, brought into being to dominate, where they do not monopolise, the production and distribution of products. Such cartels, or trusts, formal or informal, maintain, it is held, 'equilibrium' and, thus, equate to the Triple Alliance and the Triple *Entente* of the late nineteenth and early twentieth centuries, for example.

At the same time, these are practices which cannot but offend the primacy of *raison d'etat* (as understood in the Treaty of Westphalia) and render spurious the 'free market.' In particular, the economic variants proscribe serious, or real, competition between enterprises on deterrence-based grounds, namely, as John Kenneth Galbraith derisively frames it, out of 'a sensitive concern for the action that the prices they set will precipitate from their rivals.'[31] Explicitly, therefore, the activity in question is a form of managed, or suppressed, conflict in the guise of its opposite, a deception which is covered adequately by the Hobbesian definition of war in terms of 'the known disposition thereto.' In other words, it conceals itself only until the very moment that the war-prepared-for, and the hostile takeover planned for, discloses its 'known disposition,' on which occasion both alliance and cartel are, as revealed by John Vasquez's work on the former, contributory causes, rather than systemic inhibitors, of that which they seek to avoid.[32] Suggestively, then, they may be regarded as instruments of peace and perfect competition, respectively, only in a Biercean sense.

This is especially the case at the level of hyper-threat to the system in general – that posed by the superpowers (and their systems of alliances) and the large transnational, or multinational, corporations. Accordingly, while it is as true to state that nuclear war has so far been avoided, as it is to affirm that a great many transnational corporations have continued to exist for close to a century, the theoretical justifications for both deterrence and general competitive equilibrium are torn. This is not to say that alliances, or cartels, are without effect; rather, it is to say that, notwithstanding all attempts to bring them within the ambit of the respective theories derived from abstract assumptions about human nature, they remain not only obstinately outside these theories, but with an obstinacy matched only by the refusal of economic and strategic theorists to admit their virtually religious adherence to a profound contradiction. As Thomas Balogh wrote: 'The modern history of economic theory is a tale of the evasions of reality.'[33]

This denial of reality, of course, has also to be denied in the war theory of the nuclear powers, as in economics of oligopoly, because, to admit to it on the scale that is practised would in most circumstances constitute fulfilment of the classic definition of madness. Accordingly, in the face of a mounting body of evidence that nuclear deterrence theory is seriously deficient,[34] madness is evaded by the intrusion of the concept of 'existential deterrence'[35] – which pays homage to the view that, notwithstanding these deficiencies, it is possible to attribute the lack of superpower war to a general uneasiness about their possession by an enemy whose intentions are ultimately unknowable. The corresponding evasion by economics is the 'as if' recourse, meaning that it is essentially irrelevant whether or not certain necessary and sufficient conditions for competitive general equilibrium are met, if the outcome can be said to accord with the predictions of the theory. That, in both cases, this equates predictions based on the ideal with predictions based on conditions which profane the ideal, on no higher authority than it's being 'acceptable in practice' to neoclassical theorists, is thought not to disqualify either the evasions or the comparisons.[36] Not for the first time, therefore, the preposterous nature of a problematic and response defined within Hobbesianism is borne out; and not for the first time is it deserving of the Lockean ridicule:

> As if when men, quitting the state of Nature, entered into Society, they agreed that all of them but one should be under the constraint of laws; but that he should still retain all the liberty of the state of Nature, increased with power, and made licentious with impunity. This is to think that men are so foolish that they can take care to avoid what mischiefs may be done to them by polecats or foxes, but are content, nay think it safety, to be devoured by lions.

By implication, what is at stake is the standing of the theories of war and economics here canvassed, albeit within their respective but congruent discourses, as intellectual constructions. At the mundane level, both are clearly transfixed by game theory, especially two-person game theory, in a world demarcated by the 'givens' of mutual antagonism, scarce resources and zero-sum solutions. In such a world, as Charles Hampden-Turner characterises it, both sides will 'naturally' – which is to say, predictably and defensively – engage in behaviour that is typical of a 'large scale neurosis, wherein the two sides, neatly separable, mutually frustrating and rigidified by fear will respond predictably and defensively to each other's inputs.'[37] Creativity, trust, and enhancing relationships are, therefore, immediate casualties if this circumstance persists; indeed, fidelity to the models of the prisoner's dilemma in strategy and neo-liberal rational economic behaviour guarantees such an outcome.

The difficulty for economic theory, however, is that, miserable as these outcomes are, they tend to conform to Tolstoy's observation that, whereas all happy marriages are happy in the same way, each unhappy one is unhappy in a particular way. Expressing the problem another way, despite endless 'applications' neither body of theory possesses a record of prediction which justifies its pretensions. Strategic theory failed, of course, in the case of the dissolution of the Cold War, and the break up of the Soviet Union and the Eastern Bloc – in other words, its *raison d'être*. Economic theory's inadequacies are, collectively, of a similar magnitude although less confined to a single event. From the vantage point of the 1970s, it had failed to see the following developments in the previous twenty-plus years: the rise of the multinational corporation, the rise of Japan as a major economic power, and the emergence of inflation as a major problem of all industrial nations. A similar exercise conducted in the mid-1990s reveals that the vision is little changed: neither the decline in productivity suffered by all Western powers in the early 1970s, nor the striking loss of global economic leadership by the US, nor the more recent Japanese recession, nor the ERM-induced turmoil in Europe was foreseen.[38]

The issue, though, is not that the failure of the theories in question is evidence of an all-too-human lack of the gift of prophecy; rather, it is whether or not their standing might be more appropriately understood as something other than that which they claim to be themselves. More significantly, might there not be advantage in seeing them as belief systems, as theories of life of a particular type – the type being fundamental-religious? This should not surprise: no way of thinking can successfully evade its intellectual forerunners, and, in the case of modernity, a significant component of the carry-through was the need for certainty which religion provided. Religious, no less, because their most important aspects of both belief and certainty turn upon appeals to the invisible, which are, ultimately, no more nor less than the explanations-by-mystification which serve in so many areas of conservative politics.

McGeorge Bundy's 'existential deterrence' – the indefinable fear which excludes all doubts from the rationale for the possession of nuclear weapons which the scientific case cannot caulk – is, thus, but fitting company for the 'unwritten Constitution,' the 'mystery' of the Church, the 'magic' of the monarchy, the 'secret reserves' of insurance companies, the 'invisible earnings' of the financial service sector, and the 'hidden hand' of the free market. And, significantly, John Kenneth Galbraith writes of the popular belief that economists are priest-like by virtue of having privileged access to the 'assumed mystery of money,' of the 'near biblical standing' some economic theories require; indeed, of the 'necessity for faith' which George Gilder urged upon those of his readers who were unpersuaded by his arguments.[39]

Religious by way of being seamless belief systems, as well. In nuclear deterrence this was never so apparent as when, in 1985, the New Zealand Labour government led by Prime Minister David Lange refused to approve the visit of the USS *Buchanan* to a New Zealand port on the grounds that it could not determine whether the vessel accorded with the country's nuclear-free legislation and policies. In doing so, it sought to achieve the twin security goals of remaining an ally of the US, but rejecting nuclear defence in general by rejecting in particular the previously understood, but unwritten, 'right' of the United States to have elements of its navy visit its allies' ports without informing the host as to the nuclear status of the vessel(s) in question.

For the United States, New Zealand was held to be in default of obligations inherent in the ANZUS Treaty, despite the fact that the wider purpose of that treaty was the defence of democracy, and hence the distinct probability that democratic pluralism would, from time to time, and place to place, determine that variations in the embrace of informal extensions to the treaty would need to be tolerated. The argument applied was not dissimilar to that which fundamentalist theologians deploy: so heinous is the enemy, so grave is the danger, so imperative is unity, that the belief system cannot be allowed to be seen as a cafeteria from which choices can be made within the dictates of faith without inducing a crisis in the alliance as a whole. Individual conscience in the form of the sovereign right to dissent was, accordingly, declared to be intolerable, and therefore, denied.[40] Dissent, then, met with the full fury reserved for the apostate (even if such an actor happens to have been, in virtually all other alliance matters, a model subordinate partner): excommunication in the form of the suspension of the security provisions of the treaty.

Although numerous areas of economic theory-as-practice suggest themselves, the principal contemporary example is to be found in the toleration of national differences by the World Trade Organization (WTO), the economic equivalent of the United Nations, whose decisions on the interpretation of the GATT are final and unappealable. As Brecher and Costello note, its powers of dispute settlement, exercised in secret, not only authorise retaliation, but also pre-empt:

democratic self-government at local, national, regional, and global levels by defining such matters as environmental and consumer protection, labour law, worker health and safety protection, food safety policies, national industrial planning, plant closing legislation, and restrictions on foreign ownership of industries as 'non-tariff barriers to trade.'[41]

As the formal, institutional, realisation of neo-liberal economics, the WTO, therefore, bears the same relation to the expanded GATT doctrine of global free trade as the Western alliance system to nuclear deterrence theory, and the Curia to the Roman Catholic Church, their appellate status recognised in terms of the last-mentioned, in the saying: *Roma locuta est, causa finita est,* [42] the main difference being that the authority to pronounce infallibly on matters of right and wrong behaviour is derived from scientism in the case of the former, and from the New Testament in the case of the latter. This distinction is, in any case, beside the point: under all three dispensations difference is stigmatised as dissent, and dissent is punished. In formal terms it is a question of beliefs and principles; of the certainty which reposes in received truths, and their perpetuation; and of the salvation which is extended by faithfully following commandments and precepts, authoritatively interpreted: of creed, classically defined, in other words.

What the Council of Nicaea (called by the Emperor Constantine in 325 to settle the doctrinal dispute between the Arians and the Orthodox on the person of Christ) was to Christian belief, the Uruguay Round of 1986, which embarked on a new commitment to globalising the economy under conditions which were propitious to corporate interests in the West in general, and the United States in particular, is to Free Trade. Where the former produced the Nicene Creed, the latter delivered the GATT of 1994, and thereby, the WTO. To remain faithful to the metaphor, they conjoin a new doxology with irredentist hope, both being thought to demand euphony in commitment as in expression, thus explaining why confessional differences are so intolerable. To venture one final congruency, both of these momentous gatherings occur in times of crisis, and it is not at all fanciful to discern in each response the injunctive desperation of the requiem's *De Profundis.* [43]

War and economics by these measures are not only congruent, but discourses of mass violence derived from modernist certainty, resting on, and ultimately requiring, religious discipline. For many, this is no doubt another paradox of modernity, being the exact conjunction of dogma and force which provoked the original Cartesian project of transcending the destructive excesses of religious belief through scientific certainty at the end of the Thirty Years War; for others, it is the equally assured, logical conclusion of the same thing.

8 *Romanita*

Reformation and Counter-Reformation in neo classical Economics/neo-liberalism (Economics-as-religion)

REVIEWING THE PRESENT

The present and recent past are best understood as *religiose* moments. This is to say that, in the world's increasing embrace of neo-liberalism (and its core the theories of neoclassical economics) over the last two decades or more, for its political-economic salvation, there was a recognition of both grievous error, in the form of extensive state intervention in the economy, and the need to excise it and return to the purity of the free market as informed by the theories of neoclassical economics. Essentially it involved a classical return, *ad pristinum statum* (the state as it should originally have been), and to the *status rectitudinus* (the state as it should be). At first, and at best, this was no more than an insurgency against palpably failed and failing regimes – in some cases corrupt regimes – in the name of individual conscience, but it rapidly became, or at least was represented as, something more: the penitential struggle for redemption by a contrite people following their fall. Politically and intellectually, this mandated no less than a search, or, to be more precise, a rediscovery; and almost inescapably, because of the nature of the movement in question, it brought into being what Eugene Honee describes as a 'double regularity of distortion and discovery.'[1] Such was the character of political-economic reformation theory and practice from (say) the early 1970s until the advent of the Thatcher government in the United Kingdom, and the Reagan Administration in the United States of America. To the extent that it was imbued with the spirit and cast of mind of Martin Luther and John Calvin, at its inception at least, the project is to be understood as Reformation.

To the further extent, however, that it fused the Protestant commitment to taking God (the market) very seriously, with the Catholic commitment to taking the Church (the profession of economics) very seriously indeed, the historical character of this *religiose* moment in extension is more precisely understood as Restoration and Counter-Reformation.[2] Restoration comes to mind in the understanding of the World Trade Organization (WTO) as the re-establishment of a universal Church on the basis of a parliamentary convention underwritten – indeed, strongly persuaded – by force. Whereas the previous occasion, in the early 1660s, had secured the English monarchy, restored the established (Anglican) Church, and with it, church government by bishops, at the same time as it ensured defeat for contending confessions, and increased the political power of the propertied classes, the latter similarly legitimates the administration of global trade and the unequal distribution of global wealth in favour of the already industrialised states through the Uruguay Round of the GATT, with its ladder of escalatory sanctions against all dissenters.

Even this framing falls slightly short of the acute understanding that is made possible by persisting in the historical correspondence. The WTO, we know, was established for the very purpose of interpreting the Word as laid out in the GATT texts, and conversely, to prosecute any attempts to introduce, reintroduce, or tolerate competing or co-existent political-economic ideas and practices. Functionally, it is to be little distinguished from the Reformation rejection, and then anathematisation of, the Hellenic dimension of Renaissance culture, scholastic philosophy, and the greater part of post-apostolic Christianity. But, of even greater significance, its uncompromising nature is entirely consistent with that regime of confessional imperialism known in this century as the *romanita* – which, defined narrowly, is the spirit or influence of the authority of the Roman Catholic Church, and the acceptance of papal policies. Its ways pre-date this usage, of course, and are, accordingly, as well known as they are historically effective and politically infamous: in the words of Morris West, legislation, admonition, fiat, sustained throughout *by magisterium, auctoritas, potestas* – the office, the authority, the power to use them both. In terms of a broader political and social understanding, however, it is a form of atavism, a reinscription of an ancient habit of 'prescribing a juridical solution to every human dilemma, and then stamping every solution with a sacred character under the seal of the *magisterium*.'[3] By any comprehension it is a return to rule by a form of political-economic absolutism.

Dogmatic renewal, conservative and reactionary in its hue, appears, therefore, to define the particular character of the present. Borrowing from Richard Tarnas, we can see that the proponents of neoclassical economics/neo-liberalism, like those of the Reformation, successfully waged their insurgencies against all incumbent regimes in the name of personal freedom, but, in their success, they institutionalised and routinised their vision – thus incarcerating it.[4] What began, in declaratory and philosophical terms at least, as a celebration of individual conscience, became a temporal power which is served by, and is dependent upon, a belief system. Indeed, this was inevitable since the rise of neoclassical economics coincided with, and was primarily dependent on, the restorative needs of the United States. And, because of its absolutism, dialogue with the *romanita*, like the dialogue between the various, competing absolutisms regnant in Europe between the posting of Luther's 95 theses on the door of Palast Church in Wittenberg in 1517 and the Peace of Westphalia 131 years later, conforms to Stephen Toulmin's graphic portrayal of the latter years in this period: 'active, bloody, and strident.'[5]

That the theory and practice of neoclassical economics should be identified as religiose should not surprise; nor, at some levels of analysis should it be seen as original. Writing of their 'inability to see government as the justifiable force of the citizen,' and their blindness to 'an actively organised pool of disinterest called the public good,' John Ralston Saul refers to the 'religious devotion' which market theorists such as Friedrich von Hayek brought to their work.[6] Notably, from within the profession, a respected econometrician, Edward E. Leamer, wrote two articles on his own specialist area which unambiguously point to an identification with religious belief and the clergy. Thus he locates within econometrics a comfortable dichotomy between a 'celibate priesthood of statistical theorists, on the one hand, and a legion of inveterate sinner-data analysts, on the other.'[7] Both, indeed the whole profession it seems, in its pursuit of scientific objectivity, have fallen prey to a 'false idol.'[8] He continues in this vein:

> The priests are empowered to draw up lists of sins and are revered for the special talents they display. Sinners are not expected to avoid sins; they need only confess their errors openly....

> Even more amazing was the transmogrification of particular individuals who wantonly sinned in the basement [where economic modelling was carried out] and metamorphosed into the highest of high priests as they ascended to the third floor [where economic theory was taught].[9]

Nevertheless, what might be seen as both original and politically potent is the casting of economics within a sustained analogy with the Reformation and its *alter ego*, the *romanita*. To do so is to discern, first, the strength of their common objective – the ultimately futile compulsion to know the mind of God, and its economic equivalent, the Market – in effect to accommodate to a more sophisticated form of ignorance. It is, then, to understand the common persistence of what John D. Caputo defines, in the context of Catholicism, as Eucharistic Hermeneutics: in the New Testament, the accuracy and authenticity of the divine plane are effected by the celebration of the Eucharist, itself a repetition of the Last Supper and the post-Easter appearance of Christ to the Apostles on the road to Emmaus (and his interpretation of the scriptures with great clarity[10]); in these times, suggestively, it is the conflation of the US victories in World War II and the Cold War which provide the redemptive auto-hermeneutics in the texts of Western economics. (Here, Luther's rediscovery of the Judaic purity in early Christianity is complemented by economics' rediscovery of the late nineteenth- and early twentieth-century neoclassical texts in the sense that both were prized as the basis for intellectual, spiritual, and later, material, independence). Finally, it is be alive to the duality of Eucharistic Hermeneutics because in its ability to silence the dissenter within the idiom of her or his choice, dissent is broken upon the back of dogma. For this Caputo reserves the term 'terroristic hermeneutics.'[11]

Even then, it becomes necessary to acknowledge not just the correspondences between the two historical movements, but also the inversions which make a mockery of neoclassical economics' pretensions to being, in any real sense, a reformation. It is to understand that, just as the Reformation declared itself to be about the liberation of the individual conscience, it contained within itself a totalising evangelical impulse no different to that which imbues modernity in general, and capitalism in particular. The conviction that salvation is to be achieved through a certain type of confession is unlikely to be modest, especially in ages in which a communications revolution is being effected.[12] Neither a Church proclaiming to be One, Holy, Catholic, and Apostolic, nor another preoccupied with humanity's nature and God's judgment, should be thought other than superficially different on this question. By the same criterion, neither should an economic belief system thought to have the same salvational powers as both of these declared they had. That this required no change by the Catholic Church (since it was by definition universal), and an emulation of it, evangelically speaking, by the Reformation churches, was, in a way, logical: both believed the other to be in error, to be risking the mortal souls of their co-religionists by advocating heresy. In economics' arrogation to itself of the totality of economic inquiry, when it covers only the mainstream, authorised, neoclassical study of capitalist economic theory and practice, we can find, coterminously, the arrogance of Rome, in harness with apostolic zealotry.

Significantly, in the case of both the Reformation and the turn to doctrinaire neoclassical economics, closure was imposed but for profoundly different reasons. The effect of the Treaty of Westphalia, which followed decades of war, made a major concession to difference as well as conscience by allowing the rulers of Europe not only to establish the denomination of their respective territories, but also to be indifferent to the views of other creeds in other territories; the Uruguay Round of the GATT, however, preceded as it was by over four decades of a Cold War defined by a neo-Augustinian dualism, effected an inversion by restoring at the global level what the Peace of Westphalia, and before it, the Treaty of Augsburg (1555), and the Edict of Nantes (1598), had been studiously determined to avoid – an absolute moral sovereign.

Such are the dominant colourings, shapes, and themes of the turn to neo-liberalism/ neoclassical economics which demand greater attention if the dangers inherent in it for global politics are to be understood. In turn, therefore, seven facets within four foci of traverse from reformation to *romanita* will be addressed: the first three – the rejection of error, reformation, and renewal – are encompassed within a project that might be seen summarily as the resumption of the divine. The analysis then embraces the role and importance of thinking and acting as a religion, of which the resumption of the divine is symptomatic for the religious and economic movements undertaking it. Indeed, within this specific focus on the religious nature of economics, both are unsurprisingly integrated to the significant extent that they induce theological and political-economic theory and practice of a conservative character. Relatedly, but given separate and particular emphasis in this context is the regime of terroristic silence which is threatened, and actually imposed, should a dilated sense of dissent exceed the contours of a misleadingly described free will and individual conscience. It follows that the paradoxes which reformation gives rise to, and their attendant inversions and discontinuities which exist beyond them, comprise an appropriate and necessary termination. When taken together with the other six foci, they make plain that what has occurred is less reformation – in the common contemporary sense of improvement or progress – as a return to a discredited and unacceptable former state of affairs.[13]

THE RESUMPTION OF THE DIVINE: REJECTION OF ERROR, REFORMATION, AND RENEWAL

John Kenneth Galbraith has observed that 'financial genius is before the fall.'[14] A similarly invariable rule, in religion as in economics, is that Reformation and Counter-Reformation are always after the fall, the fall itself being the consequence of, to use another of Galbraith's apposite phrases, 'a serious commitment to error.'[15] The rejection of error which accompanies reformation, moreover, is tridental, comprising the radical excision of faults and abuses in the godhead, the self, and the mediations between them both. To this end it is to be noted that both the Reformation and neoclassical economics are optimistic concerning their respective understandings of the external deity, the austere God of Judaeo-Christian tradition and the free market, but entirely pessimistic in relation to the construction of the individual within the discourse of the extant religion. Thus rejected is the autonomous individual of Thomistic theology, who participates in 'God's infinite and free essence, and assert[s] the positive, God-given autonomy of human nature,' and correspondingly, all concepts of the individual other than Rational Economic Man, on essentially the same grounds; namely, that they miss the point about both the Almighty and the individual's necessary subjection to it: it is obedience to God's will that is imperative, and it is obedience to it that constitutes true freedom and joy, not the freedom to act in accordance with a fallen nature and an 'inherently ineffective and perverse' human will. Further, learning, as well as accommodation to and incorporation of existing traditions of belief into an organic religious faith and practice relevant to time and place are renounced as nothing other than apostate interventions between the individual and God.[16]

Mediation is by these accounts an error in itself and the cause of proliferating error. In the 'contamination' of scholastic theology by Greek philosophy is the precedent for the renunciation of all classical economic thought revised by such heretical formations as Keynesianism, and welfare statism. Moreover, driving these renunciations is the animus for a creed which is too worldly in that it both influences the temporal realm and recognises it, accepts it, as an integral theatre of operations. Two consequences of immense importance follow from this turning away: the first is that the puristic enthusiasm which governs them drives out the potential for critique from a human perspective because both 'contaminations' leaven the metaphysical with the critical;[17] the second is that they are, intentionally, attempts to move beyond the human standpoint for the purpose of, in Caputo's formulation, 'reattaching... to an absolute Origin.' In this they display a neurotic preoccupation with the gap, the loss of an absolute intimacy, between an imperfect humankind and the Almighty which they believe will be overcome if only a point – always in the past – can be found 'where heaven and earth intersect and some moment in time gets charged with eternity and absolutely foundational value.'[18]

This attempt to resume the divine by merging with it is as recurrent a theme in religion as it is in economics and licenses two appropriate equivalences; the first being that the judging God of the Reformation and the austere Market are indistinguishable in their origins, the roles they serve, the commitments they extract, and the mercies they bestow. While the former affirms the God of Abraham and Moses as 'supreme, omnipotent, and transcendent,' and takes its collective name ('Christian') from the corporeal expression of that God, the latter's 'theological' and 'classical' faith proclaims a Being that is equally totemic – 'free marketeer' being the badge of identity – and without fault. Here, Peter Preston's analysis of the modes of economic-theoretical engagement with regard to the market provides an extremely valuable complement to the sources consulted on economics and religion in general and the Reformation's view of God in particular.[19]

In the first instance, both the God of the Reformation and the Market are the historical results of quite specific episodes, a fact which nevertheless has failed to deter their claim that 'their categories, values, and mores alone are eternally valid.'[20] They exist, therefore, as givens, 'largely independent of human kind, whose multiple individual efforts generate [them] as a kind of all embracing epiphenomena.' Similarly, knowledge of the type which would allow a designed, intelligent engagement is humanly 'unavailable *a priori*;' all that might be forthcoming is sufficient enlightenment to the individual so that she or he might be accommodated to their purposes. [21] This being the case, Church and State are excluded from any substantial directive role in religion and economics, respectively; indeed, such are their inadequacies that any attempt to do so is deserving of contempt. Both, accordingly, are confined within the parameters of the liberal, minimalist institution which, while extending to the faithful the right to a wide-ranging belief about their objects of veneration, anathematise all understandings of the subject of veneration which do not conform with the proclaimed, essential, revised, standard individual. In effect this is a double return to the Monophysite heresy of the sixth century; then, however, the debate, and subsequent schism, was limited to the claim that there is only one, inseparable nature in the person of Jesus, whereas, in the rise of neo-liberalism, both the Market and its human subject are progressively linked with a single understanding of God.

Such a construction of a model of humankind, with its concern to describe the world as it is and ought to be, deploys for its own purposes what is termed 'philosophical anthropology.' By its light, furthermore, a model of ethics is derived against which all behaviour might be measured, or at least judged against the criteria of an externally supplied Rule. Effectively, what obtains is a 'theo-tendential' orientation whereby all reality is seen according to the measure it reflects the ideal of the model – the God in whose image and likeness humankind is made, and the rational, calculating individual, depending on the immediate context. Thus virtue rooted in faith and economic efficiency correspond as the respective practices which externalise the metaphysical axes of intelligibility provided by the original model.[22] Disasters which befall individuals and groups are, therefore, the result of 'some abuse' which, by definition, resides somewhere external to the market – effectively, in the impiety of those groups and individuals.[23]

Clearly common in this formulation is the nature of the individual. For both Reformation Protestantism and the Market this is a problematic construct because they posit a person who is defined by their private wants which are to be saved in the next life and satisfied in this one. Yet, at the same time, she or he is both the cause and the effect of the relevant god, being systemically necessary for both individual demand (which is assumed) and its satisfaction. (Expressed another way, if there was no demand for an afterlife in paradise, and if there were no consumer wants *à la* capitalism in the first place, then neither God nor the market would be required to satisfy them.) Within this conflation of assumption and objective, the nature of the individual is further reduced by holding that she or he accepts that the satisfaction of the assumed demands be reduced to the single index of price – which translates as an unremitting faith in both God and the Market. The individual in question is, therefore, a diminished being as regards sovereignty in the eyes of the Reformation and Economics. Contrary to the free will which is conceded by both the Reformation and popular neo-liberal notions, the sovereignty with which the individual is invested dissolves immediately on the reflection that, given the above conflation, she or he is more accurately understood as the essentially passive receiver of stimuli in a productive system which creates the very wants it satisfies.[24]

The second consequence of the attempt to resume the divine is the identification of prayer and work as synonymous in their respective realms; both serve as supremely cognitive utilities. To be sure, it has long been recognised that work, like prayer, is a moral activity, but the extent to which they are almost identical exercises in discipline and subordination is not so well understood. Both are external expressions of faith, which, by their devout practice provide temporal assurance to the autonomous individual that she or he is living virtuously according to a pre-existing, supreme order. To the extent that these practices are buttressed by authority (scriptural and scientific), and spiritual well-being and wealth are held to be consequent upon them, reassurance is available; it is equally inescapable that, to the extent that inequality exists in the distribution of benefits, the causes are internal, with the subject, and not with either God or the Market, both of whom are without fault.

Additionally, because prayer-as-an-expression-of-faith and work are conversations with the Origin, they are concerned with how individuals are to live, and how they are to give an account of themselves. More precisely, conducted in the spirit of the appropriate subordination, both are the living rejection of indulgences by and through an activity embedded in the godhead. Indeed, unless one already knows the provenance of the following statement, could one confidently know whether the description 'a moral obligation that projects religious behaviour onto the everyday world' defines prayer or work?[25]

Since nearly all people work, and work is a moral obligation, there is something clerical about work. Through an emphasis in Weber, again, we understand the moral ideal of hard work as a calling, and, through this association, summon up Luther's notion that the body of the church consists of the 'priesthood of all believers,' who are analogous in their labour to the contemplative orders of the Christian church whose central calling was to pray.[26] Prayer and work, furthermore, tend to be disciplined and regular, for which comparison we need look no further than the extraordinary conjunction of both in the term 'office' – which, in its many but complementary meanings blurs the distinction between the two activities. While it is true that a distinction *can* be made in terms of the one being (religiously) a divine service, and the other being (secularly) a place of business, the difference collapses as the common extensions embrace meanings such as the performance of a task, a duty or service, or religious or social observance.

Within this identity where prayer and work merge, and for the same acknowledged purpose, there are no grounds for the religiously or economically pious to refuse to perform their office. Just as no prayer goes unheard, no work is too degrading or insignificant because, whatever the tasks, as exercises in virtue, they create the possibility of an undeserved redemption; it follows that the obligation to pray and to work is absolute, and the refusal to do so is a refusal of the grace – defined as the free and unmerited favour of God and the Market – necessary for entry into paradise in the next life, or for continued participation in the cycle of wants and satisfaction in the present.

Expressed negatively, not to pray or compete is to be guilty of the sin of presumption by implying that redemption and satisfaction will be realised without in any way acknowledging the need for an external manifestation of the requisite faith. Even then, grace is a commodity which can be denied by God and the Market (since it is a concession in their gift), but the opportunities to receive it cannot be refused by any individual needing to remain in communion with both.

In this light, grace and disposable income equate, and with a certain irony. In Reformation theology, grace is absolutely degraded by God's inscrutable calculation as to whether an individual has faith, and the uncertainty of this outcome is an unceasing torture for her, or him, throughout life. The Market imposes a different, but no less chronic, dissatisfaction; or rather, it is more correct to reiterate that the Market's success is monument to the conscious and enduring way it creates, organises, and orchestrates the wants it purportedly satisfies, *ad infinitum*. The rejection of error is thus a rejection of most of the comforts which make life more bearable in favour of an existence defined by austere suspension.

If life as it is lived is a continual deferral to a future objective, the regime under which life is lived is a continual deferral to some point in the past. The movement, in the first instance, is away from the present with its moral decline and abandonment of truth, in obedience to the injunction penned by Paul in his letter to the Romans – *Nolite conformari huic saeculo, sed reformamini* (do not conform to this world , but reform Thyself)[27] – to a period of authenticity co-located with a canon of order which can only be found in the past. Second, it is a movement designed primarily to renew, and thus potentially redeem, the individual, the inner person; social reform, it is held, proceeds from this in a causal relation.[28] Under this 'law of the return' the tendency is to revert to the earliest examples of the norm that is being sought, which, almost automatically, will involve a distortion arising from the compound of intense disaffection with the present, and a vision of an innocent, pure, unspoilt *ecclesia primitiva*. In the Reformation, specifically for Lutherans, the return was codified in the Judaeo-Christian *Confessio Augustana*, and can be seen, accordingly, as slightly exceptional to the law;[29] in the reformation of economics the same qualification applies to the extent that it alighted, less in a primitive utopia and more in that 'point in the past where heaven and earth intersect' defined by mathematical economics and Rational Economic Man, or, to put it more obviously, at the meeting between God's mechanics and the lower being made in His image and likeness.

Strictly speaking, if reformation connotes a return to 'either a predetermined norm or a former state', economics did not engage in one, whereas it might legitimately be said to have engaged in a transformation. At issue here is a certain looseness of terminology in which reformation and transformation have become a synonym for each other.[30] As has been argued elsewhere in this book, one of the closest (of perhaps many) approximations to a neo-liberal economic state was the Scottish clan system which expired at the Battle of Culloden in 1746 but, globally, there has simply been no, albeit rough, precedent for the global regime that is neo-liberalism.[31] This, however, does not invalidate the comparison; rather, it points to the pitfall of distorted discovery noted by Honee in the attempted return to an idealised past state in religion and, as evidenced in the foregoing, economics.

THE RELIGIOUS NATURE OF ECONOMICS

To argue that the reformation engaged in by economics closely followed the Protestant Reformation by attempting to resume the divine, and that various constructions within economics and religion are status, role, and functional equivalents of each other, still leaves open the question of how we might understand economics in terms other than those it provides for itself. The proposition here is that the answer is surprisingly clear: economics is not *like* a religion; it *is* a religion, and it is politically prudent to understand it as such. Beyond a brief definitional exegesis, this argument is framed by further referring to economics as a system of a particular type of belief, the role and importance of that belief, and the integration of it with conservative thematics in Christian (especially Reformation) theology.

For present purposes religion is minimally defined as comprising a belief in, and a recognition of, by humankind, some higher unseen power which has control of its destiny, and is entitled to obedience, reverence, and worship. Such recognition, furthermore, is thought to be self-evidently true, and exclusive of any competing beliefs, such as those bequeathed by custom. Confessing this belief – i.e. accepting and declaring it as *the* standard of spiritual and practical life with maximum human fidelity – is an absolute obligation. Such a recognition, also, explicitly contains the admission that humankind is severely limited in its ability to understand the world, in whole or in part, with a clear consciousness, and has, paradoxically, and according to an imperfect 'rational' process, constituted a realm of infinite explanatory power which nevertheless cannot be accessed. The term 'religion' also extends to the particular system of such belief.

To begin with, there is virtually no serious challenge to the proposition that economics is a system of belief. Moreover, what its reformative project suggests – that it is religious in character – is conceded by some of the discipline's most knowledgeable and authoritative figures. Leamer's clerical metaphor was cited earlier, but it is in the commentaries of John Kenneth Galbraith that are found some of the most telling insights into its essentially ecclesiastical identity, the latter's work being especially accessible via a penetrating and wide-ranging essay by Warren J. Samuels. Through (once again) philosophical anthropology Galbraith is unequivocal in regard to its origins and utility:

> Man cannot live without an economic theology – without some rationalisation of the abstract and seemingly inchoate arrangements which provide him with his livelihood. For this purpose the competitive or classical model had many advantages. It was comprehensive and internally consistent. By asserting that it was a description of reality the conservative could use it as the justification of the existing order. For the reformer it could be a goal, a beacon to mark the path of needed change. Both could be united in the central faith at least so long as nothing happened to strain unduly their capacity for belief.[32]

Elsewhere, as Samuels demonstrates, Galbraith attributes a generally Reformationist, specifically Anglican cast to the tolerance which this economic theology extends: 'Within a considerable range he [Man] is permitted to believe what he pleases. He may hold whatever view of this world he finds most agreeable or otherwise to his taste.'[33] But the unmistakable conclusion drawn by Galbraith is that the supporting faith reposing in economics, which defines nothing less than existence itself, is as comprehensive as any practised in the monastic orders, as Charles H. Hession discovered:

> The economic system of belief comprises a cosmology, a metaphysics, a set of goals, an apologia, a vision (in the Schumpeterian sense). It is a definition of reality which mediates between man and man and between man and the unknown.[34]

Notably excluded from these beliefs, and thereby accentuating the dimension of faith, is any claim that they constitute a correspondence theory of truth, something that the positivism which lies at the heart of economics proclaims, despite the fact that positivism itself comprises a set of beliefs; rather, they are seen as the logical consequence of mastering a set of beliefs within economic instruction and learning.[35] Given the manifest inadequacies (anthropological, methodological, political, social, gender, and empirical) of the discipline of economics to describe anything remotely approaching the world of everyday life, contested as it might be, all this is as it should be. It is perhaps the only available reassurance born of the manifest necessity of simultaneously remaining in communion with a profession which is highly valued by the academy and by government, while acknowledging to oneself and one's colleagues that the basis for this esteem is profoundly similar to that extended by states to their established churches, namely, the gratitude of 'guilded constituency' for being provided with a 'justifying contrivance' of high practical value by an intelligentsia which is commonly believed to have 'privileged access to the assumed mystery of money.'[36]

This should not surprise for other reasons as well. The criterion of correspondence misses the point that economic belief, like religious dogma, serves immediate and crucial questions of identity, professionalism, and privilege that far outweigh, for priests as for economists, their contributions to understanding the world. It is the willingness to confess the requisite belief system (which Samuels also terms discourse on the basis of Galbraith's analyses),[37] and for this belief system to be sanctioned by the state, not its consequences and absurdities that, in the case of economics, defines and socialises individuals as consumers, workers, and citizens in a particular system.[38] Economists benefit from their confessional piety by deploying it strategically for 'the exclusion of lines of thought that are hostile or unsettling to the discipline or, a related matter, to an influential economic or political community.'[39]

It is a wise precaution and one totally understandable in that repository of neo-liberalism, the United States of America, especially in the context of its dominant religious beliefs. Neoclassical economics, and its currently elaborated ego, neo-liberalism, shares with (what Harold Bloom describes as) the American Religion such an identical demand for faith that it is not an exaggeration to say that, at the very least, they are mutually supporting; on an equally close examination, a more intimate relation is detectable wherein the determining strands of religious and economic belief are but extrusions from that fusion of beliefs known as American Gnosticism, a form of knowing:

by and of an uncreated self, or self-within-the-self, and the knowledge leads to freedom, a dangerous and doom-eager freedom: from nature, time, history, community, other selves.[40]

At the heart of this religion lies the fear of dying, which by Bloom's account infuses all denominations in the USA, and a 'mindlessness' that, among the fundamentalists, takes the form of a 'vicious' anti-intellectualism, which, in combination produce an idea of the self as a 'primordial Adam' (a Man before there were men and women). This is reinforced by the extraordinarily widely held conviction by people in the USA that God loves them personally (in contra-distinction to both Spinoza's remark that this was an unreasonable expectation, and to the Hebrew Bible which records that this favour was extended only to King David), and to wilder claims still which justify the term 'fantasifaction.' In sum, and in a phrase, stances which 'engender parodies of religion.'[41] If a more practical demonstration of the fusion of these two belief systems into the life world of America is needed, the instance to be cited is the realisation of American Gnosticism/neo-liberalism in the selfishness which has come to mark the national political economy.

Since the American religion preceded neoclassical economics, and since the discipline of economics, as argued persuasively by Dorothy Ross, had always to make its peace with the former (as expressed in that other great fusion, American Exceptionalism), Marx's observation in *The Eighteenth Brumaire* is that men learning a new language always begin by translating it back into the language they already know is most apposite.[42] If, as is the case, the precedent was, or contained, to put the matter delicately, serious implausibilities, then the auguries for the credibility of the succeeding belief are correspondingly poor, even if their acceptance with, and by, faith is correspondingly assured. Of this operant principle Christopher Hitchens writes:

> It's a curious thing in American life that the most abject nonsense will be excused if the utterer can claim the sanction of religion. A country which forbids an established religion by law is prey to any denomination.[43]

Much of the nonsense within capitalism is so sanctioned out of this accommodationist stance. Where Reformation Protestantism was once informed by a strict Calvinism which dwelt on 'the 'evil' inherent in people, on human powerlessness before the sovereignty of God, and on the difficulties in achieving salvation, and thus 'armed the self against the seductions of secular culture [the pursuit of commercial success to the fore] and alerted it to the dangers of spiritual decline and weakness,' its constancy was undermined by its own logic.[44] That logic, based as it was on the rights of an individual conscience and the Calvinist mandate for urgent action in every aspect of people's lives gave rise to an unpredictable dialectic. While the former was, over time, politically and scientifically liberating (though isolating because highly individualistic), the latter, in the absence of sacramental justification, and the presence of predestination-induced anxiety, gave rise to a solitude which craved its own substitute – the notion that the Reformation Christian 'could find signs of his being among the elect if he could successfully and unceasingly apply himself to disciplined work and his worldly calling.'[45] Economically, in conjunction with other historical developments, it created a highly productive economy in which both economic desire and economic benefits were increasingly democratised.[46] The self at the centre of this movement, thereby, became 'the measure of things, self-defining and self-legislating.'[47]

In the context of the Reformation and the 'priesthood of all believers,' the political-economic shift was essentially sacerdotal in character: the favoured circumstances were befitting of a priest, and indeed, in the excessive recognition of them it was possible to ascribe not only authority but a supernatural competence to those so chosen. Self was thus debased into selfishness, and, as Bloom puts it, 'the believer's freedom from others into the bondage of others.'[48] Profit, accordingly, was blessed, while duty, self-denial, and the guilt of gratuitous consumption were banished within a perverse understanding of Calvinism's vocation to realise the Kingdom of God on Earth.[49] Ultimately, and again in context, the preposterous reigned as wisdom – illustrated in Tarnas' reflection that, over time, 'the Protestant doctrine of justification through the individual's faith in Christ seemed to place more emphasis on the individual's faith than on Christ – on the personal relevance of ideas, as it were, rather than on their external validity.'[50] From William Graham Sumner's early twentieth-century esteem for millionaires as not only socially beneficent but also a 'product of natural selection,' via the privileged status in the 1980s accorded to the works of George Gilder and Arthur Laffer, to the similar status presently accorded to the historically damaging doctrine of *laissez-faire* in general, and the work of Charles A. Murray in particular, the record is one of affirmation. Though sometimes subject to wane, overall it reveals no shortage of instances in which economic doctrines beyond the serious regard of, in Galbraith's phrase, 'anyone of sober mentality,' are concomitantly mystified and acclaimed towards the end of giving acceptability, grace and justification, however transparent, to the position of the economically contented, and their 'uninhibited accumulation of wealth.'[51]

TERRORISTIC SILENCE

What this understanding of economics-as-religion omits must now be included, namely, the inducement to religion which is provided by the pessimistic understanding inherent in the Reformation view of the relation between the 'terrible righteousness of an angry God' and individual women and men in their fallen and corrupt state. In effect, economics and religion, and thus economics-as-religion, are but the elaborated consequences of the logic of the individualism of conscience and the terrible predicament imposed by that transformation: isolation – from the previously all-enveloping Church, and before God; and alienation from other women and men. So acute are these conditions experienced that 'terror' is the term Tarnas uses to describe them.[52] Moreover, it is terror which is an inescapable condition of life as defined by the Reformation. Once the God of Abraham and Moses is accepted it follows; alternatively, if that understanding of God is not accepted, or if the concept of God itself is not accepted, then terror ensues through the advent of chaos. In economics, accordingly, to live without explanations invested with authority of phenomena central to life is to reproach humankind's curiosity and ego.[53] One therefore either believes in a God because one is convinced that a God exists, or one believes in a God because a God is socio-strategically necessary.

The choice or disposition here is immaterial to the effect, which is both generally palliative and specifically analgesic in relation to the pathological nature of the human condition. Palliative because, in all common understandings of the word it is applicable: it gives superficial, or temporary relief; it serves to extenuate or excuse certain offences, and it alleviates the symptoms of the condition to which it is applied without curing it. Analgesic because, when administered with sufficient care and quantity, it removes the ability to feel pain. And pain there evidently is. As Luther was terrorised before the unrelenting gaze of God, individuals exposed to the unblinking scrutiny of the Market suffer from such *post-partum* anxiety that, according to Joan Robinson (who in turn was relying on Freud), their belief in it is to be understood as a return to the security once offerered by the womb.[54] In this Robinson is generally supported by both, *inter alia*, Adam Smith and Galbraith. It is the purpose of 'philosophy,' according to Smith, to:

> introduce order into [the] chaos of jarring and discordant appearances, *to allay the tumult of the imagination*, and to restore it, when it surveys the great revolutions of the universe, to that tone of tranquillity and composure, *which is most agreeable to itself*, and most suitable to its nature.[55]

For Galbraith the introduction or restoration of agreeability then produces a psychic balm, an elision of any need to continually negotiate the present and which, therefore, frames all (in)action: 'Better the accepted patterns of life than the terrible costs of thought and choice.'[56]

Even then, what remains unsaid is the ultimate sanction of the community of believers against dissenters. For Reformation Protestantism (as, indeed, for the Christianity which preceded it), to seriously doubt its core teachings, or to revise them without approval and to give voice to that doubt or revision, was to invite denunciation, and in all likelihood, the charges of either apostasy, or heresy, or both. In that event the effective sentence imposed was to be silent among the community via the withdrawal of not only the licence, but also the idiom in which the dissent or the injury might be heard, as captured here by Caputo:

> It follows therefore that just as he who breaks with the bishop is no longer authorised to break the bread [of the Eucharist] so one who breaks with the bishop is no longer authorised to teach or interpret, to speak or to write.[57]

Just as Christianity, pre- and post-Reformation, is littered with examples of the execution, or attempted execution, of this punishment, so too is the history of economics – from the American Exceptionalist conformism of (American) marginalism, with its dismissal of scholars who espoused unacceptable politico-economic views, such as James Allen Smith, Edward Bemis, Richard Ely, Scott Nearing, Henry Wade Rogers, and E.A. Ross, to the inability of Thorstein Veblen to even obtain a position on the grounds of irreligion, to the Cold War persecution of academics hostile to capitalism, to even John Kenneth Galbraith's advice to aspiring economists *not* to follow his dissentient path if they wish to have a successful career in the discipline of economics – the sanction of excommunication has been ever-present and imposed.[58]

Excommunication, however, results only from public practice, from the proclamation that certain acts are the empirical manifestation of the ideas with which they are integrated. Expressed in another way, to avoid the sanction, there is no requirement that the ideas change so long as public practice may be said to accord with the relevant dogma, thus achieving what Tarnas refers to as 'the modern mind's sense of the interiority of religious reality.'[59] In this move dogma and freedom of conscience co-exist, but effectively, the latter is purchased at the cost not only of its silence on the former, but also its concession to deny that difference even exists. The religious and economic monologues which remain, therefore, are then permitted to worship God and the Market according to the same criterion – namely that they are unchallenged in their status as a 'cosmic constant.'[60]

That being the case, the dominant theme of thought and action which emerges is one of passivity, a quite logical disposition if it is already accepted that the extant system is, cosmopolitically, the only one possible. At the same time this conclusion is also an inevitable return to the foundational belief which holds that, since both God and the Market are inscrutable, and the fate of any individual is already known to God, choice is an illusion – in other words to a reacquaintance with the Reformation doctrine of predestination and the economic doctrine of rational expectations. In which case Reformation theology and neoclassical economics alike are but dutiful commemorations in the spirit of M. Pangloss.

PARADOXES, INVERSIONS, AND DISCONTINUITIES

In the light of all such efforts to enforce a paradosis, it is seemingly absurd to discover phenomena in economic theory and practice that exhibit contradictions and conflicts which are contrary to the preconceived notions of what is reasonable or possible in the respective religious systems of belief. Yet this became the case in post-Reformation Protestantism with its reliance on 'scripture alone,' just as it is the case in the discipline of economics and its parsimonious, mathematicised core, most particularly in regard to their common obsession with mediation or, more explicitly, the imperative to dispense with all intercessions and supplements between individuals and the Origin in order to transcend the humanly compromised standpoint and adopt a divine one.[61] What emerges is that neither the Reformation nor economics succeeded in turning fully away from that which they most reviled largely because such a turn was, in all likelihood, impossible, but in any case was impotent against the inescapability, the tyranny if you like, of their respective constructions of God.

Intending a 'priesthood of all believers' who would know God through scripture alone and worship without graven images, Protestants very quickly elevated Luther to the role of oracle and some venerated cheap engravings of him, even in his lifetime; for his part, Luther saw nothing amiss with an evangelism which employed 'yellow-press language [which was] vivid beyond crudity in images.'[62] Economics conforms in all significant regards: in the devotion to their ideas, and based on a selective and reductionist reading of them at that, it has made apostles (pioneering missionaries authorised to lead reform) of its intellectual founders while requiring a priesthood to subsequently interpret them to the wider, vulgar audience. In both processes it is forgotten that any reliance on a text is coterminously a reliance on the limitations of a form which by nature is subject to 'a certain uncertainty… about its authenticity, its sense,' and that the purpose of the text in the first place is 'to try to fill in or supplement a dangerous gap, to represent a Presence that has disappeared,' and thus, that it stands 'between the outside and the inside, between the founding act, the absolutely authorising Origin and everyone who depends on the Origin.'[63] To this end Christianity, no matter its confessional coloration and economics, no matter its mathematical rigour, are irremediably mediated against their own first principles, and attempts to deny that this is so are attempts to deny that the habits and spirit of the *romanita* which were once so reviled – *magisterium, auctoritas, potestas*, priests, and the mystifications they wield and serve have, in the words of Nizzar Qabbani's banned poem, 'crept through our weaknesses like ants.'[64] But where the excesses of the Reformation noted above implied a knowledge of the benefits of images as propaganda among barely literate classes of the population rather than a capitulation to the Catholic counter-offensive, the moves in economics delimit its Reformation content: its paradoxes, as now detailed, establish a character both convivial with the medieval tradition of Christianity which saw monks as a 'moral elite' committed to the strict practice of their understanding of its ideals, and equally at home in the tradition of Catholicism's Counter-Reformation, replete with assiduous censorship, heroic missionary work, the Inquisition, mystical writings, and a super-elite intellectual caste in the form of the Jesuits.[65] Of this transition Caputo appropriately concludes:

> This result confirms a warning that Derrida issues in *Truth in Painting* to beware of those who promise to give us something unmediated, who would dispense with screens and mediations in order to put us in direct contact with the Origin, for we will later on find ourselves visited with the most massive mediations, with bishops and long robes and police all over the place.[66]

If ecclesiolatry is a sufficient condition by which we would know that Derrida's forebodings have been realised, then the evidence is to hand in economics. Not only is an excessive reverence for its 'learned and priestly circle' practised, but such veneration is virtually demanded in a manner which recalls Olsen's description of the attempts by reformers in the post-Gregorian period to subject the church to the disciplines of the coenobitic life by 'monasticising' its history and practices.[67] Of this advent and its advocacy there is probably no better example than in the considerable writings of Paul Krugman.

Like John Kenneth Galbraith, Krugman supports the general proposition that the educational and scientific estates are a civilising force in the world, but where the latter departs from the former is in his intense differentiation between professionally authorised economists with whom he proudly identifies, and invading commentators on economics who are, for him, irretrievably Other. To read Krugman is to be made aware at every turn that, in the great debates, he is more conscious of this difference than he is of their shared identity with other citizens, intellectuals, or (say) political economists. Consequently he is unequivocal about the need to think and scrutinise economics from a single totalising position.[68]

Krugman's concern is that of the eleventh-century pope, Gregory VII, a reformer, certainly, but who was concerned not so much to innovate, but rather to renew norms and laws which had fallen into desuetude.[69] Their particular and common concern is with the interdiction of the appointment of bishops by the king – for which read the emergence of non-economists as significant contributors to the national discourse on economics, the similar prominence accorded to economists who are variously derided as 'misguided,' or guilty of 'careless (or "sloppy") math,' and President Clinton's decision to listen to and even appoint some of them as advisers.[70] Krugman's response accords more with Pius IV, Innocent III, and Ignatius Loyola (though it also owes something to Gregory XVI); specifically, he seeks nothing less than a 'conversion offensive' which would consciously reorganise the discourse of economics from top to bottom in order that it might constitute a common culture and profess a common faith, remarkably akin to the transformations wrought in the Catholic Church throughout the nineteenth century.[71] In both cases, of course, the return is not so much to pre-existing traditions so much as to a 'decor' which conceals a problematic reality – for the Church, a distorted Middle Age Christianity; for Krugman, to the insights of Hume and Ricardo (without any mention of the epistemological reservations of the former which would undermine Krugman's, and neoclassical discipline's scientific pretensions).[72]

The prescriptions for Krugman in this time of crisis and for Paul III in the face of the Reformation, though apparently similar, are profoundly dissimilar. Sixteenth-century militant Catholicism produced the Jesuits who, in time, became 'the most celebrated teachers on the Continent' – a justly deserved plaudit based on their immersion in an education comprising:

> not only teaching of the Catholic faith and theology, but also the full humanistic program from the Renaissance and classical era – Latin and Greek letters, rhetoric, logic and metaphysics, ethics, science and mathematics, music, even the gentlemanly arts of acting and fencing – all in the service of developing a scholarly 'soldier of Christ:' a morally disciplined, liberally educated, critically intelligent Christian man capable of outwitting the Protestant heretics and furthering the great Western tradition of Catholic learning.[73]

By any criteria, the comparison with Loyola's Jesuits is embarrassing, because Krugman's imagination is so impoverished that his vision of reform is, like numerous pontiffs before him, no more than a backward glance which Paul III would have found contemptible. But perhaps that misses the point, which is that his intentions, at least, would have been blessed by Paul III.

To counter the economic 'heretics' of the Clinton era – *inter alia*, James Fallows, Jeffrey Garten, Robert Kuttner, Edward Luttwak, Ira Magaziner and Mark Patinkin, Clyde Prestowitz, Robert Reich, Lester Thurow, the World Economic Forum, and even Apple Computer's John Sculley and the best-selling fiction writer, Michael Crichton – and to rescue the damage inflicted on the otherwise attentive public of the United States of America by their, and like-minded, contributions published in *The American Prospect* and *The Atlantic,* and/or broadcast on *McNeil–Lehrer,* and ultimately to counter the 'extremely primitive' level of ensuing public discussion, Krugman's response is extraordinary. He proposes to 'vaccinate' undergraduates via a 'basic training [and] solid grounding in the principles of international trade' in order that they will 'respond intelligently' to what he describes as pervasive international economic nonsense.[74] As he develops his proposal it is clear that he is arguing for the ordination of a putative social, and no doubt political, elite, in the spirit of the enabling legislation for the Council of Economic Advisers (who, it is specified, must be professional economists) by lamenting the damaging extension of the advisory circle on economics to other discourses.

In view of the high percentage of college graduates among the citizens in the United States, this proposal can be seen as Reformative because, without doubt, its objective is 'the priesthood of all believers' – believers who have been cultivated in, and fortified by, the sacramental experience of selective exposure to Hume and Ricardo prior to their professional deployment. Not for them an *education* (from *educere*, to lead, or draw, out), but the *instruction* (from *instruere*, to build in), of the seminary. And here Krugman is adrift on a sea of professional conceit because he clearly believes that the power, or capacity, to produce certain desired effects is governed by the theological formula *ex opere operantis* – 'by the efficiency of the celebrant' when, more correctly, efficacy proceeds from *ex opere operato* – 'by the efficiency of the ceremony itself.' Thus disclosed it is more than a fixation with the need to return economics to a position of eminence; it is, more significantly, the guise taken by Counter-Reformational reform within the re-subordination of the body of the Church to its traditional rule and teachings.

If, as is argued earlier, we should understand the Market as the God-equivalent in economics, then Krugman's representation is even more appropriately situated this way. While there is no doubt that all lay people can orient, or convert themselves to the market, be subject to its inscrutable ways, and even offer penance for infidelities to it, they cannot escape the fact that they are, for all their experience, uninstructed and formally unlearned. By default they are not the elect; they lack that critical 'experience of the God' which is provided by highly pressurised and disciplined training culminating in a searching examination upon, and the official certification of, a spiritual and intellectual conversion which is known as the *metanoia*.

It is this view of economists as *confrères* in a contemplative order which forces a brief return to John Kenneth Galbraith's 'assumed mysteries' in economics. Quite apart from their installation in society at a superior and demarcated position on the basis of their own criteria, what is being effected is the contemplation of the Market in such a way that mystification is ensured and accepted in a spirit of appropriate humility, a not difficult achievement given that knowledge of the Market – sufficient to enable planning, for example – is assumed to be unavailable *a priori*. In combination, what both effect is an 'exorcising and masking of power' by deferring to the realm of the ultimately unknowable those questions (unemployment and vast disparities in wealth, for example) which most demand a human answer, and in the process transforming them into questions of faith rather than political questions. Thus John Ralston Saul writes of the way in which managerial decisions which brutalise their victims while enriching shareholders are sanctified:

> Efficiency is… one to watch for. This minor shop floor characteristic has been promoted to near membership in the Holy Trinity. Notice that it is efficiency we always hear about and not effectiveness. Effectiveness is about content and policy delivery. Efficiency is just an abstract and primarily negative term.[75]

It would perhaps be difficult to find a more exemplary case in the Counter-Reformative project of neo-liberalism than this, in which the necessary 'passivity before the inevitable' is rendered possible through the proselytising efforts of economists. Correspondingly it is sought by their acolytes through an appeal to such a mercenary concept that, for one of the contemporary period's more accessible and philosophically attuned critics, it bears comparison to what is arguably Christianity's most impenetrable doctrine.

But the comparison is even more invidious in the light of the overall processes in which economics is now clearly engaged. As time passes these transport it further and further into the *romanita*. Again, the most notable of these are best understood in contra-distinction to the Reformation. Recall, in Tarnas' formulation, that the Reformation sought to reclaim 'the unalterable word of God in the Bible' and thereby fostered 'a new stress on the need to discover unbiased objective truth, apart from the prejudices and distortions of tradition.' Crucially, this gave rise to 'the growth of a scientific mentality' which was undeterred from reappraising all claims and all wisdom, even those which had given rise to its advent in the first place. Moreover, in the contemporary dialectic between the literal meaning of Scripture and the new rationality, an 'impossible tension' was created as the latter increasingly contradicted the former, leading speedily to a dichotomy between faith and reason. Reconciliation was possible only by consigning faith and its relevance to the individual mind, while science was installed as the intellectually superior, and practically more significant account of the external, physical world.[76] Thus, that 'fundamental element in the genesis of the Reformation' which was marked by a 'spirit of rebellious, self-determining individualism, and… the growing impulse for intellectual and spiritual independence,' and which eventually became so potent that it could challenge the Roman Catholic Church, also became so potent that it gave rise to a triumphant secularism, 'disenchanting the world of immanent divinity' on the way, and inverting the intentions of its founders.[77]

Consider now the economic reformation. It was born of the dialectical overthrow of political economy by Newtonian science, an imitative project based on the apparent exemplar of late nineteenth-century physics (which itself was held to be luminous through its foundation in the formal logics of mathematics). When in time, and especially now, economics' confrontation with the same nemesis of the Reformation – positivist science – demonstrates its inferiority, the disciplinary response follows the latter's precedent, at least in the style of its response: it defines as irrelevant those influences (initial conditions, culture, history, and society) which contribute most to its inadequacies; begs the existence of that which is most contested (virtually all of its free-market assumptions in general and the 'as if' claim in particular); either proscribes science if it is embarrassing to its self-identity (as in the injunction to avoid the discussion of mathematics, methodology, and philosophy) or, persists in practising it in a debauched, parodying way (use of convenient data sets); or, failing all else, makes explicit what the previous recourses imply by appealing directly to faith (as did George Gilder in proposing that regressive taxation was necessary for the rich, just as poverty was a necessary inducement for the poor to succeed).

In sum, the fate of economic science is that of post-Reformation religious belief: to the extent that it entails the type of rigour associated with its exemplar, Newtonian physics, it is exiled from secular life and relegated to the status of a conscience belief which describes a desirable but unachievable state of affairs, a resident of greater or lesser prominence in the mind only. Faith, on the other hand, which suffered this fate at the hands of the post-Reformation scientific revolution, is the reserved prerogative of economics and, according to its own dispensation, that which distinguishes and gives precedence to its adherents. Both the religious and the economic Reformation, therefore, are to be seen as movements which adopted a defining confession which, when dialectically opposed to the consequences directly proceeding from that confession, not only de-essentialised that confession, but reassumed the confessional privileges which were the first cause of their grievance. Effectively, they engaged in an Orwellian inversion. For the Reformation this involved the double blasphemy of substituting, first, the individual for Christ, and second, science for faith; religion became secular. In economics it took the more straightforward form of a stance which, while demanding faith, denied that it was denying science; economics became religiose. And in a most surprising manner, one which recalls both the pre-Reformation selling of indulgences by the Dominican friar, Johann Tetzel, on the instructions of the Medici pope, Leo X, to raise money for the building of St Peter's Basilica, and the subsequent anti-intellectualism of contemporary Catholicism and Protestantism which found common cause in their condemnation of Copernicus' astronomy for impiety.[78]

If any processes imply the use of the term 'discontinuities,' then these must be seen among them. Equally, they must be seen as broadly consistent with a tradition of discontinuity in Christianity and Economics which results from their confrontation with unforeseeable ideas, persistent claims of everyday life, and, most of all, with details they refuse to recognise in the pursuit of a 'single, assured, and reassuring style.'[79] More particularly, they are to be seen as arising from the claim to embrace both the Origin of the existence they seek to describe, and the relation to that Origin of everyone who depends on it, within an account ostensibly authorised by the Origin, and thus, within a fixed text – one within such a firm interpretive context 'that the river of interpretations will always flow within fixed borders.'[80] Recall for a moment, for Christianity, this guarantee against plurivocity is found in the post-Easter appearance of Jesus to the disciples on the road to Emmaus, the defining occasion on which he interpreted the Scriptures with great clarity for them, performed the sacrament of the Eucharist and, of insurmountable significance, demonstrated that he had indeed risen from the dead. Caputo describes the overall meaning of the encounter for the 'fixed border' tradition of Christianity:

> this story is a text about the text [the New Testament]. It is a kind of self-instruction that the text leaves behind, a kind of auto-hermeneutics inscribed in the text, something like the stage instructions that a playwright inscribes in his text, by means of which the text itself instructs us about how it is to be read. The reading must always be entrusted to the hands of the one whose hands break the bread, which is pre-eminently the hands of the bishop, or the hands of the ones whom the bishop consecrates.[81]

Recall too, that, imitatively, Economics affirms itself through a single authorised account of the Market-as-Origin, the installation of Rational-Economic-Man-as-Imitation-of-Christ, and the formal, transformative logic of mathematics-as-Eucharist and prophylactic against error. The sacramental symmetry is complete. Through the transubstantiative/consubstantiative ritual of religion, bread and wine are converted into the body and blood of Christ; acting in accordance with the tenets of the Market-as-Origin, Economics works the miracle of common man's transformation into Rational Economic Man and celebrates the exemplary Presence.

Recall, also, that which is lost unless the detail of a close reading is given the attention it deserves, namely that these theological miracles were never authorised and never intended to effect the consequences they did. Caputo describes the foremost among these:

> The idea behind Jesus's ministry, the exegetes think, was not Jesus but the father, *abba*.... He came to give glory to the father who was greater than him. The followers of Jesus however ignored what Jesus had in mind; they did not follow what Jesus taught but began instead to teach Jesus himself, and him crucified. Had the followers of Jesus followed Jesus, there would be no Christianity because Christianity was not Jesus's idea, not what Jesus taught, and it is almost certainly something that, had Jesus lived, we can well imagine he would have opposed. The birth of Christianity depended on the death of its author, not because he died for our sins and in order to establish his church, but because had he lived he would have opposed the idea of such a church.[82]

Correspondingly, had the followers of one of the metaphorical fathers of modernity, René Descartes, whose quest for certainty through formal logic subsumes Economics, and one of that discipline's canonical thinkers, Leon Walrus, taken them seriously, it does not overstate the case to say that much of what was done in their names would not have been done; that the institutionalisation of their misappropriated ideas followed from the wilfulness of their followers; and that, accordingly, their projects were hijacked. Thus, what might have been understood in the first instance was that, far from being the 'unfolding of a pure *esprit* untouched by the historical events of his time,' Descartes' contribution to philosophical development was his attempt to escape the seemingly interminable political and theological chaos of the Thirty Years War by providing the peoples of Europe with a hope of reasoning their way out of it.[83] His project to place human knowledge on 'foundations' that are 'clear, distinct, and certain' necessarily had an appeal and an urgency but, of greater significance, it needed to be understood as an historical response to an historical issue, not, as posterity has regarded it, a divinely ordained prescription for the retreat from the oral to the written, the particular to the universal, the local to the general, and from the timely to the timeless.[84]

Hence we can acquire a perspective on Walrus, whom Heilbroner and Milberg laud as 'the commanding figure' of the marginalist movement in neoclassical economics. He applied himself to the purpose celebrated by those who have misread Descartes – highly disengaged, abstract science – and these were other, and greater (in his view), than that to which his practical political concerns were bent. It is, therefore, significant to record that Walrus was 'quite indifferent – even hostile – to the practical application of general equilibrium analysis to political life, despite his own lifelong interest in questions of agrarian socialism.'[85] Moreover, in his preoccupation with Descartes' quest and exaggerated legacy of certainty as defined in, and through, mathematics there is that inattention to Caputo's 'devilish details,' especially by his disciples – in the form of mathematics' own historicity, and, after Gödel, infinite crises of certainty – which might have cautioned against their subsequent turn to *romanita*.[86] They might even have noted, as has Napoleoni, the counter-theological content of the Walrusian model of the market economy – which can be manipulated so as to obviate the need for a market in the first place, and so suggests that knowledge sufficient to allow economic planning is possible.[87]

Writ large, the attention to detail would have established a profound absence common to pre-Reformation Christianity, Reformation Protestantism, Counter-Reformation Catholicism, and Economics: no umbilical connection to the Origin in whose name they proclaim truth, despite rejection, reformation, and renewal. The inescapable fact is that the Origin, to the extent it ever was an Origin, has absconded, leaving Christians and Economists with their irrational terror of open spaces. Christians, we are assured, know their God through a multi-authoured, multi-translated account of his Word, but to take this seriously is to sooner or later confront the fact that a gap, or 'a bit of an abyss' inevitably exists between Him and even his first interlocutor.

> Christians are always already latecomers, always the latter-day disciples, always arriving too late for the origin, after a crowd (*ecclesia*) has already gathered. [They] are the *ecclesia* of those who come too late for the Origin and too early for the *parousia*. [88]

Economics knows this agoraphobia well, or rather, through its numerous and demonstrable failures it is well acquainted with the consequences of re-forming itself into the disciple of *economics* from political economy according to the rationalist dream of purity in human reasoning. It alighted upon certainty through the veneration of physics, and linear Newtonian science in general, almost at the precise moment that they were being overthrown in favour of uncertainty, a quantum reality, and the acceptance of science as a mediation, or in a biblical sense, as science was passing from its old, to its new, Testament. Within Caputo's description, it merely joined the growing assembly convoked by the scientific revolution over the previous two-and-a-half centuries. And within the example bequeathed by Descartes, it moved away from greater or lesser intellectual scepticism and the tolerance of ambiguity, and towards not just certainty, but that consummation of the demand for certainty which Toulmin defines as the 'belief in belief itself.'[89] All of which might be unremarkable if Economics had not, and did not, justify its juridical solutions to every human dilemma by an appeal to a Presence which has manifestly withdrawn and was, and remains, insufficiently understood even by its exegetes.

Understanding the religious path that Economics has followed is to understand that Economics in its early neoclassical stage of development, like the Reformation, was given to a condition which some might describe as the 'unreturned glance,' whereby the faith in the efficacy of the return overwhelmed the self-awareness which made the return necessary in the first instance. Equally and less forgivingly, this is a condition of 'deliberate blindness,' and it is in this sense that we should understand late twentieth-century Economics. Like the Counter-Reformation, it is juridically inhuman, politically oppressive and reactionary, and scandalously anti-intellectual. Both became alienated from concerns which were essentially social and political in their respective assertions of certainty. In this process their belief systems were made obligatory if communion with other members of the faithful was to be maintained; at the same time they effectively incarcerated, or at least, consensually isolated these systems to the point where, accustomed to flattery in the guise of obligation, both scorned critical knowledge of themselves. Or, where that knowledge was difficult to evade because it came from on high and within, as in Leamer's caustic observations on the contradictions in the discipline, the response is that encapsulated by Camus in his reflection on the grotesque habits of modern times: 'They admit sin and refuse grace.'

But here we are talking of people, an intellectual movement, who believe that they experience the *metanoia*, not for them intellectual existence in a 'twilight space, of flickering images, a space in which the withdrawal leaves its trace behind, like a fissure in a surface left behind by something, *je ne sais quois*, which has passed through it and disappeared.'[90] This is, after all, a regime enthralled by *magisterium, auctoritas, potestas*. For all that, the admission of sin and the refusal of grace suggest a more appropriate conclusion, one that resonates with both the debilitated Church of the pre-Reformation and the undisguised exploitation of the papacy by the Medicis: the substitution of *metanoia*. by *agnosia* (the failure to recognise).[91] Given that Economics effected a reformation (Honee's 'double regularity of distortion and discovery'); given also that it was able to consciously and profoundly proclaim itself as separate from its predecessor's heritage, concerns and practices, the extant impetus and condition may indeed be spiritual, but it is essentially one characterised by the ability to see objects, including the self, yet not to identify them. Neuroscientifically, this results from damage to the visual cortex; intellectually, in the case of Economics, it is an acquired, which is to say, learned, collapse of the higher integrative processes for complex form recognition.

Conclusion

The new age of religious wars: neo-liberalism, neo-Clausewitzianism and the American way of war

Apocryphal accounts, if not rigorous historical research, has it that, in 1781, when Cornwallis surrendered to Washington at Yorktown, the British military band in attendance played the tune, 'The World Turned Upside Down': either way, it would not be out of place today. It was, then, a lament for the strategic failure which the ceremony formalised, but it was also, in its origins which date back to the 1640s, a protest ballad against the (Cromwellian) destruction of favourite English Christmas traditions. In no small way it was a song expressing a longing for, or celebration of, inversions of the established order. It was not out of place then, and it is as apt today in a world in which inversions abound.

Consider these prompts from the general narrative of post-Cold War world history:

> Between 1989 and 1991 the Soviet Union and the Eastern Bloc disintegrated without serious anticipation in the West in general, and the US intelligence community in particular – whose Director of Central Intelligence-designate was, in the course of his own confirmation hearings in the Senate, shown to have an extensive personal record of arrogance, exaggeration, poor judgement, corruption of the intelligence assessment process, deceit, dishonesty, dereliction of duty, selective amnesia and even fantasy, yet found to be a right and proper person for the position; the aforementioned event was, however, greeted as an earnest of God's favour, as was, implicitly, the massacre which became *Desert Storm*, and George Bush's 1992 State of the Union address proclaimed it as such; the Pentagon, accordingly, periodically constructs visions of the future in terms of a simple, linear extrapolation from what the Cold War would have been without the Soviet Union, replete with the objective of hegemony over all powers – enemies, adversaries, allies and friends, First World to Third World – alike; the global political economy, meanwhile, has become prisoner to the 'new capitalism' which is hostile to any form of state or interstate regulation, unleashing its own demons within the processes of market globalisation – in the form of arms proliferation, ecological disasters, declining democratic values and practices, famine, and accelerating social and economic polarisation within, and between states and regions.

About these 'events that really happened' the most striking impression, to this observer, is the remarkable ease with which they have been integrated into a view that holds such things to be either mere aberrations (the Gates' hearings), or worse, an accurate representation of the way things are, or should be (co-option of God in the Cold War and in *Desert Storm* triumphalism, and the Pentagon documents). There is little or no appreciation that they might all be the entirely and chronically consistent outcomes of but parallel strands of a modernist theory of domination which, ultimately, tends initially towards the annihilation of those it reduces to the status of objects.

The concession to there being some understanding is indebted to Russell F. Weigley's *The American Way of War*, a 1973 study by a leading military historian which, drawing on Clausewitz and a leading German interpreter, Hans Delbruck, argued that the total destruction of the enemy – first of its armed forces, but often of the whole fabric of its society – is a characteristic of United States military strategy and policy.[1] Weigley's thesis is based on his historical analysis of the subject from the time of the American Civil War, and thus was not dominated by the rise of the United States to global strategic pre-eminence in the early years (and somewhat beyond) of the nuclear age. Interestingly, however, though Weigley finds the origins of US strategy and policy in the Civil War, the historical scholarship which addresses the military campaigns against the Native Americans demonstrates a virtually identical tradition with its genesis in the early seventeenth century.[2] Notwithstanding this difference in temporal frameworks, the conclusion is inescapable that, insofar as national security strategy and policy are concerned, the US is clearly exceptional: for most countries with but a marginal strategic advantage, victory in war, if it is achieved, is the result of attrition, exhaustion, or erosion of the will to fight, and therefore, absolute victory is only a theoretical, and not an operational possibility. Accordingly, most wars fought by most countries are fought for limited causes and realise only incremental gains. The wealth of resources on the other hand, and the unlimited aims fostered by the ideology of American Exceptionalism allowed the US to realise the overthrow of its enemies, rather than their submission, which weaker powers knew they had to accept as victory. Though likely unacquainted with this ideology, Clausewitz was nevertheless fully aware of the mind-set in general and he warned that those who would pursue the objective of absolute victory need not only to 'presuppose a great physical or moral superiority, or a great spirit of enterprise,' but also *'an innate propensity to extreme hazards.'*[3] This is particularly the case when, throughout the twentieth century, examples proliferate of apparent victories in which the costs were frequently inordinate and the triumph illusory.

In this context it is significant that now, three decades after Weigley's thesis was propounded, the experience of economic globalisation recalls its central tenet; namely, that US strategy – the framework by which it seeks both peace and security for itself and its allies – is essentially one of annihilation, derived from, and sustained at almost every turn by the historical development of the United States. Throughout, my argument has been that a parallel exists in the logical conclusions to economic globalisation theory and practice; indeed, if we accept that *security strategy*, properly defined, subordinates and coordinates all dimensions of national life, and that the political-economic dimension is integral to any sensible definition of security, then the character of that strategy – sometimes known as *grand strategy* – will necessarily be the animating force for thinking and acting. Specifically, under the reign of the dominant discourses of war and economics, the most that can be hoped for is a respite from thinking in terms of certain forms of war, but not, it seems, the need to think in forms of war *per se*.

If that is the case, then the form of war we should recall for the purposes of locating so much of the death, destruction, and dislocation which is contextualised by contemporary economic globalisation is revolution. While it is commonplace to see the overturning of the Keynesian consensus in the West, and traditional political economy elsewhere as a revolution, the nature of that revolution is not so readily disclosed until the particularities of the turning moments, and the transformation they effect, are brought to the fore. In the first instance, therefore, we need to understand that the trends are extremal, creating the United States as not only the world's first hyper-power, but a power that, unlike any other through the successful unification of its theories and practices of nation, global military power, and religion, in a quest for nothing less than universality and historical fulfilment that is appropriately described by Johan Galtung as Manifest Theology.[4] To oppose it, therefore, is to live in the shadow of the consequences of opposing the institutional embodiment of God's will: *extra ecclesiam nulla salus* ('outside the church there is no salvation').

Opposition, unsurprisingly, is currently minimal; indeed, it is remarkable just how normalised, routinised, rationalised, and legitimised the processes and consequences of this revolution are. Thus, though it is unquestionably a violent imperial movement, many people of a hitherto liberal caste of mind – highly intelligent people moreover – have even provided its apologetics by appealing to its ultimate benevolence in the context of the evolving US geostrategy following the terrorist attacks of 11 September 2001.[5] Some, to be sure, have suggested the beginnings of a counter-revolution by defecting, but examples of daring in the face of accommodation are rare.[6] In the name of virtue and, not least, professional advancement, the reigning piety among the intelligentsia requires the affirmation of the contemporary prerogatives of power, and the denigration of a sceptical disposition and dissent. Religion and science are, accordingly, again co-mingled under the worst of circumstances and with the worst of consequences: the pre-digested faith demanded of the former infuses the unexamined certainties of the latter, effectively robbing doubt of its dignity and placing off-limits the spirit of rigorous inquiry eloquently encapsulated in the old Italian proverb: *chi piu sa, memo crede* ('who knows more believes less').

Needless to say, such an admixture creates confusions. In economic life, it is required that the state be sufficiently virile and stable to establish and maintain the requisite conditions for the existence of a market – namely, the presence of law and the absence of war – while abdicating from any interventionist role in that market. The state's personality, in other words, must be militarily assertive and economically withdrawn, while its intelligence must be sufficiently undemanding in order that it may deny that there is any conflict between them, even to the point of contradiction. Thus, the predicate rational economic personality which dominates Economics at all levels of abstraction, personal and national, is now found not to inhabit the world of America's adversaries, personal and national. Or, to put it starkly, deterrence, conventional and nuclear, which was held to be responsible for peace between the superpowers during the Cold War, when the margin of strategic advantage enjoyed by the US was highly contested, is now thought to be inadequate for the purposes of containing Iraq, North Korea, Libya, and Iran at a time when their strategic inferiority to the United States is unquestionable.[7] Quite simply, the world is held to be, at one and the same time, economically calculating and strategically insane; with equal conviction the latter condition imposes itself upon the national consciousness and is held to require the adoption by the United States of a national strategy of pre-emptive strikes, employing, if necessary, nuclear weapons, 'to combat weapons of mass destruction.'[8] Such an eccentric, isolated, and bifurcated response, with its deferral of responsibility to alien influences, and devoid of human sensitivity, is not unknown in the studies of the mind, but there it goes not by the term 'security strategy,' but, and more properly, classical, or clinically defined schizophrenia.[9]

As if this were not enough, confusion also arises from observers generally being insufficiently aware of the Neo-Clausewitzian strands interwoven through contemporary US thought. At the most fundamental level they miss its trinitarian character which is constituted, in the first instance, by the traditional political strand, and which they have no difficulty in identifying and understanding, but they fail to recognise the two other strands which, in synergy, multiply the 'innate propensity to extreme hazards.' Put another way, it is the consequence of not understanding how, in the US, thought and deed are constantly in flux between the poles of the common, or vulgar, and the Exceptionalist. And the key to understanding this is always to be aware that, for practical purposes, they are both, simultaneously. Thus, it is conceded that, for the United States, sovereignty is, or might as well be understood as absolute; that the US holds that its interests are clearly discernible, and that war, far from being unthinkable, is a rational, normal – indeed, legal – instrument of achieving or safeguarding these interests. This, of course, reproaches the various politico-legal doctrines anathematising war which emerged after 1945 but the critical understanding afforded by extending an inquiry into US strategy seldom extends any further than making this point, or rationalising the departure in many cases.

Going further we can facilitate a deeper inquiry by asking a few simple, illustrative questions: does it really matter to the United States whether Belize, or Kiribati, or Grenada, or the Ivory Coast have market economies? Or whether Bolivia, Brazil, Chile, and Venezuela are ruled by democratically elected left-of-centre governments? Or whether the socialist government of Nicaragua came to power in a popular revolution against the 43-year regime of the despot, Anastasio Somoza Garcia? Or whether successive democratically elected governments in New Zealand want to adopt a non-nuclear policy yet remain in an alliance with the US? In the realisation that, for the United States, the answer is yes, lies a key: most states, on sober reflection, concede that, overall, human identity rather than difference is the hallmark of the international community; for the US, the opposite is true, and it has the power to act accordingly, for its own good, and, so the rationale goes, for the good of others. It does so, moreover, in what is really a paranoid world of implacable, permanent, and ubiquitous enemies and gives rise to the peculiarly American character of neo-Clausewitzianism which catalysed Anatol Rapoport's study of US strategy at the high point of the Vietnam War.[10]

War, in these terms, be it economic or conventional-strategic, is perforce not only political but also an extended act of eschatological and cataclysmic violence executed within the authorising power of self-anointed messiansism. At the time of course, the US was engaged in one of its redemptive struggles on behalf of the 'Free World,' a term which, after 11 September 2001, was displaced by 'Civilisation.' The purpose then, as now, was to maintain a certain type of political-economic order convivial to the 'Free World' in the international system; by extension revolts against that order were, by definition, unacceptable challenges to be met with whatever force was deemed necessary to destroy them. Such revolts are compound threats: in the first instance, as a particular challenge to the system; in the second, as an exemplar which, if followed, would lead to wider insurrections. They therefore represent, and are understood as, a cataclysmic threat at two levels, the ethnocentric and the global – respectively, to the United States itself as the 'Applied Enlightenment,' and to humanity as a whole, which the United States has vouchsafed to defend.

By definition, the 'Free World' cannot be at fault, or as the saying has it, 'part of the problem:' it seeks only to defend itself from hostile intentions and acts, the origins for which are located either elsewhere in global space, or within political-economic structures yet to be transformed into reasonableness by Enlightenment values and practices. If this should require war of one type or another, then it is to be understood in messianic terms as a necessary eschatological violence to save the world from itself. Undertaken in the name of a unifying philosophy by a predestined agent the ensuing victory will lead to the emergence of a rational and peaceful world order. Should this be considered fanciful it might be worth also considering that only a nation so committed to the mutual suicide pact which was nuclear deterrence, so committed to retaining and developing its own weapons of mass destruction while denying the right of all others to possess them, and so preoccupied with the metaphysics of 'grand design' at a time of its own manifest decline could be so deeply indebted to the sophomoric and rhapsodic consolations provided by Francis Fukuyama and his end-of-history thesis.

Clearly, economic globalisation is revolution, but it is also much more than revolution superficially understood as an emancipatory project; indeed, it is the revolution which Albert Camus agonised over as the type which, having ushered in unchecked liberty, in this case by way of the 'free market,' gives rise to totalitarianism. At its core is a triple debasement of the human which mocks the very suggestion of the eschatological. It starts with the abstraction so beloved of those who would describe the world in an equation. Understood politically, abstraction is a preference for obliterating difference and merely suggesting the human almost as though the world and its people in everyday life actually looked like, and functioned as, a Miro painting. Above all, it is the precursor to indifference because those who thrive on abstraction do not much care whether it does or it doesn't.

If the world of full humanness is denied, then those who are denied are consigned to silence. Whether they speak, or hold their peace is irrelevant: they will not be heard. There exists, therefore, a schism of indifference between the imperial *romanita* and the sterile legalisms which are imposed from without, and those living in the world with their consequences, the principal of which is the legitimised murder undertaken in the name of economic reform. To the extent that humankind accommodates to this state, it lives, consciously or unconsciously, only in a permanent state of humiliation, which is to say, without solace or confidence in itself beyond the absurdities sanctioned by neo-liberalism. But this is not so much an end-state as a phase, or further episode, in grand strategic failure whose precedents allow us deeper understanding, if not greater optimism, concerning the future of neo-liberalism.

To say this is to say that the times are not unique. Without any form of invidious comparison whatsoever, it is possible to identify remarkably similar periods in history; indeed, this work was introduced by noting how closely the present resembled the age of religious wars which began in the sixteenth century, a theme which has been maintained throughout. Now, after developing it, the raiments of the period are more highly defined. That a form of religious war is underway is affirmed, but the type of war has revealed itself, too. It is a crusade which, in every aspect affecting strategic competence, recalls the original adventure in recklessness given the name in the eleventh century. As historians of the period advise us, the First Crusade, as evidently is this one, was led by rulers given to neither the introspection which would have tempered their belief in absolutes, nor the caution which would have bridled their ambition. In turn they addressed generally ignorant, unreflective, and frequently criminal audiences in need of simple reasons for believing that their inner zeal and the senseless, sanctimonious slaughter that they committed against people was a redemptive act, *Deus hoc vult* ('as God will it'). In the end, failure: the costs were ruinous, not least for the rulers themselves, and the reigning theology of the day was unable to provide the basis for any relevant and lasting political organisation.

Throughout the intervening millennium nothing has changed. The basest of reasons and the most threadbare philosophy have justified crusades and religious wars to the point of their being a semi-permanent feature of the global landscape. At the heart of them all is some dogma demanding absolute allegiance and exclusivity – effectively, the surrender of conscience and judgment – in the name of a reigning divinity or truth. In many periods the *casus belli* was infidelity to dominant Christian doctrine while, in others, it could be reduced to antagonistic absolutes residing in the monotheisms of Christianity and Islam respectively. In the current period it is the transubstantiation of a variant of political-economic thinking into an externality demanding service and obedience on the traditional bases found in its predecessors – faith, revelation, or circumstantial discretion. But in point of historical fact, and as a guide for action in the world, it is not only profoundly lacking, but a mortally dangerous fixation of a great power upon itself, a terrible sadness well captured by Robinson Jeffers:

> Unhappy country, what wings you have!…
> Weep (it is frequent in human affairs),
> weep for the terrible magnificence of the means,
> the ridiculous incompetence of the reasons,
> the bloody and shabby
> Pathos of the result.[11]

Epilogues

Epilogue 1

Neo-liberalism and the empirical record – theorising global strategic economic incompetence

A CASE TO ANSWER

I begin with two propositions. The first is unexceptional – that the purpose of political action, and hence the criterion by which all political action must be judged, is that it is undertaken to either improve the conditions under which we live, or to prevent those conditions from deteriorating further. The second should be equally unexceptional; namely, there are some human undertakings that are so horrendous in their conception and their consequences that our human mind demands not only an explanation of them, but a search for authorship, a rendering of an account to those whose responsibility for them can only be described as something else – as guilt for their ever having occurred in the first place. Consider just three, relatively unproblematic events which have brought this need for interrogation, against the specified criterion, to the fore.

★★★

On the great British memorial at Thiepval, the Somme, and on the Menin Gate at Ypres (by way of just two examples), are found, respectively, the names of 73,000, and 55,000 British soldiers; in both cases they record those who were, and remain, classified as 'missing,' but that is just an euphemism for the fact that, 30 years before the atom bombs dropped on Japan turned the very ground into a photo-sensitive plate, and so recorded the last nanosecond of many people's existence, thousands of tons of high explosives on the Western front were de-realising people in similar numbers as were exterminated at Nagasaki and Hiroshima.[1] And for what purpose? In the Battle of the Somme, the British captured just 45 square miles of territory in five months at a cost of 8,000 men per square mile; in the course of three years of fighting across the entire Western front no offensive succeeded in budging the line by more that 10 miles. Reflecting on the industrialised mass slaughter that it was, D.H. Lawrence wrote that it was 'not strife, it was murder'; reflecting on its causes, Norman Dixon was equally troubling in his assessment:

> Only the most blinkered could deny that the First World War exemplified every aspect of high-level military incompetence. For sheer lack of leadership, inept decisions, ignoring military intelligence, underestimation of the enemy, delusional optimism and monumental wastage of human resources it has surely never had its equal.[2]

There was a case to answer.

★★★

By the end of 1990, it was atypical of US scholarly reviews of the preceding 40 years to conclude that the Inchon landings of September 1950 were 'the last major victory for American arms.'³ From the record, which includes the débâcle in Indo-China and the more than 120 specifically designated rescue and other missions in that conflict, through still more rescue missions – such as those in support of the *Mayaguez* and the hostages in Teheran, and interventions-cum-invasions such as those in Beirut, Grenada and Panama – the armed forces of the United States performed in a manner which allowed neither confidence in themselves nor on the part of allies operating with them, or in receipt of a US security guarantee. The basic data and analytical literature attesting to this were available, cumulatively, over the four decades in question, and were, moreover, marked by four characteristics: first, the database was broadly agreed on; second, the analyses were provided by specialists from across the political spectrum; third, there was broad agreement among their findings; and fourth, their judgments were made on the basis of criteria established by the US military itself and on which there was a consensus among similar analysts and military forces outside the United States. An exemplary conclusion was reached by Richard Gabriel's study:

> The American military is in serious trouble. Its recent historical record, to say nothing of its disastrous performance in Vietnam, has been marked far more often by failure than success. Its military plans have been unrealistic and unsuccessful. The officer corps by any historical standard is lacking in the spirit and expertise that have characterised the more successful officer corps in history. *Worse, it is infected by habits and values which are characteristic of many of the worst officer corps in history. The record is clear that the officer corps has failed the single test of a successful army, the ability to perform well in the field of battle.*⁴

There was a case to answer.

★★★

Significantly, but only indicatively in terms of publicly acknowledged failures, down the years, the intelligence agencies of the United States did not foresee: the first Soviet atomic bomb; North Korea's invasion of South Korea in 1950; Korean revolt of 1956; the launching of Sputnik in 1957; Fidel Castro's victory and the subsequent placement of Soviet missiles in Cuba; the massive Soviet effort in the mid-1960s to match the US in strategic missile numbers and capabilities; the 1973 Middle East war; India's acquisition of a nuclear capability in 1974; the overthrow of the Shah of Iran in 1979; the Soviet invasion of Afghanistan in the same year; the disintegration of its principal focus and *raison d'être*, the Soviet Union in 1992; the Asian financial crisis of 1997 and the Indian nuclear tests of May 1998, etc. Then, on 11 September 2001, four civilian airliners were hijacked and three of them flown into government and public buildings in the US as part of a terrorist strategy. In all between 3,000 and 4,000 innocent people were killed in a period of less than one hour. The US intelligence community – funded, in 2001, to a level of at least US$30 billion annually, consisting in at least 39 organisations, and having access to at least 75,000 personnel, also failed to foresee or prevent these attacks.

There is a case to answer.

★★★

Now consider an ongoing event which, in its dimensions of destruction of life and ecology, dwarfs all three of the above, is a determinant of the third, and yet does not move the collective curiosity and conscience (let alone outrage) of the West: on 11 September 2001, the neo-liberal strategy of economic globalisation had been underway for approximately 20 to 25 years; to say the least, the Structural Adjustment Programs of the World Bank (WB) and the International Monetary Fund (IMF) had been in the ascendant. The state of the world this project had brought about was, compared to the 20 years prior to 1980, significantly worse: according to analyses by the Washington, DC-based Center for Economic and Policy Research, whereas just 13 per cent of the world's countries experienced a per capita growth increase of at least five percentage points, more than three-quarters of the world's countries experienced a growth *reduction* by that much; indeed, in 18 countries, Brazil and Mexico among them, per capita wealth would have nearly, or more than, doubled had the countries in question maintained their pre-IMF/ WB strategies, which concentrated on meeting local needs through the development of their own productive capacity.[5]

Confirmation of this general malaise was provided by the United Nations Development Program which found that the bottom 20 per cent of the world's poor, in less than four decades following 1960, have seen their fraction of global wealth steadily decline from a paltry 2.3 per cent to an even paltrier 1.1 per cent in 1998.[6] On 11 September 2001 this quintile of some 1.2 billion people was struggling to survive on US$1 or less, while lacking access to safe drinking-water and adequate sanitation, or, to put the matter starkly and in perspective, in the course of that day, while the world was rightly shocked, lamented the loss of life from the attacks, and was moved to anger against their perpetrators, and solidarity with the USA (as evidenced by the outpourings of the media, messages from world political and religious leaders, rock concerts, military mobilisation, and the promise of war), the Food and Agriculture Organisation reported that, as per normal in the age of neo-liberalism, the daily mortality continued: around 36,615 children died from conditions resulting from extreme poverty and resultant starvation.

There is a case to answer.

★★★

THE CASE

The substance of this fourth case, clearly, concerns the sustained assault on life and the conditions under which it is lived under the regime of increasing neo-liberalism, especially in the context of its promise that those who follow it will, in human time, not only live in greater comfort, but die with nobler dreams than would be the case if alternative political-economic arrangements were followed. This is why, after all, the entire resource base of countries was to be adjusted to a 'new economy' constructed according to a grand strategic vision – and why deregulation, privatisation, and the adoption of market economics, and the embrace of the great free trade initiatives such as the Uruguay Round of the GATT, the establishment of the World Trade Organization, the North American Free Trade Agreement, Asia Pacific Economic Consultation were not just desirable but imperative in the first place. Conversely, it is why, given the sustained nature of contrary outcomes throughout the world, the initial question must address the competence of this regime to rule, or rather, its incompetence in the face of circumstances beyond its comprehension and control, but not, it seems, its ambitions.

In other words, if the disasters arising in the time of neo-liberalism are not *ex machina* 'acts of God,' then they are direct consequences of theories-as-practices, and theorists-as-grand-strategists. In a phrase, the comprehensive failures of chosen means to achieve the identified ends. *Individual, idiosyncratic,* or *temperamental* incompetence is not, therefore, even a remotely possible explanation even though the purpose of the following analysis is to explain how a relative minority of global economic strategists came to be able to wreak so much havoc upon humankind. Accordingly, the focus of explanation will be upon the organised collective which is constituted by the body of theorists (and other advocates of their theories) whose ideas are faithfully and systematically realised in policy as the daily, lived reality for the great majority of people on the planet. Thus, though it is the case that the collective is made up of individuals, it is also the case that they share a common discourse – neo-liberalism – and the common foundation to this discourse which is the discipline of neoclassical economics. As with the pigs in Orwell's *Animal Farm*, however, it is readily conceded that not all economists are equal in their authority, influence, power, and rights; consequently, for present purposes, the defining, common characteristics of these strategists are their immersion in, commitment to, and actions in the pursuit of economic globalisation determined by the discourse of neo-liberalism, regardless of whether or not they were formally instructed in it. As John Maynard Keynes famously and practically reminded us in his *General Theory*, anyone who thinks that she or he simply received their inspiration from the air is in reality merely distilling her or his views 'from the work of some academic scribbler of a few years back.'

Notwithstanding the human need to alleviate the conditions arising from strategic failure by understanding their root causes, the need for this inquiry also arises out of an additional four special reasons. The first is that the responsible organisations are a magnet to a class, or social category, of people who, when they occupy positions of authority, ensure that disaster follows (notwithstanding their undoubted educational opportunities), while the second is that the nature of their organisational commitment serves to accentuate the characteristics which entail disaster. Third, since the organisations in question are, almost like the military forces of the state, seldom, if ever (and then only with great difficulty) accountable to even a democratic political process in a timely way, they are virtually beyond recall. Finally, and demonstrably like the military, there is an integral relationship between wrong decisions and untold misery;[7] indeed, the fastness of the link and the magnitude of the consequences surpasses the incompetence-caused misery of any campaign in military history. (In this, the role of technology in the service of incompetence plays the same role as it does in war, with the costs rising exponentially the more that its cutting edge is applied.)

Interrogated more closely for types, or varieties of incompetence, the empirical record throws up three: administrative, planning, and deliberate wastage (of human beings).[8] Within and across these categories, it is possible to abstract incompetence into a further seven aspects which broadly apply wherever the general phenomenon is found and documented, as it was in the earlier treatment of *triage*, or wherever Economics itself is subjected to scrutiny, as it was in the succeeding chapters. They are as follows:[9]

1   A serious wastage of human resources which is, in turn, derived from certain attitudes of mind reinforced by the discipline of economics.
2   A fundamental conservatism, including, of course, a refusal to admit past mistakes or even to learn from the experience they provide.
3   A tendency to ignore information – or even to be adequately informed of the situation in which neo-liberalism was to be imposed, the two corollaries of which are a tendency to underestimate the difficulties and resistance to the imposition of neo-liberalism, and, when committed, an obstinate persistence along a given line of action despite strong and comprehensive evidence to the contrary.
4   A preference for what might be called policy-rape – which is to say, a belief in, and a preference for the imposition of neo-liberalism from above under conditions inimical to the establishment of informed democratic consent.
5   An undue readiness to find scapegoats for setbacks and reproaches to neo-liberalism.
6   The suppression or distortion of information, or data, which would (or should) challenge the confidence and morale of self-critical neo-liberals.
7   A belief in mystical forces as the source of misfortune, rather than a necessary acknowledgment that disastrous situations are the result of incompetence.

The case which the neo-liberals have to answer, then, is demanded by the consequences of the strategy and means of economic globalisation, and the incompetence of those identified as the leaders, or executors, of that strategy. But it goes beyond this 'what' question to the question of 'how' we understand these outcomes of neo-liberalism in a systematic way; in other words, if we accept that the well-documented and enduring consequences of neo-liberalism can only be the result of incompetence (for any suggestion to the contrary beggars the imagination), then it behoves us to ask what it is in neo-liberalism that engenders them. Of necessity, therefore, what is sought is a theory of global economic strategic incompetence based on the identification of historically sustained conditions which derive from equally historically sustained antecedent patterns of thought and behaviour, and which reside in Economics. Accordingly, to borrow from a related (and inspiring) proposition of Norman F. Dixon's, the argument in the following pages is that the probability of incompetence arises in significant part from the unfortunate if unavoidable consequences of creating a profession of economists, the existence of which, as previously and currently configured, tends to produce a levelling down of human capability, at once encouraging to intellectual mediocrity, but cramping and hostile to the comprehensive embrace of human interests.[10]

THE ARGUMENT

As inferred at several points previously, the foundation for this attempt to account for the complex interaction between economists and the discipline of Economics (including projects informed by the latter) is Dixon's *On the Psychology of Military Incompetence*,[11] which, because of the differences which exist between Economics and the profession of arms, has been adapted in places, but not so as to disqualify the attempt in the first place. Essentially, Dixon reviews the quality of British generalship in a period running from the Crimean War, through, *inter alia*, the Boer War, the First World War, the Inter-War period, and into the Second World War (paying special attention to the débâcles of Singapore and Arnhem and seeks to explain the ways in which a certain profession operates – an objective shared by this analysis).

But the similarity extends beyond ambition into not only the character-types that are drawn to the profession, but also to the habits of mind and action which result under certain stimuli. The phenomenon to hand is that of almost remote, or solitary individuals seeking acceptance and an evasion of their alienation, by the means of advancement and success in a public vocation demanding skill or training, and offering esteem. This is not to say that the military officer class and economists are indistinguishable from each other; rather, it is to say that the professional-disciplinary requirements of both are such that the framework for understanding their theories and practices is very similar, if not identical, and that, where differences in the framework exist, they relate to the content of the various sub-categories, but not at all to their appropriateness and validity. Thus, it is apparent that both military officers and economists are dominated by a 'complex of rules, conventions and ways of thinking which, in the course of time, ossify into outmoded tradition, curious ritual, inappropriate dogma... and "bullshit."'[12] In relation to the former, the phenomenon is well known as militarism, in the latter, we might refer to it as 'economism' – the super-imposition of the dictates of the putative science of Economics upon the study of political economy in particular, and life more generally. By extension, we find that within the condition of *anxiety*, a common contributor to both military and economic strategic incompetence, the respective forms that it takes are, quite naturally, peculiar to each.

Many, no doubt, will find the attempt to compare military incompetence with economic strategic incompetence simply outrageous for the same, or very similar reasons that many oppose the attempt to show that the loss of life and destruction caused by neo-liberalism is not only warlike, but so often exceeds the costs of wars in the twentieth century. Honesty compels the admission that Dixon is of this view himself on the basis that, whereas wrong military decisions could result in mega-deaths – which is true – what he calls wrong 'academic decisions' are so 'trivial and unimportant ... that it would be arrogant to discuss them in the same breath.'[13] But even in 1976, the year of his major work's publication, he was surely wrong, and remains wrong to this day, quite possibly because then, as now, the world of commerce was agreeably, but misleadingly configured by an indulgent popular discourse in the global North in terms which excluded its violence. Furthermore, the very term 'mega-death' was not given its currency by a soldier, but by someone closer to the academic side of life – the nuclear strategic theorist,

Herman Kahn, and Kahn was not alone in the academy historically, contemporaneously, or since, as Keynes was determined to emphasise.

Thus, unless we accept the proposition that the ideas and theories – and in particular, canonical ideas and theories – developed and transmitted in, and therefore legitimated by universities, have no consequences, it is preposterous to conclude that bad academic decisions are 'trivial and unimportant.' Not only is it reproached by the historical record of the unity of purpose between the state and the university-as-institution, but the logic of denial requires that academics, and the universities which nurture them, be seen as irrelevant – a proposition which was rejected over 2,400 years ago, when Socrates was put to death by the Athenians on baseless charges of impiety for teaching and defending his philosophical views to the youth of the city.

Economics, in any case, is an aggressive and destructive discipline that, like the university more generally, is able to disguise its character by the indulgences extended to it by foolish, less-than-critical observers of its practices. While many examples exist which illustrate this, one of the better ways is to recall that, right from the earliest days of United States nuclear strategy, the disciplinary disposition of Economics allowed it to furnish game theorists to the national security state so that the costs and benefits of nuclear war could be rationally calculated. The most famous of these was John von Neumann, a believer in an 'ultimate solution' to economic questions, who not only enthusiastically embraced the game-theoretic challenge presented by nuclear weapons, but, following upon the first successful detonation of a hydrogen bomb by the US, advocated the immediate nuclear annihilation of the Soviet Union according to the axioms of game theory. In some quarters, von Neumann's intellectual contribution to world peace was a cause for wonder – he was even lauded as superhuman by some colleagues – it took the psychologist, Jacques Ellul, to place his thought processes in perspective: when 'techo-logic' so dominates the pattern of thought and action, it is likely to eliminate certain vital elements of consciousness, resulting in a diminished awareness of what it is to be a human being.[14]

Outrage at the comparison of military incompetence with economic strategic incompetence also fails to take into account the convergence in their respective ways of thinking and associating. A perusal of the business and economics section of any large mainstream bookshop reveals that 'the new economy' is revelling in its claims to be also the 'new war,' and nowhere is this more obvious than in the appropriation of the work of the fourth-century BCE Chinese strategist, Sun Tzu. Essentially what is presented in these treatises is economic-strategic advice to executives and educators on the analogous and equivalent nature of the world of business and the world of war, and the ways to reconfigure commerce accordingly.[15] To the extent that their arguments might have a common implicit or explicit conceptual origin or inspiration, they seem to have internalised Edward Luttwak's propositions that the geoeconomic is displacing the geostrategic as the most likely mode of international conflict, and that an essential equivalence exists between them:

> In geoeconomics the firepower is capital, market penetration replaces foreign bases and garrisons.... The equivalent of strategic nuclear weapons... are things like

industrial and investment policies. The everyday tool, powerful but enormously flexible, is market access.[16]

For those still to be convinced further evidence is to hand in the form of contributions from contemporary military strategists across a broad spectrum. In the late 1990s, for instance, there were the lyrical and extremely insightful writings of the Zapatista leader Sub-Commandante Marcos, whose geostrategic analysis of neo-liberalism concluded that it is a world system whose objectives and consequences constituted the fourth world war.[17] Then, almost simultaneously, there was the international travelling forum entitled *World Masters of Business* which, in August 1997, offered a 'once in a lifetime chance to see, hear and meet [such] great business leaders as former President and CEO of both Ford and Chrysler, Lee Iacocca, and former *Desert Storm* commander, General Norman Schwarzkopf: the latter's fee – between A\$130,000–A\$190,000 – being justified on the grounds that his address, "From the War Room to the Board Room," would bring together his unique insights into the military-business synergism by 'the most in-demand authority on these subjects in the world today.'[18]

For those in the United States Marine Corps still to attain Schwarzkopf's standing, training in the very arts of modern warfare decision-making that he was being lauded for was to be provided to 15 of their number by secondment to the floor of the New York Mercantile Exchange; there, they would face the 'ultimate test' (experienced by traders every day) in the form of having to make split-second decisions in the face of 'a blizzard of information – often misleading – about factors like accidents, weather, economic trends and even war.'[19] More recently, internet websites such as *War, Chaos, and Business* have emerged which explicitly link features, articles, and presentations on the theme of manoeuvre conflict in general, and manoeuvre warfare in particular, to business strategy in such a way that a fusion of (by way of example only) Sun Tzu, 'agility,' 'fast decision cycle time,' 'mission orientation,' and trust are universally applicable – to the US Marine Corps, to Japanese industrialists, and to General Electric.[20]

We find as well a resounding echo of Jomini's arrogant claim that the fundamental principles of war are unchangeable, independent of the weapons employed, and timeless in an equally arrogant 1991 speech by Lawrence Summers to a World Bank–IMF annual general meeting in Bangkok, Thailand:

> The laws of economics, it's often forgotten, are like the laws of engineering. There's only one set of laws and they work everywhere. One of the things that I've learned in my short time at the World Bank is that whenever anybody says, 'But economics works differently here,' they're about to say something dumb.[21]

Vignettes of this nature could be cited almost *ad infinitum* but those adduced are, I believe, indicative of the general case that is being advanced here; namely, that, armed with a knowledge and understanding of the incompetence on display in military disasters, the more disconcerting is the growing familiarity which comes from knowing and understanding incompetence in neo-liberal globalisation through a lens which captures the enduring features and explanations of their performances.

In brief, therefore, I am proposing that, as per Dixon, a critical understanding of the mental or emotional state of the strategists of globalisation is central to the question of their incompetence on the basis that such an inquiry more satisfactorily explains the seven constituents which were listed above – in summary form, cognitive dissonance, the tendency to pontificate, and the inability to adjust the riskiness of decisions to something approaching the real situation. All of them, as Dixon recounts from the relevant bodies of knowledge, 'are a product of such neurotic disabilities as extreme anxiety under stress, low self-esteem, nervousness, the need for approval, and general defensiveness.'[22] The progression of the argument, therefore, is to the point where these outcomes are seen as logical and natural consequences of the attraction of certain people to Economics, and their subsequent mental state within that discipline. It is, perforce of this, necessary to ground this argument in the disciplinary organisation of Economics before, successively, incorporating its phobic preoccupations with disorder (both generally and specifically), disciplinary honour, an anti-feminine outlook, professional achievement, and the embrace of authoritarianism.

THE TERRIBLE PARADOX OF ECONOMICS: WHERE LIKE ATTRACTS LIKE

If we assume that people are not indifferent to the profession in which they spend their lives, we cannot dispense with the related proposition that people are drawn to certain careers and professions for reasons that have to do with who they are – the combination of their physical and psychological make-up, in other words. Grant this unexceptional proposition and its corollary, and it can also be safely assumed that people become economists because Economics satisfies what they most want in the form of lifestyle, discipline, status, rewards, and overall expression of personality. Indeed, this is the nature of a profession: its members, by their entry to it and their progress within it, are making the statement: 'This I believe and will live by.' In some cases, the *profession* of belief is public and explicit – as in the obligations medical doctors swear to discharge in the Hippocratic Oath; in others it is implied but none the less binding if only because the profession, if it takes professional identity seriously, requires and ensures compliance, one way or the other, for the great majority of its members.

In the case of Economics, the first defining characteristic worthy of mention in this regard is its excessive belief in the applicability of the methods of physical science to the understanding of human behaviour – what is known as *scientism* – a sub-culture which hampers rather than facilitates an understanding of the global political economy. More comprehensively approached:

> We see it as an ever-increasing web of rules, restrictions and constraints, presided over by an elite, one of whose motives [is] to preserve the status quo. We see it... as the natural product of a fundamentally jealous, class-conscious hierarchy whose nostalgia and basic conservatism ensure that the present must always bear the hallmark of the past. And we see it as remarkably similar in many respects to the ethos of the prototypical Victorian upper-class family group, where absolute obedience and submission to authority are traded for security and dependence.[23]

Scientism is quite a magnetic quality in Economics. Given that there is a need in any society, particularly the society of states, and most particularly within the dominant states of that society, to be able to describe and explain the production and distribution of wealth, the ability to do so within a discourse redolent of physics fuses many motivations. It is, depending on the moment, a labour of patriotic devotion, as much as worthy public service; at all times, however, it is also a source of upward mobility and personal wealth. Equally, but depending on an economist's position within the relevant hierarchy, it brings forth an opportunity to exert political influence, most frequently over the lives of generations of people who are total strangers and presumably towards whom she or he has no hostile feelings. These in themselves are troubling intimations which only increase when a deeper appreciation of the attractions of scientism is forthcoming.

Stated succinctly, scientism provides a defence against certain anxieties, and, by extension, attracts people with those anxieties and who are disposed to the quality of defence it affords. Within the discipline, they form a community of sufferers as much as a community of scholars who are joined, first, by the expectation, and then the realisation of the effective therapeutic gain which scientism extends to its devotees. What needs to be noted, however, is that this does not cure or suppress the condition of anxiety so much as it provides a convivial, secure, and supportive environment in which people with anxieties can not only operate, but operate through approved outlets for their anxieties, and as their anxieties might determine, in socially acceptable ways. [24]

In Economics, the causes of anxiety are readily identifiable inasmuch as they are logical extensions of the nature of Economics as a discipline, and as a profession, though the latter is a particular case of a besetting condition with professions themselves. To approach the former is merely to recall that Economics was born on the cusp of an intellectual revolution which ensured the destruction of its seventeenth-century, Newtonian foundations. Choosing to turn its face from this, it has, throughout its history, retained a Cartesian vision of a world which is constant, permanent, simple, static, and invulnerable. In pursuit of this excessively abstract universe it uncritically (mis)appropriated whole areas of a discipline in débâcle (mathematics), and the superseded axioms of another (physics), made explicit its refusal to confront the former, and chose data to suit its aspirations, concepts and constructs on an opportunistic basis, in the course of which, progressively and rapidly, their emptiness became as obvious as the discipline's comprehensive inadequacy to the phenomena it sought to understand.

In evolutionary terms, its aspirations were always unrealisable; it never rose above being a pastiche of *ad hoc* stratagems and became, unsurprisingly, practically irrelevant. In the history of technology and science this is unique, but for the worst of reasons. Preceding the development of scientific thinking around 600 BCE, the Babylonians and the Egyptians at least had the former: certain things – in astronomy, geometry, and medicine, for example – 'worked' but the explanations for their doing so were mythological. It was only under the pre-Socratic Greeks that explanations entirely from the natural world were first ventured. Modernity has not consigned this condition to the past. In the world of the twenty-first century, while it is commonplace for physicists to use quantum mechanics, leading physicists, Nobel Prize winners among them, readily concede that they do not understand it, or how it could be what is. Yet Economics, which defines itself as the science of the production and distribution of wealth, has neither escaped its theoretical confusion despite its strenuous efforts to the contrary, nor approached Antiquity's consolation of providing consistent, reliable, policy-usable outcomes, nor even thought it necessary to adopt physics' humility.

For Economics, reminders of these failures are constant because records are kept and, significantly, they are made available in quality and quantity, and from sources that must be taken seriously. And while it might be the case that avoidance and denial are possible in the early stages of experience, it must also be the case that they eventually penetrate and take up residence in the conscious or self-conscious. Putting the matter bluntly, any evolving awareness of sustained failure – and remember, this is a failure which springs significantly from the organised suppression of the unpredictable elements of human creativity – necessarily induces a chain of anxieties which begin with the fear of disciplinary-professional supersession, which then leads into the fear of ongoing failure and social disapproval, and, ultimately, the encompassing fear of disorder resulting from the release of proscribed instinctual forces which the overthrow of the discipline will entail (notwithstanding that they exist and have effect anyway). At stake is a personal-professional identity, years of accumulated intellectual capital, and the return on investment that this promises, always provided that nothing changes. The question, then, is this: in the absence of large-scale defections from the discipline, what mechanisms exist within it which allow economists to cope with rising levels of anxiety born of their own incompetence? The first and clearest answer, in a single word, is 'bullshit.'[25]

'BULLSHIT' (GENERALLY)

In Economics, as in the military, bullshit is omnipresent and ubiquitous. In both, moreover, it is the outgrowth of taking an unexceptional, general principle – that any life worth living depends upon the preservation of a minimum level of order – and elevating it to the level of an obsessional neurosis.[26] At this level the phenomenon involves an excessive socialisation process marked by the ritualistic observance of the dominance–submission relationships of the Economics hierarchy, extreme orderliness, and a preoccupation with outward appearances (a common tendency in many societies), all of which are thought to have their origins in the formative years of those affected. In the modern university, with its increasing vocational mission, it would be surprising if any of these outcomes were otherwise. Where professional instruction and theoretical (albeit politically and socially irrelevant) perfection are the goals, and positivism is the method, then there too are hierarchy, order, and the exclusive concentration on things which can be measured or counted, or, more precisely, things that Economics holds can be counted. And there, too, the social and intellectual benefits which might accrue from necessary discipline are transported into habits of mind which, to cite Dixon, 'put themselves far beyond reasoned thought.' The most noticeable consequence of this conversion of a means into an end is the establishment and reinforcement of conservatism in thought and deed. [27]

More deeply understood, at work here are three common but interrelated denominators: *constraint, deception,* and the *substitution for thought.*

It is essentially by constraint that [bullshit] seems to combat disorderliness, whether this be of appearance, conduct or thought, but in doing so it necessarily conceals what is really the case.[28]

Thus, what in the military is thought to be necessary in order to maintain a certain fighting cohesion under the very real pressures of combat is, in Economics, thought necessary in order to present a unified disciplinary front to the incipient chaos of the world when left to its natural urges. The imperative born of this is the conditioning of the economist-subject to recognise only certain stimuli presented by the world, to label or categorise them, and then to respond to them, but only in the approved way, which is to reduce them to those simple terms of which Economics can speak. In this way, response is not only guaranteed, but it is fast, certain, and automatic – a remarkable achievement given that those responding are not required to have had any experience of the situations in which they are operating. Possessed with the 'supernormal' capacity thought to reside in the pure and parsimonious language of mathematics – which is stimulus in itself – the instinctual response is only heightened. At the same time, however, both the normal and the heightened responses suffer, correspondingly, from the same disadvantages of all instinctual behaviour: it is fallible, inflexible, and undiscerning.[29]

Yet, for all of these untoward effects, Economics prospers; without exaggeration, furthermore, it prospers precisely because it is so faithful to its own variant of bullshit, or rather, it supplies a form of bullshit which is in constant and heavy demand. What appears to be, and is, blind obedience to reductionism and a suppression of initiative, is lauded by the Economics hierarchy, by way of promotion and consultancies, as development of the professional economic character and intellect, a celebration which then increases the dependency of those so advanced on the hierarchy.[30] That the patterns which are required to be followed are no more than rituals, and obsessive rituals at that, is irrelevant: in their execution, an aura of certainty is established by faithful repetition. Since disciplinary disintegration and professional irrelevance are the causes of anxiety, anxiety reduction is the objective, and since difference is the forerunner to disorder, all measures which reduce the implacable hostility of diversity to conformity are valid.[31]

BULLSHIT (MORE PARTICULARLY)

The bullshit of Economics imposes two transformations. In the first, by way of a professionally sanctioned inversion, it renders the diversity of humanity and nature as undesirable, and certainly unhelpful; in the second, and through the same means, it holds as dangerous everything that is free, uncontrolled, and spontaneous.[32] Both are 'unnatural' to the extent that people are not born with such dispositions; indeed, as Dixon illustrates, the contrary is very much in evidence: people actually take delight in the richness of difference which surrounds them. Both, moreover, make casualties of economists, as explained by K.J.W. Craik:

[A] form of adaptation is thus achieved by narrowing and distorting the environment until one's conduct appears adequate to it, rather than by altering one's conduct and enlarging one's knowledge till one can cope with the larger, real environment.[33]

The process, then, is one of socialisation within Economics, or, more specifically, the disciplinary equivalent of 'potty training.' Because of its processes, especially the inversions involved, it is more properly described as 'the development of the so-called anal character.'[34]

This can take four forms. In the first, there is a complementary relationship between the perceived threat of destruction and the occurrence of compensatory devices to preserve orderliness. Ritual, therefore, assumes considerable significance: it reduces the natural human feelings which the human world arouses while encouraging and legitimating those under threat to indulge their compulsive neurotic tendencies. In the second, a compulsive concern with cleanliness – usually in the form of increasing theoretical refinement and rigour irrespective of the authenticity and relevance of the outcome – and with obedience to the hierarchy is manifest in attempting to meet the threat of disorder. In the light of the first two forms, the third form is worrying since, at origin, the reasons for economists needing to react this way are lost to their consciousness, and thus, they resist all attempts to rationally modify their behaviour.

The final form the status of Economics takes is derived from the fact that it is, simultaneously, an outlet for, and a bulwark against, indiscipline and disorder: it thus attracts people who have difficulty in reconciling these conflicting needs in themselves, and who, therefore, overvalue aggression, order, and obedience, not least within a socially acceptable framework which obscures the nature of the mutual accommodation.[35] We therefore have a frightening paradox in which those who would prescribe wealth-creation and wealth-distribution theories and practices for a world of infinite complexity, are the very people whose dispositions are antithetical to such a project, and who, therefore, are least well equipped to do it all, let alone successfully. For all of that, bullshit only comprises 'an array of relatively mindless acts' and does not by any means exhaust Economics contributions to its own incompetence, nor does it preclude the possibility that some contributions related to bullshit might be more thoughtful – disciplinary character and its offshoot, professional honour, for example.[36]

HONOUR

Dixon reminds us that the distinction to be borne in mind about honour (in contradistinction to bullshit) is that, though it too is a device for maintaining order, quelling anxiety, and regulating aggression, it is 'more concerned with a system of ideas, a code of thought and a set of inhibitions,' all of which are 'apparently inescapable products of large-scale organised aggression.'[37] Even then, Economics differs from many other younger organisations which are aggressive – for example, the younger military organisations – by opting to control instinct by character rather than by intellect – the latter being scarcely credible in the light of both its scrupulous exclusions of the human, and its abdications in the field of scientific knowledge. Nevertheless, the relevant code of honour is observed and breaches of it provoke either guilt or shame, depending on whether one has merely transgressed, or transgressed and been found out, respectively.

In Economics, as in the military, shame is the more distressing emotion, since it is public, and the more likely, since great steps are taken, via such devices as bullshit, to relieve the onset of guilt. And the fact that Economics is not ravaged by defections despite its record in economic globalisation is a tribute to its efficacy. Conversely, defecting from Economics would be the source – and probably the only imaginable source – of shame inasmuch as it would be not only a public admission of wrongdoing, but an act of flight in the face of a threatening situation which if followed by others in sufficient numbers would culminate in a rout. [38]

Shame is possible, but its progenitor is unique; specifically, it is not possible as a result of any incompetence derived from faithfully practising the discipline. To the contrary: 'So long as the individual accepts its demands he is proving himself... as brave, a rightful member of the elite.'[39] And this is what might be regarded as a monastic obligation in that it extracts a lifelong 'initiation rite' from which no discharge is possible if membership is to be maintained. It is, thus, a tribute to the solvent qualities of disciplinary honour that incompetence cannot induce shame because it is not as though the record of Economics in globalisation is unknown to vast populations. Clearly, there must be an inhibitor to shame which can prevail against a record of such extraordinary proportions, and there is: vanity.[40]

It is an entirely understandable acquisition, and the key to understanding it is the belief that economists have in their intellectual and professional superiority, enhanced in particular by notions that they are scientists who know the mysteries of money, both being affirmed, in their view, by, among numerous acknowledgments, the existence of a Nobel Prize in Economics and the requirement that the Council of Economic Advisers to the US President be composed solely of their profession. Vanity, here, easily gives way to snobbishness – a snob in this context being a vulgar specialist who is overly impressed, and therefore seeks to identify with, superior sciences. Snobs enthusiastically seek the status of the superior class of sciences irrespective of whether either deserves the standing in the first place. But even on attaining it, they are not content unless their arrival entails an explicit dissociation from those held to be inferior.[41] But this only constitutes another double inversion, equally understandable if the appropriation of mathematics and the aping of physics are brought back to mind.

In the first instance snobbishness is most generally a symptom of inferiority, low self-esteem, and inadequacy; in the second it is a form of behaviour which is 'irrational, compulsive and self-defeating,' a source of 'at best amusement, at worst ridicule, contempt or even dislike.' Being compulsive, however, it is also incapable of being curbed.[42] Understood in this way, Economics is a front, or, more colloquially, all front. Though considerable measures are taken to present a confident face to the public gaze, the measures themselves betoken underlying conditions of insecurity. The possibility exists, therefore, that an awareness of extra-Economics criticisms were imperfectly suppressed in the formation of the professional character, that there are weevils of doubt which bore into the discipline's foundations and its façade of confidence, but that none of this makes any difference to its practitioners in the long run.

Perversely, to the extent that it is realised, it only creates other avoidance mechanisms in the form of ultra-sensitivity to criticism – a refusal to listen to what can be heard with ease – and outright hostility to the feminine. In relation to the former, to listen would be to contemplate the follies of a pose totally out of keeping with reality; far better to repeat the foundational mantra that the market is perfect, and thus, that all misfortunes derive from infidelity to it. Accordingly, defending the foundation is both duty and a matter of honour; criticising it is a misplaced endeavour, and in any case, wrong-headed by definition; suggesting alternatives, by the same logic, is irrelevant, and victims, also by definition, deserving of their fate since it is undoubtedly the result of deviating from perfect principles.[43] Blame will certainly be apportioned, but to others, and elsewhere – to scapegoats – whether it be to 'crony capitalists' for the Asian financial crisis of 1997, or the Argentine government for the collapse of the national economy at the end of 2001. The required reflex in Economics is the same as it was for armies of the late eighteenth century facing failure on the battlefield, namely, Francis Grose's *Advice to Officers* of 1762 being most pertinent:

> When at any time there is a blundering or confusion in a manoeuvre, ride in amongst the soldiers and lay about you from left to right. This will convince people that it was not your fault.[44]

Importantly, in the execution of this reflex it matters not whether dutiful followers have faithfully executed the neo-liberal prescriptions that were held up to them as exemplary principles of life-order, if disaster befalls the project, it will be they, and not the prescriptions that will be found wanting. Consult any accessible source on human psychology on this behaviour and by any definition it will be fairly classified as neurotic – the individuals exhibiting it cannot help themselves even though in the recesses of their minds there is a kernel of certain knowledge that it is self-damaging. Unhindered, it persists and elaborates, not being satisfied with assuming superiority, it needs as well to exclude, the object of which is the feminine, and with which is associated threats to the integrity of science through the breakthrough of unacceptable impulses.[45]

Since the inferior position that women are subjected to in Economics is well documented, we need only remember that the feminine is understood therein as a threat to all that is scientific. To put the argument another way, so entrenched is the male sex-role identification in Economics that all things feminine threaten to *effeminise* it – to render it passive, dependent, and indecisive. Admitting the feminine, therefore, is to admit to inadequacy and to lose the reassurance extended by the profession's warrant as to its members' competence and masculinity.[46]

On this basis, and taken together, the prerequisites for professional achievement within Economics is a guarantee of disaster: it requires a monkish subordination to the discipline's psychopathology. And, as with monks, the fear of failure within the community is translated into a fear of failure professionally, though this is exacerbated by the already existing sense of inferiority in economists. Economic theorems and propositions are therefore notorious for their seemingly endless qualifications in their search for a statement which will not be offended overmuch by actual conditions. When examined closely, one of the most common of these, necessary to the narcissism economic mathematics – 'assume a continuum of traders' – is revealed to be no more than patent rubbish because the world it requires has never existed, yet it is an essential if Economics is to 'speak' at all.

Assumptions of this nature are but one symptom of the general fear. Others include the segmentation of knowledge (found in all professions) which allows success – if success is defined as reasonably accurate, short-term predictions – the reliability of which is directly proportional to the reduction of the focus in time and space, and the simplicity of the task at hand. Once mastered, this quintessentially conformist technique will assure its adepts social acceptance, limited achievement, and professional advancement at the cost of minimal, diffuse, and remote responsibility – the fusion of which will be an exemplary model of development for others. The negative corollary, however, is that those it attracts are in no way suited for national, let alone global projects; indeed, the tragedy which is neo-liberal globalisation is testimony to this (but also of the other disqualifications found in Economics).[47]

THE STRANGE (DISCIPLINARY) ATTRACTOR: AUTHORITARIANISM[48]

Of a profession which demands, explicitly and institutionally, adherence in thought and deed to the beliefs of neo-liberalism as described in these pages, we are entitled to ask whether the anxiety-relieving devices such as the release of aggression, bullshit, discipline, hierarchical structures, and rigid conventions have not been purchased at some higher cost than is immediately apparent, and/or are made possible by underlying patterns which have not yet been addressed. The answer is all very readily suggested when the toll of death and destruction (which prompted this analysis in the first place) is brought back to mind: it is in holocaust proportions. Acknowledge this, and the fact that it is a consequence of the deliberate and sustained application of neo-liberalism, and the conclusion to be drawn is that it is a form of vicarious killing – 'systematic and bureaucratised murder' taking refuge under the disguise of a totally inappropriate anodyne description, 'structural adjustment programs.'

The Holocaust prompted research, especially in the United States, into its causes and concluded that, central to any explanation was a phenomenon labelled the Authoritarian Personality.[49] Such a personality exhibited nine predispositions, virtually all of which are to be found in Economics 'personality,' as follows:[50]

1 *Conventionalism:* rigid adherence to conventional middle-class values – a virtually inescapable requirement of Economics.
2 *Authoritarian submission:* submissive, uncritical attitude towards the idealised moral authorities of the group which provides identity – a prerequisite for advancement.
3 *Authoritarian aggression:* punitive attitudes and policies towards those who violate conventional values – nowhere better expressed than in the conditions under which World Bank and International Monetary Fund assistance is made available.
4 *Anti-intraception:* opposition to the subjective, the imaginative, and the tender-minded – explicit in the insistence on a certain definition of science, in the types of exclusions (through abstractions and simplification) found in concepts and theories, and the hostility towards women.

5 *Superstition and stereotypy:* a belief in magical determinants (the 'hidden hand' and the externalising of 'the market') of the individual's fate and the disposition to think in rigid categories (Rational Economic Man, for one).

6 *Power and toughness:* a preoccupation with dominance-submission, strong-weak, leader-follower dimensions; the identification with power-figures, an over-emphasis upon the conventional attributes of the ego, exaggerated assertion of strength and toughness – again manifest in the invocation of science, but also in the fusion of corporate and military identities, and in the association of the requirements of neo-liberalism with corporate and national survival.

7 *Destructiveness and cynicism:* generalised hostility and vilification of the human – a predisposition which covers a concern for human rights, the environment, social dislocation, or cultural extinction in trade relations, no matter whether articulated by trade unions, non-governmental organisations, or church groups.

8 *Projectivity:* the belief that wild and dangerous things can go on in the world – effectively, the projection outwards of Economics' belief that unless the world is disciplined according to its own strictures, disorder will result.

9 *'Puritanical' prurience:* an exaggerated concern with things sexual – expressed variously as the general exclusion of women, the even more focused inhospitability to homosexuals, but more widely than this, as the traditional contempt for the lower orders, who, it is said, are large in number because they engage in what John Kenneth Galbraith refers to as 'unduly prodigious intercourse.' Such a view obviates the need for greater understanding and compassion by giving both refusals a moral underpinning.

Of the above, the most crippling predispositions, and the most fearful in terms of their consequences, is the confinement of thinking to 'rigid formulae and inflexible attitudes' and the intolerance of difference, unusual ideas and contradictions which come from without the approved structures. The authoritarian's response to such challenges is to fall back upon simplicity and order, or, as Roger Brown phrased it: 'If he has a problem the best thing to do is not to think about it and just keep busy.'[51] Ultimately, the world is emptied of its ambiguities and is reduced to the point where it exists as 'an image as simplistic as it is at variance with reality.'[52] This is obsessive behaviour by any criteria, and a consummate working example of the 'closed mind,' but the implications for national and global politics of economists holding positions of power or authority are equally stark: incompetence will invariably accompany their appointments, and it will continue, possibly in an intensified form. Authoritarians in power will foster other authoritarians to succeed them; their lack of humane feelings towards others will cause them to continue in habits wasteful of human life; no amount of information will force them to change their minds, and, at the apex of whatever authority structure they are located in, the lack of a higher authority to be subordinate to will effect an intensification of their disciplinary personality.[53]

★★★

Since it was a starting assumption of this analysis that economists are intelligent people, there is a desperate need to revise it in the light of the above because economism – that super-imposition of Economics on life – surely questions my initial wisdom (and generosity). Even if the spirit of generosity is retained, the conclusion is unchanged because, where overriding authoritarianism defines a profession, it 'will actually predispose an individual towards entering the very career wherein his restricted personality can wreak the most havoc.'[54] Indeed, the disciplinary claim upon economists is such that Einstein's description 'the herd mind' is not inappropriate to describe an entire profession that is repelled by personal freedom, egalitarianism, and creativity, and takes delight in conforming to theories and practices which are dehumanising – in which case it is appropriate to remember that he thought such people received their great brain 'by mistake – the spinal cord would have been sufficient.'[55]

Epilogue 2
Economics as mental illness – a satire?

INTRODUCTION

For many years I have accepted as an article of faith that, in a full life one should wholeheartedly attempt everything at least once – with three exceptions: incest, line-dancing, and Economics (defined as being, talking to, or thinking like, economists – which is to say becoming a subscriber to the discourse of neoclassical economics, regardless of whether this was the result of academic or professional instruction, or a vocational bent). The reasons for the first two were always obvious but the proscription against the last mentioned eluded me; until recently. And then, with the enlightening and liberating force of a spiritual conversion following the sight of God's face – what the Greeks described as the *metanoia* – it, too, became obvious: economists and Economics are, within the Galenic psychiatric tradition,[1] and in differing degrees, autistic, compulsive, delusional, emotionally withdrawn, hallucinatory, isolate, obsessional; in a word, mad. Indeed, according to this tradition, it is now mandatory to preface any serious discussion of Economics and economists with the form of words 'let us assume a continuum of insanity.'[2]

Conceded immediately is the charge that such an approach breaches the principal criterion honoured in the best tradition of high scholarship, namely, that it should be unobtrusive.[3] But equally, it must be understood that the charge is disingenuous: it implies that unobtrusive scholarship will be accorded its merits. And perhaps it is, because it is generally the case in politics, global and domestic, that it is ignored. And if it bothers no one, why should it not be accorded the same status as, for example, conversational Latin – a subject dimly understood to reflect the lustre of historical, but certainly not current relevance. Conceded also is the risk which Gary Mongiovi outlines in the following terms:

> The folklore of the market has so deeply penetrated our collective intuition that to doubt the rationality, desirability or inevitability of capitalism is to identify oneself as a naïve – or dangerous – eccentric.[4]

For all of that the particular nature of this inquiry is emboldened by the need to ask questions which mainstream international relations/global politics scholarship routinely ignores. At issue is the need to explain the perplexing and mysterious persistence – the enigma – of the Economics community in general, and that of mainstream political science/international relations in particular, to proclaim the salvational ideology of neo-liberalism in the face of evidence that it is inimical to the interests of the great majority of citizens globally. Other, related, questions follow closely: why is it that, in the midst of the immiseration that is occurring, untrained (and certainly uneducated), stupid people are getting rich while educated, trained, and skilled people are being laid off, in many cases never to work again; what does this tell us about the study, and pursuit of, wealth? Why is it that, in the midst of this immiseration, one of Australia's leading advertising agencies, Lintas, developed an advertisement calling for recruits into the industry which featured the message *you only need half a brain to get into advertising?*[5] (The significance of this claim in relation to economics will be dealt with below, in the discussion of schizophrenia.) Relatedly, why is it that the dominant discourse which informs these developments, neoclassical economics, is masculinised to such an extent that it routinely discriminates against women, professionally and, in much greater numbers, as subjects of economic research; moreover, it does so with what it is pleased to describe as 'scientific rigour.' And why is it that I find more insight into the political-economic travails of the economically developed West in the writings of Lewis Lapham and Hunter S. Thompson than I do in the myriad offerings within the 'unobtrusive' tradition of settled scholarship?

At issue, therefore, is the need to psycho-pathologise Economics in the hope that a more compelling understanding of the overall neo-liberal project which it serves might emerge. As indicated, the mode selected for this is satire, or at least it tends in the direction of satire – that which, through sarcasm irony, ridicule, and humour seeks to expose prevailing vices or follies. But it goes further, as Lewis Lapham has eloquently outlined. By provoking the 'not-so-gentle smile' it seeks, variously and progressively, to send 'humour on a moral errand,' to commit the crime of political arson, and ultimately, to effect 'death by ridicule.'[6] And, if candour is to prevail, extinction is the objective. Though many are the proposals to recover Economics as a gentler, more caring political study of political economy, the emergence of the latter, it will be argued, cannot be effected by the transformation of the former: as a popular and humorous account of rural Ireland has it, there are some destinations that you cannot get to if you start from the place you're currently in. By extension, women who are currently in the professional discipline of Economics are subject to a compounded jeopardy of madness on two fronts: they are not only ineluctably within the jealous domain of men, an exceedingly small number of exceptions notwithstanding, but both are also in the thrall of a discipline whose precepts and practices are consistent with some of the most obvious and incontestable symptoms of psychopathology; women who would enter such a profession are thereby warned.

A word on form is no doubt relevant at this point. As promised in this epilogue's title, it is, questionably, satire, although the particular nature of the satire employed owes much to the *exemplum* of the Middle Ages – a brief narrative or oral presentation intended to convince an audience: it uses rhetoric and narrative effects for the purpose of seizing the imagination on an important topic (back then, salvation). In turn, it can amuse, but more often than not it dramatises and terrifies in order to impart the salutary lesson that change is imperative. In short, it fashions the weapon of speech into a thing that affords instruction, example, and moral reflection on matters of everyday life in an innovative way.[7]

Nor is this out of place today. Originally, the *exemplum* was directed against the Albigensians (Cathari), who, in the name of purity of spirit, were opposed to the material world in a way strikingly similar to one of the Manichean divisions between modern economists. Thus we should note that the medieval heretics of southern France were hierarchically organised into 'the perfect' (who practised a rigidly ascetic way of life and had direct entry into heaven upon their deaths), and the 'believers' (who lived under less severe discipline), and that contemporary economists – in particular econometricians – have found this a most desirable precedent. From within the profession, the respected econometrician, Edward E. Leamer, has emphasised the broad, unambiguous identification with religious belief and the clergy in his own area of specialisation, and, of more significance in the context of this epilogue, the no less clear dichotomy between a 'celibate priesthood of statistical theorists (the "perfect" whose professional advancement is assured), on the one hand, and a legion of inveterate sinner-data analysts, on the other (whose professional status is somewhat problematic).'[8]

From these brief prefatory remarks it will be apparent that satire, even humorous satire, has a serious purpose which is at once derived from, and directed against, the lived reality of everyday life as experienced and otherwise known by the writer. After all, in the absence of religious disputes, fashionable travel literature, and the pretensions of the Royal Society, *Gulliver's Travels* would most likely have gone down in literary history as merely a funny work of fantasy. It is, because of this, a dangerous recourse, as Swift's biographies make clear: he is, today, seen as immoderate and simply too indignant, and the fact that he ended his days under the care of guardians appointed by the Irish Commission of Lunacy is thought to be no less than his unnatural outrage at the governing conditions of his time guaranteed.

This is indeed ironic because those most likely to hold such a view are also most likely to be complicit in its cause. Thus, of great concern to any student of politics from a human perspective is the now chronic and global susceptibility to a condition – advanced, doctrinaire neo-liberalism – which is symptomatic of a range of neuroses and psychoses and of which denial and delusion are the most prominent symptoms. What is so often witnessed is the phenomenon, described by Carterette and Friedman as the 'Cocktail Party' Effect in which unwanted messages from, for example, the poor, women, children, the unemployed and the under-employed, are rejected by the ears through a process which distinguishes signals by the locality and/or quality of the voice, the latter including, for example, the gender of the speaker.[9] Accordingly, the documented pathologies of neo-liberalism are ignored, and the behaviour patterns associated with their origin remain unreformed in spite of the advances in treatment which afford favourable prospects for remission.

As obviously warranted, this analysis seeks both to identify a schedule of symptoms, and to locate them within the appropriate clinical categories of mental illness. Effectively, this is to return us to a reconsideration of the debilities of modern consciousness, almost as though, at each parting from certainty, whether it be from God and the Church, or even the Keynesian consensus, a form of fractalisation occurs: the antecedent condition is equivalent to the dominant condition; it might not exactly replicate the dominant condition, but it will have the same general features no matter from what perspective it is examined. By this path we can take the insanity of Economics seriously.

MODERN CONSCIOUSNESS AND THE ORIGINS OF ECONOMICS' MADNESS

To begin, we might understand that Economics is not being singled out prejudiciously by this approach for the simple reason that, as a self-defined modernist discipline, it inescapably assumes the characteristics of that which called it into being. And because, under certain circumstances, insanity is an integral condition of modern consciousness, it is only appropriate that such a genealogy be acknowledged. To this end two of the more persuasive accounts of modernity are deployed here in the manner effected by Richard Tarnas. In the first instance he approaches the intellectual condition of modernity through the concept of the Post-Copernican Double Bind, which he says 'brought forth what was perhaps the pivotal insight of the modern Mind':

> The Copernican shift of perspective can be seen as a fundamental metaphor for the entire modern world view: the profound deconstruction of the naïve understanding, the critical recognition that the apparent condition of the objective world was unconsciously determined by the condition of the subject, the consequent liberation from the ancient and medieval cosmic womb, the radical displacement of the human being to a relative and peripheral position in a vast and impersonal universe, the ensuing disenchantment of the natural world.[10]

Moreover, because the Copernican revolution extended beyond astronomy into philosophy and religion, it was, simultaneously, a 'primordial event' and the 'epochal shift and of the modern age... world destroying and world constituting.'[11] Where Copernicus initiated the estrangement of modern consciousness from a previously reassuring cosmology, Descartes' ontology, expressing philosophically the 'experiential consequences' of this divorce, provided the bridge between the former's relativised universe and Kant's epistemology which culminated in the 'relative and unrooted' nature of human knowledge. Result: 'the post-Copernican dilemma of being a peripheral and insignificant inhabitant of a vast cosmos, and the post-Cartesian dilemma of being a conscious, purposeful, and personal subject confronting an unconscious, purposeless, and impersonal universe, with these compounded by the post-Kantian dilemma of there being no possible means by which the human subject can know the universe in its essence.'[12]

At this point, Tarnas, and this epilogue accordingly, suggest a 'striking resemblance' between this state of affairs and the condition that the anti-psychiatrist, Gregory Bateson, also describes as a double bind, defined as 'the impossibly problematic situation in which mutually contradictory demands eventually lead a person to become schizophrenic.'[13] [Bateson's work was centred on the proposition that 'family processes' – a schizophrenogenic parent, for example, whose verbal assurances of love and care to her/his child are betrayed by the nonverbal context (hostile eyes, rigid body) in which the assurance is conveyed – can drive a child in the family to bizarre and incomprehensible behaviour.] Adapted to the plight of modern consciousness, the Batesonian formulation of the four basic premises necessary for the construction of a double bind are as follows:

> (1) The human being's relationship to the world is one of vital dependency, thereby making it critical for the human being to access the nature of that world accurately.(2) The human mind receives contradictory or incompatible information about its situation with respect to the world, whereby its inner psychological and spiritual sense of things is incoherent with the scientific metacommunication.(3) Epistemologically, the human mind cannot achieve direct communication with the world.(4) Existentially, the human being cannot leave the field.[14]

Crucially, as Bateson discovered, serious psychopathological consequences follow from the pressure upon the human being to distort his/her perceptions of both inner and outer realities in order simply to cope. What impedes its remarkability is the fact that it is 'less immediately conspicuous simply because it is so universal.'[15]

When the inner reality is distorted via the repression or denial of feelings, the resultant condition ranges from apathy to psychic numbing; if they are inflated, the emergent form is one of narcissism or egocentrism. Alternatively, the outer world will be accepted as either predominant and capitulated to as the only reality, or seen as an objectified foil for self-assertion. The strategy of flight provides a third escape – through, *inter alia, the* quite familiar avenues of compulsive economic consumption, cults, ideologies, alcoholism and drug addiction. And, where avoidance mechanisms prove unsustainable, a comprehensive catalogue of mental disturbance is required to detail the ensuing state(s):

> anxiety, paranoia, chronic hostility, a feeling of helpless victimisation, a tendency to suspect all meanings, an impulse toward self-negation, a sense of purposelessness and absurdity, a feeling of irresolvable inner contradiction, a fragmenting of consciousness. And at the extreme, there are the full-blown psychopathological reactions of the schizophrenic: self-destructive violence, delusional states, massive amnesia, catatonia, automatism, mania, nihilism.[16]

The modern world, according to Tarnas, 'knows each of these reactions in various combinations and compromise formations, and its social life is notoriously so determined.' Worthy of special mention in this context is the dominant university stream of analytical philosophy, which, accurately enough, he describes as 'a severe obsessive-compulsive sitting on his bed repeatedly tying and untying his shoes because he never quite gets it right...' What is worse, and this is where Tarnas' adaptation of Bateson is contributive to both a wider and more profound understanding of the psychiatric double bind, is the complicity of the modern human being in her/his own condition. This is to say that, unlike the helpless child who was Bateson's focus, the modern human being has relentlessly pursued his/her emancipation from, and control of, nature through what is known as the scientific method. Explanations of nature are, therefore, required to be concrete, predictive, and thus, impersonal, mechanistic and structural. Extending these requirements further, the explanations on offer are necessarily 'cleansed' of all human qualities. For all of that – indeed, because of all of that – the world remains uncertain and incomplete, an intellectually justifiable state of affairs according to a narrative based on the sanction of the intellectual tradition of the last 300 years, which is to say, according to the specifically modern cast of mind.[17]

THE SOLITUDE OF ECONOMICS AS CONTRIBUTING CAUSE

Economics experienced the triple estrangement of modern consciousness: cosmologically, it lived no longer at 'home' (in political economy) but in a rearranged universe; ontologically, it was neither an inhabitant of the natural sciences, nor indigenous to them – it was an appropriator, or coloniser, of them – and politically compelled to settle within them for its future prosperity; and epistemologically, that place was increasingly the perspective which revealed the world to it. Economics and economists could console themselves that they resided in Utopia, but they were only etymologically correct: for all their contrivances that they were creating the perfect location, they were distant, isolated and, in point of fact, occupied no place. Economics lived, therefore, 'beyond the Pale,' and it had, and could take liberties, accordingly. But this was because life beyond the Pale was a reproach to scientific order – essentially lawless, and colonists, though they were subjects, were not there afforded the protection of the regnant authority on the reasonable ground that they paid no taxes to it. Thus it could, and did, run the risk of lonely exile by refusing to acknowledge, or even to be aware in the first place, that life essentially within the Pale – its role model to be precise – was changing profoundly. In all, advantageous conditions for the emergence and promotion over time of a more or less normalised paranoia within the compass of Samuel Johnson's damnation:

> Solitude is dangerous to reason without being favourable to virtue.

> Remember that the solitary mortal is certainly luxurious, possibly superstitious and probably mad.

Of this nothing more true can be said about the late nineteenth-century origins of the discipline of modern Economics than that it was an unmistakable case of (Newtonian) 'physics envy.' What impressed economists of the time were the notions upon which the classical Cartesian–Newtonian cosmology had been built, and which had lent to science in general, and physics in particular, the capacity to not only know the world through what Richard Tarnas describes as its 'supreme cognitive effectiveness,' but also to explain it with 'rigorously impersonal precision.'[18] In these terms physics had developed over two centuries to the point where it was the exemplar, *par excellence*, of the belief that it was possible to observe the world objectively; that the world was to be understood as, essentially, a machine; and that, therefore, a strict mechanistic causality governed all phenomena.

By extension, if the world accorded to what was, essentially, Newtonian mechanics, it was also, essentially, static; and being static, it was also, with the exercise of extreme detachment and the expenditure of sufficient scientific effort, subject to prediction and control. Above all, it was, as near as could be imagined in human temporality, an entity in perpetuity, existing for all time – where 'for all time' conveyed an existence coterminous with that of the Earth and its solar system itself. The modern discipline of Economics was thus naturalised, and heralded as but another instance of the unity to be found throughout the universe, in the life of humans as in the ways of the non-human world.

And there is nothing more paradoxical about these origins than that, though they reflected the historical development of natural science, they were embraced as universally valid for all forms of social inquiry by economists. Which is another way of saying that, by borrowing a tool-box from the natural sciences in order to understand human interaction and relationships, Economics embarked on an enthusiastic and dogmatic path to fundamentally misunderstanding its own subject matter. Nor was this predicament in any way alleviated by revolutionary developments in the theoretical foundations of physics which, in the very period that Economics was co-opting it, caused in physicists, according to Werner Heisenberg's prophetic words, 'the feeling that the ground would be cut from science.'[19] Indeed, for a long time prior to the quantum revolution, effectively throughout the nineteenth century, scientists drawn to such new subjects as historical chemistry, historical geology, systematic biology, physiology, ecology, and evolution, found themselves to be poorly served by methods or forms of explanation whose relevance was most appropriate only to 'objects and systems that were in fact inert, inanimate, and unthinking.' In the study of these new phenomena, the *practices* of the natural sciences required and embodied such crucial departures from the mechanistic theories of seventeenth-century physics – including historiographical reflection, and questions of good and bad modes of bodily operation – that their results could not truthfully be described as the 'coldly factual products of "alue-free" reason.'[20]

In a foretaste of the discipline of Economics' habit of cognitive dissonance when faced with a universe of facts which does not accord with its most cherished intellectual constructs, the new discipline of Economics adopted the only course available to it, if it was to maintain its pretensions as a science in Cartesian and Newtonian terms – it ignored the challenges to certainty as if they were no more than epiphenomenal. Economics was not alone in either the habit of avoidance, or the obsession with its status: as Dorothy Ross has argued, persuasively, and in reference to sociology, political science, and history, American social scientists after the Civil War made strenuous efforts to sustain fixed laws of nature and of history, and, when that was found not to be possible, to subject capitalism, democracy, and science to both scientific and technological control, and America's millennial identity, known more widely as American Exceptionalism.[21] In the context of this analysis, the fusion of American Exceptionalism with the American discipline of Economics is of extraordinary significance because not only does it locate the embeddedness of the latter in the specific historical experience of the United States, but the other social sciences are to be understood as intellectual reinforcements for economics, as complementary components of a shared meta-narrative.

In any other discipline idiosyncrasies of this type would in a short time incur a compelling disqualification from being treated seriously on any topic of political significance, let alone having a privileged voice on virtually all of them. But mainstream Economics has not only avoided such opprobrium, but flourished to the point of being the dominant social science in late-twentieth-century America if the displacement of other types of social scientists by economists from major positions of bureaucratic and political authority is any indication.[22] Explaining this seemingly outrageous success is not difficult, but it does require an extraordinarily high tolerance of further paradoxes which compound those already existing – of a putative science arising from a combination of intellectual vanity, ahistoricism, and a metaphysical commitment to universalising a model which is exceptionalist in its own terms. Thus, it needs to be understood that, from the 1930s on, the status of mainstream Economics in the United States was less influenced by the intellectual content of its theories than it was by historical developments and ideologies which reproach the corpus of beliefs which gird neo-liberalism.

ECONOMICS AS MENTAL ILLNESS

By way of introduction to this stage of the argument, a few qualifications are in order. First, it is not asserted that all economics presents as mental illness; correspondingly, neither is it asserted that all economists – defined loosely as people (business people, academics, policy-makers, market analysts, etc.) who practise a discourse of economics – are mad. Rather, rigour demands that the proposition in this epilogue embraces only the claim that neo-liberalism, with its core of neoclassical Economics, is symptomatic of insanity, and that, accordingly, a strong presumption of insanity attaches to practitioners of this discourse. This might seem a redundant qualification, but it is a necessary one nevertheless because of the universalising habit of economists to allow to stand, and even to promote, the notion that the category of 'economics' is exhausted by the currently globalising version of capitalist Economics (which itself is currently dominated by neoclassicism). This noted, it is also necessary to embed Economics within the conditions of modern consciousness which Tarnas elaborated, and which, as I suggested earlier, can be understood as a fractal. Thus the double bind is rediscovered in a particular form in that discipline, and virtually in front of our eyes, or at least on the basis of a short-term acquaintance. We find in Joan Robinson's seminal work, therefore, an argument which advances the thesis of Economics-as-mother: individuals, on finding themselves exposed to the unblinking scrutiny of the market, suffer from such a post-partum anxiety from tradition that their recourse to the all-encompassing certainties of neoclassicism is to be understood as a return to the security once offered by the womb.[23] Batesonian schizophrenogenic conditions are then manifest in the economists' vital dependency on the economy (market) whose communications he/she must assess accurately; the contradictory or incompatible information received from the Mother (economy) at different levels (i.e. the fact that reality does not conform to theory); the lack of abilities and opportunities for clarification that might resolve the contradictions; and finally, the impossibility of the economist escaping the relationship with the Mother (economy).

One example might suffice at this point, drawn from the great exemplar of capitalism, the United States of America, when it was undergoing continental expansion, because it is able to indicate that important developments in economic thinking were inseparable from endemic Batesonian conditions, in particular the anti-intellectualism and violence which together constituted the significant predicate conditions for neo-liberalism. We find, then, that John Bates Clark, the country's metaphorical father of neoclassical economics, turned from ideas equated with socialism to equilibrium theory and the celebration of capitalism as much because of the escape it provided from both the need for worker revolution (in his view) and the conservative reaction to leftist social thought, as he did because of its intellectual rigour. To this end his university appointments and standing were secure in comparison to others, such as Richard T. Ely and Henry Carter

Adams, whose oppositional Christianity and more extended advocacy of socialism he actively discouraged and cautioned them against on pain of the harassment they duly received in their university posts until such time as they capitulated to the paths sanctioned by American Exceptionalism.[24] But the condition of succour was intellectual disfigurement: as he freely admitted, in order to maintain the concordance between American Exceptionalism and an American political economy undergoing destabilising change, he put *'actual changes out of sight, intentionally and heroically.'*[25]

Later, Richard Hofstadter, from an historical perspective, drew conclusions which captured the contradictions in which Clark, Ely, and Adams, as ostensibly free intellectuals, were confined: 'business in America at its highest levels appealed not merely to greed and the lust for power but to the imagination; alluring to the builder, the gamester, and the ruler in men, it offered more sport than hunting and more power than politics.'[26] Moreover, if John Maynard Keynes is an accurate chronicler of his times, the financial sectors of the US and Britain in the 1930s were little different, as Paul Ormerod reports:

> Many individuals attracted to these markets, Keynes argued, are of a domineering and even psychopathic nature. If their energies could not find an outlet in money making, they might turn instead to careers involving open and wanton cruelty. Far better to have them absorbed on Wall Street, or in the City of London than in organised crime.[27]

It is little wonder, on such evidence, that self-disclosed insanity, even psychopathy, within the profession of Economics is, if not commonplace, at least, frequently commented upon.

SELF-DISCLOSURES OF MADNESS IN ECONOMICS.

More prosaically and typically, however, the mode of self-disclosed insanity in Economics has taken two forms: evasions-through-denials, such denials covering a spectrum from the methodological to the quintessentially human; and dementia in the market. The former is well defined by the extension of Hahn's injunction to avoid the discussion of mathematics in Economics to the more encompassing realm of methodology, or philosophy, in Economics. It is variously seen as either a 'waste of time,' or contrary to common sense; in either case, methodology is discouraged 'explicitly and boldly.' As well, there is a 'clear reluctance' on the part of mainstream economic journals to publish articles in the area, and funding agencies to underwrite relevant research. As Lawson writes of the situation in the UK, 'the training currently provided and recommended for Economics students tends to be more or less devoid of any explicit methodological content.'[28] Given the insubstantial nature of its foundations this might be thought an appropriate response, a method of avoiding an embarrassing acquaintance with doubt, akin to those communities and societies which discouraged their lower echelons from acquiring excessive education for fear that it would encourage challenges to the established order by redistributing knowledge, and hence, power. Indeed, the degree to which mainstream economic analysis excises from its professional deliberations the inescapable context of its being recalls John Ralston Saul's view that its 'greatest desire is to generalise and institutionalise a syndrome resembling Alzheimer's disease.'[29]

The travesty only continues when recourse is made to the expanded critique of *Homo Economicus* from the standpoint of a feminist understanding of Economics. To this end there is a need, in the first instance, to understand it as a male-dominated discipline, a discipline which faithfully, but mistakenly, extends the masculinised world view which overtook science in the sixteenth and seventeenth centuries. Surveying the aspirational literature of the time by such luminaries as Henry Oldenburg (an early secretary of the Royal Society) and Francis Bacon, as well as offerings which represent the historical development of Economics, and then drawing upon numerous recent analyses employing literary criticism, historical interpretation, and psychoanalysis, Julie Nelson produces abundant proof of both the gendered nature of Cartesian thought and the 'identification of science with masculinity, detachment, and domination, and of femininity with nature, subjectivity, and submission.' The critical issue of individual choice, central to neoclassical theory, illustrates this character admirably: the material world, and the existence of real persons and things within it – such things as childhood, bodily needs, human connectedness, and nature – are displaced in favour of the detached *cogito*, possessed only by man.[30] Such a theoretical eccentricity then isolates Economics from one of the most easily verifiable facts of life, as expressed by Diana Strassmann: 'human beings begin (and often end) life in a state of helplessness and unchosen dependency.'[31]

Strassman, however, is alerting us to a great deal more than the vulnerability of a tenet of neoclassical theory to a counter-factual argument; effectively she prefigures that larger, and more dangerous enterprise of exclusion within Economics which, in its highest form, simply conjures women and the feminine out of existence. Because of the mainstream disciplinary preference for economic interactions involving money to the exclusion of all other economic interactions, women, who perform the greater proportion of uncompensated domestic, and all reproductive labour, cannot even qualify as economic actors. Women are, thereby, made invisible through an incomplete treatment of the economy in which women as subjects of economic study are significantly absent, through approaches which are blind to a social, rather than an individual framework of analysis. And this says nothing of the need to not only include women, but to do so in terms of the contexts in which they are most likely to be located – dependence, interdependence, tradition, and power (although these same dimensions could, with advantage, be introduced to mainstream, male-oriented economic analysis).[32]

The partiality of the dominant mode of economic representation, therefore, is incomplete, but it is more than that as well: it is preferential and, in the injury it does to women's labour, vicious. It compounds their degrading within Cartesian science with the arbitrary refusal to hear, see, and speak the obvious role of women in the economy, an inclusion which, as Block argues, would radically potentialise economics as an area of social inquiry.[33] Specifically, this partiality acts to distort their contribution to national economies by denying it in the multi-purpose and universally adopted United Nations System of National Accounts, a characteristic of neoclassical thinking explored at length, and with deep insight by Marilyn Waring.[34] When it is considered that the economist, Robert Eisner, on the basis of 1981 figures, estimated that unpaid housework in the

United States economy would account for 33 per cent of GDP, this is as bizarre as it is offensive.[35]

Moreover, the self-absolving plea that the assumptions of Economics are only assumptions, and relatively innocent ones at that, fails, as Strassmann demonstrates, because these same assumptions disguise the value judgments inherent in the decisions, policies, and ultimately, the views of the world and the material conditions which flow from them.[36] In the denial of this nexus is found another instance of the confusion between the popular addiction to a narrow self-knowledge framed by professional self-consciousness, and a deeper awareness of the self and its relations afforded by an understanding of the origins of historical and social habit – a refusal which, far from being harmless, not only affirms (Lord) Thomas Balogh's rebuke that '[t]he modern history of economic theory is a tale of the evasions of reality,'[37] but also recalls Jung's verdict that it 'adds stupidity to iniquity.'[38]

It is, therefore, difficult to resist the inductive leap that, as a consequence of this orientation, the male domination of Economics as a discipline and profession is also in evidence. At the mundane level of awards it can be gauged by 'the extent to which women have been absent from the ranks of prestigious economists who have played a significant part in shaping the discipline.'[39] Consider the treatment of Margaret Reid, as lamented by Michael Steinberger:

> By any measure Margaret Reid was a giant among economists. Long before the economics of the home was deemed worthy of analysis by most of her peers, Reid did path breaking studies on the division of labour and consumption of goods within the household. That these topics are now the focus of some of the most innovative research in economics is a powerful tribute to Reid, who died in 1991 at the age of ninety-five. Yet *seldom has such a distinguished career received so little acclaim.*[40]

More recently, and more widely, the institutional forces at work are evidenced by the under-representation of women among those who receive advanced degrees in Economics, or who are appointed to the faculties of colleges and universities, especially to senior positions.[41] Through a system which is insensitive to many women via the fact that, typically, appointment to a tenure track position (and thus, the tenure review process itself) coincides with the advent of their principal child-bearing years, thus jeopardising the former if the latter is pursued, albeit temporarily. As the research of Colander and Woos has demonstrated, the option of a fractional appointment for women in this period, when, and where available, is but poor redress since women are then penalised by being paid significantly less than their predominantly male colleagues, and are, on the basis of their decision, often discriminated against in the tenure decision.[42] Within the discipline of Economics in universities and colleges in the United States, as of 1994, women occupied only 5 per cent of full professorships and just 10 per cent of all existing faculty positions – extremely revealing for a discipline with a well-honed (and as we will see, misplaced) mathematical conceit given that women comprise nearly 50 per cent of all mathematics majors.[43]

Further testimony in support of the general proposition that the discipline of Economics is misogynist appears in a recent account by a leading historian and philosopher of Economics, Donald N. McCloskey:

> It is a fact that there is not a single prominent economist who is also an avowed homosexual, although, given the reported percentages of men and women with homosexual experiences, there must be hundreds upon hundreds of gays and lesbians in our field.[44]

What McCloskey is raising in this unusual critique (the more so because, within it, he announces his intention, since realised, to become, 'under medical supervision,' a woman) is that the discipline to which he has given his professional life is, prima facie, a discipline of oppressive silences. It demands, or easily imparts the requirement, that the subjective 'I' exist in straitened conditions if that identity needs to be understood in terms which it has decided are feminine – bodily needs, human connectedness, and nature. As Donald/Deidre contemplates it: 'It makes you wonder whether a discipline that ignores love and friendship might be a little nuts.'[45]

The gendered nature of economic thought which follows from the gendered nature of Cartesian thought provides little support for those who would defend Economics against McCloskey's suggestion. Indeed, one of the most immediate consequences of this genealogy ought to be the replacement of *Homo Economicus* with *Vir Economicus*. The explanation here is simple: although the former literally means 'economic human,' the gendered nature of Economics demands that a more accurate, or more truthful term be used to cover the male-dominated phenomena in question: the suggestion, accordingly, is the latter, where *vir* is the Latin word for 'male adult' or 'husband.'[46] Deploying the term *Vir Economicus* would, therefore, capture the stereotypical male celebrated in market Economics: 'rule-driven, simplemindedly selfish, uninterested in building relations for their own sake. A cross between Rambo and an investment banker.'[47]

For a mainstream political science audience reared to forgive, and even to revere, the intellectual meanderings of Samuel P. Huntington, and thus his profound sorrow for the decline of authority, and the public's willingness to challenge 'the legitimacy of hierarchy, coercion, discipline, secrecy, and deception,' much of the above might be seen as the all-to-be-expected grievances which 'minorities' and 'special interests' articulate within the 'democratic distemper.'[48] In which case it is appropriate to note that one of Huntington's Harvard colleagues, the renowned economist, John Kenneth Galbraith, has identified madness as a common feature resident in the great speculative episodes of the financial markets over the last three centuries. Not only does he survey the more notorious disasters they have witnessed, he is able to account for the generational recidivism involved only by recourse to such terms as 'recurrent speculative insanity,' 'speculative dementia,' 'mass insanity,' 'mass escape from reality,' 'mania of speculation,' and 'serious commitment to error.'[49] To this end he has also provided a rudimentary typology of the three underlying causes of the condition – euphoria ('the mass escape from reality'); the extreme brevity of the financial memory; and the specious association of money and intelligence – and the dominant types of dementia operating on each occasion – individual, institutional, collective, and compelled.[50] So profound and so permanent are these features that prognosis is easily forthcoming: within the bounds of the economic culture in question it is incurable, for two reasons:

> In the first place, many people and institutions have been involved, and whereas it is acceptable to attribute error, gullibility, and excess to a single individual or even to a particular corporation, it is not deemed fitting to attribute them to a whole community, and certainly not to a whole financial community.

> The second reason that the speculative mood and mania are exempted from blame is theological. In accepted free-enterprise attitudes and doctrine, the market is a neutral and accurate reflection of external influences; it is not supposed to be subject to an inherent and internal dynamic of error. This is the classical faith.[51]

To summarise, self-disclosure reveals the socially pathetic condition of a community who forgot life's address. Clinically and more significantly, it records the chronic and general presence of mental illness in neo-liberal economists. Though, occasionally, their belief systems and behaviours are those also found in the syphillitically brain-damaged (in the period of quaternary or neurosyphillis), the absence of both physical evidence – chancres, lesions, and damage to the skin, lymph nodes, mucous membranes, cardiovascular and central nervous systems – and any evidence that it is sexually, or congenitally, transmitted, or even contractible via wounds, requires that this explanation be abandoned. We nevertheless need to explain what is, beyond all doubt, a dangerously altered state inducing abnormal levels of commitment and claim, the veneration of the market suggesting a possible approach: it is at least mildly and interestingly suggestive of paranoia since, although it does not embody claims of intercourse with God, it clearly embraces claims of constant communication with It. In this task of a more detailed and more nuanced understanding we now turn to the various categories available in psychiatry and psychology.

ECONOMICS BY CATEGORY OF MADNESS: FROM THE GENERAL TO THE SPECIFIC

The immediate problem we face in this venture is the richness of the possible categories of mental illness in which we might locate neo-liberal economists. As seen through their denials and evasions, they are clearly *delusional* in their construction of a reality which is radically incomplete as the basis of an explanatory and predictive science. Moreover, unlike normal beliefs which are modified in the light of experience and information, neo-liberal beliefs are held despite all evidence and arguments brought against them; as well, it is not uncommon for them to constitute a coherent system. Furthermore, they are to be distinguished from simply over valued ideas and beliefs (which can be found in 'normal' scientific communities) by the reaction of their adherents to challenges – whereas the former tends to provoke anger, the latter, indicative of pathology, tends to bland or otherwise inappropriate responses.[52]

At the same time, the obsession with abstract formal models and mathematics, the compulsion to marketise the world, the phobias concerning non-market alternatives, and the less well-published, but long-established, condition of erectile impotence require neo-liberals to be understood as *neurotic*.[53] As noted earlier, these habits are both maladaptive and distressing, yet, strangely, more or less fixed and resistant to modification, through processes of learning which are available to the community at large.[54] Since current investigation of neuroses turns on the study of mental mechanisms, and their origins in past experience and current behaviour, those of economists seem most likely to be the result of disciplinary training undertaken at the university level, reinforced by subsequent professional economic life and its imperatives. Fortunately, however, the full-blown *obsessive-compulsive* neurosis is relatively rare, being usurped by the simple obsessional personality found most commonly in certain scientists, typesetters, proofreaders, and clerks of an excessively orderly disposition (the anally retentive). But where 'normal' daily life is dominated by ruminations about abstract problems and the manipulation of words and numbers, and where the subject is absorbed by his/her delusions, as economists' lives are, the prognosis is poor: depression frequently accompanies this neurosis, and the best treatment available will only reduce, rather than eliminate, the full impact of the patient's disabilities.[55]

For a yet more specific classification it is necessary and useful to refer to the range of illnesses and symptoms in which the patient's basic competence as a person is called into question by her/his misapprehension and misinterpretation of reality – namely, *psychosis*. The World Health Organization lists eight specific psychoses of which four are, on the basis of current evidence, irrelevant to the generality of neo-liberals: senile, pre-senile, arteriosclerotic, and alcoholic. [The pronounced neo-liberal tendency towards thinking and behaving in a manner consistent with Alzheimer's disease is seriously challenging this view, to the extent that it has encouraged innovative psychiatric and psychological research proposals, but in the context of this epilogue these need not concern us here.] Conversely, the other four, functional psychoses – *schizophrenia, manic-depressive psychosis, involutional melancholia, and paranoia* – are already known to be extremely relevant to neo-liberalism even though there is considerable controversy within the psychiatric profession as to whether there are any convincing specifiable physical causes for them. Again, for current purposes, the resolution of this conundrum is not necessary, especially since there are at least two non-medical conceptions of psychosis in circulation, one of which holds that, in principle, they are little different to neuroses, while the other – post-Laingian school – is of the view that psychotics are the victims of the schizophrenogenic power of the politics of society and/or the family, as per the formulation proposed by Bateson.[56]

Refining the offerings further on the basis of neo-liberal economic discourse, schizophrenia and paranoia warrant the closest attention. The former commends itself on the basis that it is a relatively common, evenly distributed, condition, affecting nearly 1 per cent of the world's population, appreciably more, therefore, than the population of economists. As well, it is the most important single cause of chronic psychiatric disorder, yet the subjective experiences and observable alterations in behaviour which characterise it are very variable.[57] Symptomatically, these include a comprehensive range of the required behaviours of the neo-liberal: in the beginning, commanding voices are heard, commenting on, or repeating his/her thoughts (market outcomes); thought processes develop a vagueness and illogicality (Galbraith's euphoria); speech becomes almost incomprehensible (the journal *Econometrica*[58]), and a loss of coordination between different psychic functions, particularly the cognitive (intellectual) and the conative (emotional) aspects of the personality, (the ignorance of love and friendship).

This last-mentioned pathology is complemented, if not confirmed, by evidence that suggests schizophrenics have difficulty processing incoming information, both auditory and visual, and the relevant from the irrelevant. Over a prolonged period, apathy, eccentricity, and isolation result, as almost any of the current critical works on the discipline of Economics will attest to: in the mainstream there is neither the willingness to abandon its dishevelled and discredited abstractions, nor recognition of the need to embrace a multi-disciplinarity which could potentially revitalise the study of the pursuit and creation of wealth.

For such a socially damaging disease, it is sad to report that cures are unlikely although various palliative treatments have been attempted with varying success – for example, the drug chlorpromazine, special diets, and massive doses of Vitamin B.[59] Probably more important, though, has been the increased public tolerance of madness since the late 1950s, and the growing realisation by psychiatrists of the detrimental effects of life in nineteenth-century asylums, which together have resulted in novel attempts to both de-institutionalise, and re-institutionalise, schizophrenics within a liberal treatment regime.[60] To advance the former, traditional institutions underwent a transformation from a sombre custodial, to a seemingly enlightened open-door/community therapy/ early discharge, function (while ultimately and legally retaining the sanction of confinement should a relapse occur).[61] But in the single institution of the modern university both transformations and all possibilities were open to the neo-liberals who, with tenure, seized power in the name of 'The New Dumb.' At one and the same time, they could be schizophrenic, relapsed, incurable, and tolerated. Dr Hunter S. Thompson has written of them:

> The standard gets lower every year, but the scum keeps rising… and they have no sense of humour. They are smart, but they have no passion. They are cute, but they have no fun except phone sex and line dancing…. They are healthy and clean and cautious and their average life-span is now over 100 years.[62]

Paranoia, too, is a mode of existence common to a great number of more or less normal people; indeed, its significance extends from this feature.[63] And from the fact that, when it is unmistakably present in powerful political elites, it is allowed to reign virtually unchallenged. (To this extent it might be an even greater cause for concern than the schizophrenics since many of them are, by choice, institutionally localised.) Some occupations, however, are more fortunate in this regard than others. For an example outside of Economics we need look no further than James Jesus Angleton, former CIA chief of counter-intelligence for over 30 of the more than 40 years he spent in the CIA and its predecessor, the OSS. He has been described, even by a professional admirer, as a man who went 'dotty' and 'subtly mad.'[64] By other accounts, such as that by Tom Mangold,[65] he was a chain-smoking insomniac and drunk, a second-rate analyst and a first-rate charlatan, a projector of omniscience and certainty and, over time, a person whose paranoia increased exponentially.[66] These traits notwithstanding, he was, in so many ways, unexceptional. As historian of the CIA, John Ranelagh, has noted: 'Counterintelligence is a very specialised and sophisticated activity. It has an *in-built paranoia* which sooner or later overwhelms every counterintelligence officer and Angleton himself was not immune'.[67] Moreover he wasn't even an economist: at Yale he majored in English, and was greatly taken with formalist literary criticism which he subsequently used as the basis for the development of counter-intelligence methodology and theory.[68]

In present-day life an almost identical indulgence has been extended to Michel Camdessus, head of the IMF. Despite his organisation's abysmal double record of failure with Structural Adjustment Programs (SAPs) over a period of 15 years – they have not only failed to bring prosperity, but also caused their target countries to regress – he now advances the proposition that the time is nigh for the introduction of a 'second generation of reforms.' In one of the more outstanding examples of the refusal to learn from experience, let alone be shamed by it, he even admitted to a group of US church leaders that realising the benefits of this new macro-economic initiative might require the '*sacrifice of a generation.*'[69]

To the fore here are both the traditional, or etymological, and the contemporary clinical, symptoms of paranoia. Nothing need be said of the former other than to note that, given the circumstances surrounding Camdessus' proposition, and its highly probable consequences, he would appear to be quite literally 'out of his mind.' Turning to the latter, the degree to which this is the case is most troubling. Through the promise of another phase of SAPs, Camdessus, first, is advancing a coherent, internally consistent, but, as history records, entirely delusional belief in market Economics. Second, his proposal at this juncture of economic debilitation in the global South establishes his belief system as a persistent and chronic condition, one that almost certainly indicates a fixation at some infantile stage of development during which the self is its own love object, the period of undergraduate training in Economics being the most likely source of this. Third, coming at a time when the IMF is the object of widespread, serious, and justified criticism, Camdessus' proposal reflects an excessive self-confidence indistinguishable from hubris, a self-worth as a techno-rationalist Elect which the rest of the world refuses to endorse, a disconcerting and embarrassing assertion of the innate superiority of neo-liberalism identical to (as Galbraith confirms) religious messianism, and all are held without him in any way recognising that he is ill. In all, the symptoms in evidence are those of true paranoia, a rare disease, not amenable to any known treatment.[70]

Complicating matters, however, is the fact that internally consistent delusions of grandeur occur in other psychoses as well, most notably schizophrenia. Furthermore, when found in the presence of other symptoms such as emotional withdrawal and the pattern of arrested intellectual growth, primarily (80 per cent) in males, which define the autistic character of economists, the clinical diagnosis precludes true paranoia, but permits a finding of *paranoid schizophrenia*, indicating the breadth of mental pathology to be found in economists.[71] In an attempt to reveal the inescapably endemic nature of them in economists a *coup de grace* will be attempted via the history of scientism in Economics (physics as the model/mathematics as the means) which is their vocation.

SCIENTISM AS DEFINING SYMPTOM

It is almost commonplace to record that 'physics envy' seduced political economy away from its roots in society towards the end of the nineteenth century. The success of science, particularly physics, as an exemplar of the ability to control conditions and predict outcomes, promised a rational understanding of the economy through the eye of mathematics (with which physics was braided), which, of course, required a reconfiguration of the study in terms of the methods by which it was to be understood. In the prevailing view, mathematics was to give to Economics, and thus to economists, the relevance and, therefore, the professional status with government, industry, and community, which had progressively been accorded scientists since the age of Newton. Since, in Modernity, mathematics was the highest distillation of truth – exact, unshakeable, and infallible – all that remained for the transformation to be effected was to establish the necessary axioms, isolate the relevant variables, and apply the appropriate mathematics which would reveal economic truth with a clarity without historical precedent.

This turn to physics was ironic because physics was itself beginning its turn to a world much less congenial to the type of professional, policy-oriented certainty that was Economics' objective. Even more ironic, however, was that the associative jealousy which obsessed Economics not only occluded an awareness of the quantum revolution in physics, but also the uncertainties in mathematics, as a multi-discipline itself. It was as though, in the process of becoming something that was, by definition, an ahistorical area of inquiry, Economics was excused from seriously investigating the intellectual history of its new habitat for signs of contradiction and decay. Had it done so it is possible that the embrace of mathematics might have been less warm, because, throughout the nineteenth century, a revision of its claims and pretensions, themselves a reflection of its strange evolution since classical times, most notably in the development of 'strange geometries' and 'strange algebras,' had become imperative. Destroyed in the process was one of mathematics' principal conceits – that the mathematical laws of science were truths and that mathematical design was inherent in nature. Thus, like Newtonian physics in the face of the quantum revolution, mathematics was suffering a long overdue debility of identity, forced on it by the accumulated contradictions in the behaviour of mathematicians which were no longer tenable. Reflecting on this, the historian of mathematics, Morris Kline, writes:

> mathematics had developed illogically. Its illogical development contained not only *false proofs, slips in reasoning, and inadvertent mistakes* which with more care could have been avoided. Such blunders there were aplenty. The illogical development also involved *inadequate understanding of concepts, a failure to recognise all the principles of logic required, and an inadequate rigour of proof;* that is, intuition, physical arguments, and appeal to geometrical diagrams had taken the place of logical arguments.[72]

Nineteenth- and early twentieth-century mathematicians, moreover, were not only aware of this, but published their misgivings. Of ideal concepts such as proof and absolute rigour, Alfred North Whitehead lectured that they had 'no natural habitat in the mathematical world.' And throughout the last 200 years, the consensus seems only to have grown, with a foremost American mathematician, E.H. Moore, concluding in 1903 that mathematics were a function of the historical epoch in which they were constructed, a view essentially shared previously by Hermann Hankel, Richard Dedekind, and Karl Weierstrasss, and subsequently by some of the greatest mathematicians in the last 100 years – Hermann Weyl and, irony of ironies for Economics, Nobel prize-winning physicist, Percy W. Bridgman. As well, in the interim, Kurt Godel effected what Kline terms a 'débâcle,' by demonstrating that, while mathematics consisted of several schools, each in disagreement with the others, none of the logical principles accepted by the several schools could prove the consistency of mathematics. Even worse for the status of mathematics was an emergent character of confusion in which disagreement between the various constructions attended both the question of what might properly be designated as mathematics, and, within the constructions, of what might be the proper superstructure.[73]

As if these developments were not unsettling enough, research throughout the twentieth century has pointed to a disconcerting (for mathematicians, and, thus, economists) conclusion of Copernican significance: monkeys, though they have no formal language, can do mathematics. *Homo sapiens* has been displaced from the centre of the sentient universe. The turn-of-the-century possibility that this was true took the form of a Russian trotting horse, 'Hans,' counting answers to arithmetic questions by tapping the ground with a hoof; over time, furthermore, suggestions that 'Hans' was telepathic were raised and investigated, most notably in the 1911 book, *Clever Hans*, by O. Pfungst. This served to discredit the claims of numeracy and telepathy on the basis, *inter alia*, of unwitting gestures being made by the questioners, and there matters rested until the release of findings from a Columbia University study by Elizabeth Brannon and Herbert Terrace, in the journal *Science*, in October 1988.[74] What this showed was that two rhesus monkeys, with the Shakespearean names of 'Rosencrantz' and 'Macduff,' had demonstrated a fundamental grasp of numeracy, implying that a competence that was once thought to define the superiority of people over the 'lower' animals could now be thought of as a skill which reduced people to more adept primates (in general), and equated economists with other species who can grasp simple concepts of counting.

Notwithstanding this relegation, which admittedly took nearly a century to be realised, there was immediate and particular import for Economics in the status of two branches of mathematics which, it is widely agreed, have made seminal contributions to the development of the discipline – differential calculus (in relation to the extremal nature of economic theory), and statistics (the manipulations of which are at the heart of macro-economic predictions of probable states of the economy as a result of policy change). Neither, it has to be said, have been treated more kindly than mathematics in general in the search for certainty. Calculus, as the result of its faults, became the focus of 'rigorisation' in the mid-nineteenth century and after, but the efforts ultimately failed to achieve this end. Even the best efforts by David Hilbert failed to establish its predicate, or first order logic. Of this Kline notes that the search for certainty has produced only an 'unending' process of undecidable propositions.[75]

Statistics also underwent a developmental phase in the nineteenth century – from being seen and used in an ancillary role, as servants of argument, to being accorded the dominant role in the search for the laws of nature. Eventually they were thought capable of deciding 'whether the universe was a deterministic system of laws, or whether it was the product of the operations of blind chance.'[76] The answer, if it qualifies as such, is that nature is 'not at all determined, but rather chaotic.' The best approach to certainty in nature that statistics can provide is by way of predicting a most probable state under specified conditions, but, for all of that, nature remains independent of mathematical laws.[77] In any case, statistics do not, in themselves, explain why certain states are more, or less, probable. In the end, as Mary Douglas highlights in Ian Hacking's work, statistics are historically sensitive; they cannot be divorced from the political culture and the associated style of reasoning in which they are manufactured, the neglect of which caveat he demonstrates with many examples, effectively attributes 'autonomy' to statistics and results, *inter alia*, in the 'reckless use of the law of large numbers for finding facts about human behaviour.'[78]

For all of its existence, therefore, mathematical Economics has relied on the certainty and scientific status of a discipline whose troubles constitute, according to Kline, 'a mockery of the hitherto deep-rooted and widely reputed truth and logical perfection of mathematics.' Neoclassical economics has, therefore, throughout its lifetime and of its own volition, proceeded into serious error and ridicule since it insists on fate-sharing with a form of science, which we are reminded, is endangered and, because of this, dangerous:

> the lack of a proof of consistency still hangs over the heads of mathematicians like the sword of Damocles. No matter which philosophy of mathematics one adopts, one proceeds at the risk of arriving at a contradiction.[79]

In this light the criticisms social critics and some critical economists make of Economics, to the effect that it privileges the mathematical over the material and the interpretive, are somewhat beside the point because they imply that, in general, the status of science as a producer of knowledge is unassailable, and that, in particular, mathematics is beyond reproach as a judge in the field of Truth and Knowledge. What eludes them is a prior matter of extraordinary importance, the logical and philosophical exhaustion of science, which Bruce Wilshire outlines in the following terms:

> the term good 'talks' to us on the inner level of the self. But it cannot be taken in as a whole by science and defined in the required precise and predictive sense, so it cannot figure in the truths that scientists discover. Science by itself cannot tell us how to educate, not even how to educate as persons those who are to be scientists. In fact, although science is considered the paramount way of knowing, it cannot establish what nearly everyone assumes: that it itself is good.[80]

Thus the extremely valid charges against Economics made by Tony Lawson – that the discipline is guilty of uncritically, and in a widespread manner, appropriating mathematics for systems or conditions for which they are not suited – is a fourth, and only fourth, order criticism, being degraded, if you will, by the need to understand the long-standing and significant critiques which attend, in descending order, science, mathematics in general, and the prevailing, conventional attitude of economists to mathematics.[81] Thus, fourth, it is significant because it locates the misappropriation within a third order critique which, in simple terms, is the foregrounding of a disciplinary disposition best described as a form of contemptible anti-intellectualism.

The basis for this claim is that, historically, Economics has contrived successfully, and at the highest levels to celebrate itself as an 'unworldly' area of mathematical inquiry at the same time that its adherents lower down in the professional hierarchy represent their knowledge as essential to sound government. Nobel prize-winning economist Gerard Debreu, in his 1990 presidential address to the American Economics Association, provides one of the more outstanding contemporary examples of the former, proposing an 'acid test' for articles in economic theory, namely 'removing of all their economic interpretations and letting their mathematical infrastructure stand on its own.'[82] For others, outsiders, such a criterion is warranted on the basis that, for all of Economics' immersion in virtually every area of state policy, 'the theory and its development have been as insulated from empirical influences as geometry ever was before Einstein,' implying thereby that, since it fails by the criteria of policy utility, it might as well be given residence in the neighbourhood it most covets and, accordingly, be regarded as 'a branch of mathematics.'[83] But contempt is also courted because the abnegation of the world, so dear to Debreu's 'acid test,' has been joined not only with exhortations to use mathematics but, at the same time and in the recommendation of Frank Hahn, to 'avoid discussion of "mathematics in economics" like the plague.' Such advice, furthermore, is proffered on the basis of assertion rather than argument, but appears to have succeeded for the most part none the less.[84]

If we examine this development from the perspective of mental illness we find, in the first instance, an atavistic intrusion into the study of the economy by way of a form of uncontrolled excitement, over-activity, and obsessive behaviour – which is to say, a mania – about counting and the symbolic numbers of arithmetic which first appeared around 1200. The principal difference being that, then, it was not considered to be progress.[85] Second, we find that, rather than a turn to science, the late nineteenth-century imitation in Economics, of physics, through mathematics, is merely a cute return to religion: Newton wrote eloquently of how God 'was a skilled mathematician and physicist.'[86] And while this is not to say that Newtonian physics can only be appreciated and pursued through theism, the lack of certainty in mathematics (on which subject economists are silent), and the worshipful attitude to mathematics throughout history, from the Pythagoreans and the Platonists through to such adepts as Georg Cantor (who framed modern set theory on the claimed basis of a vision vouchsafed to him by God, and ended his days in an asylum for the insane),[87] and economists themselves, there is, again, that strong presumption that economists were seeking to evade the terror of modern consciousness through a religious consolation in delusion.

More than this: they constructed what Brian Rotman identifies as 'fortress mathematica.' Reviewing separate biographies of the mathematicians Paul Erdos and John Nash, he more generally makes a compelling case for the discipline as the refuge from (in simple and direct terms) the imprecision and impurity of everyday life, for people who believe that 'the book of the universe was written (by God) in the language of mathematics.' Failing that, it also suffices, as 'a secular divinity, a god of the atheists.'[88]

And who, or more precisely, what does the fortress protect? Consider Erdos, 'number theorist and combinatorialist extraordinary.' On the basis of extensive research he was:

> eccentric, socially dysfunctional, obsessive, childishly egocentric, helplessly dependent on fellow number freaks to feed him, transport him, put him up and put up with him… [yet] monkishly pure.

Nash, on the other hand, as befits a person with a 'vast distorted universe whispering in his head,' which included alien beings, and messages from extraterrestrials who were trying to recruit him to save the world:

> thought himself to be the emperor of Antarctica as well as the left foot of God, and was possessed by paranoid formulas and fearful ravings about punishment, humiliation and triumph.

Furthermore, and of paramount importance for current purposes, was the lucid and prescient answer he gave to a colleague, the Harvard mathematician, George Mackey, about how he could believe such things: they 'came to me the same way that my mathematical ideas did. So I took them seriously.'[89] Thus, in their detachments and withdrawals from the world, strategies of precedent already well framed by Bertrand Russell and G. H. Hardy, they were, in a manner of speaking, unremarkable in their common illness. Their contemporary, Kurt Godel, claimed to have extrasensory perception of mathematical entities, but starved himself under the paranoid delusion that people were putting poison into his food; and their successor is probably to be found in the Unabomber, Theodore Kaczynski, in whom the intellectual certainty of mathematics is transposed into a system of unchallengeable moral truth arraigned against technology.[90]

Identity rather than difference which, therefore, defines economists and mathematicians; in the pursuit of an unachievable certainty under the unforgiving regime of modern consciousness they both withdraw to a place where the world is so arranged that they do not have to experience its flux and complexity. Ironically, for Kaczynski at least, technology can achieve this end passably well (as Max Frisch warned us), but the conviction that a pure, frugal, and formal language and logic exists, which transcends legitimate uncertainty, ambiguity and disagreement, and which will yet capture the intrinsic order in all things, universally, holds the greatest guarantee. The Unabomber, after all, killed less people in all of the attacks from his own mental and physical wilderness than an average IMF economist in charge of a SAP from behind the barriers of neo-liberal theory.

CONCLUSION

The implicit question that recurs throughout this survey is one which, regrettably, cannot be answered definitively – namely, whether Economics is a site of mental illness, or whether, as seems to be the case in so many if its manifestations, it is a mental illness in its own right. Further research will also be needed to establish whether, for example, people become economists because they are mentally ill, or become mentally ill once they have accepted neo-liberalism as an authentic response to everyday life. Similarly, on the basis of the scientific literature, there is no reliable way of determining why, and how, the various forms of mental illness are distributed among economists of almost identical training and background. About all that might authoritatively be deduced is that economists enjoy a catholic affinity with most of the categories of insanity: they are generally psychotic, and, within this description, are more likely than not best located within the sub-categories describing a paranoid condition. Thus, of the proposition that Economics, economists, neo-liberalism, and mental illness are positively correlated there is no escape; indeed, for women as for men, one either evades or vacates the first two constituents of the constellation, or is wilfully complicit in the intellectually degenerative conditions which inevitably follow.

Economists, we should understand, are peculiarly modern, being afflicted with that contradictory state of mind which admits sin and continues to commit it; refuses contrition yet maintains hope; has contempt for the richness of the world yet wants to prescribe for it, and all in the face of the most destructive consequences imaginable to others. Globally their theories and practices are the habits of premeditated serial killing. By any normal calculation, two equally definitive consequences should have been observed: their discipline should have collapsed under the weight of its accumulated insanity, criminality, and stupidity as, or before, they abandoned it. That neither occurred returns us, initially, to the understanding of insanity prevalent in the first half of the nineteenth century, namely, that the strategic role was played by the will. Then later, Cowles Pritchard made a contribution in favour of the emotions by introducing the claim that an 'apparently unimpaired state of the intellectual faculties' could be influenced by 'morbid perversions of the feelings, affections, [and] habits' resulting in what he called 'moral insanity.' Though still subsequent work, in particular that provoked by Henry Maudsley and continued to the present, contrarily posited a 'tyranny of organisation' – a genetic determinism – rather than the will, as being responsible for insanity, all bodies of thought help us to an interim understanding of economists within insanity.[91] The role of the will, in the case of economists, is not in doubt; their various acts of voluntary anti-intellectualism are numerous and irrefutable. The unrepentant attitude to the global destruction caused by neo-liberalism would lead us to the same conclusion in respect of Pritchard's indicators. And while the question of whether these are genetically determined must remain open in the context of research which emphasises the importance of environmental, as much as hereditary, factors, as causes of felony, it is significant that a consensus exists, albeit divided at the level of causality, and thus, responsibility: such categories of people and patterns of thought as they describe, and within all of which are found economists and economic thinking, respectively, are, to the extent permitted by the sciences of the mind, clinically insane across a wide spectrum of the conditions referred to under this rubric, and dangerous, no matter the historical or contemporary approach favoured to account for the condition.

Although trend is not necessarily coterminous with destiny, nothing but the most profound pessimism must attach to the proposition that Economics will be transformed into an authentic study of the human, let alone that it might be rendered convivial to women. Expressed differently, while it might be the case that all possibilities are as open to Economics as to any other area of intellectual activity, Economics itself is not open to all possibilities. The reason is simple: so long as science observes its Cartesian engendering, and so long as Economics conceives itself as a science, women will be reduced, professionally and subjectively. Openness would be so transformative that Economics would endanger what it so desperately (if inappropriately) rejoices in: a predictive, disembodied, ahistorical, and decontextualised area of inquiry. Thus, preposterously, it remains what it is on the basis of a series of what Dante Aligheri described in the singular as *il gran rifiuto* – the great refusal – in which case consistency might allow us to regard Economics as he regarded that other sorrowful place of the lost: *lasciate ogni speranza voi ch' entrate!*[92]

Notes

Introduction

1   Sub-Commandante Marcos, 'The Fourth World War has Begun,' *Le Monde Diplomatique*, English edition, August–September 1997, http://www.monde-diplomatique.fr/en1997/08-09/marcos.html, accessed 27 October 1998.

2   As cited in Richard Tarnas, *The Passion of the Western Mind: Understanding the Ideas that Have Shaped Our World View* (New York: Ballantine Books, 1991), p. 412.

3   I beg an indulgence in the interests of achieving a dramatic effect – that of the illusion that I was writing only of the present: all of the historical features contained in the narrative to this point are taken, and only slightly adapted from Karen Armstrong, *The Battle For God: Fundamentalism in Judaism, Christianity and Islam* (London: HarperCollins, 2001), p. ix; Richard S. Dunn, *The Age of Religious Wars, 1559–1715*, 2nd edn (New York: Norton, 1979), pp. 1–9 and 59; and Michael A. Mullett, *The Catholic Reformation* (London: Routledge, 1999), pp. ix–xi and 1–28.

4   As cited in Neil Postman, *Conscientious Objections: Stirring Up Trouble About Language, Technology, and Education* (New York: Knopf, 1988), p. xiii.

5   Morris West, *A View From the Ridge: The Testimony Of A Pilgrim* (Sydney: HarperCollins, 1996), p. 109 (hereafter cited as West, *A View From the Ridge*).

6   Ibid., p. 114.

7   Tom Nairn, *The Break-up of Britain: Crisis and Neo-Nationalism* (London: NLB, 1977), p. 233.

8   From Morris West's play, *The Heretic*, as cited in West, *A View From the Ridge*, p. 101.

9   Werner J. Dannhauser, 'On Teaching Politics Today,' *Commentary* 59 (3 March 1971): 75.

10 The quotation and development of the idea is from Paul Bove, *In The Wake Of Theory*, (Hanover and London: Wesleyan University Press/University Press of New England, 1992), pp. ix and 136.

11 Timothy W. Like, *Screens of Power: Ideology, Domination, and Resistance in Informational Society* (Urbana and Chicago: University of Illinois Press, 1989), pp. 7–9.

12 This is, appropriately, the subtitle of the anthology edited by John Trumpbour, *How Harvard Rules* (Boston: South End, 1989).

13 August Strindberg, 'A Workers Catechism,' as cited in Michael Rosen and David Widgery, *The Chatto Book of Dissent* (London: Chatto & Windus, 1991), pp. 425–426.

14 See Lewis Lapham, 'Painted Fire,' in *Waiting for the Barbarians* (London: Verso, 1997), pp. 125–131.

15 John O'Donohue, 'Chosen,' in *Echoes of Memory* (Cliffs of Moher, County Clare, Ireland: Salmon Publishing, 1994), p. 58.

1 Neo-liberal war: *casus belli*, promises of progress, strategies of dominance, fraud

1 Carl Sandburg, 'Storm Over the Land,' from *Abraham Lincoln: The War Years 1861–1865* (London: Readers Union/Jonathan Cape, 1944), p. 27.
2 A so-called Great Office of State, which first appeared in the reign of David II, but has remained unfilled since the death of Gavin, Marquess of Breadalbane, in 1922.
3 Jeff Faux, 'The Party of Davos,' *The Nation*, 13 February 2006, pp. 18–22 (hereafter cited as Faux, 'The Party of Davos').
4 John Gray, 'The Global Delusion,' *The New York Review of Books*, 27 April 2006, p. 23; the citation from Lynn is found at the same page as well as Barry C. Lynn, *End of the Line: The Rise and Coming Fall of the Global Corporation* (New York: Doubleday, 2005), p. 254.
5 An insect's exoskeleton (integument) serves not only as a protective covering over the body, but also as a surface for muscle attachment, a watertight barrier against desiccation, and a sensory interface with the environment.
6 Wilfrid Laurier, Speech to the House of Commons, 16 March 1868, in Oscar Douglas Skelton, *Life and Letters of Sir Wilfrid Laurier* (Toronto: Oxford University Press, 1921), p. 321, as cited in John Ralston Saul, *The Unconscious Civilization* (Ringwood, Vic: Penguin, 1997), p. 194.
7 *Discriminate Deterrence: Report of The Commission On Integrated Long-term Strategy* (Washington, DC: United States Department of Defense, 1988), hereafter cited as *Discriminate Deterrence*.
8 *Defense Planning Guidance* (a draft Department of Defense Report, subsequently revised) published in *The New York Times* on 8 March 1992 (hereafter cited as *DPG 1992*).
9 *Air Force 2025*, A Report prepared by the 2025 Support Office, Air University, and developed by Air University Press, Educational Services Directorate, College of Aerospace Doctrine, Research and Education, Maxwell Air Force Base, Alabama, 1996 (hereafter cited as *Air Force 2025*).
10 United States Space Command, *Vision for 2020* (1997) (hereafter cited as *Vision for 2020*).
11 *Global Trends 2015: A Dialogue About the Future With Nongovernment Experts* (Publication approved by the National Foreign Intelligence Board under the authority of Director of Central Intelligence, 2000 (hereafter cited as *Global Trends 2015*).
12 *The National Security Strategy of the United States of America*, published by the authority of the President of the United States, 2002 (hereafter cited as *NSS 2002*).
13 *Mapping the Global Future: Report of the National Intelligence Council's 2020 Project* (The National Intelligence Council, 2004) (hereafter cited as *Mapping the Global Future*).
14 *Quadrennial Defense Review Report, 2006* (Washington, DC: United States Department of Defense, 2006) (hereafter cited as *QDDR 2006*).
15 The above passage is not arguing that what is now referred to as neo-conservatism in US strategy began as late as 1988; rather, since the time frame of this paper commences in 1988, it is arguing that the essence of neo-conservative strategy was already in official documents. Moreover, it is this writer's judgment that the essential elements of neo-conservative strategy are to be found as far back as the turn of the twentieth century.
16 Paul Kennedy, 'Not So Grand Strategy,' a review of *Discriminate Deterrence* (above), *The New York Review of Books*, 12 May 1988, p. 5.
17 *Discriminate Deterrence*, pp. 13–15.
18 Ibid., pp. 15–16.
19 Jeffrey Record, 'The Bush Doctrine and War With Iraq,' *Parameters* (spring 2003): 4–6.
20 Jared Diamond, *Collapse: How Nations Choose to Fail or Survive* (Camberwell, Victoria: Allen Lane/Penguin, 2005) (hereafter cited as Diamond, *Collapse*, pp. 486–525).
21 Ibid., pp. 486–490.

22 John Vidal and Tim Radford, 'One in Six Countries Facing Food Shortage,' *Guardian*, 30 June 2005, http://www.truthout.org/issues_05/063005EA.shtml, accessed 1 July 2005.

23 The Worldwatch Institute, *Vital Signs 2005: The Trends That Are Shaping Our Future* (New York: W.W. Norton, 2005), p. 15 (hereafter cited as *Vital Signs 2005*).

24 Diamond, *Collapse*, pp. 490–491.

25 For a summary of these drivers, see Michael T. Klare, 'The Permanent Energy Crisis,' TomDispatch.com, http://www.truthout.org/docs_2006/021006P.shtml, accessed 11 February 2006 (hereafter cited as Klare, 'The Permanent Energy Crisis'). For more sustained analyses see: Michael T. Klare, *Blood and Oil: How America's Thirst for Oil is Killing Us* (London: Penguin, 2004); Jeremy Leggett, *Half Gone: Oil, Gas, Hot Air and the Global Energy Crisis* (London: Portobello, 2005), and Matthew R. Simmons, *Twilight in the Desert: The Coming Saudi Oil Shock and the World Economy* (Hoboken, NJ: Wiley, 2005).

26 Juliet Eilperin, 'Climate Shift Tied to 150,000 Fatalities,' *The Washington Post*, 17 November 2005, http://www.truthout.ord/issues_05/111705EA.shtml, accessed 18 November 2005. Almost identical findings were published nearly one year earlier by the German Advisory Council on Global Change; see Geoffrey Lean, 'Melting Ice "Will Swamp Capitals," *Independent*, http://www.truthout.org/docs_03/120903H.shtml, accessed 9 December 2003.

27 Ibid.

28 Philip Thornton, 'West's Failure Over Climate Change "Will Kill 182 Million Africans" *Independent*, 15 May 2006.

29 Greenpeace, 'World Bank, Pentagon: Global Warming Red Alert,' Global Policy Forum, http://www.globalpolicy.org/socecon/bwi-wto/wbank/2004/0222pentagon.htm, 22 February 2004, accessed 13 February 2006 (hereafter cited as Greenpeace, 'Global Warning Red Alert').

30 Ibid.

31 Peter Schwartz and Doug Randall, *An Abrupt Climate Change Scenario and its Implications for United States National Security*, October 2003 (hereafter cited as Schwartz and Randall, *An Abrupt Climate Change Scenario*). See also Mark Townsend and Paul Harris, 'Now the Pentagon Tells Bush: Climate Change Will Destroy Us,' *Observer*, 24 February 2004, http://www.observer.guardian.co.uk/print/0,3858,4864237-102275,00html, accessed 13 February 2006 (hereafter cited as Townsend and Harris, *Observer*, 24 February 2004).

32 Schwartz and Randall, *An Abrupt Climate Change Scenario*, pp. 1–2.

33 Ibid., p. 5.

34 Ibid., p. 9.

35 Greenpeace, 'Global Warning Red Alert,' p. 3.

36 As cited in Amanda Griscom, 'Pentagoners: Apocalyptic Pentagon Report on Global Warming Could Spur Action on Capitol Hill,' *Grist Magazine: A Beacon in The Smog*, http://www.grist.org/cgi-bin/printthis.pl.

37 Townsend and Harris, *Observer*, 24 February 2004.

38 Arianna Huffington, 'The Pentagon Sounds The Alarm On Global Warming; Isn't President Bush Listening?', Common Dreams News Centre, 25 February 2004, http://www.commondreams.org/views04/0225-13.htm.

39 Diamond, *Collapse*, pp. 491–494.

40 Klare, 'The Permanent Energy Crisis.'

41 Joseph Chamie, '21st Century Demographics: Highs and Lows,' *Globalist*, 14 July 2005, http://theglobalist.com/DBWeb/printStoryId.aspx?StoryId=4629, p. 1 (hereafter cited as Chamie, '21st Century Demographics').

42 Patricia Reaney, 'Africans Forgo Basics to Save Children,' Reuters, 13 December 2005, http://www.truthout.org/issues_05/121305HA.shtml.

43 *Vital Signs 2005*, p. 15.

44 Chamie, '21st Century Demographics,' p. 5.

45 Ibid., pp. 3–4.

46 *Foreign Policy* and the Fund for Peace, States Index, *Foreign Policy* (July–August 2005), pp. 56–57.

47   This takeover is discussed at length in Michael McKinley, 'The Co-option of the University and the Privileging of Annihilation,' *International Relations* 18(2): 151–172.

48   The role of the university in decline and its effects on education and understanding receive an excellent historical treatment in Jane Jacobs, *Dark Age Ahead* (New York: Vintage, 2004).

49   Paul Ormerod, *The Death of Economics* (London: Faber and Faber, 1994), note 15, p. 208, as cited in Roger Tooze and Craig N. Murphy, 'The Epistemology of Poverty and the Poverty of Epistemology in IPE: Mystery, Blindness and Invisibility,' *Millennium* 25 (winter 1996): 685.

50   Ibid., pp. 686–687.

51   Ibid., pp. 688–689.

52   Vandana Shiva, 'How To End Poverty: Making Poverty History and the History of Poverty,' *Znet Commentary*, 11 May 2005, http://www.zmag.org/sustainers/content/2005-05/11shiva.cfm.

53   Lewis Lapham, 'Notebook: Apes and Butterflies,' *Harper's Magazine*, May 1992, p. 8. This article was prompted by the almost simultaneous publication, in the *New York Times*, in early March 1992, of a speech given by the President of Czechoslovakia, Vaclav Havel, and the Defense Planning Guidance document.

54   Ibid., p. 10.

55   Richard Rorty, 'Moral Universalism and Economic Triage,' http://www.unesco.org/phiweb/uk/2rpu/rort/rort.html, p. 14 (hereafter cited as Rorty, 'Moral Universalism and Economic Triage)'.

56   I am aware that the scriptures cited above, and many others, also serve to console the poor and have done; my concern, however, is to explain the disposition of the affluent rather than the resignation, such as it might be, of the poor.

57   Richard Rorty, 'A Queasy Agnosticism,' *Dissent* 52 (autumn 2005): 94.

58   Ibid., p. 93.

59   David K. Shipler, *The Working Poor: Invisible in America* (New York: Vintage, 2005), p. 6 (hereafter cited as Shipler, *The Working Poor*).

60   'Pentagon Plan to Fight Wars in Turn,' *New York Times*, as syndicated in the *Sydney Morning Herald*, 31 May 1993.

61   *Mapping the Global Future*, pp. 7–8 of 12, http://www.cia.gov/nic_globaltrend2020_es.html, accessed 3 February 2006.

62   Conor Cruise O'Brien, *On the Eve of the Millennium: The Future of Democracy Through an Age of Unreason* (New York: The Free Press, 1994), pp. 163 and 146, respectively.

63   David Lewis, '1,000 Congolese Civilians a Day Are Dying,' Reuters, 9 December 2004, http://www.truthout.org/docs-04/121004J.shtml, accessed 10 December 2004, and 'High-tech Genocide,' http://www.earthfirstjournal.org/articles.php?a=883, accessed 9 February 2006.

64   *QDDR 2006*, p. 27.

65   *The National Security Strategy of the United States of America*, opening paragraph. Numerous other references in accord with doctrinaire neo-liberalism are found throughout this document and there is also special attention given to it exclusively in Chapter VI, 'Ignite A New Era Of Global Economic Growth Through Free Markets and Free Trade,' pp. 17–20.

66   David Gordon (Vice Chairman of the National Intelligence Council), 'Mapping the Global Future,' *the Globalist*, http://www.theglobalist.com/DBWeb/printStoryId.aspx?StoryId+4383, accessed 12 February 2005.

67   *Human Development Report 2005: International Cooperation at a Crossroads; Aid, Trade and Security in an Unequal World* (New York: The United Nations Development Programme (UNDP), 2005), pp. 1–2.

68   As cited in Faux, 'The Party of Davos', p. 18.

69 Paul Cammack, '*What the World Bank Means by Poverty Reduction, and Why it Matters,*' *New Political Economy* 9 (June 2004): 190 (hereafter cited as Cammack, '*What the World Bank Means by Poverty Reduction*').

70 Ibid., pp. 190–192.

71 Ibid., p. 192.

72 James D. Wolfensohn, 'People and Development,' *Annual Meetings Address*, World Bank, 1 October 1996, in IMF, *Summary Proceedings of the Fifty-first Annual Meeting of the Board of Governors* (IMF, 1996), p. 26, as cited in Cammack, '*What the World Bank Means by Poverty Reduction,*' p. 196.

73 World Bank, *World Development Report 1990: Poverty* (Oxford: Oxford University Press, 1990), p. 1, as cited in Cammack, '*What the World Bank Means by Poverty Reduction,*' p. 191.

74 See: Peter Drahos with John Braithwaite, *Information Feudalism: Who Owns the Knowledge Economy?* (London: Earthscan, 2002). See also Peter Drahos and Ruth Mayne, *Global Intellectual Property Rights: Knowledge, Access and Development* (Basingstoke, Hampshire: Palgrave Macmillan/Oxfam, 2002), and Renee Marlin-Bennett, *Knowledge Power: Intellectual Property, Information and Privacy* (Boulder, CO: Lynne Rienner, 2004).

75 See: John Cavanagh and Sarah Anderson, 'A Bad Idea that Failed,' *Foreign Policy* (September–October 2002): 58–59 and 62–63; Jeff Faux, 'NAFTA at 10: Where Do We Go From Here?' *The Nation*, 2 February 2004, pp. 11–14 (hereafter cited as Faux, 'NAFTA at 10'); Public Citizen, 'Another Americas is Possible: The Impact of NAFTA on the US Latino Community and Lessons for Future Trade Agreements,' August 2004, http://www.citizen.org/documents/LatinosReport.pdf, accessed 9 March 2006, and Public Citizen, '(Consolidated) Trade Adjustment Assistance (2003–present),' http://www.citizen.org/trade/forms/taa_search.cfm?dataset=3.

76 Ibid.

77 As cited in Faux, 'NAFTA at 10,' p. 11.

78 Eric Alterman, 'A Spectacular Success?', *The Nation*, 2 February 2004, p. 10.

79 Philippe Martin, 'The Privilege of American Debt,' *Liberation*, 6 February 2006, http://www.truthout.org/docs_2006/020706H.shtml, accessed 8 February 2006, in conjunction with Martin Crutsinger, 'US Trade Deficit Hits All-time High,' *Associated Press*, 10 February 2006, http://www.truthout.org/docs_2006/021006C.shtml, accessed 11 February 2006.

80 Mark Trumbull, 'Giant Trade Gap: No End in Sight,' *Christian Science Monitor*, 10 March 2006, www.truthout.org/docs_2006/031006N.shtml, accessed 13 March 2006.

81 Joseph, Stiglitz, 'This Can't Go On Forever – So It Won't,' *Guardian*, 1 January 2005, http://www.truthout.org/docs_05/010405X.shtml, accessed 18 January 2005.

82 Brett Arends, 'Economic "Armageddon" Predicted,' *Boston Herald*, 23 November 2004, http://www.truthout.org/docs_04/112804K.shtml, accessed 28 November 2004.

83 Ian Dew-Becker and Robert Gordon, 'Where Did the Productivity Growth Go?' as cited in Paul Krugman, 'Graduates versus Oligarchs,' *New York Times*, 27 February 2006, www.truthout.org/docs_2006/022706Z.shtml, accessed 28 February 2006.

84 Paul Krugman, 'Always Low Wages. Always', *New York Times*, 13 May 2005, www.truthout.org/docs_2005/051305H.shtml, accessed 15 May 2005. See also David Cay Johnston, 'Richest Are Leaving Even the Rich Far Behind,' *New York Times*, 5 June 2005, www.truthout.org/docs_2005/060505E.shtml, accessed 6 June 2005.

85 Paul Craig Roberts, 'Nuking the Economy,' *Counterpunch*, 13 February 2006, Information Clearing House, www.informationclearinghouse.info/article11897.htm, accessed 14 February 2006.

86 Ibid.

87 Peter S. Goodman, 'White-collar Work: A Booming Export,' *Washington Post*, 2 April 2003, as cited in Christine Ahn (ed.), *Shafted: Free Trade and America's Working Poor* (Oakland, CA: Food First/Institute for Food and Development Policy, 2003), p. 64.

88 Paul Harris, '37 Million Poor Hidden In The Land Of Plenty,' Information Clearing House, http://www.informationclearinghouse.info/article11985.htm (hereafter cited as

Harris, '37 Million Poor Hidden In The Land Of Plenty'), in conjunction with Trudy Lieberman, 'Hungry in America,' *The Nation*, 18–25 August 2003, p. 17.

89 Harris, '37 Million Poor Hidden In The Land Of Plenty.'

90 Genaro C. Armas, '29 Million Americans in Working Poor Families,' Salon.com, http://www.truthout.org/docs_04/101304C.shtml, accessed 13 October 2004.

91 Harris, '37 Million Poor Hidden In The Land Of Plenty.'

92 Dan Frosch, 'Your Money or Your Life,' *The Nation*, 21 February 2005, pp. 11–14.

93 Wallace C. Peterson, *Silent Depression: The Fate of the American Dream* (New York: Norton, 1994).

94 This controversial term (at least in regard to suggesting that it is, or might be applicable to the United States) is used advisedly: it is understood that a tendency towards fascism is not fascism itself, and it is also understood that forces other than neo-liberalism – many of them hallmarks of the Administrations of George W. Bush – are responsible for these trends. Nevertheless, after due consideration, its use here is justified, particularly given the persuasive power found in the following works: Geoff Boucher, 'The Resistable Rise of Postmodern Neo-Fascism,' *Arena Magazine* 82 (April–May 2006), pp. 29–33; Umberto Eco, 'Ur-Fascism,' *New York Review of Books*, 22 June 1995, pp. 12–15; Jeff Gates, 'Modern Fashion or Global Fascism?' *Tikkun* 17 (January 2002): 30–32; Bertram Gross, *Friendly Fascism: The New Face of Power in America* (Boston: South End Press, 1980); Lewis H. Lapham, 'Notebook: On Message,' *Harper's Magazine*, October 2005, pp. 7–9; Ann Norton, 'Is it Fascism Yet?', *Adbusters: Journal of the Mental Environment* 14 (January–February 2006); John Pilger, 'Fighting Fascism Then, and Now,' truthout/Perspective, http://www.truthout.org/docs_2005/071705Y.shtml, 17 July 2005, accessed 18 July 2005; Gary Alan Scott, 'The Rise of Fascism in America,' Information Clearing House, http://informationclearinghouse.info/article12713.htm, 12 April 2006, accessed 18 May 2006; and Craig Winters, 'Blood on Our Hands,' Information Clearing House, http://informationaclearinghouse.info/article12765.htm 17 April 2006, accessed 18 May 2006.

95 James K. Galbraith, 'The Predator State,' Mother Jones, May/June 2006, as published in Information Clearing House, http://informationclearinghouse.info/article12880.htm, 29 April 2006, accessed 18 May 2006.

2 *Triage*: a survey of casualties in the neo-liberal combat zone

1 The above categories and notes are compiled from Medical Response to Terrorism, URL: <http://206.39.77.2/dmer/triage/categories.html>.

2 As cited in Soren Ambrose, 'IMF Bailouts: Familiar, Failed Medicine for Asian Tigers,' Corporate Watch website: http://www.igc.org/trac/corner/worldnews/other/other83.html.

3 William Greider, *One World, Ready or Not: The Manic Logic of Global Capitalism* (New York: Simon & Schuster, 1997), p. 12 (hereafter cited as Greider, *One World, Ready or Not*).

4 Jeremy Brecher and Tim Costello, *Global Village or Global Pillage: Economic Reconstruction From the Bottom Up* (Boston: South End, 1994), p. 30 (hereafter cited as Brecher and Costello, *Global Pillage*).

5 Robert Cox, 'The Crisis in World Order and the Challenge to International Organization,' *Cooperation and Conflict* 29(2): 103 (hereafter cited as Cox, 'The Crisis in World Order').

6 Ibid., pp. 103–105.

7 Ibid., p. 105.

8 Ibid., p. 105.

9 Robert Heilbroner, *Visions of the Future: The Distant Past, Yesterday, and Tomorrow* (New York: The New York Public Library and Oxford University Press, 1995), p. 82 (hereafter cited as Heilbroner, *Visions of the Future*).

10   Robert B. Reich, *The Work of Nations* (New York: Vintage, 1992), p. 8, as cited in Brecher and Costello, *Global Pillage*, p. 18.

11   *New York Times*, 21 May 1989, as cited in Brecher and Costello, *Global Pillage*, p. 31.

12   William H. Davidow and Michael S. Malone, *The Virtual Corporation: Structuring and Revitalising the Corporation for the 21st Century* (New York: HarperCollins, 1992), as cited in Greider, *One World, Ready or Not*, p. 25.

13   Ibid., p. 22, in conjunction with Vary T. Coates, 'Transition to the New Millennium,' paper presented to the Annual Convention of the International Studies Association, Washington, DC, 30 March 1994, p. 2 (hereafter cited as Coates, 'Transition to the New Millennium').

14   Greider, *One World, Ready or Not*, p. 23.

15   Ibid., p. 22.

16   Vary Coates, 'Transition to the Millennium,' Paper presented to the 35th Convention of the International Studies Convention, Washington, DC, February 1995, p. 2; and Joel Kurtzman, *The Death of Money* (Boston: Little, Brown, 1993), p. 64 (hereafter cited as Kurtzman, *The Death of Money*). Note: although estimates of the above figures vary, the range of the magnitude by which total global foreign exchange trading exceeds the total global trade in goods and services has attracted a somewhat elastic consensus – namely, between 20 and 50 times.

17   Kurtzman, *The Death of Money*, p. 17.

18   Greider, *One World, Ready or Not*, p. 23.

19   Fishman, 'The Joys of Global Investment,' pp. 36–37.

20   Brecher and Costello, *Global Pillage*, p. 30.

21   Greider, *One World, Ready or Not*, p. 24.

22   Fishman, 'The Joys of Global Investment,' p. 37.

23   Ibid., pp. 24–25.

24   Kurtzman, *The Death of Money*, p. 17; Fishman, 'The Joys of Global Investment,' p. 38; and Eric Helleiner, *States and the Reemergence of Global Finance: From Bretton Woods to the 1990s* (Ithaca: Cornell University Press, 1994), pp. 8–12.

25   Ibid., pp. 58–59. See also: Walter Russell Mead, 'Bushism, Found: A Second-term Agenda Hidden in Trade Agreements,' *Harper's Magazine*, September 1992, pp. 38–43 (hereafter cited as Mead, 'Bushism, Found'); and Lori Wallach, 'Hidden Dangers of GATT and NAFTA,' in Ralph Nader, William Greider, Margaret Atwood *et al.*, *The Case Against Free Trade: GATT, NAFTA, and the Globalization of Corporate Power* (San Francisco: Earth Island, 1993), pp. 23–64.

26   Brecher and Costello, *Global Pillage*, pp. 58–59.

27   Testimony of Ralph Nader before the Trade Subcommittee of the House Ways and Means Committee, 2 February 1994, as cited in Brecher and Costello, *Global Village*, p. 60.

28   Heilbroner, *Global Visions*, p. 84, and Paul A. Laudicina, *World Out Of Balance: Navigating Global Risks to Seize Competitive Advantage* (New York: McGraw-Hill, 2005), p. 24.

29   Sarah Anderson and John Cavanagh, 'Top 200: The Rise of Corporate Global Power,' Institute for Policy Studies, http://www.ips-dc.org/reports/top200text.htm, accessed 19 May 2006.

30   Stephen Lendman, 'The Corporate Control of Society and Human Life,' Information Clearing House, 25 April 2006, http://informationclearinghouse.info/article12842.htm, accessed 19 May 2006.

31   Richard J. Barnet, 'Stateless Corporations: Lords of the Global Economy,' *The Nation*, 19 December 1994, p. 756 (hereafter cited as Barnet, 'Stateless Corporations)'.

32   Clara Jeffery, 'The Perks of Privilege: How the Rich Get Richer,' *Mother Jones*, May–June 2006, p. 25 (hereafter cited as Jeffery, 'The Perks of Privilege').

33   Jeremy Rifkin, *The End of Work; The Decline of the Global Labor Force and the Dawn of the Post-market Era* (New York: Jeremy P. Tarcher/Putnam, 1995), p. 168 (hereafter cited as Rifkin, *The End of Work*).

34   Barnet, 'Stateless Corporations,' p. 755.

35 United States Department of Labor, Bureau of Labor Statistics, *News*, 'Union Members Survey,' 20 January 2006, http://www.bls.gov/news.release/union2.nr0.htm, accessed 19 May 2006.

36 International Confederation of Free Trade Unions, *Annual Survey of Violations of Free Trade Unions 1995* (Brussels: ICFTU, June 1995), p. 7 (hereafter cited as ICFTU, *Survey 1995*).

37 International Confederation of Free Trade Unions, 'Dispatch' (briefing notes accompanying the *Survey* (above)), 14 June 1995 (hereafter cited as ICFTU, 'Dispatch').

38 ICFTU, *Survey*, p. 8.

39 Brecher and Costello, *Global Pillage*, p. 72.

40 Cox, 'The Crisis in World Order,' p. 107.

41 Ibid., p. 109.

42 United Nations Development Programme (UNDP), *Human Development Report 2005* (New York: UNDP/Oxford University Press, 2005), p. 3 (hereafter cited as *Human Development Report 2005*).

43 Ibid., p. 4 in conjunction with Jessica Williams, *50 Facts That Change The World* (Cambridge, UK: Icon, 2004), pp. 46–51; 250–255 and 2–7 (hereafter cited as Williams, *50 Facts*).

44 Patrick Markee, 'Debt Heads,' a review of Catherine Caufield, *Masters of Illusion: The World Bank and the Poverty of Nations* (New York: Holt, 1997), *The Nation*, 17 March 1997, pp. 38–39 (hereafter cited as Markee, 'Debt Heads').

45 Ibid., p. 39.

46 Ibid.

47 'Poverty: Casting Long Shadows,' published by the United Nations Department of Public Information [DPI/1783/POV – February 1996], and republished by the Robinson Rojas Archive at <http://www.rrojasdatabank.org/pvshadow.htm>, and Sarah Macfarlane, Mary Racelis and Florence Muli-Muslime, 'Public health in developing countries,' *The Lancet* 356, 2 September 2000, pp. 841–846.

48 For brief accounts of this phenomenon see Richard Horton, 'How Sick is Modern Medicine?' (a review of James Le Fanu, *The Rise and Fall of Modern Medicine*) (Carroll and Graf, 2000), in the *New York Review of Books*, 2 November 2000, pp. 46–50, esp. p. 50; and Abigail Zuger, 'Infectious Diseases Rising Again in Russia,' *New York Times*, 5 December 2000.

49 The World Food Programme considers 2,100 calories per day sufficient to sustain an average adult; its threshold for malnourishment, as applied in the above figures, is 1,800 calories, or less, per day.

50 Christopher Wren, 'U.N. Report Maps Hunger "Hot Spots", *New York Times*, 9 January 2001.

51 Robert D. Kaplan, *The Ends of the Earth: A Journey at the Dawn of the 21st Century* (New York: Random House, 1996), pp. 11–13 (hereafter cited as Kaplan, *The Ends of the Earth*).

52 Walden Bello, 'Global Economic Counterrevolution: How Northern Economic Warfare Devastates the South' (hereafter cited as Bello, 'Global Economic Counterrevolution') in Danaher (ed.), *50 Years Is Enough*, p. 18.

53 Ibid., in conjunction with Walden Bello, with Shea Cunningham and Bill Rau, *Dark Victory: The United States, Structural Adjustment and Global Poverty* (London: Pluto/Food First/Transnational Institute, 1994), pp. 52–53 (hereafter cited as Bello *et al.*, *Dark Victory*); and *Human Development Report 1996*, p. 17.

54 As cited in Bello *et al.*, *Dark Victory*, p. 51; and *Human Development Report 1996*, p. 19, Budhoo, *IMF/World Bank*, pp. 21–22.

55 Branko Milanovic, *Worlds Apart: Measuring International and Global Inequality* (Princeton, NJ: Princeton University Press, 2005), p. 78 (hereafter cited as Milanovic, *Worlds Apart*).

56 Ibid., and pp. 149–154.

57 *Human Development Report 2005*, p. 3.

58 As cited in Edward S. Herman, 'Immiserating Growth: The First World,' *Z Magazine* (January 1995), p. 47 (hereafter cited as Herman, 'Immiserating Growth').

59 Rifkin, *The End of Work*, pp. 188–189.
60 Herman, 'Immiserating Growth,' p. 45, and Gene C. Gerard, 'Tax Cuts for the Rich – Housing Cuts for the Poor,' *CJOnline.com/Topeka Capital–Journal*, http://cjonline.com/stories/042206/opi_gerard.shtml, accessed 23 May 2006. Gerard's statistics are sourced from the National Law Center on Homelessness and Poverty.
61 Jeffery, *The Perks of Privilege*, p. 24.
62 Rifkin, *The End of Work*, p. 198.
63 Ibid., p. 178, and '1 of 8 Kids in America Is Hungry,' *New York Newsday*, 27 March 1991. (The latter is a report of a study conducted by the Food Research and Action Center.)
64 As cited in Rifkin, *The End of Work*, pp. 178–179.
65 Richard G. Wilkinson, *Unhealthy Societies: The Afflictions of Inequality* (London: Routledge, 1996), and *The Impact of Inequality: How to Make Sick Societies Healthier* (New York: The New Press, 2005).
66 James K. Galbraith, 'The New Dialectic,' *The American Prospect* (summer 1994): 10–11.
67 Rifkin, *The End of Work*, pp. 214–215.
68 Ibid., pp. 210–211.
69 Elizabeth White, 'Number of US Inmates Rises Two Per cent,' Associated Press, http://www.truthout.org/docs_2006/052206R.shtml, accessed 23 May 2006.
70 Rifkin, *The End of Work*, p. xvii.
71 As cited, ibid., pp. 208–209.
72 As cited, ibid., p. 213.
73 Ibid., pp. 211–212.
74 David M. Gordon, 'Chickens Home to Roost: From Prosperity to Stagnation in the Postwar US Economy,' ch. 2 in Michael A. Bernstein and David E. Adler (eds), *Understanding American Economic Decline* (Cambridge: Cambridge University Press, 1994), pp. 71–76 (hereafter Gordon's work will be cited as 'Prosperity to Stagnation in the Postwar Economy,' and the collection in which it appears will be cited as Bernstein and Adler, *Understanding American Economic Decline*).
75 Rifkin, *The End of Work*, p. 213, and Dennis Wagner, 'Private Security Guards Play Key Roles Post-9/11,' *Arizona Republic*, 22 January 2006.
76 Martin Van Creveld, *The Transformation of War* (New York: Free Press, 1991); also referred to in Rifkin, *The End of Work*, pp. 215–216.
77 Paul Virilio and Sylvere Lotringer, *Pure War* (New York: Semiotext(e), 1983), p. 104.
78 The Commission on Integrated Long-term Strategy, *Discriminate Deterrence* (Washington, DC: US Government Printing Office, January 1988), hereafter cited as *Discriminate Deterrence*).
79 See: United States Space Command, *Vision for 2020*, available from US Space Command, Director of Plans, Peterson AFB, CO 80914–3110, or <www.spacecom.af.mil/usspace> and Central Intelligence Agency, *Global Trends 2015: A Dialogue About the Future With Nongovernmental Experts* <http://www.cia.gov/cia/publications/globaltrends2015/index.html> (hereafter cited as *Global Trends 2015*).
80 *Global Trends 2015*, p. 6.
81 Michael A. Bernstein, 'American Economics and the American Economy in the American Century: Doctrinal Legacies and Contemporary Policy Problems,' ch. 11 in Bernstein and Adler, *Understanding American Economic Decline*, p. 392 (hereafter cited as Bernstein, 'Economics and Contemporary Policy Problems').
82 Margaret Spillane, 'Northern Exposure,' *The Nation*, 19 June 1995, p. 872.
83 Greider, *One World, Ready Or Not*, p. 18.
84 Fishman, 'The Joys of Global Investment,' p. 40.
85 Ibid., pp. 39–42.
86 As cited in Christopher Hitchens, *Prepared for the Worst* (London: Hogarth, 1990), p. 95.
87 Lester C. Thurow, 'Companies Merge; Families Break Up,' *New York Times*, 3 September 1995.

88 Jacques Attali, *Millennium: Winners and Losers in the Coming World Order* (New York: Times Books/Random House, 1991), as cited in Bello, 'Global Economic Counterrevolution,' in Danaher (ed.), *50 Years Is Enough*, pp. 114 and 19.

89 Ibid., p. 14.

3 American decline and the ascendancy of Economics: neo-liberalism as new containment doctrine and theory of globalisation

1 For just one comprehensive and historical account see James Chace and Caleb Carr, *America Invulnerable: The Quest for Absolute Security from 1812 to Star Wars* (New York: Summit, 1988).

2 See: Paul Kennedy, *The Rise and Fall of the Great Powers: Economic Change and Military Conflict From 1500 to 2000* (London: Unwin Hyman, 1988); Valdas Anelauskas, *Discovering America As It Is* (Atlanta: Clarity, 1999); Morris Berman, *The Twilight of American Culture* (New York: Norton, 2000) and *Dark Ages America: The Final Phase of Empire* (New York: Norton, 2006); Jane Jacobs, *Dark Age Ahead* (New York: Vintage, 2004); Eric Larsen, *A Nation Gone Blind: America in an Age of Simplification and Deceit*, (Emeryville, CA: Avalon, 2006) and Robert Pollin, *Contours of Descent: US Economic Fractures and the Landscape of Global Austerity* (London: Verso, 2003).

3 Robert D. Hormats, 'The Roots of American Power,' *Foreign Affairs* 70(3) (1991): 137–138 (hereafter cited as Hormats, 'The Roots of American Power').

4 *After the Thaw: National Security Objectives in the Post-Cold War Era*, Hearing before the Committee on the Budget, United States Senate, One Hundred First Congress, First Session, 12 December 1989 (Washington, DC: US Government Printing Office, 1990), p. 9.

5 Robert Heilbroner, 'Lifting the Silent Depression,' *New York Review*, 24 October 1991, p. 6 (hereafter cited as Heilbroner, 'Lifting the Silent Depression').

6 John Lyons, 'Battle Hymn of a Republican', *Sydney Morning Herald*, 4 January 1992.

7 Felix Rohatyn, 'The New Domestic Order?,' *New York Review*, 21 November 1991, p. 6 (hereafter cited as Rohatyn, 'The New Domestic Order?').

8 Ted Robert Gurr, 'America as a Model for the World?: A Sceptical View,' in *PS: Political Science and Politics*, XXIV (December 1991): 664–666.

9 Jean Beaudrillard, *America*, translated by Chris Turner (London: Verso, 1989), p. 88.

10 United States Information Service, Official Text, 'Bush Outlines New World Order, Economic Plans,' 29 January 1992.

11 Richard Falk, 'Reflections on Democracy and the Gulf War,' *Alternatives* 16 (spring 1991): p. 263 (hereafter cited as Falk, 'Reflections on Democracy and the Gulf War').

12 As cited in Willam Irwin Thompson, *Passages About Earth: An Exploration of the New Planetary Culture* (London: Rider and Company, 1975), pp. 67–68.

13 As cited in Jeremy Brecher and Tim Costello, *Global Village or Global Pillage: Economic Construction From the Bottom Up* (Boston: South End, 1994), p. 32 (hereafter cited as Brecher and Costello, *Global Pillage*).

14 For the figures cited, see Jon Lottman, 'Pentagon Passions,' *The Nation*, 12 December 1994, p. 713 (on the global military budget); and 'The Militarizing of Domestic Policy,' *Z Magazine*, February 1995 (for the remainder); the two-war strategy was confirmed as late as the four-year defence review which was released in May 1997 (Jennifer Hewett, 'Minor Defence Cuts Still Leave US Able to Fight on two Fronts,' *Sydney Morning Herald*, 21 May 1997).

15 Linda Rothstein, Lauren Spain, and Danielle Gordon (compilers), 'A Sense of Proportion: Or, When is Enough Enough?', in *Bulletin of the Atomic Scientists*, September–October 1995, pp. 32–33, and 61 (hereafter cited as 'When is Enough Enough?').

16 John Agnew and Stuart Corbridge, *Mastering Space: Hegemony, Territory and International Political Economy* (London: Routledge, 1995), pp. 127 and 132–133 (hereafter cited as Agnew and Corbridge, *Mastering Space*).

17   Joseph S. Nye, Jr., *Bound To Lead: The Changing Nature of American Power* (New York: Basic Books, 1990), pp. 31–32 (hereafter cited as Nye, *Bound to Lead*); and Richard J. Barnet and John Cavanagh, *Global Dreams: Imperial Corporations and the New World Order* (New York: Simon & Schuster, 1994), p. 423 (hereafter cited as Barnet and Cavanagh, *Global Dreams*).
18   Nye, *Bound to Lead*, pp. 31 and 182.
19   Agnew and Corbridge, *Mastering Space*, pp. 134–135.
20   Felix Rohatyn, 'Becoming What They Think We Are,' *The New York Review of Books*, 12 April 1990, p. 6.
21   Evans and Grant, *Australia's Foreign Relations*, p. 6.
22   Stanley Hoffman, 'An American Social Science: International Relations,' *Daedalus: Journal of the American Academy of Arts and Sciences* 106(3) (1977): 45.
23   Ross, *The Origins of American Social Science*, p. 406.
24   Agnew and Corbridge, *Mastering Space*, p. 128.
25   D. Michael Shafer, *Deadly Paradigms: The Failure of US Counterinsurgency Policy* (Leicester: Leicester University Press, 1988), p. 45 (hereafter cited as Shafer, *Deadly Paradigms*).
26   Gordon, 'Prosperity to Stagnation in the Postwar Economy,' pp. 66–67, and Martin Walker, *The Cold War and the Making of the Modern World* (London: Fourth Estate, 1993), pp. 22–23, and 141.
27   Gordon, 'Prosperity to Stagnation in the Postwar Economy,' pp. 67–69.
28   For a succinct account of these developments, see the entry 'Finance International,' in Joel Krieger (ed.), *The Oxford Companion to Politics of the World* (New York: Oxford University Press, 1993), pp. 302–304.
29   Cox, 'The Crisis in World Order,' p. 103; .Dorothy Ross, 'An Historian's View of American Social Science,' *Journal of the History of the Behavioral Sciences* 29 (April 1993): 101; and Robert Heilbroner and William Milberg, *The Crisis of Vision in Modern Economic Thought* (Cambridge: Cambridge University Press, 1996), p. 8.
30   Joan Edelman Spero, *The Politics of International Economic Relations*, 4th edn (London: Routledge, 1994), p. 92, and Sylvia Ostry and Richard R. Nelson, *Techno–Nationalism and Techno–Globalism: Conflict and Cooperation* (Washington, DC: Brookings Institution, 1995), pp. 1–10.
31   Most interesting and relevant in this discussion is the final chapter 'Epilogue: Facing the Future Again,' in Stephen Toulmin, *Cosmopolis: The Hidden Agenda of Modernity* (Chicago, IL: University of Chicago Press, 1990), esp. pp. 203–206 (hereafter cited as Toulmin, *Cosmopolis*).
32   Brecher and Costello, *Global Pillage*, p. 58.
33   Gordon, 'Prosperity to Stagnation in the Postwar Economy,' pp. 70–72, esp. p. 72.
34   As cited in Robert Merrill, 'Simulations and Terrors of Our Time,' in David J. Brown and Robert Merrill (eds), *The Politics and Imagery of Terrorism* (Seattle: Bay Press, 1993), p. 27.
35   See Melvyn P. Leffler, *A Preponderance of Power: National Security, The Truman Administration, and the Cold War* (Stanford, CA: Stanford University Press, 1992).
36   Ibid., pp. 71–76.
37   'When is Enough Enough?', pp. 32–33, and 61.
38   Jeremy Rifkin, *The End of Work: The Decline of the Global Labour Force and the Dawn of the Post-market Era* (New York: Tarcher/Putnam, 1995), p. 32 (hereafter cited as Rifkin, *The End of Work*).
39   Marilyn Waring, *Counting For Nothing: What Men Value And What Women are Worth* (Wellington, New Zealand: Allen & Unwin, 1988), p. 8.
40   Jochen Hippler, *Pax Americana? Hegemony or Decline* (London: Pluto/Transnational Institute, 1994), p. 15 (hereafter cited as Hippler, *Pax Americana?*).
41   Walden Bello, with Shea Cunningham and Bill Rau, *Dark Victory: The United States, Structural Adjustment and Global Poverty* (London: Pluto/Food First/Transnational Institute, 1994), pp. 72–73 (hereafter cited as Bello *et al.*, *Dark Victory*).
42   Ibid., pp. 80–81.

43 Ibid., pp. 72–81; James Ferguson, *Grenada: Revolution in Reverse* (London: Latin American Bureau, 1990), and Anthony Payne, Paul Sutton, and Tony Thorndike, *Grenada: Revolution and Invasion* (New York: St Martin's Press, 1984).

44 Bello *et al.*, *Dark Victory*, pp. 82–83.

45 Ibid.

46 For two particularly informative accounts of TRIPs, see Peter Drahos, 'Global Property Rights in Information: The Story of TRIPs at the GATT,' *Prometheus* 13 (June 1995): 6–19 (this ref. pp. 13 and 15, hereafter cited as Drahos, 'TRIPs at the GATT,' and Lincoln Wright, 'Patents Blunder Could Cost $4b,' *Canberra Times*, 18 April 1996 (which includes an interview with Drahos) (hereafter cited as Wright, 'Patents Blunder).' The above account relies heavily on these two sources, particularly the former.

47 Drahos, 'TRIPs at the GATT,' pp. 7 and 16.

48 Ibid., pp. 6–7.

49 Brian Martin, 'Against Intellectual Property,' *Philosophy and Social Action* 21 (July–September 1995): 9 (hereafter cited as Martin, 'Against Intellectual Property').

50 Wright, 'Patents Blunder.'

51 Martin, 'Against Intellectual Property.'

52 As cited from a report by the (Canadian) Rural Advancement Foundation, in Vandana Shiva and Radha Holla-Bhar, 'Piracy by Patent: The Case of the Neem Tree,' in Jerry Mander and Edward Goldsmith (eds), *The Case Against the Global Economy and For a Turn Toward the Local* (San Francisco, CA: Sierra Club, 1996), p. 156.

53 Drahos, 'TRIPs at the GATT,' p. 15.

54 As cited in 'Copyrighting a Human Life,' *Greenpeace Australia News* 6 (autumn 1996): 2.

55 Ibid.

56 Ibid., pp. 8–12, and 16.

57 Ibid., pp. 12–13.

58 Ibid., p. 10.

59 Ibid., p. 11.

60 Drahos, 'TRIPs at the GATT,' pp. 8 and 12.

61 Peter Wilmshurst, 'Scientific Imperialism,' *British Medical Journal* 314 (22 March 1997): 840.

62 Ibid.

63 Ibid.

64 Bello *et al.*, *Dark Victory*, pp. 83–84, and George A. Lopez, Jackie G. Smith, and Ron Pagnucco, 'The Global Tide,' *Bulletin of the Atomic Scientists* (July–August 1995): 35.

65 Bello *et al.*, *Dark Victory*, p. 84.

66 Nicola Bullard, 'Here Comes the GATS Attack!' *Focus on Trade* <http://focusweb.org> topical email <http://www.topica.com/lists/hkpd_trade@igc.topica.com/read>.

67 Ibid.

68 Ibid.

69 As cited in GATSwatch, 'What is GATS?' at http://www.gatswatch.org (accessed 27 April 2006).

70 Ibid.

71 Sarah Anderson, Institute of Policy Studies, January 2001, 'NAFTA at 7,' <www.corpwatch.org/issues.trade/background/2001/ipsnafta/.html>.

72 Ibid., plus (for Scott source) B. Kite, 'Free Trade? Someone Always Has to Pay,' a *BusinessWeek online* commentary, distributed by the Black Radical Congress <http://www.businessweek.com/bwdaily/dnflash/may2001/nf2001052_941.htm>.

73 See David E. Sanger, 'Bush Links Trade With Democracy at Quebec Talks,' *New York Times*, 22 April 2001; and Marc Lacey, 'Bush Chides Critics and Declares Freer Trade a Moral Issue,' *New York Times*, 8 May 2001.

74 An element of conditionality, or, to be specific, temporary conditionality as regards the FTAA's eventual operation was introduced into this assessment because the November

2005 deadline for assenting to the agreement at the Fourth Summit of the Americas in Mar del Plata passed because of resistance from Argentina, Bolivia, Brazil, and Venezuela. It thus met with a similar fate as the Andean Free Trade Agreement (AFTA), and the Central American Free Trade Agreement (CAFTA), both of which also stalled in late 2005. The advent of several Latin American left-of-centre governments, attuned to the costs of these agreements, will ensure that this situation continues, at least in the short term. This is reinforced by a belief that their ratification in the US is also inopportune given the political vulnerability of President George W. Bush because, traditionally, US presidents always need to bargain with recalcitrant members of Congress from a position of political strength. At the same time, the longevity of the Latin American governments and their attitudes to FTAs is, as usual in their region, problematic. Thus, in the various statements issued by official sources in Washington and the Hemisphere, there is a notable sense of optimism, even inevitability that the real question to be posed is not if, but when these agreements will become operational.

75   See 'NAFTA for the Americas: Q & A on the FTAA (Free Trade Agreement for the Americas),' *Multinational Monitor*, April 2001, pp. 17–21; Duncan Cameron, 'Ten Reasons to Oppose the FTAA' <http://www.corpwatch.org/issues/trade/background/2001/dcameron.html> and the Council of Canadians, 'The FTAA and the Threat to Democracy' <http://www.corpwatch.org/issues/trade/background/2001/cocftaa.html>.

76   Chakravarthi Raghavan, *Recolonialization: GATT, the Uruguay Round, and the Third World* (Penang: Third World Network, 1993).

77   See Heilbroner, *Visions of the Future*, p. 75.

78   Bernstein, 'Economics and Contemporary Policy Problems,' p. 363.

79   Allan Bloom, *The Closing of the American Mind: How Higher Education has Failed Democracy and Impoverished the Souls of Today's Students* (New York: Simon & Schuster, 1987), p. 371.

80   Richard Tarnas, *The Passion of the Western Mind: Understanding the Ideas That Have Shaped Our World View* (New York: Ballantine, 1991), p. 356 (hereafter cited as Tarnas, *The Passion of the Western Mind*).

81   As cited, ibid.

82   Toulmin, *Cosmopolis*, pp. 148–149.

83   Dorothy Ross, *The Origins of American Social Science* (New York: Cambridge University Press, 1991), hereafter cited as Ross, *The Origins of American Social Science*.

84   Bernstein, 'Economics and Contemporary Policy Problems,' p. 362.

85   Ibid., pp. 362–365.

86   Ibid., p. 364.

87   Michael A. Bernstein, 'American Economics and the National Security State, 1941–1953,' *Radical History Review* 63 (autumn 1995): 10 and 20 (hereafter cited as Bernstein, 'American Economics').

88   Barry M. Katz, *Foreign Intelligence: Research and Analysis in the Office of Strategic Services, 1942–1945* (Cambridge, MA: Harvard University Press, 1989), pp. 8–9, as cited in Bernstein, 'American Economics,' p. 12.

89   Bernstein, 'American Economics,' p. 14; and Bernstein, 'Economics and contemporary policy problems,' pp. 365–370.

90   For a comprehensive history of the Truman Administration's strategy, see Melvyn P. Leffler, *A Preponderance of Power: National Security, the Truman Administration, and the Cold War* (Stanford, CA: Stanford University Press, 1992).

91   Bernstein, 'Economics and Contemporary Policy Problems,' p. 371.

92   Bernstein, 'American Economics,' pp. 17–18.

93   Bernstein, 'Economics and Contemporary Policy Problems,' p. 372.

94   Bernstein, 'American Economics,' pp. 18–19.

95   Sam Bowles, 'Hardly a Surprise,' as cited in Lawrence S. Lifschultz, 'Could Karl Marx Teach Economics in the United States,' John Trumpbour (ed.), *How Harvard Rules* (Boston, MA: South End Press, 1989), pp. 283–284.

96 As cited, ibid., p. 284.
97 Bruce L. R. Smith, *The RAND Corporation: Case Study of a Nonprofit Advisory Corporation* (Cambridge, MA: Harvard University Press, 1969), pp. 12–13, as cited in Bernstein, 'American Economics,' p. 16.
98 Ibid., p. 18.
99 Ibid., pp. 373–375.
100 Ibid., p. 375.
101 Ibid., p. 377, as derived from: William Appleman Williams, *Empire as a Way of Life: An Essay on the Causes and Character of America's Present Predicament Along with a Few Thoughts About an Alternative* (New York: Oxford University Press, 1982).
102 Data abstracted from J. Phillips, 'The Economic Effects of the Cold War,' as cited in Anthony Woodiwiss, *Postmodernity USA: The Crisis of Social Modernism in Postwar America* (London: Sage, 1993), p. 69.
103 For example, Ken Jowitt, *New Worlds Disorder: The Leninist Extinction* (Berkeley: University of California Press, 1993).
104 John Kenneth Galbraith, 'The Rush to Capitalism,' *The New York Review of Books*, 25 October 1990, p. 51 (hereafter cited as Galbraith, 'The Rush to Capitalism').
105 John Kenneth Galbraith, 'Which Capitalism for Eastern Europe?', *Harper's Magazine*, April 1990, pp. 19–21 (hereafter cited as Galbraith, 'Which Capitalism for Eastern Europe?').
106 Galbraith, 'The Rush to Capitalism.'
107 Ibid.
108 Bernstein, 'Economics and Contemporary Policy Problems,' p. 391, and Jon Weiner, 'Yeltsin's American "Advisers,"' *The Nation*, 16 December 1991, p. 761 and pp. 778–780.
109 Bernstein, 'Economics and Contemporary Policy Problems,' p. 378.
110 Bello *et al.*, *Dark Victory*, pp. 10–17.
111 Waldon Bello, 'Global Economic Counterrevolution: How Northern Economic Warfare Devastates the South,' in Kevin Danaher (ed.), *50 Years Is Enough: The Case Against The World Bank and the International Monetary Fund* (Boston, MA: South End, 1994), pp. 14–19 (hereafter cited as Bello, 'Global Economic Counterrevolution,' and Danaher (ed.), *50 Years Is Enough*, respectively).
112 Bruce Rich, *Mortgaging the Earth: The World Bank, Environmental Impoverishment and the Crisis of Development* (London: Earthscan, 1994).
113 Bello, 'Global Economic Counterrevolution,' p. 19.

4 The Americanisation of the new Economics: American Exceptionalism and American religion

1 Regis Debray, *Teachers, Writers, Celebrities: The Intellectuals of Modern France*, trans. David Macey (London: Verso, 1981), p. 29 (hereafter cited as Debray, *Teachers, Writers, Celebrities*). Note: the reference to this work is not complete without an acknowledgment to the source in which I was first made aware of it, and which is used in its own right later in this chapter, namely, Paul Bove, *In the Wake of Theory* (Hanover, NH: Wesleyan University Press, 1992), hereafter cited as Bove, *In the Wake of Theory*.
2 There is no denying that the use of the term 'America' interchangeably with 'the United States' inflates an identity already exaggerated; moreover it is an abstraction which is complicit in the usurpation by the United States of an identity which could not possibly be represented by a single entity: two continents, over 20 countries, and dozens of languages, cultures and economies preclude this. Similarly, neither 'North America' nor the relatively non-specific 'United States' are real alternatives: the former, strictly, includes Canada, while the latter, according to the entry in my passport which allowed me to travel to Acapulco, where this essay was first presented as a conference paper, could include

Mexico (*'Estados Unidos Mexicanos'*). Nevertheless, of all these, 'America,' in particular, is common usage, even in the best of circles, and, to the extent that these realms come under the critical purview of this essay, I have retained their nomenclature since to do otherwise would be to impose a humility of expression upon them that they never thought worth practising. 'America', in this sense, I would ask you to accept in good faith, is used with no little irony.

3   Edward Mead Earle (ed.), *Makers of Modern Strategy: Military Thought from Machiavelli to Hitler* (Princeton, NJ: Princeton University Press, 1971), p. viii.

4   Bruce Wilshire, *The Moral Collapse of the University: Professionalism, Purity, and Alienation* (Albany: State University of New York Press, 1990), p. 41, and pp. 42–43 (hereafter cited as Wilshire, *The Moral Collapse of the University*).

5   Ibid.

6   John Agnew and Stuart Corbridge, *Mastering Space: Hegemony, Territory, and International Political Economy* (London: Routledge, 1995), p. 47 (hereafter cited as Agnew and Corbridge, *Mastering Space*), and Robert D'Amico, 'What is Discourse?,' *Humanities in Society* 5 (summer and autumn 1982): 210 (hereafter cited as D'Amico, 'What is Discourse?'), respectively.

7   Ibid.

8   Paul Bove, 'Discourse,' in Frank Lentricchia and Thomas McLaughlin (eds), *Critical Terms for Literary Study* (Chicago, IL: University of Chicago Press, 1990), pp. 57–59 (hereafter cited as Bove, 'Discourse'), and Alec McHoul and Wendy Grace, *A Foucault Primer: Discourse, Power and the Subject* (Melbourne: Melbourne University Press, 1993), p. 34 (hereafter cited as McHoul and Grace, *A Foucault Primer*).

9   Agnew and Corbridge, *Mastering Space*, p. 47.

10 Ibid.

11 Bove, 'Discourse,' pp. 54–55, and McHoul and Grace, *A Foucault Primer*, pp. 30–31.

12 Bove, 'Discourses,' p. 56.

13 Ibid., p. 54.

14 Ibid., pp. 51–52.

15 Michel Foucault, 'Politics and the Study of Discourse,' *Ideology and Consciousness* 3 [FR 1968], p. 15, as cited in McHoul and Grace, *A Foucault Primer*, p. 49.

16 Alan Ryan, 'Twenty-first Century Limited', *New York Review*, 19 November 1992, p. 24.

17 'The Myth of American Diversity', from 'Being an American', an essay by Louis Menand, in the 30 October 1992 issue of *The Times Literary Supplement* (London); and Barry Alan Shain, *The Myth of American Individualism: The Protestant Origins of American Political Thought* (Princeton, NJ: Princeton University Press, 1994), hereafter cited as Shain, *The Myth of American Individualism*.

18 Dorothy Ross, 'An Historian's View Of American Social Science,' *Journal of the History of the Behavioral Sciences* 29 (April 1993): 99–112, esp. 99–101 (hereafter cited as Ross, 'An Historian's View Of American Social Science').

19 Richard Pipes, 'Team B: The Reality Behind the Myth,' *Commentary* 82 (October 1986): 29, as cited in Loch K. Johnson, *America's Secret Power: The CIA in a Democratic Society* (New York: Oxford University Press, 1989), p. 301.

20 D. Michael Shafer, *Deadly Paradigms: The Failure of US Counterinsurgency Policy* (Leicester: Leicester University Press, 1988), pp. 43–78, esp. 44–47 (hereafter cited as Shafer, *Deadly Paradigms*).

21 Edward Said, *Culture and Imperialism* (New York: Knopf, 1993), pp. 287–288 (hereafter cited as Said, *Culture and Imperialism*).

22 William E. Connolly, *Political Theory and Modernity* (Oxford: Blackwell, 1988), pp. 144–145.

23 Ibid.

24 D'Amico, 'What is Discourse?' p. 210.

25 Dorothy Ross, 'Modernist Social Science in the Land of the New/Old', in Dorothy Ross (ed.), *Modernist Impulses in the Human Sciences, 1870–1830* (Baltimore, MD: The Johns Hopkins University Press, 1994), pp. 171–172 (hereafter cited as Ross, 'Modernist Social Science in the Land of the New/Old').

26　Ross, *The Origins of American Social Science*, p. 475.

27　Ross, 'Modernist Social Science in the Land of the New/Old,' p. 171.

28　As cited in Ross, 'An Historian's View Of American Social Science,' p. 104.

29　Ross, 'Modernist Social Science in the Land of the New/Old,' p. 174.

30　Ibid., p. 176; and Ross, 'An Historian's View Of American Social Science,' p. 106.

31　Ibid., pp. 176, and 182; and Ross, 'An Historian's View Of American Social Science,' p. 107.

32　Ibid., pp. 105–110.

33　The introduction of the term American Neo-Exceptionalism seems such an obvious one that this writer finds it remarkable that there is no reference to it in the literature consulted, and cited herein. Possibly, however, given the enormous quantity of works on the general areas of American history and identity, such a reference exists; accordingly, the assurance is offered that the writer, rather than ignoring it, is simply unaware of it.

34　Ross, 'An Historian's View Of American Social Science,' p. 106.

35　Ibid., pp. 108–109.

36　Ibid.

37　Quite apart from the specific sources cited from place to place in this section, a number of others also contributed to the understanding of American Exceptionalism; among the works so consulted are: James Chace and Caleb Carr, *America Invulnerable: The Quest for Absolute Security from 1812 to Star Wars* (New York: Summit, 1988); Richard Drinnon, *Facing West: The Metaphysics of Indian Hating and Empire Building* (New York: Schocken Books, 1990); Glenn P. Hastedt, *American Foreign Policy, Past, Present, Future* (2nd ed) (Englewood Cliffs, NJ: Prentice Hall, 1991); Richard Hofstadter, *The American Political Tradition and the Men Who Made It* (New York: Random House, 1989); Michael H. Hunt, *Ideology and US Foreign Policy* (New Haven, CT: Yale University Press, 1987); Ross, *The Origins of American Social Science*, 'An Historian's View Of American Social Science,' and 'Modernist Impulses in the Land of the New /Old;' Shafer, *Deadly Paradigms*, and Donald M. Snow, *National Security: Enduring Problems in a Changing Defence Environment* (2nd ed) (New York: St Martin's Press, 1991).

38　David Mayers, *George Kennan and the Dilemmas of US Foreign Policy* (New York: Oxford University Press, 1988), p. 248.

39　Todd Gitlin, '*Unum* versus *Pluribus*,' *The Nation*, 6 May 1996, p. 28.

40　Anders Stephanson, *Manifest Destiny: American Expansion and the Empire of Right* (New York: Hill & Wang, 1995), p. xiii (hereafter cited as Stephanson, *Manifest Destiny*).

41　Stanley Hoffman, *Gulliver's Troubles, Or the Setting of American Foreign Policy* (New York: McGraw–Hill, 1968), p. 126, as cited in D. Michael Shafer, *Deadly Paradigms*, p. 135.

42　Stephanson, *Manifest Destiny*, p. xii.

43　Seymour Martin Lipset, *American Exceptionalism: A Double-Edged Sword* (New York: Norton, 1996), p. 20 (hereafter cited as Lipset, *American Exceptionalism*).

44　Chace and Carr, as cited in above note, pp. 318–319.

45　Lewis Lapham, 'Painted Fire,' *Harper's Magazine*, 1 November 1996, p. 11.

46　Two works cited in this section were *Richard Hofstadter, The Paranoid Style in American Politics and Other Essays* (Chicago, IL: University of Chicago Press/Phoenix, 1979), pp. 145–187 (hereafter cited as Hofstadter, *The Paranoid Style in American Politics*), and Walter Russell Mead, *Mortal Splendor: The American Empire in Transition* (Boston, MA: Houghton Mifflin, 1987), pp. 3–49 (hereafter cited as Mead, *Mortal Splendor*).

47　Mead, *Mortal Splendor*, p. 3.

48　Daniel J. Boorstin, *Hidden History: Exploring Our Secret Past* (New York: Random House, 1987), pp. xviii–xxvii.

49　Robert N. Bellah, 'Civil Religion in America', *Daedalus* 96 (winter 1967): 3 (hereafter cited as Bellah, 'Civil Religion in America').

50　Ibid., pp. 1–8.

51   Quoted in Michael Kazin, 'The Right's Unsung Prophet,' *The Nation*, 20 February 1989, p. 245, and as cited in Lipset, *American Exceptionalism*, p. 18.

52   Bellah, 'Civil Religion in America,' p. 18.

53   Ibid., pp. 9–18.

54   For a further consideration of these themes, see: Michael J. Shapiro, 'Narrating the Nation, Unwelcoming the Stranger: Anti-immigration Policy in Contemporary "America",' *Alternatives: Social Transformation and Humane Governance* 22 (January–March 1997): 14–18.

55   Bellah, 'Civil Religion in America,' p. 7.

56   Seymour Martin Lipset, 'Religion and American Values', ch. 4 in *The First New Nation* (New York: 1964), as cited in Bellah, 'Civil Religion in America', p. 12.

57   Ibid., p. 8.

58   Harold Bloom, *The American Religion: The Emergence of the Post-Christian Nation* (New York: Simon & Schuster, 1992), pp. 30 and 267 (hereafter cited as Bloom, *The American Religion*).

59   Garry Wills, *Under God: Religion and American Politics* (New York: Simon & Schuster, 1990), pp. 15–16, and 381 (hereafter cited as Wills, *Under God*).

60   George Marsden, *Fundamentalism and American Culture: The Shaping of Twentieth-century Evangelism, 1870–1920* (Oxford: Oxford University Press, 1980), p. 6, as cited in Wills, *Under God*, p. 19.

61   Ibid., pp. 381–382.

62   Ibid., pp. 382–384.

63   For two short, critical accounts on both of these characteristics see Gore Vidal, 'Notes on our Patriarchal State,' *The Nation*, 27 August–3 September 1990; and Gore Vidal, 'Monotheism and its Discontents,' *The Nation*, 13 July 1992.

64   Wills, *Under God*, p. 382.

65   Bloom, *The American Religion*, pp. 21–22.

66   Ibid., front inside dust cover, which is a more succinct account than the relevant passage on p. 15.

67   Wills, *Under God*, p. 387, note 5. See also Andrew M. Greeley, *Religious Change in America* (Cambridge, MA: Harvard University Press, 1989).

68   Bloom, *The American Religion*, p. 37, and Wills, *Under God*, p. 16; the material presented above is a composite schedule derived from poll data summarised in both works, but which is derived from Gallup and Castelli, *The People's Religion*.

69   Richard G. Hutcheson, *God in the White House: How Religion Has Changed The Modern Presidency* (New York: Collier-Macmillan, 1988), pp. 240–242.

70   For an account of these see Calvin Exoo, 'Cultural Hegemony in the United States' in Calvin F. Exoo (ed.), *Democracy Upside Down: Public Opinion and Cultural Hegemony in the United States* (New York: Praeger, 1987), pp. 11–16 (chapter hereafter cited as Exoo, 'Cultural Hegemony in the United States,' and the full work as Exoo (ed.), *Democracy Upside Down*).

71   William Leach, *Land of Desire: Merchants, Power, and the Rise of a New American Culture* (New York: Pantheon, 1993), pp. 3–12 (hereafter cited as Leach, *Land of Desire*).

72   Ibid., p. 192; see also pp. 191–224.

73   Ibid., p. 386.

74   Ibid., pp. 16–25.

75   Wilshire, *The Moral Collapse of the University*, pp. xx and 255–256.

76   Ibid., p. 255–256.

77   Ibid., p. 175 for Dewey, and p. 187 for Buber.

78   Ibid., pp. 190–191 (for all except Silone). For Silone see Michael Walzer, *The Company of Critics: Social Criticism and Political Commitment in the Twentieth Century* (London: Peter Halban, 1989), pp. 101–116, and 230 (hereafter cited as Walzer, *The Company of Critics*).

79   Wilshire, *The Moral Collapse of the University*, pp. 41–43.

80   Ibid., p. 42–43, and 59–158.

81 Thompson, *The Imagination of an Insurrection*, pp. 233–234.

82 John Garnett, 'Strategic Studies and its Assumptions,' in John Baylis, Ken Booth, John Garnett and Phil Williams, *Contemporary Strategy: Theories and Concepts*, Vol. 1 (New York: Holmes and Meier, 1987), p. 5.

83 See, for example, Charles Hampden-Turner, *Radical Man: The Process of Psycho–social Development* (Cambridge, MA: Schenkman, 1970), pp. 1–15 (hereafter cited as Hampden-Turner, *Radical Man*).

84 Thompson, *The Imagination of an Insurrection*, p. 233.

85 William Irwin Thompson, *Passages about Earth: An Exploration of the New Planetary Culture* (London: Rider, 1975), p. 14 (hereafter cited as Thompson, *Passages about Earth*).

86 For a discussion of this institutional schizophrenia see F. G.. Bailey, *Morality and Expediency: The Folklore of Academic Politics* (Oxford: Blackwell, 1977).

87 Lewis Perry, *Intellectual Life In America: A History* (Chicago, IL: University of Chicago Press, 1989), p. 436 (hereafter cited as Perry, *Intellectual Life in America*).

88 Ibid., pp. 437–438.

89 Ibid., p. 440.

90 Ibid., p. 438–443. [See also Stanley Aronowitz, *Science as Power: Discourse and Ideology in Modern Society* (Minneapolis: University of Minnesota Press, 1988), pp. 3–34; Peter T Manicas, *A History and Philosophy of the Social Sciences* (Oxford: Blackwell, 1987); and Michael Ryan, *Marxism and Deconstruction: A Critical Articulation* (Baltimore, MD: The Johns Hopkins University Press, 1984).]

91 Ibid., p. 440.

92 Ibid.

93 Ibid., p. 439. [See also and especially, Thompson, *Passages about Earth*, pp. 10–29.]

94 Ibid., pp. 442–443 (brief extracts from the article are cited).

95 Ibid., p. 441.

96 Ricci, *The Tragedy of Political Science*, p. 48.

97 Dorothy Ross, *The Origins of American Social Science* (Cambridge: Cambridge University Press, 1992), p. 472.

98 Dorothy Ross, 'An Historian's View of American Social Science,' *Journal of the History of the Behavorial Sciences* 29 (April 1993): 104 (hereafter cited as Ross, 'An Historian's View of American Social Science').

99 Ibid., pp. 472–473.

100 Ibid., p. 474.

101 Dorothy Ross, *The Origins of American Social Science*, pp. 472–473.

102 Michael Ryan, *Marxism and Deconstruction: A Critical Articulation* (Baltimore, MD: Johns Hopkins University Press, 1982), p. 149.

103 Ibid., pp. 133–156.

104 For a more fulsome account of this approach see Edward W. Said, 'Opponents, Audiences, Constituencies and Community,' in Hal Foster (ed.), *Postmodern Culture* (London: Pluto, 1985), p. 144.

105 Said, *Culture and Imperialism*, pp. 291 and 285 respectively.

106 Wilshire, *The Moral Collapse of the University,*' p. 48.

107 William H. Epstein, 'Counter-intelligence: Cold-War Criticism and Eighteenth-century Studies,' *English Literary History* 57 (spring 1990); 63–64, and 71 (composite citation) (hereafter cited as Epstein, 'Counter-intelligence').

108 Ibid., p. 64.

109 Jane Flax, *Thinking Fragments: Psychoanalysis, Feminism, and Postmodernism in the Contemporary West* (Berkeley: University of California Press, 1991), p. 40.

110 Ibid., p. 73.

111 Pierre Bordieu, as cited, ibid., p. 65.

112 Ibid., p. 248.

113 Said, *Culture and Imperialism*, p. 303.

114 Peter T. Manicas, *A History and Philosophy of the Social Sciences* (Oxford: Blackwell, 1988), pp. 210–211.
115 Ralph Waldo Emerson, as cited in Merle Curti, *American Paradox: The Conflict of Thought and Action* (New Brunswick, NJ: Rutgers University Press, 1956), p. 28.
116 Ibid., p. 29.
117 John Trumpbour, *How Harvard Rules: Reason in the Service of Empire* (Boston, MA: South End Press, 1989), hereafter cited as Trumpbour, *How Harvard Rules*.
118 Robert N. Bellah, 'The New Religious Consciousness and the Secular University,' *Daedalus* 103 (autumn 1974): 110–111.
119 See Michael Ryan, *Marxism and Deconstruction: A Critical Articulation* (Baltimore, MD: The Johns Hopkins University Press, 1982), pp. 132–158; and Bruce Wilshire, *The Moral Collapse of the University: Professionalism, Purity, and Alienation* (Albany: State University of New York Press, 1990), pp. 21–34.

5 *Suprema a situ*: Economics in the university and the world

1   Supreme by site, or location.
2   Stephen Toulmin, *Cosmopolis: The Hidden Agenda of Modernity* (Chicago, IL: University of Chicago Press, 1992), p. 104 (hereafter cited as Toulmin, *Cosmopolis*).
3   Ibid., p. 79.
4   Toulmin, *Cosmopolis*, pp. 199–200.
5   Werner Heisenberg, 'Planck's Discovery and the Philosophical Problems of Atomic Physics,' in *On Modern Physics* (New York: 1962), p. 20.
6   Werner Heisenberg, 'The Representation of Nature in Contemporary Physics,' in Rollo May (ed.), *Symbolism* (New York: 1963), p. 215.
7   As cited in Paul Ormerod, *The Death of Economics* (London: Faber and Faber, 1994), p. 67 (hereafter cited as Ormerod, *The Death of Economics*).
8   Toulmin, *Cosmopolis*, pp. 194 and 200–201; and Ormerod, *The Death of Economics*, pp. 11, 36, 41, and 42.
9   Dorothy Ross, 'An Historian's View of American Social Science,' *Journal of the History of the Behavioral Sciences* 29 (April 1993): 107–108, and 110 (hereafter cited as Ross, 'Historian's View'); and 'Modernist Social Science in the Land of the New/Old,' ch. 7 in Dorothy Ross (ed.), *Modernist Impulses in the Human Sciences 1870–1830* (Baltimore, MD: Johns Hopkins University Press, 1994), pp. 176 and 182 (hereafter cited as Ross, 'Modernist Social Science').
10   Ross, 'Historian's View,' pp. 107 and 109.
11   Ibid., pp. 108–109.
12   Ibid., pp. 106–107.
13   Michael Pusey, *Economic Rationalism in Canberra: A Nation Building State Changes its Mind* (Cambridge: Cambridge University Press, 1991), pp. 42–44 (hereafter cited as Pusey, *Economic Rationalism*).
14   Robert W. Cox, 'The Crisis in World Order and the Challenge to International Organisation,' *Cooperation and Conflict* 29(2): 105.
15   Paul Ormerod, *Butterfly Economics* (London: Faber and Faber, 1998), pp. 72–73 (hereafter cited as Ormerod, *Butterfly Economics*).
16   Ibid., p. x.
17   Morris Kline, *Mathematics: The Loss of Certainty* (Oxford: Oxford University Press, 1980), pp. 4–5, and 313 (hereafter cited as Kline, *Mathematics: The Loss of Certainty*).
18   Brian Martin, 'Mathematics and Social Interests,' in Arthur B. Powell and Marilyn Frankenstein (eds), *Ethnomathematics: Challenging Eurocentrism in Mathematics Education* (Albany: State University of New York Press, 1997), p. 156 (hereafter cited as Martin, 'Mathematics and Social Interests').

19 Ibid., p. 165.
20 David Bloor, *Knowledge and Social Imagery* (London: Routledge & Kegan Paul, 1976), chs 5–6, as cited in Martin, 'Mathematics and Social Interests,' pp. 157–158.
21 Ibid.
22 Ibid., pp. 159–160.
23 Nick Herbert, *Quantum Reality: Beyond the New Physics* (Garden City, NY: Anchor Press/ Doubleday, 1985), pp. 15–28.
24 Kline, *Mathematics: The Loss of Certainty*, pp. 5–6 and 307–327.
25 Felipe Fernandez-Armesto, *Truth: A History and a Guide for the Perplexed* (London: Transworld, 1997), p. 190.
26 Ibid.
27 Kline, *Mathematics: The Loss of Certainty*, p. 310.
28 Mary Douglas, 'Faith, Hope and Probability', a review of Ian Hacking, *The Taming of Chance* (Cambridge: Cambridge University Press, 1990), *London Review of Books*, 23 May 1991, p. 6 (hereafter cited as Douglas, 'Faith, Hope and Probability').
29 Kline, *Mathematics: The Loss of Certainty*, p. 348.
30 Douglas, 'Faith, Hope and Probability,' p. 6.
31 Kline, *Mathematics: The Loss of Certainty*, p. 310.
32 Bruce Wilshire, *The Moral Collapse of the University: Professionalism, Purity, and Alienation* (Albany, NY: State University of New York Press, 1990), p. xviii.
33 Tony Lawson, *Economics and Reality* (London: Routledge, 1997), p. xiii (hereafter cited as Lawson, *Economics and Reality*).
34 Gerard Debreu, 'The Mathematicization of Economic Theory,' *American Economic Review* 81: 1–7, as cited in Julie A. Nelson, 'The Study of Choice or the Study of Provisioning?: Gender and the Definition of Economics' (hereafter cited as Nelson, 'Gender in the Definition of Economics'), in Marianne A. Ferber and Julie A. Nelson (eds), *Beyond Economic Man: Feminist Theory and Economics* (Chicago, IL: Chicago University Press, 1993), p. 26 (hereafter cited as Ferber and Nelson (eds), *Beyond Economic Man*).
35 Alexander Rosenberg, *Economics – Mathematical Politics or Science of Diminishing Returns?* (Chicago: Chicago University Press, 1994), p. 247 (hereafter cited as Rosenberg, *Economics*).
36 Ibid., pp. 12–13.
37 Fred Block, *Postindustrial Possibilities: A Critique of Economic Discourse* (Berkeley, CA: University of California Press, 1990), p. 21 (hereafter cited as Block, *Postindustrial Possibilities*).
38 R.E. Lucas, 'Econometric Policy Evaluation: A Critique,' in K. Brunner and A.H. Meltzer (eds), *The Phillips and Labour Markets* (1976), pp. 22–23 (hereafter cited as Lucas, 'Econometric Policy Evaluation') as cited in Lawson, *Economics and Reality*, p. 6.
39 E.E. Leamer, 'Specification Searches: Ad Hoc Inferences With Non-experimental Data' (New York: Wiley, 1978), p. vi (hereafter cited as Leamer, 'Specification Searches') as cited in Lawson, *Economics and Reality*, pp. 6–7.
40 Ibid., p. 7.
41 Lawson, *Economics and Reality*, p. 9.
42 Ibid., pp. xiii and 42.
43 Block, pp. 21–33.
44 Rosenberg, *Economics*, pp. 231–233.
45 T.W. Hutchison, 'On the History and Philosophy of Science and Economics,' in his *Knowledge and Ignorance in Economics* (Chicago, IL: University of Chicago Press, 1977), pp. 34–61, as cited in Deborah A. Redman, *Economics and the Philosophy of Science* (New York: Oxford University Press, 1993), p. 108 (hereafter cited as Redman, *Economics and the Philosophy of Science*).
46 Lawson, *Economics and Reality*, p. 12; see also pp. 10–13.
47 John Ralston Saul, *The Unconscious Civilization* (Ringwood, Victoria: Penguin, 1997), pp. 4–5 (hereafter cited as Saul, *Unconscious Civilization*).

48   Ross, 'Historian's View,' p. 109.
49   Ibid., p. 110.
50   Jeremy Rifkin, *The End of Work: The Decline of the Global Labour Force and the Dawn of the Post-Market Era* (New York: Tarcher/Putnam, 1995), p. 19.
51   As cited in William Leach, *Land of Desire: Merchants, Power, and the Rise of a New American Culture* (New York: Pantheon, 1993), pp. 229, 232, and 233.
52   Ibid., p. 385. (The remainder of this paragraph also contains ideas that appear in the chapter entitled 'Legacies' but is also common to many works critical of consumerist economics and to the general stock of ideas relevant thereto.)
53   Toulmin, *Cosmopolis*, pp. 179–180.
54   Ormerod, *The Death of Economics*, pp. 205 and 211.
55   Ibid., pp. 6, 45–46, and 57.
56   For a brief summary of Axelrod's 1984 work *The Evolution of Co-operation*, in this context, see: ibid., pp. 34–35.
57   Ormerod, *Butterfly Economics*, p. 72.
58   Ibid.
59   Toulmin, *Cosmopolis*, p. 125.
60   Julie A. Nelson, 'The Study of Choice or the Study of Provisioning?: Gender and the Definition of Economics' (hereafter cited as Nelson, 'Gender and the Definition of Economics'), in Ferber and Nelson, *Beyond Economic Man*, pp. 24–26.
61   Diana Strassmann, 'Not a Free Market: The Rhetoric of Disciplinary Authority in Economics' (hereafter cited as Strassmann, 'Not a Free Market'), in Ferber and Nelson, *Beyond Economic Man*, p. 63.
62   Marianne A. Ferber and Julie Nelson, 'Introduction: The Social Construction of Economics and the Social Construction of Gender' (hereafter cited as Ferber and Nelson, 'Introduction'), in Ferber and Nelson (eds), *Beyond Economic Man*, pp. 2–4.
63   Donald N. McCloskey, 'Some News That At Least Will Not Bore You,' *Eastern Economic Journal* (autumn 1995), reprinted in *Lingua Franca* (May–June 1996), and reprinted again in *Harper's Magazine* (July 1996), pp. 21, and 24–25.
64   Ibid.
65   Donald N. McCloskey, 'Some Consequences of a Conjective Economics,' in Ferber and Nelson, *Beyond Economic Man*, p. 79.
66   Ibid.
67   Ferber and Nelson, 'Introduction', in Ferber and Nelson (eds), *Beyond Economic Man*, pp. 4–6.
68   Helen E. Longino, 'Economics for Whom?', in Ferber and Nelson (eds), *Beyond Economic Man*, pp. 166–167; and Block, *Postindustrial Possibilities*, p. 30.
69   Strassmann, 'Not a Free Market,' in Ferber and Nelson, *Beyond Economic Man*, pp. 55–56.
70   See Saul, *Unconscious Civilization*, pp. 51–52.
71   John Kenneth Galbraith, *The Good Society: The Humane Agenda* (Boston, MA: Houghton Mifflin, 1996), p. 75 (hereafter cited as Galbraith, *The Good Society*).
72   Robert Kuttner, 'The Limits of Markets,' *The American Prospect* (March–April 1997): 28–29 (hereafter cited as Kuttner, 'The Limits of Markets').
73   Ibid., pp. 28–31.
74   Block, *Postindustrial Possibilities*, pp. 21–22, and 26–27.
75   Ibid., pp. 27–28.
76   Ibid., pp. 41–42.
77   Ibid., p. 46.
78   Ibid., p. 29.
79   Ormerod, *Butterfly Economics*, pp. 20–21.
80   Ibid.
81   Ibid., pp. 29–30.
82   Saul, *Unconscious Civilization*, p. 123.

83 Galbraith, *The Good Society*, p. 76.

84 Ormerod, *The Death Of Economics*, p. 63.

85 Kuttner, 'The Limits of Markets,' p. 30.

86 Galbraith, *The Good Society*, p. 60.

87 Robert Heilbroner and William Milberg, *The Crisis of Vision in Modern Economic Thought* (Cambridge: Cambridge University Press, 1995), p. 26 (hereafter cited as Heilbroner and Milberg, *Crisis*).

88 Dorothy Ross, *The Origins of American Social Science* (Cambridge: Cambridge University Press, 1991), p. 462 (hereafter cited as Ross, *Origins*).

89 Ibid., pp. 454–456; esp. p. 456.

90 John Agnew and Stuart Corbridge, *Mastering Space: Hegemony, Territory, and International Political Economy* (London: Routledge, 1995), pp. 199–201 (hereafter cited as Agnew and Corbridge, *Mastering Space*).

91 Ormerod, *The Death of Economics*, pp. 46 and 48.

92 Agnew and Corbridge, *Mastering Space*, pp. 200–201.

93 Allan Bloom, *The Closing of the American Mind: How Higher Education Has Failed Democracy and Impoverished the Souls of Today's Students* (New York: Simon & Schuster, 1987), p. 371 (hereafter cited as Bloom, *The Closing of the American Mind*).

94 Galbraith, *The Culture of Contentment* (Sinclair-Stevenson Ltd) (hereafter cited as Galbraith, *The Culture of Contentment*), p. 3; also pp. 78–108.

95 Ibid., pp. 96–97. The other two requirements are the need 'to selectively defend the need for 'general limitation on government as regards the economy', and the need 'to justify a reduced sense of public responsibility for the poor' (see pp. 95–98).

96 Ibid., pp. 80–81, as cited in William Graham Sumner, *The Challenge of Facts and Other Essays*, edited by Albert Galloway Keller (New Haven, CT: Yale University Press, 1914), p. 90.

97 Ibid., pp. 101–105.

98 Ibid., and p. 80.

99 Ormerod, *The Death of Economics*, pp. 43–52.

100 Ibid., pp. 71–72.

101 Ibid., pp. 53–56.

102 John Kenneth Galbraith, *A History of Economics: The Past as the Present* (London: Penguin, 1989), p. 287 (hereafter cited as Galbraith, *A History of Economics*).

103 Ibid., p. 138.

104 Ormerod, *The Death of Economics*, p. 166.

105 Ibid., p. 124.

106 Ormerod's summation of findings in Partha Dasgupta and Geoffrey Heal, *Economic Theory and Exhaustible Resources*, in *The Death of Economics*, pp. 75–76.

107 John McCrone, *Going Inside: A Tour Round a Single Moment of Consciousness* (London: Faber & Faber, 1999), p. 10 (hereafter cited as McCrone, *Going Inside*).

108 Ibid., pp. 302–303.

109 Ibid., pp. 303 and 305.

110 Ormerod, *The Death of Economics*, p. 76.

111 Gerald P. O'Driscoll and Mario J. Rizzo, *The Economics of Time and Ignorance* (London: Routledge, 1996), pp. xv–xvi.

112 Ibid., p. xvi.

113 Ibid., p. 76.

114 Ross, *Origins*, pp. 106–118.

115 As cited in Ross, 'Historian's View,' p. 107.

116 Ibid., p. 196, as cited.

117 Ibid., pp. 62 and 71.

118 Galbraith, *A History of Economics*, pp. 102 and 286.

119 Ormerod, *The Death of Economics*, p. 78.

120 Ibid., p. 80.
121 Ibid., pp. 80–81 and 89.
122 Ibid., p. 89.
123 Ibid., p. 89.
124 Ibid., pp. 90–91.
125 As cited, ibid., p. 91.
126 Ibid., p. 82.
127 Ibid., pp. 82–84.
128 Ibid., p. 86.
129 Ibid., pp. 86–87.
130 Galbraith, *A History of Economics*, p. 286.
131 Ormerod, *The Death of Economics*, p. 106.
132 Ibid., pp. 104–105; and Robert Heilbroner, *Twenty-first Century Capitalism* (Concord, Ontario: Anansi, 1992), pp. 3–4.
133 Ibid., pp. 107–108.
134 Heilbroner and Milberg, *Crisis*, p. 74.
135 As cited in Toulmin, *Cosmopolis*, p. 177.
136 Ibid., pp. 177–178.
137 Ibid., p. 178.
138 Galbraith, *The History of Economics*, pp. 263–264, and Ormerod, *The Death of Economics*, p. 108.
139 Ormerod, *Butterfly Economics*, p. 65.
140 On illiteracy, see Jonathan Kozol, *Illiterate America* (New York: Plume, 1985); and on a-literacy, defined as 'the ability without the inclination, to read' see the Librarian of Congress' estimate in Neil Postman, *Conscientious Objections: Stirring Up Trouble About Language, Technology, and Education* (New York: Knopf, 1988), pp. 64 and 111.
141 A large volume of survey-based literature exists on this subject, but in the above context it might suffice to cite the National Geographic Society's 1988 survey of 18 to 24-year-olds in nine countries in which the US was allocated the equal sixth position (with UK) above Italy and Mexico, but below Sweden, West Germany, Japan, Canada, and France. Among the findings relating to the US were: 75 per cent did not know where the Persian Gulf was; 45 per cent could not identify Nicaragua on a map; 25 per cent could not identify the Pacific Ocean or the Soviet Union; less than half could identify Japan on a map; 50 per cent could not identify South Africa on a map (and 45 per cent did not know that apartheid was the official government policy there; and 14 per cent could not identify their own country on a map.) [NB: the number tested in all countries was 10,820, and the maps in question were unmarked.] This report was carried in *The Australian*, 29 July 1988. The condition is, apparently, both chronic and worsening: in the 2002 survey, the US scored second to last (above Mexico), with only 17 per cent being able to find Afghanistan, while the whereabouts of the US itself defeated 11 per cent, the Pacific Ocean 29 per cent, Japan 58 per cent, France 65 per cent, and the UK 69 per cent. Worse, less than 15 per cent could locate Iraq or Israel, and 33 per cent thought that the population of the US was between one and two *billion*. Four years later still, the US was still only ranked above Mexico and, despite Hurricane Katrina's devastation to the southeastern US in 2005, nearly half could not locate Mississippi, and one-third could not locate Louisiana on a map of the US; the same number could not identify the compass direction 'northwest.' Tested on places beyond the borders of the US, the percentage able to locate Afghanistan had fallen to 10 per cent and 47 per cent could not locate India, and 74 per cent wrongly thought that English was the most commonly spoken native language (when it's Mandarin Chinese). On a map of the Middle East, 63 per cent were unable to locate Iraq and 70 per cent found the location of Iran and Israel too difficult. See: 'Survey Reveals Geographic Illiteracy,' *National Geographic News*, 20 November 2002, http://news.nationalgeographic.com/news/2002/11/1120_021120_GeoRoperSurvey.html and 'Young Americans

Geographically Illiterate Survey Suggests,' *National Geographic News*, 2 May 2006, http://news.nationalgeographic.com/news/2006/05/0502_060502_geography.html, both accessed 4 May 2006.

142 Ormerod, *The Death of Economics*, p. 108, and *Butterfly Economics*, pp. 65–66.

143 Ormerod, *The Death of Economics*, p. 108.

144 Ibid., p. 109.

145 Ibid., pp. 109–110.

146 Ibid., p. 109.

147 Ormerod, *Butterfly Economics*, p. 89.

148 Ibid., pp. 79–80.

149 Ibid., pp. 81–90.

150 Galbraith, *A History of Economics*, p. 263.

151 Daniel R. Fusfield, *The Age of the Economist* (7th edn) (New York: HarperCollins, 1994), p. 170 (hereafter cited as Fusfield, *The Age of the Economist*).

152 Heilbroner and Milberg, *Crisis*, pp. 78–79.

153 Lawson, *Economics and Reality*, p. 75.

154 Ormerod, *The Death of Economics*, pp. 99–101.

155 As cited in Nelson, 'Gender and the Definition of Economics,' in Ferber and Nelson, *Beyond Economic Man*, p. 27.

156 Lucas, 'Econometric Policy Evaluation,' as cited in Lawson, *Economics and Reality*, p. 25, as cited in Lawson, *Economics and Reality*, p. 72.

157 David F. Hendry, 'Econometrics: Alchemy or Science?', *Economica* 47 (November 1980): 396, as cited in Redman, *Economics and the Philosophy of Science*, p. 121.

158 Oskar Morgenstern, *On the Accuracy of Economic Observations* (2nd completely revised edn) (Princeton, NJ: Princeton University Press, 1963), as cited in Redman, *Economics and the Philosophy of Science*, p. 121.

159 Lawson, *Economics and Reality*, p. 70.

160 Saul, *The Unconscious Civilization*, p. 4.

161 Ibid., pp. 119–120.

162 Ibid., p. 123.

163 Ibid., pp. 125–126.

164 Ibid., p. 126.

165 Ibid., p. 133.

166 Ibid., p. 146.

167 Ibid., p. 151.

168 Ibid., pp. 151–152.

169 Ibid., pp. 149–161; and Michael A. Bernstein and David E. Adler (eds), *Understanding American Economic Decline* (Cambridge: Cambridge University Press, 1994), pp. 383–384.

170 Ormerod, *The Death of Economics*, pp. 175–176.

171 Ibid.

172 Caroline Postelle Clotfelter (ed.), *On the Third Hand: Humor in the Dismal Science, An Anthology* (Ann Arbor: University of Michigan Press, 1999), p. 52.

173 As cited in Ormerod, *Butterfly Economics*, p. 60.

174 Alfred Marshall, *Principles of Economics* (Amherst: Prometheus Books, 1997), p. 42.

175 Commutative: a series of numbers taken in any order will come to the same result.

176 Associative: numbers which, grouped differently, produce the same total.

177 Development of points essentially made by Ormerod, but placed in a slightly different context here (p. 210).

178 Ibid.

179 See Toulmin, *Cosmopolis*, pp. 154 and 199; see also the reference (p. 171) to David Hilbert's work showing that, contrary to the metaphysical commitments of neoclassical economics in general, and its asserted concordance with nature in particular, pure

mathematics 'can be viewed as a body of formal operations that does not refer to our experience of nature.'

180 Heilbroner and Milberg, *Crisis,* pp. 3–4.
181 Lawson, *Economics and Reality,* pp. 4–5, and 14.
182 Strassmann, 'Not a Free Market,' pp. 54–55.
183 Heilbroner and Milberg, *Crisis,* pp. 105–108.
184 Ibid., pp. 109–113.
185 Toulmin, *Cosmopolis,* pp. 169–170.
186 Barry Alan Shain, *The Myth of American Individualism: The Protestant Origins of American Political Thought* (Princeton, NJ: Princeton University Press, 1994), p. 325.
187 Ibid., as cited.
188 As cited in Paul Bove, *In the Wake of Theory* (Hanover: Wesleyan University Press/ University Press of New England, 1992), p. 110 (hereafter cited as Bove, *In the Wake of Theory*).
189 As cited in Milan Rai, *Chomsky's Politics* (London: Verso, 1995), p. 139 (hereafter cited as Rai, *Chomsky's Politics*).
190 Rai, *Chomsky's Politics,* pp. 149 and 161.
191 See, for example, J.E. King, *Economic Exiles* (New York: St Martin's Press, 1988); Michael Parenti, *Against Empire* (San Francisco, CA: City Lights, 1995); Ellen W. Schrecker, *No Ivory Tower: McCarthyism and the Universities* (New York: Oxford University Press, 1986); Lawrence C. Soley, *Leasing the Ivory Tower: The Corporate Takeover of Academia* (Boston, MA: South End Press, 1995); John Trumpbour, *How Harvard Rules: Reason in the Service of Empire* (Boston: South End Press, 1989); and Dorothy Ross, *Origins.*
192 Paul Hollander, *Anti-Americanism: Critiques at Home and Abroad 1965–1990* (New York: Oxford University Press, 1992).
193 Ibid., pp. 127 and 161.
194 In this, the university is behaving no differently on questions of economics than it does on questions of national security; indeed, when the historical record is interrogated, the university is seen to have an affinity for producing and reproducing theories of destruction. For an account see Michael McKinley, 'The Co-option of the University and the Privileging of Annihilation,' *International Relations* 18(2): 151–172.

6 Equivalence and convergence: neo-liberal globalisation as war and militarisation

1 Francis Fukuyama, *The End of History and the Last Man* (London: Penguin, 1992), (hereafter cited as Fukuyama, *The End of History*).
2 Samuel P. Huntington, *The Clash of Civilizations and the Remaking of World Order* (New York: Simon & Schuster, 1996) (hereafter cited as Huntington, *Clash of Civilizations*).
3 Michael Rosen and David Widgery (eds), *The Chatto Book of Dissent* (London: Chatto & Windus, 1994), p. 5 (hereafter cited as Rosen and Widgery (eds), *The Chatto Book of Dissent*).
4 Here, the term is defined in accordance with the basic elements of a definition offered by Hans-Henrik Holm and Georg Sorensen – namely, 'the [uneven] intensification of economic, political, social, and cultural relations across borders.' See *Whose World Order? Uneven Globalization and the End of the Cold War* (Boulder, CO: Westview Press, 1995), p. 1. At the same time, it would be misleading not to acknowledge two emphases within the overall process. The first is its dominant economic-prescriptive aspect of globalisation as the economic theory and practice that the greatest productive efficiency will be achieved with the free movement of capital, technology, goods, and services throughout the world, for the purpose of taking advantage of the cheapest conditions of production and supply of labour. The second is the simultaneous and synonymous project of globalisation-as-modernisation-as-Westernisation, wherein the non-Western world engages in interminable,

and therefore hopeless, mimicry of the West in order to conform to the strictures of (Western-defined) survival. See Serge Latouche, *The Westernization of the World* (Cambridge, UK: Polity Press, 1996). All elements, it should be noted, are either made possible in the first place, or intensified, by what Eleonore Kofman and Gillian Youngs describe as 'supraterritoriality' – by which is meant the advent of such speed in communications, etc., that distance and territory are, for all intents and purposes, eliminated. See *Globalization: Theory and Practice* (London: Pinter, 1996).

5   Melvyn P. Leffler, *A Preponderance of Power: National Security, the Truman Administration, and the Cold War* (Stanford, CA: Stanford University Press, 1992), hereafter cited as Leffler, *A Preponderance of Power.*

6   John Lewis Gaddis, *The Long Peace: Inquiries into the History of the Cold War, 1945–1950* (New York: Columbia University Press, 1985), pp. vii and 21, as cited in Lynn Eden, 'The End of US Cold War History?,' *International Security* 18 (summer 1993): 194 (hereafter cited as Eden, 'The End of US Cold War History?').

7   See, for example, Joyce Kolko and Gabriel Kolko, *The Limits of Power: The World and United States Foreign Policy, 1945–1972* (New York: Harper & Row, 1972); and Fred L. Block, *The Origins of International Economic Disorder: A Study of United States International Monetary Policy from World War II to the Present* (Berkeley: University of California Press, 1972), as cited in Eden, 'The End of US Cold War History?', pp. 190–198.

8   Walter Russell Mead, 'On the Road to Ruin: Winning the Cold War, Losing the Economic Peace,' *Harper's Magazine,* March 1990, pp. 60–61.

9   For an account of this experience see: William Leach, *Land of Desire: Merchants, Power, and the Rise of the New American Culture* (New York: Pantheon, 1993) (hereafter cited as Leach, *Land of Desire).*

10 Ibid., pp. 233–242.

11 Ibid, p. 37.

12 As cited in Jeremy Rifkin, *The End of Work: The Decline of the Global Labor Force and the Dawn of the Post-market Era* (New York: G.P. Putnam's Sons, 1995), p. 20.

13 David C. Korten, 'The Limits of the Earth,' *The Nation,* 15–22 July 1996, p. 15 (hereafter cited as Korten, 'The Limits of the Earth)'.

14 As babies, clan chiefs were wet-nursed by the wife of a low-ranked member of the clan.

15 John Prebble, *Culloden* (Penguin, 1967), pp. 35–37, and 45 (hereafter cited as Prebble, *Culloden).*

16 Prebble, *Culloden,* p. 43.

17 John Kenneth Galbraith, *A Short History of Financial Euphoria* (New York: Penguin, 1993), pp. 12–13.

18 Paul Krugman, *Pop Internationalism* (Cambridge, MA: MIT Press, 1996), p. 6 (hereafter cited as Krugman, *Pop Internationalism.*)

19 For two of the more prominent of these see Lester C. Thurow's *Head to Head: The Coming Battle Among Japan, Europe and America,* and Richard Bernstein's *The Coming Conflict With China.*

20 Leach, *Land of Desire,* pp. 384–385.

21 Andrew L. Shapiro, *We're Number One: Where America Stands – and Falls – in the New World Order* (New York: Vintage, 1992), p. 87.

22 Prebble, *Culloden,* pp. 35–36 and 45–46.

23 Ibid., p. 32.

24 Liam de Paor, *Divided Ulster* (Harmondsworth: Penguin, 1971), p. 2.

25 Prebble, *Culloden,* p. 38.

26 Ibid., pp. 34 and 36.

27 Ibid., pp. 46–47.

28 Ibid., p. 39.

29 Bruce Wilshire, *The Moral Collapse of the University: Professionalism, Purity, and Alienation* (New York: State University of New York Press, 1990), p. 41 and 43 (hereafter cited as Wilshire, *The Moral Collapse of the University).*

30 Ibid., pp. 41–43, and pp. 255–256.
31 Paul A. Bove, 'Discourse,' in Frank Lentricchia and Thomas McLaughlin, *Critical Terms for Literary Study* (Chicago, IL: University of Chicago Press, 1990), pp. 50–54.
32 Wilshire, *The Moral Collapse of the University*, p. xx.
33 Prebble, *Culloden*, p. 34.
34 Wilshire, *The Moral Collapse of the University*, p. 153.
35 Ibid., pp. 48 and 72. The Larson citation appears on p. 134, and is taken from Magali Sarfatti Larson, *The Rise of Professionalism: A Sociological Analysis* (Berkeley: University of California Press, 1977), pp. 23–24.
36 Robert Kuttner, 'Peddling Krugman,' *The American Prospect*, September–October 1996, p. 79 (hereafter cited as Kuttner, 'Peddling Krugman').
37 Paul Krugman, *Pop Internationalism* (Cambridge, MA: MIT Press, 1996), pp. 69–73 (hereafter cited as Krugman, *Pop Internationalism*).
38 Ibid., pp. 78, 83, and 108; and Kuttner, 'Peddling Krugman,' p. 81.
39 Prebble, *Culloden*, p. 53.
40 Krugman, *Pop Internationalism*, pp. 80–82, and 130.
41 Ibid., pp. 124–125.
42 Ibid., pp. 89–90.
43 For an account of the significance, and implications, of Hume's work in relation to empiricist-based knowledge, see Jim George, *Discourses of Global Politics: A Critical (Re)Introduction* (Boulder, CO: Lynne Rienner, 1994), pp. 51–55 (hereafter cited as George, *Discourses of Global Politics*).
44 Paul Bove, *In the Wake of Theory* (Hanover, NH: Wesleyan University Press, 1992), p. 78 (hereafter cited as Bove, *In the Wake of Theory*).
45 Wilshire, *The Moral Collapse of the University*, pp. 21–22, 79, 229, and 232.
46 Adapted from Robert L. Heilbroner, *The Nature and Logic of Capitalism* (New York: Norton, 1985), p. 117.
47 Richard B. Freeman, 'Toward an Apartheid Economy?,' *Harvard Business Review*, September–October 1996, pp. 114–121 (hereafter cited as Freeman, 'Toward an Apartheid Economy?').
48 Ibid., pp. 118–119.
49 James Hillman, *The Myth of Analysis: Three Essays on Archetypal Psychology* (New York: 1978), p. 250, as cited in Wilshire, *The Moral Collapse of the University*, pp. 147–148.
50 Ibid., p. 147, as cited.
51 Joseph M. Hassett, *Yeats and the Poetics of Hate* (Dublin: Gill & Macmillan, 1986), pp. 80–86.
52 Warren J. Samuels, *Essays in the History of Heterodox Political Economy* (London: Macmillan, 1992), p. 295 (hereafter cited as Samuels, *Essays in the History of Heterodox Political Economy*).
53 Ibid.
54 The character Giordano Bruno, in Morris West's play, *The Heretic* (London: Heinemann, 1970), p. 38.
55 Michael A. Bernstein, 'American Economics and the American Economy in the American Century: Doctrinal Legacies and Contemporary Policy Problems,' in Michael A. Bernstein and David E. Adler (eds), *Understanding American Economic Decline* (New York: Cambridge University Press, 1994), pp. 362–363 (hereafter cited as Bernstein, 'American Economics,' and Bernstein and Adler (eds), *Understanding American Economic Decline*, respectively).
56 Ibid., pp. 361–384.
57 Richard J. Barnett, 'Stateless Corporations: Lords of the Global Economy,' *The Nation*, pp. 754–756 (hereafter cited as Barnett, 'Lords of the Global Economy').
58 Glen Falls, *Post-Star*, 11 March 1994, and *New York Times*, 11 March 1994.
59 Jeremy Brecher and Tim Costello, *Global Village or Global Pillage: Economic Reconstruction From the Bottom Up* (Boston, MA: South End Press, 1994), pp. 29–30.
60 Barnett, 'Lords of the Global Economy,' p. 755.
61 Paul Ormerod, *The Death of Economics* (London: Faber and Faber, 1994), pp. 12–13 (hereafter cited as Ormerod, *The Death of Economics*).

62 See, respectively, Edward N. Luttwak, 'From Geopolitics to Geoeconomics: Logic of Conflict, Grammar of Commerce,' *National Interest* (summer 1990): 17; and Peter Kornbluh and Malcolm Byrne (eds), *The Iran-Contra Scandal: The Declassified History* (New York: New Press, 1993), pp. 123–125.

63 George, *Discourses of Global Politics,* pp. 111–134.

64 Neil Postman, *Technopoly: The Surrender of Culture to Technology* (New York: Alfred A. Knopf, 1992), pp. 139–140.

65 Ibid., p. 140.

66 Major-General Smedley D. Butler, as cited in Rosen and Widgery (eds), *The Chatto Book of Dissent,* pp. 287–288.

67 Richard A. Gabriel and Paul L. Savage, *Crisis in Command: Mismanagement in the Army* (New York: Hill & Wang, 1978), pp. 59–63, and 144–150; and Edward N. Luttwak, *The Pentagon and the Art of War* (New York: Simon & Schuster, 1985), pp. 24, and 138–139.

68 'US Marines Get a Lesson from War St.', *The Sydney Morning Herald,* 2 December 1995, ex *Newsday.*

69 Robert Heilbroner, *Visions of the Future: The Distant Past, Yesterday, and Tomorrow* (New York: The New York Public Library/Oxford University Press, 1995), p. 82.

70 Elizabeth Rubin, 'An Army of One's Own,' *Harper's Magazine,* February 1997, p. 54.

71 Ibid., pp. 44–55.

72 Ibid., p. 55.

73 Ibid.

74 As cited in Barnett, 'Lords of the Global Economy,' p. 754.

75 Robert Dreyfuss, 'The New China Lobby,' *The American Prospect,* January–February 1997, pp. 30–37; Chalmers Johnson, 'Breaching the Great Wall,' *The American Prospect,* January–February 1997, pp. 24–29; and Ken Silverstein, 'The New China Hands: How the Fortune 500 is China's Strongest Lobby,' *The Nation,* 17 February 1997, pp. 11–16.

76 Ibid., p. 756.

77 Walter H. Capps, *The Unfinished War: Vietnam and the American Conscience,* rev. edn (Boston, MA: Beacon Press, 1990), p. 1; and Michael Maclear, *Vietnam: The Ten Thousand Day War* (London: Eyre Methuen, 1981), p. 386.

78 Indicatively, the *New York Times* reported, 'in Manhattan the income gap between the rich and the poor is greater than in Guatemala, and within the US is surpassed only by a group of 70 households near a former leper colony in Hawaii' (as cited in *Z Magazine,* February 1995, cover page). For accounts and evidence of these claims, see, for example, the relevant sections in the following: Michael A. Bernstein and David E. Adler (eds), *Understanding American Economic Decline* (Cambridge: Cambridge University Press, 1994); Jeremy Brecher and Tim Costello, *Global Village or Global Pillage: Economic Reconstruction From the Bottom Up* (Boston, MA: South End Press, 1994); Victor Bulmer-Thomas (ed.), *The New Economic Model in Latin America and its Impact on Income Distribution and Poverty* (New York: St Martin's Press, 1996); Robert Cox, 'The Crisis in World Order and the Challenge to International Organization,' *Cooperation and Conflict* 29(2); Kevin Danaher (ed.), *50 Years Is Enough: The Case Against The World Bank and the International Monetary Fund* (Boston, MA: South End Press, 1994); John Kenneth Galbraith, 'The New Dialectic,' *The American Prospect* (summer 1994); Edward S. Herman, 'Immiserating Growth in the First World,' *Z Magazine,* January 1995; Serge Latouche, *In the Wake of the Affluent Society: An Exploration of Post Development* (London: Zed Books, 1993); Ozay Mehmet, *Westernizing the Third World: The Eurocentricity of Economic Development Theories* (London: Routledge, 1995); Wallace C. Peterson, *Silent Depression: The Fate of the American Dream* (New York: Norton, 1994); Jeremy Rifkin, *The End of Work; The Decline of the Global Labor Force and the Dawn of the Post-market Era* (New York: Jeremy P. Tarcher/Putnam, 1995); and John E. Schwarz and Thomas J. Volgy, *The Forgotten Americans* (New York: Norton, 1992).

288 *Notes*

79 Statistics as cited in Davison Budhoo, 'IMF/World Bank Wreak Havoc on Third World,' in Kevin Danaher (ed.), *50 Years Is Enough: The Case Against The World Bank and the International Monetary Fund* (Boston, MA: South End Press, 1994), pp. 21–22.

80 James F. Dunnigan and Albert A. Nofi, *Dirty Little Secrets: Military Information You're Not Supposed To Know* (New York: Morrow, 1990), pp. 381–382.

81 This, of course, begs the question as to whether the lack of intention makes any sense at all when the conditions of war, and the weapons used, are virtually guaranteed to render meaningless notions of discrimination between the antagonists.

82 As cited in *The Sydney Morning Herald*, 8 June 1996.

83 Esther Schrader, 'A Giant Spraying Sound,' *Mother Jones*, January–February 1995, pp. 34–37, and 72–73.

84 Danielle Knight, 'The Global Politics of Pesticide Use in Brazil,' *Z Magazine*, January 1997, pp. 41–46.

85 Ibid., and William Appleman Williams *et al.*, *America in Vietnam: A Documentary History* (New York: Norton, 1975), pp. 302–303. Comparison is based on statistics provided in both works.

86 'Toward an Apartheid Economy?', p. 119; and Max Hastings, *The Korean War* (New York: Simon & Schuster, 1987), pp. 304 and 329.

87 Paul Ormerod, *The Death of Economics* (London: Faber and Faber, 1994), pp. 61 and 196.

88 See, respectively, *The American Way of War: A History of United States Military Strategy and Policy* (New York: Macmillan, 1973), p. xxii, and John Kenneth Galbraith, *A Short History of Financial Euphoria* (New York: Penguin, 1993), p. 16.

89 Jeremy Rifkin, *Beyond Beef: The Rise and Fall of the Cattle Culture* (Melbourne: Viking, 1992), pp. 170–175 (hereafter cited as Rifkin, *Beyond Beef*).

90 Asa Wahlquist, 'Beefing Up our Trade is Almost Green,' *Sydney Morning Herald*, 26 March 1992. The Worldwatch paper also makes the point that beef farming in Australia and sheep farming in New Zealand are considerably less energy-intensive because the animals there are raised purely on grass.

91 Rifkin, *Beyond Beef*, p. 1.

92 Peter Singer, *Animal Liberation* (2nd edn) (London: Jonathan Cape, 1990), p. 168, in conjunction with 'Dutch Drowning in Pig Manure,' *Sunday Star–Times* (New Zealand), 31 December 1995 (ex *Sunday Times*, London).

93 Joni Seager, 'Operation Desert Disaster: Environmental Costs of the War,' in Cynthia Peters (ed.), *Collateral Damage: The 'New World Order' at Home and Abroad* (Boston, MA: South End Press, 1992), p. 198 (hereafter cited as Seager, 'Operation Desert Disaster').

94 Arthur H. Westing, *Ecological Consequences of the Second Indochina War* (Stockholm: Stockholm International Peace Research Institute, 1976), pp. 1, 10, and 86.

95 See Ramsay Clark and others, *War Crimes: A Report on United States War Crimes Against Iraq – Reports to the Commission of Inquiry for the International War Crimes Tribunal and the Tribunal's Final Judgment* (Washington, DC: Maisoneuvve Press, 1992), p. 214.

96 Seager, 'Operation Desert Disaster,' p. 211.

97 Rifkin, *Beyond Beef*, p. 225.

98 As cited in Richard Hofstadter, *Anti-intellectualism in American Life* (New York: Vintage, 1963), p. 50.

99 Ibid., p. 50.

100 Ormerod, *The Death of Economics*, p. 7.

101 Davison Budhoo, 'IMF/World Bank Wreak Havoc on Third World,' in Kevin Danaher (ed.), *50 Years Is Enough: The Case Against The World Bank and the International Monetary Fund* (Boston, MA: South End Press, 1994), pp. 18–22.

102 Ibid., p. 19, and as cited in Walden Bello, 'Global Economic Counterrevolution: How Northern Economic Warfare Devastates the South' in Kevin Danaher (ed.), *50 Years Is Enough: The Case Against The World Bank and the International Monetary Fund* (Boston, MA: South End Press, 1994), pp. 18–22.

103 Herbert C. Kelman and V. Lee Hamilton, *Crimes of Obedience: Toward A Social Psychology of Authority and Responsibility* (New Haven, CT: Yale University Press, 1989), pp. 23 and 29.
104 As cited, ibid., p. 5.
105 Eric Markusen and David Kopf, *The Holocaust and Strategic Bombing: Genocide and Total War in the 20th Century* (Boulder, CO: Westview Press, 1995), pp. 210–237.

7 Congruence: Economics as war

1 Ricardo Trumper and Lynne Phillips, 'Cholera in the Time of Neoliberalism: The Case of Chile and Equador,' *Alternatives* 20 (1995): 167.
2 Edward Mead Earle, *Makers of Modern Strategy: Military Thought from Machiavelli to Hitler* (2nd printing) (Princeton, NJ: Princeton University Press), p. viii.
3 Michael Pusey, *Economic Rationalism in Canberra: A Nation Building State Changes its Mind* (Cambridge: Cambridge University Press, 1991), p. 21 (hereafter cited as Pusey, *Economic Rationalism*).
4 Ibid., p. 22.
5 In the contemporary global political economy literature numerous terms are deployed to describe neoclassical economic theory-as-practice on a global scale. Thus (to name a few) 'neo-liberalism,' 'economic rationalism,' 'free market liberalism,' 'free trade,' and 'transnational liberalism' all appear, depending on the proclivities of the author. The resulting confusion can be reduced, however, by understanding that, with due allowance being made for different emphases and stylistic preferences, the phenomenon which they describe is, essentially, the same – namely, to paraphrase Robert Cox, the legitimation of capitalism's 'instinct …to free itself from any form of state or interstate control or intervention [by way of] deregulation, privatisation, and the dismantling of state protection for the vulnerable elements of society' (Robert W. Cox, 'The Crisis in World Order and the Challenge to International Organization', (*Cooperation and Conflict* 29(2): 105.
6 Paul Ormerod, *The Death of Economics* (London: Faber and Faber, 1994), p. 182–183.
7 Oliver MacDonagh, *Ireland: The Union and its Aftermath* (rev. and enl. edn) (London: George Allen & Unwin, 1977), p. 165.
8 Azar Gat, *The Origins of Military Thought: From the Enlightenment to Clausewitz* (Oxford: Clarendon Press, 1991), pp. 106–189 (hereafter cited as Gat, *Origins*), and Roman Kolkowicz, 'The Strange Career of the Defense Intellectuals,' *Orbis* 31 (summer, 1987): 170–180 (hereafter cited as Kolkowicz, 'Defense Intellectuals').
9 Paul Ormerod, *The Death of Economics* (London: Faber and Faber, 1994), p. 45 (hereafter cited as Ormerod, *The Death of Economics*); and Stanley Aronowitz, *Dead Artists, Live Theories, and Other Cultural Problems* (New York: Routledge, 1994), pp. 257–276 (hereafter cited as Aronowitz, *Live Theories*).
10 Aronowitz, *Live Theories*, pp. 259–261.
11 Anatol Rapaport (ed.), Carl von Clausewitz, *On War* (Harmondsworth: Penguin, 1968), Editor's Introduction, p. 63 (hereafter cited as Rapaport (ed.), *On War*); Gat, *Origins*, p. 168; and Kolkowicz, 'Defense Intellectuals,' p. 179.
12 John Kenneth Galbraith, *The Culture of Contentment* (London: Sinclair-Stevenson, 1992), pp. 78–108, esp. pp. 78–79 (hereafter cited as Galbraith, *Contentment*); and Alan Ryan, 'Professor Hegel Goes to Washington' (a review of Francis Fukuyama's *The End of History and the Last Man*) *New York Review of Books*, 26 March 1992, pp. 12–13.
13 Gat, *Origins*, pp. 223–224.
14 Raymond Aron, as cited in Eric Markusen and David Kopf, *The Holocaust and Strategic Bombing: Genocide and Total War in the 20th Century* (Boulder, CO: Westview Press, 1995), p. 38 (hereafter cited as Markusen and Kopf, *The Holocaust and Strategic Bombing*).
15 This concept is developed at length in Markusen and Kopf, *The Holocaust and Strategic Bombing* , pp. 195–209.

16 Ibid., pp. 201–202.

17 Ibid., p. 202.

18 Ibid., pp. 203–205, on strategic bombing; and pp. 195–201, on the Holocaust.

19 See, for example, Gar Alperowitz, *Atomic Diplomacy: Hiroshima and Potsdam* (rev. edn) (London: Pluto, 1994).

20 As cited in Enrique Dussel, *The Invention of the Americas: Eclipse of 'the Other' and the Myth of Modernity* (New York: Continuum, 1995), p. 63 (hereafter cited as Dussel, *Invention*).

21 Ibid., pp. 64–66.

22 Ibid., pp. 66–67.

23 Douglas C. North, *Institutions, Institutional Change and Economic Performance* (New York: Cambridge University Press, 1990), p. 110, as cited in Ozay Mehmet, *Westernizing the Third World: The Eurocentricity of Economic Development Theories* (London: Routledge, 1995), p. 12 (hereafter cited as Mehmet, *Westernizing*).

24 Francis Fukuyama, 'The End of History?', *The National Interest* (summer, 1989): 3–4, as cited in Mehmet, *Westernizing*, p. 13.

25 Ibid., p. 13.

26 Jacques Attali, from his book, *Millennium: Winners and Losers in the Coming World Order*, as cited in Walden Bello, 'Global Economic Counterrevolution: How Northern Economic Warfare Devastates the South,' in Kevin Danaher (ed.), *50 Years is Enough: The Case Against the World Bank and the International Monetary Fund* (Boston, MA: South End Press, 1994), p. 14 (works hereafter cited as Bello, 'Global Economic Counterrevolution,' and Bello, *50 Years is Enough*).

27 Ibid., p. 19.

28 Conor Cruise O'Brien, *On the Eve of the Millennium:: The Future of Democracy Through an Age of Unreason* (New York: The Free Press, 1994), pp. 163 and 146, respectively.

29 Pusey, *Economic Rationalism*, p. 10.

30 Galbraith, *Contentment*, pp. 80–81.

31 John Kenneth Galbraith, *A History of Economics: The Past as the Present* (London: Penguin, 1991), p. 287 (hereafter cited as Galbraith, *History*).

32 John Vasquez, *The Power of Power Politics* (New Brunswick: Rutgers University Press, 1983), pp. 219–220.

33 Thomas Balogh, *The Irrelevance of Conventional Economics* (London: Weidenfeld & Nicolson, 1982), p. 32, as cited in Galbraith, *History*, p. 189.

34 For just one comprehensive account, see Honore M. Catudal, *Nuclear Deterrence – Does it Deter?* (Atlantic Highlands, NJ: Humanities Press, 1985).

35 Morton H. Halperin, *Nuclear Fallacy: Dispelling the Myth of Nuclear Strategy* (Cambridge, MA: Ballinger, 1987), p. 102.

36 Galbraith, *History*, pp. 183–184; and Paul Ormerod, *The Death of Economics* (London: Faber and Faber, 1994), p. 77.

37 Charles Hampden-Turner, *Radical Man: The Process of Psycho-Social Development* (Cambridge, MA: Schenkman, 1970), p. 12 (hereafter cited as Hampden-Turner, *Radical Man*).

38 Ormerod, *The Death of Economics*, pp. 104–105; and Robert Heilbroner, *Twenty-first Century Capitalism* (Concord, Ontario: Anansi, 1992), pp. 3–4.

39 Galbraith, *Contentment*, pp. 88–89, and 101.

40 For an account of the New Zealand–US *impasse* on this matter, and in the terms outlined, see Michael C. Pugh, *The ANZUS Crisis, Nuclear Visiting and Deterrence* (Cambridge: Cambridge University Press, 1989).

41 Jeremy Brecher and Tim Costello, *Global Village or Global Pillage: Economic Reconstruction From the Bottom Up* (Boston, MA: South End Press, 1994), pp. 58–59. See also Lori Wallach, 'Hidden Dangers of GATT and NAFTA,' in Ralph Nader *et al*, *The Case Against Free Trade: GATT, NAFTA, and the Globalization of Corporate Power* (San Francisco and Berkeley, CA: Earth Island Press and North Atlantic Books, 1993), pp. 23–64.

42 'Rome has spoken, the cause is ended.'

43 Which begins: 'Out of the depths I have cried unto thee, O Lord; Lord hear my voice.'

8 *Romanita*: Reformation and Counter-Reformation in neoclassical Economics/neo-liberalism (Economics-as-religion)

1   Eugene Honee, 'The Relation of Old and New and the Phenomenon of *Reformation*,' in J.B.M. Wissink (ed.), *(Dis)Continuity and (De)Construction: Reflections on the Meaning of the Past in Crisis Situations* (Kampen, The Netherlands: Pharos, 1995), pp. 30 and 45 (hereafter cited as Honee, 'The Relation of Old and New and the Phenomenon of *Reformation*').

2   For this acerbic and neat distinction I am grateful to J.S. McClelland, *A History of Western Political Thought* (London: Routledge, 1996), p. 174.

3   Morris West, *Lazarus* (Port Melbourne, Victoria: William Heinemann Australia, 1990), pp. 67, 9, and 105, respectively (hereafter cited as West, *Lazarus*).

4   Richard Tarnas, *The Passion of the Western Mind: Understanding the Ideas That Have Shaped Our World View* (New York: Ballantine, 1991), pp. 233–243 (hereafter cited as Tarnas, *The Passion of the Western Mind*).

5   Stephen Toulmin, *Cosmopolis: The Hidden Agenda of Modernity* (Chicago, IL: Chicago University Press, 1990), p. 79 (hereafter cited as Toulmin, *Cosmopolis*).

6   John Ralston Saul, *The Unconscious Civilization* (Ringwood, Victoria; Penguin, 1997), p. 88 (hereafter cited as Saul, *The Unconscious Civilization*).

7   Edward E. Leamer, 'Specification Searches: Ad hoc Inferences with Non-experimental Data' (New York: John Wiley and Sons, 1978), p. vi, as cited in Tony Lawson, *Economics and Reality* (London: Routledge, 1997), pp. 6–7 (hereafter cited as Leamer, 'Specification Searches: Ad hoc Inferences with Non-experimental Data').

8   Edward E. Leamer, 'Let's Take the Con Out of Econometrics,' *American Economic Review* 73 (March 1983): 36, as cited in Deborah A. Redman, *Economics and the Philosophy of Science* (New York: Oxford University Press, 1991), pp. 120–121.

9   Leamer, 'Specification Searches: Ad hoc Inferences with Non-experimental Data'), p. vi.

10 John D. Caputo, 'Bedeviling the Tradition: On Deconstruction and Catholicism,' in J.B.M. Wissink (ed.), *(Dis)Continuity and (De)Construction: Reflections on the Meaning of the Past in Crisis Situations* (Kampen, The Netherlands: Pharos, 1995), pp. 15–18 (hereafter cited as Caputo, 'Bedeviling the Tradition').

11 Ibid., p. 18.

12 The present surely needs no explanation of this claim; neither, probably, does its predecessor, but just in case it does, the reference is to the woodcut and movable type. For a brief account, see: Felipe Fernandez-Armesto, *Millennium: A History of Our Last Thousand Years* (London: Black Swan, 1996), pp. 276–277 (hereafter cited as Fernandez-Armesto, *Millennium*).

13 For a brief account of the meanings of reformation in the above context see Honee, 'The Relation of Old and New and the Phenomenon of *Reformation*,' pp. 39–40.

14 John Kenneth Galbraith, *A Short History of Financial Euphoria* (New York: Viking, 1990), p. 17 (hereafter cited as Galbraith, *A Short History of Financial Euphoria*).

15 Ibid., p. 16.

16 References to the Reformation in this section are from Tarnas, *The Passion of the Western Mind*, pp. 237–238.

17 Ibid., p. 234.

18 Caputo, 'Bedeviling the Tradition,' pp. 15–16.

19 Peter Preston, 'Modes of Economic–Theoretical Engagement,' in Roy Dilley (ed.), *Contesting Markets: Analyses of Ideology, Discourse and Practice* (Edinburgh: Edinburgh University Press, 1992) (hereafter cited as Preston, 'Modes of Economic–Theoretical Engagement).'

20 Ibid., p. 60, and S. Pollard, *The Idea of Progress* (Harmondsworth: Penguin, 1971), pp. 138–139, as cited, ibid., p. 58.

21 Ibid., pp. 57–58.

22 Ibid., pp. 65–66.

23 Galbraith, *A Short History of Financial Euphoria*, pp. 23–24.

24   Preston, 'Modes of Economic–Theoretical Engagement,' pp. 66–67.
25   Max Weber, on the Protestant ethic, as cited in Alan Wolfe, 'The Moral Meanings of Work,' in *The American Prospect*, September–October 1997, p. 85 (hereafter cited as Wolfe, 'The Moral Meanings of Work').
26   Tarnas, *The Passion of the Western Mind*, p. 239.
27   Rom: 12.2, as cited in Honee, 'The Relation of Old and New and the Phenomenon of *Reformation*,' p. 37.
28   Ibid., pp. 36–41.
29   Ibid., p. 40.
30   Ibid., pp. 37–39.
31   Michael McKinley, 'Globalisation as War: Equivalence and Convergence in the Theory and Practice of Neoliberalism,' paper presented to the 38th Annual Convention of the International Studies Association, Toronto, Canada, 21 March 1997.
32   John Kenneth Galbraith, *American Capitalism* (rev. edn) (Boston, MA: Houghton Mifflin, 1956), p. 17, as cited in Warren J. Samuels, 'Galbraith on Economics as a System of Professional Belief,' in his *Essays in the History of Heterodox Political Economy* (New York: New York University Press, 1992), p. 294 (hereafter cited as Samuels, *Essays in the History of Heterodox Political Economy*).
33   John Kenneth Galbraith, *The Affluent Society* (Boston, MA: Houghton Mifflin, 1958), p. 7 (hereafter cited as Galbraith, *The Affluent Society*) as cited in Samuels, *Essays in the History of Heterodox Political Economy*, p. 295.
34   Charles H. Hession, *John Kenneth Galbraith and His Critics* (New York: Mentor, 1972), p. 195, as cited in Samuels, *Essays in the History of Heterodox Political Economy*, p. 295.
35   Ibid., p. 294.
36   John Kenneth Galbraith, *The Culture of Contentment* (London: Sinclair-Stevenson, 1992), pp. 80, 104, and 88–89, respectively (hereafter cited as Galbraith, *The Culture of Contentment*).
37   Samuels, *Essays in the History of Heterodox Political Economy*, pp. 6 and 350.
38   John Kenneth Galbraith, *The New Industrial State* (Boston, MA: Houghton Mifflin, 1967), p. 370, as cited in Samuels, *Essays in the History of Heterodox Political Economy*, p. 302.
39   John Kenneth Galbraith, *Economics, Peace and Laughter* (New York: New American Library, 1972), p. 56, as cited in Samuels, *Essays in the History of Heterodox Political Economy*, p. 295.
40   Harold Bloom, *The American Religion: The Emergence of the Post-Christian-Nation* (New York: Simon & Schuster, 1992 (hereafter cited as Bloom, *The American Religion*), p. 49.
41   Ibid., pp. 15, 17, and 257–258.
42   Dorothy Ross, *The Origins of American Social Science* (New York: Cambridge University Press, 1991), hereafter cited as Ross, *The Origins of American Social Science*.
43   Christopher Hitchens, 'Standing Tall,' in *Prepared for the Worst* (London: Hogarth; 1990), p. 277.
44   William Leach, *Land of Desire: Merchants, Power, and the Rise of a New American Culture* (New York: Pantheon, 1993), p. 195 (hereafter cited as Leach, *Land of Desire*).
45   Tarnas, *The Passion of the Western Mind*, pp. 245–246.
46   Leach, *Land of Desire*, pp. 3–12.
47   Tarnas, *The Passion of the Western Mind*, p. 243.
48   Bloom, *The American Religion*, p. 258.
49   Leach, *Land of Desire*, pp. 229–230 in conjunction with Tarnas, *The Passion of the Western Mind*, p. 245.
50   Tarnas, *The Passion of the Western Mind*, p. 243.
51   Galbraith, *The Culture of Contentment*, pp. 80–108.
52   Tarnas, *The Passion of the Western Mind*, p. 245.
53   Galbraith, *The Affluent Society*, as cited in Samuels, *Essays in the History of Heterodox Political Economy*, p. 295.

54 Joan Robinson, *Economic Philosophy* (London: C.A. Watts, 1962), as cited in Preston, 'Modes of Economic–Theoretical Engagement,' p. 65.

55 Adam Smith, 'History of Astronomy,' in *Essays on Philosophical Subjects (and Miscellaneous Pieces)*, ed. W.P.D. Wightman; part of *The Glasgow Edition of the Works and Correspondence of Adam Smith* (Oxford: Clarendon Press, 1980), pp. 45–46, as cited in Robert Heilbroner and William Milberg, *The Crisis of Vision in Modern Economic Thought* (Cambridge: Cambridge University Press, 1995), p. 16 (hereafter cited as Heilbroner and Milberg, *The Crisis of Vision in Modern Economic Thought*).

56 John Kenneth Galbraith, *Economics and the Public Purpose* (Boston, MA: Houghton Mifflin, 1973), p. 226, as cited in Samuels, *Essays in the History of Heterodox Political Economy*, p. 296.

57 Caputo, 'Bedeviling the Tradition,' p. 18.

58 See David Colander and A.W. Coates (eds), *The Spread of Economic Ideas* (Cambridge: Cambridge University Press, 1989), p. 34; Michael Parenti, *Against Empire* (San Francisco, CA: City Lights, 1995), pp. 175–196; and Ross, *The Origins of American Social Science*, pp. 172–218.

59 Tarnas, *The Passion of the Western Mind*, p. 243.

60 Heilbroner and Milberg, *The Crisis of Vision in Modern Economic Thought*, p. 83.

61 Caputo, 'Bedeviling the Tradition,' p. 16.

62 Fernandez-Armesto, *Millennium*, p. 276.

63 Caputo, 'Bedeviling the Tradition,' p. 17.

64 Nizzar Qabbani, 'Footnotes to the Book of the Setback' (1967). The full text is available in Michael Rosen and David Widgery (eds), *The Chatto Book of Dissent* (London: Chatto & Windus, 1994), pp. 101–105.

65 For such an explanation regarding the Reformation, see Fernandez-Armesto, *Millennium*, p. 276; for the account on the Counter-Reformation refer to Tarnas, *The Passion of the Western Mind*, pp. 246–247.

66 Jacques Derrida, *La verité en peinture* (Paris: Flammarion, 1978), pp. 372–373, as referred to in Caputo, 'Bedeviling the Tradition,' p. 18.

67 G. Olsen, 'The Idea of the *Ecclesia Primitiva* in the Writings of the Twelfth-century Canonists,' *Traditio* 25(1960): 61–86, here p. 67, as cited in Honee, 'The Relation of Old and New and the Phenomenon of *Reformation*,' p. 44.

68 Here, I am relying heavily on an essay which originally appeared in the *American Economic Review* (May 1993): 23–26, but appears as ch. 8 ('What Do Undergrads Need to Know About Trade?') in Paul Krugman, *Pop Internationalism* (Cambridge, MA: MIT Press, 1996), pp. 117–125 (hereafter cited as Krugman, *Pop Internationalism*).

69 Honee, 'The Relation of Old and New and the Phenomenon of *Reformation*,' p. 43.

70 Krugman, *Pop Internationalism*, pp. 3–33, 69–84, and 129–154.

71 Honee, 'The Relation of Old and New and the Phenomenon of *Reformation*,' p. 45, and Krugman, *Pop Internationalism*, pp. 117–125.

72 Ibid., pp. 45, and 124–125, resp.

73 Tarnas, *The Passion of the Western Mind*, pp. 246–247.

74 Krugman, *Pop Internationalism*, pp. 3–33, 69–84, and 117–125.

75 Saul, *The Unconscious Civilization*, pp. 126–127.

76 Tarnas, *The Passion of the Western Mind*, pp. 242–243.

77 Ibid., pp. 234, and 241–243.

78 Ibid., pp. 252–253.

79 Caputo, 'Bedeviling the Tradition,' p. 14.

80 Ibid., pp. 15–18.

81 Ibid., pp. 17–18.

82 Ibid., pp. 28–29.

83 Stephen Toulmin, *Cosmopolis: The Hidden Agenda of Modernity* (Chicago, IL: University of Chicago Press, 1990), pp. 70–71 (hereafter cited as Toulmin, *Cosmopolis*).

84 Ibid., pp. 30–35, and 70–71.

85 Heilbroner and Milberg, *The Crisis of Vision in Modern Economic Thought*, p. 2.
86 Morris Kline, *Mathematics: The Loss of Certainty* (Oxford: Oxford University Press, 1980), pp. 4–5, 310, 313, 307–327, and 348.
87 C. Napoleoni, *Economic Thought in the Twentieth Century* (London: Martin Robertson, 1972), as cited in Preston, 'Modes of Economic–Theoretical Engagement,' p. 65.
88 Caputo, 'Bedeviling the Tradition,' p. 21, and pp. 21–23.
89 Toulmin, *Cosmopolis*, p. 55.
90 Caputo, 'Bedeviling the Tradition,' p. 21, and p. 23.
91 See Susan Greenfield, *The Human Brain: A Guided Tour* (London: Weidenfeld & Nicolson, 1997), pp. 49–50.

Conclusion: the new age of religious wars: neo-liberalism, neo-Clausewitzianism and the American way of war

1   Russell F. Weigley, *The American Way of War: A History of United States Military Strategy and Policy* (New York and London: Macmillan/Collier, 1973) (hereafter cited as Weigley, *The American Way of War*).
2   See, for example, Ward Churchill, *A Little Matter of Genocide: Holocaust and Denial in the Americas, 1492 to the Present* (San Francisco, CA: City Lights Books, 1997), and Richard Drinnon, *Facing West: Indian Hating and Empire Building* (New York: Schocken, 1990).
3   Weigley, *The American Way of War*, p. xxii.
4   Johan Galtung, 'U.S. Foreign Policy as Manifest Theology,' in Glenn Hastedt (ed.), *One World, Many Voices: Global Perspectives on Political Issues* (Englewood Cliffs, NJ: Prentice-Hall, 1995), pp. 16–31.
5   See, for example, Christopher Hitchens, 'Imperialism: Superpower Dominance, Malignant and Benign,' Slate <http://slate.msn.com/?id+2075261> posted 10 December 2002, and Michael Ignatieff, 'The Burden,' *New York Times*, 5 January 2003.
6   Probably the most notable defection is that of Joseph Stiglitz, the 2001 Nobel Laureate in Economics and former Chief Economist at the World Bank; see his apologia, *Globalization and its Discontents* (London: Allen Lane/Penguin, 2002).
7   According to the Center for Defense Information, the United States defence budget is more than 26 times as large as the combined defence spending of the seven countries traditionally identified as America's most likely adversaries – Cuba, Iran, Iraq, Libya, North Korea, Sudan and Syria; as well, the United States and its closest allies (including NATO, Australia, Japan and South Korea) spend more than two-thirds of all global military spending <http://www.cdi.org/issues/wme/> accessed 17 July 2002.
8   *National Strategy to Combat Weapons of Mass Destruction.*
9   Richard L. Gregory (ed.), *The Oxford Companion To The Mind* (Oxford: Oxford University Press, 1987), pp. 697–699.
10 Carl Von Clausewitz, *On War*, edited, with an Introduction by Anatol Rapoport (Harmondsworth, Middlesex: Penguin, 1968) (hereafter cited as Rapoport, *Clausewitz*). The significance of this edition is the editor's own significant contribution, by way of his introductory essay to the understanding of contemporary Clausewitzian thinking within US strategic theory and practice – a development he articulates as a related, but faithful departure from the original, and thus as *neo*-Clausewitzian; see pp. 11–78. The analytical framework of this section relies heavily on Rapoport's approach.
11 Robinson Jeffers, 'Eagle Valor, Chicken Mind.'

Epilogue 1: neo-liberalism and the empirical record – theorising global strategic economic incompetence

1   For this and related matters see John Laffin, *British Bunglers and Butchers of World War One* (Melbourne: Macmillan, 1989), p. 5.
2   Norman F. Dixon, *On the Psychology of Military Incompetence* (London: Jonathan Cape, 1976), p. 80 (hereafter cited as Dixon, *Military Incompetence*).
3   Paul Seabury and Angelo Codevilla, *War: Ends and Means* (New York: Basic Books, 1989), p. 128.
4   Richard A. Gabriel, *Military Incompetence: Why The American Military Doesn't Win* (New York: Hill & Wang, 1985), p. 37.
5   Russell Mokhiber and Robert Weissman, 'Corporate Globalization and the Poor,' ZNet Commentary, 08-08-01, http://www.zmag.org/Sustainers/content/2001-08/09mokhiber.htm.
6   Jerome Binde, 'Challenges to Meet in the New Millennium,' *New Straits Times*, 25 August 1998, http://library.northernlight.com/BM19980825010047157.html?no_highlight=1&.
7   These reasons have been adapted from Dixon, *Military Incompetence*, pp. 20–21. A fuller explanation of this adaptation – which is a central feature of this analysis – will be found in the following pages.
8   Ibid., pp. 153–154.
9   Adapted from Dixon, *Military Incompetence*, pp. 152–153. The original cites 14 aspects, but, because the economic globalisation material is of a type amenable to synthesis in a particular way, I have omitted a small number of Dixon's schedule altogether, and amalgamated others without, I believe, any loss of relevance or force of argumentation.
10 Ibid., p. 19. The above argument draws heavily on – indeed, in some phrases is identical to – Dixon's thesis on military incompetence; at the same time, because my subject matter and purposes are different, I have had to modify the original thesis somewhat – thus, although I cannot cite it verbatim, I wish to acknowledge it fulsomely.
11 For full publication details see note 2.
12 Ibid., p. 169.
13 Ibid., pp. 19 and 21.
14 Paul Strathern, *Dr Strangelove's Game: A Brief History of Economic Genius* (London: Hamish Hamilton, 2001), pp. 301–302.
15 For a recent offering of this school of thought, see Chou-Hou Wee, Kai-Sheang Lee and Bambang Walujo Hidajat, *Sun Tzu: War and Management – Application to Strategic Management and Thinking* (Singapore: Addison-Wesley, 1996).
16 Edward N. Luttwak, Centre for Strategic and International Studies In Washington, quoted in Thomas A. Stewart, 'Sometimes Force is the Necessary Path to Peace,' *Fortune*, 26 July 1993, pp. 122–130, as cited in Titus Alexander, *Unravelling Global Apartheid: An Overview of World Politics* (Cambridge, UK: Polity Press, 1996), p. 57.
17 Sub-Commandante Marcos, 'The Fourth World War has Begun,' *Le Monde Diplomatique* (English edn), <http://www.monde-diplomatique.fr/en/1997/08-09/marcos.html>.
18 Various publicity and sales brochures from the World Masters of Business Seminar, held at the Sydney Entertainment Centre, 7 August 1997, provided by Sales Pursuit Results, 22–24 Hutchinson Street, Surry Hills, NSW 2010, Australia.
19 'US Marines Get a Lesson from War St,' *Sydney Morning Herald*, 2 December 1995 (ex *Newsday*).
20 URL: <http://www.belisarius.com>.
21 Lawrence Summers as recorded, 19 October 1991, by the Australian Broadcasting Corporation's programme, *Background Briefing*, by Kirsten Garrett, broadcast by the ABC's Radio National on 3 and 10 November 1991, transcribed from that tape, and cited in Susan George and Fabrizio Sabelli, *Faith and Credit: The World's Secular Empire* (London: Penguin, 1994), p. 106.

22   Dixon, *Military Incompetence*, p. 168.
23   Ibid., pp. 169–172 (esp. p. 172).
24   Ibid., pp. 173–174.
25   Ibid., pp. 176–188.
26   Ibid., p. 192.
27   Ibid., pp. 177–179.
28   Ibid., p. 179.
29   Ibid., p. 180 (adapted).
30   Ibid., pp. 182–183.
31   Ibid., pp. 184–187.
32   Ibid., pp. 185 and 189–190.
33   K.J.W. Craik, The *Nature of Explanation* (Cambridge, UK: Cambridge University Press, 1943), as cited in Dixon, *Military Incompetence*, p. 189.
34   Dixon, *Military Incompetence*, p. 189. For those sceptical of the influence of this early developmental discipline, and Dixon is alive to exactly this objection, on p. 195 of his work he summarises a potent argument in support of his thesis (which, on the basis of my understanding of economics, I hold to be applicable in the above analysis).
35   Ibid., p. 192.
36   Ibid., p. 194.
37   Ibid., pp. 194–195.
38   Ibid., p. 197.
39   Ibid., pp. 199–200.
40   Ibid.
41   Ibid., p. 201.
42   Ibid., p. 202.
43   Ibid., p. 205.
44   Ibid., p. 206 (as cited).
45   Ibid., p. 207 (adapted).
46   Ibid., pp. 208–209 and 213 (adapted)
47   Ibid., pp. 244 and 254–255 (adapted).
48   *Attractors* emerged from the study of complex systems and became more well known in the further emergence of the study of Chaos, wherein they became *Strange* Attractors: the former represent the states to which any system eventually settles, depending on the overall properties of that system. They tend, therefore, to constitute a restricted, or localised, or specific mode of behaviour in the set of conceivable behaviours. The cultural equivalent of attractors in complex physical systems are social systems such as tribes, states, religion, class, ideologies, and professions. *Strange* Attractors, however, seem to have the same general descriptive properties in Chaos Theory as in Economic Theory: first, they are abstract constructions; second, they look strange because, when depicted, they are indeed strange; third, by attracting nearby trajectories (predispositions, if you like), they reconcile contradictory effects which subsequently, however, diverge rapidly – and all of this exhibits a sensitive dependence on initial conditions (in this case the psychological make-up of the economist).
49   Dixon, *Military Incompetence*, p. 256.
50   Ibid., p. 258. Note: all nine predispositions have been taken from this work; the elaborations of them are not.
51   Roger Brown, *Social Psychology* (New York: Macmillan, 1965), p. 504, as cited in Dixon, *Military Incompetence*, p. 261.
52   Ibid.
53   Ibid., p. 286 (adapted).
54   Ibid., p. 278.
55   Ibid., p. 173 (as cited).

Epilogue 2: Economics as mental illness – a satire?

1   So named after the Greek physician who elaborated the system of the four temperaments (choleric, melancholic, phlegmatic, and sanguine) which is still used in various forms in the contemporary period.

2   In the advancement of this argument heavy reliance will be placed upon Richard L. Gregory, with O.L. Zangwill, *The Oxford Companion To The Mind* (Oxford: Oxford University Press, 1987) (hereafter cited as Gregory, *The Mind*).
      NOTE: Care should be exercised in referring to footnotes which appear in passages describing a symptom of mental illness and the corresponding condition in economists: where possible I have attempted to keep such matters separate, but, for the sake of readability and effect, there are many passages where this has not been possible. Accordingly, I would advise that nowhere in Gregory's *The Mind* are there any references to economics or economists: the connections between his descriptions of mental illness and the location of economists within them is my construct alone.

3   As with several points made in this chapter, this observation owes much to a valued contribution to the understanding of the modes and rituals of academia in the form of a novel by John Kenneth Galbraith – *A Tenured Professor: A Novel* (Boston, MA: Houghton Mifflin, 1990), p. 49 (hereafter cited as Galbraith, *A Tenured Professor*).

4   Gary Mongiovi, 'Whose Economy Is It?' [a review of Doug Henwood, *Wall Street: How It Works and for Whom* (London: Verso, 1997), *The Nation*, 8–15 September 1997, p. 29].

5   Karin Bishop, 'Star Search,' *Sydney Morning Herald*, Employment section, 5 December 1998, p. 1.

6   Lewis Lapham, 'Painted Fire,' in *Waiting for the Barbarians* (London: Verso, 1997), pp. 125–131.

7   Jacques Le Goff, *Your Money Or Your Life; Economy and Religion in the Middle Ages* (New York: Zone, 1990), pp. 13–14.

8   Edward E. Leamer, 'Specification Searches: Ad hoc Inferences with Non-experimental Data' (New York: John Wiley & Sons, 1978), p. vi, as cited in Tony Lawson, *Economics and Reality* (London: Routledge, 1997), pp. 6–7 (hereafter cited as Leamer, 'Specification Searches: Ad hoc Inferences with Non-experimental Data').

9   E. C. Carterette and M. P. Friedman, 'Perceptual Processing,' *Handbook of Perceptions* 9 (New York and London, 1978).

10   Tarnas, *The Passion of the Western Mind*, p. 416.

11   Ibid.

12   Ibid., pp. 417–419.

13   Gregory, *The Mind*, pp. 657–658. See, *inter alia*, also Gregory Bateson, 'Towards a Theory of Schizophrenia,' in *Steps to an Ecology of Mind* (London: 1956).

14   Tarnas, *The Passion of the Western Mind*, pp. 419–420.

15   Ibid., p. 420.

16   Ibid., pp. 420–421.

17   Ibid., pp. 421–422.

18   Richard Tarnas, *The Passion of the Western Mind: Understanding the Ideas That Have Shaped Our World View* (New York: Ballantine, 1991), p. 356 (hereafter cited as Tarnas, *The Passion of the Western Mind*).

19   As cited, ibid.

20   Toulmin, *Cosmopolis*, pp. 148–149.

21   Dorothy Ross, *The Origins of American Social Science* (New York: Cambridge University Press, 1991) (hereafter cited as Ross, *The Origins of American Social Science*).

22   Bernstein, 'Economics and Contemporary Policy Problems,' p. 362.

23   Joan Robinson, *Economic Philosophy* (London: C.A. Watts, 1962), as cited in Preston, 'Modes of Economic–Theoretical Engagement,' p. 65.

24   Dorothy Ross, *The Origins of American Social Science* (Cambridge: Cambridge University Press, 1992), pp. 106–118.

25   Dorothy Ross, 'An Historian's View Of American Social Science,' *Journal of the History of the Behavioral Sciences* 29 (April 1993): 107 (hereafter cited as Ross, 'An Historian's View').
26   Richard Hofstadter, *Anti-intellectualism in American Life* (New York: Vintage, 1963), p. 50.
27   Paul Ormerod, *The Death of Economics* (London: Faber and Faber, 1994), p. 7.
28   Tony Lawson, *Economics and Reality* (London: Routledge, 1997), p. 12 (hereafter cited as Lawson, *Economics and Reality*); see also pp. 10–13.
29   John Ralston Saul, *The Unconscious Civilization* (Ringwood, Victoria: Penguin, 1997), pp. 4–5 (hereafter cited as Saul, *Unconscious Civilization*).
30   Julie A. Nelson, 'The Study of Choice or the Study of Provisioning?: Gender and the Definition of Economics' (hereafter cited as Nelson, 'Gender and the Definition of Economics') in Ferber and Nelson, *Beyond Economic Man*, pp. 24–26.
31   Diana Strassmann, 'Not a Free Market: The Rhetoric of Disciplinary Authority in Economics' (hereafter cited as Strassmann, 'Not a Free Market'), in Ferber and Nelson, *Beyond Economic Man*, p. 63.
32   Ferber and Nelson, 'Introduction', in Ferber and Nelson (eds), *Beyond Economic Man*, pp. 4–6.
33   Helen E. Longino, 'Economics for Whom?', in Ferber and Nelson (eds), *Beyond Economic Man*, pp. 166–167; and Block, *Postindustrial Possibilities*, p. 30.
34   Marilyn Waring, *Counting for Nothing: What Men Value and What Women are Worth* (Wellington: Allen & Unwin/Port Nicholson Press, 1997). Complementing Waring's view, though not from a feminist perspective is a recent work by two Australian economists, Dick Bryan and Michael Rafferty, *The Global Economy in Australia: Global Integration and National Economic Policy* (St Leonards, NSW: Allen & Unwin, 1999), which argues that, under economic globalisation, the national accounting system cannot be said to describe the thing known as the 'national economy.'
35   Statistics as cited in Michael Steinberger, 'The Second Sex and the Dismal Science: The Rise of Feminist Economics,' *Lingua Franca* (November 1998): 61 (hereafter cited as Steinberger, 'The Second Sex and the Dismal Science').
36   Strassmann, 'Not a Free Market,' in Ferber and Nelson, *Beyond Economic Man*, pp. 55–56.
37   Thomas Balogh, *The Irrelevance of Conventional Economics* (London: Weidenfeld & Nicolson, 1982), p. 32, as cited in Galbraith, *History*, p. 189.
38   See Saul, *Unconscious Civilization*, pp. 51–52.
39   Marianne A. Ferber and Julie Nelson, 'Introduction: The Social Construction of Economics and the Social Construction of Gender' (hereafter cited as Ferber and Nelson, 'Introduction'), in Ferber and Nelson (eds), *Beyond Economic Man*, pp. 2–4.
40   Steinberger, 'The Second Sex and the Dismal Science,' p. 57.
41   Ferber and Nelson, 'Introduction,' p. 2.
42   The relevant work of David Colander and Joanna Wayland Woos is abstracted in Steinberger, 'The Second Sex and the Dismal Science,' p. 60.
43   Steinberger, 'The Second Sex and the Dismal Science,' p. 64.
44   Donald N. McCloskey, 'Some News That At Least Will Not Bore You,' *Eastern Economic Journal* (autumn 1995), reprinted in *Lingua Franca* (May–June 1996), and reprinted again in *Harper's Magazine* (July 1996), pp. 21 and 24–25.
45   Ibid.
46   Donald N. McCloskey, 'Some Consequences of a Conjective Economics,' in Ferber and Nelson, *Beyond Economic Man*, p. 79.
47   Ibid.
48   For a brief account of the views expressed in Huntington's works to the late 1980s, see John Trumpbour, *How Harvard Rules: Reason in the Service of Empire* (Boston, MA: South End Press, 1989), pp. 71–76.
49   John Kenneth Galbraith, *A Short History of Financial Euphoria* (New York: Viking/Penguin, 1993) (hereafter cited as Galbraith, *Financial Euphoria*).
50   Ibid., pp. 12–13; and Galbraith, *The Tenured Professor*, p. 68.

51 Ibid., p. 23.

52 Gregory, *The Mind,* p. 184.

53 The recent widespread availability of Viagra has both served to reduce the anxiety associated with neo-liberalism, and to make possible a less intrusive, survey-based, research project which could be carried out, in its initial stages, by the relevant GP.

54 Gregory, *The Mind,* pp. 549–550.

55 Ibid., pp. 568–569.

56 Ibid., pp. 657–658.

57 Ibid., pp. 697–698.

58 Paul Ormerod reports what he terms a 'perhaps apocryphal' story from Romania under the communist dictatorship of Nicolae Ceausecu: the authorities banned all imported economic journals from the West on ideological grounds, with the exception of *Econometrica* on the grounds that it was so abstruse as to be of no conceivable relevance to anything (Ormerod, *The Death of Economics,* p. 43).

59 Ibid., p. 698.

60 Ibid., pp. 654 and 699.

61 Ibid.

62 Hunter S. Thompson, *Better Than Sex: Confessions of a Political Junkie – Trapped Like a Rat in Mr Bill's Neighborhood* (Doubleday: Sydney, 1995), p. 126.

63 Richard Hofstadter, *The Paranoid Style in American Politics and Other Essays* (Chicago, IL: University of Chicago Press, 1964), p. 4.

64 Thomas Powers, 'The Truth About the CIA,' *New York Review,* 13 May 1993, pp. 52–53.

65 Tom Mangold, *Cold Warrior – James Jesus Angleton: The CIA's Master Spy Hunter* (New York: Simon & Schuster, 1991).

66 William H. Epstein, 'Counter-intelligence: Cold-War Criticism and Eighteenth-century Studies,' *English Literary History* 57 (spring 1990): 84–85 (hereafter cited as Epstein, 'Counter-intelligence').

67 John Ranelagh, *CIA: A History* (London: BBC Books, 1992), p. 134.

68 Epstein, 'Counter-intelligence,' p. 84.

69 Soren Ambrose, 'IMF Bailouts: Familiar, Failed Medicine for Asian Tigers' Corporate Watch website: http://www.igc.org/trac/corner/worldnews/other/other83.html.

70 Gregory, *The Mind,* pp. 576–577.

71 Ibid., pp. 63–64, and 576.

72 Morris Kline, *Mathematics: The Loss of Certainty* (Oxford: Oxford University Press, 1980), pp. 4–5, and 313 (hereafter cited as Kline, *Mathematics: The Loss of Certainty*).

73 Ibid., pp. 5–6, and 307–327.

74 Rick Weiss, 'Scientists Say Yes, We Have Sum Bananas,' *Sydney Morning Herald,* 24 October 1988 (ex *Washington Post/Guardian*); and John von Radowitz, 'Mathematics Mere Monkey Business, Say Scientists,' *Canberra Times,* 24 October 1998.

75 Kline, *Mathematics: The Loss of Certainty,* p. 310.

76 Mary Douglas, 'Faith, Hope and Probability', a review of Ian Hacking, *The Taming of Chance* (Cambridge: Cambridge University Press, 1990), *London Review of Books,* 23 May 1991, p. 6 (hereafter cited as Douglas, 'Faith, Hope and Probability').

77 Kline, *Mathematics: The Loss of Certainty,* p. 348.

78 Douglas, 'Faith, Hope and Probability,' p. 6.

79 Kline, *Mathematics: The Loss of Certainty,* p. 310.

80 Bruce Wilshire, *The Moral Collapse of the University: Professionalism, Purity, and Alienation* (Albany, NY: State University of New York Press, 1990), p. xviii.

81 Tony Lawson, *Economics and Reality* (London: Routledge, 1997), p. xiii (hereafter cited as Lawson, *Economics and Reality*).

82 Gerard Debreu, 'The Mathematicization of Economic Theory,' *American Economic Review* 81: 1–7, as cited in Julie A. Nelson, 'The Study of Choice or the Study of Provisioning?: Gender and the Definition of Economics' (hereafter cited as Nelson, 'Gender in the

Definition of Economics'), in Marianne A. Ferber and Julie A. Nelson (eds), *Beyond Economic Man: Feminist Theory and Economics* (Chicago, IL: Chicago University Press, 1993), p. 26 (hereafter cited as Ferber and Nelson (eds), *Beyond Economic Man*).

83 Alexander Rosenberg, *Economics – Mathematical Politics or Science of Diminishing Returns?* (Chicago, IL: Chicago University Press, 1994), p. 247 (hereafter cited as Rosenberg, *Economics*).

84 Ibid., pp. 12–13.

85 Le Goff, *Your Money or Your Life*, pp. 68–69.

86 Morris Kline, *Mathematics in Western Culture* (London: Penguin, 1990), p. 298.

87 Jim Holt, 'The Monster and other Mathematical Beasts,' *Lingua Franca*, November 1977, pp. 76–77.

88 Brian Rotman, 'Fortress Mathematica,' *London Review of Books*, 17 September 1998, pp. 25–26.

89 Ibid., p. 25.

90 Ibid., p. 26.

91 Gregory, *The Mind*, p. 373.

92 'Abandon All Hope You Who Enter!' (*Inferno* iii. 1), from the inscription at the entrance to Hell.

Bibliography

Agnew J. and Corbridge, S. (1995) *Mastering Space: Hegemony, Territory and International Political Economy,* London: Routledge.

Ahn, C. (ed.) (2003) *Shafted: Free Trade and America's Working Poor,* Oakland, CA: Food First/ Institute for Food and Development Policy.

Air University (1996) *Air Force 2025.* A Report prepared by the 2025 Support Office, and developed by Air University Press Educational Services Directorate, College of Aerospace Doctrine, Research and Education, Maxwell Air Force Base, Alabama.

Albert, M. (1993) *Capitalism vs. Capitalism: How America's Obsession with Individual Achievement and Short-term Profit Has Led It to the Bank of Collapse,* trans. P. Haviland, Introduction by F. G. Rohatyn, New York: Four Wall Eight Windows.

Alexander, T. (1996) *Unravelling Global Apartheid: An Overview of World Politics,* Cambridge, UK: Polity Press.

Alperowitz, G.(1994) *Atomic Diplomacy: Hiroshima and Potsdam* (rev. edn), London: Pluto.

Ambrose, S., 'IMF Bailouts: Familiar, Failed Medicine for Asian 'Tigers,' Corporate Watch website. Available HTTP:< http://www.igc.org/trac/corner/worldnews/other/other83. html> (accessed 18 December 2006).

Anderson, S. (2001) 'NAFTA at 7,' Institute of Policy Studies, January. Available HTTP: <www.corpwatch.org/issues.trade/background/2001/ipsnafta/.html> (accessed 7 February 2001).

Anderson, L. (2000) *Genetic Engineering, Food, and our Environment A Brief Guide,* Melbourne: Scribe Publications.

Anderson, S. (ed.) (2000) *Views from the South: the Effects of Globalization and the WTO on Third World Countries,* Foreword J. Mander, Afterword A. Mittal, Canada: Food First Books, LPC Group.

Anderson, S. and Cavanagh, J. 'Top 200: The Rise of Corporate Global Power,' Institute for Policy Studies. Available HTTP: <http://www.ipsdc.org/reports/top200text.htm> (accessed 19 May 2006).

Anelauskas, V. (1999) *Discovering America As It Is,* Atlanta: Clarity.

Argyrous, G. and Stilwell, F. (eds) (1996) *Economics as a Social Science Reading in Political Economy,* Marrickville, NSW: Pluto Press.

Armas, G.C. '29 Million Americans in Working Poor Families,' *Salon.com.* Available HTTP: <http://www.truthout.org/docs_04/101304C.shtml> (accessed 13 October 2004).

Armstrong, K. (2001) *The Battle For God: Fundamentalism in Judaism, Christianity and Islam,* London: HarperCollins.

—— (2001) *Holy War: The Crusades and their Impact on Today's World,* New York: Anchor Books.

Aronowitz, S. (1988) *Science as Power: Discourse and Ideology in Modern Society,* Minneapolis: University of Minnesota Press.

—— (1994) *Dead Artists, Live Theories, and Other Cultural Problems,* New York: Routledge.

Aronowitz, S. and DiFazio, W. (1994) *The Jobless Future: Sci-Tech and the Dogma of Work,* Minneapolis: University of Minnesota Press.

Athanasiou, T. (1998) *Divided Planet: The Ecology of Rich and Poor,* Athens: The University of Georgia Press.

Attali, J. (1991) *Millennium Winners and Losers in the Coming World Order,* trans. from French L. Conners and N. Gardels, New York: Times Books.

Atwood, M. *et al.* (1993) *The Case Against Free Trade: GATT, NAFTA, and the Globalization of Corporate Power,* San Francisco, CA: Earth Island.

Ayittey, G.B.N. (1999) *Africa in Chaos,* New York: St Martin's Griffin.

Bailey, F.G. (1977) *Morality and Expediency: The Folklore of Academic Politics,* Oxford: Blackwell.

Bairoch, P. (1993) *Economics and World History: Myths and Paradoxes,* London: Harvester Wheatsheaf.

Bakan, J. (2004) *The Corporation: The Pathological Pursuit of Profit and Power,* New York: Free Press.

Barber, B.J. (1995) *Jihad vs. McWorld,* New York: Times Books Random House.

Barber, W.J. (1967) *A History of Economic Thought,* London: Penguin Books.

Barnet, R.J. and Cavanagh, J. (1994) *Global Dreams: Imperial Corporations and the New World Order,* New York: Simon & Schuster.

Barry, B. (1978) *Sociologists, Economists & Democracy,* Chicago, IL: The University of Chicago Press.

Barry, T. (1995) *Zapata's Revenge Free Trade and the Farm Crisis in Mexico,* Boston, MA: South End Press.

Baudrillard, J. (1989) *America,* trans. C. Turner, London: Verso.

Baum, G. (2001) *Nationalism, Religion and Ethics,* Montreal and Kingston: McGill-Queen's University Press.

Bauman, Z. (1998) *Globalization: The Human Consequences,* Oxford: Polity Press.

Baylis, J. and Smith, S. (eds) (2001) *The Globalization of World Politics: An Introduction to International Relations,* (2nd edn), Oxford: Oxford University Press.

Beck, U. (2000) *What is Globalization?,* trans. P. Camiller, Malden, MA: Polity Press.

—— (2000) *Risk Society: Towards a New Modernity,* London, Thousand Oaks, New Delhi: Sage.

Bell, S. (ed.) (2000) *The Unemployment Crisis in Australia: Which Way Out?,* Cambridge: Cambridge University Press.

Bellah, R.B. (1967) 'Civil Religion in America,' *Daedalus,* vol. 96, winter.

—— (1974) 'The New Religious Consciousness and the Secular University,' *Daedalus,* vol. 103, autumn.

Bellamy Foster, J. (1999) *The Vulnerable Planet A Short History of the Environment,* New York: Monthly Review Press.

Bello, W. (1994) 'Global Economic Counterrevolution: How Northern Economic Warfare Devastates the South,' in K. Danaher (ed.), *50 Years Is Enough,*

Bello, W., with Cunningham, S and Rau, B. (1994) *Dark Victory: The United States, Structural Adjustment and Global Poverty,* London: Pluto/Food First/Transnational Institute.

Bello, W., Bullard, N. and Malhotra, K. (eds) (2000) *Global Finance: New Thinking on Regulating Speculative Capital Markets,* Dhaka, Bangladesh: Zed Books.

Bendaña, A. (1996) *Power Lines: U.S. Domination in the New Global Order,* New York: Olive Branch Press.

Berman, M. (2000) *The Twilight of American Culture,* New York: Norton.

—— (2006) *Dark Ages America: The Final Phase of Empire,* New York: Norton.

Bernstein, M.A. and Adler, D.E. (eds) (1994) *Understanding American Economic Decline,* Cambridge: Cambridge University Press.

Bernstein, R. and Munro, R.H. (1998) *The Coming Conflict With China,* New York: Vintage Books.

Beynon, J. and Dunkerley, D. (2000) *Globalization: The Reader,* London: The Athlone Press.

Bhagwati, J. (2000) *The Wind of the Hundred Days, How Washington Mismanaged Globalization*, Cambridge, MA: The MIT Press.

Bishop, K. (1998) 'Star Search,' *Sydney Morning Herald*, Employment section, 5 December, p. 1.

Black, M. (2002) *The No-nonsense Guide to International Development*, Oxford: New Internationalist Publications Ltd in association with Verso.

Blank, R.M. and McGurn, W. (2004) *Is the Market Moral? A Dialogue on Religion, Economics & Justice*, Washington, DC: Brookings Institution Press.

Block, F. (1990) *Postindustrial Possibilities: A Critique of Economic Discourse*, Berkeley, CA: University of California Press.

Bloom, A. (1987) *The Closing of the American Mind: How Higher Education has Failed Democracy and Impoverished the Souls of Today's Students*, New York: Simon & Schuster.

Bloom, H. (1992) *The American Religion: The Emergence of the Post-Christian Nation*, New York: Simon & Schuster.

Bloor, D. (1976) *Knowledge and Social Imagery*, London: Routledge & Kegan Paul.

Boorstin, D.J. (1987) *Hidden History: Exploring Our Secret Past*, New York: Random House.

Boucher, G. (2006) 'The Resistible Rise of Postmodern Neo-Fascism,' *Arena Magazine*, vol. 82, April–May, pp. 29–33.

Boulding, K.E. (1970) *Beyond Economics: Essays on Society, Religion and Ethics*, Michigan: Ann Arbor Paperbacks, The University of Michigan Press.

Bourdieu, P. (1998) *Acts of Resistance Against the Tyranny of the Market*, trans. from the French R. Nice, New York: The New Press.

Bourdieu, P. *et al.* (1999) *The Weight of the World Social Suffering in Contemporary Society*, trans. by P. Parkhurst Ferguson, S. Emanuel, J. Johnson and S. T. Waryn, Oxford: Polity Press.

Bove, P. (1992) *In the Wake Of Theory*, Hanover and London: Wesleyan University Press/ University Press of New England.

Brecher, J. and Costello, T. (1994) *Global Village or Global Pillage: Economic Reconstruction From the Bottom Up*, Boston, MA: South End Press.

Brecher, J., Childs, J.B. and Cutler, J. (eds) (1993) *Global Visions, Beyond the New World Order*, Montréal: Black Rose Books.

Brockway, G.P. (1995) *The End of Economic Man* (3rd edn), New York: W. W. Norton.

Brown, L.R. (1995) *Who Will Feed China? Wake-up Call for a Small Planet*, New York: W. W. Norton.

Brown, S. Congressman (2004) *Myths of Free Trade: Why American Trade Policy Has Failed*, New York: The New Press.

Bryan, D. and Rafferty, M. (1999) *The Global Economy in Australia: Global Integration and National Economic Policy*, St Leonards, NSW: Allen & Unwin.

Buckman, G. (2004) *Globalization: Tame It or Scrap It?*, London and New York: Zed Books.

Budhoo, D. (1994) 'IMF/World Bank Wreak Havoc on Third World', in K. Danaher (ed.), *50 Years Is Enough: The Case Against the World Bank and the International Monetary Fund*, Boston, MA: South End Press.

Bullard, N., 'Here Comes the GATS Attack!', *Focus on Trade*. Available HTTP: <http:// focusweb.org> topical email. Available HTTP: <http://www.topica.com/lists/ hkpd_trade@igc.topica.com/read> (accessed 4 June 2004).

Bulmer-Thomas, V. (ed.) (1996) *The New Economic Model in Latin America and its Impact on Income Distribution and Poverty*, New York: St Martin's Press.

Burbach, R. (2001) *Globalization and Postmodern Politics From Zapatistas to High-tech Robber Barons*, London, Sterling, Virginia: Pluto Press, Kingston, Jamaica: Arawak Publications.

Burbach, R., Núñez, O. and Kagarlitsky, B. (1997) *Globalization and its Discontents: The Rise of Postmodern Socialisms*, Chicago, IL: Pluto Press.

Burke, W.T. (1969) *Towards a Better Use of the Ocean*, Stockholm: Almqvist & Wiksell.

Cameron, D., 'Ten Reasons to Oppose the FTAA'. Available HTTP: <http://www.corpwatch. org/issues/trade/background/2001/dcameron.html> (accessed 3 July 2004).

Cammack, P. (2004) 'What the World Bank Means by Poverty Reduction, and Why it Matters,' *New Political Economy*, vol. 9, 2, pp. 189–211.

Capps, W.H. (1990) *The Unfinished War: Vietnam and the American Conscience* (rev. edn), Boston, MA: Beacon Press.

Caputo, J.D. (1995) 'Bedeviling the Tradition: On Deconstruction and Catholicism,' in J.B.M. Wissink (ed.) *(Dis)Continuity and (De)Construction: Reflections on the Meaning of the Past in Crisis Situations*, Kampen, The Netherlands: Pharos.

Carnoy, M., Castells, M., Cohen, S.S. and Cardoso, F.H. (1993) *The New Global Economy in the Information Age*, University Park, PA: The Pennsylvania State University Press.

Carterette, E.C. and Friedman, M.P. (1978) 'Perceptual Processing,' *Handbook of Perceptions*, vol. 9, New York: Academic Press.

Castles, F., Geritsen, R. and Vowles, J. (eds) (1996) *The Great Experiment Labour: Parties and Public Policy Transformation in Australia and New Zealand*, Auckland: Auckland University Press.

Catudal, H.M. (1985) *Nuclear Deterrence — Does it Deter?*, Atlantic Highlands, NJ: Humanities Press.

Caufield, C. (1996) *Masters of Illusion: The World Bank and the Poverty of Nations*, New York: Henry Holt.

Cavanagh, J., and Anderson, S. (2002) 'A Bad Idea that Failed', *Foreign Policy*, September–October, pp. 58–65.

Central Intelligence Agency, *Global Trends 2015: A Dialogue About the Future With Nongovernmental Experts*. Available HTTP: <http://www.cia.gov/cia/publications/globaltrends2015/index.html> (accessed 12 September 2006).

Chace, J. and Carr, C. (1988) *America Invulnerable: The Quest for Absolute Security from 1812 to Star Wars*, New York: Summit.

Chamie, J. (2005) '21st Century Demographics: High and Lows', *the Globalist*, 14 July. Available HTTP: <http://theglobalist.com/DBWeb/printStoryId.aspx?StoryId=4629> (accessed 6 August 2005).

Chilcote, R.M. (ed.) (1999) *The Political Economy of Imperialism Critical Appraisals*, Boston, MA, Dordrecht, London: Kluwer Academic.

Chossudovsky, M. (1997) *The Globalisation of Poverty Impacts of IMF and World Bank Reforms*, London: Zed Books.

Chou-Hou Wee, Kai-Sheang Lee and Bambang Walujo Hidajat (1996) *Sun Tzu: War and Management – Application to Strategic Management and Thinking*, Singapore: Addison-Wesley.

Churchill, W. (1997) *A Little Matter of Genocide: Holocaust and Denial in the Americas, 1492 to the Present*, San Francisco, CA: City Lights Books.

Clairmont, F.F. (1996) *The Rise and Fall of Economic Liberalism: The Making of the Economic Gulag*, Goa, India: The Other India Press.

Clark, I. (1997) *Globalization and Fragmentation: International Relations in the Twentieth Century*, Oxford: Oxford University Press.

Clark, R. and others (1992) *War Crimes: A Report on United States War Crimes Against Iraq — Reports to the Commission of Inquiry for the International War Crimes Tribunal and the Tribunal's Final Judgment*, Washington, DC: Maisoneuvve Press.

Clinch, F., Convery, F. and Walsh, B. (2002) *After the Celtic Tiger Challenges Ahead*, Dublin, Ireland: O'Brien.

Clotfelter, C.P. (ed.) (1999) *On the Third Hand: Humor in the Dismal Science, An Anthology*, Ann Arbor: University of Michigan Press.

Coates, V.T. (1994) 'Transition to the New Millennium,' paper presented to the Annual Convention of the International Studies Association, Washington, DC, 30 March.

—— (1995) 'Transition to the Millennium' paper presented to the 35th Convention of the International Studies Convention, Washington, DC, February.

Cohen, D. (2006) *Globalization and Its Enemies*, Cambridge, MA: The MIT Press.

Colander, D. and Coates, A.W. (eds) (1989) *The Spread of Economic Ideas*, Cambridge: Cambridge University Press.

Collire, G., with Quaratiello, E.L. (1994) *Basta! Land and the Zapatista Rebellion in Chiapas*, Foreword P. Rosset, Monroe, OR: Food First Book.

Connolly, W.E. (1994) *Political Theory and Modernity*, Oxford: Blackwell.

'Continuity and Change in the Westphalian Order' (2000) *International Studies Review*, 'Special Issue,' vol. 2, 2, summer.

Cooke, J. (1998) *Cannibals, Cows & the CJD Catastrophe*, Sydney: Random House.

'Copyrighting a Human Life' (1996) *Greenpeace Australia News* 6, autumn.

Council of Canadians, 'The FTAA and the Threat to Democracy.' Available HTTP: <http://www.corpwatch.org/issues/trade/background/2001/cocftaa.html> (accessed 12 September 2006).

Cox, R. (1994) 'The Crisis in World Order and the Challenge to International Organization,' *Cooperation and Conflict*, vol. 29, 2.

Coyle, D. (2002) *Sex, Drugs & Economics: An Unconventional Introduction to Economics*, New York, London: Texere.

Curti, M. (1956) *American Paradox: The Conflict of Thought and Action*, New Brunswick, N.J.: Rutgers University Press.

D'Amico, R. (1982) 'What is Discourse?', *Humanities in Society*, vol. 5, summer and autumn.

Danaher, K. (ed.) (1994) *50 Years Is Enough: The Case Against The World Bank and the International Monetary Fund*, Boston, MA: South End Press.

Danaher, K. (1999) *10 Reasons to Abolish the IMF & World Bank*, New York: Seven Stories Press.

Dannhauser, W.J. (1971) 'On Teaching Politics Today,' *Commentary*, vol. 59, 3, March.

Dannin, E.J. (1997) *Working Free: The Origins and Impact of New Zealand's Employment Contracts Act*, Auckland: Auckland University Press.

Dasgupta, P. and Heal, G. (1994) 'Economic Theory and Exhaustible Resources,' in P. Ormerod (ed.) *The Death of Economics*, London: Faber and Faber.

Davis, M. (2001) *Late Victorian Holocausts: El Niño Famines and the Making of the Third World*, London: Verso.

Dawkins, K. (1997) *Gene Wars: The Politics of Biotechnology*, New York: Seven Stories Press.

Debray, R. (1981) *Teachers, Writers, Celebrities: The Intellectuals of Modern France*, trans. D. Macey, London: Verso.

'Defense Planning Guidance' (1992) *New York Times*, 8 March.

Derber, C. (1998) *Corporation Nation: How Corporations Are Taking Over Our Lives and What We Can Do About It*, New York: St Martin's Press.

Desai, M. and Redfern, P. (eds) (1995) *Global Governance: Ethics and Economics of the World Order*, London: Pinter.

Diamond, J. (2005) *Collapse: How Nations Choose to Fail or Survive*, Camberwell, Victoria: Allen Lane/Penguin.

Dicken, P. (1992) *Global Shift: The Internationalization of Economic Activity* (2nd edn), New York: Guilford Press.

Dilley, R. (ed.) (1992) *Contesting Markets: Analyses of Ideology, Discourse and Practice*, Edinburgh: Edinburgh University Press.

Discriminate Deterrence: Report of the Commission On Integrated Long-term Strategy (1988) Washington, DC: United States Department of Defense.

Dixon, N.F. (1976) *On the Psychology of Military Incompetence*, London: Jonathan Cape.

Dobkowski, M.N. and Wallimann, I. (1998) *The Coming Age of Scarcity: Preventing Mass Death and Genocide in the Twenty-first Century*, New York: Syracuse University Press.

Doremus, P N., Keller, W.W., Pauly, L.W. and Reich, S. (1998) *The Myth of The Global Corporation*, Princeton, NJ: Princeton University Press.

Douglas, M. (1991) 'Faith, Hope and Probability,' a review of Ian Hacking, *The Taming of Chance*, Cambridge: Cambridge University Press, 1990, in *London Review of Books*, 23 May.

Dowd, D. (1997) *Against the Conventional Wisdom: A Primer for Current Economic Controversies and Proposals*, Oxford: Westview Press.

—— (2000) *Capitalism and its Economics: A Critical History,* London: Pluto Press.

Drahos, P. (1995) 'Global Property Rights in Information: The Story of TRIPs at the GATT,' *Prometheus,* 13 June, pp. 6–19.

Drahos, P. with Braithwaite, J. (2002) *Information Feudalism: Who Owns the Knowledge Economy?,* London: Earthscan.

Drahos, P. and Mayne, R. (2002) *Global Intellectual Property Rights: Knowledge, Access and Development,* Basingstoke, Hampshire: Palgrave Macmillan/Oxfam.

Dreyfuss, R. (1997) 'The New China Lobby,' *The American Prospect,* January–February.

Drinnon, R. (1990) *Facing West: The Metaphysics of Indian Hating and Empire Building,* New York: Schocken Books.

Duffy, E. (1997) *Saints & Sinners: A History of the Popes,* New Haven, CT: Yale University Press in association with S4C.

Dunkley, G. (1997) *The Free Trade Adventure, The Uruguay Round and Globalism – A Critique,* Melbourne: Melbourne University Press.

—— (2004) *Free Trade Myth, Reality and Alternatives,* Dhaka: University Press.

Dunn, R.S. (1979) *The Age of Religious Wars, 1559–1715* (2nd edn), New York: W. W. Norton.

Dunnigan, J.F. and Nofi, A.A. (1990) *Dirty Little Secrets: Military Information You're Not Supposed To Know,* New York: Morrow.

Dussel, E. (1995) *The Invention of the Americas: Eclipse of 'the Other' and the Myth of Modernity,* New York: Continuum.

Dwyer, A. (1994) *On the Line Life on the US–Mexican Border,* Nottingham: LAB.

Earle, E.M. (ed.) (1971) *Makers of Modern Strategy: Military Thought from Machiavelli to Hitler,* Princeton, NJ: Princeton University Press.

Easton, B. (1997) *In Stormy Seas: The Post-war New Zealand Economy,* Dunedin: University of Otago Press.

—— (1997) *The Commercialisation of New Zealand,* Auckland: Auckland University Press.

—— (1999) *The Whimpering of the State Policy after MMP,* Auckland: Auckland University Press.

Eco, U. (1995) 'Ur-Fascism,' *New York Review of Books,* 22 June, pp. 12–15.

Eden, L. (1993) 'The End of US Cold War History?,' *International Security,* vol. 18, summer.

Edwards, L. (2002) *How to Argue with an Economist,* Port Melbourne, Victoria: Cambridge University Press.

Ehrlich, P.R. and Ehrlich, A.H. (1990) *The Population Explosion From Global Warming to Rain Forest Destruction, Famine, and Air and Water Pollution – Why Overpopulation is our #1 Environmental Problem,* Australia: Simon & Schuster.

—— (1996) *Betrayal of Science and Reason: How Anti-Environmental Rhetoric Threatens Our Future,* Washington, DC: Island Press/Shearwater Books.

Ellis, B. (1998) *First Abolish the Customer: 202 Arguments Against Economic Rationalism,* Victoria, Australia: Penguin Books.

Ellwood, W. (2001) *The No-nonsense Guide to Globalization,* London: NI Verso.

Enderwick, P. (ed.) (1998) *Foreign Investment: The New Zealand Experience,* Foreword D. Brash, Palmerston Nth, NZ: The Dunmore Press.

Engler, A. (1995) *Apostles of Greed Capitalism and the Myth of the Individual in the Market,* London: Pluto Press.

Epstein, W.H. (1990) 'Counter-intelligence: Cold-War Criticism and Eighteenth-century Studies,' *English Literary History,* vol. 57, spring.

Evans, G. and Grant, B. (1995) *Australia's Foreign Relations: In the World of the 1990s,* Carlton, Victoria: Melbourne University Press.

Ewald, P.W. (2000) *Plague Time: How Stealth Infections Cause Cancers, Heart Disease, and Other Deadly Ailments,* New York: The Free Press.

Exoo, C.F. (ed.) (1987) *Democracy Upside Down: Public Opinion and Cultural Hegemony in the United States,* New York: Praeger.

Falk, R. (1991) 'Reflections on Democracy and the Gulf war,' *Alternatives,* vol. 16, spring.

—— (1995) *On Humane Governance Toward a New Global Politics,* Oxford: Polity Press.

Falls, G. (1994) *Post-Star,* 11 March.

—— (1994) *New York Times,* 11 March.

Farmer, P. (2005) *Pathologies of Power: Health, Human Rights, and the New War on the Poor,* Berkeley, Los Angeles: University of California Press.

Faux, J. (2004) 'NAFTA at 10: Where Do We Go From Here?,' *The Nation,* 2 February, pp. 11–14.

—— (2006) 'The Party of Davos,' *The Nation,* 13 February.

Ferber, M.A. and Nelson, J. (eds) (1993) *Beyond Economic Man: Feminist Theory and Economics,* Chicago, IL.: Chicago University Press.

—— (1993) 'Introduction: The Social Construction of Economics and the Social Construction of Gender,' in M. A. Ferber and J. Nelson (eds) *Beyond Economic Man: Feminist Theory and Economics,* Chicago, IL.: Chicago University Press.

Ferguson, J. (1990) *Grenada: Revolution in Reverse,* London: Latin American Bureau.

Fernandez-Armesto, F. (1996) *Millennium: A History of Our Last Thousand Years,* London: Black Swan.

—— (1997) *Truth: A History and a Guide for the Perplexed,* London: Transworld.

Flax, J. (1991) *Thinking Fragments: Psychoanalysis, Feminism, and Postmodernism in the Contemporary West,* Berkeley: University of California Press.

Forrester, V. (1999) *The Economic Horror,* trans. from French, Malden, MA: Polity Press.

Foss, M. (1997) *People of the First Crusade,* Chicago, IL.: Arcade Publications.

Frank, T. (2001) *One Market Under God: Extreme Capitalism, Market Populism and the End of Economic Democracy,* London: Secker & Warburg.

Franklin, H. (1985) *Cul De Sac: The Question of New Zealand's Future,* Wellington: Unwin Paperbacks in association with the Port Nicholson Press.

Freeman, R.B. (1996) 'Toward an Apartheid Economy?,' *Harvard Business Review,* September–October, pp. 114–121.

Friedman, T. (2000) *The Lexus and the Olive Tree,* London: HarperCollins.

Frosch, D. (2005) 'Your Money or Your Life,' *The Nation,* 21 February, pp. 11–14.

Fukuyama, F. (1992) *The End of History and the Last Man,* London: Penguin.

Furedi, F. (1994) *The New Ideology of Imperialism,* London: Pluto Press.

Fusfield, D.R. (1994) *The Age of the Economist* (7th edn), New York: HarperCollins.

Gabriel, R.A. (1985) *Military Incompetence: Why The American Military Doesn't Win,* New York: Hill & Wang.

Gabriel, R.A. and Savage, P.L. (1978) *Crisis in Command: Mismanagement in the Army,* New York: Hill & Wang.

Galbraith, J.K. (1969) *The New Industrial State,* Harmondsworth: Penguin Books.

—— (1977) *The Age of Uncertainty,* London: British Broadcasting Corporation.

—— (1983) *The Voice of the Poor: Essays in Economic and Political Persuasion,* Cambridge, MA: Harvard University Press.

—— (1987) *Economics in Perspective: A Critical History,* Boston, MA: Houghton Mifflin.

—— (1989) *A History of Economics: The Past as the Present,* London: Penguin.

—— (1990) *A Tenured Professor: A Novel,* Boston, MA: Houghton Mifflin.

—— (1990) 'Which Capitalism for Eastern Europe?,' *Harper's Magazine,* April, pp. 19–21.

—— (1990) 'The Rush to Capitalism,' *New York Review of Books,* 25 October.

—— (1992) *The Culture of Contentment,* London: Sinclair-Stevenson.

—— (1993) *A Short History of Financial Euphoria,* New York: Penguin.

—— (1993) *American Capitalism The Concept of Countervailing Power,* New Brunswick: Transaction Publishers.

—— (1993) *A Short History of Financial Euphoria,* New York: Whittle Books in Association with Viking.

—— (1994) 'The New Dialectic,' *The American Prospect,* summer, pp. 10–11.

—— (1994) *The World Economy Since the Wars: A Personal View,* London: Sinclair-Stevenson.

—— (1995) *Money Whence It Came, Where It Went*, London: Penguin.

—— (1996) *The Good Society: The Humane Agenda*, Boston, MA: Houghton Mifflin.

—— (1999) *The Affluent Society* (new edn), London: Penguin.

—— (2006) 'The Predator State,' *Mother Jones*, May/June. Available HTTP: <http://informationclearinghouse.info/article12880.htm> (accessed 18 May 2006).

Galbraith, J.K. and Salinger, N. (1979) *Almost Everyone's Guide to Economics*, London: Penguin.

Galeano, E. (1973) *Open Veins of Latin America: Five Centuries of the Pillage of a Continent*, New York: Monthly Review Press.

Gallup, G. and Castelli, J. (1989) *The Peoples Religion: American Faith in the 90s*, London: Macmillan.

Galtung, J. (1995) 'U.S. Foreign Policy as Manifest Theology,' in G. Hastedt (ed.) *One World, Many Voices: Global Perspectives on Political Issues*, Englewood Cliffs, NJ: Prentice-Hall, pp. 16–31.

Garnett, J. (1987) 'Strategic Studies and its Assumptions,' in J. Baylis, K. Booth, J. Garnett and P. Williams (eds), *Contemporary Strategy: Theories and Concepts*, vol. 1, New York: Holmes & Meier.

Garrett, L. (1994) *The Coming Plague: Newly Emerging Diseases in a World out of Balance*, New York: Farrar, Straus & Giroux.

—— (1996) *Microbes Versus Mankind: The Coming Plague*, New York: Foreign Policy Association.

—— (2000) *Betrayal of Trust: The Collapse of Global Public Health*, New York: Hyperion.

Garten, J.E. (1992) *A Cold Peace: America, Japan, Germany, and the Struggle for Supremacy*, New York: Times Books.

Gat, A. (1991) *The Origins of Military Thought: From the Enlightenment to Clausewitz*, Oxford: Clarendon Press.

Gates, J. (2000) *Democracy at Risk: Rescuing Main Street From Wall Street*, Cambridge, MA: Perseus Publishing.

—— (2002) 'Modern Fashion or Global Fascism?,' *Tikkun*, 17, January.

GATSwatch, 'What is GATS'?. Available HTTP: <http://www.gatswatch.org> (accessed 27 April 2006).

George, J. (1994) *Discourses of Global Politics: A Critical (Re)Introduction*, Boulder, CO: Lynne Rienner.

George, S. (1986) *How the Other Half Dies: The Real Reasons for World Hunger*, London: Penguin.

—— (1992) *The Debt Boomerang: How Third World Debt Harms Us All*, London: Pluto Press.

George, S. and Sabelli, F. (1994) *Faith and Credit: The World Bank's Secular Empire* London: Penguin.

Giddens, A. (1998) *The Third Way: The Renewal of Social Democracy*, Malden, MA: Polity Press.

—— (1999) *Runaway World: How Globalisation is Reshaping our Lives*, London: Profile Books.

Gill, S. (1991) *American Hegemony and the Trilateral Commission*, Cambridge: Cambridge University Press.

Gills, B., Rocamora, J. and Wilson, R. (1993) *Low Intensity Democracy: Political Power in the New World Order*, London and Boulder, CO: Pluto Press.

Giroux, H.A. (2004) *The Terror of Neoliberalism: Authoritarianism and the Eclipse of Democracy*, Boulder, CO: Paradigm Publishers.

Gitlin, T. (1996) *'Unum* versus *Pluribus'*, *The Nation*, 6 May.

Glendinning, C. (1996) *Off the Map*, Boston, MA and London: Shambhala.

Goldman, K. (1994) *The Logic of Internationalism: Coercion and Accommodation*, London and New York: Routledge.

Goodman, A.E. (1993) *A Brief History of the Future*, Boulder, CO: Westview Press.

Gordon, D., 'Mapping the Global Future,' *The Globalist*. Available HTTP: <http://www.theglobalist.com/DBWeb/printStoryId.aspx?StoryId+4383> (accessed 12 February 2005).

Gorringe, T. (1999) *Fair Shares: Ethics and the Global Economy*, London: Thames & Hudson.

Gould, J.M. (1996) with members of the Radiation and Public Health Project, *The Enemy Within: The High Cost of Living Near Nuclear Reactors*, New York: Four Walls Eight Windows.

Gray, J. (1998) *False Dawn: The Delusions of Global Capitalism*, London: Granta Books.
—— (2006) 'The Global Delusion', *The New York Review of Books*, 27 April.
Greeley, A.M. (1989) *Religious Change in America*, Cambridge, MA: Harvard University Press.
Greenfield, S. (1997) *The Human Brain: A Guided Tour*, London: Weidenfeld & Nicolson.
Greenpeace (2004) 'World Bank, Pentagon: Global Warming Red Alert,' *Global Policy Forum*. Available HTTP: <http://www.globalpolicy.org/socecon/bwi-wto/wbank/2004/0222pentagon.htm> (accessed 22 February 2004).
Gregory, R.L., with Zangwill O.L., (1987) *The Oxford Companion To The Mind*, Oxford: Oxford University Press.
Greider, W. (1997) *One World, Ready or Not: The Manic Logic of Global Capitalism*, New York: Simon & Schuster.
Griscom, A., 'Pentagoners: Apocalyptic Pentagon Report on Global Warming Could Spur Action on Capitol Hill,' *Grist Magazine: A Beacon in the Smog*. Available HTTP: <http://www.grist. org/cgi-bin/printthis.pl> (accessed 12 September 2006).
Gross, B. (1997) *Friendly Fascism: The New Face of Power in America*, Boston, MA: South End Press, p. 19.
Gurr, T.R. (1991) 'America as a Model for the World?: A Sceptical View,' *PS: Political Science and Politics*, 24, December, pp. 664–666.
Hadenius, A. (ed.) (1997) *Democracy's Victory and Crisis*, Cambridge: Cambridge University Press.
Hahnel, R. (1999) *Panic Rules: Everything You Need to Know About the Global Economy*, Cambridge, MA: South End Press.
Halperin, M.H. (1987) *Nuclear Fallacy: Dispelling the Myth of Nuclear Strategy*, Cambridge, MA: Ballinger.
Hamilton, J.M. with Morrison, N. (1990) *Entangling Alliances: How the Third World Shapes Our Lives*, Cabin John, MD/Washington, DC: Seven Locks Press.
Hampden-Turner, C. (1970) *Radical Man: The Process of Psycho-social Development* Cambridge, MA: Schenkman.
Hampden-Turner, C. and Trompenaars, F. (1993) *The Seven Cultures of Capitalism: Value Systems for Creating Wealth in the United States, Britain, Japan, Germany, France, Sweden, and The Netherlands*, London: Piatkus.
Hancock, G. (1989) *Lords of Poverty: The Freewheeling Lifestyles, Power, Prestige and Corruption of the Multi-billion Aid Business*, London: Macmillan.
Hassett, J.M. (1986) *Yeats and the Poetics of Hate*, Dublin: Gill & Macmillan.
Hastedt, G.P. (1991) *American Foreign Policy, Past, Present, Future* (2nd edn), Englewood Cliffs, NJ: Prentice Hall.
—— (ed.) (1995) *One World, Many Voices: Global Perspectives on Political Issues*, Englewood Cliffs NJ: Prentice Hall.
Hastings, M. (1987) *The Korean War*, New York: Simon & Schuster.
Hauchler, I. and Kennedy, P.M. (1994) *Global Trends: The World Almanac of Development and Peace*, New York: Continuum.
Hazledine, T. (1998) *Taking New Zealand Seriously: The Economics of Decency*, Auckland: HarperCollins Publishers New Zealand.
Heilbroner, R. (1985) *The Nature and Logic of Capitalism*, New York: Norton.
—— (1986) *The Worldly Philosophers: The Lives, Times, and Ideas of the Great Economic Thinkers* (6th edn), New York: Touchstone Book Published by Simon & Schuster.
—— (1988) *Behind the Veil of Economics: Essays in the Worldly Philosophy*, New York: W.W. Norton.
—— (1991) 'Lifting the Silent Depression,' *New York Review*, 24 October.
—— (1992) *Twenty-first Century Capitalism*, Concord, Ontario: Anansi.
—— (1995) *Visions of the Future: The Distant Past, Yesterday, and Tomorrow*, New York: The New York Public Library and Oxford University Press.
—— (1996) *Teachings from the Worldly Philosophy*, New York: W. W. Norton.

Heilbroner, R. and Milberg, W. (1995) *The Crisis of Vision in Modern Economic Thought*, Cambridge: Cambridge University Press.

Heilbroner, R. and Thurow, L. (1994) *Economics Explained: Everything You Need to Know About How the Economy Works and Where It's Going*, New York: Touchstone Book, Simon & Schuster.

Heisenberg, W. (1962) 'Planck's Discovery and the Philosophical Problems of Atomic Physics,' in *On Modern Physics*, New York.

—— (1963) 'The Representation of Nature in Contemporary Physics,' in R. May (ed.), *Symbolism*, New York.

Held, D. and McGrew, A. (2002) *Globalization/Anti-globalization*, Malden, MA: Polity Press.

Held, D., McGrew, A., Goldblatt, D. and Perraton, J. (1999) *Global Transformations: Politics, Economics and Culture*, Oxford: Polity Press.

Helleiner, E. (1994) *States and the Reemergence of Global Finance: From Bretton Woods to the 1990s*, Ithaca, NY: Cornell University Press.

Hellyer, P. (1999) *Stop. Think. Globalization*, Toronto, Canada: Chimo Media.

Henderson, H. (1988) *The Politics of the Solar Age: Alternatives to Economics*, Indianapolis, Indiana: Knowledge Systems, Inc.

Henwood, D. (1997) *Wall St*, London, New York: Verso.

Herbert, N. (1985) *Quantum Reality: Beyond the New Physics*, Garden City, NY: Anchor Press/Doubleday.

Herman, E.S. (1995) 'Immiserating Growth: The First World,' *Z Magazine*, January.

—— (1995) *Triumph of the Market: Essays on Economics, Politics and the Media*, Boston, MA: South End Press.

Hettne, B. (ed.) (1995) *International Political Economy: Understanding Global Disorder*, Halifax, NS: Fernwood Books Ltd; Cape Town: Sapes SA; Dhaka; University Press Ltd; London and New Jersey: Zed Books.

Hewett, J. (1997) 'Minor Defence Cuts Still Leave US Able to Fight on Two Fronts,' *Sydney Morning Herald*, 21 May.

Heycox, K. (1991) *A Question of Survival: Environmental Issues for the 1990s*, Crows Nest: ABC Books.

'High-Tech Genocide', *EarthFirst! Journal*, vol. 25, 5. Available HTTP: <http://www.earthfirstjournal.org/articles.pho?a=883> (accessed 9 February 2006).

Hippler, J. (1994) *Pax Americana? Hegemony or Decline*, London: Pluto/Transnational Institute.

Hirschman, A.O. (1992) *Rival Views of Market Society and other Recent Essays*, New York: Penguin.

Hitchens, C. (1990) *Prepared for the Worst*, London: Hogarth Press.

—— (1990) 'Standing Tall,' in *Prepared for the Worst*, London: Hogarth Press.

—— 'Imperialism: Superpower Dominance, Malignant and Benign,' *Slate*. Available HTTP: <http://slate.msn.com/?id+2075261> posted 10 December 2002 (accessed 5 January 2003).

Ho, M-W. (1998) *Genetic Engineering Dream or Nightmare: The Brave New World of Bad Science and Big Business*, Bath, UK: Gateway Books.

Hocking, B. and McGuire, S. (eds) (2004) *Trade Politics* (2nd edn), London: Routledge Taylor & Francis Group.

Hoffman, S. (1977) 'An American Social Science: International Relations,' *Daedalus: Journal of the American Academy of Arts and Sciences*, vol. 106: 3.

Hofstadter, R. (1963) *Anti-intellectualism in American Life*, New York: Vintage.

—— (1979) *The Paranoid Style in American Politics and Other Essays*, Chicago, IL: University of Chicago Press/Phoenix.

—— (1989) *The American Political Tradition and the Men Who Made It*, New York: Random House.

Hollander, P. (1992) *Anti-Americanism: Critiques at Home and Abroad 1965–1990*, New York: Oxford University Press.

Holm, H-H. and Sorensen, G. (1995) *Whose World Order? Uneven Globalization and the End of the Cold War,* Boulder, CO.: Westview Press.

Holt, J. (1977) 'The Monster and other Mathematical Beasts,' *Lingua Franca,* November.

Holton, R.J. (1998) *Globalization and the Nation-State,* London: Macmillan.

Homer-Dixon, T.F. (1993) *Environmental Scarcity and Global Security,* New York: Foreign Policy Association.

Honee, E. (1995) 'The Relation of Old and New and the Phenomenon of *Reformation,*' in J. B. M. Wissink (ed.), *(Dis)Continuity and (De)Construction: Reflections on the Meaning of the Past in Crisis Situations,* Kampen, The Netherlands: Pharos.

Hoogvelt, A. (1997) *Globalisation and the Postcolonial World,* Basingstoke and London: Macmillan.

Hoover, K.R. (2003) *Economics as Ideology: Keynes, Laski, Hayek, and the Creation of Contemporary Politics,* Lanham, MI: Rowman & Littlefield.

Hopkins, A.G. (ed.) (2002) *Globalization in World History,* London: Pimlico.

Hormats, R.D. (1991) 'The Roots of American Power,' *Foreign Affairs,* vol. 70: 3.

Horne, D. (1986) *The Public Culture: The Triumph of Industrialism,* London: Pluto Press.

Horne, D. (ed.) (1992) *The Trouble with Economic Rationalism,* Newham, Victoria: Scribe.

Horton, R. (2000) How Sick is Modern Medicine?,' a review of James Le Fanu, *The Rise and Fall of Modern Medicine* (Carroll and Graf, 2000), in *The New York Review of Books,* 2 November.

Huffington, A. (2004) 'The Pentagon Sounds the Alarm On Global Warming: Isn't President Bush Listening,' *Common Dreams News Centre,* 25 February. Available HTTP: <http://www.commondreams.og/views04/0225-13.htm> (accessed 6 April 2004).

Hunt, M.H. (1987) *Ideology and US Foreign Policy,* New Haven, CT: Yale University Press.

Huntington, S.P. (1996) *The Clash of Civilizations and the Remaking of World Order,* New York: Simon & Schuster.

Hutcheson, R.G. (1988) *God in the White House: How Religion Has Changed The Modern Presidency,* New York: Collier-Macmillan.

Hutton, W. (2003) *The World We're In,* London: Abacus Books.

Iadicola, P. and Shupe, A. (2003) *Violence, Inequality and Human Freedom,* Lanham: Rowman & Littlefield.

International Confederation of Free Trade Unions (1995) *Annual Survey of Violations of Free Trade Unions 1995,* Brussels: ICFTU, June.

—— (1995) 'Dispatch' (briefing notes accompanying the *Survey*), 14 June.

Jackson, B. (1994) *Poverty and the Planet: A Question of Survival,* London: Penguin.

Jacobs, J. (2004) *Dark Age Ahead,* New York: Vintage.

Jawara, F. and Kwa, A. (2003) *Behind the Scenes at the WTO: The Real World of International Trade Negotiations,* London: Zed Books.

Jay, P. (2000) *The Wealth of Man,* New York: Public Affairs.

Jeffery, C. (2006) 'The Perks of Privilege: How the Rich Get Richer,' *Mother Jones,* May–June.

Johnson, C. (1997) 'Breaching the Great Wall,' *The American Prospect,* January–February.

Johnson, L.K. (1989) *America's Secret Power: The CIA in a Democratic Society,* New York: Oxford University Press.

Jowitt, K. (1993) *New Worlds Disorder: The Leninist Extinction,* Berkeley: University of California Press.

Kanth, R.K. (1997) *Against Economics: Rethinking Political Economy,* Aldershot: Ashgate.

Kanth, R.K. and Hunt, E.K. (eds) (1991) *Explorations in Political Economy: Essays in Criticism,* Savage, MI: Rowman & Littlefield.

Kaplan, R.D. (1996) *The Ends of the Earth: A Journey at the Dawn of the 21st Century,* New York: Random House.

—— (2000) *The Coming Anarchy: Shattering the Dreams of the Post Cold War,* New York: Random House.

Karliner, J. (1997) *The Corporate Planet: Ecology and Politics in the Age of Globalization,* San Francisco, CA: Sierra Club Books.

Kazin, M. (1989) 'The Right's Unsung Prophet,' *The Nation*, 20 February.

Keegan, W. (1993) *The Spectre of Capitalism: The Future of the World Economy After the Fall of Communism*, London: Vintage.

Keen, S. (2001) *Debunking Economics: The Naked Emperor of the Social Sciences*, Annandale, NSW: Pluto Press.

Kegley, C.W. Jr. (1995) *Controversies in International Relations Theory: Realism and the Neoliberal Challenge*, New York: St Martin's Press.

Kegley, C.W. Jr. and Wittkopf, E.R. (2004) *World Politics: Trends and Transformation* (9th edn), Belmont, CA: Thomson Wadsworth.

Kelman, H.C. and Hamilton, V.L. (1989) *Crimes of Obedience: Toward A Social Psychology of Authority and Responsibility*, New Haven, CT: Yale University Press.

Kelsey, J. (1995) *Economic Fundamentalism: The New Zealand Experiment – A World Model for Structural Adjustment?*, London, East Haven, CT: Pluto Press.

—— (1999) *Reclaiming the Future: New Zealand and the Global Economy*, Wellington: Bridget Williams Books.

Kennedy, P. (1988) 'Not So Grand Strategy,' *New York Review of Books*, 12 May.

—— (1988) *The Rise and Fall of the Great Powers: Economic Change and Military Conflict From 1500 to 2000*, London: Unwin Hyman.

Kennedy, P., Messner, D. and Nuscheler, F. (eds) (2002) *Global Trends and Global Governance*, London: Pluto Press.

Keyman, E. Fuat (1997) *Globalization, State, Identity/Difference: Toward a Critical Social Theory of International Relations*, New Jersey: Humanities Press.

Kim, J.Y., Millen, J.V., Irwin, A. and Gershman, J. (2000) *Dying for Growth: Global Inequality and the Health of the Poor*, Monroe, Maine: Common Courage Press.

King, J.E. (1988) *Economic Exiles*, New York: St Martin's Press.

Kite, B., 'Free Trade? Someone Always Has to Pay,' a *BusinessWeek online* Commentary, distributed by the Black Radical Congress. Available HTTP: <http://www.businessweek.com/bwdaily/dnflash/may2001/nf2001052_941.htm> (accessed 30 May 2001).

Klak, T. (ed.) (1998) *Globalization and Neoliberalism: The Caribbean Context*, Baltimore, MD: Rowman & Littlefield.

Klare, M.T. (2004) *Blood and Oil: How America's Thirst for Oil is Killing Us*, London: Penguin.

Kline, M. (1980) *Mathematics: The Loss of Certainty*, Oxford: Oxford University Press.

—— (1990) *Mathematics in Western Culture*, London: Penguin.

Knight, D. (1997) 'The Global Politics of Pesticide Use in Brazil,' *Z Magazine*, January, pp. 41–46.

Kofman, E. and Youngs, G. (eds) (1996) *Globalization: Theory and Practice*, London: Pinter.

——(ed) (2003) *Globalization: Theory and Practice* (2nd edn), London and New York: Continuum.

Kolko, J. and Kolko, G. (1972) *The Limits of Power: The World and United States Foreign Policy, 1945–1972*, New York: Harper & Row.

Kolkowicz, R. (1987) 'The Strange Career of the Defense Intellectuals,' *Orbis* 31, summer.

Kornbluh, P. and Byrne, M. (eds) (1993) *The Iran-Contra Scandal: The Declassified History*, New York: New Press.

Korten, D.C. (1995) *When Corporations Rule the World*, Connecticut: Copublication of Kumarian Press, Inc., and Berrett-Koehler Publishers.

—— (1998) *Globalizing Civil Society: Reclaiming Our Right to Power*, New York: Seven Stories Press.

—— (1999) *The Post-corporate World: Life After Capitalism*, Connecticut: Copublication of Kumarian Press, Inc., and Berrett-Koehler Publishers.

Kozol, J. (1985) *Illiterate America*, New York: Plume.

Krieger, J. (ed.) (1993) 'Finance International,' in *The Oxford Companion to Politics of the World*, New York: Oxford University Press.

Kristof, N. and WuDunn, S. (1999) *The Japanese Economy At The Millennium Correspondent's Insightful Views*, New York: Foreign Policy Association.

Krugman, P. (1994) *The Age of Diminished Expectations* (revised and updated edn), Cambridge, MA: The MIT Press.
—— (1995) *Peddling Prosperity: Economic Sense and Nonsense in the Age of Diminished Expectations,* New York: W.W. Norton.
—— (1996) *Pop Internationalism,* Cambridge, MA: MIT Press.
—— (1998) *The Accidental Theorist And Other Dispatches from the Dismal Science,* New York: W. W. Norton.
—— (1999) *The Return of Depression Economics,* New York: W.W. Norton.
Küng, H. (1997) *A Global Ethic for Global Politics and Economics,* trans. J. Bowden, London: SCM Press.
Kurtzman, J. (1993) *The Death of Money,* Boston, MA: Back Bay Books, Little, Brown.
Kuttner, R. (1996h) 'Peddling Krugman,' The American Prospect, September–October.
—— (1997) 'The Limits of Markets,' *The American Prospect*, March–April.
Lacey, M. (2001) 'Bush Chides Critics and Declares Freer Trade a Moral Issue,' *New York Times*, 8 May.
Laffin, J. (1989) *British Bunglers and Butchers of World War One,* Melbourne: Macmillan.
Laidlaw, C. (1999) *Rights of Passage: Beyond the New Zealand Identity Crisis,* Auckland: Hodder Moa Beckett.
Lang, T. and Hines, C. (1993) *The New Protectionism: Protecting The Future Against Free Trade,* London: Earthscan Publications.
Lapham, L. (1992) 'Notebook: Apes and Butterflies,' *Harper's Magazine,* May.
—— (1996) 'Painted Fire,' *Harper's Magazine,* 1 November.
—— (1997) 'Painted Fire,' in *Waiting for the Barbarians,* London: Verso.
—— (2005) 'Notebook: On Message,' *Harper's Magazine,* October.
Lappé, F.M. and Collins J. (1988) *World Hunger: 12 Myths,* London: Earthscan Publications.
Larsen, E. (2006) *A Nation Gone Blind: America in an Age of Simplification and Deceit,* Emeryville, CA: Avalon Publishing Group.
Latona, B. (1994) *A New World Order: Economics for a Peaceful Planet,* Taree: W J Latona.
Latouche, S. (1993) *In the Wake of the Affluent Society: An Exploration of Post-development,* London: Zed Books.
—— (1996) *The Westernization of the World,* Cambridge: Polity Press.
Laudicina, P.A. (2005) *World Out Of Balance: Navigating Global Risks to Seize Competitive Advantage,* New York: McGraw-Hill.
Lawson, T. (1997) *Economics and Reality,* London: Routledge.
Le Goff, J. (1990) *Your Money Or Your Life: Economy and Religion in the Middle Ages,* trans. P. Ranum, New York: Zone.
Leach, W. (1993) *Land of Desire: Merchants, Power, and the Rise of a New American Culture,* New York: Pantheon.
Leakey, R. and Lewin, R. (1996) *The Sixth Extinction: Biodiversity and its Survival,* London: Weidenfeld & Nicolson.
Leffler, M.P. (1992) *A Preponderance of Power: National Security, The Truman Administration, and the Cold War,* Stanford, CT: Stanford University Press.
Leggett, J. (2005) *Half Gone: Oil, Gas, Hot Air and the Global Energy Crisis,* London: Portobello.
—— (ed.) (1990) *Global Warming: The Greenpeace Report,* Oxford: Oxford University Press.
Lentricchia, F. and McLaughlin, T. (eds) (1990) *Critical Terms for Literary Study,* Chicago, IL: University of Chicago Press.
Leslie, J. (1998) *The End of the World: The Science and Ethics of Human Extinction,* London: Routledge.
Levitt, S.D. and Dubner, S.J. (2005) *Freakonomics: A Rogue Economist Explores the Hidden Side of Everything,* London: Allen Lane, an imprint of Penguin.
Lieberman, T. (2003) 'Hungry in America,' *The Nation,* 18–25 August.
Lifschultz, L.S. (1989) 'Could Karl Marx Teach Economics in the United States,' in J. Trumpbour (ed.), *How Harvard Rules,* Boston, MA: South End Press.

Lipset, S.M. (1996) *American Exceptionalism: A Double-edged Sword*, New York: W.W. Norton.

Longino, H.E. (1993) 'Economics for Whom?', in M.A. Ferber and J. Nelson (eds), *Beyond Economic Man: Feminist Theory and Economics*, Chicago, IL: Chicago University Press.

Longworth, R.C. (1998) *Global Squeeze: The Coming Crisis for First-World Nations*, Chicago, IL: Contemporary Books.

Lopez, G.A., Smith, J.G. and Pagnucco, R. (1995) 'The Global Tide,' *Bulletin of the Atomic Scientists*, July–August.

Luke, T.W. (1989) *Screens of Power: Ideology, Domination, and Resistance in Informational Society*, Urbana and Chicago, IL: University of Illinois Press.

Luttwak, E.N. (1985) *The Pentagon and the Art of War*, New York: Simon & Schuster.

—— (1990) 'From Geopolitics to Geoeconomics: Logic of Conflict, Grammar of Commerce,' *National Interest*, summer.

—— (1999) *Turbo-capitalism: Winners and Losers in the Global Economy*, New York: HarperCollins.

Lynn, B.C. (2005) *End of the Line: The Rise and Coming Fall of the Global Corporation*, New York: Doubleday.

MacCullogh, D. (2004) *The Reformation: A History*, New York: Viking.

MacDonagh, O. (1977) *Ireland: The Union and its Aftermath* (rev. and enl. edn), London: George Allen & Unwin.

MacEwan, A. (1999) *Neo-liberalism or Democracy? Economic Strategy, Markets, and Alternatives for the 21st Century*, Sydney: Pluto Press.

Macfarlane, S., Racelis, M. and Muli-Muslime, F. (2000) 'Public Health in Developing Countries,' *The Lancet*, vol. 356, 2 September, pp. 841–846.

Maclear, M. (1981) *Vietnam: The Ten Thousand Day War*, London: Eyre Methuen.

McChesney, R.W. (1997) *Corporate Media and the Threat to Democracy*, New York: Seven Stories Press.

McClelland, J.S. (1996) *A History of Western Political Thought*, London: Routledge.

McCloskey, D.N. (1985) *The Rhetoric of Economics*, Madison: The University of Wisconsin Press.

—— (1993) 'Some Consequences of a Conjective Economics,' in M. A. Ferber and J. Nelson (eds), *Beyond Economic Man: Feminist Theory and Economics*, Chicago, IL: Chicago University Press.

—— (1995) 'Some News That At Least Will Not Bore You,' *Eastern Economic Journal*, autumn, reprinted in *Lingua Franca*, May–June 1996, and reprinted again in *Harper's Magazine*, 1996, July.

McCrone, J. (1999) *Going Inside: A Tour Round a Single Moment of Consciousness*, London: Faber and Faber.

McHoul, A. and Grace, W. (1993) *A Foucault Primer: Discourse, Power and the Subject*, Melbourne: Melbourne University Press.

McKinley, M. (1997) *Globalisation as War: Equivalence and Convergence in the Theory and Practice of Neoliberalism*, paper presented to the 38th Annual Convention of the International Studies Association, Toronto, Canada, 21 March.

—— (2004) 'The Co-option of the University and the Privileging of Annihilation,' *International Relations*, vol. 18: 2.

McMurtry, J. (1999) *The Cancer Stage of Capitalism*, London and Sterling, VI: Pluto Press.

McRae, H. (1995) *The World in 2020 Power, Culture and Prosperity: A Vision of the Future*, London: HarperCollins.

Madeley, J. (1999) *Big Business, Poor Peoples: The Impact of Transnational Corporations on the World's Poor*, London: Zed Books.

Mander, J. and Goldsmith, E. (eds) (1996) *The Case Against the Global Economy and For a Turn Toward the Local*, San Francisco, CA: Sierra Club Books.

Mangold, T. (1991) *Cold Warrior: James Jesus Angleton: The CIA's Master Spy Hunter*, New York: Simon & Schuster.

Manicas, P.T. (1987) *A History and Philosophy of the Social Sciences*, Oxford: Blackwell.

Mapping the Global Future: Report of the National Intelligence Council's 2020 Project (2004) Available HTTP: < http://www.cia.gov/nic_globaltrend2020_es.html> (accessed 3 February 2006).

Marcos, Sub-Commandante (1997) 'The Fourth World War has Begun,' *Le Monde Diplomatique*, English edn, August–September. Available HTTP: <http://www.monde-diplomatique.fr/en1997/08-09/marcos.html> (accessed 27 October 1998).

Markee, P. (1997) 'Debt Heads,' a review of Catherine Caufield, *Masters of Illusion: The World Bank and the Poverty of Nations*, New York: Holt, *The Nation*, 17 March.

Markusen, E. and Kopf, D. (1995) *The Holocaust and Strategic Bombing: Genocide and Total War in the 20th Century*, Boulder, CO: Westview Press.

Marlin-Bennett, R. (2004) *Knowledge Power: Intellectual Property, Information and Privacy*, Boulder, CO: Lynne Rienner.

Marshall, A. (1997) *Principles of Economics*, Amherst: Prometheus Books.

Martin, B. (1995) 'Against Intellectual Property,' *Philosophy and Social Action*, vol. 21, July–September.

—— (1997) 'Mathematics and Social Interests,' in Arthur B. Powell and Marilyn Frankenstein (eds), *Ethnomathematics: Challenging Eurocentrism in Mathematics Education*, Albany: State University of New York Press.

Martin, H-P. and Schumann, H. (1998) *The Global Trap: Globalization and the Assault on Democracy & Prosperity*, trans. P. Camiller, London: Zed Books.

Mayers, D. (1988) *George Kennan and the Dilemmas of US Foreign Policy*, New York: Oxford University Press.

Mead, W.R. (1987) *Mortal Splendor: The American Empire in Transition*, Boston, MA: Houghton Mifflin.

—— (1990) 'On the Road to Ruin: Winning the Cold War, Losing the Economic Peace,' *Harper's Magazine*, March.

—— (1992) 'Bushism, Found: A Second-term Agenda Hidden in Trade Agreements,' *Harper's Magazine*, September.

Meadows, D.H., Meadows, D.L. and Randers, J. (1992) *Beyond The Limits: Global Collapse or a Sustainable Future*, London: Earthscan Publications.

Mehmet, O. (1995) *Westernizing the Third World: The Eurocentricity of Economic Development Theories*, London: Routledge.

Menand, L. (1992) 'The Myth of American Diversity,' in 'Being an American,' an essay in *The Times Literary Supplement*, London, 30 October.

Merrill, R. (1993) 'Simulations and Terrors of Our Time,' in D. J. Brown and R. Merrill (eds), *The Politics and Imagery of Terrorism*, Seattle: Bay Press.

Mészáros, I. (1995) *Beyond Capital*, Finland: WSOY.

Milanovic, B. (2005) *Worlds Apart: Measuring International and Global Inequality*, Princeton, NJ: Princeton University Press.

Milbank, J. (2002) *Theology and Social Theory Beyond Secular Reason*, Cambridge, MA: Blackwell.

Milhevc, J. (1995) *The Market Tells Them So: The World Bank and Economic Fundamentalism in Africa*, London: Zed Books.

Mirowski, P. (1995) *More Heat than Light: Economics as Social Physics, Physics as Nature's Economics*, Cambridge: Cambridge University Press.

Mittelman, J.H. (ed.) (1996) *Globalization: Critical Reflections*, Boulder, CO, and London: Lynne Rienner.

—— (2004) *Whither Globalization? The Vortex of Knowledge and Ideology*, New York: Routledge.

Moffett, G.D. (1994) *Global Population Growth: 21st Century Challenges*, Ithaca, NY: Foreign Policy Association.

—— (1999) *Corporate Predators: The Hunt for Mega-Profits and the Attack on Democracy*, Monroe, Maine: Common Courage Press.

—— (2005) *On the Rampage: Corporate Predators and the Destruction of Democracy*, Monroe, Maine: Common Courage Press.

Monbiot, G. (2000) *Captive State: The Corporate Takeover of Britain*, London: Macmillan.

—— (2003) *The Age of Consent: A Manifesto for a New World Order,* London: Flamingo.

Mongiovi, G. (1997) 'Whose Economy Is It?' [a review of Doug Henwood, *Wall Street: How It Works and for Whom,* London: Verso], *The Nation,* 8–15 September.

Mullett, M.A. (1999) *The Catholic Reformation,* London: Routledge.

Murphy, C.N. and Tooze, R. (eds) (1991) *The New International Political Economy,* Boulder, CO: Lynne Rienner.

Nader, R. *et al.* (1993) *The Case Against Free Trade: GATT, NAFTA, and the Globalization of Corporate Power,* San Francisco, CA: Earth Island Press.

Nairn, T. (1977) *The Break-up of Britain: Crisis and Neo-Nationalism,* London: NLB.

Nelson, J.A. (1993) 'The Study of Choice or the Study of Provisioning?: Gender and the Definition of Economics,' in M.A. Ferber and J.A. Nelson (eds), *Beyond Economic Man: Feminist Theory and Economics,* Chicago, IL: Chicago University Press.

—— (1993) 'Gender and the Definition of Economics,' in M.A. Ferber and J.A Nelson (eds), *Beyond Economic Man: Feminist Theory and Economics,* Chicago, IL: Chicago University Press.

Nelson, R.H. (2001) *Economics as Religion; From Samuelson to Chicago and Beyond,* University Park: Pennsylvania, State University Press.

Nijar, G.S. (1998) *TRIPS (Trade-related Intellectual Property Rights) and Biodiversity – The Threat and Responses: A Third World View,* Penang, Malaysia: TWN.

Nikiforuk, A. (1992) *The Fourth Horseman: A Short History of Epidemics, Plagues and Other Scourges,* London: Phoenix.

Norton, A. (2006) 'Is it Fascism Yet?', *Adbusters: Journal of the Mental Environment,* 14 January–February.

Nye, J.S. Jr. (1990) *Bound To Lead: The Changing Nature of American Power,* New York: Basic Books.

O'Brien, C.C. (1994) *On the Eve of the Millennium: The Future of Democracy Through an Age of Unreason,* New York: The Free Press.

O'Donohue, J. (1994) 'Chosen,' *Echoes of Memory,* Cliffs of Moher, County Clare, Ireland: Salman Publishing.

O'Driscoll, G.P. and Rizzo, M.J. (1996) *The Economics of Time and Ignorance,* London: Routledge.

Oldstone, M.B. (2000) *Viruses, Plagues, and History,* New York: Oxford University Press.

Ong, A. (2006) *Neoliberalism as Exception: Mutations in Citizenship and Sovereignty,* Durham, NC: Duke University Press.

Ormerod, P. (1994) *The Death of Economics,* London: Faber and Faber.

—— (1998) *Butterfly Economics,* London: Faber and Faber.

—— (2005) *Why Most Things Fail Evolution, Extinction and Economics,* London: Faber and Faber.

Ostry, S. (1997) *The Post-Cold War Trading System: Who's on First?,* Chicago, IL: The University of Chicago Press.

Ostry, S. and Nelson, R. R. (1995) *Techno-nationalism and Techno-globalism: Conflict and Cooperation,* Washington, DC: Brookings Institution.

Otero, G. (ed.) (1996) *Neo-liberalism Revisited: Economic Restructuring and Mexico's Political Future,* Boulder, CO: Westview Press.

Pagels, E. (1989) *Gnostic Gospels,* New York: Vintage.

Parenti, M. (1995) *Against Empire,* San Francisco, CA: City Lights.

—— (1996) *Dirty Truths: Reflections on Politics, Media, Ideology, Conspiracy, Ethnic Life and Class Power,* San Francisco, CA: City Lights .

Pascal Zachary, G. (2000) *The Global Me – New Cosmopolitans and the Competitive Edge: Picking Globalism's Winners and Losers,* London: Nicholas Brealey.

Pauly, L.W. (1997) *Who Elected the Banks? Surveillance and Control in the World Economy,* Ithaca, NY, and London: Cornell University Press.

Payne, A., Sutton, P. and Thorndike, T. (1984) *Grenada: Revolution and Invasion,* New York: St Martin's Press.

Perkins, J. (2004) *Confessions of an Economic Hit Man,* San Francisco, CA: Berrett-Koehler Publishers.

Perloff, J. (2002) *The Shadows of Power: The Council on Foreign Relations And The American Decline*, Wisconsin: Western Islands.

Perry, L. (1989) *Intellectual Life In America: A History*, Chicago, IL: University of Chicago Press.

Peterson, W.C. (1994) *Silent Depression: The Fate of the American Dream*, New York: W.W. Norton.

Petras, J. and Veltmeyer, H. (2001) *Globalization: Unmasked Imperialism in the 21ˢᵗ Century*, London: Fernwood Publishing/Zed Books.

Pettman, R. (1996) *Understanding International Political Economy with Readings for the Fatigued*, Boulder, CO, Lynne Rienner.

Pilger, J. (2002) *The New Rulers of the World*, London: Verso.

Polanyi, K. (1957) *The Great Transformation: The Political and Economic Origins of Our Time*, Boston, MA: Beacon Press.

Pollard, S. (1971) *The Idea of Progress*, Harmondsworth: Penguin.

—— (1997) *The International Economy since 1945*, London: Routledge.

Pollin, R. (2003) *Contours of Descent: U.S. Economic Fractures and the Landscape of Global Austerity*, London: Verso.

Ponting, C. (1991) *A Green History of the World*, London: Penguin.

Postman, N. (1988) *Conscientious Objection: Stirring Up Trouble About Language, Technology, and Education*, New York: Knopf.

—— (1992) *Technopoly: The Surrender of Culture to Technology*, New York: Alfred A. Knopf.

Powers, T. (1993) 'The Truth About the CIA,' *New York Review*, 13 May.

Prebble, J. (1967) *Culloden*, Penguin.

Preston, P. (1992) 'Modes of Economic-Theoretical Engagement,' in Roy Dilley (ed.) *Contesting Markets: Analyses of Ideology, Discourse and Practice*, Edinburgh: Edinburgh University Press.

Preston, R. (1994) *The Hot Zone: A Terrifying True Story*, New York: Random House.

Public Citizen, '(Consolidated) Trade Adjustment Assistance (2003–present).' Available HTTP: <http://www.citizen.org/trade/forms/taa_search.cfm?dataset=3> (accessed 9 March 2004).

—— 'Another Americas is Possible: The Impact of NAFTA on the US Latino Community and Lessons for Future Trade Agreements' (2004) August. Available HTTP: <http://www.citizen.org/documents/LatinosReport.pdf> (accessed 9 March 2006).

Pugh, M.C. (1989) *The ANZUS Crisis, Nuclear Visiting and Deterrence*, Cambridge: Cambridge University Press.

Pusey, M. (1991) *Economic Rationalism in Canberra: A Nation Building State Changes its Mind*, Cambridge: Cambridge University Press.

Pusey, M. (2003) with the assistance of S. Wilson, N. Turnbull and T. Fattore, *The Experience of Middle Australia: The Dark Side of Economic Reform*, Cambridge: Cambridge University Press.

Quadrennial Defense Review Report (2006) Washington, DC: United States Department of Defense.

Quigley, W. P. (2003) *Ending Poverty as We Know It: Guaranteeing a Right to a Job at a Living Wage*, Philadelphia, PA: Temple University Press.

Raghavan, C. (1993) *Recolonialization: GATT, the Uruguay Round, and the Third World*, Penang: Third World Network.

Rai, M. (1995) *Chomsky's Politics*, London: Verso.

Ranelagh, J. (1992) *CIA: A History*, London: BBC Books.

Ransom, D. (2001) *The No-nonsense Guide to Fair Trade*, London: Verso.

Rapaport, A. (ed.) (1968) Introduction, Carl von Clausewitz, *On War*, Harmondsworth: Penguin.

Rapley, J. (2004) *Globalization and Inequality: Neoliberalism's Downward Spiral*, Boulder, CO: Lynne Rienner.

Reaney, P. (2005) 'Africans Forego Basics to Save Children,' *Reuters*, 13 December. Available HTTP: <http://www.truthout.org/issues_05/121305HA.shtml> (accessed 2 January 2006).

Record, J. (2003) 'The Bush Doctrine and War With Iraq,' *Parameters*, spring.

Redman, D.A. (1993) *Economics and the Philosophy of Science,* New York: Oxford University Press.

Rhodes, R. (1997) *Deadly Feasts: Tracking the Secrets of a Terrifying New Plague,* New York: Simon & Schuster.

Ricci, D. (1984) *The Tragedy of Political Science: Politics, Scholarship, and Democracy,* New Haven, CT: Yale University Press.

Rich, B. (1994) *Mortgaging the Earth: The World Bank, Environmental Impoverishment and the Crisis of Development,* London: Earthscan.

Richardson, J.L. (2001) *Contending Liberalisms in World Politics Ideology and Power,* Boulder, CO: Lynne Rienner.

(2003) *The Hydrogen Economy,* Oxford: Polity Press.

Rifkin, J. (1992) *Biosphere Politics: A Cultural Odyssey from the Middle Ages to the New Age,* San Francisco, CA: Harper San Francisco.

—— (1992) *Beyond Beef: The Rise and Fall of the Cattle Culture,* Melbourne: Viking.

—— (1995) *The End of Work: The Decline of the Global Labor Force and the Dawn of the Post-market Era,* New York: Jeremy P. Tarcher/ Putnam.

—— (1998) *The Biotech Century: Harnessing the Gene and Remaking the World,* New York: Jeremy P. Tarcher/Putnam.

—— (2000) *The Age of Access: How the Shift from Ownership to Access is Transforming Modern Life,* London: Penguin.

Roberts, P.C. (2006) 'Nuking the Economy,' *Counterpunch,* 13 February, Information Clearing House, Available HTTP: <www.informationclearinghouse.info/article11897.htm> (accessed 14 February 2006).

Robertson, R. (2003) *The Three Waves of Globalization: A History of A Developing Global Consciousness,* London: Zed Books.

Rodrik, D. (1997) *Has Globalization Gone Too Far?,* Washington, DC: Institute for International Economics.

Rohatyn, F. (1990) 'Becoming What They Think We Are,' *New York Review of Books,* 12 April.

—— (1991) 'The New Domestic Order?,' *New York Review,* 21 November.

Rorty, R., 'Moral Universalism and Economic Triage.' Available HTTP: <http://www.unesco.org/phiweb/uk/2rpu/rort/rot.html>(accessed 12 September 2006).

—— (2005) 'A Queasy Agnosticism,' *Dissent,* vol. 52, autumn.

Rosen, M. and Widgery, D. (1991) *The Chatto Book of Dissent,* London: Chatto & Windus.

Rosenberg, A. (1994) *Economics — Mathematical Politics or Science of Diminishing Returns?,* Chicago, IL: Chicago University Press.

Rosenberg, J. (2000) *The Follies of Globalisation: Polemical Essays,* London, New York: Verso.

Ross, D. (1991) *The Origins of American Social Science,* New York: Cambridge University Press.

—— (1993) 'An Historian's View Of American Social Science,' *Journal of the History of the Behavioral Sciences,* vol. 29, April.

—— (1994) 'Modernist Social Science in the Land of the New/Old,' in D. Ross (ed.) *Modernist Impulses in the Human Sciences, 1870–1830,* Baltimore, MD: The Johns Hopkins University Press.

Ross, E.B. (1998) *The Malthus Factor Population, Poverty and Politics in Capitalist Development,* London: Zed Books.

Rothstein, L., Spain, L. and Gordon, D. (compilers) (1995) 'A Sense of Proportion: Or, When is Enough Enough?,' *Bulletin of the Atomic Scientists,* September–October.

Rotman, B. (1998) 'Fortress Mathematica,' *London Review of Books,* 17 September.

Rubin, E. (1997) 'An Army of One's Own,' *Harper's Magazine,* February.

Rudd, C. and Roper, B. (eds) (1997) *The Political Economy of New Zealand,* Auckland: Oxford University Press.

Rugman, A. (2001) *The End of Globalization: A New and Radical Analysis of Globalization and What it Means for Business,* London: Random House Business Books.

Russell, M. (1996) *Revolution: New Zealand From Fortress to Free Market,* Auckland: Hodder Moa Beckett.

Ryan, A. (1992) 'Twenty-first Century Limited,' *New York Review,* 19 November.

—— (1992) 'Professor Hegel Goes to Washington', (a review of Francis Fukuyama's *The End of History and the Last Man*), *New York Review of Books,* 26 March.

Ryan, M. (1982) *Marxism and Deconstruction: A Critical Articulation,* Baltimore, MD: The Johns Hopkins University Press.

—— (1984) *Marxism and Deconstruction: A Critical Articulation,* Baltimore, MD: Johns Hopkins University Press.

Sachs, W. (ed.) (2001) *The Development Dictionary: A Guide to Knowledge as Power* (8th impression), Johannesburg: Witwatersrand University Press, London: Zed Books.

Said, E.W. (1985) 'Opponents, Audiences, Constituencies and Community,' in Hal Foster (ed.), *Postmodern Culture,* London: Pluto.

—— (1993) *Culture and Imperialism,* New York: Knopf.

Sampson, A. (1973) *The Sovereign State: The Secret History of ITT,* London: Cornet Books, Hodder Fawcett.

Samuels, W.J. (1992) *Essays in the History of Heterodox Political Economy,* London: Macmillan.

Sandburg, C. (1944) 'Storm Over the Land,' in *Abraham Lincoln: The War Years 1861–1865,* London: Readers Union/Jonathan Cape.

Sanger, D.E. (2001) 'Bush Links Trade With Democracy at Quebec Talks,' *New York Times,* 22 April.

Saul, J. Ralston (1997) *The Unconscious Civilization,* Ringwood, Victoria: Penguin.

—— (2005) *The Collapse of Globalism and the Reinvention of the World,* Camberwell, Victoria: Viking.

Schott, J.J. with Buurman, J.W (1994) *The Uruguay Round: An Assessment,* Washington, DC: Institute for International Economics.

Schrader, E. (1995) 'A Giant Spraying Sound,' *Mother Jones,* January–February.

Schrecker, E.W. (1986) *No Ivory Tower: McCarthyism and the Universities,* New York: Oxford University Press.

Schwartz, P. and Randall, D. (2003) *An Abrupt Climate Change Scenario and its Implications for United States National Security,* October.

Schwarz, J.E. and Volgy, T.J. (1992) *The Forgotten Americans,* New York: W.W. Norton.

Seabrook, J. (1990) *The Myth of the Market: Promises and Illusions,* Devon: Green Books.

Seabury, P. and Codevilla, A. (1989) *War: Ends and Means,* New York: Basic Books.

Seager, J. (ed.) (1990) *The State of the Earth: An Atlas of Environmental Concern,* London: Unwin Hyman.

—— (1992) 'Operation Desert Disaster: Environmental Costs of the War,' in C. Peters (ed.), *Collateral Damage: The 'New World Order' at Home and Abroad,* Boston, MA: South End Press.

Sennett, R. (1998) *The Corrosion of Character The Personal Consequences of Work in the New Capitalism,* New York: W. W. Norton.

Shadows of Tender Fury: The Letters and Communiqués of Subcomandante Marcos and the Zapatista *(1995) Army of National Liberation,* trans. F. Bardacke, L. López, and the Watsonville, California, Human Rights Committee, Introduction by J. Ross, Afterword by F. Bardacke, New York: Monthly Review Press.

Shafer, D.M. (1988) *Deadly Paradigms: The Failure of U.S. Counterinsurgency Policy,* Leicester: Leicester University Press.

Shain, B.A. (1994) *The Myth of American Individualism: The Protestant Origins of American Political Thought,* Princeton, NJ: Princeton University Press.

Shanks, H. (ed.) (1993) *Understanding the Dead Sea Scrolls: A Reader from the Archaeology Reviews,* New York: Vintage.

Shapiro, A.L. (1992) *We're Number One: Where America Stands – and Falls – in the New World Order,* New York: Vintage.

Shapiro, M.J. (1997) 'Narrating the Nation, Unwelcoming the Stranger: Anti-Immigration Policy in Contemporary "America",' *Alternatives: Social Transformation and Humane Governance*, vol. 22, January–March.

Shipler, D.K. (2005) *The Working Poor: Invisible in America*, New York: Vintage.

Shiva, V. (2005) 'How to End Poverty: Making Poverty History and the History of Poverty,' *Znet Commentary*, 11 May. Available HTTP: <http://www.zmag.org/sustainers/content/2005-0/11shiva.cfm> (accessed 11 May 2005).

Shiva, V. and Holla-Bhar, R. (1996) 'Piracy by Patent: The Case of the Neem Tree,' J. Mander and E. Goldsmith (eds), *The Case Against the Global Economy and For a Turn Toward the Local*, San Francisco, CA: Sierra Club.

Silverstein, K. (1997) 'The New China Hands: How the Fortune 500 is China's Strongest Lobby,' *The Nation*, 17 February.

Simmons, M.R. (2005) *Twilight in the Desert: The Coming Saudi Oil Shock and the World Economy*, Hoboken, NJ: Wiley.

Singer, P. (1990) *Animal Liberation* (2nd edn), London: Jonathan Cape.

—— (1993) *How Are We to Live? Ethics in an Age of Self-interest*, Melbourne, Victoria: The Text Publishing Company.

Sklar, H. (ed.) (1980) *Trilateralism: The Trilateral Commission and Elite Planning for World Management*, Boston, MA: South End Press.

Skousen, M. (1991) *Economics on Trial: Lies, Myths, and Realities*, New York: IRWIN Professional Publishing.

Snarr, M.T. and Snarr, D.N. (eds) (1998) *Introducing Global Issues*, Boulder, CO, and London: Lynne Rienner.

Snooks, G.D. (1993) *Economics Without Time: A Science Blind to the Forces of Historical Change*, London: Macmillan.

Snow, D.M. (1991) *National Security: Enduring Problems in a Changing Defence Environment* (2nd edn), New York: St Martin's Press.

Soley, L.C. (1995) *Leasing the Ivory Tower: The Corporate Takeover of Academia*, Boston, MA: South End Press.

Soros, G. (1994) *The Alchemy of Finance: Reading the Mind of the Market*, New York: Wiley & Sons.

—— (1998) *The Crisis of Global Capitalism Open Society Endangered*, London: Little, Brown & Company.

Sowell, T. (2006) *On Classical Economics*, New Haven, CT: Yale University Press.

Spero, J. E. (1994) *The Politics of International Economic Relations* (4th edn), London: Routledge.

Spillane, M. (1995) 'Northern Exposure,' *The Nation*, 19 June.

Steinberger, M. (1998) 'The Second Sex and the Dismal Science: The Rise of Feminist Economics,' *Lingua Franca*, November.

Stephanson, A. (1995) *Manifest Destiny: American Expansion and the Empire of Right*, New York: Hill & Wang.

Stiglitz, J. (2002) *Globalization and its Discontents*, London: Allen Lane/Penguin.

Stopford, J., Strange, S. with Hensley, J. S. (1991) *Rival States, Rival Firms: Competition for World Market Shares*, Cambridge: Cambridge University Press.

Strassmann, D. (1993) 'Not a Free Market: The Rhetoric of Disciplinary Authority in Economics,' in M. A. Ferber and J. A. Nelson (eds), *Beyond Economic Man: Feminist Theory and Economics*, Chicago, IL: Chicago University Press.

Strathern, P. (2001) *Dr Strangelove's Game: A Brief History of Economic Genius*, London: Hamish Hamilton.

Stretton, H. (1999) *Economics: A New Introduction*, Sydney: University of New South Wales Press.

Stubbs, R. and Underhill, G.R.D. (eds) (1994) *Political Economy and the Changing Global Order*, Basingstoke, London: Macmillan.

Sub-Commandante Marcos, 'The Fourth World War has Begun,' *Le Monde Diplomatique,* English edn. Available HTTP: <http://www.monde-diplomatique.fr/en/1997/08-09/marcos.html> (accessed 4 April 2001).

Sumner, W.G. (1914) *The Challenge of Facts and Other Essays* (ed.) Albert Galloway Keller, New Haven, CT: Yale University Press.

'Survey Reveals Geographic Illiteracy' (2002) *National Geographic News,* 20 November. Available HTTP: <http://news.nationalgeographic.com/news/2002/11/1120_021120_GeoRoper Surey.html> (accessed 4 May 2006).

Suzuki, D. (1993) *Time to Change,* St Leonards: Allen & Unwin.

Synott, J. (2004) *Global and International Studies: Transdisciplinary Perspectives,* Southbank, Victoria: Thomson Social Science Press.

Tarnas, R. (1991) *The Passion of the Western Mind: Understanding The Ideas That have Shaped Our World View,* New York: Ballantine Books.

Taylor, P.J. (1999) *Modernities: A Geohistorical Interpretation,* Oxford: Polity Press.

Teeple, G. (1995) *Globalization and the Decline of Social Reform,* New Jersey, Toronto: Humanities Press, Garamond Press.

Teivainen, T. (2002) *Enter Economism, Exit Politics Experts, Economic Policy and the Damage to Democracy,* London, New York: Zed Books.

The Commission on The Integrated Long-Term Strategy (1988) *Discriminate Deterrence,* Washington, DC: US Government Printing Office, January.

'The Militarizing of Domestic Policy' (1995) *Z Magazine,* February.

The National Security Strategy of the United States of America (2002) published by the authority of the President of the United States.

The Worldwatch Institute (2005) *Vital Signs 2005: The Trends That Are Shaping Our Future,* New York: W. W. Norton.

Thomas, C. (1987) *In Search of Security: The Third World in International Relations,* Boulder, CO: Lynne Rienner.

Thomas, C. and Wilkin, P. (eds) (1999) *Globalization, Human Security & the African Experience,* Boulder, CO, and London: Lynne Rienner.

Thompson, H.S. (1995) *Better Than Sex: Confessions of a Political Junkie – Trapped Like a Rat in Mr Bill's Neighborhood,* Sydney: Doubleday.

Thompson, W.I. (1967) *The Imagination of an Insurrection: Dublin, Easter 1916,* New York: Harper & Row.

—— (1975) *Passages About Earth: An Exploration of the New Planetary Culture,* London: Rider.

Thornton, P. (2006) 'West's Failure Over Climate Change "Will Kill 182 Million Africans",' *The Independent,* 15 May.

Thurow, L.C. (1992) *Head to Head: The Coming Economic Battle Among Japan, Europe and America,* New York: William Morrow.

—— (1995) 'Companies Merge; Families Break Up,' *New York Times,* 3 September.

—— (1996) *The Future of Capitalism: How Today's Economic Forces Shape Tomorrow's World,* New York: William Morrow.

Tillman, R.H. and Indergaard, M.L. (2005) *Pump & Dump: The Rancid Rules of the New Economy,* New Brunswick: Rutgers University Press.

Tomlinson, J. (1999) *Globalization and Culture,* Oxford: Polity Press.

Toohey, B. (1994) *Tumbling Dice, The Story of Modern Economic Policy,* Port Melbourne, Victoria: William Heinemann.

Tooze, R. and Murphy, C.N. (1996) 'The Epistemology in IPE: Mystery, Blindness and Invisibility,' *Millennium,* vol. 25, winter.

Toulmin, S. (1990) *Cosmopolis: The Hidden Agenda of Modernity,* Chicago, Il: Chicago University Press.

Trumpbour, J. (ed.)(1989) *How Harvard Rules: Reason in the Service of Empire,* Boston, MA: South End Press.

Trumper, R. and Phillips, L. (1995) 'Cholera in the Time of Neoliberalism: The Case of Chile and Ecuador,' *Alternatives*, vol. 20.

United Nations Development Programme (UNDP) (2005) *Human Development Report 2005*, New York: UNDP/Oxford University Press.

United States Department of Labor, Bureau of Labor Statistics, 'Union Members Survey' (2006) *News*, 20 January. Available HTTP: <http://www.bls.gov/news.release/union2.nr0.htm> (accessed 19 May 2006).

United States Space Command, *Vision for 2020* (1997) Available HTTP: <www.spacecom.af.mil/usspace> (accessed 12 September 2006).

'US Marines Get a Lesson from Wall St' (1995) *Sydney Morning Herald*, 2 December, ex *Newsday*.

Van Creveld, M. (1991) *The Transformation of War*, New York: Free Press.

—— (1999) *The Rise and Decline of the State*, Cambridge: Cambridge University Press.

Vasquez, J. (1983) *The Power of Power Politics*, New Brunswick: Rutgers University Press.

Vidal, G. (1990) 'Notes on our Patriarchal State,' *The Nation*, 27 August–3 September.

—— (1992)'Monotheism and its Discontents,' *The Nation*, 13 July.

Virilio, P. and Lotringer, S. (1983) *Pure War*, New York: Semiotext(e).

Veseth, M. (1998) *Selling Globalization: The Myth of the Global Economy*, Boulder: CO, and London: Lynne Rienner.

von Radowitz, J. (1998) 'Mathematics Mere Monkey Business, Say Scientists,' *Canberra Times*, 24 October.

Wagner, D. (2006) 'Private Security Guards Play Key Roles Post–9/11', *Arizona Republic*, 22 January.

Wahlquist, A. (1992) 'Beefing Up Our Trade is Almost Green,' *Sydney Morning Herald*, 26 March.

Walker, M. (1993) *The Cold War and the Making of the Modern World*, London: Fourth Estate.

Wallach, L. (1993) 'Hidden Dangers of GATT and NAFTA,' in R. Nader *et al.*, *The Case Against Free Trade: GATT, NAFTA, and the Globalization of Corporate Power*, San Francisco and Berkeley, CA: Earth Island Press and North Atlantic.

Wallach, L. and Woodall, P. (2004) *Whose Trade Organization?*, New York: The New Press.

Wallach, L. and Sforza, M. (1999) *Whose Trade Organization? Corporate Globalization and the Erosion of Democracy*, Washington, DC: Public Citizen.

Walzer, M. (1989) *The Company of Critics: Social Criticism and Political Commitment in the Twentieth Century*, London: Peter Halban.

Waring, M. (1988) *Counting For Nothing: What Men Value And What Women are Worth*, Wellington, New Zealand: Allen & Unwin.

Watts, S. (1997) *Epidemics and History: Disease, Power and Imperialism*, New Haven, CT: Yale University Press.

Weatherford, J. (1997) *The History of Money*, New York: Crown Publishers.

Weigley, R.F. (1973) *The American Way of War: A History of United States Military Strategy and Policy*, New York: Macmillan.

Weiner, J. (1991) 'Yeltsin's American "Advisers",' *The Nation*, 16 December.

West, M. (1970) *The Heretic*, London: Heinemann.

—— (1990) *Lazarus*, Port Melbourne, Victoria: William Heinemann Australia.

—— (1996) *A View From the Ridge: The Testimony Of A Pilgrim*, Sydney: HarperCollins.

Westing, A.H. (1976) *Ecological Consequences of the Second Indochina War*, Stockholm: Stockholm International Peace Research Institute.

Wilkinson, R.G. (2005) *The Impact of Inequality: How to Make Sick Societies Healthier*, New York: The New Press.

—— (1996) *Unhealthy Societies: The Afflictions of Inequality*, London: Routledge.

Williams, J. (2004) *50 Facts That Change The World*, Cambridge: Icon.

Williams, W.A. (1982) *Empire as a Way of Life: An Essay on the Causes and Character of America's Present Predicament Along with a Few Thoughts About an Alternative*, New York: Oxford University Press.

William Appleman Williams *et al.* (1975) *America in Vietnam: A Documentary History,* New York: W. W. Norton.

Wills, G. (1990) *Under God: Religion and American Politics,* New York: Simon & Schuster.

—— (2000) *Papal Sin: Structures of Deceit,* New York: Doubleday.

Wilms-Wright, C. (1977) *Transnational Corporations: A Strategy for Control,* Fabian Research Series 334, London: Fabian Society.

Wilmshurst, P. (1997) 'Scientific Imperialism,' *British Medical Journal,* vol. 314, 22 March.

Wilshire, B. (1990) *The Moral Collapse of the University: Professionalism, Purity, and Alienation,* Albany: State University of New York Press.

Wolfe, A. (1997) 'The Moral Meanings of Work,' *The American Prospect,* September–October.

Womack, J. Jr. (1999) *Rebellion in Chiapas: An Historical Reader,* New York: The New Press.

Wood, G.A. and Leland, L.S. Jr. (eds) (1997) *State and Sovereignty: Is the State in Retreat?,* Dunedin: University of Otago Press.

Woodiwiss, A. (1993) *Postmodernity USA: The Crisis of Social Modernism in Postwar America,* London: Sage.

Index